INVENTING GOD

OMNI WELFARE TRUST

In the Service of Writers, Authors, Scholars, Academicians and people connected with literary community, who wish to publish their literary or other works

Gate No.1, Mezzanine Floor
Central Wing, Thapar House
124, Janpath, New Delhi-110001

INVENTING GOD

V.D. MADAN

OMNI WELFARE TRUST

Universal
Law Publishing Co. Pvt. Ltd.
NEW DELHI - INDIA

2014 Edition

ISBN: 978-93-5035-463-6

Published by

Universal
Law Publishing Co. Pvt. Ltd.
NEW DELHI - INDIA

A-58, G.T. Karnal Road Industrial Area,
(Near Azadpur Metro Station), Delhi-110033
Tel. : 011-47082254, 27458529, 27215334 Fax : 011-27458529
e-mail: unilaw@vsnl.com

- Showroom : C-27, Connaught Place, New Delhi-110001
- Sales : sales@unilawbooks.com
- Editorial : edit@unilawbooks.com
- Website : **www.unilawbooks.com**

Join us on Facebook
www.facebook.com/unilawbooks

Under the auspices of
OMNI WELFARE TRUST

Computer Typeset at Aesthetic and *Printed* at Glorious Printers, Delhi.

Sarvam Khalvidam Brahmn

(All this is Brahmn)

Ayam Atma Brahmn

(This Self is Brahmn)

Isavasyam Idam Sarvam

(God Permeates all Creation)

—The Upanishads

"God is described as
Sabda Brahmamayi, Characharamayi
Jyotirmayi, Vangmayi, Nitayanandamayi
Paratparamayi, Mayamayi, Sreemayi"
(Embodiment of Sound, Mobility and Immobility, Light, Speeh, Eternal Bliss, Perfection, Delusion and Wealth)

—Sri Sathya Sai Baba

Divine Dream and Humble Offering

"All dreams related to God are true. Whenever I appear in a dream, it is to communicate something to the individual; it is not a mere dream, as is generally known. It is a real appearance," said Bhagwan Sri Sathya Sai Baba in one of His divine discourses. I am one of those fortunate ones who happened to have such an experience. On 10th November, 2006, at 11.45 A.M., after the morning Darshan, while I was having my usual nap, Bhagwan Sri Sathya Sai Baba appeared in my dream. He drew my attention by pointing out His right hand index finger to a book held in His left hand with all pages blank and cover page entitled, "**Inventing God**", and directed me to write it.

It is a well-known experience of the Sai devotees that whenever and whatever, Sai Baba wills, gets it accomplished through whosoever He chooses to do so. I feel extremely fortunate, and hence, record my deep gratitude to Swami, as He is popularly addressed, for having identified me and chosen me for such a sacred and auspicious work. Here I must make it clear that I do not see myself as an author nor do I consider myself a spiritual schclar nor even a Sai Devotee in the sense defined by Baba. Indeed, Sai Baba Himself is the original author of this book since He only conceived the idea, seeded it into my mind and nurtured it with His divine grace. He conceptualized the thematic structure of the book and wrote it by using me as His instrument. All its themes and contents are presented in accordance with His divine commands communicated to me through His visions, thoughts and dreams.

This book is, therefore, submitted as my most reverential and humble offering at the divine lotus feet of Bhagwan Sri Sathya Sai Baba who demystifies knowledge and dispels darkness.

Remaining at the Divine Lotus feet of Bhagwan Sri Sathya Sai Baba.

V.D. MADAN
(A Humble Mortal)

"God is the innermost Self in all beings which are all his gross manifestations. He is the Science of the Self which is Divine knowledge (Atman Vidya or Brahmn Vidya or Brahmn Gyan). He is the beginning, the middle and also the end of all beings. He is the material as well as the efficient cause of the Universe. God is with form, without form and also transcending all these. He alone knows who and what He is".

—Swami Ramakrishna 'Paramhans'

Contents

Foreword

The world has witnessed countless fascinating phenomena since the dawn of civilization. The 'starry heavens above' and the human ingenuity below have both inspired man to go where no one has ever gone before. The stupendous advancement in the field of science, researches in anthropology and behavioural studies, creative evolution in the field of fine arts and literature, and above all, mind boggling explosion in quantum of knowledge, have been all brave attempts to portray the human spirit that triumphs over all trials and tribulations – natural as well as man-made. Human pursuits and achievements have been succeeding each other in cyclic order.

However, the bottom line of all human endeavours has been to have a tryst with destiny. As one fathoms the **modus vivendi** (thoughts and feelings) and **modus operendi** (action) of man, one is simply struck by a mental archeology which creates both 'awe' and 'impulse'. A relentless, passionate longing has enabled the present generation to skyrocket into outer space, even opting for one way voyage to the Mars. It is this yearning that has stimulated the modern nuclear scientists to explode the proton – explore the essence of the God's particle (Higgs-Boson) and recreate, rather manufacture complete creatures from stem cells. The acquired sophistication in instruments and their use through nanotechnology speaks volumes for the glorious advancements made by mankind in various spheres.

Truly, the scientists have found out answers to many daunting problems regarding life by decoding, in Eddington's phraseology, 'Strange footprints on the shores of the unknown'. But **have they really been able to discover or invent or reconstruct a happy world? Is not the world today suffering from an all engulfing turmoil**? In fact their so called conquest of outer space has simply underlined the basic urge for quest into inner space, individually or collectively. There is a dire need of finding a sweet sojourn, 'the happy home' that provides safe refuge to the wayward, baffled humanity. While the 'intellectuals are smugly satisfied in 'exploding the obvious' through scientific enterprise, the common man finds true deliverance in religio-spiritual experiences.

Obviously today's man has seen through the futility of the modern day 'pleasure haunts' and other escapades. Slowly but surely the hitherto all-pervading sensate culture is making way for the supra-sensuous ideational culture, helping man to realize the reality within.

Hailing this epochal shift in the central concern from materialistic order of life to the idealistic one and, that too in the religio-spiritual genre, Prof. V.D. Madan, has in his voluminous work tried to encapsulate issues that directly or indirectly relate to all those who intend to seek true happiness. The work entitled 'Inventing God' very succinctly and honestly unfolds all the related themes and sub-themes which a genuine seeker is confronted with. In this task, the author has projected various perspectives which the believers and even the non-believers are likely to delve into. There is graphic description of the existential anxiety and the spiritual predicaments that modern man finds himself in. It provides meticulous analyses of the varied perceptions and experiences that mirror the present-day response to the stabilizing traditions and the radical changes in the usual ways of looking at things. Reading between the lines, one is sure to tread along the path that meanders through the social crises and the antinomies that characterise human pilgrimage to sublimity. As if providing counter malady to the divine symphony, the author has painstakingly assessed the validity of the astrophysics and formulations related to varied branches of modern scientific know-how which he finds falling short of answering questions about the **Ultimate Reality**. The text has also given ethical auditing of various theories of evolution that dot the march of humanity, leading to the similar conclusion. Without making any attempt to sell a particular ideology or a philosophy, this work places and examines the available arguments for and against all the possible perceptions or even assumptions advanced to deal with theological or spiritual dimensions. The sub-stratum remains predominantly philosophical.

Following methodology that approximates dialectics, Professor Madan raises all the relevant questions regarding the universe and its efficient and final cause, humanity and its relation with divinity, the status and functions of an anthropomorphic God, the occasional emergence of various incarnations (avtar) and the nature of the highest reality – the Brahmn of the Vedantic philosophic tradition. He also essays to portray the physical and metaphysical dimensions of human existence. Respecting all the religio-philosophical traditions regulating human thoughts, actions and aspirations, he unassumingly evinces his full faith in the catholicity and universal liberalism of the Hindu culture which is not confined to the pricints of a founded or organized religious tradition. There is a profusion of the well-worded quotes from the ancient Indian scriptures, the Bhagvat Gita, in particular, along with the undergirding of the Upanishadic grandstand. He has also made copious use of the relevant extracts from the most widely read column of "The Speaking Tree" which regularly appears in the popular daily – The Times of India. Realizing his limitations in following the exactitude of a research work, he records his indebtedness to all those authors of the classics or other scholarly works he advances in support of his contentions and arguments.

While discussing different, even contrasting, views on the various problematic points, the author has made judicious use of the celebrated sayings of Sri Sathya Sai Baba which is undoubtedly the hallmark of this book. These sayings unmistakenly uphold and glorify the finest fruition of Indian culture which believes in universal good and upliftment of humanity without any discrimination, pride or prejudice. Perhaps the most ticklish as well as valuable aspect of this subject is to traverse the distance between various levels of philosophical consciousness that buttress Hindu religious outlook. **How to bridge the gulf between human consciousness and the Supreme Consciousness? How to account for the assumptions regarding God, the Creator and the unqualified Brahmn? Are there any superhighways or springboards which can catapult a human being to merge with the Supreme soul or become the same – the Journey from Tattvam Asi (That Thou Art) to SOHAM (That I am)**? These issues are of perennial nature in religious as well as philosophical parlance and impact the human attitude towards life and the world.

Without any strict adherence to a particular philosophical world view, the author of this book, follows a line of religious thought which is integrative, inclusive and holds divinity as well as humanity in a single embrace, much to the satisfaction of the devotees of various religious faiths and the SAI TRILOGY. There is an axiomatic acceptance of the highest conceived authority – Brahmn of the Advait Vedantic Tradition which stands Supreme, unmanifest, Transcendent yet Immanent, all Existence-Consciousness and Happiness – SAT-CHIT-ANAND. God's incarnations and various Divine Messengers/Prophets are held as manifest forms of the Supreme Reality, the efficient (Creator) and the final (Purpose) cause of this whole creation. It is immanent God (Paramatman) that resplendently permeates humanity (Jivatman).

It needs to be realized here that one can endlessly continue hairsplitting in logico-philosophical debates but religiosity or spirituality defies such attempts. In almost all religious matters, God constitutes axiomatic truth, and it serves the purpose for which the believers invoked Him, the atheists and agnostics notwithstanding. All religions more or less follow the same line of thought. Even while straddling the two distinct realms of Reason and Faith one could leave it for the rationalists and techno-rationalists to indulge in never-ending debate regarding the nature and proof of the existence of God, and opt for the path of faith that becomes the solace of one's life and of the final end as well. God is that one power that cushions all human predicaments and provides security and comfort to all those who fall upon the thorns of life and bleed. Also, it is in this context that the doctrines of various divine incarnations, messengers and prophets acquire significance.

Without being assertive or apologetic, Prof. Madan adheres to the protein philosophy of Hinduism and evinces full faith in the theory of incarnation as propitiated in the Gita. Besides, this enables him to live out his unmitigated faith in Sri Sathya Sai Baba as God incarnate along with His incarnation, earlier as Shirdi Sai Baba and the future Prema Sai.

As I thumbed through the pages of the script, I was somewhat intrigued by the very title of the book – INVENTING GOD. More so because the book has been thematically entrenched in the conception of God as an *apriori* proposition which means it is prior to any knowledge or consciousness that constitutes the conceptual capital of the human beings. **How can God, which is premised as the first cause of creation, be 'created' or invented by any agency, much less the mortals?** However, I got answer to my philosophical discomfort in the argument that God transcends everything created including human thought and imagination. That He exists is *an **inferred judgement**, not a proven reality*. Human faith 'creates' Him, as a *practical necessity* – the human beings consecrate Him in Thought and Action.

Prof. Madan has yet another over-riding reason to opt for the title – 'INVENTING GOD' as he has simply carried out a mandate from no other authority than Sri Sathya Sai Baba Himself, who inspired him to take up this task with this title of the book. For a devotee, it is a divine intervention. That he (Madan) being a mathematician, devoted more than seven years to complete the task of this nature – formidable, yet engaging, is a testimony to the dedication required to live out **His Will**.

OM SHANTI, SHANTI, SHANTI !

R.P. SHARMA
Formerly, Head, Department of Education and
Dean, Faculty of Education, University of Delhi
Delhi-110 007 (India).

Acknowledgements

This book, in reality and in its entirety, is authored by Bhagwan Sri Sathya Sai Baba Himself who, being the Yogeshwara, the Lord of the present Yuga (Epoch) would get things done with His divine will. It is a well-known experience of the devotees that Swami would dive deep in the ocean of universal knowledge and fish out anything including the contents of the book to be written. My role has been limited to that of compilation and the underpinning of His gospels, discourses and teachings, even that too could happen with His grace only. Perhaps due to some good deeds (Karmas) done by me earlier either in the present life or in my previous/past life (lives), Bhagwan Sri Sathya Sai Baba selected me, out of a huge galaxy of spiritual seekers and scholars, to undertake the venture of writing this book. Throughout the process of thinking, collections of relevant material for the book and consequently penning down its contents, the inspirational guidance has been ignited in me by my beloved Sai Baba. Indeed, He has been the motivating force for the ideas and thoughts that together got manifested as a book of this form. I, therefore, first of all, register my most profound gratitude to Bhagwan Sri Sathya Sai Baba for having honoured me as the writer and compiler of this pious work. So long as there is breath in my body, I pray to Him to continue guiding me and helping me with His divine grace to enable me to join the ranks of those who venture to quench their thirst for His Realization.

The challenging task of producing this book that too on a theme, so abstract and so difficult, could not have been possible but for my incidental and circumstantial landing in the world of Sai phenomenon. Indeed, it was merely because of my destiny that I happened to get into the spiritual company of a Sai devotee couple namely Mrs. Molly Guha and Mr. A.K. Guha, an IAS officer, who became instrumental in motivating me and my family into the Sai phenomenon without whom our divine experience with Bhagwan Sri Sathya Sai Baba would not have been possible. I, therefore, along with my wife record my deep gratitude to Mrs. and Mr. Guha who showed my family and me the way to Sai Baba which consequently turned out to be a divine boon manifesting in many forms including this book.

I would like to express my special sense of gratitude to my revered teacher preceptor and philosopher friend Prof. R.P. Sharma, formerly, Dean, Faculty of Education, and Head, Department of Education, University of Delhi (Delhi) not only for his guidance and advice in the consultation of literature pertaining to the spiritual philosophy and in clarifying the philosophical meanings of various spiritual terms and terminologies but also for acceding to my request to honour me by accepting my humble offer to review the book, and write its Foreword.

I would also like to put on record my deep gratitude to my Sai Brother, Sh. G. Ramachandran, a learned spiritual scholar, formerly a Joint Secretary in the Govt. of India, who gave very useful suggestions for its initiation. Further, I would like to express my sincere gratefulness to all my Sai Brothers particularly Shri S.B. Raman Rao, a highly evolved spiritual scholar and devotee of Bhagwan Sri Sathya Sai Baba, and Dr. Hem Raj Seth, another ardent Sai Devotee, a scientist, and a Homeopath among others, for their help and encouragement in the preparation of this book. Also, I must thank Alexander R. Prowse ARMS PS of England, an ardent devotee of Bhagwan Sri Sathya Sai Baba, for preparing the cover design of the book.

Finally, I would like to put on record my gratitude to my family members for their cooperation in the preparation of this book. I am equally thankful to the Omni Welfare Trust for providing me the necessary financial support and M/s. Adam Smith Associates for word-processing/computer typing work related to the book.

To the best of my knowledge and belief, the references of various scholarly works have been appropriately given in the list of references at the end of the book. Yet, some references may have been omitted inadvertently due to the reasons beyond my control for which, I offer my sincere apologies. The referential materials which have been of great help to me in the preparation of this book also include, among others, various articles published on the week days "Speaking Tree" column and the weekly (Sunday) edition of the "Speaking Tree Supplement" of the esteemed newspaper, *"The Times of India"* during the last one decade. Repetitions in some sections became imperative in order to give a sense of completeness and also in the context of the relevant aspect of the idea which in any case may have been the focus. Resemblance, if any, in the subject-matter of the book with some other published work, may be coincidental but certainly not intentional. In any case, for my part I maintain a comfortable refuge in the protected bliss of my ignorance of all the omissions and errors, if any.

Introduction

On a first sounding, the title of the book, "**Inventing God**" looks baffling as a mysterious riddle defying any understanding. Interestingly and curiously enough, the subject has been prompted by the very transcendental Being who is beyond all inventions, discoveries, learnings and findings. Thus, in order to get a possible peep into the subject, I opened up the Oxford dictionary and came across certain statements extracted as under:

"Inventing something means making or designing or creating something new that did not exist before. Discovering something means finding something that already existed but remained hidden or unknown, and came to be known for the first time. Learning something means comprehending it by study or enquiry, while finding something means achieving or obtaining or getting something by chance or by a flash of an idea".

The basic critical question would arise: **Is God a subject matter of invention or discovery or learning or finding**? Or, **is God a state of felt experience and realization happening outside the scope of any invention**, **discovery**, **learning** and **finding**? A variety of thoughts seemingly arose in my mind namely the following:

- 'Human beings invent God', means human beings create God. The implication of this thought is the existence of human beings prior to God, and the ephemerality of eternity.
- Human beings may not invent but only discover – not God but Godhood or Divinity inherent in everyone, and the eternal nature of Divinity.
- All beings including the human beings are divine creations as a play of God's sport (Leela). What, then, is the impelling need for the human creation of God? Moreover, there is the theory of vacuum. Can that vacuum or emptiness be filled through invention of God or through discovery of Godhood?
- Perhaps invention or discovery of God cannot be viewed in isolation. Discovery of the eternal follows the invention of the ephemeral – indeed a vertically downwards spiritual movement.

- God's "presence" existing before, now and after. So it cannot be invention of any non-existent phenomenon before.
- God is 'present' in everyone for ever. So, it cannot be mere discovery prior to others' experience.
- God's "presence" transcending human enquiry and study. So it cannot be mere learning.
- God's 'presence' to be experienced on sustained meditation (sadhana). So, it cannot be just by chance, study or enquiry.

In short, is God the process of invention, discovery, learning and finding? At the same time, Godhood (divinity) may outgrow any single or individual process within an overall invention, discovery, learning and finding. But then there is Divinity (God) both beyond and within the processes – a strange paradox indeed. God cannot be a paradox.

To resolve such puzzling questions, I happen to consult and share the divine dream with some Sai brothers Sh. S.B. Raman Rao, Dr. Hem Raj Seth and Sh. G. Ramachandran as well as my philosopher friend and preceptor Prof. R.P. Sharma who told me that there is a very thin difference between the words invention and discovery in the context of God-realization. They all encouraged me to interpret the title "**Inventing God**" as something more than realization of God, say recreating the idea of Godhood in mind, and going ahead to obey the divine command given by Bhagwan Sri Sathya Sai Baba in the divine dream.

To be more sure, I thought of writing a letter to Swami. As is the practice and belief, I wrote the letter describing the divine dream and carried it with me while going for the Holy Darshan with the feeling that if Swami accepts this letter, I will go ahead and make efforts to pen down whatever my capabilities and capacities permit me to do. As usual Swami came to give the holy Darshan but passed quickly through the place where I was sitting for Darshan. I presumed that I need not worry about writing the book. However, after going a little distance away from me, Swami took a quick about-turn, came straight to me and took my letter with a sweet divine smile. Thus, I concluded that I should undertake the venture of writing this book with Swami's divine grace and blessings.

The word of Sai Baba is a divine command, a 'Vedvakya' for me. This book is a divine work born out of divine inspiration. Bringing out this work in print would be carrying out His divine mission of spreading inner light, spiritual love and the eternal truth sustaining the whole existence.

The book has six chapters beginning with a prologue and culminating in an epilogue. The first chapter highlights various spiritual predicaments in the modern human society with a focus on spiritual crises and paradoxes in relation to the divine perceptions. Chapter 2 on Astrophysics and Metaphysics deals with cosmic evolution, biological evolution (creation) and the spiritual evolution. Hinduism and its philosophy form the backbone of chapter three centred around the Hindu culture, Hindu scriptures and Hindu philosophical systems. Supreme Reality, that is, the Brahmn and its manifestations; and the Trinity Principle along with divine incarnations together constitute what may be termed as the central theme of Chapter 4. There have been several divine messengers, personalities and prophets all over the world ever since with the advent of the present aeon (Kaliyuga) who tried their best to revive the spiritual values and to awaken the humankind through their preachings and doctrines. The profiles, miracles and doctrines of a few such divine messengers/prophets have been briefly sketched out in Chapter 5. The last chapter 6 entirely revolves around the Sai phenomenon beginning with the advent of Shirdi Sai Baba, reincarnated as Sri Sathya Sai Baba and the predicted future Sri Prema Sai Baba. It also highlights the mission of the Sai phenomenon with a divine message to the modern world. Inventing God interpreted as Realizing or Recreating God in the mind, the book concludes in the Epilogue which provides the possible answers to the questions raised in the Prologue.

"Each soul is potentially divine. The goal is to manifest this divinity within by controlling nature, external and internal. Do this either by work or by worship or psychic control or philosophy, by one or more or all of these, and be free"

—Swami Vivekananda

Prologue

While brooding over the mysterious Universe, people sometime raise their heads and gaze at the boundless immensity of the star-studded sky with amazement and curiosity. Suddenly, few questions arise in their minds: **What is this Universe**? **Who created this Universe**? **How was it created**? **When was it created**? Such questions among others continue to be explored even to-date by the greatest scientists and cosmologists of the world. Despite their tremendous mastery over science and technology, they have still done not more than the tiniest fraction ever imagined on exposition of the mystery of the universe. Bewildered by the overpowering sense of the wondrous phenomenon of the universe, people try to find the answers to their curious queries from the spiritualists, scientists, sages and seers. The abstract, philosophical and spiritual knowledge, which deals with creation of the Universe, when properly understood, helps them to move little by little, along a path of developing faith in some supreme divine power called God. Certainly such exploratory efforts lead them to the quest of God.

Several types of explanations and enunciations are given by the sages and spiritualists on the subject of God. A large number of books and articles are getting published describing the concept of God. In fact, the topic of God has been under debate for centuries. But there does not seem to be a common understanding of the phenomenon of God as to **What is God**? **Who is God**? And **Where is God**? Such questions have been puzzling the minds of both believers and non-believers, scientists and rationalists, scholars and even the spiritualists. Paradoxically enough, almost all communities and human races have been worshipping God in their own ways with some forms visualized by them in their respective visions.

Ancient races and the tribals all over the world, whether in India, Africa, Australia or, South America, visualized God carved on a piece of rock or wood, sometimes with a frightful glare. The people, who have had some experience of tribal civilization, must have found them believing in some higher or supernatural power termed as God. Millions of temples, churches and mosques all over the world are dedicated to the worship of God. Some adore God with form and some meditate on God without form, while there are others who believe in God both with form and without form. It is difficult to say as to which is true God, God with form or God without form or both. In a country like India people merely adore a huge multiplicity of deities representing one or other form of God, while the more enlightened and thoughtful spiritualists have reduced the whole puzzle to a choice between personal and an impersonal God, a personified and non-personified God.

If God is considered to be the Supreme Power, there has to be only one concept of God. There are various forms of divine Beings who are treated as God by several people. As such God may be viewed differently by different people. God may be many things even to the same person at different stages of his spiritual evolution. For instance to an ordinary believer, God is invariably a personal deity while to some, God may look like an individualized Being who is usually pictured with a human or an angelic figure, someone to whom the believers/devotees can pray and to whom they can make requests for personal gains and favours. For an intellectually and spiritually enlightened person, God may look like a Divine Power superior to human beings and a Super Power which permeates the Universe. To the Vedantists of Advaita genre, Brahmn, the highest absolute reality, without any epithets or names, defies logic and is, therefore, not acceptable. They often use negative appellations such as 'Neti, Neti' etc. for referring to the absolute reality *i.e.* Brahmn.

One of the most puzzling issues that have been baffling both cosmologists and spiritualists is about the origin and mystery of the Universe. While spiritualists believe that the Universe goes through endless cycles of appearing and disappearing, the cosmologists, however, trace its origin to a Big Bang and its end to a Big Crunch. Some spiritualists link it with Siva's Cosmic Dance believed to be synchronized to the creation and dissolution of the Cosmos.

According to the Vedanta philosophy, Creation is associated with the primordial sound, 'AUM' (written as OM also) about which Bhagwan Sri Sathya Sai Baba says, "**Every little movement results in a sound, you may not be able to hear, because the range of the ear is**

limited. The falling of the eyelid over the eye makes a sound and the dropping of dew on a petal makes a sound. The sound caused by primal movement that is believed to have resulted in enveloping Brahmn by self-evolved Maya is the Pranavaa or OM". This means **OM** symbolizes the birth of the universe. In the beginning there was nothing but the Great Void, the true Absolute, wherein all was silent, still and empty. There was eternal darkness. This silence of the Absolute was broken by '**OM**', the sound of God as enunciated by the spiritualists.

Looking into the various religious practices, no matter in what community or in what faith, it can be found that God is worshipped usually pictured as personified individual, visible or invisible being, with or without form who, it is believed, answers to the prayers of the devotees. Their faith, however, gets shaken when the concept of God as some divine Power, is analyzed in a critical manner by the scientists and the rationalists. The two notions, one that of God as an individual being, and the other that God is some Divine Power, create confusion in the minds of the believers. This confusion mostly arises because of the dependence of religious people on feelings and sentiments alone particularly when there is no proper test for Truth in such a dependence. On the other hand, when they begin to believe in the concept of God as Power, then faith in their original idea of personified God tends to shatter. Apart from this confusion, there is a class of religious enthusiasts who claim to have seen God as if they knew God before hand. Likewise some atheists take pride in pronouncing loudly that they do not believe in God as if they know God and as if such an attitude is a great achievement. Thus, God is a subject which has unquestionably been under debate rather than perhaps properly comprehended. But then, there is a need to invent a universal way to know the truth which will always be appealing and which is acceptable by all.

Strangely enough people keep on changing their concepts, whether as a believer or a non-believer, a sage or a scientist under different circumstances. Moreover, the whole concept of God entirely depends upon the situation, and the idea that suits is the one which helps most. Thus, for some persons, the compulsive conclusion is that concept of God is relative, which means there is no absolute, ultimate and final idea of God. Mostly, human beings are not able to conceive God as He really is, but only as they imagine Him to be. At the same time, if the concept of God is accepted as relative, then it must be admitted that the use of the term 'must' conceptually presupposes (conjures up) the existence of entities other than God also.

Very often devotees experience some holy presence in a religious centre like a temple, church or a mosque especially when they offer prayers with some picture or no picture in their minds of what they believe God to be. Such a pious feeling and a pictorial vision of God is a mental image which has come down to them by tradition, through thousand of years, perhaps, and strongly supported by the force of some organized religions or some idea of God sketched by some artist as suggested by the priests. It is just possible that such an idea, sketched by the artists comes and must eventually go off, may get changed and reshaped. Indeed, an idea need not be a reality and from the stand point of deep enquiry, may prove to be an illusion. An illusion cannot be reality while reality indeed means something that is eternally true.

Believers generally have some idea of God which they believe to be true. How is it that the religions all over the world have been exercising such a spell over the people? It is, perhaps, primarily because of their faith in some higher power or Supreme Being, the power which helps them and protects them. Even some scientists also believe that such higher power exists and helps or guides them. The spiritual scholars believe in God and through their deep concentration or meditation, they are able to visualize some Supreme Power which they believe to be outside of themselves. This gives them the guidance, help and some sort of spiritual consolation which they believe they find in a temple or church or mosque or in their faith or in their idea of God. It, however, hardly matters where from such a power comes so long as they are realistic and believe in some external deity or power. It also does not matter if they are ready to change their idea when they begin the quest of truth, that is to say, when they are interested to understand the inner reality of the life and of the universe. Then they will see that God is to be found not in particular form, but in all forms; not in any particular place, but everywhere; not through any particular faith, cult or religion, but through any religious mode; not at any particular religious centre like a temple, mosque or church but at any place and everywhere. They must be prepared to get enlightened that the actual avenue to find God is not only outside themselves but also within themselves.

In the present era of technological advancement, people have begun to gain intelligence and knowledge at an extraordinary pace. As a result, they are restless and are not able to still their mind. They are keen to know everything including the reality of God through an easy and short-cut method. Ancient methods and traditional ways are neither sufficient for them nor appear to be convincing to them. They want to know the ultimate truth as to what is this Supreme Being called God.

They want to hear voices, the voices of men who have been privileged to experience God face-to-face or who can demonstrate their convincing spiritual experience. Modern men are not willing to understand that Truth is not a creed, and not a set of statements to be swallowed like a pill. They must first divest themselves of such a notion of the Truth. Even the goal of the scientists is also to know the ultimate Truth so that they understand the beliefs upon which mankind has been fed for millions of years. Indeed, the scientists will find the same Truth which the sages and the spiritualists have already realized because there is only one ultimate Truth.

What are the scientists going to discover or invent about God? Indeed, the scientists have already begun to perceive that there is no room for a personified God in the Universe. They have started realizing that the present Universe is only a part of the whole and a part cannot be greater than the whole, nor the creation can be greater than the creator. They are fully convinced that since there is creation, there must be a creator just like there must be a builder of a building. Is this creator the Supreme Power beyond the form? If so, then God must be an Infinite Force. The scientists are trying to explore this infinite entity. This is the only difference which is likely to be in the conceptualization of God – the Infinite. The scientists may not name this infinite entity or the Supreme Power as God. They may give some other name, say, Higgs Boson, the God Particle. They are not willing to agree with the priests and theologians who take God both as personified and non-personified. They are, however, convinced that God is some most intelligent life force and the Supreme Power, and all the evolutionary cycles of this Universe are merely demonstrations, displays and the outworkings of this Supreme Power. Bhagwan Sri Sathya Sai Baba says, "**God is the Creator. He created everything in the Cosmos. But He did not retain within His hands the responsibilities relating to His creation. He gave to human beings all capabilities. But He laid down a condition relating to the use of these capabilities. Men are free to live as they like. They can utilize all the material objects in creation. There can be no objection in this from anyone, not even from God. But the Divine has declared there is no escape from the consequences of one's action. This has to be properly understood**".

Scientists do believe that the origin of the Universe is some source out of which the multiplicity of objects, beings and forces have emerged. They believe that there is only one source, and everything else has sprung, developed or evolved out of that root source. In view of this, scientists are bound to admit that the Infinite Power, which is God, is a single force – there is only one such force, only one God and not more than one. Since this is an Infinite Force (Power), and not something which can be enclosed in a box or encased in a form or any shape whatsoever, scientists will have to look for God outside their laboratories. It does not mean that they will have to fly out in the sky to find such a God. In fact, they have to turn inwards to their minds, to their ownselves after they have tried all their scientific methods or experiments. In the pursuits of such a scientific quest of God, and to search the ultimate Supreme Power which must be at the root of everything, it is possible that the scientists may discover to their amazement that they are just confirming the spiritual gospels which have already been given by the spiritual scholars declaring the existence of a Supreme Power which is termed as God.

How did the creation come into being? **Where did it come from**? **What is the origin and purpose of creation**? Such questions and many more in relation to the existence of God have been raised several times before and are continuously being asked to-date. These questions along with other related queries are demanding appropriate and satisfactory answers. The answers are expected from both science and spirituality. It is believed that right at the basic level, science and spirituality seem to disagree in both abstraction and generalization. While science has been exploring the Universe without taking human beings into consideration, the spirituality considers Universe with human being as the central focus. The primary reason to this disagreement being that spirituality revolves around the concept and **the domain of consciousness** which is more relevant to human beings.

The Indian philosophy of spirituality has consistently been emphasizing the realization of the **self** while treating human personality as the 'subject', not an 'object'. It has been asserting self-consciousness, self-analysis and free-will as the exclusive domains of a human being. The orthodox Hindu philosophy truly and fairly represents postulations of human personality in relation to God contrasting the unorthodox views of Buddhism and Jainism. The six systems emanating from the Upanishads represent various philosophical positions with regard to the notions of existence of God and the Universe. Upanishads, containing sum and substance of the whole Vedic knowledge treat human personality as the confluence of the Cosmic Powers. This knowledge reveals Brahmn as the Supreme Reality which is Satyam, Jnanam, Anandam *i.e.* Truth – Consciousness – Bliss. The main focus of the Upanishandic knowledge is centered on the perception of the 'I' principle *i.e.* 'I' consciousness, the Atman and various states of consciousness. These are generally known as the progressive stages of spiritual advancement of the individual self from the waking state through dream state to dreamless deep-sleep state leading to Turiya. The main aim is to raise the level of human consciousness to the realization of the Brahmn which is the same as Self-realization or Cosmic consciousness. Contrasting the Upanishadic philosophy, Jainism treats spirituality in terms of matter both in size and shape. The sanctified self is considered as self-sufficient all-knowing inward being. Buddhism conceptualizes human being in terms of what looks to be temporary along with the temporariness of the world structured in terms of matter, sensation, perception, mental constraints and consciousness, and its transitory character.

Vedanta is the only spiritual philosophy which presents a full and complete picture of God and the Universe including human beings. While science feels shy of discussing the question of consciousness, the Vedantic philosophy forcefully asserts that consciousness pervades the entire universe. Science finds it difficult to relate the gross matter with the consciousness (Brahmn). However, Vedantis and other spiritualists are able to relate this energy with the gross matter. Indeed, the universe contains both sentient and insentient beings which coexist because of the Cosmic Power which remains unchanged. This Cosmic Power is the substratum of the whole universe including creation called the Brahmand. Both matter and energy that exist in the universe, have this Cosmic Power as their origin – the only source.

There are various views as to how the Universe came into being. Science believes that energy is the foundation of this Universe and all that is visible around is a gross manifestation of this energy. Vedanta too proclaims that the ultimate is the energy – termed as Cosmic or Divine Power which is infinite and timeless. It is a state of Pure Consciousness or Absolute Awareness which is also referred to as the Brahmn which is Eternal, and from which everything emerges and merges back into it. It is a case of one becoming many. According to Bhagvat Gita, which emphasizes that everything flows from the Brahmn, called the Cosmic Power. The creation of the Universe followed the emergence of unmanifested matter and spirit, what in Vedanta is named as **'Prakriti'** and **'Purusha'**, which the scientists and spiritual philosophers refer to as physical or inanimate energy (Prakriti) and animate or consciousness energy (Purusha) respectively. The spirit or Purusha is often termed as Consciousness Energy which is present in both sentient and insentient beings. A debate on this concept of sentient and insentient beings is continuously going on at the religious and philosophical levels. A detailed account of this discussion is given in the classic work, "Message of the Lord", listed in the reference. **Bhagwan Sri Sathya Sai Baba says, "Generally it is considered that the natural sciences are concerned only with matter, and metaphysics and the metaphysical are inextricably related to each other. The unique greatness of the Upanishads consists in proclaiming this basic unity".**

According to the holy Bible, the first creation was Light, and thereafter came all other beings. God, a single unit as existence, created Light out of Himself or out of His own Being just as a spider spins a web out of its own body. The web is not different from the spider's body, it is indeed a part of it. Thus, likewise God created Light out of His own being, which means Light, is not different from God. In other words this Light is God Himself. This view also corresponds to the opinion given in the ancient Hindu Scriptures, which say that in the beginning was Brahma – one of the triadic or triple manifestations of the eternal Brahmn, which means the "Creator", who made light, and out of light, emerged all other beings. The ancient Egyptians used to worship sun because according to them, sun was the father of all creation. To them, light or the sun was divine power being present and visible everywhere in the universe. The latest research has discovered increasing evidence that all matter is the condensation of radiant energy, that is, of light. Indeed, scientists have proved in the laboratory that it is possible to convert light into matter, and matter into light, as said by Albert Einstein. In other words, the structure of the present material universe which is considered as matter-solid, a hard substance, can dissolve and become the light, a collection of electrons, protons and neutrons. This also vindicates the ancient belief of the Hindu philosophers who said, **"God is Light, and all the material objects are nothing but condensation of the radiant energy of light".** This implies that God is present everywhere, in everything, in every living being. The whole material Universe is made out of God and is filled with Him. Thus, God is Infinite and the Universe has been created out of God by God Himself. Is this, then, a more satisfactory conception than the theological notion of personified God? Is it more appropriate to believe intuitionally that God is an Infinite Power – the Power at the back of all forces, which exists everywhere, within everything and every being? **If it is so, then is it not true that such a conception of God is somewhat similar to the ancient Vedantic view of God**? Such a view is, indeed, built not only on the basis of ancient faith or intuition but supported by intellect and reason. Such a view should be considered as final and absolute not merely a relative one which is going to get changed or wiped out. As such, therefore, the mind should come to rest on this notion of God, and the debate should come to an end. But this is not the case since pursuits of God and Universe continue even to-date.

When the spiritualists practice meditation, they eventually begin to experience certain visions of God in their hearts and minds as some sort of divine light. The spiritualists get immersed in this light and they feel it as the highest realization. Indeed, this is the highest divine experience which a human being can have, especially those who strive to seek God. Such spiritualists when they return from such a state of divine realization back to their ordinary human consciousness, they describe this experience of theirs as a vision of God as the light or of hearing an inner voice or something that has been revealed to them within that light. This means they look upon that light as a state or a situation within which they had to look for something, to find a form, the form of God. But then God is an Infinite Power and hence cannot be considered like the human beings who speak, nor can He be limited by definite forms or shapes. Indeed, it is contradictory to think of God as an Infinite Power with a definite shape, and then attempt to visualize that God can be so limited as to be seen and heard. What perhaps, in reality, may be happening is that the meditator or the spiritualist is so illumined by the divine light that he posits his ordinary consciousness into the Cosmic Consciousness to know the truth – the Ultimate Truth. While the meditator has made some amazing discovery, yet he is not willing to stop by the wayside and the search continues. For most of the meditators, such an experience may be sufficient, but then for several others this glorious experience may not be the end of search, for soon another path may open up – a path which leads to the Ultimate Truth, the Supreme Reality. In that path, there is neither Light nor Darkness, nor even an Experience, because by then, the meditator has learnt to transcend time. The quest continues till he is able to find the Eternal Brahmn which has neither any beginning nor any end nor any form.

Various questions related to creation have been discussed and debated by the most sublime minds in each century. The answers they arrived at have been varied. Here are a few examples. "A life without introspection is not worth living," asserted the Greek philosopher Socrates around 400 B.C., while in the mid-1880s, evolutionist Charles Darwin spoke of "survival of the fittest". Thousands of slogans, pledges, oaths and mottos have been chanted across continents throughout the world. **Whose ideology is 'correct'? Which maxim reflects the highest and most lofty truth? Which slogan can bear the test of eternity? Are there any peaks to ascend higher than Everest? Are there any planets to voyage towards beyond the solar system? Are there any worlds**

beyond this present world? Are there any depths deeper than oceans, beyond the heart's and the mind's? Socrates was forced to drink hemlock, Darwin's theory collapsed long back, Hillary scaled the Everest, America put man on the moon. What next? A thousand more slogans and goals! A thousand more efforts and journeys! A thousand more struggles, undertakings and fantasies! The search will continue endlessly till the goal is achieved.

Human beings may eventually succeed in harnessing all the resources of the universe. They may even encounter intelligent life forms in other parts of the universe, befriend them, and hopefully, strive for the common benefit of all species. But achieving one goal after another, realizing fantasy after fantasy, a thoughtful person finally asks: '**What is the end of all this**?' The heart experiences no peace in the spinning maze of events that surround it. Mindless indulgence of desires brings with it only frustration, anxiousness and regret. The search for the zenith, yearning for a climactic and eternal joy that seemingly evades the advancements, remains tantalizingly out of reach. Where must people hunt and chase if they wish to fulfil this aspiration and realize this alluring and unrelenting dream? The outward search has gone on long enough. People must now turn and seek within, in the very core of their existence, where lies the substratum of consciousness which has made all materialistic pursuits and enterprises possible. The stream of consciousness they experience within themselves throughout their lives ties together all events of physical existences like the silken string that holds together a necklace. In its realization, they will meet their journey's end, the Omega point, a place of final rest and the dawn of a new existence in the divine Self and the beautiful, blissful Lord within. The human soul perpetually peers outward towards mundane objects of the five senses, but never looks inwards to see itself. Such a soul is the most ignorant of all since it is surrounded by the expanding process of globalization, a reality in many spheres, especially in the fields of space technology and communication system.

There is, however, a big gap between globalization suffused with technological advancements on one hand, and the human society devoid of the spiritual awareness, on the other. This calls for harmonious development of the human society based on technology and spirituality. Technology is creating only an environment of functional information and knowledge globalization. The web-site surfing seems to be alienating itself from the holistic pattern of thinking and creating isolated information islands. The awesome power of television and Internet are tragically being used to promote the cult of violence and vulgarity – rather than to inculcate the message of harmony, spiritual insights, and moral values. Huge amounts of money go into the production of feature films and tele-serials which revel in mindless horror and hedonism, thus polluting spiritual; and cultural environment. **Can something be done to divert this brazen exploitation of the dangerous tool of information technology towards its proper harnessing as a powerful instrument for social and spiritual transformation**? It is only through spiritual awareness that the much-desired cultural change in the mind-set of the people can be brought about. The holistic harmony lies in the deepest recesses of human consciousness. It is here that people will ultimately find the divine light, which according to the Bible enlightens every mind, and is known as the Roohani Noor of Islamic Sufis, the Ek Onkar of the Sikh Gurus, and the light of the Atman (Soul) of the Vedanta. In the on-going chaos and confusion that surrounds humanity, it is this spiritual light that can give the right direction, wisdom and the maturity to march forward keeping pace with the developmental process and technology advancement.

To the question, "***Where is God?***", the simple answer is, "***God is everywhere, God is in everything. God is Omni-present.***" To yet another question, "**Who is God**?", the answer given is that God is supernatural, immortal, an Omnipresent, Omnipotent and Omniscient power, that permeates the lives and affairs of the living beings including the human race, and the nature. The best answer to this question is given by Sri Sathya Sai Baba who invariably says, "*I am God. You are also God. The only difference is that I know that I am God but you don't know that you are God.*" To another question, "***What is God***?", the answer is that God is the totality of all the creations that exist, and considered as a harmonious and orderly system. Finally, to the question, "**Where can God be seen**?", The answer is, "God can be seen through His manifestations of creation, protection and dissolution synonymous with the process of the Universe."

The above questions have been explored in terms of their spiritual meanings which are hugely deep and profoundly philosophical. It has been said that if man is God's greatest creation, then so is God man's greatest discovery. As the French philosopher Voltaire put it, even if there is no God, it would be necessary to invent one, otherwise the world can't move on an even keel. The world of heart and art should not be a closed book to rationality. It is a point at infinity, the place where the parallel lines meet. The idea of existence of God conveniently answers many troubling questions to solve the increasingly intricate and bewildering problems of life. It is an idea with tremendous appeal. It is interesting to examine the way the idea of God has figured in the lives of those who think themselves as the most rational of all human beings; mathematicians and physicists included among others.

There have often been mystical beliefs about the mystery and beauty of natural laws or mathematical theorems to be having some objective correlation of a divine order. Some mathematicians and physicists have somewhat surprisingly been the staunchest of believers, going so far as to prove the existence of God through rigorous mathematical arguments. Notable amongst mathematicians who could reconcile their profession with faith in God was a French mathematician B. Pascal (1623-62). He was the inventor of notion of probability, the idea of which to a certain extent does not fit well with the idea of God. Only in a universe that is not preordained, can one have the play of chance. Otherwise every phenomenon unfolds according to some divine master-plan. Pascal came up with a somewhat ingenuous argument supporting belief in God. According to him even if one does not know that God exists, the benefits of believing in His existence far outweighs the possible drawbacks of such a belief. He gave a cost-benefit analysis that would convince many corporate managers of today. Another mathematician who tried to prove the existence of God was L. Euler (1707–83), a great Swiss mathematician of the 18th century. *The eminent British scientist Isaac Newton (1642-1727) did not believe in the concept of the Trinity,* yet he gave his mind increasingly over to speculations about the unfathomable mysteries of God. Another British mathematician, Stephen Unwin recently said that the odds on God's existence are two-to-one in favour if one believes in a mathematical probability theorem. Stephen, a graduate of London's Imperial College used the 200 year old Bayes Theorem, named after Thomas Bayes, an 18th century mathematician who was also a Presbyterian minister; to calculate that there is a 67 per cent chance that God exists. Unwin weighed the existence of evil and suffering against miracles, divided into supernatural events and miracles that occur when prayers are answered. He also factored free will, innate goodness and sense of morality and the many arguments for and against God's existence.

Different people have different views about God. It is immaterial so long as they have an understanding that these are merely views and thoughts and vary from individual to individual, place to place, time to time. The seekers continue evolving through various thoughts and ideas which lead them to the ultimate and highest concept of God. When they reach that state, their ideas melt away and they realize harmony with God, instead of thinking about Him. Once they really realize God and they become one with Him, their knowledge and intelligence get merged into God. Indeed, thoughts put a veil between them and God. When this veil is torn aside, they become one with God. Everybody can find a way to seek God because God is omni-present, omni-scient and omni-potent. But one must begin to search and look, and the proper place is within, not outwards. One must look inwards and seek that sacred feeling of realization within the heart – the spiritual self within. Once that is done, one can look outwards again and see God in everything, in everybody and at every place. Bhagwan Sri Sathya Sai Baba emphasizes by saying that a person discovers (or invents) God only by the Grace of God, the opportunity to make a discovery is a privilege, and the discovery itself is a gift of God or Prasadam. Mathematicians routinely dabble in the infinite, and have demonstrated that given an infinity, there is always a greater infinity, and thus God is the boundless spot of mathematical thought. Mathematicians are also comfortable with the idea of Nothingness or Vacuumness or Emptiness (Shunyata) – another concept important in the Indian philosophical thought. It is then perhaps no wonder that **Indians invented zero – a number that denotes the presence of an absence**. Amongst mathematicians, there is a philosophical divide as there are some who believe that they discover mathematical truths pre-existing in some Platonic world, or in God's mind, and thus they are merely deciphering His mind. They see themselves crouched in deep darkness, being privileged occasionally to see trembling shadows of higher truths, or brief flashes that illumine and make visible though briefly, a perfect world.

The idea of God is so subtle that it has fallen through the finest sieves mathematicians and physicists have come up with. In any case spirituality is a matter of experience rather than learned disquisition. 'God is an enigma before which the hubris of the intellect is tamed, and its finitude exposed!' The human beings, instinctively, sense deep down in their minds, the existence of a deeper power governing the destiny of the universe. Somewhat in a similar manner, giant telescopes initially glimpsed the fact that the distant galaxies in the universe were receding and that the universe itself was expanding. These telescopes tried to catch a fleeting glimmer of a power beyond and behind all that is perceived, a power that guides the course of all that is around, and determines all that ever will be. It is this universal backdrop that man has traditionally referred to as God. It is this universal principle that Albert Einstein tried to explore in his search for a unified field theory. Such a unified field theory, the famous scientist thought, would explain all gravitational and electromagnetic phenomena; and all that is invisible in the universe could be explained as the result of the interplay of the forces of gravitation and electromagnetism. It is a similar theoretical and logical framework that the famous British Cosmologist Stephen Hawking attempted in his 'theory of everything'. It is this underlying spirit of universal governance that the eminent British mathematician and philosopher Bertrand Russell tried to reach through his enunciation of the principles of deductive logic and mathematics. *But can God be understood, comprehended or even vaguely glimpsed by the human mind*? God is beyond all the forms of the world and of time. God may be with the world but He is not of the world. Albert Einstein's general theory of relativity makes the profound point that to understand the effects of gravitation, there is a need to view the universe as a four-dimensional world coursing through time. Similarly, **to experience the divine, there is a need to** grow into supramental and spiritual dimensions.

Indeed, science has itself come to a stage of direct confrontation with some mysterious phenomenon which has been occurring to some persons and creating thereby doubts in the minds of the scientists and rationalists. There have been several cases of life after death. Some persons could speak something of their previous lives. They could speak even of the houses and surroundings where they had lived in their previous lives. They could talk of some incidents with confidence which on verification were found to be true. Such occurrences, therefore, raise a question which must strike these rational and scientific minds that is, if the maxim of incarnation and reincarnation is not true, what is then the truth behind this phenomenon? Even the scientific experiments have failed to explain this mystery. **When the intellect, divorced from intuition and consciousness, is held down by desire and ego; when science, swollen by pride and self-deception about its vaunted powers, is painted as the prophet; when rationality, swayed by its aggressive power of logic and argument, leads the mankind to a cynical materialism; when the social scenario wedded with lust and pleasure seeking liberation, becomes the supreme status of life; and when religion discards its philosophy and idealism of spirituality, then the divine souls appear on the earth to cure humanity of the maladies of its disaster, disillusionment and depression, and to guard and guarantee its ultimate redemption. Can the truth of the presence of divinity, however covered and hidden it may be within the beings, sentient or insentient, be denied even on logical and/or scientific grounds?**

Chapter 1
Spiritual Crisis and Divine Mystery

Maladies of disillusionment and disbelief have descended all over the world. Human society is enveloped by desires, passions and egotisms swollen by arrogance into self-deception about its own boasting habits. Science accompanied by rationality, and painted as the modern prophet is pushing the society into a cynical materialism and pleasure-seeking liberation. Human values are being devalued, religion is being despised and spirituality is being ridiculed. The modern civilization is afflicted with materialistic greed. It is pitifully unable to refrain the human beings from becoming ravenous beasts. Indeed, the modern society is confronted with a serious spiritual crisis. What is happening all over the world presents a scenario of the rule of conjoined animality and cunningness, of violent energies and explosive passions, and of jungle-struggle mentality and inescapability from bestial thoughts. How can real peace come until people realize the need of spiritual guidance on self-training and self-improvement? Those who are trying to seek the needed spiritual guidance are not too many, those who attain it are very few. Spirituality as a noble ideal is far from realization. This chapter throws light on the social crisis faced by the human society. It points out some spiritual paradoxes and explores a few perceptions of the divine mystery.

1.1 Social Crises

Modern youth is yet to learn to discipline its violent passions, its aggressive attitudes and destructive tendencies. It is a plain fact that the ethical way of living is beyond the vision and mind of the modern youth today. Their views lack trust not only in the higher values but also in the idea of divine powers. They have become the victims of their inflated egos. They are deeply drunk with the desires of material achievements and glamour. They have become slaves to self-created vicious environments, sinful conventions and crowd mentality. Tendencies of aggressive rationality, rabid materialism and extreme selfishness are so rampant in the present times that people glaringly reveal the terrible intensity for evil. They are savagely causing unprecedented ethical destitution and moral infirmity.

Politicians are clamouring for seats of power; scientists are rapidly inventing nuclear weapons of mass destruction; media professionals are hurting sensitivity of the people by distorting facts; intellectuals are generating social tensions and economists are glued to their serried ranks of figures. The clergy men are puzzling people through misinterpretation of holy scriptures. Leaders all alike are misleading the people by their biased contentions, conflicting views and contradictory explanations. The result is that there is chaos and confusion. People do not know where to turn for truth, what to believe in the present, what to expect in the future. They are bewildered by the staggering news-headlines and the sensationalism created by the electronic media. Terrible occurrences of terrorists' attacks on the innocent people and mass-killing due to riots are causing huge depression in the human minds. Natural disasters, rapid happenings of tsunamis and epidemics are forcing people to lose faith in the spiritual values and truths. The course of events is compelling them to surrender to the cynical attitudes and beliefs. The distress and woes have demolished the religious faith of many while the current social environment has made several other indifferent and apathetic postures towards spirituality. Mostly people are preoccupied with a totally materialistic approach to a life based on commercial or financial considerations.

Human Society, shocked in its nerves and wounded in its feelings, is passing through the ordeal of a crisis whether to fall morally through a negative reading of its experience or to rise through a positive understanding of spirituality. It is not willing to understand that craving for materialism increases egoism and stimulates arrogance, while the spiritual quest arouses love and peace. It is true that human beings have complex characteristics since the good and evil both are mixed and together reside in them. Hence, their conduct under the prevailing circumstances is equally complex. Despite the miseries of life, the moral effects on humanity do not show enough of character advancement.

Social standards are getting more materialistic than before, the individuals more than ever, are devoted to the body's luxuries and mind's pleasures. The wide degradation of values is leading to the downfall of ideals causing thereby frustration and apathy. When the religious sanctions of morality become ineffective, when faith and reverence lose their purpose and meaning, then it is inevitable that society will have to face chaos and conflict. The human beings feel either disgusted or disappointed and forget the moral and spiritual values in reckless pleasure-seeking pursuits. The craving of physical excitement and the tendency towards the unrestrained acceptance of animal impulses are finding transient solace in cynicism and sensualism. The hard fact remains that the moral character of human beings is getting largely degraded, and ambitions are getting more materialistic than ever before. Consequently the modern society considers spiritual practice to be unproductive and declares that it has no time for spiritual pursuits. A certain section of the intellectuals sneer at spirituality as compulsive escapism, never understanding that it is they who are the real escapists. Their vision of life definitely gets out of focus and they treat a genuine spiritual seeker either as a naive fool or a designing hypocrite. Such an attitude of life leads to anguish and despair, and leaves the people high and dry on the shores of doubt and skepticism about the existence of a divine power.

When virtue is mocked and virtuous people are ridiculed, when the false, cruel and diabolic become powerful, then it is not surprising to find the minds of human beings getting suffused with doubts in spiritual ideals and disrespect to moral values. However, there are others who are optimistic with the firm hope that inspite of all such sufferings and horrors, a new humility would emerge which would acknowledge and revere a higher power called the divine power. History shows that it is especially at such times of widespread distress, social upheaval and shattered values of ethical crisis and moral challenge, that larger and loftier perceptions of life are sought and new spiritual movements are born. Swept by waves of pessimism, when people would start seeking religious consolation or comforting prophetic messages or spiritual experiences, then and only then will begin a conscious search for the meaning and purpose of life. Then and only then, the spiritual quest will start emerging. Then and only then, more and more people will seek spiritual truth to know the meaning of inner life. It is natural for a generation, influenced by unparalleled conflict and unprecedented evils, to lose faith in the divine power or spiritual wisdom. That is what is exactly happening to so many people in the present times. The people are so preoccupied with the external circumstances of their lives that they neglect its real and higher purpose. Their analyses of historic events and of human evolution are either entirely untrue or quite misleading. This is because they lack knowledge of the divine laws governing the causation of events all over the universe and the process of its evolution.

Under such circumstances and in such a social environment, it is quite natural for people to lose faith in God. People should try to analyze the causes behind these conflicts and evils instead of losing their faith in God. However, they are not able to do so because of their lack of self-confidence and faith in God. Hundreds of thousands of people blindly and eagerly follow a political leader who provokes these conflicts and leads them to ultimate destruction, whereas a very few people will follow an inspiring spiritual leader who leads them to the path of truth and righteousness. People having faulty sense of values are entirely ignorant of the spiritual values. Not having enough faith in divinity they put their faith in the destructive forces. People stuck deep in vulgar materialism cannot see the truth of the spiritual philosophy. They consider themselves fleshy bodies whose primary interests are acquiring material wealth. With such a wrong conception of human nature, they remain under the illusions of extreme egoism. The evils of bitter hatred flourish among them. Under the influence of such attitudes and having become so accustomed, they believe darkness to be light. The real struggle today is therefore, between the great illusion of the material concept of life and the real truth of the spiritual awareness. The illusion of materialism asserts that the human beings are here on earth solely to satisfy their temptations of body luxuries and gratify their lusty desires. Billions of people get illusioned under the impact of materialistic modes of life. They believe that their existence is only physical and nothing more. They forget that they are not only creatures compounded of body, passions and bestial thoughts but also of spiritual intuitions. It is, therefore, imperative that a social structure should be founded on the firm base of essential ethics, moral and spiritual values. A materialistic civilization becomes outwardly impressive but remains inwardly impoverished. Until the men and women tame their tempers, control their desires, leash their lust and curb their cruel mentalities, the menacing evils and destructive conflicts are sure to continue dominating the social environment. To overcome this socio-spiritual crisis, people have to modify their materialistic tendencies and create an atmosphere of social harmony which is possible only when the spiritual environment prevails around.

There can be no adequate answers to the questions of socio-spiritual crisis without first finding appropriate answers to the larger questions of life itself, which include among others the questions such as: "**What is a human being?**" "**What are the real objectives for which an organized human society exists?**" "**What are the final ends to be achieved through appropriate means?**" Unless the correct and befitting answers to such questions among several others are worked out, the human society shall only be roaming in dark and wasting energies quite aimlessly, and shall gravely harm the human stuff of which the very society is comprised of. Ignorance of the answers to these questions among several others is the primary cause of the present socio-spiritual crisis.

Without spiritual awareness, the society may stumble in the dark from one disaster to a more horrible catastrophy. The problems apparently may look to be linked with the socio-economic crisis, and therefore may need to be tackled by socio-economic measures. But the root cause of these problems remains the lack of moral and spiritual values. No solution can be a fundamental and permanent one which ignores morality and spirituality. Political, economic and social reforms by regimentation or by legislation cannot and will never lead to the desired solutions to meet the socio-spiritual crisis. Appropriate policies and principles need to be propounded and designed on the spiritual basis. The reforms cannot, by themselves, lead to the true social harmony. This is not to say that they are not needed, for they may lead to partial or transient satisfaction. They are useful palliatives which may give some temporary relief to the society but cannot provide a permanent cure. A human society or a nation which is solely focused on industrial or agrigarian economy, and which does not recognize a human being as a spiritual being or the universe as an outworking divine phenomenon, breeds psychic perils for its people. Even if its planners provide a more satisfactory place in which the general mass of people can lead a prosperous life as is the case with the so-called developed societies of Europe, Australia and America, they cannot provide the ideals for which their peoples have to live to fulfil their higher purposes or objectives. Those realists and rationalists who dismiss the application of worthy spiritual ideals as being nothing more than dreamers' catchwords and impracticable slogans, delude themselves. The failure to build a society free of socio-spiritual crisis is primarily a moral disaster. But prior to the social and moral reforms, there has to be spiritual reform. This is the fundamental solution to the socio-spiritual crisis. The ultimate remedy lies with the development of faith in the Supreme Reality, the God – the ultimate truth at the core of spiritual awareness.

To be agnostic and atheist can be the choice or inherent nature of an individual. But to deny flatly, and that too without any logic, the existence of God, is neither reasonable nor acceptable. No doubt, it is difficult to prove the existence of God in the way in which a mathematical theorem is proved. It is equally, rather much more difficult, to prove that God does not exist. In fact, non-belief in the existence of God or atheism demeans the humanity, while denying God's existence generally destroys the human nobility. Atheism takes a low view of humanity. A world without respect and reverence for God is meaningless. It will be a dungeon of horrors and demons. To the non-believers one could say that if this is the world ridden with so many problems, imagine this world without the idea of that supreme overseeing power; it would be a royal road to catastrophe wherein ignorant armies clash in the encircling gloom. Indeed, idea of God is needed, not so much as a panacea for life's ailments and problems, but a much more fundamental value. Humanity has huge potential which is demonstrated in many ways and through several achievements such as miraculous inventions, astounding discoveries and amazing creativities for its progressive evolution. But it is equally and more importantly desirable that it should develop a strong potential for moral and spiritual evolution for peace and harmony in the human society. This is just possible with a faith in a Supreme Divine Power called God.

The current fast life is causing tremendous nervous tensions which is driving the modern society specially the youth to seek relief through artificial stimulants, intoxicating liquors and narcotic drugs. Among them, the weaker-willed young boys and girls get themselves maimed in the end. Hypnotized by modern materialism, increased prosperity and aggressive technology, the human society today is breeding mental depression, cultural disaster and nauseating vulgarity. Big builders, manipulative industrialists, shrewd scientists, enterprising merchants, astute financiers in collusion with top educationists, irresponsible writers, corrupt politicians, and cynical journalists and media – professionals, are causing destructive effects on the human nervous system, creative talents and moral character. Today, science and technology have made human life comfortable but equally, if not more, restless. The need for a poised, serene and spiritual attitude is imperative. Spirituality is the only way out to overcome this social crisis. Spiritual philosophy is not against the uprising of industrialization or materialistic progress which is inevitable and essential. It simply advocates the need for a properly balanced and harmonized way of social existence. The ascetic notions idealized by the philosophers like Tolstoy, Tagore and Gandhi are not against the balanced industrialization or material prosperity but its excessive greed undermine the importance of the ways needed to cultivate the spiritual basis for liberating the human mind. Indeed, science and technology have opened up great possibilities for the socio-economic development of the mankind, but spiritual evolution alone provides the real basis for social harmony. It does not mean to forsake the scientific materialism for discovering the spiritual truth. People who are driven to an enforced and continuous preoccupation with the problem of earning a livelihood for supporting their families, would be foolish indeed if they do not give it preferential importance. There is nothing wrong if people are able to acquire material comforts, modern conveniences, a good home, decent clothes and healthy food. The wrong begins only when materialism becomes the only focus of life acquired at the cost of spiritual values or in violation of moral integrity. The ideal way is a properly proportioned synthesis of the two modes of life namely the materialism and spirituality. The fundamental needs of adequate food, clothing, shelter and living comforts always have to be provided. It is true that the need of earning a livelihood has always been the most important need for existence. Spirituality, however, does not mean extreme asceticism. Higher standards of living and the multiplication of desires are not at all to be treated as evils in themselves, but if left unaccompanied by spiritual discipline, they may become evils and regrettable demons. Good homes, adequate food and economic prosperity do not prevent anyone from attaining spiritual awareness and noble ideas.

No living man today can escape good and bad effects of the scientific development. The technological advancements and industrial developments are inevitable if the human society has to make an over-all progress. It is a necessary phase of human evolution. The work of science and rationality has helped people in removing the absurd superstitions, parasitic rituals and blind faith in traditional customs. The good done by the faith in orthodox ways, has been undone by their harmful effects due to superstitions. Science has put the human beings on their guard against the superficial view, the exaggerated emphasis and fallacious tendencies. However, science has also weakened faith in a higher power. Its doctrine based on the physical phenomenon, along with its interpretation of the universe and nature has promoted excessive worship of materialism at the cost of faith in a divine power. Modern scientific progress has given the human personality width without depth and fluency without wisdom. While it has demolished the myths and blind beliefs, it has equally destroyed the spiritual faith. This chaotic scenario prevailing in the modern society needs to be overcome by achieving a balance between the materialistic progress contributed by science on one hand, and the social harmony through spiritual practice on the other. Excessive materialism and extreme logical reasoning is steadily pushing the modern civilization into a great moral peril.

Exponents of science and technology have become over-enthusiastic while picturizing the paradise of applied science and glamorous technology. They do not realize that the moral and spiritual values are the real and eternal powers of the human society. The self-styled advocates of the paradise of machines and inventions do not feel the need of a parallel inner change in humanity. These self-deceived dreamers think that scientific progress and industrial advancement will solve all the problems of their living. Yet the more they burn incense at the alters of modern materialistic progress, the more the destiny mocks at them by giving them gigantic blows of natural disasters. The more they identify their highest good with physical and intellectual development alone, the more do both primitive and rationalist forces arise to shatter that development. They fail to see that the rationality when ascending to its purest metaphysical stretch, becomes impersonal and ennobles a person, but when it descends into its murkiest materialistic depth, it becomes selfish and cunning, and converts the best into the beast.

The naïve belief that science alone can improve the human personality is falling rapidly by the wayside. There is a realization even among the scientists themselves that the so-called scientific progress is meaningless since it does not provide mental peace and leaves the heart still empty when it is also equally responsible for the dreadful progress of hand grenades, intercontinental ballistic missiles, remote-controlled bombs, and atomic weapons. There is a smug satisfaction that everything is getting better and better by the progressive advancements of science and technology. It is, however, being realized that the technological progress is not compensating the spiritual regress, drawing attention to the glaring disparity between science and spirituality. The current era, though may not be described as unspiritual, yet harbours a culture which sing songs in praise of romantic industrial and technological innovations. The so-called advancement is necessary and proper to a great extent, but, beyond limits, it breads greed, selfishness and loss of faith in the higher divine power.

Having more aeroplanes, latest luxury cars, and several types of electronic gadgets overshadows the inner reality and the depth of human personality. Scientists are going out and investigating the outer planets and the whole universe, except themselves, since they have no time and tendency to look at their own selves. The lack of spiritual feeling, and the indifference towards the spiritual experience, is bound to show its negative consequences in all their ventures suffused with violence and war, greed and lust, and hate and jealousy. These are the bitter fruits of the loss of faith in a higher divine power and loss of belief in those who commune with it. It is merely the scientists and the rationalists who believe that they can eventually make the earthly life exactly as they want it to be by the powers of scientific knowledge and social rationality.

As stated earlier, the development of science and technology is not an evil phenomenon in itself. It is inevitable and even essential to some extent for the evolution of human activity. But their misuse is emerging as an evil. It has created an unbalanced situation tilted towards one-sided extremism at the cost of faith and spirituality. Modern society needs a spiritual complement to the impressive achievements of science. It needs a new spiritual dynamism to balance the extreme advancement of science so as to nourish mind and soul simultaneously. It is often questioned why the existing religious modes have not been able to check the growth of materialism. This is partly because the religious practices, over the times, have become devitalized and uninspiring. A new spiritual impulse is needed to revive the core values of life. What is important is that the spiritual impulse needs to be seeded in every heart? The time has come that humankind must wake up to this purpose and become aware of the spiritual truths.

Human beings are generally considered to be rational animals with several distinct features such as their faculty of speech, their erect physical postures and their sphere of mental operations to help them in discrimination between right and wrong. Moreover, human beings are the only species gifted with full consciousness and memory which is their exclusive privilege. Their potentialities still further enable them to surpass the animals in a totally different way to lead them to an altogether higher world of being. There are no living beings other than the human beings who can reason abstractly and attain metaphysical thought. It is the human beings who are bestowed with the power to become conscious of themselves as spiritual being. If the human beings are nothing other than the materialists and rationalists, then they should be quite contented with their mental finitude and their physical appetites. It is wrong and erroneous to think of human beings as nothing more than the bodies. On the contrary **human beings, which include scientists and intellectuals also, has valuable characteristics which elevate and distinguish them from animals: faith in the unseen higher power called God, humility, reverence and the capacity to pray to**

God. No other living beings on the earth other than the human beings are able to invent, discover, discriminate, communicate and contemplate the mysteries of nature, universe and concept of God, much less than the idea of their own spiritual beings with an intuitive feeling to the full blooming of the higher experience of the self which is generally called the soul within. It is this that links them to the Universal Mind or the God, and gives them a ray of the ultimate experience.

It is a question of faith that all things in nature and the universe are being guided by an Infinite Mind. Only intuition can tell quite definitely that this belief is true. There is no other path confronting science than the path leading from physical reality to the metaphysical truth, from observation to illumination found by the mind, from concrete results to their abstract meaning, and from the materialistic physics to the mentalistic meta-physics. It is then and only then that the soul's reality can be known, and the Spiritual Self can reveal its nature. Then and only then the questions such as: **What is God**? **Who is God**? **Where is God**? **Why should one believe in God**? among many more, get answered and the truth gets revealed. Reason must check feeling but it must not be allowed to replace feeling. Intellect with intuition is a blessing to human beings only up to a certain degree, beyond that it turns into a veritable curse for them. The sturdy struggle of reason against feeling and self-interest against self-realization is an unending process. Faith is the foundation. It is an axiom on which the human edifice is to be raised.

There is, and there can be one and only one Universal Truth which is called God. It is eternal. It is realized and discovered in many ways. It reveals and manifests in various forms. It never changes or evolves. Only its form of manifestation changes. Before it appears in the world, it must find human minds sufficiently prepared to be able to receive it and sufficiently developed to be able to grasp it. It appears in the form of divine incarnations or prophets or seers. This happens as and when the world is confronted with a spiritual crisis and large-scale turmoil. The cosmic laws survive even amidst the greatest catastrophes and chaos. It is because of the cosmic laws that the sun rises everyday and the planets move in a perfect order without ever colliding with one-another in accordance with certain laws of planetary motion, termed as Kepler's Laws after the name of an Austrian astronomer J. Kepler (1571-1630). It is to be noted that these are divine cosmic laws not evolved but only discovered by Kepler. Thus, Kepler cannot be given the credit of originating these laws. If there were no such laws, their discovery by the use of human free-will would be meaningless. Human life receives its full significance only when such a will can be exercised. These cosmic laws are the divine laws which express the will of God. It is, therefore, natural for the human beings to seek to know what these cosmic divine laws are, and who is that God who generates and governs these laws.

Spiritual crisis, as and when it occurs, is a world crisis. It is not merely a continental or national crisis. It touches the whole humanity, and not merely a section of it. Such an external phenomenon is in line with the extraordinary internal phenomenon which brings a turning point in the spiritual evolution – something of the inherent divine phenomenon. The divine phenomenon does not work quite like an architect at work. The divine phenomenon should be understood to mean not only an architectural plan or pictorial drawing board but the inherent necessity whereby its manifestations follow a certain order. Everything in the cosmos is passing through various stages of unfoldment. Since it originates as a divine phenomenon, all the possibilities of such an unfoldment from lowest to the highest are inherent in it, they do not have to be planned for they are already existent as a part of the divine phenomenon.

Why should the law of change dominate the world of physical forms as well as human affairs? Why cannot a permanent socially and spiritually stable system be created and maintained for ever so as to pre-empt the recurring socio-spiritual crisis? For answers to such fundamental questions, there is a need to investigate the secret structure of every atom which is nothing but 'a ceaseless vibration'. Similarly, every human mind is a perpetual birth place of a progeny of ideas. This is the very nature of the human mind. But these observations remain half-truths unless they are augmented with the basic fact that behind every atom in every human mind, there is an everlasting stillness or Silence of God. This is the rhythmic evolution – a feature of the divine, of which human evolution is the most important component. Human evolution works through three successive phases: the physical, the intellectual and the spiritual. For the human entity to develop its capacities, it has to combine its self-centeredness with all the three phases – namely the physical capacities, mental capabilities and spiritual potentialities. The spiritual component of the human evolution is the only way to remove obstacles of its own animalistic and demonic tendencies to overcome the spiritual crisis.

As and when the spiritual crisis arises, humanity is led to the cross-roads. It needs to pause and think. The cosmic journey has to choose whether or not it has come to the end of its severest evolutionary cycle. Deeper into darkness, it will not be allowed to go. Higher into light it cannot go. Forces both inside and outside themselves wage a titanic war for its right and wrong guidance. The result is clash and conflict within the humanity itself. All the evils in humanity's character emerge on the surface. Horror and violence, lust and greed, fear and hate, envy and jealously get openly glorified. Strengthened with sins and sloths, destruction and disasters become inevitable. This is the time when the humanity begins to renounce its ego and surrender sovereignty in favour of the Divine. The change in thought and feeling as a preface to a change in humanity's tragic fortunes is an absolute necessity. The change of heart becomes inevitable. Negative attitudes need to be curbed and evil deeds need to be stopped. Spiritual practices have to take over to overcome the social crisis. A total change of the attitudes, a large renunciation of the materialistic outlook and a quick reversal of spiritual indifference become the only ways to ensure a transformation of the humanity. This has been the divine message, for such times. Thousands of years ago, India's sacred book, **'The Bhagvat Gita'** proclaimed that peace and prosperity will return on the earth only when a divine being appears to show the path of truth and righteousness – the two foundational axioms of spirituality, and convince the humanity that its ultimate destiny is to become spiritualized.

Humanity in socio-spiritual crisis can find a way to come out of critical times only through spiritual values. The divinity within the human beings always exist. Only its presence within the self is to be realized. The faith, which humbly acknowledges the existence of this divine power is a true instinct planted in the heart of humanity. It is supported by realization although for a moment it may be throttled by the excessive use of logic and rationality. Let there be no shame in kneeling down in prayer for realization of such a faith and communion with the divine power. A great and holy mystery lies enshrined in such a socio-spiritual crisis. When humanity finds itself with its back against an impassable wall, when it seems to reach the utmost limit of disasters, when the agony of utter helplessness crushes it down, then it stands close, very close, to the door. "Knock and it shall be open unto you", means a total concentration on the divine is what is required. Since self-surrender to the Divine in the fullest humility is all that is required. Relief will mysteriously appear and the rescuing hands will emerge. Courage will rise and the strength to support will come. That is the stage of realization of the presence of the Divine, that is the invention of God.

The reality behind this divine phenomenon of pains and pleasures, fortunes and misfortunes, agony and malady is attributed to the consequences of actions/deeds done earlier. This reality is an infinite wisdom inherent in the cosmic plan which momentarily (temporarily) gets overshadowed. The whole creative movement of this wonderful cosmos is a constant reminder of the Universal Mind whose presence is everywhere and expression of whose genius is visible everywhere. This Universal Mind manifests in every part or element of the cosmos and it is behind the life of every creature. This supreme, infinite and all knowing Universal Mind is always at work and it never rests. Spiritual philosophy openly admits that mostly circumstances, events and happenings, whether pleasurable or painful, are certainly divine doings in accordance with the divine constitution. It is, therefore, certainly true that there are situations when there is no other alternative (option) except the humble submission to the divine will with the faith that divine wisdom is interlinked with their occurrences. Tragedies and troubles happen under a divine law which brings most of them as the consequence to the unworthy deeds and thoughts.

Human beings are ordained in accordance with their own actions. Their destiny is self-earned, partly during the present times and partly in past times or wholly during the present or the past. Nobody is punished or rewarded by God who sits remote from the struggles and strives carried out by the human beings in their own way. Everybody has to bear the consequences of his/her deeds in accordance with the provision of the divine constitution. People earn punishment because of their own sins and misdeeds. The divine laws are impelling everything and everyone onward and upward. Those who are spiritually shortsighted (or poor) do not know what is good for them. Sometimes sufferings come to the people under the evolutionary law of the divine will to help them develop better character, evolve moral qualities and foster more intelligence. This is termed as a process of illumination when the pain of sorrow, frustration or depression is realized. It is only in that moment, that the mind is put to test to overcome its bitterness, and mitigate its pain of suffering it perceives. It is only then that the divine power is there to befriend it. For the person who is striving to become spiritually conscious, the distresses and sorrows provide him/her a stimulus to learn the aspects of truth and/or righteousness. Human actions are largely determined and their corresponding consequences are mostly destined accordingly by no other power than the human beings themselves. Failure to understand such a cosmic law, and the defiance to disobey it are responsible for the sorrows and miseries.

Pure religion is the faith by human beings in a secret and invisible divine power higher than themselves. Its proper functions are: to instill into its believers a firm belief in a higher divine power and to sustain it; to bring people into communion with this divine power and to inculcate in them the path of devotion; to make them better in character and nobler in conduct; and to relieve them of miseries and sufferings. Religion teaches the people not only that God exists but also what is their relationship with God. Religion is the most widespread, the most popular, and the most fundamental source of righteous conduct. It is consequently the most powerful means of reforming the human society. Its inescapable duty is to foster faith in God. However, religious fanatics seem to have failed it, though partially, in respect of the religious functions and practices. Some of the causes of the partial failure of religions may be attributed to the fact that the religious people have not been true to themselves. The real aim has been often contradicted by their paradigms. Pure religion teaches its followers to overcome prejudices and animosities towards others. Unfortunately fundamental principles of each and every religion have been deeply and darkly stained with unreligious thoughts and unfaithful practices. Another cause that can be attributed is that the modern society, especially the younger generation, wants to investigate for themselves in order to use their own judgment on the basis of the evidences available to them and not blindly accept them as religious truths. Two tremendous factors namely progressive science and aggressive rationality seem to have influenced the religious thinking process. The modern youth wants to examine scientifically and understand rationally the religious philosophy and its paradigm. Scriptural writings and religious discourses no longer impress the young minds while beliefs, rituals and traditions do not appeal to them.

While rationalism to some extent liberates religion from its superstitions and degenerates religious practices, the extreme opposition to religion becomes a retrogressive factor and leads to rabid materialism which declines faith in the divine power called God. It is a historic fact that there have been conflicts resulting into loss of human life, it is equally true that religious clashes have also been accompanied by social upheavals. When disbelief in religion flourishes and morality vanishes, when human aspects of society deteriorate, then no real peace and lasting moral progress is possible. Despite defects in religious practices, an organized religion does bring about enough good to the society. When the religious principles are not binding, when the religious ethics is set aside and when the religious philosophy is denounced, then a dangerous situation becomes inevitable. The adverse effects of disbelief in the existence of divine power manifest in moral crisis and selfishness leading to chaos and confusion. Pure religion itself is divine and enduring, but religious dogmas and rituals generate human exploitation.

The skeptics lose faith in model teaching about God, and they develop misplaced notions about spirituality. Such persons, then, become not only religiously irrational but also socially irrelevant.

Why is there conflict among religions? Swami Vivekananda said: **"Every religion has three components – philosophy and ethics, mythology and rituals, celebrations and ceremonies. The more evolved followers focus on the philosophical aspects of faith, novitiates tend to be drawn to mythology. Still others tend to settle for ritualistic and ceremonial aspects of religion. All the three are valid forms on the path of the seeker, provided mythology and ritual do not overshadow or obliterate the philosophy that is the core**." Indeed, there need not be any conflict or competition when it comes to matters of faith and religion. But due to the argumentative nature of the religious people, they rarely tend to agree with what someone else holds to be the truth. No two people can fully agree on what they mean by the term 'God'. To each of them, the concept of a Supreme Power has come to mean whatever, they want it to mean, or whatever they have been told about it, learnt, or know from their own experiences.

Is it possible to establish a direct connection with the Divine Power called God? Perhaps that would depend upon what is meant by the term God. Some people feel that God exists only in a remote, inaccessible place called Heaven, with unlimited powers and a most accurate judgmental nature, and think that attaining to the Supreme Power is possible only after having led a virtuous life or die first to have a direct experience of God. But if they were to broaden the definition of God to see God as the energy source behind creation, then they can indeed have the divine experience, every minute of their living.

Vedanta talks of an infinite God, in the form of Brahmn, which is all-pervading and which in its manifest form (Prakriti) is the reason and cause for creation, maintenance and destruction of all that is seen and which being energy is formless and shapeless, unbound by time and space. It is nowhere and everywhere. It resides in every hearts, in human beings in animals, insects, rocks, mountains and the sky, for instance. It is Omniscient, Omnipresent and Omnipotent. Most religions would agree with the definition that God is indeed infinite and all-powerful.

At the root of every religion there are core concepts. But when the believers move from core concepts towards the mythology or ritualistic part of religion, things become different and divergent. If a person is truly religious, irrespective of his religious inclinations, he would see the unity in diversity and the oneness of all life on earth. Why the believers don't see that all this is because the mythology and rituals of religion have overshadowed the principles which got mistaken for the core values of the religion itself, and which eventually have become the religion. This is the myth that Swami Vivekananda constantly tried to demystify. The core principles of all religions are easy to list and most are familiar namely: faith in God, love, compassion, honesty, altruism, selflessness, forgiveness, sensitivity, sympathy or empathy, sharing, caring, kindness, charity, protection of virtues, the effort to overcome negative qualities, prayer and gratitude for all that they have.

Thus, it is highly desirable to develop a proper understanding of religion. Its great conventions, traditions, methods and forms need to be expounded in a positive manner. Religious practice needs to demonstrate its usefulness on the social scene. This is possible only when its sponsors and exponents begin to make religion relevant to the modern society, meaningful to the social need, helpful to overcome the moral crisis and instrumental to social harmony. Both rationality and science are capable of giving the human society material and mental support for survival, but none can give precisely what religion alone gives. Scientific factor and logic cannot of themselves nourish the soul of a human being. The transcendental needs of the soul can never be replaced by any substitutes of science or rationality. A grave error made by the scientists and rationalists is that they are often the first to oppose and the last to accept any manifestation of the living spirit of the Divine Power. This they do so when they can find help from nowhere else. Spiritual harmony is an inward and not an outward fact of life. It must grow by itself out of an awakening to the fact that disharmony is the cause of constant misery and suffering. The ideals of self-discipline, self-improvement and sense-control are indeed practical, sensible and essential. These ideals uphold the dignity of human life, proclaim the divine potentialities and inculcate the reality of the moral order.

Divine Revelation is possible even in the present age as it was possible in the previous epochs or aeons open to every caste, every race, every community, and every nation. It is universally potential since God is not only Omni-potent but also Omni-present and Omni-scient. That which is Omni-present cannot be the property or monopoly of a particular race, people or sect. The spiritual seekers born anywhere in the world can realize God anywhere, in anything, at any time and by any mode of worship or by following any religion. It is wrong to believe that philosophy holds one religion better than the other. An idea or paradigm or institution or religion which appeals and effectively helps an individual to adopt a spiritual path, cannot be dismissed as worthless or inferior merely because it does not attract or appeal some individuals in any way. An appropriate and deep study of comparative religions of the world can wipe out bigotry and misgivings about various religious teachings and practices. The ultimate source of all authentic religious truths is one and the same – the Higher Self called the Divinity, and that this explains why the best ideas of such truths are common to different people and different epochs. It is obligatory to hold every religion in high esteem, no matter what particular one is followed or thought of or pondered over, by feeling its reality and obeying its spiritual or religious principles.

The appearance of a spiritual teacher or a religious leader or a prophet indicates the existence of one and the same source of creative and transformative divine power. The work of a prophet or a divine messenger is essentially two fold: to plant a gift of divine grace in the hearts of the people so that it gets transmitted down through some centuries in ever-widening ripples; and to give the divine message which prudently caters to the needs of that time or appeals to the thought – forms of the people. The dissemination of the divine grace or divine message gets bedimmed with the passage of time, not because of its inherent power but because of the generational decadence which is somewhat natural. However, the prophet truly possesses the divine power to bestow grace, whereas after the lapse of centuries many who speak in his name mostly lack the divine impact. Consequently the religions evaporate during the long lapse of centuries. For this an evolutionary path needs to be laid down for the human beings that leads them from the foundational base of their character upward to the noblest. It should be designed to raise them far above the level of sub-conscious or unconscious or semi-conscious animality. Spirituality, the core philosophy of every religion is the first right step in this direction. But sooner or later, the followers must continue their journey and go all the way along that road. The real requirement, however, which spirituality or for that matter religion expects from the human beings is faith – simple and firm, the faith that a divine power exists and sustains everything. Faith is essential for an intimate affinity with God. It is only through this intimate affinity based on the firm faith that one can find a reflection of the divine power and 'invent God'.

1.2 Spiritual Paradoxes

Simultaneous logical validity of two apparently irreconcilable consistencies is what may be termed as a paradox. The paradoxical situations not only look to be true when put together but they also constitute a greater truth than either of them alone can hold. When a paradox prevails, logic gets diluted or it fails. Paradox tends to transcend logic, whereas logic inferentially sustains paradox. This is quite common in spiritual parlance.

According to logic, not only one side of an assertion should be given the weightage but equally the other side should not be ignored particularly when both sides of the same assertion look to be valid, consistent and interlinked. The two sides are sometimes respectively called the Absolute Reality and the Relative Reality. The Absolute Reality in the context of spirituality is the truth known as God while the Relative Reality is that truth which a human being generally knows or sees, termed as the Universe. In the sense of Absolute Reality, the Universe is merely a mental construct, an illusion (maya) which to the human mind, appears to be real. An individual soul, being a part of the Supreme Soul – the Universe, cannot perceive the Brahmn (the Supreme Soul). This is a spiritual paradox which reflects the essence of the Absolute Reality verses the Relative Reality, while both Absolute and Relative are accepted realities. Moreover, God, in the sense of Absolute Reality transcends 'religiosity' as is commonly known but in the sense of Relative Reality, God abides in all religions.

To the puzzle, whether God is immanent or God is transcendent, the appropriate explanation would be neither this only nor that only because God is both immanent and transcendent. Thus, the paradox denies, "either/or", kind of approach but encourages "both/and" type of approach. God is described as the essence of light and also as mystery (darkness).

God – the Almighty, the Brahmn is referred as 'Kalatit' (timeless or beyond time) transcending time while in another sense, the Brahmn means the infinite extending over countless time. In the former sense, Brahmn has neither any beginning nor any end. Hence it is designated as 'Anaadi' and 'Anaant". 'Ana' here denotes 'sans', 'adi' for beginning, and 'ant' for the end. But in another sense, Brahmn is designated as 'Adi' (from the very beginning) and described as Adi Brahmn (Primal Being) or 'Brahmn Ant' (Last Being). The former sense refers to the Absolute or Supreme Reality while the later sense pertains to the Relative aspect of the same Reality. This is also a paradoxical situation. Further 'Kaal' means 'Death' because over the time, things die or vanish. God, however, is considered to be 'Akaal' *i.e.* immortal. But God is also considered to be the cause of mortality of His Creation. This means that the death (end) of time or the death of the death, both are relative aspects of the same Absolute Reality. Again, in the sense of Absolute Reality, God is 'the one' (ekai) but in the Relative Sense, He is many (anekai), for He is all pervasive through the multiplicity of His creation termed sometimes as one in many and many in one *i.e.* multiform spectacle, or a paradoxical spectacle.

Every form of life or creation is finite and limited. It involves sorrows and joys. Every human being aspires for happiness unmixed with sorrow, a life unbroken with death, a health unafflicted by sickness, a freedom unhindered by restrictions, a knowledge unfermented by questions, and a harmony without instability. This paradoxical riddle, which confronts every human being, may be viewed from many points of view, of which two are most prominent: one that there is the practical, personal, obvious and immediate aspect; and the other that there is the metaphysical, impersonal, profound and ultimate aspect. The fact, however, remains that very few individuals are really in a position to contemplate their own lives and fortunes with the genuine detachment demanded by the metaphysical approach. The reason being that the human view is naturally based upon the finite reactions, limited senses, short-range perceptions and low perspectives. Three reasons are evident enough: first, people rarely stop to weigh their own distresses against those of others; second, they are inclined to lament their hard fate, and rarely balance their troubles against their outcomes; and the third, when their personal situation works out to their advantage, they are often satisfied with their achievements, but if it does not, they become discontented with the world as it is and blame God. This is due to their failure to view life from a spiritual perspective with its special features namely: the truth of the law of 'Karma'; and the path of spirituality.

The question, however, arises: **Why does God**, if **He exists, permit such spiritual paradoxes?** Why are virtuous and noble human beings oppressed and stifled under the duress of evils, vicious and wicked forces which brutalize and degrade them? Such worse conditions of sufferings due to cruelties make the sufferers feel in utter despair that either God does not care for them or even God Himself does not exist at all. It is, then, they ask: "**Where are the signs of the Divine Existence in such happenings**? Indeed, there can be no correct answers to such questions unless the human minds are cleared of such confusions which arise not only in the mind of a gross materialist but even in the mind of a spiritual seeker or in the mind of an enlightened rationalist. Many people get prompted by their compassion for the suffering creatures and human beings which lead them to disbelieve or lose faith in the very existence of God. But such 'compassionate' disbelievers should not be led to believe also, in their limited, finite and dim understanding that the Universal and Infinite Intelligence called God is capable of making any mistake. Such paradoxical impressions about God need not suggest that life's sorrows and sufferings are meaningless or purposeless in the divine framework.

Does it occur to the doubters or disbelievers that the normal attitude towards sufferings, destruction and death is not the attitude with which the divine system works? Whether a painful experience, is **really an evil or a virtue,** is **largely relative to the** specific character of **the situation or the sufferer**? The answers to such questions could be in the form of counter questions namely: **Why does the same nature, which gives pleasing summer showers and soothing cool breezes, also gives scorching hot summers and biting cold winters? Why do same universal laws, which bring the bright light of the day give deep darkness of the midnight? Why does the same Infinite Power, which upgrades the human beings through their fumbling steps towards self-realization, permit them to fall and bruise themselves? If the goal of humanity is to unfold spirituality, and to achieve that goal, if it is driven by the pressures of sufferings and pains, then why should the Divine Power permit such drastic and painful happenings**? Those who take the trouble and look deep beneath appearances for realities, may even see in these very happenings the vindication of the divine's care for humanity and demonstration of its dexterous working in the universe. The tides of fortune and misfortune, pleasure and pain, prosperity and poverty, ebb and flow are for all. Nobody can alter this divine law, as nobody can afford to ignore it. It is this tantalizing realization that constitutes the general human experience. Either in reflective moods inspired by such living experiences or prompted by several other happenings in the world, people feel vaguely that there must be some kind of grander and nobler being than the limited earthly common human being, which is non-apparent and invisible to them. But when sufferings or sorrows emphasize the tremendous contrast between the two, then only arises the stirring question of exploring that nobler and grander force. Then and only then, the quest for the search or invention of that higher power or Divine Being begins. What is this mysterious paradox?

God is called "**The Merciful**", as and when fortunate events happen to people while opposite epithet as, "**The Merciless**" is used for the same God if unfortunate events take place. If people feel grateful to God for pleasant things, they should equally and logically be grateful to Him for the unpleasant things also. But they are not. To say that the divine powers of God have created a crisis of human destiny in order to enable human beings to face the inner challenge is true. To say that human conduct has created it, is also true. The two complementary situations must be put together to get the whole truth about the pleasant and unpleasant events which overtake the humanity. It would be wiser, therefore, to stop attributing both good and bad to God, and ascribe them to the true source, which is mostly in the human beings themselves. This is a **psychological paradox** which has been created by the people themselves and not by God or His divine power. People usually ask for divine blessings in the form of material benefits and worldly advantages. Such people do not know that the divine blessings can come even in the form of physical sorrows and worldly misfortunes also. A deeper reflection, however, during the course of time may enable them to perceive the hidden joy in the apparent sorrow. The today's sufferers may become tomorrow's seekers. The divine paradigm of human therapeutic treatment involves the use of sorrows and sufferings as some of unavoidable cures. In the great epic of Mahabharata, Kunti, the queen mother of the five Pandava brothers pleads with Lord Krishna and urges Him to give her sons more sufferings and hardships lest they forget God. For, the divine wisdom ordains the divine laws which in turn ordain that the human beings must pass through the tests of hardships leading them to the path of God-realization.

The real meaning of sufferings gets revealed only when its complete picture is brought out including both bright and dark sides. If the governing laws of the universe were not beneficient, there would be no hope for humanity. But on the contrary, there is every reason for the better hope since evils and virtues of life have only a passing existence relative to the pains and pleasures of life. Existence of both good and bad laws is controlled by the systemic and systematic divine laws. **How could a universe be visualized without virtues and vices, light and darkness, joy and sorrow, pain and pleasure**? If sufferings and sorrows were the only way out for spiritual development, then the divine phenomenon could rightly be accused of being merciless rather than being merciful. Indeed, to refuse a place for suffering in the divine plan when people judge it solely by their finite and limited human capacities, is to detract from an objective analysis of the divine phenomenon. This is another paradoxical situation which may be termed as 'judgmental paradox'.

Divine incarnations such as prophets and messengers among others leave a divine message for the people to follow for their spiritual upliftment. This divine message eventually takes the shape of an institutionalized doctrine or religion. Spiritual philosophy is the common base of every religion. Spirituality is for everybody including the religious preachers or followers of any type. Spiritual philosophy extends religion beyond its sectarianism, for it rectifies and eliminates the limitations of religion. Religion is most suitable to the masses while its philosophy is best suited to the intellectuals. The real purpose of codified religion is to lead the common people step by step from the lower to loftier stages of spirituality. The spiritual philosophy includes and contains religion as a cult of worshipping God, but is not itself limited to religious codes and practices. The frontiers of spirituality are much wider and its explorations are much deeper. **Religion, metaphysics, mysticism and philosophy are the four basic features of spirituality. Religion engages and strengthens faith in God, metaphysics develops the intellect, mysticism motivates intuition and philosophy leads to the highest stage of awakening and realization.** It is again paradoxical to note that while divine incarnations, prophets and messengers of various religions preached love and harmony, their priests have been found propagating wrongly and misinterpreting religious doctrines.

The scriptures of Hinduism like Ramayana and Mahabharata firmly stemmed in the Vedic roots promote peace and harmony. They do not mention any kind of creation and discrimination of communities on the basis of castes. What has been stated in Manusmriti is not to be interpreted as creation of castes but merely an observation of the four types of tasks that were prescribed. Unfortunately, it were the later Hindu priests and protagonists who in close collaboration with the then ruling classes created discrimination and hatred among the four categories of people to suit their selfish and vested ends. As a result, religion and caste were used as instruments of class conflicts in Hinduism to achieve territorial, commercial and material gains. As a result more blood was shed in the name of caste and religion which to-date continues in various parts of India. Thus, while Hinduism as a spiritual philosophy advocates tolerance, truth, righteousness, love and peace, its religious preachers, and some fanatic elements, most often, propagate hatred against those who do not subscribe to their view point. This is a paradoxical situation in Hinduism.

A somewhat similar religious paradox exists in the case of various organized monolithic religions of the world *viz.* Buddhism, Zoroastrism, Christianity, Islam and Sikhism among several other cults and creeds. While founders of these religions were simple and humble beings. They were indeed divine prophets and messengers who gave the message of love and harmony to all. The Buddha, Mahavir, Jesus, Mohammed and

Nanak promoted love, peace and harmony. The tradition of tolerance is well-known in Christianity like Hinduism. Also, the Quran repeatedly affirmed peace and harmony and asserted no compulsion in religion. Most religious scriptures took shape after their founders were gone. It was Ashoka who, 200 years after the Buddha, expanded the preaching of Buddhism too far off places, St. Peter and St. Paul gave shape to Christianity much after the crucifixation of Jesus Christ. But for the first four Khalifs, the message of Prophet Mohammed would have remained a hidden philosophy of desert. But for the works of later Sikh Gurus, Nanak might have remained just one of the mystic sage or a saint. All such religions took shape containing the original message of their founders to promote peace and harmony which unfortunately get misdirected because of the vested interests of the priests and the rulers. The easy targets of caste-based and religion-based discriminations have been the poor and ignorant. Thus, the original message of peace and harmony given by the divine prophets and messengers is distorted by some of their followers to serve their vested interests. This is again a paradoxical face of various religions or their followers.

The phenomenal advancement of science during the last three centuries of the second millennium, together with the dominant impact of extreme rationality increasingly made religion and spirituality irrelevant to the needs of the human society. This trend got augmented by the advent of modern information and communication technology during the last leg of twentieth century. The spiritual vacuum created by excessive technological advancement on one hand, and the socialist ideologies, on the other, generated an acute thirst for the human needs of religious philosophies and ethics. Thus, paradoxically enough, the new millennium, which contributed to the tremendous advancement of science and technology, also saw the powerful revival of religion and spirituality as an essential ingredient of social harmony. Yet, another paradox is the renewal of faith in some supreme divine power called God by the ever increasing number of people thronging to the religious discourses, travelling to various places of pilgrimage. At times tens of millions of people gather at just one place to celebrate an auspicious occasion or listen to their revered religious or spiritual leader. This is perhaps the most perceptible dichotomous situation of the convergence of science and spirituality.

An impression is, sometimes, generated that a total acceptance of the divine will and passive resignation to each situation or event linked with the will of God, deprives the human beings of the chance to struggle and develop intelligence. Blind acceptance of every event and apathetic submission in the face of every situation means failure to exercise one's own free will. For, every time a mechanical submission presumable to the will of God, may, on occasions, cause self-deception, laziness and selfishness. It questions the assertion that they are necessarily God's will and, therefore, unchangeable. **There is a paradox here**: On one hand, there is the choice of the benumbing mystical belief of leaving everything to the will of God, and on the other, there is an arrogant materialistic idea of everything being done by human beings.

Sages and spiritualists believe that all this happens because of God's sweet will, while the rationalists and non-believers say that events follow a pattern either due to chance or free will. This dichotomic conflict between the God's will and free will has been going on from time immemorial, and may continue till either faith in God overtakes the logic or otherwise logic prevails upon faith. Several attempts have been made to reconcile the two theories.

The rationalists wrongly assume the concept of God as someone sitting in the high sky with a Supreme powerful computer with the capacity of operating and controlling trillions of commands every nano second. That is how they perceive the Universe. The spiritual scientists and philosophers on the contrary believe that there is Supreme Being called the Brahmn who alone exists and everything else is its manifestation including the whole Universe. In its impersonal aspect, it is pure Existence (Truth)-Consciousness-Bliss (Sachhidanand) who is the controller of all things in the Universe through its three manifestations of Generation, Organization and Dissolution caused by its Supreme inscrutable power, called Maya or Shakti. Hence, there can never be a free will. Swami Vivekananda Said, "Free will means nothing – sheer non-sense." The free will is only the crazy dance of their senses for their respective objects, powered by the existence of **Atman** (Soul or Spirit).

The Brahmn is the impelling force both at micro and macro-levels. Brahmn as God is the conscious principle at the macro level behind the Universe where as this conscious principle, at micro-level, is the Omniscient (Antaryamin), pure consciousness and hence Brahmn itself. While God is the personalized aspect of the Brahmn in a manifest Universe, there is an inherent identity between individual soul (consciousness) and God, the cosmic consciousness. At the micro-level whatever the individual souls do, the source of their action is Atman whereas at macro level, God is the mover of energy itself which makes the Universe to function. Not a blade of grass can move without His will.

Religion asserts unity of human efforts with the divine grace, and the surrender of consequences to the Higher Will. Such an attitude gives up the expectations and anxiety about the results, and thus keeps its inner peace, working harmony and mental contentment. Leaving everything to the Will of God and doing nothing of their own Will make the human beings lazy and lethargic. Such a negative attitude of life termed as extreme asceticism cannot be termed as religious. A balance needs to be maintained between the worldly needs and the religious goals.

In this case, the exhortation by the Bhagvat Gita, the song celetial, dispels all the confusion talked about. It succinctly classifies that any action done with an eye on the results (desirable or undesirable) would rob an action of its moral quotient, the righteous action should be done for its own sake and not for profit. To say that 'honesty is the best policy' is only a pragmatic stance and not virtuous one. Poverty is not the gateway to spirituality neither excessive richness leads to the path of disbelief in God. The better way calls for an appropriate synthesis of materialism with spiritualism. Materialistic acquisitions or possessions are not necessarily anti-spiritual. Wealth and luxury are no obstacle to the quest of spiritual wisdom. There is no evil in the desire and pursuits of materialistic possession. Evils begin only when the inner spiritual goal of life is discarded for the sake of sensual pleasure and physical luxuries. Spiritual philosophy neither advocates extreme asceticism nor excessive materialism. Attending to basic needs of life is as important as treading the path of spirituality. Human beings should realize that life is not to be wasted in the quest of material or sensual pleasures lest the values of a higher purpose of life breakdown and faith in the higher power is lost. Total concentration only on materialism, leads to a self-deceptive outlook culminating only in dangerous and painful disillusionment. The heaviest self-retribution comes when the Supreme Reality is treated as the extreme triviality. A humble submission to the Supreme Reality – God with a firm faith in Him based on reflective and profound thinking does not prelude the intelligent self-effort. The submission which spirituality asserts is perceptive and not blind. Plato's precept to Aristotle says, "**Be sure that all punishment which is inflicted upon human beings is not to be treated as tyranny of God, but that it is correction and instruction**". Virtues and vices are two in-built features of human activity. Their vivid interest between the two makes a person much more conscious of the relevance of the higher divine power called God. Without the experience of both, the human being cannot distinguish good from evil, bliss from curse and truth from falsehood. The consciousness of the sound can be realized only in comparison with the consciousness of the silence. The world-process is inescapably a paradoxical interplay and inter-struggle between the creative and destructive forces, between the vices and the virtues, and between the evil and good.

Human beings have enough freedom to chalk out their own destiny. Both virtues and vices are mixed into their temperaments and attitudes. When the vices increase in volume and become massive in strength, they inevitably lead to consequences which are dangerous and destructive. The terrible and sinful reality of the evil, and its horrifying havoc in human life cannot be denied. The type of vices, which are so prevalent in the form of evils, glorify brutality, justify oppression, ridicule religion and deride consciousness. People often ask: "**Why does the Higher Divine Power, which is universally regarded as beneficient, permit these vices to threaten humanity**"? A parallel and closely linked question arises: "**Could the World-Idea of His Divine Power be completely accomplished for humanity without the existence of vices**"? This again is a situation of religious paradox. If the Divine Power has to bring every human entity to full moral, intellectual and spiritual realization, the range of human experience has to be adequately wide and evenly contrasting. Restricting this range to the virtues and to restrain the human experience only to the non-evil, would render impossible the full purpose of human consciousness. This is after all not merely a matter of morality but equally of knowledge and consciousness. There is indeed no other way than the prevalent one – a mix of virtues and vices, in which humanity could have found all the conditions necessary for the development of all its faculties. The mere fact that the higher Divine Power allows the existence of vices and evils shows that it is temporary and utilitarian but inevitable in the functioning and management of the universe. **The need, therefore, is to explore some glimmering of this paradoxical pattern of the universe – management with a view to understand as to why do good and decent people face distress resulting from the evil activities of vicious persons, why there is so much crime and violence in the world, why the vices are so abundant, occurring in a divinely ordered system**?

The materialistic view treats vices as a by-product of the social environments and unavoidable circumstances which can be set right by the mere setting right the social functioning and living conditions. According to some spiritual philosophers, the evils and vices have something to do with the divine phenomenon. The free will of the people has created so much of the evils and distress in the world is obvious but the situation itself could not have emerged without the will of the higher Divine Mind. With partial or total freedom for the human beings to act, they are not given choice to select a certain race, a certain country, a particular family, a particular economic status, a condition of good health or ill-health, and an abundance or lack of energy, intellect, will and intuition. All this is dictated by nature, Karma-based fate or the cosmic plans, designed by the higher divine power called God under which no human entity can deviate from this cosmic plan, with complete autonomy, and determine its course with total freedom. The freedom of total entities is limited as their power is dependant. The human beings do not possess absolute free will. It is controlled by the inexorable cosmic will and divine constitution with provisions of Karma-based consequences, since the whole cosmos is emanation of the Divine Mind. Therefore, it is not only the ignorance or misuse of the free-will of the human being that accounts for the human vices but also the cosmic plan of the divine constitution itself, which is something beyond the control and operations of their will. This is God's world which is His manifestation. Therefore, whatever good or bad, evil or virtue, pleasant and unpleasant, which looks to be man-made, is not entirely true. Everywhere, there are signs of the Divine Power working. But the human eyes, that are not spiritually opened, naturally fail to see them. What people see in the present world's scenario and past history depends upon what they are in themselves. They have to find deeper meaning in their own nature. The discovery of a divine self in their own heart will be a pointing finger to the invention of a divine mind behind the whole universe to which they belong.

As the human entity evolves in knowledge and consciousness, it changes its view as to what is bad, what is evil or what is not evil, what is right or wrong. Its highest change results from the discovery or invention of the divine self when the relativity of vices becomes perfectly clear and visible. **If, from one of the philosophical points of view, vice is an illusion and if the virtue is the opposite of vice, surely must not virtue itself then be an illusion**? The answer is that there are two types of '**virtue**': '**relative**' and '**absolute**'. The relative virtue is true opposite of 'vice' and is illusory. The absolute virtue is the one which is a quality of the One Infinite Absolute Power, this is the real virtue. Both virtues and vices have been assigned roles in human development from its very origin. They have not appeared by accident or by any unexpected mishap. They have not been introduced against the Divine Will by some satanic power. The fall into sin and the experience of the consequent pain are integral parts of the Cosmic Plan. They are neither cosmic accidents nor cosmic mistakes. The Divine Wisdom is as much at work in them as anywhere else. What is at fault is human perception, human impatience and human limitation. All seemingly wrongs and apparent evils must have a rational place in the Cosmic Order including the sufferings and joys, sorrows and pleasures. They cannot be considered as mistakes in the divine planning and its universal functioning. The Cosmos is to be grasped as a single whole in the infinite consciousness of the Divine Mind. If there is a single supreme principle of Being in the cosmos, if all things and all creatures have emanated from it and if the whole universe or creation is the manifestation of the Will of that Supreme Power, then what in the workings of this cosmos are called the vices or evils as well as what are called sufferings and sorrows also have emanated from the same source. Since this Supreme Power is the only ever-existing one, it follows that vices and evils are only transient appearances which are doomed to appear and vanish altogether. Only then does the duality of the two opposite forces become apparent. The idea of light can be formed only by the notion of darkness along with it. A manifested cosmos is not possible without this duality. The theological notion, that there is a fundamental duality of virtues and vices working right around the tortuous phenomenon of the universe, needs to be properly analyzed. According to the philosophical analysis, virtues and vices are relative. There is no ultimate virtue nor ultimate vice. The vice in a person is as innate as the virtue. The vice in the end is forced to secure the purpose of virtue.

According to another philosophical view, victory of the evil forces is only a temporary phase because of their limited power. If the sinners were supposed to commit sin by the divine plan or the divine will, they would perpetrate any crime assuming it to be God-ordained, in which case the foundations of morality would collapse. This would, then, be inconsistent with the ethical teachings of all great prophets, seers and incarnations. Religious philosophy does not deny the existence of vices and evils but only their absoluteness. Religious ethics always opposes such forces and accepts only their relative relevance. The attribution to God's will does not in any way shift the responsibility which indeed belongs to the human activity. The paradox here is that human being is considered as the doer of actions, and yet God is saddled with the responsibility for them. It is only after an appropriate analysis of the vices from the religious, metaphysical and mystical angles combined, can clear the real picture. In the realm of human conduct, evil is a relative reality which is found everyday and therefore, has to be overcome either by non-cooperation with it or by non-submission to it so as to elevate the character of humanity. Forgiveness of sins is a reality but it is meant for those who are willing to learn from the lessons of their suffering. They must, however, bear the consequences of their bad actions (karma) for otherwise the law of 'karma' would become erratic and unreliable, and the experience it brings would be valueless. This is because it becomes operative only after the repentance of sins, and change of conduct. It has to be understood with full conviction that wrong-doing has to be abandoned completely and one has to get prepared for self-improvement.

If the appearance of a vice is an ordained phase of human activity, its liquidation is equally ordained to succeed it. This is again a paradoxical situation. Although vice is present everywhere but it will prevail no-where. It is not an eternal principle. A cosmos, divinely born and divinely sustained, containing vices and evils, is something which cannot be comprehended so easily or judged logically at the first glance. Instead of seeking their origin in the universe, it is better to seek their root in the human consciousness, for it is only the human beings who represent a corruption of human values, an alienation from the higher self and a misdirection of the free will. Somewhere in the exercise of human free choice, a cycle of sinful thought, feeling and action comes into being. But as it has a beginning, so shall it have an ending. The sinful kingdom of hell is within the human beings. Therefore, the sinless kingdom of heaven must be found by each individual being and it must be found within himself or herself. That the sinners may one day become saints, the evil life may one day get transmitted into the virtuous one, is not only a possibility but an acknowledged truth. Examples of the great seer Balmik who wrote the original Ramayan, and Angulimal who became the saint are well-known. **This is the process of self-realization, self-introspection and self-analysis which eventually leads to the invention of Divine within one-self.**

According to some spiritual philosophers, the Supreme Divine Power is the universe itself. There is no place in space where it is not present and there is no moment of time when it does not exist. That is why it is omni-present and infinite. But such a perception is found to be vaccus by some other philosophers. For, according to them, the universe is limited by the bounds of space and time. If the Supreme Divine Power is visualized as the Universe, then it becomes limited in space and limited to a time-frame (time-period), which means it no longer remains boundless or infinite and beyond time. But putting the Supreme Divine Power within the bounds of space and time means it is being subordinated to its own manifested universe and if it is to be subordinated to its own manifested universe, then it cannot be omni-present and infinite. Indeed, **this is a paradoxical situation and a mystery-may be the divine mystery.**

According to another perception, the Supreme Divine Power is one and has produced many out of itself. It means One becomes multitude, and continuously manifest itself into several living universes and living creatures. But, then it can never exhaust itself for it never really loses anything by this process – a finite part taken out of infinity does not affect the infinite characteristic of its infinity. A verse in the Isoupanishad proclaims that even the microcosm taken out of the macrocosm is a whole in itself and the remaining macrocosm continues to remain the whole. A spoon of water taken from an ocean does not diminish its immensity. Such a phenomenon looks mysterious to the human mind and thus, remains beyond its comprehension. The only conclusion that can be drawn is that the Supreme Divine Power is not only in the universe but also metaphysically beyond it. The infinitude of the universe indicates the infinite which transcends the universe. Thus, the cosmos is truly a self-revelation of the Supreme Divine Power but an intellectual insight into its nature and meaning and in its reality remains mystery.

Yet, another perception, as claimed by some spiritualists, of this Supreme Divine Power is to visualize it in two ways. If considered only as an infinite and transcendent being wrapped up in the static contemplation of its own perfection, remote and aloof from the current finite universe, then it reveals only half of the truth. If it is considered as the universal energy working entirely within every cell creating, promoting and destroying tier after tier of its space-timed universe, inspiring an evolutionary endeavour in countless series of creatures, then only the one half gets revealed while the other half remains veiled. Reconciliation of these two opposing halves poses an immense difficulty and it generates a philosophical paradox.

Metaphysics finds a fixed time duration to be inadequate, a fixed limited space to be contradictory, a fixed material substance to be inconsistent, and therefore it rejects time-space-matter phenomenon as being nothing more than a relativity-based appearance, and not being ultimate reality. A universe of changing phenomenon stamped by relativity cannot be an absolute reality, and God is nothing that can be caught in a space-time-matter network. The ultimate reality must be absolute where-in there is no relativity, no time, no space and no distance. Such an absolute timeless, space-less and matterless universe would be utterly empty when viewed from outside. It would look like blank nothingness, an emptiness bereft of all content, shape, time and space. Such a perception is that of an empty set or a null-set or a void set in the language of Mathematics which has no element in it, yet it plays an important and crucial role to the illustration of some subtle mathematical ideas and notions. Such a phenomenon is inconceivable, except by negating all properties which leave a vast void that is paradoxically its only existence which hears no sounds, sees no forms, observes no movements and performs no actions. It cannot be called an existence because there is nothing in it and nobody at all there to exist either as an experience or inexperienced thing, neither as a thinking being nor as the thoughts themselves. There is no room for personality whether sub-human, human or super-human. It seems indistinguishable from complete non-existence. Such a perception of the void initially looks to be repulsive to the human sense. If the absolute is so different from all that is known as existence which may not be rightly described as nothing, then it gives the notion of a formless, featureless and attributeless. Void is indeed incomprehensible by the intellect and can only reveal its profound meaning to a higher faculty of insight. It is admittedly not easy for the form-ridden consciousness to accept the notion of formless as the reality, that of emptiness as measurable. It is only by giving up all that is transient and by negating all that is familiar that its real perception can be grasped. The void is really blindness, nameless and not be-ness which fills the actuality it represents. This may be termed as another philosophical paradox.

By asserting that all is darkness, the void actually indicates the existence of its own light. The notion of an absolute void is unthinkable for even if everything else is eliminated, the thinking mind would still be there. Its metaphysical meaning of "**nothing**" is only an illusion for it is a removable reality, that of utter non-existence is therefore fictitious and that of non-absoluteness is equally illusory. Thus, there is a paradox where the void is unique as much as the idea of fullness against it. Everything visible to the naked eye seems to have emerged out of the invisible which cannot therefore be a mere nothing. The void is empty of individual and separate appearances but not of the universal reality. The materialist notion of matter which spreads out to fill out empty space as water spreads out to fill out an empty reservoir may be matched against the notion of the void that it is both potential stuff and potential space. If every vestige of the universe were to be removed from it, be it all its plants and creatures, its planets and stars, the ineffable mysterious emptiness would even then remain in its primal and unmanifest state. If there is nothing that is relative in the void, this is not the same as nothingness. The Real is still there, transcending all relativity, beyond the senses of all creatures just as the body of a person cannot be separated from his mind. Thus, the universe exists during its period of manifestation in this void like a cloud in the sky. Paradoxically, the void means a pure phenomenon devoid of all colours, forms, feelings, tastes, smells, senses and sounds which means the cessation of earthly consciousness. Likewise the Absolute Divine Power in its primal state has no attributes, no birth, no death, no desire, no will, no passion, no target, no shape, no appropriate name, no visible perceptible or conceivable individuality, no possible magnitude, it is not a thing graspable by human mind or thought which is constituted of experienced reality, the phenomenal reality only. The reason, why, in the utter stillness of the void, there is no past, present or future, no time orders, no space constraints, no forms, no manifestation or dissolution of the universe either. Does such a phenomenon exist only for and within the imagination of the individuals within them, not for the formless (void) Divinity? This is a mysterious paradox.

Philosophers think that the phenomenon of feelings, senses, emotions, desires, etc. are mind-related features, and since mind-essence is invisible, intangible and incomprehensible, it does not mean all such attributes and characteristics are non-existent. These things are not to be denied or discarded but need to be understood in a proper perspective. They are the transient form which the everlasting mind-essence takes. Mind is not mere emptiness but the very reality itself behind the earthly-experience. The universe is real, it is vivid to the human eyes, ears, fingers and yet it is nothing less than an appearance of the Supreme Divine Power. The Void or Vacuum is only a blank nothingness from the materialist standpoint, whereas it is the fundamental reality – the basis of all manifested existence from the mentalist point of view. It is also the universal state before arising of the Universal Existence. Though paradoxically, yet perfectly true, the Void, the Nothing which is never experienced directly, is the ultimate reality whereas the All, the Everything which is commonly experienced is an appearance of it. Everyone sees the universe-appearance but few realize the truth behind it. The visible universe is not a self-existent or self-supporting reality for it depends on the original Void-Mind and indeed arises from it and merges back into it. People are used to think in terms of measurable or quantifiable forms so habitually that they lose the power of thinking in terms of the dimensionless and formless Being which is the unseen reality of all these forms. This is a riddle or a strange mental paradox before the human beings.

Presently the exploration of the universe and the divine truth have been two eternal quests. Cosmologists are flying farther and farther into the space and plumbing deeper and deeper into the oceans to know about the universe. For uncovering the divine mystery, spiritualists have been groping in dead darkness. World is passing through the Kaliyuga, the last aeon of the four aeons of the Universe as enunciated by

Hinduism, the previous three being the Satyayuga (Kritayuga), Tretayuga and Dwaparyuga in succession. Hindu spiritualists call the Kaliyuga as the hot bed of sins and vices where religion is stifled, Imposters invent and propound a number of hedonistic cults and creeds. People are mostly addicted to greed and passion. The teacher and taught are like the blind and the deaf: the former cannot see, the latter cannot hear. Parents teach their children the art of earning money by fair or foul means. Almost everybody follows a conduct of his own imagination. There is total lawlessness. The meanest, if he is rich, is considered to be the noblest. Leaders practice sin, terror, perversity, malice, arrogance, infatuation and lust while their followers pervade the whole society. Hypocrites, practice prayer and charity, and they perform sacrifices and undertake vows with unholy designs. Common people are afflicted with diseases and are conceited. In short, Kaliyuga is the store house of misery, sins and chaos.

However, Hinduism also believes in a redeeming feature of Kaliyuga. According to the Hindu religious leaders, Kaliyuga has many virtues also, of which the most important is that in Kaliyuga, the escape from the circle of birth and death is easy. The goal of liberation or God-realization is reached easily and solely by chanting God's name, in Satyuga, people used to meditate for years and ages to achieve the goal of God-realization. In Tretayuga, people used to perform various types of sacrifices (yagnas) to escape rebirth while in Dwaparyuga, they used to dedicate their actions to God. But in the present ongoing Kaliyuga, all that people have to do is to chant God's name to achieve the aim of liberation from the cycle of birth and rebirth. Thus, no other aeon can compare with Kaliyuga provided people have faith in God, chant His name and follow the path of righteousness while performing their duties and doing their actions. Thus, it can be implied that in the Kaliyuga where conditions are not conducive to spiritual evolution, the easier methods are available such as chanting the name of God, fixing Him in mind and tiding across the ocean of emotions (Bhav-sagar). Isn't it an irony or may be an example of divine paradox in the sense that the effort required for liberation or God-realization is inversely proportional to the spiritual intensity in the ongoing Kaliyuga.

1.3 Divine Perceptions

The word **'GOD'**, to a philosopher is perceived as the ultimate principle of all beings within or beyond the intellectual expression or reach, unique, unlimited, absolute and eternal, whereas to a theologist or a spiritualist, God means the ultimate principle of the manifested world of creation which exists in relation with the universe and the human entity – which is qualitatively describable, and which is ever active. Thus, the first version is assumed to mean that God stands alone in uniqueness whereas the second version means that God is eternal in relation with the world which is its own creation. Second is considered as an aspect of the first, a timeless God in time and for a time, while first version is forever beyond time and space. Except for human interpretation, the two versions of God are not treated totally distinct entities. Indeed, it is not possible to understand the true concept of God unless the two-fold nature of the divine mystery is understood. While it is, in its most abstract and most remote aspect, the immeasurable, all-transcending and attributeless void, yet it is also, in its more concrete and nearer aspect, animating everywhere – the immanent life and mind of the universe. Thus, God is assumed to be both the No-thing and the Every-thing. God is beyond all thought and outside all imagination. It is not possible to have an exactly correct perception of God other than its description by analogy based on human experience, the concept of endless time and boundless space and of their coexistent phenomenon. The concept of time is generally compartmentalized into three stages namely past, present and future. The common idea of time makes it a continuum and picturise it in the form of an endless straight line, coming from the infinite past, running through the present and culminating into the indefinite future.

Everything, from microscopic cell up to a human being leading to the gigantic cosmos is believed to be a preconceived systematic pattern of a circuitous phenomenon, moving spirally at various levels. According to this belief, a living plant, and a human body all follow the same law of evolutionary growth. Various stages and their forms of this growth show intelligence behind them infinitely beyond the comprehension of a human mind. Those who deny its existence are considered to be emotionally charged rather than being intellectually penetrative. They need to understand the nature and purpose of various seasons, the creative power of the sun, movement of the planets in an orderly manner without ever clashing with one another, and the intelligent and meticulous systemic management of the universe so that they can come to the belief that a higher power directs all. The universe is not bereft of life and sense. It has both. There is within and behind every bit of it, a directing mind and a governing divine principle. This omni-present divine principle of life and the creative cosmic power are one and the same – God. In rocks, soil, plants, creatures, human beings, stars and planets, the evidence of incomprehensible intelligence and unbelievable omnipotence of the same divine power is visible. If the universe were quite lawless, if the universal events and movements such as the sun's rising or setting, planetary motion and seed's growth, were happening in a haphazard manner, it could hardly continue with its existence. Even those microscopically tiny organisms called the cells, out of which plants, animals and human bodies grow, contain latently characteristics of some invisible but ordered energy drawing its strength from the same divine power. The process continues with a perfect pattern, by orderly and evolutionary states, and through millions of births and rebirths.

Let no one underestimate the infinite wisdom of the Universal Mind merely because it is beyond the comprehension of a finite human mind – be it of a great scientist, scholar or an intellectual giant. Nothing has happened in the world's history or could have happened or will happen in the future without the ultimate sanction of the will and wisdom of the Universal Mind. There is a definite and well-defined divine purpose behind human existence, a rational order within the universe itself and a beneficient Universal Mind as the real ruler of both. Every plant, every creature and every living being demonstrates the cosmic intelligence in the progressive stages from seed to flower and from fetus to full size creature with an inevitable evolutionary process. This Universal Mind is believed to be the origin of all existence. Just as it is in the very nature of the sun to radiate light, so it is in the very nature of the Universal Mind or Soul to manifest the cosmos. Everything in the universe and the entire universe itself is an inevitable expression of the Universal Mind which is all conscious, all-knowing and all-present beyond the comprehension of the finite human mind. Spiritual philosophy holds the view that this Universal Mind is the Supreme Divine Power which is Omni-present, Omni-scient and Omni-potent.

Human beings try to personify this Omni-present, Omni-potent and Omni-scient Universal Mind as a person like themselves and name it as God. Accordingly they attribute human activities to God. They find it easier to understand the concept of humanized God who can look somewhat like them, may be bigger and more powerful than they are, and who behaves like them. In their visualization of God as a glorified and magnified person, they worship and adore God as a deity since they find it difficult to understand the real concept of the invisible God. This is called anthropomorphic conception of God. Even the scientists, in their wisdom of acquiring knowledge through experimentation, try to conceptualize this anthropomorphic image of God what the religionists call a personified or personalized or humanized God. As a result, they are not able to intellectually grasp its vast and infinite Divine Power. They forget that the human attributes do not and cannot ameliorate fully the nature of the Omni-present, Omni-potent and Omni-scient Universal

Being. Indeed, the Divine Power sustaining the Cosmos is beyond the comprehension of a limited human mind, equally so of a scientist who is believed to be oriented towards logic and rationality in place of faith. The spiritual scholars and religionists, however, because of their faith in the Supreme Being, believe in both personified and non-personified forms of God. The personified God is the one who incarnates like Rama, Krishna or Jesus or Shirdi Sai Baba or Sri Sathya Sai Baba. Growing intelligence and pervading ethics yield an ever higher ideal of God. Human beings can realize God within their own consciousness whatever idea of God inspires their efforts, influence their thoughts and guide their attitudes. They have this idea, which is beyond all ideas, the Absolute Truth. Some may be inclined to doubt its existence, others may flatly deny it, but no one will ever be able to write off this Infinite and Absolute Reality.

The human beings in every age and land have vigorously engaged themselves in the quest of this divine power. The philosophic doctrine of the Being of God is based upon the solid foundation of the versions of those who have succeeded in this quest and come closest to God. Its truth has been known to, and verified by, the wise, the mature and the inspired of all periods in all parts of the world. Like billions and trillions of plants are rooted in one and the same earth, millions and billions of human beings and creatures are rooted in one and the same universal being.

God and its creation are so interwoven that the two cannot possibly be separated. God is the undivided universal basis of all experience, all thought, all life and all existence. The profoundest sense of the word God means that there must be one Infinite source of all the universe, and of all the life in the universe, and of all the consciousness in that life. In their highest perception of the universe, the spiritualist seers find that the guiding idea behind such an unlimited entity, is the divine presence which exists, knows, cares and guides. There is a power, invisible, universal, immortal, original, ineffable and transcendental which surrounds everyone and spreads everywhere. The organization of human life overlooks the ultimate aim of human birth, which is to realize the divinity in each heart. It is the singular and only duty of a human entity to discover its original place and purpose in the whole Universal Idea. Even its so-called conquests of nature, exploration in the planets and space, experimentation and invention of new ideas etc. all bring out its own best potentialities and lead the magnificent efflorescence. Yet the mental situation of the human race today seems to be so dark that pessimists and rationalists ask the questions: "**What is God**"? "**Where is**

God"? "**Who is God**"? Several intellectuals and scientists have attempted to explore such questions among others related to the invention of God but only a few, a very few have qualified to answer them on the basis of having explored the innermost consciousness of their own psychological being and discussed their kinship to God. They are the few who have in perfect confidence, through their own experience, realized that this innermost self is divine and is linked with God.

The believers believe that the divine power is not absent from the world nor from any situation which can develop in the world. The divine law controls every situation. It is God's will which has set a course for human beings leading them from darkness into light, from ignorance into knowledge, from wickedness into goodness, from helplessness into powerfulness, and above all from animality into rational humanity, and then to infinitive divinity. The infinite and boundless cosmos consisting of the universes, galaxies, and solar systems came into existence because of the creative divine power of God. The manifestation of the cosmos occurred infinitely and eternally as a reflection of the infinite and eternal nature of that Supreme Power. The world is limited and finite whereas the Universal Being is unlimited and infinite. This Universal Being unfolds a tip of the iceberg of its infinitude, of its timelessness and of its spacelessness. The Universal-Mind never loses any part of itself nor gains anything when something is taken from it or is added to it because it is truly infinite. Therefore, there is no moment when it is not, and no place, where it really is not. This is a divine mystery and to get an intellectual understanding of the Universal Being, the intellectuals have to explore this mystery.

To explore the divine mystery and to comprehend the concept of the Supreme Power, it is important to first clear the mind of all false notions and false concepts. For this, every principle and every phase of life must be washed off the doubts and impact of unhealthy social environment and unfounded conceptualizations seeded into the human mind. Human beings have been making strange visualizations of the Supreme Divine Power – called the God, in their minds for their worship or solace. They are imbued with the belief that God is a bigger anthropomorphic being – somewhat more powerful and more knowledgeable – a gigantic human being with big hands, big eyes and big ears and so on. With such an illogical view of God, the vicissitudes of fortune and misfortune, and happiness and misery are attributed to the arbitrary will of this anthropomorphic God, who could get annoyed or pleased with a particular individual. The anthropomorphic view of

God is comforting and acceptable to most people because it brings God closer to them in as much as it makes God like themselves. **Is such a God, who is merely a projection of the human mind, acceptable to the modern person**?

Anthropological vision of God is cherishable and acceptable to the present millennium minds which are nourished on the developed scientific reasoning and broadened with modern rational outlook. The very notion of modern human personality based on different senses is imperfect and incomplete, and hence is liable to falsify the Supreme Power the way it is visualized within the limited range of human ideation. Thinking of God in this way as a glorified and expanded human being, will make people think of Him in the same space-time order as of their own. When the Supreme Power or Mind is reduced to be visualized to fit in the finite space-time continuum to which the human beings are conditioned, the notion of God gets demolished. The Supreme is infinite and cannot fit in the finite dimensional space because the moment people begin to talk of this Cosmic Mind as 'He" or "Him", they begin to turn it into an idol or a deity. The use of a masculine pronoun anthropomorphizes God and reduces this loftiest of all possible concepts to a hugely stunted stature. For this reason, the term "It" being neuter and impersonal is a better and fitter appellation of God than "He" and "Him". Those awed by conventional thought may at first feel such a neuter pronoun to be sacrilegious as derogatory but when they become accustomed to its use, they realize that it is neither sacrilegious nor derogatory but preferable to the use of a masculine pronoun like "He" or "Him" for God. The usage of "It" makes the concept of God more lofty, more pure and more abstract which honours it as the sublime principle, called the Brahmn by Adi Shankaracharya. It may be noted here that to the Vedantists of Advaita genre, qualifying Brahmn, the highest absolute reality without any epithets or names, defies logic, and is therefore not acceptable; they use negative appellations such as 'Neti Neti' etc. for referring to the absolute reality *i.e.* Brahmn.

To consider God as a Deity is to stretch it away from the earth and far beyond the skies as an extra-cosmic being, turning it into a big scientist or a phantom who made the universe out of nothing – just a few thousand years ago – that too by an outburst of sudden activity rather than a gradual process of evolution. Were God an infinite being standing alongside a world so arbitrarily created, and were the world something really isolated, and then God's infinitude would no longer be possible, for, the world's independent reality would limit God from the outside. As earlier asserted, the reality is that this Supreme Reality called God neither has a beginning nor has an end. It never started in vacuum. It has always been in existence, for otherwise the concept of a creator of and apart from the universe becomes a superfluous one. No God-like Being or being-like God has made the universe. For it is not a thing or an item to be manufactured or shaped but a process which is continuous and eternal like the motion of a point on a line or a plane. Even if an external God is postulated as a creator of the universe, and if discovery of its origin is explored, then it will become obligatory to proceed further and postulate a second God who is the creator of the first one. The process will not stop even there. It will be then desirable to postulate a third God who created the second. And so on, there shall be a sequence of creators of Gods which must be extended endlessly backwards. This is obviously a most unsatisfactory situation because it offers no solution to the question of the invention of God. The only rational way to conceptualize God is some self-existent power and visualize the universe as a thought within God and God as the existence within the universe.

Another belief is that God is a separate entity, an individual personality among several other living beings but only bigger and better than all of them. This is again related to the anthropomorphic version mentioned earlier. The difficulty with this version is that it chalks out a line of demarcation between what is God and what is not God. It signifies a separate identity of God from other living beings. Such a demarcation of God from other living beings deprives it of its characteristics of being omni-present, universal being and infinitude.

The common error in all such beliefs is to turn the infinite into finite, the impersonal into personal and the cosmic into the parochial. It does not seem to be the ultimate truth. An infinitely large being is not necessarily same as a truly infinite being. If God is to possess a personality and if it is to exist alongside of or outside other beings, then it will necessarily possess all limitations that are generally associated with human beings, and then it will no longer be the Supreme. The problem is that all human visualizations and conceptualizations are rooted in some sort of experience, and human experience cannot transcend conceptualizations which are nothing but reflections of human perceptions. Then how do people justify human faith in God, that is, attributeless beyond time and space – beyond human imagination? The answer lies in the very question itself, in the sense that and individual's perception of any entity enable him/her to include or logically infer reality that transcends experience. Objects lead to ideas which are abstract. However human minds are so focused that they can affect abstraction and then experience those obstruction by objectifying or personifying any idea or a principle. In the present case the idea of the infinite attributeless God, that is Brahmn, is arrived at only through inferences but is understood only through concretization or personification. Incarnation of God, the Highest Divine Principle in the human form is arrived at not only through inferences but also through experience.

God appears and incarnates as a person or a living being according to the Hindu scriptures for two-fold reasons. **First**, God appears as a person for the benefit of humanity who cannot hope to enter into its direct transcendental awareness which is beyond the comprehension level of the limited human mind and which when revealed through the personified human form can be easily grasped or seen by direct experience. The personified form of God provides an opportunity not only to realize its existence but also to receive its direct grace. This is clearly hinted in "The Bhagvat Gita" where Lord Krishna says, "**I reveal my grace in different forms and aspects solicited by the different seekers**". It is only through direct experience of a personified God, that people can have its holy sight (Darshan) directly or through visions or intuitions, feelings or ideas, dream experience or mentally-impressed visuals. The personified God speaks to the people in the way they can understand, and respond to those who cannot grasp its impersonal form. God manifests in the particular form sought by the aspirants and seekers which to them is most appealing and is easily understood. This does not mean, however, that God divides itself into various beings just as the sun remains intact while manifesting itself into sun-rays or sun-beams which it reflects on the surface of the earth or on the ocean waves. **Second**, the appearance of God in its personified form is really an instrumental device to concretize the concept of God, communicate the divine messages to the people to follow the path of truth, righteousness, love, peace and non-violence, to wipe out injustice and cruelty being inflicted on the innocent by the tyrants and cruel rulers, and to demolish the sin and criminality so as to reform or transform the human society and re-establish the path of 'Dharma' – propriety and righteousness. Incarnations of God as Rama in the TretaYug, Krishna in the Dwapra Yug and the Sai phenomenon in the current Kaliyug or other appearances of divine messengers or prophets like Buddha or Jesus Christ or Hazrat Mohammed as the chosen divine beings or various divine personalities like Sri Guru Nanak Dev, Lord Mahavir, Zoroastra and several others are the living examples of the personified divine with the messages of love and peace. In other words, **there has never been a time when the world was without a personified divinity or God in this sense and has never been bereft of the presence of God**.

Thus, Divine Power appears in several different ways to help the troubled hearts or seeking minds. The sinners and the sufferers, the ignorant and the scholars are not excluded from its grace. Indeed, the idea of the existence of God cannot be denied. The yearnings of billions of believers down through the ages have not been in vain. They had their firm faith in the existence of God. Three types of divine perceptions are generally believed in Hinduism:

- A building or a structure does not arise of its own unless there is someone who constructs it. In this case a human being, who is generally called an architect or a civil engineer, belongs to a higher order of existence than the house or building itself. Likewise the universe full of suns, galaxies, stars, planets, nature and creatures could not have come into existence, had there been no Maker or Creator of it. Just as a house-builder uses bricks, water, sand and cement for his work, so does God who is believed to have used a substance called "**matter**" for the creation and construction of this universe. God is one thing and matter is another. Consequently, God stands apart from the Universe just as the house-builder stands apart from the built-up house. The relevance of this illustrative example is its acknowledgement of the existence of a higher order of being. The draw-back in this view is that it conceptualizes God in the form of a magnified living (human) being. Further it makes God a particular object among other objects and sets it apart from its creation or the universe. In its highest form, such a perception regards God as an infinite Being but still places it outside of and apart from the universe. Such a view is better but metaphysically unsound. This anthropomorphic perception has been propounded by an Indian philosopher and thinker, Sh. Madhavacharya.
- The second perception sets up God as the life of the universe through and through, its very soul. This removes the drawback or shortcoming mentioned in the first perception by removing the anthropomorphic image of God. It places the universe within God, who thus becomes its immanent principle. The followers of this belief no longer look outside God but within themselves as their inmost soul. This view recognizes the contemporary existence of a higher power which not only creates things both animate and inanimate, but also plans their organization meticulously and maintains a balance. The short-coming of this

perception, however, is that it still has not annulled matter but retains a duality of spirit and matter. If the first perception is termed as duality, then this second perception can be interpreted, at the most, a qualified duality or qualified non-duality. The second perception still keeps separate the identities of two principles as eternally co-existent and eternally conflicting. This perception was postulated by Sh. Ramanujam another Indian philosopher and a great spiritual scholar.

The third and final progressive perception about God can be reached only when the human intelligence reaches its full maturity. It evolves an idea about God which takes into itself all that is true in the earlier two beliefs and at the same time transcends them – a belief which expresses completely what the first two beliefs express it partially. The belief in God, who is outside the universe, is as natural for non-metaphysical minds as the belief in a God, who manifests the Universe, is natural for metaphysical reasons. The third perception, therefore, considers the universe as the self revelation of God, not merely something made by it. There is only a single reality – called Brahmn the Supreme Reality *i.e.* **God is the Creator of Universe and Universe is the manifestation of God**, where matter and mind, thoughts and things, living beings both animate and in-animate, creatures and human beings, plants and trees, stars and planets etc. are all its manifestations. This is a perception which is generally termed as non-duality or monism conceptualized by yet another Indian saint and philosopher Shri Adi Shankaracharya. This view enunciates that God does not exist separately outside or alongside the universe but very much in it and as it. The universe has not been arbitrarily created by outside intervention but is self-born through the hidden activity of God. There is no intervention of an outside being simply because there is no outside being. The universe is a self-active system based on the heritage of 'Karma' and all karmic forces/energies are like parts of a vast machine which is automatically operational and which does not need any separate or outside operator to operate it. The 'Karma' forces are set in motion spontaneously. There was no special reason for an external power to make a universe out of matter but there was every reason why it had to make it out of its own self because the latent 'karmic' impressions within it had to manifest themselves.

The universe is believed to be as inseparable from the Universal-Force (God) as a person's ideas are inseparable from his/her own mind.

The life force which is behind the creation in the form of a tree leaf or an ant is one and the same life force which is behind the form of the universe. This force is Universally-present as one and the same everywhere in all respects and is called God. He is the very essence of the universe, who is all embracing, all-merciful and all-knowing *i.e.* who is omni-present, omni-potent and omni-scient. The cosmos is nothing but the self-externalization of this Universal Force which is self-existent. The universe is a manifestation of this Universal Force, vested with sense and sanity – it is alive and conscious. However, its consciousness need not be visualized only in the anthropomorphic form. Also consciousness is not confined only to the human beings who think, know, feel and experience things. Other beings are not denuded of consciousness. If bright flowers and grey minerals have no brains like the human beings, this does not mean that they are not conscious but the difference is that their consciousness is of a different form – distinct from that of the human beings, may be inferior or lower to that of the human being. The way some plants distribute their seeds, and the way in which they protect their seeds against premature destruction is as much a tribute to the presence of universal intelligence (consciousness) as the way in which human beings or animals or insects or reptiles or other species protect themselves to sustain their lives. Sir Jagdish Chander Bose – one of the greatest scientists of India, amply demonstrated by strict laboratory methods that how plants react to events in their environment in a manner which shows a certain measure of understanding or consciousness. Similarly, modern scientists have established the intelligence/consciousness revealed by minerals and their salts when their molecules group themselves into precise crystalline patterns although neither crystals nor plants have evolved organized brains like the human beings.

Consciousness exists in every being whether big or small because some fragment of the cosmic mind (divine power) is itself the life-force which strifes to attain self-maturity inherent in every finite form ranging from that of a so-called dead stone or a mineral so-called inorganic matter to that of a living human being and beyond. In other words, the life-force or the consciousness is as much present in a piece of stone as in an animated living being. But the stone cannot rise to the consciousness of its own essence, whereas the human being has always the potential of doing so. All this explains why biologists are able to discover an amazing intelligence at work in the intricate formation and orderly maintenance of living organisms. It also explains why physicists are able to find an extra ordinary sagacious behaviour in the energies they investigate, and why nature reflects a rational functioning throughout its vast domain. The scientists are able to detect not only the intelligent system at the base of Nature but also in the various forms taken by minerals, acids, gases and liquids. The presence of such orderliness in the cosmos shows enough evidence of a hidden and veiled mainspring of life and mind (consciousness), will and intelligence while the universe reveals that it is being held in an intelligent and unambiguous order. There is a well-defined system, genuinely coherent, and there is a regulated gradual evolution of the level of consciousness rising from stone to flower and from beast to human being through higher and higher levels of integration in this universal existence. It is an eternal law which tends to adjust the individual operation to the universal operation in a perfect harmony with its own integral balance. Every part is bound to the whole. It is indeed comforting to perceive that the universe has such a significant equilibrium at its secret core – called the Universal-Force, the invisible God.

A few questions arise: **Why has the universe been brought into existence at all? Why has the cyclic process of creation, protection and dissolution in the universe been evolved? Why are there the stars and galaxies, suns and planets, living beings both animate and inanimate? and Why there is life and death cycle?** Intellectuals or scientists are bound to explore such questions among several others including even their own existence. Indeed, some endless secret force is driving the world onwards and upwards with some kind of purpose or aim. According to Bhagvat Gita, the world is not devoid of its significance and without a superior cause. A few interpretations of this divine phenomenon are also given in the following way:

One of the most prominent ideas given by the meta-physicians and spiritualists is that the universe is a game of the Infinite Universe-Being called God which it plays for its self-delight and self-pleasure. If this view is accepted, then it means that the universe is to be regarded as a big playground or a good theatre or a vast game-chamber with God as the only game-watcher who is enjoying the game on the play-ground or a show in the theatre or even the mobilities or activities of the swarming multitudes of helpless beings. Another view is that the universe has not been brought into existence nor it has been created. It arose because it must. The Universe-Force or Universe-Being (God) must obey the everlasting constitution of its own being, and periodically manifest or reabsorb in accordance with the law of 'karma' enunciated as the eternal and fundamental base of the divine constitution. This law, however, is not imposed from outside because there is nothing outside of this universe. This law is its inner necessity which is beginningless and endless because the Universe-Being is itself a beginningless or endless phenomenon.

Thus, the question why this universe has been brought into existence is the one which will continue to arise so long as the reality of its being (existence) is not brought into lime light. If the universe exists according to some general law of karma, then it is a perpetual process of self-production, self-profusion and self-dissolution system of appearing, disappearing and reappearing intermittently in cosmic cycles (epochs) that it has neither any beginning nor any end. If the universe was never brought into existence but has always been in existence and the Universe-Being intermittently reincarnates itself, then it is like a revolving wheel which forever circulates on itself. No scientist or mathematician ever calculated it, no philosopher's insight has ever penetrated its process of beginning or re-beginning of this cosmic circular motion. It is the very nature of the universe to exist eternally in the sense that it is utterly beyond the limit of the time-series without a beginning and an end, it is, therefore, futile to ask why it was created. The question itself becomes unanswerable because it is unaskable. This question no longer arises and therefore can no longer be asked and hence answered. The fact that the universe is a perpetual self-actuating process is something which preludes the questioner from asking such a question. Alternate space-time manifestation and withdrawal of the universe are as inseparable from the Superior Power as breathing is inseparable from life.

The Supreme Power is understood to have no self-motive for itself in its manifestation as the universe. But it does not mean that it has none for its innumerable creatures particularly the human beings vested with an appropriate level of consciousness. Indeed, the creation and existence of creatures is not purposeless although human beings have been assigned a special role to achieve a specific goal. They have to comprehend what the human life is for. The cosmic evolution is a continuous process. It goes on, therefore, not only for the sake of Supreme Divine Power but also for the sake of the living beings, since it is purely karmic. The Supreme Divine Power is providing an opportunity to the human beings of realizing their existence and developing a quest for a sublime goal of achieving loftier levels of divinity. This is one of the main purposes behind the universe-manifestation focused on the development of self-consciousness and the unfolding of higher consciousness.

Remembrances of the past, anticipation of the future, and moment-to-moment living in the present are believed to be common traits among the human beings, while for the Supreme Divine Power, past, present, and future are co-equal because it sees the universe in itself and itself in the universe because it is present everywhere in everyone and everything. The Supreme Divine Power embraces all possible time-series and space-orders because it is conscious of the universe as being within itself whereas the human beings are conscious of it as being outside themselves and can function only in one state at a time in a specific time-order and in a specific space-setting, because of the mental division of time and space within them. To the Supreme Divine Power, all things, all knowledge and all orders of consciousness are equally present at a single glances for they are all one to it since its existence is eternal and endless. The Supreme Divine Power knows everything and the way in which the time-space phenomenon appears and is experienced by its time-space creation. The human beings cannot stretch out their time-space perception even to a tiniest fraction of the extent of that of the Supreme Divine Power. Human knowledge is relative to their consciousness. How can they know the ultimate nature of consciousness which totally transcends all such relativities? They cannot rightly judge the level of divine consciousness by human standards. It is unrealistic and un-philosophical to try to bring the infinite Supreme Divine Power into their limited finite time-space experience. What is an immeasurable cosmos to a human mind is just a minor fine element in the perception of the Supreme Divine Power. With the limited human faculty, the human beings cannot grasp such a supreme truth. What is an eternity to human mind is just a single instant in the mind of the Supreme Divine Power. The sages and spiritual scholars project these ideas of infinity and eternity as a circle moving on itself like the wheel of a vehicle, sometimes modified into the shape of an ever-evolving Swastika-Wheel symbol of the Hindus. The Supreme Divine Power is perceived to manifest and operate in a multitude of different time-space orders without making the human beings aware of what it is doing. All this magnificient and spectacular monism or non-duality is truly and literally incomprehensible to the human conceptual thinking. It is inconceivable to human mind because it is abstract and unlimited. Thus the perception of a humanized and personified God gets filled with inconsistencies and contradictions, the moment human beings try to put God in their own finite and limited time-space dimension. This fact has to be considered and acknowledged that the Supreme Divine Power is the self-manifested universe which is beginningless and endless which makes it unpicturable formless God.

The debate, whether or not God exists, is as old as the human civilization itself is. Yet centuries and millenniums later continue to find a 'strong resonance of God'. In a recent survey conducted by an international magazine, it was found that 91% of those surveyed believed in God. Yet, the major question remains, is God real? Some believed in God as depicted by the various religious scriptures while others took a standard view of being atheists. The religious ones believe that since the scriptures talk about God, therefore, there has to be one. Further, the world is so complex, it makes sense to believe that there is indeed some guiding intelligence at the centre of it all. The rationalists, however, debunk this logic. Scriptures, they argue, have been written by human beings, and hence it is not impossible to disbelieve the perfection of these scriptures. Moreover, there is not ample evidence to suggest that there has been a divine power behind this universe. If God really existed, then atheists are more likely to ask. Why there is so much suffering, disparity and dehumanization? Why do the innocent suffer? Why is there so much religious killing in the name of God, when especially, God is supposed to be One and Same? Indeed, the believers in God have a fitting reply. They argue that God gave people the free will, and wanted them to choose. God gave an option to the people to choose whether to love Him or not. Evil exists because sometimes horrible choices are made and hence they fall short of the glory of God. The debate over God is abstract. The atheists call upon the world to get rid of religious faith and rely on rationality and science. The believers on the contrary hold a strong view based on firm faith that there is some divine force behind this universe and there exists a reality beyond the universe.

Though it may appear that the cycle of nature, the functioning of the Universe, the enormous human potential, etc. happen of their own accord, they actually manifest the presence of an unseen divine power. For rationalist or a scientist, the whole phenomenon is happening because of the law of nature. Where is the role of God? But at some point of time each individual comes to terms with this invisible divine power. Ever since life began on the earth, people have been asking themselves various questions: **Who or what made them**?, **What is their mission in the world**?, **Where do they come from**?, **Where do they go from here**?, **Why do people take birth and Why do they die**? Nobody has yet been able to find satisfactory answers to such questions among several others. All they have the sermons about a hidden divine power called God who creates life, gives different names to different creatures, decides different spans of life for them and then makes them disappear forever. The same divine power created the five basic elements namely the ether, earth, air, water and fire or there are different creators for different creations. He is called God 'Who has been appearing on the earth in various forms – incarnated as Rama, Krishna and prophets like Zoroaster, Christ, Mohammed and Nanak.

The characteristic that distinguishes a human being from all other forms of life is his inquisitive tendency to explore an invisible realm of the universe leading to the ultimate reality called God. Everyone agrees that God is same whether He is called Ishwara, Allah, Jenovah or simply God. Indeed, God is a mystery that cannot be understood; He cannot be subjected to any thought process or perceptions or some concrete knowledge. He is beyond the empirical rational understanding. God is the unknowable essence, the first cause and the final goal. He is by no means a mere idea or a useful fiction as some philosophers would depict Him.

There is a deep and appealing notion that the Universe is but the dream of God who, after a hundred Brahma years dissolves Himself into a dreamless sleep. The Universe dissolves with Him – Until, after another Brahma century, He stirs, recomposes Himself and begins again to dream the great cosmic dream. This process continues indefinitely.

"All the World's a stage, and all men and women merely players: They have their exits and their entrances", wrote William Shakespeare, one of the greatest dramatists of all time. Shakespeare visualized the whole world as a large stage, life as a play and the living beings as mere actors or participants in enacting that play. The questions, however, is: Who is the author of the play? Obviously God. This supports the Hindu view that creation is God's play (leela). God is a mystery. This Universe is a mystery. To understand God and His Universe, one has to be a spiritualist or a scientist. The spiritualists always believe that God is a divine power which exists everywhere, in every particle of the matter. Everything is divine. A spiritualist feels a strong energy field around him which he calls as Divine Energy. He feels the presence of this energy because he is receptive. Only receptive people can feel the presence of this Supreme Divine Energy while sitting, walking and talking through their inner voices or tunings.

How does a scientist feel about this divine energy? A scientist will view it as something that mystifies the world. The spiritualist treats it as the one who is real even though sages describe it variously. Can Science tell why the human beings or for that matter the living beings are here? Science, however, is concerned with 'hows' rather than 'whys'. Science has no ultimate answer to date so far as the meaning of life is concerned. Scientists are trying their best to explore such a global issue. It requires a great effort to look beyond the conditioning of their belief-systems and admit that they have yet to find appropriate answers to the above questions. The well-known, twentieth century's greatest scientist **Albert Einstein said, "A human being is a part of the whole, called by us, Universe – a part limited in time and space. He experiences himself, his thoughts and feelings as something separated from the rest – a kind of optical delusion of consciousness. This delusion is a kind of prison for us, restricting us to our personal desires and to affection for a few persons nearest to us. Our task must be to free ourselves from this prison by widening our circle of compassion to embrace all living creatures and the whole of nature in its beauty."** According to another view, the Universe is a living evolving aspect of God. Every atom contains information which is shared with the adjoining atoms that ultimately leads to a collection of atoms to become heavenly bodies, stars and planets which together constitute which is termed as the Universe.

Science has established that the Universe is a space-time phenomenon, full of galaxies planets, suns, moons and various other solid bodies. The apparent present world comprises of large and small bodies which are made of many smaller molecules which are further composed of still smaller atoms that are made of even smaller electrons and protons moving in the charged energy fields. The whole observable material is, thus, full of infinite fields of energy moving in a great vacuum or void – the great emptiness, called 'shunya' by the ancient Hindu spiritualists, that pervades and surrounds everything. All objects and living beings are just bundles of energy which eventually decay and die. Who is the source or subject of all these objects both animate and inanimate that directs them in their microscopic and macroscopic cycles of change and movement? Who or what is the force within all these object specially the living beings, that supervises or monitors or directs their continuously changing process of birth, growth, decay and death? Is this force within all animate beings and inanimate objects (things) a separate entity? This source or force, called the Cosmic Creator, without any name or form, may be yet another greater and bigger Cosmic Power or the Supreme Power who is called God by the seers, sages and prophets. Whether there is God and whether this Cosmic Power is God, is something to be believed or not. Belief essentially means assuming the existence of something which is not known. If there is something which is not known, how is it possible to know whether it exists or not. Likewise it is not even known as to when Creation began and when it is going to end. Then how is it possible to know the nature and form of the Creator? It is something like believing something that has been culturally conditioned to be believed.

The belief system started because of the absence of any logical explanation for the nature of Creation and hence its Creator. Thus, it is just a child-like answer that somebody living up in the sky and doing everything in the world is some big being who is called God. Just as there is Creation candidly visible to everybody, and there are creatures of various shapes and sizes, therefore, there must be a creator. Using a simple simile, if there is a building structure, there must be a builder. Likewise, there is a visible creation full of all sort of inanimate objects like soil, rocks etc. and animate creatures in the form of plants, reptiles, birds, animals etc., therefore the automatic corollary is that there must be a Creator. Who is this Creator and why is He called the God? According to some spiritualists, God is the highest level of all existence and of the combined consciousness of all also called Cosmic Consciousness. All the objects of creation are elements of this Cosmic Power of Consciousness. This Cosmic Consciousness split itself up in different forms and levels just as, the so called Bing Bang, as believed by the scientists, created the material universe which is ever expanding and which, after a critical time, would get back to naught due to contraction similar to the cyclic process of births and deaths. Consequently the Cosmic or Supreme Consciousness will draw back all the forms and levels of consciousness into itself. This is a divine mystery. Its basis, however, lies in the Cosmic view of God. The intimate relationship God and His cosmos is that God energizes this Cosmos and the Cosmos in return dances with the Creator in the cosmic dance of creation.

The divine phenomenon, which looks to be without forms, personalities and ideas, yet paradoxically, is the root of all forms, personalities and ideas. Apparently, there seems to be no movement, no activity in it, yet it contains the endless movement and activity. From nothing comes everything, from silence emerges sounds, from unconsciousness emanates consciousness and from invisibility appears visibility. How is it possible for the Unchanging to become the Changing, for the immobile to pass into Motion, from One Being to manifest into multiformed universe?

Nature has given a glimpse of the answer to this question. One seed germinates into a plant to give many seeds. Human mind in its unified and undivided state generates a number of thoughts and ideas, yet the mind loses nothing of its own oneness or integrity by this apparent sub-division. The one splits itself into the Many. The Universal Mind manifests itself in the evolutionary existence yet remains unimpaired, undiminished and unexhausted. The individual human mind can manifest itself in various ways. For example, in simple arithmetic, the number 100 can be expressed in various ways *viz.* 100 = 10 x 10, = 5 x 20 = 50 x 2 = 90 + 10 = 40 + 60 and so on. All these are different representations but all the ways of its representations are equivalent to the same number 100.

The seemingly Vacuum, Void or Nothingness is claimed to be the secret basis of the whole universe's existence by some spiritual philosophers. It is considered to be the original source of the emergence of the universe. It seems to be the same which is being termed as the **black hole** by the modern scientists like Stephen Hawking. It is considered to be the first and last of all creation. Its infinite nature is unalterable, its existence is immutable and in the earthly sense, its mystery is impenetrable. The universe can never be outside the Universe-Being nor the Universe-Being can be apart from the universe. It, however, manifests in different shapes and forms. Just as it is one and the same element which appears as vapour as water and yet looks different from solid ice. Then, it is one and the same invisible Universal-Being which manifests as the visible universe. The Universal-Being is incessantly restless, constantly in motion, because of its very nature of ever-striving in various ways in all the beings, animate and inanimate, moving into its original state of emergence. It is here that the divinity gets revealed by its own indescribable nature, undivided and undiscovered.

Chapter 2
Astrophysics and Metaphysics

Astrophysics and metaphysics are considered to be the two most subtle areas of interest. While metaphysics is a complete philosophy, astrophysics is an incomplete science, for metaphysics begins where astrophysics ends. Noumenology and phenomenology are the two well-known aspects of the Supreme Knowledge. Noumenology is the realm of 'being', whereas phenomenology is process of 'becoming'. Phenomenology is the science of the changeable and hence it resembles science or physics for that matter. Noumenology is the philosophical study of the unchangeable – the Eternal Reality. Philosophy is a way of an intellectual enquiry. The word 'physics' is originally derived from its Greek root: 'phusics' which means 'nature'. Thus, physicalism is the doctrine that all phenomena can be described and hence can be reduced to some empirically verifiable physical statements or propositions. Metaphysics is beyond astrophysics or for that matter beyond any variant of physics. The prefix 'meta' denotes 'beyond'. Metaphysics connotes transcendental philosophy. Accordingly, the metaphysical enquiry of the Divine Power, the Universe and the valid experience of each, is generally termed as Vedanta. Philosophy is the sweet fruit whereas Vedanta is the sweet juice of that fruit. Vedanta proves by experience that which has been postulated. Vedanta is the most fundamental and profound philosophy of Hinduism. It leads to the foundation of the Truth. It gives a complete vision of the Supreme Reality.

Science and spirituality or for that matter astrophysics and metaphysics are related to each other in more than one way. It is being assumed here that astrophysics represents science while metaphysics represents spiritualism. Astrophysics must rise to the level of metaphysics, and metaphysics must take care to ascertain facts with scientific accuracy and thoroughness. It does not mean that metaphysics is to be sieved solely through the process of scientific synthesis making it as a generalization of existing scientific knowledge. For, it would be absurd to regard such a generalization as the Ultimate or Supreme Reality. Were metaphysics to be based only on physics or science, it would then become a one-sided affair and would fail to achieve the all-embracing comprehensiveness of the Supreme Reality. It would, then become a glorified branch of physics masquerading under a different name. In any case, the scientific method cannot alone suffice for metaphysics because, being analytic, it deals with parts and thus overlooks systemic characteristics which can bring "completeness". For example, music for science is a system of sound, an important area of study in physics, which only feelings can appreciate. Science can calculate, measure and analyze quite effectively tangibles like salt and sugar, for that is its province. But it cannot effectively appreciate the intangibles like melodious music, charming beauty and aesthetics. Astrophysics or physics, as the expression of concrete reason, cannot alone lead to realization of the Ultimate or the Supreme Reality whereas metaphysics as the expression of abstractness, can do so. Its campus knows no bounds.

Astrophysics and Metaphysics have been systematically and systemically interpreted both by the scientists and spiritualists in terms of the three evolutionary processes namely the Cosmic Evolution, Creative Evolution and Spiritual Evolution enunciated in the following three sections of this chapter.

2.1 Cosmic Evolution

According to cosmology, space, matter and time together constitute what is termed as the Universe. Spirituality believes that Universe together with consciousness forms what is termed as Existence. Cosmology appears to be dealing with the some sort of ideas related to spirituality. It raises the same spiritually-related questions such as: **How did the Universe come into being? What was there before the so-called Big Bang Theory? How is it all going to end? Is there an end at all? How does creation fit into this scenario? Why is there something instead of nothing?** Indeed metaphysics deals with such questions among several others. It seems as if physics or for that matter Astrophysics or Science, in general, is bothered about the question of existence. It looks as if cosmology is offering cosmologists a backdoor entry into the faith. The fact that to some cosmologists, the Universe appears fine-tuned for the emergence of life, immediately raises the question of who is the tuner in the background doing all the fine-tuning?

The Earth, of all the planets, seems to have been exceptionally fine-tuned for creation. The composition of its environment is just appropriate for oxygen-breathing living beings, water exists in abundance, the soil is rich in minerals and adequately fertile for plant-growth. Moreover, it is at the right axis and at the right distance from the sun so as to receive the right quantum of heat and energy. It is equipped with multi-weather phenomenon. While astrophysicists would end up thinking that the whole system was a coincidence, the metaphysicists, on the other hand, believe it to be uniquely and divinely created. The solar systems and other galaxies seem to have plenty of planets which do not seem to be conducive for the life and creation similar to that of the Earth. **The living eminent Cosmologist Stephen Hawking remarks: "The laws of science, as we know them at present, contain several fundamental numbers, like the size of the electric charge of the electron and the ratio of the masses of proton and the electron. The remarkable fact is that the values of these numbers seem to have been finely adjusted to make possible the development of life."** For example, the gravitational force is a constant number. Had it been little greater or less, it would have been too difficult to sustain life-bearing planets like the Earth, and the Universe would have been different as well as difficult for survival of the creation. Indeed, even a little change in the gravitational force would have been disastrous for stars including the sun which would mean no Earth and hence no creation, whatsoever is witnessed today. **Does it mean that there is a Creator who designed the Universe with the explicit purpose of generating complexity and the emergence of intelligence along with consciousness?**

Cosmologists and astrophysicists evade answering such questions among others because the answers invariably seem to spell some Divine Supreme Power as believed by the metaphysicists. As a result, they make conjectures of weird coincidences, whereas the proponents of the Supreme Intelligent Power would believe it to be its doing. One of the finest fusions of science and theology or for that matter, of astrophysics and metaphysics, is that all of evolution has been with a purpose towards the resolution of complexity of creation and mystery of consciousness. It is not a one-off process which applies only to animate matter on Earth but to the totality of everything animate and inanimate that appeared and subsequently existed since Big-Bang. It is believed that the Universe is evolving towards higher forms of consciousness to finally become one with God. Although the astrophysicists do not believe in the divine phenomenon, yet the alternative, to-date, available to them is to openly acknowledge that the Universe, apparently so-friendly, seems to have a Divine Cause of its origin. Indeed, the other alternative could possibly be a mind-blowing proposition if the Universe had not been the only one around but just one among many billions and trillions of other Universes constituting together what could perhaps be termed as the Mega Universe or the Multiverse, containing several gazillion universes along with their physical laws all different from one another. It would be hardly possible to think of at least one universe among them containing the physical laws which could create and sustain life. Even so, what happens if the concept of multiverse is confirmed? Does it disapprove the existence of its creator? **Physics Nobel Laureate Steven Weinberg says, "I don't think that the multiverse idea destroys the possibility of an intelligent, benevolent Creator."**

While elaborating on the concept of Cosmic Evolution, **Sri Sadhguru Jaggi**, an eminent spiritual philosopher says "**The Big Bang – or Roar", is indicative of the situation when science and yoga meet. Shiva is asleep when Shakti woos Him – He gets up and roars as Rudra. Shiva is the dark one (matter) and Shakti, the Dark Energy, the two forces that science now informs us, are linked. It is a yogic explanation of the Universe, contrived at some points and convincing in others; when Shiva cools off, He becomes an ellipsoid – the linga. And it is this yogic process of linga-making and the significance of living in a consecrated space that needs further exploration."** The astronomers have discovered this invisible dark matter across the universe – a mysterious substance that cannot be seen, only sensed through its gravitational pull.

Matter only appears to be solid. It is actually pulsating with energy. This is Einstein's discovery. The energy is invisible while matter is visible. Human body or in that sense every living body of plants, trees, animals and reptiles is energy. Even mind and souls are also termed as energy. The difference lies in their rhythm and wavelengths. Such as insight into the matter brings modern physics close to metaphysics. Such a view brings the scientists and spiritualists to arrive at the same conclusion, that existence is energy. Both the object and observer are energy. **Arthur Stanley Eddington, another great scientist of the present age, has remarked, "We used to think that matter is a thing; now it is no more so. Matter is more like a thought than like a thing."**

Mutual understanding of science and spirituality is bound to play a major role in the understanding of the Supreme Reality. The recent declaration of the CERN scientists about the 'Higgs-Boson' particle that is thought to add mass to matter, making possible the clustering together of the particles to form matter and its various shapes. If one can have access to this Higgs Boson particle, then theoretically one can create matter. In other words, the Higgs Boson particle is responsible for creating matter, since, this is the one particle that gives mass to the rest of the particles that together constitute what is termed as matter. Moreover, this particle has the intelligence to create everything in the world. That is why, the Higgs Boson particle has been named as "God Particle". This particle consciousness provides infinite flexibility, infinite freedom, infinite energy and infinite intelligence to enable the human beings to move towards the goal of attaining complete awareness of their being constituted of particles. Eventually, they should be able to shift this logical reality to an unending, ever-moving, unlimited, dynamic and energetic reality of the quantum field culminating into a state of vacuum, termed Nirvana by the Buddha.

The question, however, remains, **what exactly is the Higgs-Boson particle**? As claimed by the scientists, the Universe is made up of twelve fundamental particles and four fundamental forces. One more particle was visualized by an Indian scientist Satyendra Nath Bose in 1920, who worked with Albert Einstein and who was a natural candidate for the Nobel Prize which was, however, denied to him, and instead was given to Einstein. Later in 1960, credit was earned by the British scientist Peter Higgs, being declared the pioneer for claiming the existence of such a particle, which came to be known as 'Higgs-Boson' particle. As the CERN scientists celebrate the finding of Higgs-Boson (which should be appropriately named as **'Boson Higgs'** particle), after whom the God particle is named. The so-called 'Higgs-Boson' particle explains the most important property of all matter-mass. However, the scientists have yet to identify other properties of this particle.

A few more aspects of the cosmos remain unexplained particularly the so-called dark-matter and dark-energy which together constitute most of the Universe, as declared by the scientists. Also, the most well-known gravitational force is still not fully explained. The basic question remains unanswered: **Who or what created the particles including the Higgs-Boson itself**? The answer to such a question may lead to some possible enunciations which could bring the explorers closer to what scientists call the Theory of Everything. Will this theory say everything about the Cosmic Evolution, and the phenomenon of consciousness – an infinite consciousness that spans the whole Universe which creates an individual consciousness? The whole debate leads to one and only one conclusion, by all standards, that it is some divine power called God who is inventing the God-particle and the Universe is a creation of God's mind. **The eminent British scientist Stephen Hawking says, "It is difficult to discuss the beginning of the Universe, without mentioning the concept of God..... It is quite possible that God acts in ways that cannot be described by the scientific laws. But in that case one would just have to go by personal belief."**

Cosmology provides the believers a scientific rationale for their faith. For instance, most of the scientists actually do not feel shy of using spiritual terminology, namely the 'Divine-Particle' or the 'God-Particle' as the fine tuner. They seem to have struck a resonant chord with spirituality. This means the scientists have finally developed some kind of tryst with their common cosmic destiny. They seem to have agreed that the term 'Divine-Particle' or 'God-Particle' is more appropriate which is causing everything to be as it is. The same thinking seems to have emerged in the minds of all cosmologists down the ages. They are not able to get rid of the G – word. **Einstein said, "The Lord may be subtle, but He is not malicious**". Even when the scientists say they do not believe in God, they still touch the base with God. In his latest book, Stephen Hawking flatly declares creation of something out of nothing does not require God. Yet he gives his book a semi-religious title: **The Grand Design**? Thus, the astrophysicist and metaphysicist seem to be willing to agree on the existence of some supernatural source of power which is all pervasive and from which emerges everything and merges back into it. The Vedanta philosophy of Hinduism provides a similar glimpse of the essence of the realization of Brahmn and the Universe. Creation and the creator comprise an inseparable oneness. The creator Brahmn permeates all space, matter and time, thereby upholding and administering the fundamental aspects of creation, Brahmn or the Universal Consciousness or the Cosmic Consciousness. Such a Vedic view of Brahmn and the Universe is now being echoed by the modern science also.

Quantum Physics and Cosmology are inextricably interwined. Empty space devoid of matter is vacuum. Indeed, it is not empty. According to Quantum Theory, the empty space is mysteriously full of elementary particles such as electrons among others which are identical everywhere in the Universe, no matter when or where they originate, the amount of their mass, electric charge, and spin are always exactly the same whether they are created in space or in a laboratory. The mystery of the matching particles has been solved by the physicists who found out the underlying quantum fields embedded in vacuum which give birth to the elementary particles *i.e.* the electrons. Thus, the quantum field theory came to be known as the cause of this revelation. According to eminent physicist and nobel laureate Frank Wilezek, in Quantum Field Theory, the primary elements of reality are not individual particles, but underlying fields. Thus, all electrons are the elements of an underlying field naturally called the electronic field which fills up all space and time. The same view holds true for all the fundamental particles required for the functioning of the universe. Their most mystifying property is that they are able to keep their fidelity to be the same on a universal scale at all times. According to Heisenberg's Uncertainty Principle, the quantum fields are always active namely, they are fluctuating frenetically at all points in the space in an unpredictable way. Yet on an average they have remained the same everywhere, at all times.

Most things in the life of the Universe are always changing. As space expanded, temperature got dropped from its extreme high degree to extreme low tending to below zero. Matter got clumped to form galaxies and stars. Yet the primary quantum fields did not change at all; they remain exactly the same as before the expansion of space. According to Albert Einstein, the space expands in a manner as if every point in the Universe is its centre and each centre point is moving away from each other. Thus, the field will be the same at each point of space, no matter how small or big the universe is. What does keep the fidelity of the fields intact in such a vast universe at stake for all times when they are in fact always energetically fluctuating randomly at each point? A scientific answer would be: the self-interacting dynamics of the quantum fields which appears to resemble the Self-awareness principle embedded in the primary reality of the universe. Another astrophysicist Roger Penrose contends forcefully that the mysteries of this quantum behavior and human awareness are linked.

According to the latest theory envisaged in the Nobel Awards Committee's words, "**Every physical thing in this Universe comes from a single common source**". This is what is being termed as the theory of everything. In addition to the basic forces, this common source includes various matter fields such as the electronic fields among others. The matter fields and force fields together generate everything in the Universe. What unites all of these matter fields and force fields constitutes the common source. After the development of holography in 1947, an eminent theoretical physicist, David Bohm worked for a long time on same hypotheses regarding the nature of reality. Holography is a three-dimensional photography which creates a projected image of the object – called hologram – which not only looks like the original object but can also be viewed from different angles and seen from different perspectives, just like looking at a real object. After working for a long time on the holographic hypotheses, David Bohm came to the conclusion that the Universe itself was a holographic projection of some deeper level of a distinct and more fundamental reality that was indivisible, invisible and infinitely interconnected.

According to the Quantum Theory, empty space is occupied by some quantum fields. Both scientists and cosmologists are of the view that the Universe got originated from the quantum fields which are embedded in vacuum. They generate elementary (quantum) particles which fill up the space and time. According to Albert Einstein, space, time and quantum fields cannot exist separately. They coexist since the physical reality of space is represented by a field whose components are functions of space-time. Indeed, a field is a physical property of space and space cannot exist without a field. Even, mathematically speaking, a space is always defined on a field. This implies that the quantum fields uphold the structural space-time phenomenon of the Universe while operationalizing its basic aspects. The idea of quantum fields is interpreted in the following alternative way also: The Universe is created by a trinity of electricity, magnetism and gravitation which together constitute as the three dimensions of space termed as metricity. Space with the interplay or interaction of this metricity generates the universe while the three components electricity, magnetism and gravitation together form a field which is called the unified field, same as the above termed Quantum field. As space got expanded, matter got clumped to form galaxies and stars. However, the median values of the primary quantum field never got changed. Their accuracy remained intact at all times. The phenomenon of maintaining this accuracy appears to be some sort of self-referral akin to the spiritual notion of self-awareness, embedded in the primary reality of the Universe. Scientists conjecture that all the quantum fields behave as merely different aspects of one primary field, a singular source for everything in the Universe including its creation and the creatures. This indicates that the origin of the Universe is the same single source which is termed as Brahmn by the spiritual philosophers or Vedic scholars. This is termed, by the cosmologists, as the scientific face of the abstract Brahmn.

According to the Vedanta – the confluence of science, religion and philosophy, the whole universe is a gross manifestation of an **Immutable Principle** which is essentially **Eternal** ('Sat'), **supremely Conscious** ('Chit') and deeply **Blissful** ('Anand'). It is this **Reality** which lends existence (truth), intelligence (awareness) and joy (pleasure) to all beings, and illumines all material phenomenons. This is the **Supreme or**

Divine Reality and hence, it is the essence of all that is the basic source of all energies and forces that constitute what is termed as the universe. This reality is invisible to the human eye, unthinkable by the human's mind and incomprehensible by the human's intellect. It can only be realized/cognized directly by merging the individual consciousness into the all-pervading super consciousness. Rightly, therefore, this Supreme Reality is called the '**Brahmn**' the All-pervading Supreme Being – the Almighty and Absolute. The Upanishads says, "**That which is Supreme Brahmn, is the Self, the eternal support of the Universe, subtler than the subtle. That alone Thou art. Thou art that Alone.**" In other words, the entire Universe is within God – the Ultimate Consciousness.

Brahmn, in Vedantic parlance, does not mean a person, not even a personified God but **Existence** itself, the Cause of all causes, and, therefore, reverentially addressed as the 'Supreme Being'. Brahmn is the beginningless and endless chain of cycles of involution and evolution, each such cycle constitute a 'Kalpa' – the period of Cosmic manifestation. All the attributes essential for creating the Universe are vested in Brahmn – the Supreme who is Omni-present, Omniscient and Omnipotent, that out of which all being are born, by which they are sustained and to which they ultimately return, the one which manifests in creation, protection and dissolution.

Three ontological phases are generally described in relation to Brahmn in the process of Cosmic Evolution. First phase is related to the beginning of every cycle of Creation. It is called '**Nirguna Brahmn**' – attributeless; beyond both 'being' and 'non-being': This, in fact, is the unmanifest form and therefore is also named as **Para Brahmn** or the Transcendental Reality. In the second phase, the Nirguna Brahmn becomes '**Saguna**' or the Brahmn equipped with all attributes of '**Sathyam-Jnaanam-Anatham**' where '**Sathyam**' is the Reality underlying all creation, '**Jnaanam**' stands for the Cosmic Consciousness which illumines all phenomena and, '**Anatham**' is the infinite power which ensure the continued manifestation of the Universe. In the third phase, Brahmn becomes '**Saakaara**' that is to say it assumes form and attributes. It becomes dynamic and manifests itself as the Universe of time, space and causation. Indeed, the unmanifested state of the Brahmn means an undifferentiated existence. It has neither any form nor any attributes. It is the state of neither 'nothingness' nor 'emptiness' but Brahmn holding within itself all the forces of creation, preservation and annihilation in perfect harmony and equilibrium.

The scientists believe that the universe seems to have originated from a source of unimaginably dense concentrated matter in which all the galaxies were packed together within a pin-point at a definite epoch of time. This is, more or less, in line with the Vedic Theory which says that the unmanifested Brahmn breathed its own self-effulgent consciousness; hidden within the void, it burst forth as the supreme one. It began to manifest its true identity of Infinite Existence (Being) starting thereby the creations of the universe with the potential of Primordial Energy (Adi Shakti). Thus, the self-effulgence consciousness became the primal cause of the manifestation of the universe. Vedanta substantiates this proposition with further explanation of Cosmic Consciousness as the infinite potential of super-physical energy which gradually became dynamic and active, and culminated in a physical phenomenon constituting the universe. The Vedantic theory further elaborates the nature and working of the universe as also the Supreme Intelligence which projected human being as the creature's most important creation expected to play a crucial role. Scientists interpret this phenomenon in terms of what they called the Big-Bang Theory. Out of the Cosmic Consciousness, emerged the Primordial Energy – the seed of Creation – the expanding 'Brahmanda' which literary means the Egg of Brahmn or the Cosmic Egg.

According to the Big Bang theory, the entire matter and energy forming the Universe was compressed at the beginning of creation into a voluminous mass named as Cosmic Egg by the scientists. Eventually, this cosmic egg exploded *simultaneously* releasing light, sound and heat generating the five basic elements constituting thereby the Universe. There emerged out of the explosion of the primordial four forces namely Energy (Shakti), Sound (Naada), Matter (Mahaa-Maya) and Ether (Vyoma). The cosmic sound followed by the Big Bang has been identified by Vedanta as AUM or OM, going on in the whole universe endlessly carrying the primordial power of Brahmn through the vibrating forces of Creation, Preservation and Dissolution simultaneously, and is therefore, revered as Brahmn itself. It is in this sound of OM that the unmanifested Brahmn became first manifest as the Creator. Modern science too has acknowledged this primordial sound. Thus, the Vedic Theory gives a logical account of the great event with which Creation began, consistently following its basic thesis of a Conscious Supremely Intelligent Realty as the cause of the Cosmos. Thus spiritual approach seems to be in line with the modern scientific approach. The question, however, arises: **How did creation proceed to evolve further after the beginning as commonly enunciated both under Vedic Theory and science-based Big Bang theory**?

Desire, according to Vedanta, is considered to be the root cause of whole creation. The Supreme Being – the Brahmn, having emerged in its own Reality, developed a desire to manifest itself by evolving into manifold. This bond between the Being (Existence) and its 'Becoming' manifold has been mysterious also for the spiritual seekers of Reality. Brahmn – the only Being willed to become many. The Vedantic philosophy firmly believes that the Universe, in reality, is not a **Creation** but a **Manifestation** or projection of the Brahmn itself, by itself, of itself and for itself. Thus, according to the Vedanta, the Brahmn manifested itself as the manifold universe and the whole universe is, indeed, the Supreme Brahmn itself. This manifestation is a planned Cosmic Will (Sankalpa). It has been evolving according to well-defined axioms, postulates, principles and laws which, (in a subtle way) have been recognized/realized by spiritual philosophies on one hand, and discovered by the physical sciences, (at the gross level) on the other. Even modern philosophy also acknowledges this Cosmic Truth on the basis of its research findings pertaining to para-psychology and other related areas, and consequently concluded by interpreting Cosmic Consciousness as the Consciousness of the Cosmos. Infact both scientists and psychologists are coming round to this Vedic view that Cosmic Consciousness is the most subtle and supreme energy which gradually evolved as a dynamic and active force, culminating into the Universe. The (Sankalpa) Will of the Supreme Being as a consequence of the desire to manifest itself into many, the self-aware Brahmn accompanied by Maya – the illusion of physical entity acquired a relative grossness of an infinite creative potential and came to be known as God (Ishwara), that is the Lord of all possible manifest glory. As an initial step towards this manifestation, the Supreme Consciousness, the Brahmn got overwhelmed with His Will (sankalpa), **"I was alone, and I wanted to be many to enjoy my glory and therefore, multiplied or added myself to myself"**. Accordingly, within this Supreme Energy Principle called Hirayangarbha, there emerged the Maha-Tatwa, the Supreme Principle (Element). This became the first stage in the evolutionary process of (Prakriti) Nature from the invisible Cosmic Consciousness to the visible or grass level as the infinite expansion equipped with the potential of the space-time-causation-bound Universe. From this Supreme Energy Principle, emerged the Universal Matter-Principle (Sthoola-Bhoota-Tatva).

The spiritual philosophy, which postulates the whole process of, "One becoming the Many", finds a parallel phenomenon on the physical plane discovered by science. The cosmologists now recognize that the phenomena of emergence, existence and evolution of the universe reveal an amazing systemic and systematic paradigm of organization, integration and harmony which can be expounded only by some super intelligent power. According to Vedanta philosophy, the Cosmos means more than the physical Universe – a gross manifestation of the Universal Consciousness, operating through multifarious and multitudinous forms of energy, with their cause and effect relationship intelligently designed. All these forces and energies are ultimately found to be integrated in **'Shiva-Shakti'** phenomenon which according to Vedic tradition is considered to be a two-fold unity known also as Ardha-Naarishwara (Half-Female and Half-Male Lord of the Universe), in which the male represents Consciousness and the female, Pure Cosmic Energy. The whole Universe is a manifestation of Brahmn brought about by this dual principle with Shiva as the static power potential while Shakti as the dynamic energy of movement and change, emerging in various forms. Shiva is related to the space and Shakti to time. The two together make a unified principle of Cosmic Evolution generating the process of emergence and merging symbolized as Nataraja performing the Cosmic dance of creation and annihilation simultaneously going on endlessly in the Universe. This spiritual postulation is also interpreted as under:

- The word Subtle (Sookshma) means consciousness which is aware of itself and also of things around, while gross or physical (Sthool or Jada) means neither aware of itself nor of other things around it. This is a two-fold development which has been proceeding simultaneously on the physical plane as well as on subtler plane of consciousness, involving, again, a dual principle in each case. On the physical plane, the dual causal principles are Prana (Life) and Akasha (Space). Prana, as Swami Vivekananda elaborated, is the Vital Energy or the source of all energies in the Cosmos. All the forces of gravitation, attraction, repulsion, heat, electricity or magnetism are nothing but vibrations of that Vital Energy. The other component of this dual principle, namely 'Akasha', called ether is the primal form of matter. Vibration of Prana and Akasha is the cause of all manifestation: the two operate together to evolve the material universe. "**This Akasha**"', said Swami Vivekananda "**vibrates under the action of Prana and as the vibration becomes quicker, the Akasha is lashed into all these wave forms which we call suns, planets, satellites and systems**".
- A simultaneous development seems to have taken place at the subtle level of consciousness, which also follows the dual principle. One part of this dual principle comprises of five sense

perceptions in the forms of sound, touch, sight, taste and smell. These five senses in conjunction with the interaction of Prana and Akasha, seems to have brought forth the (Pancha Sthoola Bhootas) five basic elements namely: Space with attribute of sound, Air with sound and touch, Fire with sound, touch and form, Water with sound, touch, form, taste and the earth with the attributes of sound, touch, form, taste and smell. Thus according to the Vedic scriptures, out of the Cosmic Principle, was born space, air from space, out of air came fire, from fire was born water, and finally water gave birth to Earth. The Vedic Theory postulates that the whole universe is a manifold phenomenon of evolution of both inanimate and animate, from the tiniest (ant) elementary particle to the living human beings which is an endless variety of permutation and combination of each of these five basic elements.

- "He – the Brahmn dwells in the earth, water, fire, air and space, yet they know Him not, these elements being His body", says the Vedic Theory that further explains inter-relationship of these five elements by the principle of five-fold integration. Along with these five elements, two other noteworthy cosmological aspects in Vedic Theory are described prominently. One of these refers to the sun which is glorified in the Upanishads as the sum-total of energy in all beings and the giver of heat in various forms in Nature. The rising sun fills with its rays all Pranas in the Universe and energizes with its rays all creatures. The other equally important aspect in the Vedic Theory is that the earth is surrounded by gravitation beyond which is the space in which the solar system operates in an harmonious manner – the planets, galaxies and satellites (like the Moon) keep moving in their specified and orderly orbit. Thus, according to the basic Vedic Theory, evolution including creation is the process of the Cosmic Consciousness manifesting itself as the Universe. Indeed, this is the fundamental thesis of the Vedic tradition.

With regard to the idea of the Brahmn as the Ultimate or Absolute truth, several opinions have been propounded and to date continues to be explored by philosophers and scientists. The eminent Greek philosopher Plato looked for the absolute truth. There are scientists who say that there is no such thing as absolute truth, but many truths. The Buddha said that the ultimate answer is emptiness or vacuum or void. Mathematicians interpret this philosophy in different ways. Not all mathematicians are atheists. The eminent German mathematician

Leibnitz believed so much in God that he thought that the universe was designed by Him. There are other mathematicians who are divided with regard to their faith in God. Mathematics is, indeed, an important tool to understand the cosmos and life itself. In physics there are physicists who are looking for an absolute (unified) theory. They look for atoms and find that actually atoms are not the smallest elements. Thus, they probably look for the continuum and then they hope to find the absolute theory. But then this continuum is infinite and hence veers around the realm of philosophy and spirituality. Indeed, Mathematics cannot exclude philosophy. Mathematicians do get divine inspiration. The late S. Ramanujam, the great Indian mathematician is another glaring example of a mathematician who had firm faith in God. A mathematician spends a lot of time and thinking with one self. Mathematics helps in keeping a track of the perspective, looking at different ends and processes and making a sense of fragments in a holistic manner. In that sense, Mathematics is indeed a unifying discipline, making a sense of parts. It is rooted in reality. It is also a tool to help cope with the infinity. For example, void which means 'shunya', which also philosophically means non-duality. It is realized when the mind is free from perceptions and thoughts. Shunyata is self-experienced. The mind has to be trained through concentration and meditation to realize the Shunyata. The process of employing the mind is a prerequisite for focusing on and realizing the ultimate reality which is beyond the human sensory experiences.

A recent study undertaken by the Oxford University found faith in God to be an innate trait of human beings. Stephen Hawking, however, does not agree with the report on this study. He denounces all such faiths and notions of the Divine Power. According to him, the human brain is like a computer which will stop working when its components fail. There is no heaven or life after death for the broken computers. His detractors, like James Heiser on the other hand, say, "If Hawking intends to argue that a human being is merely a biochemically programmed computer, then his position is fundamentally untenable from the outset, for if a computer is programmed, there must be a computer programmer since the computers perform only those functions for which they are programmed by some programmer. If human beings are merely computers – no matter how sophisticated – then their every 'thought' and 'action' is preprogrammed. If human beings are simply preprogrammed computers made out of meat or flesh and bones, but who is their programmer? Moreover, the very possibility of freedom of thought and action becomes illusory while debating the meaning of life is not only irrelevant, but also absurd.

Not only in respect of the process of Creation and Evolution, Science and Spirituality have found common grounds, even in the context of its doom or destiny, both are agreeable that the Universe, though with a very long life, has a sure end. Vedanta thinks in terms of 'Kalpa', an aeon, at the end of which, creation goes back into its first cause which brings it forth again, thus forming a beginningless-endless cycle of emergence and disappearance of the Universe. According to the Vedic Theory, at the time of Dissolution (Pralaya) of the Universe, the elements are withdrawn back into the Brahmn – its origin and prime source. In other words, the grossest of the five elements namely the Earth will be drowned in water, water will be submerged in fire, fire will be absorbed by air and air will vanish into space, and so on, till the Mahatatwa, Hiranyagarbha, Shiva-Shakti, and all merge back into the Brahmn. This is, as the Bhagvat Gita says, how the Universe enters into the night of the Brahmn, and then, awaits for the dawn when it will start emerging again. A somewhat similar interpretation, regarding the disappearance and reappearance of the Universe, has been given by several scientists. Indeed, there can be gaps in the interpretation and enunciation of Vedic theory pertaining to the physical manifestation of the Universe, particularly because the Vedic philosophy permeates a vast number of Upanishads, Samhitas, Sutras and so on, and often, also interwoven into their main spiritual theme.

The Supreme Reality, according to the spiritualists, is the Ultimate Reality which is a unifying concept and an existential reality. Though this reality to the scientists looks vacuous, indescribable and incomprehensible, yet it exists. The quest for understanding and realization of this reality is the common aim of both spiritualists and scientists. Spiritualists prescribe various methods to realize the existence of this reality. Scientists are striving to understand this reality by devising various scientific techniques. Indeed, there is a difference in what is perceived spiritually and what is expressed empirically or justified scientifically. Knowledge acquired through scientific reasoning and methodology is transitory, impermanent and always changing, while spiritual wisdom attained through spiritual paradigms is eternal, comprehensive and all-pervading. The two perceptions, however, need not be treated contradictory rather they must be considered as complementary. **Indeed, verified and explored knowledge of the scientists, and the experiential wisdom of the spiritualists together can constitute a strong trust in the existence of such a Supreme Reality**.

Different spiritual pursuits give rise to different perceptions about the Supreme Divine Reality. A dispassionate study of various religious scriptures down the ages reveal different versions of the Cosmic

Evolution. Various religious scriptures have given different perceptions about it. It is not known what perceptions are given in other religious scriptures, but the Hindu religious scriptures have given a comprehensive description of the Cosmic Evolution. Vedas, the ancient Hindu scriptures, say, **"Then, there was neither non-existence nor existence, — , neither air nor the sky beyond —. Death did not exist nor was the night, of the day there was no sign. Without breathing, along with self-impulse was that One — Incomprehension was covered by incomprehension. All was then incomprehensible and formless."**

Yet another philosophical scripture propounds, "That One, whose primal turbulence flashes with luminosity and reverberates with thunder reminiscent of the Big Bang Theory, creates an indeterminate amorphous state, where everything exists concentrated with limited independence, appearing as dark spot or dark hole, showing the faint stage of the creation in becoming." While describing this stage the Rig Veda says, "**By whom this space is made strong, by whom the ground is made steadfast, by whom the luminous course and the sky is made spirited – By whom the two – the space and the earth – are arranged and supported in shinning spirit, on whom the Sun shines in resplendence; to the Divine Being, I offer my obeisance**." The Upanishads say that when "That One" found Himself alone without any delight, He split Himself to fall in two parts, the male and the female – Purusha (God) and Prakriti (Shakti) – which manifested in different forms comprising of two principles: Purusha as God – the Universal or Cosmic consciousness and Prakriti as Shakti – the Cosmic Energy. **The Cosmic Consciousness is the reality of the spiritualists while the Cosmic Energy is the reality of the scientists.**

According to the Bhagvat Gita, Prakriti – the Cosmic Energy evolves the process of creation under the supervision of Purusha – the Cosmic Consciousness as her supervisor. The real creator is, therefore, the Purusha (God) Himself while Prakriti (Shakti) is His executive to carry out the process of Cosmic Evolution or creation. The five basic elements of earth, water, fire, air and ether, five senses of touch, taste, sight, smell and sound, five organs of perception (gyan indirayas), five organs of action (karma indirayas), mind, reason (Buddhi); the faculty of discrimination and ego are various evolutes or instruments of evolution used by the Prakriti. Since the cause always pervades its effects, Prakriti pervades the whole universe and its elements. The Purusha's pervasiveness is even greater than that of Prakriti. Therefore, Purusha (God), the Universal or Cosmic Consciousness pervades both Prakriti and its evolutes *i.e.* the Universe and its elements.

Sometimes, Prakriti is termed as personal and Purush as Impersonal. Sri Ramakrishna says, "**Shakti (Prakriti) stands for the personal aspect of the impersonal**." Both personal and impersonal are the two aspects of the same Reality, the integral Brahmn or the Supreme Reality. These are also known as the dynamic and static aspects of the same reality which are complementary and remain inseparably together. The dynamic aspect is the Prakriti or Shakti which is represented by the infinite creation or flow of energy. It is also termed as the **'Saguna' Brahmn** – Brahmn with attributes and form, while the static aspect of the Supreme Reality represents the timeless, spaceless and causeless substratum as the Nirguna Brahmn Unmanifest, Absolute, Attributeless Formless and Invisible. The Rig Veda again says, "The dynamic Universe is the result of intensive divine fervor, application of the mind-force to matter. The Supreme Being is described here as the Architect of the Universe, the Supreme Sculptor of the Universe who chiseled the planetary systems in as great a variety of forms, as is perceived and even beyond." Thus, the Supreme Reality is termed as something mysterious wherein, the being and becoming, consciousness and matter, subject and object, Brahmn and Maya, Unmanifest and Manifest, Absolute and Relative, Impersonal and Personal, Purusha and Prakriti, are all different expressions of the same Supreme Reality, and are held together in one embrace.

In the greatest Hindu epic the 'Mahabharata', the Brahmn, which is said to evolve the universe/cosmos, is described as an entity or a phenomenon without any beginning, without any end, is unborn and resplendent. It is difficult to be thought of or known. It is undifferentiated and timeless yet it appears in terms of time. The 'day' and 'night' of Brahmn are described; creation takes place at each dawn and what is created is withdrawn at the close of day. Hinduism has its trinity of Creator, Preserver and Dissoluter, dealing with such a conception of eternal cyclical evolution; and with the ideas of preservation and dissolution being implicit in the concept of creation. Creation could be visualized not simply as consequence of the huge Big Bang as enunciated by the scientists, but rather as both evolved and evolving process of transformation of the potentials of the Supreme Reality, that is the Brahmn, referred to as 'That One' (Tad Ekam) in Rig Veda.

According to Sri Guru Granth Sahib, through countless ages, complete darkness prevailed. In a complete void, there was no world, no firmament. The Will of the Lord alone existed, neither night nor day, neither sun nor moon; Only God in an endless trance. Neither creation nor destruction, neither coming nor going; There were no continents, no underworlds; no seven oceans, no rivers, no flowing waters; There were no higher, middle or lower planes; Neither was there heaven, nor hell; Neither death nor time; There was no world of tortures, nor region of bliss; Neither birth nor death; When He so willed, Then He created the world, and without any support sustained the firmament. He founded the continents, solar systems, underworld and from the Absolute Self, He became manifest. None knows His limit. The Atharva Veda proclaims that the All-controlling, Immortal wheel of the Universe is revolving in infinite space. The Wisdom of God, united with Energy, manages the whole Universe. On this Energy, rest and depend All regions and planets.

The above metaphysical ideas find some parallels in astrophysics, particularly with regard to the theory of the origin of matter. How can something be created from nothing? The concept of relationship of energy and matter, gives an appropriate answer to this question. The reason being that matter (something substantial, visible) can be considered as a transformation or evolution (something vacuous and hence invisible), and conversely, matter can be transformed into energy. Albert Einstein improvised it by giving a formula for interchangeability of energy into matter and matter into energy in his special theory of Relativity, while in his general theory of relativity, he propounded the indivisibility of space-time continuum. This led to the modern Unified theory or Theory of Everything being intensively explored by the modern eminent cosmologist Stephen Hawking of England, and others.

According to the cosmologists, the visible matter as the form of so-called creation, is the left over of the original Big-Bang. Recent discoveries have shockingly shown that there are some more kinds of matter which are not visible. Such matters are being named as dark matters because of their invisibility. Infact, the visible matter or creation constitutes only four per cent of the whole universe. The rest of the universe is the invisible dark energy and dark matter. The particles of this dark matter or energy create black holes which are of all sizes ranging from sub-atomic small holes (whose energy can barely light a bulb) to big-black holes of the sizes of stars. Small holes are harmless in the sense that sometimes the planet like the Earth is hit by the particles of dark matter creating thereby small holes. Such small black holes are considered to be harmless. The big black holes, on the other hand, are the graves of big and massive stars, which on dying, first explode, then collapse to a point and disappear completely from the Universe. But, before, they disappear, the big massive stars leave behind their imprints, on the cosmic fabric of space-time continuum, in the forms of black holes called the dark regions. However, Hawking's exploratory work has shown that these black holes or regions are not dark but glow as particles which mechanically move into farther reaches or domains of space. Hawking also postulated that in addition to super large black holes, corresponding to the theory of the blackholes conceived earlier by the eminent American astrophysicist Chander Shekhar of Indian origin, – a billion times more massive than even the sun, the universe could be populated by trillions of mini-black holes.

For the last several years, various theories have been advanced by the scientists with regard to the evolution of the Universe and the related notion of the divine power. These among others include the Big Bang Theory, Vibration Theory, Quantum Field Theory and Theory of Everything. In an attempt to reveal the origin of the Universe and the mystery about the divine phenomenon, eminent Scientist Einstein concluded by saying that, "**God does not play dice with the Universe**," while Stephen Hawking has been of the view, "**God not only plays dice, He sometimes throws them where they can't be seen inside the dark holes**." Whatever be the truth about the theories and views of various scientists of the world, these statements of the two renowned astrophysicists are indeed indicative of some idea of the existence of an entity called God at the back of their minds which they could not deny while enunciating their respective theories. To date both spiritualists and scientists believe in the four-dimensional continuum of space, matter, time and consciousness which, in appearance as Phenomenon and in non-appearance as Noumenon, is the Supreme Being – the Ultimate and Absolute Reality called the Brahmn.

According to the some cosmologists immediately after the Big Bang, and before anything else appeared in the Universe, primordial sound waves were heard. These could have formed the basis of 'Brahmn Nada', or 'Nada Brahmn' mentioned in the Upanishads. Thus, throughout sound has been with the evolutionary process. Indeed it is an integral part of all activities in the world. The 'Brahmn Nada' is termed as the Hindu 'Big Bang' in the modern terminology. In 'Patanjali Yoga Darshan', God (Ishwar) is defined as a Special Being who is expressed by the original word 'Pranav', it is called 'OM'. According to Swami Vivekananda, Brahmn first manifested itself as Sound, and then as Form. The Universe is that Form. The sound of the word 'OM' is a generalized form of all sounds, often termed as Brahmn Sound or 'Brahma Nada'. Vedas and Upanishads have given two astounding insights that have emerged in modern science recently. The first is the concept of endless Universe (Anantakoti Brahmanda). The second is the concept of vast aeons of time through which creation passes, with the belief that a single day of Brahma (the Creator, one of the trinities, other two being Vishnu and Mahesh) is 432 million human years long, so that his one year corresponds roughly to the age of planet earth. It is also believed that this knowledge came to the ancient seers in their enhanced states of consciousness.

The question of consciousness and its evolution has attracted some of the best minds in the world. The study of consciousness has now become an attractive area for intellectual and experiential exploration which outlines a convergence of science and spirituality. Such a concept is embodied in the extensive Hindu scriptures starting with the four Vedas and their subsequent elaborations in the Upanishads. The central theme of this concept is that underlying all physical reality, there is one abstract entity, Brahmn, with the characteristic of consciousness. Having created the Universe, Brahmn remains present everywhere to date, organizing and managing basic aspects of everything in the cosmos. Recent scientific discoveries seem to validate the concept of Brahmn. Astrophysicists and cosmologists are convinced that there is one source behind the Universe, called the unified field. Brahmn, as the Vedantic concept appears to be similar to the modern unified field of physics. It is further being realized that various types of fields, both manifest and unmanifest are nothing but different aspects of a single entity, the unified field or the Vedantic Brahmn. The earth's gravitational field is an example of a manifest field. Likewise, there are other fields manifest in the earth. If earth is taken away from its orbit, all the manifest fields will go away with it. The leftouts will be unmanifest fields in the empty space and time. Understanding this inherent primary reality of the cosmos is essential to grasp the concept of the Brahmn. The unmanifest unified field, possessing the blue-print of everything, pervades all space. Einstein showed that space, time and fields cannot exist separately, but are always magnificently interwined in their operation. At this juncture, it is quite natural to see whether the unifled field possesses the characteristic of consciousness which is an in-built part of the Universe. Quantum physics has revealed that indeed, it is so in the sense that the phenomenon of consciousness is compatible with the reality of the unified field. Infact, astrophysicists believe that consciousness and quantum fields (systems) are not only complementary but even in their separable aspects of the same underlying process, have been permeating all space and time.

In some way, science and spirituality seem to be postulating one and the same view namely that a single entity created the Universe and is still present everywhere, maintaining and governing the fundamental principles of everything in the Universe. Albert Einstein was neither a theist nor an atheist. He was of the opinion that anyone seriously involved in the pursuit of science would get convinced at some stage that a spiritual phenomenon is manifest in the laws of the Universe. There is no last word in science. Just like any other theory, the Big-Bang theory also is not perfect, as some scientists believe. Finding a reasonable way of understanding, in the philosophy of science, the beginning and the end of the Universe is yet a formidable challenge. The astrophysicists are still searching for a 'grand unified theory' that will explain all phenomena in the Universe. They continue working to formulate the theory of everything. Science is yet to provide answers for the mysteries surrounding life and death under a scientific explanation though such ideas and many more related to the existence of the Universe are candidly given in the Hindu scriptures of Vedas which have yet to find acceptability in the world of science.

According to the Vedantic philosophy, Brahmn is that from which the universe evolved, while science strongly advocates its evolution out of the Big-Bang, which, too, is not considered to be perfect according to some other scientists. It is believed that prior to Big-Bang, nothing existed, for existence needs space. Prior to Big-Bang there was no space and hence nothing existed before. Another view is that Universe and God are same. In other words, the creator is in creation and the creation in the creator or God or Universe are self-creative phenomena. May be the Big-Bang or explosion are distortions of the self-creative phenomenon. If science can help in understanding this phenomenon, then it can serve as something that invokes and inspires faith in God. Indeed, science can actually strengthen, rather than weaken the faith in God. Sir Isaac Newton, in reality demonstrated that nothing happens by blind chance, that there is always some living mover, a force behind even the motions and planetary bodies in the space. Alongside his profound scientific insights, Newton claimed that behind every law of the Universe, there is some divine power called God. In other words, there exists an intelligence which is fundamental to all the laws of science and nature. Indeed, Newton was a transcendentalist.

Referring back to the Vedantic philosophy of consciousness, an eminent mathematical physicist John Von Neumann reasoned that, whatever was happening in the Universe, was not governed by the quantum theory and therefore there had to be some non-physical element. He discovered consciousness as a vital ingredient in a quantum experiment. According to a Nobel prize-winning physicist Eugene Wigner, the very study of the external world led to the conclusion that the content of consciousness is an ultimate reality. Strangely enough, physics by looking only at the external physical world, points to consciousness as an indispensable component of a quantum experiment, while spirituality, by looking inward, explores the nature of this consciousness. Thus, astrophysics shows the way to consciousness while metaphysics investigates what consciousness is. Indeed, in spirituality through its process of meditation, there is a conscious being the spiritualist, who perceives the thoughts which emerge and merge in his/ her mind – the same consciousness which Von Neumann discovered as the perceiving element in his quantum experiment.

Thus, science and spirituality, each dealing with different phenomena, seem to be converging in consciousness. While science deals with the external world of matter, space and time, from the infinitesimally small particles which make up the atom, to the giant galaxies in outer space, spirituality looks inward, its domain being that which is not physical, which is not visible, which cuts off the senses that connect the inner world with the outer physical world and which sustains life, alertness and awareness of the world.

In the quest for ultimate reality, the scientists are crossing the borders of astrophysics and entering the domain of metaphysics. Science is generally concerned with the nature of the physical universe within space-time causality. Spirituality is the quest for the ultimate reality, the unity of existence beyond the endless pluralities of its manifestations. The well-known scientist Max Planck thought, "Science cannot solve the ultimate mystery of nature...Every advance in knowledge brings us face to face with the mystery of our own being." Earlier the ancient Indian cosmologists provided somewhat similar explanations by connecting the micro or inner and the macro or outer worlds. The Pinda-Brahmand theory articulated by them says that the body (pinda) is a replica of the Universe, Brahmand, and the microcosm is a reflection of the macrocosm. A stunning pictorial example of this assertion comes from a 16th century painting on display at the visions of the cosmos from the Milky ocean to the evolving Universe shown at the Rubin Museum of Art in London. The Universe itself appears in the form of a human being or a Vishwa Purusha in the painting. The Indian philosophical thought talks about the 'Cosmic Pot' being composed of dualities such as sthula, gross or macro and sukshma, subtle, micro or Shiva, Purusha (male) and Shakti, Prakriti (female). Scientific materialism, dating from Newton, Descartes or Laplace with atoms as the building block, had been a study of matter essentially separate from metaphysics or spirituality. Stephan Hawking says, "I think that time, space and everything else are really in us. They are just mathematical models we have made to describe the universe." It seems scientists and spiritualists, astrophysicists and metaphysicists, cosmologists and astrologists, are mingling together in a probability-wave of pure consciousness; a mathematical abstraction.

Since ages, there has been a continuous debate between the scientists or rationalists on one side, and the spiritualists or religious people on the other. Infact, this debate is between rationalists and intuitionalists spiritualists. Rationalists deny the existence of cosmic consciousness. To them rationality is a reasoning consequence of the thought process which is the natural domain of the human mind. They ought to understand that intuition is also the inbuilt process of the same human mind. This is because of the intuition which spiritualists perceive about the existence of some unexplained phenomenon, and which is termed as the cosmic consciousness. Indeed, both reasoning and intuition are the outcomes of the thought process of the same human mind. Both originate from the same source but operate in different ways. One analyses external experience while the other has the inner vision. While external experience is accepted as the reality which is outer, intuition, which is the inner reality, is treated as illusory. Spiritualists assert that some preconditions need to be fulfilled before a conscious mind can qualify to experience intuitive reality which is the ultimate reality. It would, therefore, be unfair to reject the intuitive experience as unscientific and illusory. For a rational view of God, Rigvedic hymns offer a succinct account of the nature of God in true, scientific terms. They describe God as a spiritual substance pervading the entire, infinite universe. As a spiritual entity, God is omnipresent and every material object of the universe contains this spiritual substance. The terms that denote this are 'sarvavyapak' and 'vyapta'.

Rig Veda and Atharva Veda describe God as the most subtle substance existing throughout the universe. They talk of three cardinal entities in the infinite universe. These are: (i) inanimate and eternal material nature (matter) composed of five elements – earth, water, fire, air and ether; (ii) countless souls existing as animate eternal spiritual finite entities; and (iii) one eternal, animate infinite spiritual entity called God.

The soul is subtler than the matter and God is subtler than the soul. Matter is made of particles – electrons, protons, neutrons and positrons. The soul being subtler than matter can reshape, relocate and work upon finite portions of matter, but God as the most subtle spiritual substance holds complete control over matter and souls. This control comes through centrifugal action which is directed from within outwards. God regulates the existence of soul by providing it physical body and enabling it to refine itself and evolve through enlightenment. The process of enlightenment culminates in salvation of soul. The process of refinement and evolution involves association of soul with a physical body through a process of birth, growth, ageing and death which repeats itself.

If God is understood as supreme, infinitesimal, all-pervading spiritual substance, His power over matter and soul becomes clear. Then, people would not need to regard God as an object of obeisance through blind faith; rather they would understand God scientifically. Superstition would yield place to scientific enquiry and curiosity, would be satisfied rationally. This would make way for true communion with God.

The soul, Vedas say, is endowed with limited knowledge, understanding and intellectual prowess. God, on the other hand, is omniscient. Because the soul is limited by understanding, souls residing in human bodies perceive God in multifarious ways. Out of their ignorance about the real nature of God, they begin to view the formless God through totems, images and forms. This ignorance further creates multiple schools of religion and faith, many of which differ sharply on basic precepts and premises. This is precisely the reason why there is so much strife and discord in the world in the name of religion.

If only the human beings begin to understand the simple metaphysical truths expounded in Vedas, they will easily converge to a common, shared understanding of God and God's relationship with matter and living beings. That would enhance peace, harmony and empathy among human beings and would surely make this earth a much better place to live, thus facilitating the physical, mental, intellectual and spiritual evolution of human beings towards the goal of salvation. The concept of supreme consciousness is believed to be a pre-space time reality, which for the spiritualists, is the Ultimate Reality, a unifying concept and an experiential truth. The scientists, however, demand verifiable proof or quantitative and empirical evidence. The spiritualists envisage methods that are non-empirical. They believe only their own intuitions enough to provide them glimpses of spiritual reality. Just as cosmic energy is the reality for scientists and rationalists, likewise Universal or cosmic consciousness is the reality for the intuitive minds of the spiritualists. Indeed, the quest for ultimate reality has been pursued both by the reasoning minds of the scientists and rationalists on one hand, and the intuitive minds of the spiritualists and religious people on the other. Thus, the pursuit of this ultimate reality is the common aim of both scientists and spiritualists.

The intensive search for answers to various spiritual questions and the urge to understand the meaning of life and death, led the human beings to believe in a Divine Power. Later, scientific discoveries and inventions began to shake this faith in the existence of God. Karl Marx in the 19th century, dismissed the notion of God. Later Charles Darwin dismantled the theory of creation as propounded by various religions. The German philosopher Friedrich Nietzsche proclaimed total disbelief in God while Sigmund Freud urged people to treat God as illusion and science as reality. But later science through modern physics and cosmology took a lead to the conclusion, that everything in the world is consequence of one single source from which creation itself sprang. Scientists call this source the 'unified field' with consciousness as its apparently inseparable aspect, experiencing oneness with the source of everything, which is called God by the spiritualists. Through the medium of consciousness, even the professed agnostics, atheists and scientists conceded that there has to be some element of truth in the existence of God. Quest for the Divine has been a major aspect of all religions and civilization. The divine has been explored in different ways, described in different versions and portrayed in different forms. The eternal truth has been expressed in the Rig Veda – the truth is one, wise men call it by many names. This is the inner core, the light that is within all living beings. It must be, therefore, recognized that this fundamental truth is enshrined deep within the human consciousness. No one can deny that the Universe is the outcome of an intelligent planning. It is, indeed, unique and unusual. Thus, there is indeed an intelligent planner who initiated the Universe and created it. This intelligent planner is called God.

People ask a question that if God created the Universe, then who created God? Thus, there is always a problem with a beginning. Can't it be a self-created phenomenon? Science attempts to understand how the Universe came into being and how it works. Spirituality tries to visualize the purpose and meaning of the Universe. True, science has many inconsistencies while spirituality has mysteries. For example, according to the scientists, general relativity and quantum mechanics are not consistent with each other in several ways. Yet, each of them is considered to be correct. Same is true of spirituality. For example, revelation – it is an idea, a flash of genius which cannot be proved through an experiment in a laboratory. Scientists invariably get ideas or flashes suddenly. Who gives them such ideas or flashes? God? Who knows? Scientists usually do say but they do feel the sense of some supreme power who brought them the idea or a flash. Some acknowledge this power as the Divine Power while other usually treat it just an idea. Many of such scientists create a spiritual universe of their own which is not visible. But it is there and it exists. Just because they do not know, does not mean that it does not exist.

The Universe is considered to be ever-active-something beyond what the human brain can comprehend. Accordingly to astrophysicists and cosmologists, the element of chaos is omni-present in the Universe. Just the universe came into being with the Big-Bang, it could well end in a Big Crunch, collapsing into itself. The Hubble telescope's recent images of a black hole – a voracious and vacuous 'suction tunnel', the remains of a collapsed star-identified it on the strength of the swirling gases that seem to get stucked into apparent nothingness ("Shunya" of the Hindu scriptures). Likewise the scientists conjecture that they can calculate the Universe. By the same token they say that they can observe the force that moves the cosmos. Hawking says, "If there is a God, the Supreme creator too, has to be within the Universe and follow its rules." The reasoning power due to which a human being is considered to be a superior animal, is a limited human skill. Logic or reasoning can take him only up to a certain point whereas the area of operation of intuition is boundless. He has been made to believe that science is the only medium to know the truth. But this is not the only way because science has its limitation. It is not complete. The only valid truth is that a human being is basically a consciousness. This truth was founded by the Hindu seers many centuries back and this is valid even today.

Astrophysicists and metaphysicists have been grappling with the theories of abstractness particularly with regard to the beginning of the Universe and existence of God. Vedas clearly say that before creation began, everything was shrouded in the darkness, and from that darkness came out the creation. Einstein's theory of relativity turned the Newtonian physics upside down. Newton had assumed that space and time are both absolutes: space divides objects and time divides events. He asserted that space and time will always have the same meaning for every observer in the world. In contrast, Einstein established that space and time are different manifestations differently to different observers. His theory of relativity not only proved that space and time are relative but also raises an open question as to whether absolute knowledge is attainable at all. According to Einstein, space and time are free creations of human intelligence and tools of thought. Einstein discovered that matter (mass) and energy are one and the same, and are mutually convertible. He established that although matter as gross energy is invisible and subtle, yet the two are interchangeable. This idea of space also underwent a modification. Einstein observed that space is initially defined as the interval between two solid bodies. According to Rene Descartes, space is everywhere and objects are to be considered as contained in space. Even this understanding has also undergone a transformation. Space is no longer seen as a container of objects, all matter is a condition of space and not separate from it. This has generated the already raised open questions namely: **How was the Universe created? What will be its ultimate fate? Is this the only Universe or just one of an infinite number of Universes? Was the creation inevitable? How inevitable was the origin of life? Does the Universe harbor other intelligent life forms?**

Hidden behind all these puzzling questions is the biggest mystery of all: **Why is there something rather than nothing**? In the late nineteen eighties, Stephen Hawking stipulated a unified theory as well as a possible description of all basic forces of nature and a possible key to understanding the origin of the Universe. By 1988, Hawking declared that the unified theory would help know the mind of God. Thus earth-shattering concepts such as cosmic evolution, relativity theory and quantum mechanics together with the Heisenberg's Principle of Uncertainty (that it is not possible to measure accurately, both the position and the velocity of a particle), have brought the development of Science beyond Newtonian mechanics to a realm of infinite possibilities and new truth. Laplace's determination theory states that if one knew the positions and velocities of all particles in the Universe at one time, then in principle, it should be possible to predict the future. Interestingly enough, physics seems to be taking recourse to metaphysics in the sense that physicists feel that while they are not yet in contact with the ultimate reality, experts on quantum theory have come out with ideas like what they term as, **'The mysterious vision'**, and **'The Mystic Vision'** among others, using the language of mysticism with sayings such as "Reality is unknowable; any attempt to describe it obscures as much as it illuminates". Enquiries resembling spiritual questions into the mysteries of nature and processes of the forces that create, sustain and subsume have come up recently.

Great intellectuals have devoted themselves to the pursuit of knowledge regarding the origin of the Universe and forces governing it. The body of knowledge, consisting of the four principles and six auxiliary scriptures known as Veda Shastra, explores the fundamental mysteries of the Universe. It provides most convincing answers to the questions: **How did the cosmos originate**? **What is its future**? **Who is the originator of this Cosmos**? In so doing, they satisfy the deeply felt need of humans to understand the nature and purpose of life on earth.

They explain what maintains the existence of cosmos, and what will happen after it ceases to exist. They unravel the relationship between causes and their effects, and between actions and consequences of action. They explain how energy is the foundation of matter and how matter ultimately is transformed into energy. They identify nature and roots of ignorance and give the means to remove them. They explain principles, processes and the mystery of macrocosm. They analyze what comprises the human being and how it is different (in which respect not different) from other species. In this way they tell gross from the subtle, from body, from mind and then intellect, explaining the bases on which all these three function.

2.2 Creative Evolution

When and how did life begin on earth? When were the creatures on earth born? What is the origin of life? Such questions among others have been bothering the human mind ever since human being, the greatest event of the Universe, appeared on the earth. The answers to such questions are yet being explored by the scientists and thinkers all over the world. Process of creation of life, emergence of the creatures and the role of the creator together constitute what may be termed as the Creative Evolution – considered to be unique to the planet of earth.

Science believes that the creative evolution or what may be termed as Biological Evolution began about 11 billion years ago after the Big-Bang with the appearance of the first life cell on earth a little more than three billion years ago. From this cell, a steady process of life evolved leading to its human form about 25000 years ago. Then began the psycho-social phase in which human consciousness began to manifest and develop in various directions until the full-fledged human being – intelligent, rational and endowed with sense of discrimination emerged about 10,000 years ago which strangely coincides with the Vedic-period in Indian history.

The creative evolution is considered to be a two way process of inorganic and organic evolution. The infinite cosmic consciousness as enunciated earlier in section 2.1, first manifested itself as 'energy', thereafter as subtle elements which became more and more gross and gradually got condensed into diverse types and forms of 'matter'. This, in scientific terminology, is called the process of inorganic evolution. And then, began the organic evolution which reversed this process and energy started flowing while getting released from the matter. Consciousness gradually started generating itself released from the bondage of matter. From the 'dead' matter (with lowest consciousness almost tending to zero consciousness) sprang the living plant with little consciousness (more than zero consciousness) followed by the partially conscious animal and finally, fully self-conscious and intelligent human being. Thus, if inorganic evolution was **'consciousness lost'**, then the organic evolution was **'consciousness regained'**! The creative evolution is, therefore, described as the two-way process of converting matter into energy and energy into matter as also believed by Albert Einstein. It is, indeed, a two-way channel through which the Cosmic Intelligence and Energy emerge from and return to its original source – the Brahmn. The Vedic Theory also includes in its scope this process of creative evaluation in respect of two major aspects namely (a) **Emergence of life**, and (b) **Evolution of living organisms culminating in the emergence of human beings**.

According to the Upanishads, the creator created a pair of matter and energy so that the two together would, between them, produce a multiple of creatures and creation. This is further explained in the Upanishads as to show how, step by step, life developed into active, intelligent and embodied species and beings. The creative process originated in the Cosmic Consciousness. Having created the world of elements and matter, this Cosmic Consciousness became the manifest as well as the unmanifest. Latent in matter like oil in mustard seeds or butter in the curd, it became manifest through countless variety of big and small embodied forms, while itself dwelling therein as a microscopic part of the **Supreme Being,** the controller of energy, attributes in matter as well as life in the body. Prana or the vital breath, is born of the **Inner Being**, just as the shadow is born of man. In other words, the consciousness, latent in matter is the real substance from which springs the shadow of life-breath which, in turn, enters the body through the action of mind. In the same way, the vital forces, mind and all organs emerge from it. The Supreme Being, whose nature is Consciousness, penetrates the mind and assumes Prana as his sheath of subtle body.

Scientists have been striving for a long time to discover how the process of creative evolution came into being. How did life appear in matter? How does an organism produce consciousness? The mind-body problem, though vividly probed, yet remains unexplained. The present maxim of neurobiology, that all is matter, raises more questions than it answers. The Universal System behind the terrestrial evolution may, in Sri Aurobindo's view, has been outlined as under:

> There is the silent Brahmn, the Ineffable, which can only be known by the highest spiritual experience. One and the same Brahmn is the active Brahmn which manifests its inexhaustible infinity in the endless way and beyond time. This manifestation

has been and will always be on the top of the gradations of the eternal manifestation in the worlds of the three ultimate attributes, of the One, Sat or Truth (Existence), Chit or Consciousness (Awareness), Ananda (Bliss), the quintessence of supreme ecstasy. The fourth attribute (domain) of this upper hemisphere is called 'Super Mind'. It is, indeed, the manifesting consciousness of the One, the Unity-consciousness or Truth-Consciousness, the Absolute Knowledge that is the absolute truth that is the absolute power. This super-mind is not something like the limited human mind at its highest potential. It is a supra-mind which generates the human mind but which is as different from it as the sun is from the stars. It is what scientists believe to be some invisible phenomenon behind the complexities of nature of creation, what is present in it and supports it everywhere and which they name it as the real 'Mind of God'. In fact it is what the spiritualists term as 'the Brahmn' in the purest form. From the domains of the Super-Mind, descend the worlds of lower hemisphere, those with which people are more familiar: mind, life and matter. Nevertheless, all is and remains the One Supreme Truth in every categorization. Thus, "matter too is the Brahmn," and so are human life and human mind. Indeed, it is believed that there are uncountable worlds of every level of the manifestation, from the highest to the lowest, from Sat, Chit, Ananda, and the brilliances of the Super Mind to the worlds of human mind and life, higher and lower. This universe is an evolutionary phenomenon. All possibilities exist: infinite oneness becoming infinite fragmentation and vice versa; light becoming darkness and conversely; bliss transforming into sorrow and conversely while embodied in matter. This cyclic phenomenon of the emergence and disappearance of the Universe, and the organic cycling of its creation is a continuous process, governed by the eternal Brahmn. Thus, the cyclic equation Matter = Energy = Consciousness may find its acceptability and understanding by both science and spirituality.

"Consciousness is the fundamental ground of existence. It is both the observer and the observed. In this deeper understanding, the Universe is an integrated wholeness that differentiates into space, time, energy and matter on the objective side, and the subjective world of thoughts, sensory experiences, feelings, creativity, insight, love, joy and compassion on the other side," says Deepak Chopra, an eminent spiritualist philosopher. Few scientists are satisfied with the theory that creation was a mere accident, the outcome of a combustion of cosmic dust. Spiritual seekers, too, are engaged in a similar quest. They are interested in the scientific laws of nature, but wish to go even further to find the divine law that brought everything into being. While scientists search through outer instrumentation, spiritual scientists plumb the inner consciousness. Thus, the mission of both scientists and spiritualists is one and the same. They are both here to find the hidden laws of nature, the higher power that created everything.

Science and spirituality may opt for a mutual partnership. If those engaged in science spend some time in silence, looking within, they will get inspired to find answers to the questions they ask. Similarly, spiritual seekers, when they test hypotheses in the laboratory of their own body and soul, will find the answers. So one can safely conclude **that science and spirituality are two sides of the same coin. The aim of science is to uncover the deepest spiritual truths, and the aim of spirituality is to search for the cause behind scientific fact.**

Spirituality is considered to be relevant only to the sentient life. Therefore, at the very foundational level, it is important to explore how life originated, and most importantly so, since it is a process of common occurrence. It is only then that one can meaningfully examine whether mind, consciousness and spirituality are relevant to one's life. Is it necessary to figure out how something animate could appear or emerge from an inert and inanimate (non-living) material? Scientists have been attempting several types of theories including experimentation to discover the origin of life. A Greek philosopher, Anaxagoras in the 5th century B.C. propounded a theory named "**panspermia**" theory meaning the theory of "**seeds everywhere**" in which he said that the Universe has an infinite spermata everywhere which give rise to life form on reaching any suitable destination.

According to the Panspermia Theory, micro-organisms from outer space are responsible for originating life on earth and in other parts of the Universe where suitable conditions exist for sustaining them. This theory has been refined by some of the modern astronomers and experts on the theory of evolution by propounding the hypothesis which states that life forms continue to enter the earth's atmosphere even to date and may be responsible for the genetic novelty necessary for large scale evolution as well as for various types of epidemics and diseases. Also several mechanisms have been evolved by means of which life could be transported from one place to another place through space. It is conjectured that chunks of material dust blasted out of the collusion of asteroids with some planets could be carrying with them micro-organisms to the earth or other planets. These micro organisms could find earth like planets quite conducive to gain a foothold which could lead to their further evolution. Thus, according to Panspermia Theory, the seeds of the physical phenomenon such as space, time and matter might have been sown into the expanding fabric of the Big Bang of Creation which permeated the Universe and thus, in this way the seeds of life could have originated and become prevalent everywhere. Thus, gaining the root, evolution might have taken place and, in due course of time, might have generated sentient beings who further evolved to generate the non-physical entities like mind, consciousness and hence the spiritual aspects. Most of the scientists and spiritual scholars do not subscribe to the Panspermia Theory of Evolution.

Creation is an ocean of surprises. The little planet in the universe – the earth contains the variety of living and non-living beings. A few vital questions about creation arise: The first one is as to **who created this universe**? Religion says that there is a God, but the scientist hasn't fully accepted it. The second question is, **why has this universe been created**? Science is not able to answer this question, while spiritual view is that the divine power called the Brahmn being alone wanted to become many-fold, as enunciated in 2.1. The third one is, **when was this universe created**? The answer is big 'Nobody knows'. No doubt modern physicists are trying to calculate the date of creation, but they are vacillating. The fourth question is, **out of what has this universe been created**? No answer, again though both spiritualists and scientists have broken down solid mass into the atom and say it is the fundamental unit of life. Indeed, there, isn't the final answer. Thus, the four vital questions have remained unanswered till now. Efforts are being continuously made to explore the fifth and final question: **What is the role of human beings in creation**? The first possible rational answer is, human beings don't have any role at all. Like all living beings, they are born, undergo metamorphosis and die. But is that all? Are they mere waves in the ocean? Fortunately not. Why, because human beings alone ask questions. They alone can raise the above five vital questions about creation, because they are unique beings and hence have a unique role to play in creation. They can think of God, they can think of the Infinite, they can analyze, while other living beings cannot.

There are two methods: one of science and other of spirituality. Science is the study of the external, spirituality is the study of the internal. Science claims the objective study of the universe, since it has accumulated much knowledge about the earth, solar system, stars, and galaxies. It has propounded many theories. However, yesterday's theory is today's junk! Why, because the more they study, the more it's confusing, and more is left unknown. Secondly, the instrument, the mind, can't find answers to all questions through the five senses. This leads to the second path – spirituality which alone has declared that the universe is only an objective manifestation of the Brahmn – the Supreme Reality.

Spirituality is essentially the in-depth study of human personality. This study leads to supreme knowledge of everything. How? It was Swami Vivekananda, who experienced the grandest truth that the microcosm and the macrocosm are built upon the same plane, said, **"To know the human being is to know the universe. But to know the human being one doesn't need instruments. The fine instrument called mind will suffice. Using it, one has to dive deep into oneself: one should meditate. Meditation leads us to the hitherto unseen universe within.**" The inner universe, say saints, is astounding. This universe will reveal all the knowledge one needs. The knowledge of why, who, how, what, when, etc. will all become perfectly clear once one looks within. Sri Ramakrishna declared: **"A man attains everything when he discovers his true Self in himself. That also is the purpose of assuming a human body".** Adi Shankaracharya said, "**Human birth is the most precious gift of God. To expand it in vain pursuits is a colossal and stupendous waste; To utilize it to know is the greatest good. Therefore let's all sit down quietly for sometime every day, close our eyes, and dive deep within. This alone, and nothing else, will bring us knowledge, lasting peace and supreme happiness."**

The origin of creation is something which baffles every understanding. The best of human intellects have failed to throw light on this fundamental question. Did the cause appear first or the effect? What is the primeval cause? Can there be a causeless cause? The mystery that surrounds these questions agitates the human mind. **Who was his the first creator**? Similar puzzling questions confuse intelligent enquirers. Did plant precede seed or seed precede plant? Did hen succeed egg or egg succeed hen? **What is the origin of all living creatures? What is the origin of the world**? This is the most fundamental question. The answer to this question seems to be wrapped up in upmost secrecy, obscurity and mystery. To appease the agitated mind, religious prophets gave a name to that causeless cause. The name was God.

God is reckoned to be the origin or source of the world. Some axiomotise a personal God with a form. Others postulate an impersonal God without a form. The introduction of God as creator or originator is a mere proposition. An intellectual supposition. In mathematics, sometimes a problem is solved on the basis of some self-evident truth called the axiom or a postulate. This is the first step used in solving the problem. The real answer has to be derived methodically by applying the laws of mathematics. Similarly, the concept of God is a sheer proposition. Faith in the existence of God is taken to be as an axiom. It is the origin of the world. That does not solve the question. Nevertheless, the vast majority has passively accept God as creator, originator of everything. They firmly believe in the existence of the unknown divine being. To them the existence of God is obvious. To question His existence is not liked by them.

If the mystery of the unknown is to be solved, it has to be dealt with in terms of what is already known. But no one seems to heed this basic law of learning. The unknown God is described in equally unknown terminology. God is said to be infinite mercy, infinite love, omnipotent, omniscient, etc. But the human intellect cannot conceive infinity. The mass of humanity is innocent. They struggle with these unknown terms and terminologies. Little do they realize the futility of their meanings. Time passes on and they are where they are. The knowledge of God remains ever in obscurity. The intelligent become conscious of their incapacity and give up their chase. The ignorant believe that they know God. In their innocence they parrot their limited concepts to the world.

The role and goal of Vedanta is to unravel the mystery of the divine unknown called God. The Vedantic approach to the problem is logical and experiential. It explains thoroughly and clearly, the facts of life. It proceeds logically from the known to the unknown. It moves step by step from the lowest depth of ignorance to reach the highest peak of knowledge. From delusion to realization, one is made to understand, appreciate, experience and verify the ultimate truth. Vedanta does not merely give names to God. It provides the material to think. The knowledge of Vedanta serves as a pointer indicating God. One cannot capture God with words and expressions. Finite efforts cannot achieve infinite. But at the same time one cannot reach God without this knowledge. Knowledge takes one up to the furthermost point. Vedanta or for that matter, any philosophy cannot take one beyond that point. So one cannot get attached to the knowledge and remain there. Indeed one needs knowledge, makes good use of it and goes beyond it. Vedantic knowledge purifies one's mind. It makes one's mind contemplative and meditative. One must plunge into that mind, into the silence within. One will then realize God.

Although creation is perfect within itself, yet it is not possible to forget the creator. Body, mind and sentiments are three most important aspects of life. Soul is another essential aspect of life. It is the source of the other three dimensions of life. Study of soul or science of soul, called spirituality, is a dimension beyond the integrated mechanism of body, mind, sentiments and physical energy. A living being is just the combination of the five basic elements of creation namely: water, air, fire, earth and space. But this combination is so beautifully compiled that it is complete by itself. Not only this, but the rest of the existence is also constructed of the same five basic elements. All this is a part of creation. But what is the foundational source and force behind the whole creation? It is the divine energy. Swami Vivekananda said, **"Everything in the Universe is filled with the same energy, with the same intelligence, the same consciousness. Thus, the objects that we use in our life, the actions we do with this body, the persons to whom our actions are directed, are nothing but the manifestations of God"**

The Universe is full of many manifestations of the divine energy. Galaxies are made up of this energy in the form of matter consisting of vibrating atoms, electrons, protons and subatomic particles. The space between them (atoms) is emptiness. The energy, which vibrates and pulsates between the emptiness at different frequencies, is the God-force or God-power which comes directly from the cosmos to give them different forms and structures. Thus, everything that exists in the cosmos is present in space but in different forms. The God-force holds past, present and future of everything and everything is in its place. A body is made up of cells, molecules and atoms which are all components of emptiness. Space, the emptiness between two atoms, is filled with divine energy or God-force which is flowing eternally all over the body. As blood in the human body flows through veins and nerves, likewise energy flows through veins and nerves. It is also called Shakti or the energy. Intellectually, it is not easy to make a study of the empty space, the field of that Divine Power (Divya Shakti) flowing between the atoms in the body. Only an enlightened person can undertake such a study that lead him to the study of the self. Enlightenment is beyond logic.

In short, at the core of energy manifestation of life is "individual consciousness" (Atman), particle (Ansha) of the Cosmic Consciousness (Parmatma). Being pure intelligence, it is not perceptible by the gross senses. And, yet it is this very intelligence which illumines and activates every limb and every cell in the body, having permeated the body upto the very tips of finger nails and body-hair. When the living being (Jeevatman) with these limited adjuncts of body, mind and sensory system, becomes active, it is called an embodied being (Dehatma) attached to the body by its love for existence. Thus, the Atmic Principle at the core of every living being – from microbe to human being – is in reality – in no way different or apart from the Cosmic Intelligence "from which have emerged energy, matter, time, food and the seeds of various species of living beings. Thus, the original Sankalpa (Cosmic Will) of Brahmn to become manifold carries within it the whole plan and design of Creation right from its very starting point. All manifestations of energy and matter, life and living forms are only an unfoldment of that Cosmic design with a definite objective and a goal. Thus, Vedic Theory gives an account of the Cosmic consciousness evolving, through matter, into conscious, intelligent and active organisms.

Science too, while investigating into this very phenomenon along the physical plane, advocates that life emerged from matter through a series of physio-chemical processes in which light, cosmic rays, water vapour, hydrogen, etc. acting together gave rise to the building blocks of living organisms. Science further propounds that when the earth cooled and oceans were formed, life first manifested as algae, green weeds, shrubs and plants to provide oxygen and food to the moving organisms that were to follow. This theory of the science corresponds to the Vedic view which states that from the earth sprang vegetation, from vegetation sprang food, from food sprang the living being. Thus, began the process of Biological Evolution under which the organisms multiplied in varieties culminating in homospiens or human being. Indeed, science has bridged the gap between the animate and the inanimate through microbiology and biochemistry.

A human being is generally considered to be the highest form of life in the process of the Creative evolution. How is a human being considered to be a better being? What are the specific parameters that distinguish a human being from other forms of life such as animals and plants among others? Scientists and rationalists mostly believe in Darwin's Theory of Biological Evolution as the only credible scientific explanation for the origin and evolution of life on earth. But Darwin's theory is increasingly being challenged especially or mostly by those who believe that God created all of life and the Universe. They further believe that Darwin's theory of evolution cannot explain the full complexity of life on Earth, and that a supernatural designer or a supreme creator must have done the whole creation. Some also contend that Darwin's theory denies religious faith in the existence of this Supreme Power called God and embraces a materialistic worldview. They advocate the theory that creation, which is so intricately organized, can be the work of some super intelligent power. Indeed, Darwin's theory and for that matter any biological evolution theory is open to debate because of some possible spiritual reasons.

Darwin's theory stipulates that human beings evolved from apes. This notion seems to be farfetched, because for thousands and thousands of years, apes have coexisted with humans but to the best of knowledge and belief none of them have ever evolved into a human being. Moreover, biological evolution is a gradual process of step-by-step growth and development of a living being. Darwin's view, however, finds some resemblance or similarity with the Vedic spiritual view of creation which is also supported by a Greek mathematician and philosopher Pythagoras. The Vedic view believes a human being seems to be evolved from an animal, including an ape, but not as far as his body is concerned but as far as his 'being' is concerned. This view, indeed, seems to be more valid. According to its philosophy of birth and death, based on the actions or deeds of a human being, not that animal's body or an ape's body gradually evolves into a human body, but that an animal's soul or ape's soul gradually evolves (develops) and then, the soul based on its deeds of its previous birth/physical form, takes the form of a physical body in its new birth. Thus, there is no bodily or biological evolution. But, it is the spiritual evolution that takes place in a being to become a super-being. In this way, different people evolve from different animal bodies. That may be the cause of so much diversity in the shapes and behavior of human beings.

Some sort of similarity or resemblance between certain human beings and animals is invariably observed in the sense that some human beings behave like animals or resemble monkeys or apes just like Hanuman, as monkey-faced man, and Jamvant, as bear-like being, in the holy scripture Ramayana of the Hindus. Some human beings, sometimes, carry the animal instinct such as anger, aggressiveness, sense of possession, cunningness and short-memory. At the same time, there have been instances, although very rare, where the animals behave in more humane way than even the human beings do. Indeed, animal's animality and human's humanity cannot exist as one because humanity is meant to have acquired qualities which can be divine qualities. The spiritual view of the biological evolution, further gets strengthened with the Hindu's belief in cycle of life and death, sufferings and comforts, virtues and vices etc. It is considered to be equally relevant in the sense many cases of persons having the memories of their previous lives have been reported as well as described realistically in the literature on Hinduism.

An ancient philosopher-poet once said, "I died as a plant to be born as an animal. I died as an animal to be born as a man. I will die as a man to be born as an angel." This means that animals belong to a higher order of creation as compared to plants, and that human beings aptly occupy an even more superior position in the hierarchy of creation. Do plants have life and feelings? Do they suffer pain and pleasure like the human beings? Can their feelings be detected or even measured? The answer to each such question is yes. Sir Jagdish Chander Bose, a distinguished Indian scientist proved, in a international conference of physicists at Paris in 1900, that plants, being full of life, responds to pain and suffering much like humans, especially when plants are cut or transplanted. To prove this theory, Bose invented an instrument called the Resonate Recorder that was so sensitive that it could record the subtlest of changes inside a plant. Using his theory and experiments as a basis, Bose boldly challenged the blurred line between living beings and non-living beings. He demonstrated that even the so-called non-living beings (insentient beings) like rocks and metals respond to different stimuli and produce different kinds of sound *e.g.* musical (Indian) instruments like drums, tabala, dholak, harmonium as well as echoes in the hilly areas. The only things lacking at that period of time were sensitive instruments to empirically record those responses, and an open-mind to think the seemingly impossible. The genius within Bose quickly invented these instruments which are even today considered marvel of technology. In 1895, in front of a packed audience, he transmitted radio-waves that travelled through a wall to ring an electric bell 75 feet away and ushered in the world a wireless instrument. Two years later, the Italian scientist Marconi improvised the wireless work of Bose for which he (Marconi) was awarded the Nobel Prize.

The stages of creative evolution are: Prakriti, matter, sound, ether, touch, air, sight, light, taste, water, smell and earth. So the process of creation begins with empirical or fundamental matter followed by the five subtle elements, the five gross elements, the mind, the senses of knowledge, the karma indriyas and the individual self. This is how the world or the universe is believed to have been created. The further creation of human beings, animals, trees and plants is called biological creation.

The Bhagvat Gita, the most famous work on philosophy of life, describes "Atman" as an entity which leaves the old bodies at the time of death and seeks out new forms at the time of birth just like a person discards old clothes for new. Can this view be reconciled with the biological creation? Is there any common ground of the mapping of human genome and the wisdom of the Gita? While science or for that matter biology appeals mostly to the scientists, Gita is adored and liked by spiritualists and other people including a common person and the learned philosopher. An appropriate perspective of human philosophy would convince even the most skeptic scientist that science, infact, reinforces the Wisdom of Gita and makes it more relevant to the people. The relation between man and creation is that of the relationship of the microcosm to macrocosm. All beings are pervaded by consciousness. It is the consciousness that pervades and sustains the world and all its creation. Indeed, nature or the creation is nothing but God's manifestation which is visible to the world and can be experienced through senses.

A human being is equipped with the brain which is most productive. It is the only entity which can turn inwards, can go back into its own depths and search out wonderful things. Human being is considered to be the only medium through which one can attain realization of the nature of the Self – the ultimate aim of human life.

Extending the same argument, analogously, the rising, sinking and winding movements are some of the expressions of the same dynamic patterns of energy within the earth. All things grow, evolve and perish. These are seen as patterns of continuous transformation or evolution. A flower, a tree or a human body, although at different rates, transform. Indeed, all things eventually evolve and transform. The phenomenon of birth and death pertains to the body only and not to the soul. The soul is immortal. Vedic philosophy says that soul is the real self of a living being and not its vesture called the body. In the Gita, this message of the Vedic knowledge refers to the immortality and transmigration of the soul. When a soul enters a body, it is called birth, and when the same soul departs from the body, it is called the death. This is a continuous process which comes to an end only when the soul obtains liberation (Moksha) from its cycle of birth and death.

Biologists describe evolution itself as the continuous adaption of organisms or species to the environment by the integrating agencies of selection, hybridization, inbreeding and mutation. All life began in the water and only after millions of years did some forms adapt to land. Let's take a look at the ten avatars of Vishnu. His abode is in the mythical ocean of milk, an oblique reference to the cosmos; he reclines on the coils of the Adisesha, the five-headed primeval serpent, each of its heads symbolizing each of the five elements, the panchabhootha – Earth, water, energy, air and sky.

People differ from each other by just a fraction of a per cent, according to the scientists who have successfully deconstructed the human genome. The basic chemistry is almost the same among different species. For instance, what sets human beings apart from animals is only a few hundred genes. No wonder, then, that Hindu mythology is replete with stories of what seem like 'freaks' of nature – mutation and semi-mutations as reflected in exotic creatures. The story of creative evolution as enumerated in the Vedas and other scriptures is startlingly in tune with modern scientific theories.

In his Matsya (or fish) Avtaar, the first, Vishnu saves the world from the deluge. His rescue of the Saptarishis, the seven sages, ensured the survival and dissemination of the species. As Kurma or the divine tortoise, an amphibian in the second Avtaar, Vishnu lent his back to be used as the pivot on which the Gods (the Angels) and the Demons (Asuras) placed the churning rod (the Meru Mountain) with which they churned the ocean to recover some of the precious things lost in the deluge.

The third incarnation was that of Varaha or the wild boar, an unrefined land animal that rescued the earth after it had been dragged deep down the water by the demon Hiranyaksa. The fourth is an interesting mutation: Half-animal (lion) – half-human, the Narasimha Avtaar. He freed the world from the oppression of Hiranyakasipu, the demon-father of Prahlada.

As Vamana, the dwarf-like man, Vishnu in his fifth incarnation restored the power of the gods which had been undermined by the penance and devotion of King Bali. As Parasurama in his sixth avatar, he delivered humankind from the oppression of the warrior (kshatriya) rules. With the arrival of Rama as an ideal human being, evolution reached a point of refinement, both biological and civilizational. Here too, Rama as Vishnu's seventh incarnation, yet again, destroyed a wicked force personified by Ravana.

But it is as Krishna, the eighth avatar, that Vishnu steals hearts and minds. That's why it is referred to as the perfect avatar. The Lord becomes the eternal lover of the milkmaids (gopis) symbolizing pure souls in Vrindavan; but he also becomes the serious and eternal philosopher and guide when He advises Arjuna on the battlefield at Kurukshetra in the great epic of Mahabharata. This is immortalized as the Bhagvat Gita, the Song of God, a do-it-yourself manual on how to attain self-knowledge and realization. Although Krishna is the propounder of the Gita, He is at once both its substance and its goal.

Reverting to the scientific exposition of evolution, Darwin Theory of the evolution of species gives a progressive refinement of their physical structure and increasing intelligence; the long chain of progressive evolution of the species through a variety of shapes, sizes and structures in terms of genetic mutation, differential reproduction and natural selection, culminating into the emergence of the most refined species namely the human beings equipped with the most integrated and organized physical and mental structure among all the species. The Hindu tradition too has more or less similar view of the graded order of species beginning with the lowest species such as insects and worms evolving though a long series of progressively superior order of the evolution of creatures into the final form of the human beings. The vital difference, however, between the two theories is that while the Drawinian theory views evolution as progressive development of the physical and mental components of the animal, the Vedic Theory sees in it the spiritual trend towards perfection through a gradual unfolding of divinity in all beings. Consistent with its thesis, the Vedic Theory concerns itself primarily with the spiritual evolution of the individual soul (Jeevatman) and provision of an appropriate vehicle for the individual self (Jeevatman) to proceed on its upward journey through 8.4 millions of forms of organisms ('yonees') in this long chain of the evolutionary process. The measuring scale for this ascent of the individual self (Jeevatman) is based on the spiritual principle in terms of three basic attributes of Satva, Rajas and Tamas.

The earliest of all the organisms, the insects and worms are steeped in 'Tamas' or ignorance, sloth and dullness. In the evolutionary order of organisms that follows, there is a gradual diminution of 'Tamas' and a proportionate infusion of Rajas which makes the species progressively conscious and dynamic, alert and active. When 'Tamas' dominates over 'Rajas', the dynamism in the animal expresses itself in selfishness, ego, anger, desire, greed, hatred, jealousy, lust, cruelty and violence summed up in four general tendencies namely hunting for food, passing time in sleeping, living in fear of danger or attack and finally lust for procreation. The third attribute 'Satva' uses a steady process of humanization of the animal behaviour/instinct manifesting human qualities such as self-awareness and self-introspection, thinking and reasoning, selflessness and discriminating ability, self-discipline and self-improvement, love and service, peace and harmony. Under each of the three categories of these attributes namely Tamas, Rajas and Satva, species appear showing permutation and combination of different degrees of each of these three attributes (gunas) determining the inner nature of the individual soul (jeevatman) within and also the shape, size, colour and other characteristics of its physical equipment. This evolution of the individual soul (jeevatman) is, therefore, rightly compared in the Upanishads to a stream with small beginnings, passing through hills and valleys, plains and fields, gathering more and more force until it becomes a broad and big deep river winding its way only to reach ultimately its goal as well as its source – in this case, the Ocean of Cosmic Consciousness.

Evidently both science and spirituality believe in the evolutionary process of the species in somewhat comparable ways. While science postulates the physical and psychological development of the species, Vedic theory enunciates the spiritual evolution of the individual soul (jeevatman) towards its upward journey. It shows how cosmic consciousness, which apparently lay hidden in the matter, manifests itself in the plant, in animals and finally in the human beings who are well-equipped with individual consciousness and intelligence to explore the mystery of the Universe including their own appearance and role in the whole process of creation. Science is gradually realizing its limitations of its view of the evolutionary process while admitting that the phenomenon of the Creative Evolution cannot be explained solely in terms of biology, chemistry and physics. The scientific theory is also turning closer towards the spiritual theory of evolution. It agrees that life manifests in material bodies because of the working of some intelligent principle drawing its strength from Cosmic Consciousness. The cause of emergence of life must be subtler as well as more dynamic than the living organism itself because of some kind of higher integration taking place which cannot be explained totally in terms of the physical and chemical sciences. **Science to-date has not been able to explain as to why particles cease to function like matter, and ascend to the level of organized living system**. It does not satisfactorily explains as to why invariably the living body becomes dead in a split of a second, even when the cells in the body are reasonably intact with all their physical and chemical ingredients.

The physicists, psychologists and biologists are now in agreement that consciousness has been there at all time in the matter, though in a varying degree. The Vedic view is that life is a manifestation as the entry of individual soul (jeevatman) in the world with all its limited adjustments of life-breath, mind, sense-perception etc. in a seed form into the fertilized egg in the womb while death is the exit of the individual soul (jeevatman) in the same form to manifest or enter again into another body waiting for it elsewhere for its further evolution. The biologists, of late, have begun to have doubt about some of the basic assumptions in the Darwanian theory, particularly its basis in random occurrence through chance or mutation which are later stabilized by natural solutions.

Thus, accurate synchronization of body and mind in every order of evolving species, making each of its members physically as well as psychologically complete in its respective group, shows intelligent working of some non-physical principle bringing about this equilibrium in every living being. Psychologists too, have started believing that it is because of intelligent direction and guidance that each one of the hundred billion cells in every human being works in complete synchronization with all others in the whole organism. Indeed, the new trend of thought about evolution is in continuation of the same fundamental principle regarding the emergence of life in molecules, namely, that there is some intelligent principle working behind the whole process of evolution. It is being realized if the physical and psychological characteristics were the sole determining factors of evolution, then every ape in the world by now would have developed into a human being.

Another dimension of this evolution where science is turning towards the spiritual view is the nature of the mind. Darwanian theory treats mind a product of the evolving form of specie, as is evidenced in brain. The Vedic view, however, is that mind is more in nature of a bundle of thoughts, impressions, expressions and inherent tendencies (Sanskaras) which the individual soul (jeevatman) brings with it from the preceding life and is, therefore, antecedent to the type of body it inhabits. It is this mind that functions through the brain, influencing the organism's actions, nature and behaviour. Even this mind, which is subtler than the brain, is itself a gross principle illumined by the Cosmic Consciousness. This, according to Vivekananda, refers to the power of the Supreme Being that illumines all phenomena in the Universe, including the mind.

In short, the modern trend of scientific thought relating to evolution is gradually coming around the Vedic Theory according to which Cosmic Consciousness has been designing and guiding the process of evolution right from its beginning. Darwin himself admitted the extreme difficulty or rather impossibility of conceiving this unique and amazing universe, including the human beings with their capacity of looking far ahead into the future brought him at the end of the long road of his study of the evolution of species which becomes the starting point of spiritual evolution.

The notion of an atom and a particle in modern physics comes very close to the Vedic Concept of the 'Anu' and the 'Paramaanu'. Anu, as described in the Upanishads, is that substance which cannot be further sub-divided. It is the tiniest manifestation of the Supreme Being – the essence of all things both animate and inanimate. It is the infinitesimal essence of the Universe. Referring to the relationship of the 'Anu' with the Supreme Being – the Brahmn, Swami Vivekananda remarked that the whole macrocosm is only the expanded microcosm, and the microcosm is only the shrunk macrocosm. The dynamic energy giving rise to the particles inside the atom are symbolized in the Shiva-Shakti concept of the Hindu tradition. Shiva is described as the flawless reality in which Cosmic Conscious Energy (Shakti) exists in a state of quiescence. He dwells in all elements and beings, as all-pervading. Shakti is glorified as the inexhaustible reservoir of energies. All the gross and subtle elements comprising the whole world are being constantly created by Shakti. In all objects and phenomena, Shakti alone is manifest and is the only reality enveloping the whole world. Shakti or Cosmic Energy itself being the creative principle is indestructible and eternal. As a matter of fact, Shiva and Shakti are not two separate principles, but two aspects of one and the same Shivtatva/Brahmn. Shiva represents the creative reality and is the guiding power while Shakti is the working power or energy which is perceived in the atom as the ultimate base of the Universe. Shiva is changeless, stable, potential while Shakti is the kinetic creative power of movement and change that is observed inside the atom. Thus, both according to both physics and Vedic tradition, every atom (anu) and particle (paramanu) pulsates with the interactional and inter-relational activity of the unitary energy principle (wave) and the unitary matter principle (particle) which accounts for the ceaseless phenomena of creation, sustenance and dissolution at all levels of manifestation, and thus keeps the universe going.

An interesting feature of this ceaseless flow of energy inside the atom and its dynamic interplay is that the vibrating particles and their inter-action reveal a great deal of order, rhythm and harmony. The Cosmic dance of Shiva-Shakti is a symbolic dance of creation, preservation, annihilation going on from the beginning of Time into Infinity. The charm of this dance conveys the majesty and beauty, rhythm and melody, music and harmony, love and joy experienced by those who have an insight into the realm and reality of the Cosmic Consciousness which has manifested itself as the Universe.

According to Quantum Physics, the appearance of matter as solid mass is due to an ever-continuing process of interactional and inter-relational movement of energy waves inside the atom which gives them density. It is these infinitesimal particles in the atom whirling at lightning speeds that give rise to the solid mass of matter. This is in line with the Vedic Science of Matter (Padaarth Vijnana) that it is Shakti or Cosmic Energy which is manifesting itself as the material world, while Cosmic Energy itself emanates from the Cosmic Consciousness. Thus,

Vedic Theory of manifestation of the material world is in conformity with ideas of modern science pertaining to the atom and the material phenomena in the Universe. According to the Upanishads, the Divine Brahmn is immanent in every 'atom' (anu) and 'Parmaanu' (particles). All that exists in the whole universe is also contained in the least microcosm which affirms almightiness of the atom. The Divine Brahmn whose nature is beyond the comprehension and imagination of human beings is great or vast and subtle or tiny at the same time. It is spread farther than the farthest bounds and centered within the tiniest of the body. Swami Vivekananda, while giving the Upanishadic statements a scientific interpretation said (When the scientist had just started exploring the mysteries of the atom), "What the metaphysicists call 'being', the physicists call 'matter', but there is no real fight between the two; for, they are one". Though the atom is invisible and unthinkable, yet in it are all the real power and potency of the whole Universe. That is what Vedanta says of the 'atma'. This unthinkable power and potency of the invisible atom – the subtle 'Anu' is explained by the fact that the Infinite Cosmic Energy Principle of Shiva-Shakti is indivisible and, penetrating the whole Universe, it is equally Omnipotent at every point in space or time.

Spirituality as propounded by the Vedic philosophy is not a religion founded by any prophet or messenger but a system of eternal and universal truths pertaining to Creation, Creator and Creatures. Spirituality provides the right motivation to the scientists, spiritualists and scholars to unravel the mysteries of the Universe. The well-known Indian physicist and plant-psychologist, Dr. J.C. Bose was a keen follower of the Vedanta philosophy. While speaking about his famous discovery that plants and even inorganic matter have feeling of pain, pleasure and elation, his faith in the Supreme Being was endowed with the ever-evolving mystery of creation. According to an American scientist well-known for his micro-crystal research, Dr. C.A. Battista, science leads basically to the search towards knowing God in things and phenomena. John Glenn – the American astronaut who was the first to enter into the space experienced God's presence in the vastness of the Universe and the precision with which it operates. There are many more examples of scientists and mathematicians who while having intense faith in the Creator, see in the mystery of His Creation, its beauty and power. Vedic philosophy is not confined only to all 'non-material' knowledge as it is generally considered to be. It contains as much knowledge about the material Universe as physical science itself. Infact, it has much more to throw light on the unity of creation, creator and creatures and their inter-relationship. Indeed, it unravels their common foundation in the ultimate reality of Cosmic Consciousness. Vedanta, as the very word implies, is the ultimate end of human knowledge and hence the brilliant lamp that illumines all other knowledge, the human mind can conceive of.

In the theory of Creative Evolution, both science and spirituality present the basic phenomena of the emergence of the Universe out of some most subtle substratum forming progressively into grosser substances, culminating in hard matter and becoming this boundless Universe. In this long drawn process both these fields of knowledge speak of sound, space, vibration, energy, radiation and so on. There is a common agreement on the process of creation – preservation – dissolution simultaneously and continuously going on, and in the existence of billions of galaxies in the expanding Universe. Like the Quantum Theory, the Vedic Theory also enunciates the concept of atom ('anu') and the 'beyond-atom' ('paramaanu'), the latter being described as comprising of space and energy. Science, however, is yet to explain as to how or why the transition from a radiation-dominated Universe to a matter-dominated universe occurred at a particular point of time in the process of Creation or which of the two transitions occurred first. The Vedic View of the process of transition postulates that condensation of the Cosmic Energy, occurred progressively with the help of the three basic **'Energy-Attributes'** (Satva, Rajas and Tomas) – the 'trigunas', While science stresses on the material aspect, spirituality does so on the energy aspect of the same occurrence or phenomena.

This animated relationship between representative view and their seminal arguments could be summed up as under: While Vedic Theory expounds the emergence of the consciousness and life, the physio-chemical theory of science considers body, brain, nerves etc. as ingredients for the physical constitution forming an appropriate instrument for life to manifest and become active. The two theories may look to be different but essentially seem to be complementary to each other. A few aspects may be looked into this assertion:

Darwanian Theory of Evolution of species, which has been found wanting in many respects, can be interpreted in terms of Vedic Theory of the individual consciousness (jeevatma) passing through countless forms (8.4 million) of progressive manifestations of the Cosmic Consciousness in matter, plant, animal and finally culminating into the form of human being. This evolution is considered to have reached its final form as a human being because a human being is the only specie who is fully equipped physically, mentally, intellectually and emotionally to unravel the mystery of life and creation, and return to its source with a sense of achievement and satisfaction. This, indeed, necessitates going deeper into the Vedic Theory of the **Law of Karma** (*i.e.* the law of action and destiny pertaining to thought, word and deed), the theory of reincarnation of the soul under the Karmic Law and so on. Further, exploration of the phenomenon of reincarnation would give a better and deeper understanding of the meaning and purpose of life and creation.

Theory of creation, enunciated by the modern science, traces backwards the emergence of the Universe and tells almost everything about the various processes involved in its evolution but to-date it is unable to say about its origin and source. Vedic Theory of evolution of creation, on the contrary, is consistent and complete, beginning with its origin, the source, the motiving-power, the processes involved, its end and even beyond this end when the next cycle of creation begins just as the night is followed by the dawn heralding the day. What stops the modern scientists to accept this scientific and logical Vedic Theory is a mystery specially when science, itself, acknowledges the limitations/ incompleteness of its knowledge because of the constraints of sense-perception and experience. Moreover, Vedic Theory, after taking due cognizance of matter, extends its vision further beyond. No doubt, science helps to unravel the mystery of life and creation, yet the spirituality propounded Vedic Theory helps to solve the riddle of the Universe and its creator.

The scientific and Vedic postulations, when synthesized together, can mutually contribute to the exploration of this mystery surrounding the Universe and its creation. This will bring conceptual clarity about the Truth governing the Universe which science is searching for, and which Vedic theory postulates as Brahmn – the Supreme Being or the Creator. It will bring out a sublime vision of the Universe beyond matter and diversity of the phenomenon which may completely transform the modern materialistic world view as well as the mechanistic approach to spiritual evolution of life. It will help in comprehending and recognizing the human evolution as the inseparable component of Creation, and also that of its creator.

Science is now, more or less, willing to agree to Vedic view that the whole creation is manifestation of an Infinite and Immutable Principle which is Eternal (Sat), Supremely Intelligent (Chit) and Blissful (Anand) Brahmn. It is the tiniest of the tiny at the micro level and the vastest of the vast at the macro-level projecting the Universe and setting into operation its working in perfect order and harmony in accordance with the Cosmic Design. The Cosmic Consciousness and Energy designated as Shiva-Shakti, and the fastidious multiplicity of Gods and Goddesses are only embodiments of the various cosmic energies, powers and elements involved at various levels of creation ranging from subtle consciousness to gross matter. Their personification is the most effective way of making the human beings convinced of the Supreme Consciousness (Brahmn) operating through various presiding deities connected with the innumerable forces and functions involved in the boundless creation and its operation.

Accordingly, therefore, there is the Holy Trinity of Brahma – the creator, Vishnu – the preserver and Maheshwara – the destroyer looking after the management of the whole creation. These three deities are accompanied by their respective consorts namely the Saraswati (with Brahma) personifies the goddess of Wisdom; Lakshmi (with Vishnu) – the goddess of Prosperity; and Parvati (with Shiva) – the goddess of Energy (Shakti). Similarly, various other divine powers are personified such as the Sun, Earth, Air, Fire, Water, Death with their corresponding powers and functions. All these great gods provide the human beings the conceivable and perceptible divine manifestations whom they glorify and worship in reverence. The Vedic concept of the Supreme Being or Cosmic Consciousness – the Brahmn, as the Supreme Reality, has found increasing acceptance among scientists during the twentieth century. Even Darwin himself expressed his extreme difficulty or rather impossibility of conceiving this immense and amazing Universe without being impelled to look to a First Cause having an intelligent Mind. In short, science, of-late, has started conceding that a Supremely Intelligent Consciousness underlies matter at the sub-atomic level and also transcends space, time and causation.

According to the Vedic Theory, the whole universe is a gross-manifestation of the Cosmic Consciousness itself. The creation, creator and creatures are bound together in this eternal consciousness. The whole universe of space and objects came into existence due to the grosser forms. The stuff of the Universe, therefore, is that of its creator, namely consciousness only. All beings are only consciousness; so too, is the whole world, consciousness only. This consciousness being the whole universe is a unified being. In accordance with the creator's design, it presents an appearance of plurality of objects and multiplicity of forms and thereby conceals inner reality of its being. In fact, the duality of the knower and the known, the subject and object is the stage on which the whole cosmic play of knowledge and ignorance, pain and pleasure, virtues and vices and so on – goes on endlessly. The cause of this duality is **'Maya'** – divine power which casts a spell on human's mind and makes him/her feel himself/herself separate from his/her self.

The words like 'Maya' (deluding power) makes the human beings confuse the myriad objects and beings with reality, without perceiving the existence of Brahmn underlying all these forms. Maya is the illusion of taking the objects as reality which merely lies in the vision of the human beings about the shapes and structures, objects and events, names and forms etc.

Both creation and creatures including the human beings are inseparable from their creator. All the three together constitute what is term as one Reality of the Cosmic Consciousness, the Supreme Being – Brahmn glorified as **Sathyam, Shivam and Sundaram** *i.e.* Truth, Purity and Beauty of Love and Harmony. Human beings' faith in God, the creator, gave them the glimpse of His Omni-presence, Omni-science and Omni-potence. The devotional love and deep adoration of the human beings for God is the beginning of the universal religion-termed in Vedanta as the Snathan Dharma, envisioned by Swami Vivekananda as the religion of spiritual science and scientific spirituality. Ever since creatures appeared on the earth with human beings as the supreme creation of God, all along their evolution, a divine power made them grow into rational, intelligent and self-conscious beings as compared to the animals whose awareness is limited only to their body needs. Human beings have further sharpened their intelligence, imagination and outlook so as to become civilized being.

Creation has a goal and the human being have a purpose. The evolutionary process continues. It is not only psychological or anatomical but equally a moral and spiritual one. The core of the Vedic Theory, however, remains that the Universal Consciousness with its attributes of Sat (Eternal Existence), Chit (Self-Awareness) and Anand (Bliss) has itself become many in the sense it dwells in each and every being both animate and inanimate **why did the One become many**? The answer is that the One could not realize its divine glory of Sat-Chit-Anand Swaroopa in the absence of an adequate 'frame of reference' having attributes of an opposite nature. One cannot comprehend light in the absence of darkness. This explains the Sankalpa or the Divine Will of the 'One' to become 'Many' in which it assumed attributes opposite to those of the one. This Sankalpa brought forth the Universe in which Cosmic Consciousness, passing through the stages of unconscious matter, plants with very little consciousness, animals with slightly more consciousness and finally into a human being – the epitome of creation with full consciousness, having the potential to become one with the Supreme Being.

2.3 Spiritual Evolution

The dawn of new century is identified with the emergence of a global society. Impelled by technology explosion and economic liberalization, it needs a holistic harmony that stresses convergence in place of conflict, complementation in place of competition, and compassion in place of cruelty. It calls for ethics that would link the highest achievements of technology with the deepest insights of spirituality. A human being is a triune – a three-in-one phenomenon – a unique combination of soul, mind and body. Harmonious development of this triune is the only antidote to overcome the prevalent spiritual crisis. A strong grounding in both scientific knowledge and spiritual awareness is essential to overcome the prevalent global crisis in terms of the attributes of moral-development, self-control and personal-integrity. An analysis of these attributes leads to the process of introspection in terms of thoughts, words and actions – a set of principles that constitutes what may be termed as the spiritual evolution. Whether this is feasible without a composite harmony of science and spirituality, depends upon the way the 21st century responds to the challenges it is going to face.

What is spiritual evolution and what is its objective? Why spiritual evolution and what for? People generally believe that spirituality means leading a noble way of life based on truth and righteousness by following the path of honesty, integrity, charity, selflessness and such other ideals. Indeed, these are some of the important parameters of spirituality. However, these are not the be-all-end-all of spirituality. Spirituality means self-realization with detachment from the material world. The chief objective of spirituality is to transcend the limited bodily identity and experience the oneness with the Supreme Being that is called the Brahmn. What is transcendentalism? It is a philosophical doctrine that goes beyond human knowledge and surpasses human experience. It is, indeed, a divine experience. It is linked with idealism. The philosophical postulation is based on two maxims: idealism and materialism. Idealism is focused on consciousness while materialism pertains to the senses of material things, needs of body and apparent facts. Idealism believes that senses are not final in themselves and affirms ways of thinking in the higher realm of existence. Indeed, materialism ends where idealism begins. Spiritual experience cannot be attained through one or more of the five bodily senses. It can be perceived directly from inside in one's consciousness for which one has to have an intense will for it and has to switch off the material world completely. It is an experience of a state of no-mind, no-thought, calmness, serenity and inner oneness with the Supreme Consciousness. It is a Homa (fire for purification and enlightenment) of purifying and healing the inner atmosphere by burning through fire the toxic material and pollution.

Spiritual Evolution means holistic evolution which comprises of two aspects: outer or external evolution and the inner evolution. In the present epoch of science and technology, human intellect understands knowledge based on logic, reason and rational explanation. This is the knowledge of ever evolving relative things termed as material or physical or outer knowledge while the other is the knowledge of the inner self. Anything perceived through the five senses is termed as outer knowledge. But what is it that explains the energy behind these five senses and that which is within as the Knower, Perceiver or Observer? What enables the mystics or spiritualists to experience an experience? Modern science is trying to explore the tangible concepts like consciousness and awareness. But everything cannot be explained by experimentation alone.

The advancement of science and technology has made available all essential amenities as well as luxuries. Despite all this, there is unrest, chaos and stress all around. Human beings are still in search of inner peace, happiness and harmony. Material progress is not the only important aspect of human life. Total or holistic progress in terms of mind, body and soul is equally essential. In addition to Intelligence Quotient (IQ), due importance ought to be given to the Emotional Quotient (EQ) and Spiritual Quotient (SQ).

When the inner knowledge and perception of the pure-self is fully realized, all mysteries of the divine knowledge get revealed. It is indeed the evolution of the inner self concerning the mind, body and soul. It means the evolution of the 'relative self' in relation to the 'Real Self'; individual self (soul), (Jeevatma) in relation to the Universal or Cosmic Self (Parmatman, the Brahmn); the Prakriti in relation to the 'Purush'; and the cause in relation to the effect.

Modern science has found sufficient evidence in support of the concept of One Cosmic Consciousness – the Supreme Being prevalent in all objects and beings – both animate and inanimate. Their conclusion is that the whole Universe is one indivisible whole on account of the divine power which is all pervading. Once this concept of God is rightly grasped, it becomes easier to visualize the scope and content of the Universal Religion – Sanathan Dharma. The Vedic terminology 'Dharma' means the path of righteousness as the core of 'being' manifesting in thought, word and deed. This fundamental axiom has been the foundation of the Sanathan Dharma (the Universal Religion) propounded by the Vedas and practiced in India since eternity. Since the basic principle of this religion is the eternal and universal truth of the divinity in every being, it came to be known as Sanathan Dharma or the Eternal Religion or the Universal Religion. It acquired the name as Hindu Religion, the people inhabiting the region called middle east, addressed the people living on the side of the Indus River as Hindus. Infact, there is no such religion as Hinduism founded by any prophet or messenger. It is only the Eternal Religion given to the world by the Vedic scriptures. This is the secular religion in the real sense of secularism. It has been named as the scientific religion of the world by Swami Vivekananda because this religion follows the eternal (Sanatana) and Universal principles in their pursuit of God. It implies the spiritual evolution since it calls upon the people to seek the Truth of God as the Ultimate Reality, through multiplicity and duality in creation.

Spirituality lies beyond the material world of proof, beyond what can be measured or counted. It is made up of the inner life, the realm of belief, mystery, and faith. And yet for all the mystery that surrounds it, spirituality is vital to human beings. It is the foundation of most closely held values, the seat of trust and hope. Spirituality brings purpose and meaning to life, and as it evolves, one grows in wisdom and love. A spiritually evolved person begins to experience a sense of relief, a sense of connection to all of life, and a deep reverence for the Divine. He finds himself moved to prayers of gratitude and moments of spontaneous worship. Spirituality calls a human being to a life of faith, love and service.

A major casuality of modern society is the value system. There is a sharp decline in basic human values. Sai Baba Says, ***"The world is today in deep distress because the common man and his leaders are all distracted by lower desires and lower motives. Though man is inherently Divine, he lives only at the animal level. Very few live even in the native human level."*** A human being is the super form of creation – far above the other living species put together, yet he has fallen so low. Animals, birds, insects and even plants have not deviated from their nature. They have a reason and season for their living. A human being alone has neither any reason nor any season for what he does or proclaims. He is deeply involved in the crude attempt of acquiring material progress. He is failing to appreciate his own native worth and is constantly degrading himself more by exploiting advancement of science and technology for material gains. With the temptations and attractions of the materialistic world, a human being is delving deep into the desire of earning wealth and fame in the world by gaining some position of authority and leading a luxurious life under the influence of glamour and glory. In the process, he is losing mental peace. What is needed for a human being is to be conscious of the fact that every movement of his life is precious. He must tread the Spiritual path along with the worldly path, based on the ideals of Truth (Satya), Righteousness (Dharma), Peace (Shanti), Love (Prema), and Non-Violence (Ahimsa); the five ideals, enunciated by Bhagwan Sri Sathya Sai Baba, together constitute what spirituality offers a value system, and shows the way of ethical life. Caring for value-system and uplifting of living style is the true path of spirituality.

Life is made up of matter, mind and soul. Harmony in the development of body (matter), mind and soul is the focus of spirituality. The core of spirituality is the philosophy of Vedanta – a science that is founded on a scientific basis. It is the unique process of observation-hypothesis-test-theory. The only difference is that whereas the pure sciences of physics, chemistry, biology, etc., are sciences of materialism, spirituality is the science of the idealism. It is infact, the essence of living. It provides answers to questions that are related to the real goal of life, and shows the way how to achieve that goal.

Spirituality is the eternal linkage of God with the human beings. In order to identify the true features and the essence of being a human, *it is necessary to evolve a process of spirituality in living*. What distinguishes a human being from other living species is that a human species is gifted with an ability to exercise enormous power of discrimination, memory and reasoning. Amongst all the creations, only the human beings have the ability to intellectual analyze, determine their own value-system, and decide for themselves their course of action. They have the option to enhance their power of analytical ability by acquiring knowledge through learning, by attaining professional dexterity through technology, and by ensuring quality of life through basic spirituality.

In more than one way, spirituality is closely linked with technology in terms of its philosophy and productivity. Both draw their strength from the same Source-Energy which is the solid core, the stable, unchanging foundation. It is the source of all that is happening. Energy is power and dynamo, intensity and motion. Moving towards higher Self requires thinking and thinking requires energy. Energy is powerful, ever changing, always active, performing and transforming. ***Technology is a process of turning one form of energy into another, motion into electricity, fossils into heat, heat into motion. Spirituality is a process of transforming one form of energy into another but with a difference.*** Even the very thoughts, as subtle as they are, can transform energy.

Energy is source of it all. Spirit is the cause. It's always there both moving and immovable.

Spiritual energy is to be treated as an essential component of human evolution. The Divine incarnations and divine personalities can generate in themselves the power of performing what they want. This is amply demonstrated invariably through miracles done by various divine incarnations and messengers and lately by Bhagwan Sri Sathya Sai Baba in front of several skeptics and scientists. Several scientists believe that *energy has as much claim to be regarded as an objective reality as matter itself.* Everything is pulsating with energy which includes even the stones and dirt (soil) as well as animals and plants. The same force which animates the human body, the beasts, the birds and the reptiles, also vitalizes the oaks, vines, and the mineral world. Life, the occultists say, is the eternal untreated energy which has bridged all the gap yawning among the different kingdoms of nature, while science has to confess its ignorance. There is nothing to contradict the occult axiom that the same life energy animates human beings, plants, and rocks simply in different states of the one indestructible force, – the Universal Soul, – making all Nature what is termed as the living visible garment of God. This is because of the existence of some supernatural force behind the eternal process of creation, preservation and dissolution taking place every moment and everywhere.

When spirituality is nurtured and vibrant, people get connected. This connection is both a sense of relationship to the Creator, the God (Divine Force), as well as a relationship to all people and to Mother Earth (life-giving environment). Spirituality takes people beyond their ego-centered lives by expanding their hearts with compassion towards all. Spirituality forms the framework of orientation to life; it does not dwell in a realm apart. It is not an extracurricular activity. Spirituality involves a reverential attitude towards all beings because it awakens to a divine presence in all beings. In this way of seeing and doing, all beings and persons get interconnected and interdependent.

It is important to differentiate spirituality from religion. Some people have rejected religion in order to escape what they consider to be a system of oppressive rules and regulations. In the process, however, many lose the great gifts of joy and compassion that spirituality brings. Religion and spirituality are related and intertwined, but they are not the same. A person may experience spirituality without being a member of any specific religious affiliation, and even the most religious person may feel spiritually bereft. The true purpose of religion is to enhance spirituality through ritual and practice. This is accomplished when a person approaches his or her religion as a way to become aware of the sacredness of all rituals and ceremonies. Religion can become a barrier to spirituality when it insists on narrow, judgmental dogma, and estranges its followers from a sense of connection with the Divine.

Religion serves best as a vehicle to nourish and develop spirituality. It is possible, however, to get caught up in the religious practice, while losing sight of spirituality. For modern scientists, rationalists and professionals, spirituality is often a difficult subject. Their training is framed by science, logic and materialism. They depend on logical, analytical and rational approaches, and perhaps for good reason. These approaches have successfully ushered in a host of life-changing improvements in health care and technology. While honouring science and the mind, cultural tendency urges people to devalue trust in God, but the result is costly for they are left spiritually starved and out of balance.

Some of the life's most difficult questions are the spiritual ones. What is the purpose of life? What is the truth of life? What is the significance of human life? If there truly is a God who loves people, how could there be so much suffering and unfairness in the world? The fact of the matter is that materialistic addiction to the business of life prevents people from thinking about mortality and the inevitable fact of death. But when they keep themselves too busy to consider the purpose of existence, their lives cease to have meaning. Strangely, it is only when they fully accept the reality of their mortality that they truly begin to live. This is the point at which they begin to enter into and learn about the spiritual dimension of humanity. As an eminent French philosopher Pierre Teilhard de Chardin remarked, **"We are not physical beings having a spiritual experience, but spiritual beings to have a physical experience."** Spirituality is the true essence of life. It is that part of life which relates to soul and which forms a spiritual perspective connected to the Divine.

Spiritual evolution brings with it the realization of the ephemeral nature of the world and the determination to search for means to get extricated from the wheel of materialism. Three human limitations among others are attributed to this determination: limitations of sensual pleasure; limitation of rational and scientific knowledge; and limitation of human capability. Modern advancement and culture has put at people's disposal a great range of sensual enjoyments. The excessiveness of the sensual pleasures has created a crisis of confidence among the people that it is not possible to attain lasting happiness or peace as satiation of worldly pleasure gives rise of more indulgence which brings in dissatisfaction and restlessness. Sensuality knows no bounds and hence no lasting peace. The second reason is the quest for meaning and purpose of human life. The search for this meaning and purpose is one of the most distinguished features of the modern society. The third reason is the breaking of the barriers of the cultural separations of value-based ethics from materialism, of ancient with modern, of old with new. As a result, there is an intermixing of various cultures and there is a paradigm shift in thinking and attitudes of the people all over the world. Although there is an emphasis on meditation, yoga, social service, self-realization, peace of mind and various other modes of spiritual living, yet, in certain directions, the human mind stands arrested and bewildered and can no longer find its way. Indeed, the real essence of humanity is the realization of all the potentialities inherent in it, which lead to the path of spiritual evolution. The modern human society is in the throes of an evolutionary crisis with an enormous one-sided development. Human beings have created a structure of external life to serve largely their sensual instincts. This structure has now become so huge and so complex as to be unmanageable because of their very limited spiritual and moral capacity. It is, therefore, obvious that something else is needed: perhaps spirituality which would intervene and use life for a higher perfection.

Sri Aurobindo's concept of 'Supramental' is of great significance to spiritual evolution. It means Brahmn's manifestation as matter which means self-limitation or an act of involution. In other words, the matter, which seems to be devoid of consciousness, actually has Supreme Consciousness hidden in it, in a dormant form exactly as a plant lies dormant in the seed. The creation of matter was followed by evolution which is the opposite of involution. The process of evolution may be viewed as a progressive expression or revelation of the Supreme Consciousness hidden in the matter. Appearance of life on the planet earth is the first major milestone in the process of evolution. Evolution of mental consciousness is a higher revelation of the Supreme Consciousness. Infact, mental consciousness is believed to have reached its peak in human beings. However, human consciousness expresses only a fraction of the Supreme Consciousness. The evolutionary processes, in case of human beings can further enhance to the higher level of consciousness. The reason being that only human beings can rise in consciousness partly through their own spiritual efforts and partly because of their evolutionary urge of the Divine strongly planted in their minds. This has been amply demonstrated by the great sages and spiritualists like Adi Shankaracharya, Swami Ramakrishna Paramhans,

Swami Vivekananda, Sri Aurobindo and Ramanarishi among several others, across all religions and cultures including various sufis and mystics like Guru Nanak, Kabir, Rahim, Saint Gyaneshwar, Meerabai, etc. who were charged with superamental consciousness. The difference according to Sri Aurobindo, is that human level of mental consciousness is rooted in diversity while the Supramental consciousness has its deep foundations in Oneness. The Oneness, in this context, means replacement of the demonic tendencies like ego, desire, anger, greed and jealousy among others by the virtues like truth, righteousness, peace, love and non-violence among others. This, according to Sri Aurobindo, is the key for a fundamental change in human nature and its spiritual evolution.

The Supreme or Divine Reality is beyond the comprehension of the human mental capacity, even in terms of its conceptual framework. This is the divine reality which is the foundation and ultimate purpose of all beings. Human beings are capable of reflecting on this divine reality through their longing for realization of God. Human mind can understand only the realms of appearances, forms and manifestations of God and His phenomenon. Divine incarnations, prophets and divine messengers are visible manifestations or appearances of God who exemplify highest perfection of human development and the actualization of the divine power which is latent in all human beings. Indeed, the ultimate meaning and purpose of human destiny are realized through the recognition of the divine manifestations of God from time to time. These divine manifestations in the form of divine messengers are spiritual healers who prescribe spiritual medicines relevant to the diseases afflicting the human society. The divine reality of all manifestations of God is the same like the same sun that appears each day but looks to be different in different horizons. Humanity is a mirror of this divine reality while humans are endowed with reflection of divine attributes in their beings. The realization of the divine in human life is through spiritual awareness in the midst of the diversity of individuals and cultures.

Almost all religions refer to oneness of God. Prophets and spiritualists stress this traits of God in their holy scriptures where Oneness appears as the precursor of all other traits of the Divine, such as omni-presence, omni-potence and omni-scient. A close scrutiny and analysis will reveal that all the other traits attributed to God boil down to this trait of Oneness. It implies that God is one without a second and there is no other entity or substance except the Divine in the Cosmos. Indeed, God's oneness is all inclusive. It also implies that even matter does not exist in the form that is perceived with human senses. The

Universe, therefore, is not separate from God. It is included in the Oneness of God. In other words, Universe is God and God is Universe in the sense that the Universe is the visible vesture of the invisible God. In other words, only God exists as the existential reality which is Universal. It is this existential reality which is the Universality and the Oneness, the non-divisibility of the noumenon which is called God.

According to physics, all matter is energy or energy is matter in the sense that matter can be converted into energy and energy can be converted into matter. Matter is deconstructible into molecules, atoms and subatomic phenomena which takes the form of energy that dissolves into the void or emptiness of the space. This void is not actually empty. It is full of energy which is invisible, which is dynamic and being one, it pervades the whole of the void. The reverse process will lead to manifestation of energy into matter. It is this basic underlying energy phenomenon that manifests into material phenomenon at the time of its creation and absorb it back at the time of its dissolution. Indeed, nothing is really created or destroyed in the cosmos. The primordial substance or energy pervades the entire Universe. This is divine phenomenon or energy called God, Brahmn, Allah, Ishwar, Aparpurusha etc. This is the Ultimate Reality – the reality of science, logic and philosophy. Thus, Oneness of God is not an abstraction. It is a fact and the ultimate truth which is the **foundation of edifice of humanism** built by the prophets and divine messengers.

Every religion has laid down its mode of worship, its paradigm of devotion, and service for the needy, deprived and physically handicapped as the spiritual exercise or meditation (Sadhana). Such offerings to the divinity of human beings are said to be the highest worship of God. Reinforcing this great principle of worshipping God in humanity, Sri Aurobindo said, "**The fundamental idea is that mankind is the God head to be worshipped and served by Man**". This Universal religion or the "Sanathan Dharma" of the Hindus has the potential and capacity to spiritualize the ideal of unity in humanity. The Vedic prayer in this context, "Loka Samastha Sukhinah Bhawantu", prays that all beings in all the worlds be happy.

Spiritual evolution essentially relates to the human transformation through inculcation of ethical, cultural and spiritual values in life. But the divine values do not sprout of their own in human's heart. It is only through the faith in the Truth of Cosmic Consciousness as the core of human existence. This faith in the human heart is the Universal religion. As this faith takes roots in the human heart it urges him/her to shake off the evil tendencies in his/her nature on one hand, and to adopt the path of good thoughts, good words and good deeds, on the other. The progress on this path, however, depends on the intensity of human's faith and conviction about the divinity pervading in all beings. The link between this progress on the spiritual path and the values needed for human transformation is based on the human values evolved by Bhagwan Sri Sathya Sai Baba embedded with five fundamental ideals of Truth (Satya), Righteousness (Dharma), Peace (Shanthi), Love (Prema) and Non-violence (Ahimsa).

Spirituality is the science of life and action. It is the systematic and logical exposition of philosophy and knowledge. It expounds the truth and essence of life. The major role of the spiritual philosophy is to pull the people out of their infatuations and educate them about the eternities. It reveals the true knowledge of the relationship between human-human and human-divine. According to the spiritual scholars, every living being is essentially the spark of the Divine whether a saint or a sinner, whether a plant or an animal, whether a rock or a reptile. Divinity is the core of every living being but only the human beings have been gifted with the capacity to understand it and use it to live a life of perfect harmony. The spiritual philosophy has a universal appeal which is flexible and open. Some religious enthusiasts, however, brought out their over ambitious and abridged versions of spirituality leading to orthodox rituals, rigid maxims and distorted mandates propagated as religious sermons. As a result, people have been continuously infested with religious fanatism and parasitic superstitions leading to spiritual suicide. It is, therefore, essential to enlighten the people about the true perceptions of religion and spirituality in a systematic and scientific manner. Spiritual knowledge can provide the suitable way to understand the philosophy of the religions.

The most significant and remarkable attribute of the living species from an insect to a human being is that it is aware that it exists. Wherefrom, did this awareness spring? Awareness or consciousness is not just the result of a bunch of molecules coming together. It is an instinctive phenomenon that is inherent in the Universe. It existed long before life appeared, before the stars and the galaxies formed, indeed even before nature appeared in the form of plants and animals. It exists to date and will continue forever. Vedanta philosophy believes that there is an indefinable SPIRIT pervading the Universe – that is referred to as the Divine – the Supra-Mental, normally accepted as God. This spirit is not empty and vacuous; it is believed to be a source of power which manifests in many ways.

Rapid advancements in science and technology have generated the feeling that the creation is accidental. Aggressive rationality has promoted the belief that creatures are the outcomes of the nature's evolutionary phenomenon. The role of the creator – (God) the supernatural force behind the whole process of creation or evolution, protection and dissolution is being ruled out. Rabid materialism and distorted mythological versions of religions have further led to the confusion about the existence of God – the almighty. Egoistic attitudes and whims have, to a great extent, denied the truth about God. As a result, creation has been accepted as the Nature and its creatures have been treated as the elements of the evolutionary process. Questions till date are often raised about the existence and relevance of the creator. Wisemen and intellectuals have been exploring the truth about God and a grand debate continues on some of the related questions Such as: What is this Universe? Where has it come from? Why and how has it been created? Since there is creation, there are creatures, and therefore, there must be a creator. Who is this creator? Can the creator's role as God be denied? Probing of such questions among others, very often, lead to spiritual evolution, the realm of spiritual vision, and the core of spiritual philosophy.

There is a wide-spread feeling that science and spirituality are mutually contradictory. A debate, however, continues between science and spirituality. Spirituality is a philosophy, while religion is one of the ways to attain spiritual awareness. There is no need of any specific belief system in the form of a religion, cult or creed for generating spiritual awareness. Indeed, spirituality is not essentially based on any specific religious faith. Spiritual awareness is related to an individual's intuitive understanding of human values for spiritual growth. Spirituality reinforces the avenues of thought and universal knowledge to strengthen the foundations and development of value system.

Body, mind and the soul together form a powerful trinity. Body is an instrument for performing actions, mind is the faculty which discriminates between right and wrong, and the soul is that which is ever pure, unchanging and permanent. A human being is endowed with body, mind and soul which means doing, knowing and being. It is only when this trinity of body, mind and soul act together in perfect harmony that a human being can be said to exist. That human being is said to be in the animal state when the body alone acts without mind and spirit. When the body acts in association with the mind without spirit, that condition is described as imperfect. For achieving the Divine state, a human being must get installed in the Atmic (Spiritual) state, transcending the body and the mind as has been the experience of many sages like Ramakrishna and Ramana among several others. Those who delve deep into the spiritual philosophy may think that everything is God, and there is nothing else, that the Universe is a combination of matter and spirit, that there are actually three entities: God (Parmatman), the creator, the creation (Prakriti) and creatures (Pranni). According to the ancient Hindu tradition, the human being alone has the capacity to inquire, to reason and to find the way to God. In other words, the human body has been given in order to experience divinity in the physical and mental planes, and through these experiences, transcend mundane existence.

Among the hundreds of thousands of different types of species, to be born as human being is considered to be an extremely rare boon. It is difficult to appreciate what it is to be born as a human being. Before taking a human birth, the soul has to evolve through millions of different life forms in accordance with one's deeds (Karmas), as believed in the Hinduism. Thus, to gain a human birth is a very rare boon. Only the human beings have the opportunity to understand life through a wider scope. Human beings have the senses, an evolved mind and also an evolved intellect. They have the ability not only to understand the world around them, but also they have the faculty to have self-introspection. Thus, in this way human beings is the only species to have such a rare opportunity and a skill to evolve further and further.

There are various levels of human evolution. Every human being is at a different level of evolution. Every human being has a particular Self-view. For example a person may have a very low self-view a very low self-opinion. Depending upon this self-opinion, he may respond to the surroundings, in particular, and to the world, in general. A person may have a good up-bringing, a good education, and may have a good family background. His response to the world depends upon on the image or opinion he or she has built of himself/herself. One step higher in the evolutionary process, one may find oneself with a slightly evolved opinion about oneself. One may have different desires or even have an ego complex in one's mind. Such a person may fight and react to every situation in a way different from those of others. One may be aggressive or depressed or defensive on one's conduct and behaviour towards the society. On further evolution, one may show more courage and better conduct. Instead of blaming others, stars or the whole world, one may feel responsible for one's own conduct, one's happiness or one's sorrow. With such a opinion of oneself, one can gradually bring self-analysis which will lead to self-improvement. On further evolution, one attains the state of wisdom. At this stage, the intellect becomes sublime and one becomes spiritually evolved. The evolved souls at this juncture with this level of spiritual wisdom can understand the secrets of nature and the universe. Many great scientists and spiritualists have reached this stage where they understand life much better than the ordinary human beings can do. Such an evolutionary process leads one to understand the divine phenomenon embracing the whole cosmos. Enlightened in this way, one starts understanding the meaning of "Oneness" with God and identification with the entire cosmos. Such human beings are the ultimate evolved souls. The meaning and purpose of life starts evolving with the process of spiritual evolution.

The ultimate human evolution is through the spiritual evolution which lies in the realization of God or experiencing God within and around or merging in God. Human life must be utilized for going from the temporary to the permanent, from the perishable to the imperishable, and from the finite to the Infinite. These evolutionary levels of divine abstraction are generally propounded as **God** – the supreme, beyond the bounds of forms, time and attributes; **God** – the super-being with all attributes but formless; and **God** – the incarnate with both forms and attributes. Vedanta philosophy, comprising its varied versions and interpretations believes in all the three versions of divine abstractions. Nevertheless, God through incarnation, is found to be the most realistic and acceptable version all over the world. Skeptics and non-believers, however, will always remain doubtful and critical. In the ultimate analysis, God – the absolute and supreme is characterized as an embodiment of Supra-Energy manifested through the divine attributes of Creation (Brahma), Protection (Vishnu) and Dissolution (Mahesh) endowed with the mysterious powers of being Omni-Scient, Omni-Potent and Omni-Present. According to the latest version given by Sri Sathya Sai Baba, the English term 'GOD' may be abbreviated as G for Generation (Creation), O for Organization (Sustenance) and D for Dissolution (Destruction). Realization of God's existence as a human being has been amply demonstrated, witnessed and experienced over the epochs through incarnations of Rama, Krishna and in various other forms; the latest being that of the Sai Baba. The unique Divine phenomenon adored earlier as Shirdi Sai, lately as Sri Sathya Sai, and the future as Prema Sai.

One of the most important conclusions that can be drawn through the spiritual awareness is that Creative or Biological Evolution is governed by the Divine laws. These laws are not only related to socio-economic living but also to every practical activity of human life. Most important of these is the law of activity or action (Karma) which is somewhat similar to Newton's third law of motion namely. "To every action, there is a equal and opposite (Karmic)) reaction." Skeptics, however, would never agree to such logical conclusions, even though, they may encounter innumerable inexplicable phenomena that are unquestionably the manifestations of the Divine law. At the foundational level, spiritual awareness is very much like the scientific abstraction and its generalization; if at all it lacks anything, it is a mathematical formulation/scientific modeling. But then mathematics, though indispensable for astro physics, is not necessarily required in the case of metaphysics. On the contrary, spiritual exploration is based on the spirit as the central entity.

According to the Christian belief, there is a spirit-world which is an extension of the real world. The spirits in the spirit-world float through wall, invulnerable to accidents, storms, earthquakes and diseases. They cannot be buried, burnt, shot, drowned, drugged, chained, broken, suffocated, run over, infected, trapped, lashed, electrocuted, beaten, hanged, starved, operated on, manipulated or messed with. After death, one sheds one's mortal shell or earthly remains as body and appears in spirit form. It is not death or the end but a new beginning as a spiritual being where one has to cleanse one's soul of its deeds (Karma). After death, an individual's spiritual journey begins. There is no such thing as death or end of the spirit. It is the continuation of journey in the spirit-world. When an individual dies the physical death, he comes to "no man's land" where he stays for a while. From here, his spirit moves to a level where soul-cleansing begins. This is where he has to deal with his karmas – all deeds, good or bad done by him in his life and the misdemeanors that he may have indulged in while being in the earthly body. As he clears one karmic debt, he moves up one level as recognition of purity of his soul. At each level, he takes on added responsibilities to help those in need just like on the earth plane. Likewise there are nine levels: at the highest level, an individual attains divine qualities. Most great thinkers and spiritualists reach the levels four or five of these divine qualities in accordance with the karmas performed by them.

According to Vedanta philosophy, a human being experiences four states of consciousness: the waking state, the dream state, the deep-sleep state and turiya state. Indeed fourth state namely the turiya state transcends the normal empirical experiences. Thus, this is the true spiritual state, the realization of true Self. Normally speaking, a spiritualist is fully aware in the walking state, is partially aware *i.e.* semi-conscious in the dream state and blissfully unconscious in the deep-sleep state. The so-called awareness both in the waking state and dream state is called the Secondary Spiritual Awareness, whereas the deep-sleep state is known as the Primary Spiritual Awareness. According to the spiritual scholars, in the deep-sleep state, the body is not aware that it is experiencing deep sleep. However, there is an entity, distinct and separate from the gross-body, which is Primary Spiritual Consciousness or Primary Spiritual Awareness. This Primary Spiritual Awareness never switches off, is always on, and is also referred to as the Self. What switches on and off is the Secondary Spiritual Consciousness. Infact, the Secondary Spiritual Consciousness derives its capability from the Primary Spiritual Consciousness. It is the fourth state called Turiya, and said above, which lies beyond the three experiences during which a spiritualist experiences the existence of an all-pervading and eternal substratum, the 'Spirit' (Atma). This spirit is derived from the Divine Energy or Cosmic Energy, which is all pervading. The Universe, according to Sai Baba, is made up of two entities – Matter (Padartha) and Spirit (Parartha). The question is, *"How to bridge the gulf between this Divine Cosmic Energy and the mundane (gross) matter?"* Science does not admit of such an existence but if the concept of Cosmic Energy (Consciousness Energy) is accepted, then many mystic phenomena can be explained.

While the creation is full of splendor and wonders, man's achievements are no less astounding. Science has enabled man to walk on the Moon and explore the distant planets like the Mars. Because of technological advancements, man is able to launch himself into the space and go into the farthest corner of the Universe. He is able to create life into a test-tube and clone other living beings including even the human beings. Man is capable of acquiring incredible and most breath-taking achievements. Yet, something subtle is missing. He is presently not feeling inclined to do introspection and self-analysis. He is not willing to probe questions like: **"Where from came to him such extraordinary abilities"? Is there any Divine force who is guiding and helping him in his pursuits and achievements? He just wants to have the proof of the existence of Divine Energy.** He seems to believe that nothing is true unless it is proved within the framework of science. He is not willing to understand the meaning of spiritual love and peace. Sai Baba says, ***"Modern man has mastered science and technology but has thereby become the servant of mammon. He bloats over his apparent success in harnessing nuclear energy; yet, he lives as a mortal dwarf".***

Modern man has mastered science and technology. He has succeeded in generating atomic energy but is yet to harvest Atmic (Spiritual) energy. Man is proud of his modern material achievements. He fails to see the Universe around him, and refuses to realize the presence of the Almighty in the form of the Cosmos, the amazing manifestation of Divinity. On the contrary, arrogance has overtaken the mind and sense of the modern man. His monkey mind hops from one place to another which runs after sensual pleasures and is trapped in evil desires. For him, it is becoming difficult to control this terrible and agitating mind. Man's mind is far more polluted than the environment. It is the inner pollution of man which is reflected as pollution outside. It is quite difficult to harness. The solution lies in merging the mind with the Divine. Mind is essentially a bundle of thoughts. Control of mind means control of the thoughts. Mind control must be preceded by sense control. Indeed, sense control and mind control go hand in hand. The only way to control sense and mind is to place the mind in God. ***"Bend the body, mend the senses, end the mind"***, **says Sai Baba**. Mental process motivates the sense organ and the body. It draws its strength from the Atmic power which enables all the body organs to function. Mind is energized by the Atmic power. In the ultimate analysis, the power of the 'Atom' and the power of the 'Atma' are pitted against each other. Modern scientists including even the eminent Indian scientist Dr. Abdul Kalam former President of India, accepts the superiority of Atmic power over the Atomic power.

Science and spirituality both deeply influence the human society. While science improves the human life by providing material abundance, spirituality generates a feeling of cosmic kinship and provides essential inner happiness. While science has produced weapons of mass destruction, spirituality brings oneness of humanity. Amazingly, the same science which earlier challenged the very existence of God, is now, by way of astrophysics and cosmology, providing evidence that tends to support the spiritual belief in the existence of one source – a supreme power behind the phenomenon of the Universe. Science is now willing to certify that everything in this universe emerges from one single source with its roots in consciousness. Indeed, the present world, which is full of conflicts and terrorism, desperately needs the feeling of universal love that comes from the realization of existence of one common single source. Just as the highest power, called the God has not left the Universe after creating it, likewise science is trying to prove that the source is still there with the Universe. Spirituality evolves consciousness which facilitates experiencing one-ness with the source, the highest power behind everything that is called God. The scientists have starting accepting the truth of the same consciousness which enable them to infer empirically that everything comes from one source, it stands to reason out that there exists the one and only one source in reality which allows the human brain to experience. There is ample scientific evidence to prove that human consciousness in its evolved form can give relief to the distressed mind and brings supreme bliss. In that stage of supreme bliss, the human beings get attuned with themselves as whole and one with the universe.

An unnecessary ideological debate continues between science and spirituality. People are amazed by the powers of science as much as they are bewildered by the miracles of spirituality. There is no competition between the two: science is the discovery of nature outside: while spirituality is the discovery of humanity within. In the final analysis, science and spirituality are complements of each other. Science starts from the head, while spirituality originates from the heart and action (practice) takes place through the hand. Science lead to materialism through technology, while spirituality shows the way to idealism through religion. Both science and spirituality agree that there is life (energy) even in a stone. Vedantic philosophy is both scientific and spiritual. An in-depth study of the scientific literature and Vedanta would reveal that science and spirituality do not contradict each other but rather reinforce each other. A deeper analysis would reassure that contradictions as claimed, do not really exist.

- **According to science, energy is the basis** of this Universe. The Universe began its existence with an initial deposit of energy, and all that is seen around is really a gross manifestation of this energy. Further, energy by itself is subtle and invisible. Only its presence or effects can be felt. Spirituality too proclaims that the ultimate is energy referred to as Cosmic or Divine Energy. This ultimate Cosmic state of energy is boundless and timeless. It is a state of Absolute Awareness or Pure Consciousness. In other words, the ultimate in energy is nothing but the energy of Pure Consciousness or Absolute Awareness. This is the state generally referred to as *Brahmn* or *Atma*. The physical Universe got its initial deposit from this infinite reservoir.
- According to science, there are three central entities: vacuum, radiation and matter. The vacuum is the source, and from it everything flows. What is here termed radiation is nothing but electromagnetic vibration. Matter is self-explanatory. Even according to spirituality, the three primary entities are energy (radiation or efflugence), vibration and matter. Vacuum is

primordial. From the vacuum is born everything, and into the vacuum everything dissolves. Further, the vacuum is never diminished. There is a striking parallel. *Brahmn* is primordial and eternal. Everything emerges from Brahmn and merges back into it.

- At the time the emergence of the Universe, there was total uniformity; diversity came later. Thus, even in the case of the physical Universe, it was a case of "One becoming many". Needless to say that Spiritual view of the phenomenal Universe also is the same, namely, "One becoming many". Science accepts the close interlinkage between the micro and the macro, be it in the case of a plant or animal or a human being or even the entire Universe. Spirituality too holds that the microcosm is the macrocosm and *vice versa.*
- Science has its own quota of subtle entities like quantum fields, quantum correlations and so on. Spirituality of course has a rich bag of subtle entities. Science has come round to the view of observer-created physical reality. Spirituality has always maintained that the perception is created entirely by the perceiver. According to quantum philosophy, what one sees is what one can see. A Vedantin would perhaps state this aphorism as: As is the thought, so is the feeling.
- According to quantum philosophy, all entities in the Universe are really correlated to each other on account of a common origin. "There is a web of relationship to the whole. Spirituality not only accepts this web but goes one step further by identifying the whole as Atma or Brahmn. Elementary particles have an outer and an inner world. The properties they exhibit and the attributes they have are the result of a beautiful and delicate balance between the two worlds. Spirituality too cognizes both the external and the internal worlds (in the case of man), and recommends a proper balance – in the words of **Sri Sathya Sai Baba "Thoughts of God in the mind, and work of God on hand"**.

More and more parallels can be drawn to demonstrate that science and spirituality do not really contradict each other. Almost all modern sciences are tending to confirm more and more assuringly the revelations made in the texts and scriptures of Vedanta. **Sai Baba stresses this point even more forcefully: "Generally it is considered that the natural science is concerned only with matter, and**

metaphysics is regarded as being concerned with things spiritual. But the physical and metaphysical are inextricably related to each other". Why then the widely-held view that science and spirituality contradict each other? Several reasons can be given:

First, not many scientists take the trouble of making clear the distinction between enlightened spiritual philosophy and institutionalized religion which does not explain the inner meanings. Unfortunately, spiritualism is wrongly treated as ritualism, whereas spirituality ought to be treated as the spirit of Oneness. Secondly, even if scientists are prepared to concede that spirituality is plausible and attractive, there would still be a resistance to fully accepting it because of the wrong perception that it does not have the "predictive power" that scientific theories are supposed to have (at least, this is what scientists claim). Thirdly, and this in a sense is related to the prevalent objection that scientific hypotheses can be put to laboratory tests, while those of spirituality, cannot, in the manner scientists would like. In fact, scientists are proud that in science, theories can be falsified by further inquiry and experimentation. They cannot accept that there can be such a thing as Eternal Truth which is what Spirituality proclaims which can never be falsified and which exists independent of man. *Gita* gives the essence of Spirituality which is not just a mere theory but THE TRUTH. Finally, objection generally comes from physicists that while physics is quantitative, and one can express it in exact mathematical equations, spirituality or metaphysics, on the other hand, is purely descriptive and not amenable to quantification; and therefore, it is of little value. Does that mean that all scientists summarily reject spirituality, spiritual truths, and spiritual values? Not indeed, for many eminent scientists who have wandered to the very edge of science, **Einstein being one of them, do concede that there "is a Divinity that shapes our ends"**. While most scientists of this variety are willing to accept in a vague sort of way the existence of an Almighty. Noted scientist David Bohm endeavoured to construct what might be called a rudimentary mathematical theory of metaphysics. Bohm was led to this exercise because he wanted to sort out the unsatisfactory aspects of quantum physics as currently known. According to Bohm what physics reveals is not the totality but only a part of it. A deep analysis of science and technology (*both of which are dependent on measurement and quantification), and religion and philosophy (both of which are directed towards the immeasurable*) will convince that the fragmentary approach of science is not productive beyond a point. An Indian saint once declared that what man knows could be compared to a handful of earth while what he does not know is vast like the oceans. A few evolved scientists are modest enough to recognize this. For Sir

Isaac Newton, the whole universe remained unexplored and unknown despite his amazing contribution to scientific investigations.

It is crystal clear that there is no need to believe that science can explain anything and everything. It is still struggling to understand the complexities of matters related to the Spirit. Scientists dismiss spirituality because it is not quantifiable. Can everything in life be quantified? Take the case of the brain. Computer scientists have long wondered whether it is at all possible, even in principle, to construct a computer that would mimic the human brain in every possible way. In a best-seller entitled *The Emperor's New Mind,* the renowned physicist Roger Penrose has discussed this question at length. One interesting point which he makes is that computers compute, solve problems, play chess etc., by relying on algorithms or a step-by-step procedure encoded into them. No algorithm, no computer. The human brain, on the other hand, is known to perform many tasks in totally non-algorithmic fashion. In other words, even at the level of the human brain (that is the "meat machine" as opposed to the mind), one runs into the problem of not being able to quantify. Whether one likes it or not, this is a fact of life one has to live with it. Even the workings of the brains of scientists cannot be quantified! So, however much one wishes, it seems that certain matters would forever remain outside the purview of quantification. That being the case with the human brain, how then can one insist that metaphysics too must be quantifiable? Can sentiments, thoughts, emotions, feelings, etc. be quantified? Can truth, righteousness, peace, love and non-violence be quantified?

Scientists claim that they are in the quest of truth. What they mean by truth is what they call "Verification of facts". For spirituality, Truth is eternal, that which does not ever change. A scientist might argue: The law of gravitation does not ever change. Therefore it represents truth. "But did gravitation exist before the Universe came into existence? Certainly not, indeed, even at the time of the so called Big Bang, it did not. Therefore, it is not eternal and in that sense, does not quite qualify to be called the truth. It may be termed as a relative truth, in relation to the planets or heavenly bodies. There is only one truth that is Eternal, namely, God. Thus, as Sai Baba often declares, *God is Truth and Truth is God*. However, Sai Baba has also clarified that facts relating to Nature (such as scientists investigate) are true in a limited time scale. For example, scientists have been investigating the solar system and have discovered many facts about it. All these are certainly true but they become meaningful only in the context of the Sun itself. Indeed, facts which are locally true or valid for a limited period of time are referred to a relative or temporary. There is a need to distinguish and discriminate between *relative truth and Eternal Truth*. Scientists are solely concerned with the former, and as of today, refuse to contemplate the latter. Does that imply that science has no meaning or relevance? Not quite. The Universe is the vesture of God, and what science reveals are facts about a particular manifestation of God. However, science neither enquires nor sheds any light on the Eternal substratum.

If science deals with THIS (meaning *Prakriti* or *Nature*), spirituality deals with THAT (meaning God); In fact, it (spirituality) assures that THIS is the same as THAT. Science looks outwards whereas spirituality directs attention inwards. Science relies on experimentation whereas spirituality is based on experience. Science depends entirely on perception through the senses and their extensions, whereas spirituality goes beyond the senses to higher levels of perception. As Sai Baba crisply puts it, science is BELOW the senses, whereas spirituality is BEYOND the senses. Science limits itself to the framework of space-time, whereas spirituality transcends space-time. Science, as currently pursued, induces self-centeredness, ego, competition and even jealousy, whereas spirituality promotes love, peace and the dissolution of one's ego. Science is the splitting of Love, spirituality is the spreading of Love, Science digs deep into differences (though seeking common forms), whereas spirituality seeks transcendental unity in diversity. Finally, science leads to where the mind ends and spirituality is where the heart begins. Science of its own does not in any way rule out the existence or relevance of God. All that it expects is an explanatory and logical justification based on logical grounds. Indeed, science deals with the knowledge of the manifested divinity *i.e.* the phenomenal Universe whereas spirituality refers not only to the knowledge of the phenomenal Universe but also to that knowledge too which allows one to perceive the existence of the Divine substratum underlying the Universe, and that Substratum is nothing other than the Supreme Reality – the Brahmn Itself. Science explodes the obvious only, spirituality explores the final and efficient cause of the obvious and beyond.

It is fashionable these days to give credit to science for everything and rule out the relevance of God. Somehow the feeling has been created that belief in God is tantamount to being irrational. The eminent Indian physicist Chandrasekhar (who won the Nobel Prize for spectacular discoveries in astrophysics) went so far as to declare that man invented God to explain his failures and successes. This is because science has been largely dominated by the physical and materialistic attitudes of scientists. Understandably the views of modern scientists about God are considerably influenced by the even the so mundane events as recorded in history, persecution of Galileo and other atrocities perpetrated on even innocent reformers.

There has been a gradual change of view about the concept of God. The Greek philosophers Plato visualized two universes, one that of the material objects, which is well-recognized as the physical Universe and which is accessible to the senses but it is fleeting, ephemeral and even illusory. The other being a higher universe which was perfect, unchanging and inaccessible to the senses. Plato conceived of this higher universe in terms of beautiful geometric structures and mathematical forms (ideas, not objects) and held the view that the physical universe was but a pale shadow of the superior universe. In Plato's perception, the higher universe is the domain of BEING, while the lower is the domain of Becoming. Plato gave primacy to the former (shades of the Vedantic picture). Plato's student Aristotle however struck a different note.

A number of scientists regard God as belonging to the superior realm which is beyond space and time. Such a God is simple, perfect, timeless, omnipotent and omniscient. The scientists do see in their discoveries the handiwork of God. After giving shape to what is now called Newtonian mechanics, Issac Newton wrote; "*This most beautiful system of the Sun, planets and comets, could only proceed from the counsel and dominion of an intelligent and all powerful Being*". His contemporary, Robert Boyle (of Boyle's Law fame) also believed in a similar supreme power. Science, after Newton, grew at a breathtaking pace. More and more facts of Nature, which at one time were totally baffling, received a coherent logical and rational explanation. Darwin's theory and some other philosophical ideologies argued that the origin of life and the evolution of species were merely the result of random mutations and natural selection; that there was no need for a God to look after the Universe. Spiritualist, however argue what about Creation of the Universe? Can the Universe exist without a divine force? Who created the Universe?" Since there is a creation, and there are creatures the elements of creation, these must be a creator. Just as there can be no effect without a cause, there can be no creation without a creator.

The scientific version is that the Universe originated in a Big Bang, roughly about eleven billion years ago. What happened next? Two scenarios are generally visualized. In one of these, the Universe having been born in a Big Bang, goes on expanding and after a while becomes tired of expanding, starts contracting, and eventually disappears in a Big Crunch! The so-called Big Crunch is really a most remarkable phenomenon. The Big Bang phenomenon may be compared to the explosion of an ordinary bomb. In such an explosion, the fragments fly away and get widely separated, but it is inconceivable that the fragments ever come together to make up the original bomb. Yet that is what the Universe is believed to be doing; starting as an incredibly tiny drop, swelling to astronomical proportions and finally shrinking back again to an inconceivably small drop. It is true that as of now there is no firm scientific experimental evidence in support of the Big Bang or Big Crunch, but for a variety of reasons most scientists seem to be willing to accept. Isn't science creating its own mythology?

Scientists now raise another question: "If the Universe was in fact born as the result of a Big Bang, why the process stopped after the first Big Bang? Why have not been subsequent Big Bangs? Does it mean that there had to be only one – the first and last Big Bang which gave birth to the present Universe? Moreover, what was there 'before' the Big Bang?" In a strictly technical sense, the question of "before" is itself debatable because perception of time begins only after the birth of present Universe; and it is not quite so meaningful to talk about the so-called before-the-birth scenario. **There is a model for this also, known as the oscillatory universe, the Universe goes through endless cycles of birth and death. Needless to say that this picture would find similarity with Siva's Cosmic Dance, believed to be synchronized to the creation and the dissolution of the Cosmos according to the Hindu scriptures**. All these scientific explanations are mere speculations, since gaps are still to be filled in. However what stands out clearly is that at the time of so-called Big-Bang, there was no diversity of any kind – it was all one, and later that one became many. Although all this look to be perfectly logical and rational, yet the fundamental question remains unanswered. Where did the original Universe originate from and get its energy from? This, in fact, is precisely the controversy which becomes endless, each side holding on to its own view. Some argue that the energy, out of which the Universe was born, came from the Cosmos whose existence does not require a God! The Vedanta views that Cosmos as the Ultimate, call it Brahmn, the Abstract and the Formless. Out of that Supreme Brahmn, the Universe got created and is bound to Dissolve (at the time of Dissolution). So one thing is clear the traditional Hindu wisdom, like science, too talks of creation (Srishti) and dissolution (Pralaya), the equivalents to the theory of the Big Bang and the Big Crunch respectively.

Vedanta does not describe the birth and the subsequent evolution of the gross or the physical Universe in such detail as modern science does. Nor does Vedanta refute modern science. On the contrary,

Vedanta largely complements science by giving hints of the manner in which energy became available for the Big Bang to occur. Roughly speaking, it is like the emission of a particle by a quantum field. The creation of the particle, the vacuum continues as before without any diminution of its characteristics or nature. There is lot of similarity in the two mentioned expositions. From Brahmn "**Flows**" some energy out of which the Universe is born, while Brahmn itself remains unaffected, and "witnesses" in a detached manner the growth of the baby Universe. In the language of science Brahmn is the Cosmic Mother. As is well-known, in the Vedantic picture, Creation is associated with OM or AUM and about which **Sai Baba says, "Every little movement results in a sound; only you may not be able to hear, because the range of the ear is limited. The falling of the eyelid over the eye makes a sound and the dropping of dew on a petal makes a sound. The sound caused by primal movement that resulted in enveloping Brahmn by self evolved Maya is the Pranavaa or OM.**" In other words, OM is the word that symbolizes the cosmic uniformity, which subsequently resulted in the birth of the Universe. Here, it is pertinent to stress that according to Vedanta, Srishti or Creation is merely the projection of that which is **Latent** and Unmanifest in the Brahmn. Thus, from the Vedantic point of view, the term projection is preferable for describing the coming into existence of the Physical Universe.

Towards the end of the twentieth century, there has been a perceptible movement of society towards spirituality. Indeed the last three centuries of the second millennium saw a phenomenal development of both science and society. Both rationality and materialism increasingly emphasized that many of the lasting human needs had not much to do with spiritualism. Science and Socialism both propounded that all sorts of truths: social, historical, scientific and philosophical could be established without reference to spirituality or existence of God. The end of the twentieth century, however, brought home the fact that neither science nor the socialist ideology was equipped to fulfil the basic human needs of social harmony. Paradoxically enough, the outgoing century that saw the phenomenal advances in all branches of science and technology, also witnessed the powerful revival of religion and spirituality as the essential ingredients of holistic progress. It also saw the revival of faith in God linked with the perceived notions of religious, ethical and spiritual values that were destroyed directly or indirectly by the extreme scientific outlook, glaring technological advancements and aggressive rationality of socialism.

The twentieth century will be known as the century of unprecedented events – the two great world wars, the continuous cold wars, and beginning of the global economic war against poverty. Also, it will be remembered as an era of a disgusting environment of vulgarity, crimes and violence that have crushed the human values, ideals, norms and morals. Yet, at the same time, there is a satisfaction that this century left the world not only with the arrival of technology but also the revival of spirituality, and survival of universality. The twenty-first century is going to be the confluences of knowledge, technology and spirituality. A systematic and comprehensive spectrum founded on spirituality, technology and knowledge is the only way out to free the troubled world from anguish, frustration and vulgarity. The advent of modern technology is the super high way to economic and material prosperity. Global knowledge is the super-specialty platform for knowledge dissemination. Spirituality is bound to provide the guiding harmony in terms of the comparative parameters of rationality, morality and technology.

However a conflict continues on the question of rationality versus spirituality. Most intellectuals have a deep distrust of spirituality because to them it smacks of irrationality. However, many of those who have stood at the very frontier of science have felt quite differently about it. Heisenberg, for example, realized the presence of God, while he was writing the Symphony of the Universe. Likewise, Einstein spoke of a cosmic spiritual feeling that inspired him to seek beauty, order and harmony in Nature a parallel to Satyam, Shivam and Sundaram of the Vedanta Philosophy. To these giants, it was as if there existed some overpowering hidden force which induced awe and commanded respect. In contrast to those just mentioned one feels like asking as to why the rationalists of today frown upon spiritualism and spiritual experiences. Perhaps because it reminds them of religion, especially institutionalized religion, which they learned to distrust and dislike. Also most intellectuals, despite their eminence and achievement hardly ever call for philosophical reflections of spirituality. They are not oriented enough to see the grand design of the Supra-mental in seemingly mundane matters.

Science gives a good and detailed portrayal of what happened after the Big Bang (which signifies the birth of the physical Universe) while Vedanta provides what might be called the "missing link", by describing the bridge between the Cosmos and Brahmn. This offers scope for a synthesis of the two points of view to produce a unified picture of Creation. But right now this synthesis remains a dream because the hard-core rationalists and the staunch spiritualists view each other with suspicion. Whereas rationalists scoff at spirituality, some eminent scientists on the hand, have finally veered around Vedanta philosophy; a spiritual philosopher, however, may be critical of non-believers but not of science per se.

'Going back to the relative perception about God and rationalists' rejection of it, one may note that in the special theory of relativity (by which all scientists swear), there is the issue of the relative perspective of the observer. What the static observer sees is different from what the dynamic viewers see. Both spiritualists and rationalists are like the two observers in two different frames of reference. To confirm what spiritualists see, the rationalists must move over to the frame of faith and vice-versa. Many of the scientists who have professed agnosticism have been extraordinarily creative like Chandrasekhar to whom a reference has already been made, Dirac (one of the founding fathers of Quantum Mechanics), von Neuman (a mathematical wizard) and Hardy (the mentor of the Indian mathematical genius Ramanujan) were persons of impeccable character, very disciplined in their own way, and pious in a substantial manner yet they argued an outright denial of, God, and a belief that this world was nothing but an accident. How could these people being so intelligent were so oblivious to something which is so patently obvious to even the most illiterate villager? Knowledge which was the strength of these people also proved to be their weakness.

Science is based on logic and therefore most scientists hold that if God exists, one must be able to deduce His existence by sheer logic. Interestingly, many decades ago, a famous mathematician named Gödel proved an important theorem now called Gödel's theorem the essence of which is that in a logical framework, there are certain questions which simply cannot be answered. Gödel's theorem is very technical, and it was enunciated and proved in the context of understanding mathematics as a logical structure. However, it is now recognized that it has implications far beyond mathematics. Since, science is based on logic, therefore, Gödel's theorem must apply also to science. There must exist questions which cannot be answered one way or the other within the framework of the logical system that supports scientific reasoning. Using this as a basis, some have pointed out that science cannot provide the answer as to whether God exists or not. As a corollary it is pointed out that God's existence can be understood only in a larger framework that goes beyond space and time (within which science works). However, this objection is not universally accepted because the counter question is raised: "How is one to know that the question of God's existence is one of those un-decidable propositions?" Does God exist only if He can be reasoned out logically? At this stage one might wonder: "What if scientists deny God? So do many others. Let them do so. Can they prove that God does not exist? This happens to be the age of science and technology where scientists have a disproportionate leverage in relation to the state of the society. Not only individual scientists, but even the universities which are supposed to be the seats of learning have been influenced by the non-belief in the existence of God.

Rationalists pride themselves on their ability to analyze logically and in a rational manner, and yet when confronted with the question of human matters, their thinking is as much clouded and subjective as that of many others. What is required is a delicate blend of knowledge and faith. It is necessary to pursue the scientific investigations. But science should not get satisfied by scientific knowledge alone. There are innumerable other things which ought to be explored such as spiritual philosophy for which, the scientist should cultivate interest in the existence of God. Einstein once said: "Science without religion is blind; and religion without science is lame. Thus, in today's world, both science as well as spirituality are needed." Unfortunately, the loss of faith in God is a relatively recent phenomenon. Those who refuse to believe in God often say: "Truth is Beauty and Beauty is Truth". Scientists are often fond of quoting this phrase. Over two thousand years ago, Plato talked of three primary and inter-related entities namely, Truth, Goodness and Beauty. Sri Sathya Sai Baba has often remarked that what Plato referred to is already inscribed in Satyam (Truth), Sivam (Purity), Sundaram (Beauty). Truth and Beauty are related no doubt, but via Purity – the spiritual purity. However, such an equivalence finds no place in the what the modern intellectuals try to seek. They totally miss the point, and what they perceive is a dry, lifeless and limited equivalence.

Science deals strictly with the physical Universe, and its modeling starts from the instant of the Big Bang. It has not only been able to give a reasonably comprehensive description of the evolution of the Universe, it has also not been able to explain the constitution of inert matter in terms of the basic building block even though they are being deciphering these riddles. Two points on which science has not been able to shed light are: "What is awareness?" And "What is before and after life?" These questions are yet to be explored. Origin of life therefore, remains a mystery even within the framework of science. The optimal hope is that the prevailing atheistic attitude among the scientists will one day reverse. They will realize that believing in God does not deny the credit to them for their amazing achievements in science and technology. It is equally wrong to think that science per se rules out God. Science merely reveals facts pertaining to Nature; it says nothing about God. It merely restrict itself to the phenomenon of the physical universe observed within the framework of space and time, and to observations based on the conjectures and their scientific verification. Denial of God is by those, who choose to interpret scientific facts in their own particular way. Thus, one must make a clear distinction between what science itself reveals and how scientists interpret the revelations. The facts of science in no way refute the existence of God. On the contrary, one is amazed by the striking parallels between the discoveries of science and the concepts of spiritual philosophy (as contained in the *Vedanta*). In fact, this should not come as surprise, since after all, Nature is nothing but the vesture of God or a manifestation of God Himself. To put it differently, there is no reason to expect that astrophysics and metaphysics should be contradictory. As already remarked, by choice, present-day scientists limit themselves to observations and experience regarding both space as well as time. Scientists, however, dodge and avoid consciousness, giving their own reasons as well as excuses. And as long as they do so, they would tend to dismiss spirituality as well as metaphysics, as they are presently doing.

According to an article published in a recent edition of Time magazine, there is a growing credence given by the scientific community – spanning computerology and artificial intelligence to genetics and biotechnology – to what is called Singularity; the moment in the foreseeable future (around the year 2045) when human beings, with the aid of supra-human machines, will have the power to banish death forever and make themselves immortal. Indeed, there have been instances of immortal beings given in ancient Hindu scriptures *e.g.* a noble demon King Bali in Satyayuga; Hanuman, Parsurama, Vibhishna (another noble demon king of Sri Lanka), Sage Balmiki in the Tretayuga; Ashwathama (Son of Guru Dronacharya), Ved Vyas (known for compilation of the four Vedas and author of the greatest epic Mahabharata) and the sage Kripacharya of the Dwapur Yuga. It is further predicted by the scientists that with the advances made in biotechnology, it will be possible to reverse the aging process. Such a prediction is asserted on the basis of their core argument based on the advances in science and technology that are growing faster at the rate of exponential acceleration. This process of immortality, however, raises a few questions: Can the already over-crowded planet Earth endure the burden of an ever-increasing, deathless human population? Is the immortal super-humankind destined to colonize the Cosmos? What about the human consciousness? Can an artificial machine replicate the complicity of human consciousness which includes the consciousness of the self and consciousness of the consciousness itself and which separates human beings from the domain of animal kingdom? But perhaps the most haunting of all questions is whether, along with their morality, which is in any case at the lowest ebb presently, they will also lose their humanness. Indeed, it is the knowledge of human consciousness that makes them human: capable of love and sacrifice, joy and sorrow, of appreciating the beauty of nature. It is the inevitability of death that makes human life more charmful and mortal. If death is subtracted from mortality, what is left – a robot, a ghost in a deathless machine. What about the Karma philosophy which is scientifically and beautifully propounded in the Hindu philosophy?

Spiritual evolution according to Mukul Sharma: (Spiritual Theory of Evolution; Speaking Tree, 13 February, 2011, New Delhi) integrates the role of consciousness into the system of biological evolution, as held by Alfred Russel Wallace, a great 19th century naturalist, explorer and biologist who made an extremely important contribution to the theory of evolution along with Darwin. In fact, it so happened that when Darwin was about to conclude his thesis, he was surprised to receive a letter from Wallace who had independently devised a similar theory of evolution. Darwin was so impressed by Wallace's letter that he offered to share his own work with that of Wallace and eventually, both of them published a joint paper on theory of evolution. The credit, however, was given to Darwin because of two reasons. First being that Wallace was a revolutionary type of person. His views on socio-economic reforms and women's rights among several other issues did not appeal to the minds of the then ruling class. Secondly, Wallace suddenly moved towards spirituality and espoused the cause of spiritual philosophy. Wallace also maintained that broad principles of the theory of evolution were not sufficient enough to explain the intellectual traits in human beings such as reason, judgment, philosophy and metaphysics nor could they account for mathematical, artistic or musical dexterities inherent in humankind. Wallace believed that the Universe had interceded at least three times in history. The first was creation of life from inorganic matter, the second was the introduction of consciousness in higher living beings namely the human beings, and the third was the generation of higher mental faculties in the human beings. Such thoughts among others caused a conflict in Wallace's mind regarding the cold reality of the survival of the fittest. Ultimately, Wallace came to the conclusion that the Universe existed for the development of the human soul which means he came closer to the realization that there existed a divine power.

It, however, hardly matters where from the power comes so long as the man is realistic and believes in come external deity or power. If he thinks that the power of the deity is helping him, it is perfectly alright for him. It also does not matter if the man is ready to change his idea when he begins the quest of truth, that is to say, when man is interested to understand the inner reality of the life and of the universe. Then he will see that God is to be found not in particular form, but in all forms; nor in any particular place, but everywhere; not through any particular faith, cult, religion, but by any faith or religious mode; not at any particular religious centre like temple, mosque or church but at any place of worship. He must be prepared to get enlightened that the actual avenue to find God is not outside himself but within himself.

In the present era of mental advancement, man has begun to gain intelligence and knowledge at an extraordinary pace. As a result, he is restless and is not able to still his mind. He is keen to know everything including the reality of God. Ancient methods and traditional ways are neither sufficient for him nor appear to be convincing to him. He wants to know the ultimate truth as to what is this Supreme Being called God. He wants to hear voices, the voices of men who have been privileged to experience God face-to-face or who can demonstrate their convincing spiritual experience. Modern man is not willing to understand that Truth is not a creed, and not a set of statements to be swallowed like a pill. He must first divest himself of such a notion of the Truth. Even the goal of the scientists is also to know the ultimate Truth so that they understand the beliefs upon which mankind has been fed for thousands of years. Indeed, the scientists will find the same Truth which the sages and the spiritualists have already realized because there is only one ultimate Truth. In such a situation, what are scientists going to discover or invent about this question of God?

Indeed, the scientists perceive that there is no room for a personified God in the Universe because the Universe is infinite and immeasurable. They have started realizing that they are only a part of the whole and a part cannot be greater than the whole, nor the creation can be greater than the creator. They are fully convinced that since there is creation, there must be a creator just like there must be a builder of a building. If this creator is a Supreme Power beyond the form, then God must be an Infinite Force. The scientists are trying to explore His infinite creation. This is the only difference which is likely to be in a conceptualization of God – the Infinite. The scientists may not name this

Supreme Power as God. They may give some other name. They are not willing to agree to the priests and theologians who take God both as personified and non-personified. They are, however, convinced that God is some most intelligent life force, and all the evolutionary cycles of this Universe are merely demonstrations, displays and the outworkings of this Supreme Power. Bhagwan Sri Sathya Sai Baba says, **"God is the Creator. He created everything in the Cosmos. But He did not retain within His hands the responsibilities relating to His creation. He gave to human beings all capabilities. But he laid down a condition relating to the use of these capabilities. Men are free to live as they like. They can utilize all the material objects in creation. There can be no objection in this from anyone, not even from God. But the Divine has declared there is no escape from the consequences of one's action. This has to be properly understood."**

Now the moot point in this context is that whether it is possible to arrive at some conclusion and find some space common between the two ways of conceiving universe and its efficient cause, its creator. To that effect it can be argued that Brahmn is the meeting point of Astrophysics and Metaphysics. According to the eminent American physicist Max Plank, the father of Quantum Theory, matter is secondary while consciousness is primary and there is a higher power described as the Brahmn in Vedas. There are primary quantum fields, in the language of Physics, which permeate the Universe. They are Omni-present and Omni-potent like the Brahmn of the Vedas, but randomly fluctuate at every point. Their value, however, remains the same at every time. Everything is changing around these quantum fields, the Universe is also undergoing some change and new galaxies are forming, but the venues of these fields have not changed at all. These quantum fields of Physics can be described almost like the scientific face of the Brahmn. Physics, however, cannot give any metaphysical assumption but can provide a logical support to it. A spiritual scholar may be termed as a spiritual scientist who experiences oneness with the Brahmn while a scientist is a spiritual seeker who can have some inquisitiveness and keeps on searching for answers.

Everything is changing in the Universe including the Universe itself but there is one thing that is permanent and eternal and That is the Brahmn. Indeed, there arises the need to believe in some higher power that is Universal. Spiritualists always desire to communicate with that entity called the Brahmn. When this fact is realized by the scientists, everything falls into its proper place. Then the consciousness knows what to do, while science is needed to show the correct way out.

Scientists have no clue about consciousness. They have not been able to establish the idea of consciousness although some scientists do believe that consciousness is an inbuilt characteristics of awareness. But they have not evolved any instrument to measure consciousness, though they can only measure the physiological manifestation of consciousness, just as, the quotient of happiness is difficult to measure in a more definitive way than having the feeling of it.

Consciousness is something that intrigues both spiritualists and scientists. Consciousness is enlightenment where the seekers realize the truth and experience absolute bliss, Consciousness is fundamental to knowing all about the world and cosmos including birth and death. Science is baffled by the fact that every mystery of the physical world points to a further mystery. Einstein said that advancement of knowledge is the process of extracting one incomprehensible from another which has inherent deficiencies and limitations.

The Universe fundamentally appears to be working in an orderly manner although its existence seems to be abstract. Its huge cosmos is consistent in the sense that same natural laws prevail everywhere. Despite seemingly contrasting and divergent view points, science seems to be on the verge of concluding that the whole existence emerges from a single source which is called the Brahmn – the Supreme Reality by the spiritual philosophers. Thus, all this seems to indicate the existence of a higher power which is guiding the entire universe in a perfect order while maintaining coordination on an unimaginable scale. The present emerging scientific research and knowledge seem to be supporting such a spiritual belief in a supreme higher being which is at the core of everything. Some scientists are bold enough to acknowledge with wonder that the universe is intertwined with consciousness as a foundational and fundamental reality and there is a supreme power behind it. Indeed, it implies that creation, the creator and the process of creation together comprise an inseparable oneness.

A synthesis of science and spirituality by some great scholars suggests that the first and the foremost is the faith in an omni principle in which no speculation is entertained. This is the principle of Omni-presence, Omni-science and Omni-potence of a Supreme Reality or Power which is considered to be beyond the capability of human perception. This is Absolute Reality which is called Absolute Consciousness – free from any kind of conditioning. This Absolute Reality or Supreme Reality is the absolute 'Parabrahmn' or simply referred as 'Brahmn'. It is the force and source of all individual consciousness – the fundamental identity of all souls with the Universal

Soul, the spirit of the Universe and the cosmic ideation, the basis of the intelligent operations in and around the existence.

Science and spirituality are indeed the two sides of the same coin. **Science is the evolution whereas spirituality is the involution of the same thought process**. Science is experimental while spirituality is experiential. Spirituality is experienced through consciousness. The same consciousness facilitates gaining the profound scientific knowledge indicating thereby the existence of a deep and hidden relationship between the two comprehensions. **How to reconcile the two apparently disparate perceptions garnered by the same consciousness? Does there really exist an architect which works as a stabilizing force behind this magnificent phenomenon called the Universe? Can science support the spiritual belief in the existence and oneness of an abstract entity called the Brahmn which manifests through its creation**? Indeed, science has been battling all along to come to a consensuous theory of everything which, according to spirituality, is the essence of the singularity or oneness of non-duality (Advaita) where the observer, the observed and process of observation merge. Manifestation is the ability of the source to virtually express itself multidimensionality. Realization is the process of moving from awareness of the virtual reality to pure awareness. A human being as the citadel of a body equipped with the soul full of a myriad power is ever marching on to the realization of the Supreme Being – the Brahmn.

Science and spirituality are complementary, according to many spiritual scholars and scientists. Science is the discovery of one area and spirituality is the discovery of another area. In the final analysis both types of discoveries are complementary and not contradictory, because both are an experience of 'awareness'. Both scientists and spiritualists agree that this awareness exists everywhere and in everything including even the stone. Scientists consider stone as a compound of molecules which are ever-changing but are invisible. Spiritualists believe that there is some level, although very low, of consciousness even in a stone.

Albert Einstein believed in Unity not only between matter and energy but also between the material and the mystical. Declaring that "Science without religion is lame, and religion without science is blind," he said, "Everyone who is seriously involved in the pursuit of science becomes convinced that a spirit is manifest in the laws of the Universe – a spirit vastly superior to that of man." Vedanta asserts faith in the Supreme Reality called the Brahmn because faith sees the invisible, believes the incredible and perceives the impossible. Vedanta fuses the faith of religion, vision of spiritual philosophy and the rationalism of science to provide answers to various questions and offers a way to sensible living. It is a science of spirituality aimed at integral vision of life and consciousness and strives to enable the people to take an all inclusive look into the Universe and its process of working.

At this juncture one may say that the rise of science and technology is gradually leading to disappearance of spiritual values, but one needs to realize that science and spirituality, however, together can be found to be mutually complementary. Science can tell the truth of the physical world, whereas spirituality will see the same truth in the world of consciousness. Both are needed to enable people to lead a perfect human life based on scientific outlook and spiritual idealism. All have to work for the realization of spiritual values for peace and harmony.

Both science and spirituality are needed to understand the Supreme Reality. Wisdom lies in the knowledge of matter and spirit, astrophysics and metaphysics. Metaphysics is physics with a flavor of mysticism. This has been amply exemplified by the seers who were scientists par excellence as they knew the inner world of the ultimate reality and knew what to reveal for Universal application and what to restrict to few worthy minds. Vedic seer Kanad is reported to have discovered the atom (anu) long ago but did not reveal it for the simple reason of its being misused. Krishna, in Srimad Bhagavata, tells his cousin and disciple Uddhava that knowledge matures into wisdom once the physical science partakes of the science of introversion. Integration of both astro physics and metaphysics leads to the supreme wisdom – the key to comprehend the Supreme Reality. Science enhances knowledge of the physical world while spirituality takes a comprehensive view of matter and spirit. Science as such covers a part of total human experience while spirituality includes supra-intellectual and other subtle planes of human consciousness as it leads to exploration of the knowledge of the infinite which is beyond the ephemeral world of duality. Knowledge of both the outer (physical) and inner (spiritual) worlds, as given in the ancient Hindu texts like Vedas, reveals the eternal truths comprehensively which have been elucidated by Lord Krishna in the common man's language in the Geeta. The imperfection witnessed in the explicit behaviour of Man is simply a good to dive deep to discover the implicit perfection well portrayed in the Upanishadic sayings.

Chapter 3
Hinduism and Its Philosophy

From the very beginning of human civilization, four types of wars have been raging with no prospect of their abating. First, humans versus nature: Human beings have been ruthlessly exploiting nature and its endowments for satisfying their ever increasing need and greed. Secondly, humans versus animal: human beings have been equally ruthless with the animal kingdom, brutally exploiting animals by using them for hard work, by killing them and treating them as insentient beings. The third war, humans versus society: between humans and humans – hopelessly divided into races and ethnic groups, religions and cults, tribes and languages, nations and nations. The fourth war has been going on between human and human himself, that is, a human being perceiving himself as a body, mind and intellect on one hand, and on the other, as a divine spark, a component of the Universal Consciousness. The reasons for these wars are attributed to evolutional and technological developments, employing the forces of nature to race ahead in aimless competitions with a death wish. This has led to total lack of stability in the nature of social organizations in evolving appropriate ideological models with complete absence of the evolution of suitable solutions for sustaining the human society in harmony with, nature, animals and fellowmen. These reasons owe their origin to the social and empirical principles emanating from the specific disciplines such as politics, economics, psychology, sociology, law and logic among others. Unfortunately, all the civilizational and cultural issues have been delinked from spirituality – the essence of existence, and hence a human being has failed to identify himself as a part of divinity. Consequently, religion has largely become a periodic tryst of humanity with divinity while relations between human beings and society are governed by social science principles separated from spiritual philosophy.

According to some Hindu scholars and spiritual philosophers, it was many many (perhaps more than ten) thousand years ago, there lived a more progressive, highly sophisticated and hugely prosperous human civilization in the Indian subcontinent spreading over the Indus Valley in the North-West at one end, while passing through the Gangetic plains, culminating in the East and the Southern Peninsula on the other end. It was considered to be one of the most culturally rich societies of the human world. Spread over more than several millions square kilometers of area, it was considered as one of the largest at the time. It contained big cities, towns and villages with wide roads, effective drainage systems, public places of tourist interests, docks and granaries inhabitated by people wearing unmatched golden jewellery and ornaments bedecked with diamonds and pearls. Known as the Hindu Civilization, it had deep knowledge of philosophy, technology, science, art and culture. Their best known achievement has been the massive literary work in Sanskrit language accumulated and compiled as Vedic literature spanning several centuries. Indeed, Sanskrit is considered to be the ancient language of the Hindus. It seems to have maintained its prestige as the supreme language of the Vedas. Since Vedas are eternal and beginningless, Sanskrit, being their language, is also considered to be eternal and beginningless. It is, in this sense, that Sanskrit is considered to be an original language. Panini; a famous Sanskrit grammarian is reported to have transformed it as a more recognizable and reproducible language around 350 B.C.

Hinduism is like a gigantic banyan tree with its refreshing and ever growing change and variation where the pursuit of invisible spiritualism has been given priority over the visible materialism. The central focus of its philosophy has been on realization of the supreme consciousness for which various systems have been evolved. Its pluralistic tradition has always offered freedom of worshipping/adoring the divine in the name and form of one's own choice. Hinduism is pluralistic both at the level of religious practices as well as philosophical propensities. It is because of this reason, Hinduism encompasses so many sects, cults and religions. This chapter highlights Hindu Culture, Hindu Scriptures and Hindu Philosophy in its three corresponding sections 3.1, 3.2 and 3.3.

3.1 Hindu Culture

Hinduism is considered to be one of the richest cultures that flourished prior to the Christian and Islamic eras. The Greek, Roman, Egyptian, Mesopotamian, among others became mere ruins of brick and mortar, leaving no trace of their past glory. What remains are the Coliseum in Rome, the Pyramids in Egypt and temple pillars in Athens

– all of which are of archaeological curiosity and tourist interest. But the Hindu civilization is still enliven and vibrant with an unbroken continuity of its unique philosophical thoughts and features which are clearly distinct from Occidental thinking, and are of Universal interest and eternal value. Hindu philosophers and spiritual scholars did not care much for keeping records of history. Thus, there is always some speculation about the truth and historicity of the ancient Hindu scriptures like the Vedas containing Hindu philosophy of spiritualism as to when were they written and who wrote them. These spiritual sages and scholars were so self-effacing that they did not even put their names as authors of their voluminous scholarly works which, in fact, show their total mastery of intellect and wisdom. This feature of Hindu philosophers has no parallel in any other culture or religion. Their concern was solely spiritual service to humanity with a dedicated devotional love for God. With their extraordinary super-sensory perception, they evolved innumerable concepts of eternal utilitarian and spiritual values; and those too without the help of any mechanical device or technological tool which are available in abundance in the present times.

Late Dr. S. Radhakrishnan, one of the greatest philosophers of the world and the second President of India, described Hinduism as a way of life and not a religion. He considered Hinduism as an umbrella where everybody including even the atheists and agnostics, could take refuge. This inclusive and all embracing version of Hinduism has also been advocated by Late Mahatma Gandhi, who held that Hinduism allowed everyone to worship God according to one's faith or 'dharma'. Such a view enabled Hinduism to survive at pace with all other religions of the world. Such an understanding of Hinduism permits pluralism and multiplicity of several philosophies, faiths, cults and sects.

Two major combinations are, sometimes, described with regard to the major religions of the world namely the Hindic which comprises of the Hindus, Jains, Buddhists and Sikhs; and the Judaic which consists of the Jews, Christians and Muslims. The Hindic approach believes in the Supreme Soul, Self-existent, devoid of all distinguishing characteristics of complexion, caste or the like, and is exempt from birth, vicissitude, death or decay; is always alone; exists everywhere and in which all things exist; and is the resplendent one, in which all things dwell. Hinduism deals with the nature of existence, truth and awareness; Brahmn-Atman, the Supreme Being from which all things evolve – the soul, the reasoning faculty, the self, the mind which has sense of individuality, the self-esteem, the intellect – the ultimate unity of design.

Hinduism is also known as the eternal phenomenon called 'Sanathan Dharma' which is based on the philosophy of its ancient scriptures: the Vedas, Upanishads and the Puranas like Srimad Bhagvatam and the epics like Ramayana and Mahabharata among others. Sanatan Dharma is the simple, effective and practical system of Truth (Satya), Righteousness (Dharma), Peace (Shanti), Love (Prema) and Non-violence (Ahimsa).

The pursuit of righteousness, the urge for self-realization and desire for liberation are common to all paths of Hinduism. Unlike in the West, Hindu sages and seers never perceived science and spirituality as incompatible. Spirituality has been perceived as a way of knowing and understanding the philosophical knowledge. This knowledge is considered to be of two types – lower knowledge and upper knowledge. The lower knowledge is necessary for practical functioning in life. It deals with the outer world of name, form and causation. The higher knowledge is concerned with consciousness and the Absolute or Supreme Reality. Various systems of Indian philosophy have been more like various scientific theories meant to be debated rationally, explored and experienced with a view to realize higher form of consciousness, and thereby validate the corresponding systemic theory in the shape of a religion.

With a decline of the Indus valley civilization around 1300 B.C., settlers in the Gangetic plains tried to protect some of its philosophical material particularly its Vedic literature and other ancient texts. While doing so, they also reproduced some surviving mathematical treatise – the Sulbhsastras, appendices to the Vedas, written by a succession of sages and mathematicians: Baudhayana (800 B.C.), Manava (750 B.C.), Apastambha (600 B.C.) and Katyayan (200 B.C.). Perhaps the highest contribution was made around this period, when Brahmi numerals from 1 to 9 appeared which were later transformed as Hindu-Arabic numerals in the Islamic world and transmitted to Europe where they became internationally acceptable. Around 350 B.C., Panini, as mentioned earlier, produced a treatise on language, called Ashtadyayi (8 chapters and 4000 sutras) in order to distil the complete grammar of Sanskrit. Panini's work to date remains a model for grammarians of the whole world. Another most influential thinker, philosopher and political intellectual, Chanakya also known as Kautilya during 350 to 275 B.C., advised and guided the great warrior Chandragupta Maurya to overthrow the then corrupt rules of Patliputra (now called Patna) known by the names of Nandas and establish the great Hindu empire. Chanakaya's Arthashastra describes economic policies valid even for the modern times war strategies, foreign relations, administrative policies and rules of conduct while His Neetishastra is a treatise on the ideal way of human life. During this period, India produced two great philosophies also called religions – Jainism and Buddhism, the latter spread in eastern Asia. Some of the Jain philosophers were also great mathematicians. Some of the Hindus during that era excelled in music, dance and theatre work authored by artists like Bharata Muni between 200 B.C. and 200 AD. This work formed the basis of aesthic theory and expression of sentiments in performances. Around fourth century AD, Kalidasa produced great romantic poetry and Creative works such as Meghdoot, Abhigyanshakuntalam and Kumarsambhava.

During the course of time, the pantheon of Hinduism to be viewed as the Vedic religious tradition suffered many an onslaught of varied intensity and kind, by the invaders who professed to be iconoclasts on one hand and on the other, some bigoted missionaries who used noncorrosive but at times, unscrupulous means to dislodge the Hindus from their traditional (native) beliefs. Besides, there were others who projected themselves as progressive crusaders, much enamoured of western life-style and values, who till this day miss no opportunity to denounce all Hindu religious practices and beliefs. It is indeed the inherent vitality of Hinduism that it has weathered all these storms, without losing its universal values and catholicity. Hindus need to stop playing apologist for the genuine cultural and spiritual values of Hinduism. The so-called modernists need to reverse their blind and obsequious adulation of the West. The great spiritual traditions of India, in general and of Hinduism, in particular will be lost if the Hindu intellectuals and intelligentsia fail to wake up to the call of the information war and false media projection of the Hindu spiritual ethics. Ancient Hindu philosophy and culture seem to have reached lofty heights, explored grand truths and established noble traditions with a lasting and living legacy. The Hindu seers and sages, poets and musicians ensured a great grandeur and beauty. The Hindu epics embodied glorious visions and built huge temples as a testament of their majestic and artistic accomplishments in the field of art, archaeology and aesthetics. Over the long period of its ancient history, Hinduism has met many challenges from within and without. It has been responding to the changing socio-economic and political conditions. It has reinterpreted many of its doctrines and principles while reaffirming its old truths and safeguarding its cherished values. It has been playing a greater role in the lives of the people with an aim to spiritualize the human society and establish a world order of peace and harmony.

Hinduism has always taken pride in the fact that it is not a religion like any other indoctrinating religion of the world, and as such it does not have commandments. This absence is considered as a blessing in disguise, for it has left Hinduism free to evolve in accordance with its own genius and is not tied down to specific codifications and commandments. Hindu's texts and scriptures range from high philosophy to mundane rituals of worship of one's choice, none of which is exclusively sacrosanct. It is this remarkable freeness of Hinduism which has ensured its survival through the turbulence of many centuries and millennia. It is only the free-wheeling nature of Hinduism which allows harsh commentaries and heresays. Its philosophical debate is possible because there exist the holy Vedas, regarded as the Words of God as watershed for many creeds to flourish. Hinduism gives full liberty to the sages and intellectuals to pronounce their independent vision of the Ultimate or Supreme Reality and of its philosophy enunciated in its sacred literature like the Vedas and Upanishads.

Vedanta presents the real philosophy of Hinduism. Vedanta is the scientific exposition of truth. It expounds the truth methodically and logically. It does not rely on the authority of a preceptor. Its truth is its scholarly authority. No master or messiah can claim it. No single view has a hold on it. It belongs to one and all. It bears no distinction of caste or creed, community or country. Its universal applicability appeals to all lovers of truth. The study of Vedanta reveals that it is founded on its own authority. It is based on reason and logic. Vedanta does not propound anyone to live a life of renunciation. Vedanta believes in Sanathan Dharma – the Universal and time-less faith. Its precepts, principles and ideals together constitute what is termed as Hinduism. It searches for the ultimate truth and relentlessly explores answers to questions such as, "**Who is God? What is the highest absolute reality of life and the Universe (Brahmand)? What is a human being? What is the purpose of life**?

Followers of the Vedanta philosophy firmly believe that everybody has the right and freedom of adoring God in his or her own way. The ultimate aim of Hinduism is God-realization through the spiritual pursuits. Hinduism is the collective wisdom of the philosophical messages of great many seers and sages. It is more of a canopy for faiths, somewhat connected by a set of scriptures and spiritual views. It is a system which respects and accepts all paths leading to God-realization and truth-realization. Unlike many other faiths, Hinduism refuses to accept the monopoly of one belief in God, one spiritual practice or one scripture as the One and Only way to salvation and God-realization. Indeed, Hinduism is based upon the principles of acceptance, absorption, continuous evolution and expansion. It is, thus, a dynamic system of spiritual ideas and ideals. It accepts freedom of thought for all spiritual philosophy. Hinduism believes that everyone is on a journey to reach the destination of higher awareness through the cycle of birth and death while the soul continuously reincarnates to experience the effects of actions (karmas) performed in earlier incarnations which, it believes, is an automatic phenomenon. The greatness of Hinduism lies in its commitment to search for the truth and raising consciousness of the self, community and humanity.

Sanatan Dharma (Universal or Eternal Religious System) based on the eternal principles of Vedas, represents the traditional religious wisdom and its modus operandi of Hinduism. In fact, Hinduism itself is Sanatan Dharma. It has neither any beginning nor any end. Its philosophy is revealed from time to time as enunciated in its ancient scriptures of Vedas and Upanishads. It has been demonstrated through the epic of Ramayana in the Treta Yuga, and through the epic of Mahabharata in the Dwapur Yuga with Bhagvat Gita depicting the real philosophy of life and Universe which is now acknowledged by the whole world. Valmiki, the seer who wrote Ramayana, spanned sixteen traits a person must have to be a perfect human being. These are related to the sixteen self-introspective questions: **Who can possibly be full of virtues? Who is possessed of powers? Who knows what is right? Who is conscious of services done? Who is truthful of speech? Who is firm of resolve? Who is possessed of right conduct? Who is friendly to all living beings? Who is a man of knowledge? Who is powerful? Who has a singularly loveable appearance? Who has subdued his self? Who has conquered anger? Who is possessed of splendor? Who is above faultfinding? Whom do the very gods dread when his wrath has been provoked in battle?** The entire personalities of Rama and Krishna who epitomize these virtues are some of the prime examples of perfect human beings vested with such peerless qualities.

Two features of Hinduism are sometimes described in the context of its religious aspect: Sanatana Dharma – the ever-existing universal religion, and Yuga Dharma – the man made religion. A religion (dharma) conceived for a particular time period is called Yuga Dharma which changes with change of time. But even within all this, there is one eternal and Universal Sanatana Dharma also called 'Shasvata Dharma' (Eternal Religion) which never changes. Socio-economic policies and values which keep on changing, pertain to the Yuga Dharma while the spiritual principles and values which are eternal are relevant to the Sanathan Dharma. Yuga Dharmas are likely to be in conflict with each other whereas the Sanatan Dharma like Hinduism is not contradictory to any Yuga Dharma. In fact, its Sanathan Dharma aspect remains eternal.

The Hindu view of creation is no different from that of science except that it believes in the existence of the Supreme Power called Brahmn and creativity is inherent in its nature. It is a beginningless and endless continuity. It is difficult to say that a particular day has been the first day of creation or a particular creature has been the first creature, or a particular thing is the first creation of the Universe. There are millions of stars, suns and planets which are all subject to a constant and continuous process of cyclic evolution of creation, sustenance and dissolution. According to this process or law of cyclic evolution, formation, integration, disintegration and reintegration is always taking place. It is believed that first there was nothing. Then there was water followed by aquatic animals. Then there were reptiles followed by mammals; then savages followed by human beings. Some other Hindu scholars believe that life has evolved through the process of births and rebirths in the form of minerals, vegetables, lower and higher animals leading to human beings and thus, every life has passed through different species. After passing through so many lives, human form of beings appeared as embodiment of consciousness called the soul or spirit. Thus, human beings are the only species which are privileged to obtain illumination or enlightenment through awareness. Animals and other beings may be sufficiently intelligent but unlike the human beings, they continue living in the state of inertia (tamasic state). Awareness of the self, Atman and God is a special trait bestowed upon the human beings. The physical body, however, is not the ultimate and finished product of nature according to the process of cyclic evolution. The physical form of a human being has five sense organs (Gyanendriyas) and five action or motor organs (Karmendriyas), and the brain. But there is still something more than being as a being has to evolve further. This is called the sense of intuition which comes from the soul of full consciousness, a peculiar trait in human beings. Several sages, seers and divine personalities could experience this but not everyone can have such a super experience.

Several traditions, customs and rituals have been evolved in Hinduism with a view to enable a human being to adopt a virtuous life. Strangely enough death is not perceived as something final destination of the life as a journey. It is described just another event rather than seen as the beginning of another journey, where one physical body is discarded by the soul so as to be replaced by a new body like an old cloth is replaced by a new dress-material, with a view to prepare the soul (atman) to unite with the Supreme or Super Soul (Parmatma). The Rig Veda prescribes thousands and thousands of verses most suitable for the evolution of humans to follow a virtuous way of life. The underlying principal of these verses is that all species are important, and that humans have no exclusive rights to appropriate for themselves all rights or privileges to existence.

Human life has two important features: the visible physical and the metaphysical which is invisible. The individual **soul** (Jivatma) is the indestructible energy which is eternal, just as the air or vacuum inside a pot continues to exist even when the pot is broken and gets merged (united) with the air or vacuum which exists everywhere. The reason being that the individual soul merges with the Divine Energy or the Adi Brahmn from where it emerges from, while overcoming obstacles on the way. The last rites at the time of so-called death of a human being are symbolic efforts to assist in this endeavour. Just the offerings to God in a temple or at the time of some religious ceremony are meant to wash and cleanse of all impurities before it reaches its final destination. While money and worldly riches are necessary for survival, but good deeds and acts of meditation and worship are equally important. The human body needs to be protected and treated with utmost care, being the temple of individual soul – an atmic constituent of the Universal Soul. Once one physical body dies, the soul needs to be given its space to proceed on to its journey beyond. Hinduism believes that nothing exists other than the Self. There is neither bondage nor liberation for those who understand that the world is illusion (Maya). If everything is ultimately energy whether light or dark – the spark that became life has to one day get back to its origin, that is, return to the Ultimate Cosmic Energy that permeates all space. Death is merely an interval between births.

The religious and ritualistic face of Hinduism should not be confused with its philosophic face which is based on the Vedic view, which in any case, by nature has pluralistic vision that accommodates a variety of spiritualistic quests and manifestations. The philosophical face of Hinduism presents a universal vision that sees the whole of the human society as one family. It is, indeed, a genuine secular religion. Secularism does not mean the exclusion of spirituality from the worldly life. It should mean the elimination of religious conflicts that upset the social harmony. Secularism or Universalism is the fundamental aspect of Hinduism or the Sanatan Dharma. The Vedas, Upanishads and several other ancient Hindu scriptures (Puranas) are essentially focused on describing ways and means of purifying and stabilizing the human mind. They emphasize attaining peace of mind by disciplining, controlling and restraining it. Mind is the pulsation of the inner Self which arises from the Self along with the vital force, called the 'Prana' which permeates the entire physical body. From the inner self or consciousness, originates this vital life force (Prana) and with the help of the mind, it moves in the body, carries out all its functions and enables the body to experience the world through five senses of perception and five organs of action. Mind takes four forms – each with a different function. When the mind is filled with thoughts, it is called **'manas'**. When it contemplates, it is called **Citta**. When it makes decisions, it is called intellect **(Buddhi)**. When it takes on the feeling of 'iness', it is called ego **(Ahamkara)**. Together these four functions of mind constitute what is called inner psychic instrument (Antakhkarna). There are three subtle channels, called 'Nadis' in the human body that lead from the heart to the spiritual centre in the crown of the head. That is why mind is always considered to be in the head. Nevertheless, the central abode of the mind is the heart. The Self has other two aspects: light (Prakash) and understanding (Vimarsa). Light illuminates everything in the world, and understanding identifies it. Yoga and meditation brings stability of mind and can stop it from wandering.

The Hindu scholars evolved many abstract concepts which are now taken for granted, such as zero, infinity, decimals, the currently used international numerals, etc. Another amazing feature is their concept of time, including relative time. Modern science is willing to believe that India's ancient people had insights into the mysteries of creation, nature, life and so on. They did not lean on dogma or creed, but insisted on direct experience that is 'Darshana' meaning philosophy. The word 'Darshana' is used in two ways in Hinduism: one, having a sight of a divine being or a holy deity in a temple, and the other being 'philosophy'. Epistemology and logic were highly developed. Hindus took to science to check their postulations. India's sages gave equal importance to Para Vidya (spirituality) and Apara Vidya (empirical sciences). In the theology of Hindu philosophical thought, metaphysics occupies an important place. Philosophy and mysticism are two sides of the same coin. Secular and spiritual aspects of life are integrated. All these thoughts are contained in the four Vedas and several Upavedas, the 108 extant Upanishads, the two historical legends of Ramayana and Mahabharata, 18 Puranas, the Bhagvat Gita, Brahmasutras as well as the innumerable commentaries by sages, saints, philosophers and scholars. It would need several lives to read through and understand their philosophical significance.

There is a mistaken impression that Hindu scriptures are orthodox, and have no relevance to modern life. On the contrary, Hindu philosophy and teachings are essentially meant to guide the human society of any era to lead a purposeful life with less of sorrows and sufferings, and more of happiness and mental peace. The Upanishads say that these spiritual ideals and truths are meant for human welfare. Ethics and morals are more or less common to all religions and cultures. But Indian thought gives the rationale as to why one should observe righteous codes of conduct and behaviour. Further, the teachings suggest innumerable ways to rise to a higher state of being. Hinduism believes that it takes 8.4 million births (janmas) to rise from the lowest level of life to be a human being. All are different not only in looks, size and structure but also differ widely in intelligence, tendencies, values, etc. – all differentiated by the way they think and work in each cycle of birth and death. These tendencies get carried to successive births. Therefore, each needs a different route to reach Godhood. All are proceeding in the same direction: some go fast and some others slow. Therefore, provision exists for the nomadic tribal at one end and the highly evolved person at the other. All such thoughts are contained in thousands of pages of Hindu books and teachings, most of which are in verse form, that is in Sanskrit slokas. Some of the Puranas have 80,000 slokas. The vastness of literature is in beautiful verse form.

Hindu philosophical thought and wisdom are spread over thousands of books in varied forms – poems, slokas, prose, aphorisms, stories, rituals, injunction and so on. A western scholar once commented that the ancient Hindu teachings are embodied brilliantly even in the Panchatantra – tales of life and conversation in the Animal Kingdom – a fascinating way to teach morals to children and adults alike. However, it has to be conceded that Hindu literature is so vast and complex to ordinary minds that one gives up in sheer bewilderment. Crude forms of rituals and exaggerated praise of nature are at one end, and the most abstract and abstruse speculations on issues of life and death, at the other.

India is considered to be Punya Bhoomi: and also Deva Bhoomi, Karma Bhoomi and Dharma Bhoomi. That is why perhaps literally thousands of saints and sages are born in India. Even in the twentieth century, India has been having the privilege of having among several others, Aurobindo, Ramakrishna 'Paramhans', Swami Vivekananda, Ramana Rishi, Sai Shirdi Baba and Sathya Sai Baba considered to be divine personalities with millions and millions of followers all over the world. There is something unique and spiritual to India, which is relevant to people all over the world, regardless of race, religion, nationality, caste, creed or sex. This is because of the special feature of

Hinduism that its secular and spiritual aspects are visibly and manifestly integrated in its approach.

Spirituality is all pervading. Religion is considered as a personal matter between individual and God, while secular concepts govern all social relationships. In the West, philosophy is a separate discipline, while in India it is a part of spirituality which has mysticism and metaphysics as its integrated parts. It is a way of purifying, quietening and silencing the turbulent mind so as to go beyond mental consciousness. Spirituality ascribed to Hinduism is an all-embracing term used to describe Indian thought and wisdom. It is not really correct to call Hinduism a religion like Judaism, Christianity and Islam, which were founded by Prophets, or established in their name by their respective followers.

Hinduism has no historical beginning. Its teachings do not depend upon a belief or a dogma which must be accepted on the basis of faith in its purest form. It postulates God as the Supreme Reality – the Brahmn. It is more a view of life than a way of life. It is universal. Hinduism does not believe in conversion to and from other faiths. Thousands of sages and philosophers have contributed to its teachings, each based on understanding, direct experience of truth and reality. It offers its ideas to all faiths, and leaves them for their adoption in order to strengthen convictions of their own religion. It suggests a variety of methods for self-realization and service of mankind. Hinduism is freedom. It does not worry about criticism and outrage against its ideals by others.

Hindu religion is all inclusive. It accepts all religions as true. It tolerates teachings of other faiths which are even contradictory to Hindu beliefs and doctrines. It encourages other religions to propagate their faith on Indian soil. Indians gave refuge to Jews and Parsis who were driven out of their homeland. Christian missionaries were given facilities to set up and operate their missions. Though Christians converted Hindus, the latter had no interest in bringing other faiths into the Hindu fold. However some Muslim rulers of medieval period used coercive and punitive methods to convert Hindus, yet Hindus tolerated in line with the maxim of tolerance in Hinduism. This is the maxim of tolerance of the Hindus which made the Muslims realize the message of oneness and adopt India as their homeland. This attitude of the Hindus, however, has been misinterpreted as weakness of Hindus and vulnerability of Hinduism. The universal approach of Hinduism can be seen from the Vedic declarations: **"Let noble thoughts come from every side. The world is one family. Let people all over the world be happy.**

The whole world is Brahmn. Truth is one: sages call it by different names."

Hinduism declares that different religions follow different paths to reach the same God. Just as water from the clouds takes different courses as rivers but still reaches the ocean, so too all prayers and prostrations (in different religions and languages) go to the same God. The concept of integration of life is another unique feature of the Hindu philosophical thought. Everything is done with an underlying spiritual theme whether it is breathing, working, playing etc. The Hindu starts his day with a prayer to Mother Earth, "**Please forgive me for treading on you and hurting you. Please make all my actions auspicious**." Prayers to water, sun and other basic elements are made with a view to preserving the ecological balance and also for restraining people from their exploitative tendencies.

The concept of indebtedness is unique to the Hindu way of life. According to Hinduism, a human being owes three debts: One to God as He is there in every atom of a human body (being) protecting and sustaining him; the other to the sages as they guide the path to God-Realization and salvation; and the third to the parents. The debt to God can be paid back through service to humanity, the debt to the sages by following the path shown by them and to the parents by ensuring them through spiritual evolution. Some scholars attribute it to the perpetuation of family through progeny. As per the Hindu concept, a person should not only be grateful to fellowmen and to God, but also to the whole of creation including the planets and stars as well as to animals and nature. A devout Hindu starts the day expressing his gratitude to and in praise of the Sun and the planets. Similarly, wind, water, fire, earth, mountains, rivers, plants, animals and bird species – all are revered and worshipped. It is postulated that everything in the Universe is interconnected, and to that extent, all lives are affected by them and all lives affect them too.

To the non-Hindu mind, praying to such animate and inanimate things may look absurd. But to a Hindu, gratitude and obligation purify his mind and develop humility, in the sense that his life is dependent on so many entities. In contrast to the Western concept of conquering the Himalayas, Hindus pay homage to Himalayas. Instead of exploiting rivers they are revered as goddesses and mothers. Treating nature as inert matter has led to widespread brutalizing, which has now upset nature's balance and created environmental degradation. Therefore, in a sense, Hindu concepts of adoring or worshipping rivers, trees and nature in all forms help in preserving the ecological balance and prevention of environmental degradation. Seeing God in everything would help to treat nature's manifestations as partners in progress.

In the social sphere, Hinduism is the only religion which gives place of pride to women. While the Western mythology portrays a woman as the temptress or a symbol of infatuation who causes the downfall of man, the ancient Hindu gave a high place to women in society. Parasakthi – the ultimate power – is conceptualized as woman. Hindus call their country Motherland. Most male deities in Hinduism have their consorts, whom Hindus worship with equal reverence. Sri Ramakrishna revered even his wife, Sarada, as Devi. He worshipped Bhadrakali and Durga. Rama was known as Sita's husband (Sitapati), but Sita was not known as (Ramapatni) Rama's wife. Similarly, Lakshmipati, Girjavallabha, Umapati and so on. India's dances, music, painting, sculpture, architecture and art forms – all are around spiritual themes and have no conflict with secularism.

Apart from the economic and ecological aspects of Man-Animal relationship, Hindus inculcated spiritual relationship between Man and the other creations. **Inert matter plus life is plant, plus consciousness is Animal, plus awareness is Man, plus realization is God.** At the awareness level all are same, which gave rise to the concept of Non-duality, the Advaita concept of Sri Shankaracharya which has been considered as the most rational of all theories. The Atman is the same in all beings, which is the same as Paramatman, *i.e.* the Divine Principle. Hindus believe not only three levels of consciousness – waking, dreaming and deep sleep, but they have also postulated the fourth state – Turiya, a kind of super consciousness level which is beyond the five senses. According to Upanishads, Turiya is not which is conscious of the inner (subjective) world, nor that which is conscious of the outer (objective) world, nor that which is conscious of both, nor that which is a mass of consciousness. It is not simple consciousness nor is it unconsciousness. It is unperceived, un-related, incomprehensible, uninferable, unthinkable and indescribable. The essence of the Consciousness manifesting as the self in its three states, Turiya is the cessation of the whole phenomenon. It is all peace, all bliss and non-dual. This is what is known as the Fourth (Turiya) state of consciousness. This is Atman (self) and this has to be treated as the state of God-realization. Thousands of saints and sages have experienced this state of Turiya, even in this century itself. Ramakrishna, Ramana and Aurobindo are believed to have experienced the Turiya state. Ramakrishna loved Christians and Muslims in order to understand their faiths. He declared that one could attain God-realization by any route.

Sri Sathya Sai Baba has devotees from every part of the world, and He thus paved the way for a universal religion (Sanathan Dharma), which is not a substitute for the existing ones, but common to all faiths.

Hindus postulated the four Ashramas – Brahmacharya, Grihastha, Vanaprastha and Sanyasa – taking into account the spiritual and mental state of mind during the successive years of one's growth to adulthood and old age. The natural and observational evolution of caste system based on the inherent attributes of persons, has unfortunately been corrupted and brutalized with perverse connotations. The four objectives (Purushaarthas) – Dharma, Artha, Kama and Moksha – righteousness, wealth, desire and liberation, insist that Dharma should guide and restrain pursuit of Artha and Kama so as to achieve salvation (Moksha).

The Hindu philosophical ideas tell as to how to make life fulfilling and rewarding. Hinduism suggests that the best way to get happiness is to do all actions in the name of God, surrendering to Him without bothering about the fruits of actions. Such an attitude removes anxiety and tension about the outcome and makes the way for mental peace. The philosophical basis for all these is the Hindu concept of non-dualism, re-incarnation, cause-effect relationship, the three gunas – Sattwa, Rajas, Tamas – methods, Yoga, meditation and so on. Patanjali also gave excellent methods for achieving physical health and mental peace in the world.

While the materialistic Westerners accept only heredity and environment as responsible for one's physical and mental characteristics, Hindus declare boldly that the third element is the destiny (Prarabdha), inherited from the previous birth. This explains why dull parents beget brilliant children and vice-versa. Musicians and scholars are born to illiterate parents. Children are born blind and maimed though they were born to healthy parents and forefathers. There is something beyond the hereditary factor. Thus the theory of successive births and the concept of Prarabdha explain such unexplainable phenomena. Hindus consider that everybody is divine, and accept that a few realize it, while others are ignorant of it. Hinduism believes that one can feel God realization through path of devotion (Bhakti Yoga or Maarga), path of knowledge (Gyana Yoga or Maarga), and path of action (Karma Yoga or Maarga). Thus, Hindu thought and wisdom, theories and postulations, philosophy and mysticism, religion and spirituality are of Universal and eternal value. Modern civilization which has been guided by science and technology and the various social disciplines can take advantage of these principles for reducing sorrows and resolving conflicts and for gaining increasing peace and happiness. Mankind is losing a great deal by not getting a proper understanding of the relevance of Hindu teachings to modern times.

3.2 Hindu Scriptures

Hinduism has been surviving because of its deep spiritual philosophy and the knowledge-enriched **ancient scriptures**. A scripture is generally considered to be an authority of regulating and guiding human personality based on a religious faith and philosophy. The scriptures prescribe not only the temporal values like that of conduct for human behaviour, but also teach eternal spiritual values. While the temporal values are suitable for a particular cult or sect, the spiritual values are universal in character. A scripture may contain divine revelations of a prophet or a messenger or an incarnation of God. Its essence, however, lies in its revelations of the philosophical truths that are received from the divine resources. Moreover, a scripture interprets and translates the abstract teaching in a simplified way so that it is equally understandable both by scholars and ordinary persons. The teachings are reiterated and interpreted suitable to the aspirations of the seekers.

Various ancient Hindu scriptures composed in the language of Sanskrit present a rich poetic philosophy of spiritualism and idealism. The modern minds being conditioned by contemporary thought and culture lack the necessary insight into the philosophy of these ancient scriptures. What is today termed to be mythological in these ancient Hindu texts was never intended or designed to portray the actual state of things in terms of the benchmarks or the dimensional parameters of time and space with a view to maintenance of records in the modern perspective of historical evidences. These texts include not just the visible world in their scope but also the invisible worlds belonging to subtle and astral dimensions of existence. Some apparent chronological inaccuracies in these scriptures are found because of the sacredness attached to their history which takes into account the relationship between the temporal and the eternal aspects, and which is less concerned with the actual dates of the occurrence of events. This is in sharp contrast to the linear view of time held by the modern or even contemporary historians who seem to be ignorant of the relationship of time with the eternal. These scriptures are so ancient that the modern archaeological or linguistic approach would need to be replaced by an academic, intuitive and philosophical insight for arriving at an appropriate view of their authentic nature.

The seers, poets and religious leaders play an important and crucial role in communicating the scriptural messages to the people and guiding them to path of the corresponding religious philosophy. It is the religious scriptures which show a way-out for harmonious living. A scripture is the voice of a divine messenger based on his life and message. It shows the path and direction as drawn by a particular religion. It spells out the spiritual goal and lays down the norms and pattern of religious practice. The holy scriptures provide an advice and guidance in the field of religion and its philosophy termed as spirituality. Religion and philosophy are interdependent. **"Religion without philosophy is blind, philosophy without religion is lame"**, remarked, the eminent scientist Albert Einstein. It is the holy scripture where religion and its spiritual philosophy is encased. The value of a holy scripture lies in its revelations of super-sensory knowledge, which is obtained from divine sources.

There are several holy scriptures related to various religious faiths. Accordingly, there are many versions of their religious philosophies propounded and presented by their respective religious leaders. The Vedas, Upanishads, Gita, Ramayana and Mahabharata of the Hindus; the Gatha of the Parsis; the Koran of the Muslims; the Bible of the Christians; the Dhammapada of the Buddhists; the Acaranga of the Jains; the Guru Granth Sahib of the Sikhs; and the Torah of the Jews are some of the most prominent holy scriptures prevalent all over the world. But the spiritual message of all the religious scriptures is same. The goal is same to be achieved by variety of paths shown by these scriptures. "Yato Mat, Tato Path" – as many faiths, so many paths, as voiced by the great saint of India, Sri Ramakrishna Paramhans. What is needed urgently and importantly is the realization of this great truth by the world which is torn apart by the conflicts, unleashed by the fundamentalists, swearing by their own scriptures but ridiculing those of the others. It is, therefore, highly desirable for everyone to study the holy scriptures of various religious faiths in addition to one's own, if any, so as to formulate an integral opinion of different religions and follow the path of universal religion – Sanathan Dharma. A religious scripture defines the Ultimate Reality, lays down the ways of leading a spiritual life in the modern context, inspires the readers to quench their quest of the spiritual knowledge, and shows how the society should function to establish peace and harmony in the world.

Scriptures generally deal with the eternal verities like the God (creator), Soul (creature) and Nature (creation), and their inter-relationship. Scriptures are considered to be of two types in Hinduism.

The first type is termed as '**Sruti**' ('what is heard') and the second type is called '**Smriti**' (what is written). The 'sruti' is considered to be eternal and valid since it deals with the eternal verities which do not change with change of time and place. The 'smriti', on the other hand, needs continuous innovation and modifications keeping pace with the changes in the system. The Vedas are the only 'Srutis' while the rest of other religious literature – like the 'Puranas', the 'Tantras', the Epics and the 'Dharamsastras' falls into the category of 'Smriti'. Indeed, the 'smriti' texts are just interpretations or elaborations of the truths propounded in the 'Srutis'. Smritis provide simplified methods of preaching through the means of historical events, mythological stories and legends so as to make the abstract philosophy understandable to the common people. Srutis are the divine gifts and not man-made (APAURUSHEYA) and hence are the eternal truths spoken by God Himself. The Vedas are considered to be the 'Srutis'. As God is eternal, so the Srutis too are eternal.

Vedas are considered to be the ancient scriptures of Hindus. The word 'veda', is derived from the root word 'vid' which means to know. Vedas contain a vast ocean of spiritual knowledge and values as revealed to the great sages in the depth of their meditation through the divine voice of the Almighty God – the Absolute. It is in this sense that 'Vedas' are known as 'srutis' (what is heard). The Vedas are revered as the basic scriptures of Hinduism and have been accorded the highest status in the hierarchy of Hindu spiritual literature.

As stated earlier, the Hindu scriptures namely Srutis are considered as divine revelations and comprise of the Vedas while Smritis are records and interpretations of the divine revelations. Smritis are also known as detailed explanations in the form of rituals (Vidhis) and books of law (Dharam Shastra) which codify and regulate the laws that govern Hinduism. They contain detailed description of duties, manners and customs for common people to follow. The works of the sages – Manu, Yajnavalkya, Vyasa and Parasara among others together constitute the foundation of Hinduism. Traditionally, Manusmriti is considered to be relevant to Satya Yuga and, Yajnavalkasmriti to Treta Yuga. A treatise of Sankha Likhita is supposed to be moral and legal code for the Dwapara Yuga. A number of other works are also considered to be path breaking in the field of religious and Parasarasmriti for Kaliyuga enunciations. These include among others the prominent works contributed by the sages: Daksha, Samvarta, Vasishtha, Gautama, Atri and Saunaka among others. The British colonizers are reported to have used Manusmriti as the basis to form judicial laws for the Hindus. It covers all living norms for the Hindus from birth to death through marriage, married life, duties of men, women, rulers, the public, warriors and merchants among their several other categories.

Sruti, as mentioned earlier comprise of four main groups of Vedic texts namely: Rig Veda, Yajurveda, Sama Veda and Atharva Veda. In the context of performing arts, the Vedas are vividly identified as recitation from the Rig Veda, music from the Sam Veda, action from the Yajurveda and aesthetics from the Atharvaveda. Veda reflects the original ultimate sound which is eternal, all-pervading and non-destructible. Vedic mantras are not only rich in meaning but also melodious in sound (emanating from accurate chanting), something that is acquired from oral recitation. Veda chanting generates vibration of both ether and air which is supposed to have the power of healing and sanctifying the environment.

The four Vedas have also the four Upvedas and the six Vedangas all of which form an indivisible corpus of divine knowledge. The four Upvedas are: Ayur Veda, Gandharva Veda, Dhanur Veda and Sthapatya Veda. Ayur Veda is a well-known medical science, Gandharva Veda seems to be dealing with social and married life, Dhanur Veda obviously is concerned with the weapon technology, and Sthapatya Veda deals with engineering, architectural and structural endeavours including visual arts. Ayur Veda is quite popular to date perhaps because it expounds knowledge of the medical treatment of human body through three basic principles namely etiology (cause), symptom metology (symptoms) and therapeutics (treatment) medicines.

Vedas propound three principal attributes/tendencies (Gunas) prevalent in the creation or nature or Prakriti: luminosity or virtuosity (Sattwa), dynamism or activity (Rajas) and inertia or evil (Tamas). It is a permutation and combination of these three qualities that Prakriti or matter does in contact with Purusha (Brahmn) which lead to creation. Blended in various proportions, this triangular root-causative phenomenon (triguna-prakriti) influences the mind, intellect and personality of living beings and generates, thereby, in them various types of tendencies, tastes, temperaments and their functionings reflected through their physical, biological, psychological and spiritual traits. Accordingly, the three basic characteristics of thoughts, words and actions, particularly true of the human beings, are regulated by this triguna-prakriti.

Although the essence of every scripture is the same or at the most identical, yet scriptures differ in terms of their descriptions, their way of treatment of a subject-matter, in the way they are expressed and in the style of their presentation. This becomes apparent when one undertakes the study of different scriptures with an unbiased and open-mind. The common 'essence' follows like an undercurrent in all the scriptures just as the same electric current flows through the electric wire in different rooms, houses and cities and in different forms like a bulb, a fluorescent tube or running a motor. Identification of this 'essence' can wipe out religious narrowness, fanaticism and segregation, and lead to the path of the Universal Religion – The Sanathan Dharma based on truth, righteousness, peace, love and non-violence as extolled by the divine Sri Sathya Sai Baba of Puttaparthy. Scriptures are the lamp-posts guiding the human beings through the gloomy darkness of ignorance leading to the gleaming light of knowledge. The goal of these scriptures is accomplished as and when the soul beholds the Divine within the spiritual glimpse of the holy scriptures. The soul, scriptures and the supreme – one merge into One who is beyond thought, word and deed. "**The Bhakta (the devotee), Bhagvat (the scripture) and Bhagwan (the Divine) – are One, and the One in three**," said Sri Ramakrishna Paramhans. According to him, there are three types of devotees. One says, "God is up there", and he points to the sky on heaven. Another says that God dwells in the heart as the "Inner Controller". But the evolved devotee says, "God alone is everything. All things, that are perceived, are so many forms of God". Thus, God is no longer invisible. God has created all these forms so that people can see Him in those forms. This is miraculous power of God, to show Himself through all beings. For, nothing is invisible, not even the incorporeal. The intellect makes itself visible in the act of thinking. God makes Himself visible in the act of creating.

According to the annals of Hindu Philosophy, there existed an infinitely unaccountable number of Vedas. It was, however, the great sage Ved Vyas (Krsna Dvaipayana Vyasa) who edited and compiled all the Vedas into four groups each identified with his four disciples namely: **Rg-Ved** with sage Paila, **Yajurveda** with sage Vaisampayna, **Sama-Ved** with sage Jaimini and Atharva-Ved with sage Sumantu. Each Veda is divided into four sections: First section contains a collection of Mantras – Hymns in the poetic form known as a '**Ved-Samhita**'. Second section contains liturgies in prose called the **Brahmna**; Third section is focused on the ways of meditation named as '**Arayanakas**'; and the fourth and the last section comprises of the philosophical treatises – classified as the '**Upanishads**'. It is in this sense that sometimes the Upanishads are called the Vedantas as they constitute the concluding (anta) part of the Vedas. Vedanta also means the ultimate knowledge (Jnana) for 'Veda' means 'jnana' and 'anta' means the end of the frontier or the border. Conventionally, it is the Ved-Samhitra that represents a Veda. For instance Rg-veda means only the Rg-Ved Samhita followed by its corresponding Brahmnas, Arayankas and Upanishads. Each Veda has a metaphysical aspect (Janankanda) along with its mundane aspect (Karamkanda) described in various ways.

(a) **Rg-Veda-Samhita**: Of all the four Vedas/Vedic Samhitas, the Rgveda Samhita is the oldest and has a pre-eminent place in the vedic literature. It is a collection of hymns (Suktas) revealed to various sages (Rishis) at different periods of time. Accordingly, there is a variety in the styles of language, grammar and ideas along with the historical and cultural features.

Religious Aspects of the Rg-veda or Rg-veda-Samhita contain three major features namely: the vedic deities like Agni, Indra, Varuna and others; the cosmic enunciations like the origin of the universe and the real nature of human beings; and the social customs like marriage, administration, management, culture and civilization among several others. The vedic deities like Rudras, Adityas, Indra and Prajapati are assigned to the three regions of the Universe namely earth (Prithvi), heavens (Planets) and the intermediary space (Antariksa). Though these deities appear to be the personifications of the forces of nature, they are actually various manifestations of Brahmn – the Supreme Force.

The philosophical or the spiritual or ideological aspects of Rig Veda deal with the origin and repository of the Vedantic ideas of knowledge (jnana) and devotion (bhakti). It clearly establishes that Rig Veda is not merely a book of laudatory hymns as is interpreted by some people. The Rig Veda teaches monotheism (non-duality) and not polytheism as is often mistakenly assumed. However, notion of 'Sagunopsana' (God with form and attributes) is predominant. According to this Veda, God creates, protects and dissolves in accordance with a well-defined system of creation, protection and dissolution.

The Meta-Physical perceptions of the Rig Veda are based on the existence of the soul (**Atma**), as an entity, which is accepted with life here and life hereafter having been nicely harmonized. Social life is permeated with spiritual consciousness. Satya (Truth) and Dharma (Righteousness) are extolled as the basic axioms of life and immortality (Amritatva) as the ultimate goals of life. Social norms (system) such as monogamy, polygamy and swayamvara (choice of husband by the bride) are prescribed. Agriculture and animal husbandry are considered as some of the means of livelihood. Equitable distribution of wealth is highly emphasized; somewhat similar to the philosophy of socialism or communism. Culture and fine arts are encouraged. System of performing yogas evolves a high degree of perfection and contentment. It strongly advocates a knowledge imparted by the sages who used to perform the Yajnas and recite the Mantras to reveal knowledge imparted by the Devata – the deity to whom the Mantra is addressed; and the Mantra itself, composed in the form of Chhandas is recited. '**Aitraya**' and '**Kousitakee**' are the two '**Upanishads**' associated with the Rig Veda.

(b) **Yajurveda-Samhita**: The corresponding Yajurveda-Samhita of the Yajurveda is a collection of the mantras in prose which are useful in the performances of the Yajnas. It is in two major forms: the '**Krsna**' and the '**Sukla**', 'Krsna' is mixture of prose and poetry while 'Sukla' is entirely in poetry. Being more ancient, it is difficult to comprehend 'Krsna' while 'Sukla' being of more recent origin, is easier to grasp. The part of Yajurveda that was revealed to Yajnavalkya by Surya (the Sun-god) came to be known as Sukla (the Bright/White) and the earlier part was called Krsna (the Dark/Black) by the followers of Yajnavalkya, who had fallen out with his guru 'Vaisamapayana' – the first promulgator of the Yajurveda. Yajurveda-Samhita is divided into two sub-groups: One is known as Krsna-Yajurveda-Samhita and the other is known as Sukla-Yajurveda-Samhita. Though the Krsna-Yajurveda-Samhita is reputed to have had 85 branches but to-date only four are available. The Sukla-Yajurveda-Samhita, also known as Vajasneyi-Samhita is reported to have been collected and edited by the sage Yajnavalkya. It is entirely in verses and resembles the Rg-Ved-Samhita in the format. The Sukla–Yajurveda-Samhita is said to have 17 branches, but only two, the Kanva and Madhyandina, are available to-date. The well-known **Kathopanisad**, **Isavasyopanishad** and **Brhadaranyakopanishad** are the three Upanishads associated with Yajurveda.

(c) **Samaveda-Samhita**: The associated Samveda-Samhita has been highly extolled in several holy scriptures of the Hindus. However, the Samveda-Samhita is not considered as an independent entity. It is, in fact, the Rig Veda set to music. All the mantras of the Rig Veda have been transformed and expressed in the musical formats and renamed as Sama Veda-Samhita. Though it is supposed to have 1000 branches, only three are available to-date namely: **Kauthuma**, **Ranayantya** and **Jaiminiya**. Unlike the mantras of the other three Vedas, the Mantras of the Samveda known simply as 'Samans', have seven well-known 'Svaras' or musical scales of classical music (namely Sa Re Ga Ma Pah Da Ni). It can, therefore, be concluded that the origin of Indian classical music lies with the Samveda. The two well-known Upanishads associated with this Veda are **Chandogya Upanishad** and the **Kena Upanishad.**

(d) **Atharva-Veda-Samhita**, also known as Brahm-Veda, has some special features distinct from the first three Vedas. In particular, the Atharva-Veda-Samhita stands apart from the Rig Veda-Samhita. It deals more with the social and materialistic aspects such as economics, trade and commerce. This Veda designates God – the absolute as Brahmn and the whole universe as manifestation of His will. This Veda refers to heaven and hell as also, virtues and vices. It mentions the values like Satya (Truth), Diksa (Discipline) and Tapas (Austerity) that help human beings to attain perfection.

The Atharva-Veda-Samhita throws light on the societies of that time, the land in which the people lived extended from Gandhar (Afghanistan) to Magadha (Bihar) and Anga (Bengal). It also talks about the varna (social) structure by stating that the first three varnas were called Aryas and the last as Sudras. However, people lived in perfect harmony with kings as rulers, trade, commerce and agriculture as the main occupations of the people. Brahmins (the learned class, one of the four categories of people, according to Hinduism) were considered as the custodian of knowledge and spiritual guidance. Cow was considered as the most sacred animal. The institution of marriage was similar to that in the Rig-Vedic times. The **Prasna**, the **Mundaka** and the **Mandukya** are the well-known Upanishads of this Veda.

It becomes difficult to understand the Vedas because of the archaic form of language and terminology used in their texts. Hence came into existence, the six Vedangas (links of veda) six subsidiary sciences that unfold the Vedic wisdom namely: **Siksa** which deals with the modes of chanting; **Vyakarna**, the Vedic grammar; **Chandas** concurred with Vedic poetry; **Nirukta** giving the meanings and explanations of Vedic words; **Jyotisa** which means astrology dealing with the times and periods for the performance of Vedic rites/yaganas; and **Kalpa** in the form of **Sutras/phormenims** dealing with all aspects of religious rites and rituals. There have been several commentaries over the centuries on the Vedas but the one given by Adi Sankaracharya (14th century) holds a unique place not only because of the sheer volume of work but also because of the quality of its exposition. The Vedantic thought, according to Swami Vivekananda, because of the philosophy of oneness in all existence, is called the practical Vedanta.

A study of six Vedangas (limbs of Vedas) is considered to be essential to comprehend the hidden philosophical knowledge of the four basic Vedas, the use of "mantras" concerned with the ritualistic aspect of the Vedas; and Jyotisha or Astrology – which speaks with conviction and contains knowledge of the past, present and future of each and every individual on earth. Indeed, astrology is, even to-date, considered as an important area of Vedic knowledge. Bhrigu Samhita – a fascinating treatise, compiled by Sage Bhrigu in the Satya (Krita) Yuga, is an amazing store house of knowledge with five lakhs horoscopes prepared on the basis of planetary positions, making pointed predictions and giving other details of individual lives. These horoscopes contain detailed events in the lives of various individuals and form a database for further research and advanced study in the field of astrology, which, as claimed by some astrologers, can be used to prepare approximately 45 million horoscope charts. Bhrigu Samhita has shaped the principles of palmistry, horoscopy and other branches of Vedic Astrology which are used to explain the events that have happened or likely to happen. This led to the creation of the 'Nadi' literature and the 'Shastra' (the scientific body of knowledge) and much more. This literature is even to-date available in various forms in certain parts of India notably among others are Hoshiarpur in Punjab and Nadi village in Tamil Nadu, the well-known states of India.

Upanishads constitute an important part of the Vedas. They are known as the philosophical treatises having an accumulated wealth of the revealed spiritual philosophy of the Vedas. The principles and teachings that stemmed from the seers' experiences became the subject matter of the Upanishads. Exactly when the Upanishads were codified and formulated is not known to-date. Regardless of their historical origin, the authenticity and depth of spiritual philosophy contained in the Upanishads is unparalleled. The Upanishads serve as authoritative reference books for the spiritual quest. The spiritual seekers can find ample material for their spiritual inspiration or intellectual stimulation. The knowledge revealed in the Upanishads is unique. It offers a level of knowledge leading to supersensuous realization beyond the sense organs and gross mind. The Upanishads, while making passing reference to the knowledge available through the senses and mind, come closer to the Truth of truths, the Self of selfs, the Essence of being, the Supreme Reality which is the very foundation of everyone and everything whether sentient or insentient.

The Upanishads clearly expound the infinite nature of the Brahmn. When conceived in its unmanifested pure form, it is said to be transcendent – undefinable, attributeless and free from all attachments. It is that stage where there is not a trace of duality, where the subject and object become one, and where the seeker and sought get merged. The Indweller – Brahmn, gets revealed as the Immanent, the Inner Controller, the Ruler of the Universe and the Supporter of all who inhabits all being, dwells within all beings, controls all beings from within. This is the Self – the Immortal and Lord of the Universe. The **Kena Upanishad** says, "He is the Mind of the mind, Life of the life". He is the impelling force, the power that is omni-present, omni-potent and omni-scent. The **Katha Upanishad** describes it as the energy that persists before and after death. Those who know It become immortal. The **Isa Upanishad** tells how that truth pervades and interpenetrates everything in this universe. The essence of knowledge, according to the **Mundaka Upanishad**, is the one unchanging entity which, when revealed, gets known to every being. The **Taittiriya Upanishad** says that He is covered with the layers of body, senses, mind and ego, with bliss as His center. In the **Mandukya Upanishad**, figures the Turiya or the Fourth State, the eternal witness of the waking, dream and deep sleep states. The **Chandogya Upanishad** declares that, "The Infinite alone is bliss, the visible universe is Brahmn". The **Brihadaranakya Upanishad** emphasizes the Self-consciousness. The Self is all love and pure joy. This Self or Atman should be meditated upon. Finally, the **Svetasvatara Upanishad** extols devotion to the all-loving, beneficent God, who listens to the prayers, who is all compassionate, who is the dispenser of the fruits of one and all, the one who blesses all creatures and the one who is the bridge to immortality.

Knowledge of the self (self-knowledge) given in the Upanishads is indispensable for this is the true knowledge. Knowledge of the Truth prescribed in the Upanishads pertains to the knowledge of the self. Without knowledge of the self, knowledge of God is not possible, and without knowing this God, it is not possible for the living beings to exist, to breath or move even for a second. Infact, all other knowledge comes in through self-knowledge. It is because of this knowledge that people know each other, they know several others and they know the whole universe and its surroundings. The holy scriptures are like hundreds of teachers who guide the humanity to the discovery of the light which lies hidden in their hearts. It is for this reason that the seers have explained vigorously the nature of the world and individuals, and the underlying common linkage of truth between the two, often using several stories, illustrations, similes and ordinary day-to-day examples even though some of them are, at-times, abstract and archaic. The divine basis, which is externally existent, undergoes a process of manifestation. The Supreme Reality/Truth is the God (Isvara) who projects the universe from His very essence. This world, the previous world, the future world and all beings are the breath of the Infinite Reality considered to be the **Apar-Brahmn**. An individual is intimately bound with the universe. It is, therefore, equally important for the individuals to consider how they view themselves in relation to this Brahmn (God) and the world around. The Upanishads present a range of perceptions from the gross-level where human beings identify themselves with the body, as illustrated in the Chandogya Upanishad, to the more subtle levels where they identify with the life force, mind and intellect and ultimately uniting with the Supreme One (God).

The Upanishads help in the cultivation of spiritual character and moral culture. Their study sharpens the intellect, strengthens control of senses and mind, and generates the sense of discrimination and comprehension. The vedantic philosophy expounded in the Upanishads inspires neither a world-negating nor a world-hugging religion. The Upanishadic philosophy has been classified into three stages: **dualistic, qualified non-dualistic and non-dualistic based on three kinds of spiritual experiences**. First, an intimate relationship with God in which the seeker experiences a closeness to his Beloved God and maintains a sense of difference though being in-separately connected with Him. This is the stage of duality. Secondly, the seeker/devotee develops the qualified non-dualistic experience and feels himself like a wave in the vast ocean of the supreme being while himself having all the characteristics of Divinity. Third stage is that of non-duality or oneness – the individual/seeker merges into Supra-Being, the Brahmn – a kind of super consciousness experience that is very vast and deep. The human mind finds it difficult to grasp the third stage fully.

The philosophical interpretations of the Upanishads are sometimes coloured by various interpretations. But its basic fundamentals remain unchanged. In the ancient times, the Upanishads were studied by a smaller group of people, mostly the seers and the spiritual philosophers, whereas in modern times these philosophic systems have influenced the scientific thinking and rational outlook of the intellectuals of all sorts. The Upanishads, however, remain the source of all systems of Indian philosophy and the wide spectrum of spiritual experience.

The philosophy of the ancient holy scriptures of Hinduism provides a detailed view of the pre-scholastic Vedanta in which higher aspects of the divine power get amplified. The metaphysical side of the Puranas and Epics expounds the wisdom of the Upanishads with Brahmn getting identified with Narayana as the Supreme Being. The **Purusha** and **Prakriti** are depicted as working hypothesis, not existing independently by themselves but mutually dependent, forming His very body.

The ancient scriptures generally known as the Puranas, contain history, mythology and discourses on religion, philosophy, yoga, mystical attainment and spiritual realization along with several other subjects. The eighteen Puranas are devoted to the glorification of three great divine manifestations of the Supreme Being – the Brahmn namely, Brahma (the creator), Vishnu (the protector) and Shiva (the annihilator) along with their respective consorts depicted as the three forms of the Goddess namely, Saraswati, Laxmi and Parvati (Durga/Shakti) as well as Ganesha and Skanda (Subramanian) – the sons of Lord Shiva and Parvati. Also, Surya (the Sun), Vayu (the Air), Varun (Water) and Agni (the Fire) along with their leader Indra, occupy prominent places in these Puranas and receive great importance. These Puranas also deal with, in great detail, the areas of medicine, art, education, literature, grammar, ethics, politics, ritual, social laws, religious ways and observances, expositions of the philosophies of Samkhya, Yoga and Vedanta, in a variety of ways. They also provide interesting descriptions of the vivid biographies of the great sages, saints, kings and warriors who lived and moved as paragons of wisdom, power and morality.

Of the eighteen Puranas, six are devoted to each Brahma, Vishnu and Mahesh. From the point of view of the philosophical depth and spiritual profundity, Vishnu Purana and Bhagvat Purana are considered to be most important. Bhagvat Purana, in particular, deals with practically everything relevant to religion, philosophy and theology. These Puranas throw light on cosmology with an elaborate descriptions of the astronomical system of the universe, the solar system and the fourteen worlds on realms of creation. These Puranas also contain information on the size and capacity of each of the five basic elements of creation namely Earth, Water, Fire, Air and Ether.

The epics constitute an important aspect of the Hindu scriptures of which the two 'the Ramayana and the Mahabharata' are considered to be most significant in various ways. The epics show the path of Truth and Righteousness with an appeal to the sentiments of people and generate love for God and humanity, and a power to stimulate the longings of the deepest soul – the self of everyone. While Vedas glorify in their peak of sublimity looking on all things on earth with a deep concern for even the lowest to enable it to rise to the requirements of the highest attainment, the epics speak to the human beings like a father would direct or a mother would instruct or as a friend would urge or a teacher (Guru) would guide. The Ramayana and the Mahabharata including the Gita, are considered to be the two great Hindu Epics – the first by the great Sage Valmiki and the second by the great teacher / Guru Ved Vyasa who is also identified with the compilation of all the Vedas. The seven books (Kands) of the Ramayana and the eighteen books {Chapters or Adhayas} of the Mahabharata are said to represent the seven stages in the life of a human being and the eighteen steps in the effort towards perfection, respectively.

The Yoga-Vasishtha, a classical work of philosophical mysticism, emphasizes the existence of a universal consciousness linking the object of perception with its perceiver as the subject. Creation is a two-field phenomenon with universe as the object of creation, and its perceiver as the subject in accordance with the will of the creator identified with the universal consciousness – the Brahmn. According to the enunciations of Yoga-Vasishtha the universe or creation is a relative reality and does not have absolute existence by itself since its constuents, space and time, do not have any absolute meaning both being relative to the Supreme Reality – the Brahmn who is undifferentiated Existence/Truth (Sat), Consciousness (Chit), Bliss (Anand) – Satchitanand, who is everywhere, yet cannot be seen, who is formless, and who exists as the Self as everything. Yoga Vasishta is an exemplary work of thirty-two thousand verses divided in six parts designated as: Renunciation (Vairagya); Aspiration for liberation (Mumukshtva); Creation (Utpatti); Preservation (Sthiti); Dissolution (Upasama); and Salvation (Nirvana). It is a self-learning study-material presented in an instructional manner than in a way of logical argumentation or reasoning. It propounds seven stages by which the spiritual seeker can rise progressively:

- God-Desire (Subhecha) to pursue the path of truth and righteousness.
- Inner-investigation (Vicharana) into the ways and means of acquiring true knowledge.
- Mind-Attention (Tanumanasi) due to the subtlety attained by it in the practice of deep concentration.
- Realization of Spiritual Equilibrium (Sattavapatti) wherein the light of the Brahmn splashes forth like lightening in one's experience.
- Non-Attachment (Anasakti) to anything that is external to the vision of universality.
- Non-Perception of Materialism (Padartha-Abhavana) and the Perception of Radiance filling the whole universe, as if the entire existence is lit up with endless light.
- The Ultimate State (Turiya) of experience of identity with the Absolute.

Swami Vivekananda said, "**Each Soul is potentially divine. The goal is to manifest this Divinity within by controlling nature, external**

and internal. Do this either by work, or by worship, or psychic control, or philosophy – by one or more or all of these – and be free". The last of the seven stages is the stage of actual realization. It is also known as, Jeevanmukti or liberation while living. When the body drops, one attains videhmukti or disembodied salvation. The liberated soul is a master and a super-being. Its actions are universal (Mahakarta), its enjoyments are Universal (Mahabhokta), and its renunciation, too, is universal (Mahatyaga). The Yoga-Vasishtha abounds in a large number of illustrative stories which bring out vividly its philosophical aspect and its practical suggestions for spiritual practice. The meditation process, as instructed in the Yoga-Vasishta, comprises of mainly three steps:

- Affirmation of the universality of the Brahmn in one's own consciousness, thinking, speaking and discoursing of the Brahmn only known as **Brahmn-Abhayas**;
- Complete control of the mind by eliminating its desire known as **Mano-Nigraha**; and
- Restraint of the breath (Praana) by the well-known method of **Praanayama**, called Praana-Nirodha.

While Vedas and Upanishads glorify the divinity of the Absoluter Brahmn, the epics and scriptures endeavour to portrait God personified as the commanding father, loving mother, a philosopher-friend, an adoring teacher (guru) and the unique ruler of the Universe. Human life in the spiritual terms is conceptualized and consummated with God as its central focus. The spiritual achievements of the ancient seekers and sages of India are enshrined in Vedas and Upanishads.

The knowledge attained from the Vedas and Upanishads leads to the spiritual wisdom. This spiritual wisdom nourishes the Sanatana Dharma – the eternal religion with Satya (Truth) and Dharma (righteousness) as its two foundational pillars, Satya (Truth) as the goal and Dharma (Righteousness) as the means. The Vedas constitute the ultimate authority of these two eternal axioms of the Sanatana Dhrama. The goal remains unchanged since it is eternal but the means namely Dharma is subject to change according to time, place and person. The Vedas proclaim Brahmn – as the Truth and Dharam (Righteousness) as the path to achieve the desired goal. Thus, Vedas proclaim Truth and Dharma as the two important features of their philosophy. Manu, the first law-maker, expanded the scope and meaning of Dharma by augmenting it with three more values namely Artha (Wealth), Kama (Enjoyment) and Moksha (Liberation). He designed the framework for all these four values (PURUSHARTHAS) and prescribed ways for their pursuance in the form of a Manual called Manu's manual. Manu underlined the fundamental concept of Dharma and declared: **"Dharma destroys one who destroys it. It saves one who serves it. Therefore, never destroy Dharma. If it is not destroyed, it destroys none."** That is the message of Dharma Sastra.

A holy scripture is expected to be viewed from two perceptions: history and faith. The historical perceptions brings a rational approach, but that alone does not constitute the whole truth of life. Things are not measured by historical standards alone. There are human sentiments based on faith which is as good an instrument of measurement of the history of an epic. In fact, historical measurement brings dry and pedantic approach, whereas faith generates devotion which enriches a value system of life. People do not live by intellect and rationality alone. It is the faith that nourishes their lives and helps them in their spiritual progress. This, however, does not mean that intellect or rationality is to be discarded completely. It only means that faith in God has as much, if not more, a place in life as science or logic. Indeed, science has given botanical descriptions of plants and trees in nature. It has provided rational explanation of the phenomenon of nature. Even, it has given the logical description of the movement of planets including Earth which forms the basis of day and night. It has verified that the shining moon has rough surface as in the case of certain portions of the Earth. But all these scientific and logical explanations about the phenomenon of nature cannot deter faith and sensitivities of the people like the poets and writers or the human mind from appreciating the beauty of the nature or pleasant view of the full moon. No doubt, science has given a description of the human body as a carcass of differently shaped bones suffused with flesh and blood. But it cannot deter a mother from loving her child. Thus, the angle of history alone does not reveal the whole truth of life. The angle of love and faith is equally, if not more, potent in achieving the goal of life. The perception of faith has its distinct advantages over those of science. Indeed, faith has an edge over the perception of history.

History is totally concerned with the events of the past which may not be depicted as complete truth; some distortion is bound to be there even if the historian has been living during the occurrence of those events. Distortion is an inevitable component of human tendency since it operates within the frame work of changing time and space. The faith perception, on the other hand, recognizes no such limits of time and space. If the central characters Rama of Ramayana and Krishna of Mahabharata are merely viewed from the parameter of history, they have to be reckoned as those who were born on a particular date in a particular year and at a certain place. Moreover, whosoever is born must die. Thus, the parameter of history makes Rama and Krishna physically perishable like all other mortal beings. But the parameter of faith transcending time and space makes both Rama and Krishna eternal, ever present. Faith treats both Rama and Krishna beyond the bounds of time and space, and makes them the ever present reality. If Rama and Krishna were merely historical entities or personalities like several other mortal beings read and referred to in history, then they would have not been remembered and worshiped for the last several thousands of years. Moreover, if the dates and years of a particular event or existence of a human personality is not traceable, it does not mean that event did not happen or that person did not exist. It is rather, some historical deficiency.

Nevertheless an account of historical dating of Ramayana has been given by some scholars of historical research. Placing the Ramanaya in the historical context is yet an unfinished task, as witnessed by the endless debates among archaeologists, historians and literary pundits. An analysis given by Saurabh Kwatra (Speaking Tree, The Times of India) among others, is a unique attempt to use astronomy, astrology and the science of time together in elevating the status of Ramayana from an epic to a chronological reality.

Astonishingly, the ancient Indians had an accurate method of time measurement. They regularly and systematically recorded the dates ('tithis'), or days marked according to the phases of the Moon, the months, the seasons, solstices, equinoxes and the positions of astrologically relevant luminaries like the Sun, the Jupiter, the Venus and so on. In other words, the timings of events were recorded in the astronomical format. To convert this coded information on heavenly positions into a simple calendrical timeline, all that is needed is a database of ephemeris.

According to some historians and experts in ancient history of Hinduism, Sage Valmiki, the celebrated composer of the Ramayana records the birth of Rama in Uttarayana (the Divine Half-year), in the Chaitra month, in the bright fortnight, on the ninth day, in the Punarvasu Nakshatra, on a Monday, and under Karka Lagna. Valmiki further details the birth with various planetary positions in the zodiac: Sun in Mesha at 10 degrees, Mars in Capricorn at 28 degrees, Jupiter in Cancer at 5 degrees, Venus in Pisces at 27 degrees and Saturn in Libra at 20 degrees. These starry configurations are so unique that they have occurred only once so far in measurable history and this helps historians to fix the important date, the birthday of Rama, as the 4th of December, 7323 B.C. Due to the slow yet continuous precession of the Earth, Rama's birthday anniversary, celebrated as Ram Navami, has since shifted by about four months over a period of about 9300 years.

Valmiki has also beautifully described the sky at the moment when Rama left Ayodhya on his 14 year exile. He states, "Crux (Trishanku), Mars, Jupiter and Mercury have cornered the Moon, Vaishakha and Milky Way are shining in the sky". Using this additional input, astronomical rules help us to fix Rama's exile to a time when he turned 17 years of age. Another event, Hanuman's return from Lanka after locating and meeting Sita (in Sunderkanda, one of the most evocative chapters of Ramayana) can be similarly pinpointed as occurring on a full moon (Poornima) day.

Using the above techniques, the historians are believed to have recorded following pivotal events of the Ramanaya at the following dates: Rama's birth: 4th December 7323 B.C., Rama's marriage with Sita: 7th April 7307 B.C., Rama's exile: 29th November 7306 B.C. Hanuman's entry in to Lanka: Ist September 7292 B.C., Hanuman's meeting with Sita: 2nd September 7292 B.C., construction of Setu (bridge): 26-30th October 7292 B.C., the beginning of the great war: 3rd November 7292 B.C., Kumbhakarna's death: 7th November 7292 B.C., Ravana's killing by Rama: 15th November 7292 B.C., and Rama's return to Ayodhya: 6th December 7292 B.C. The last event, celebrated as Deepawali, should also have advanced by about four months, but strangely the festival of lights now falls in October-November each year. Complicated explanations have been put forth by many researchers to explain this anomaly, and most of them have been found satisfactory.

Astrological interpretations of Rama's birth chart provide further insights. In fact the matching and the mapping between his natal chart and the course of his life is so precise that it can be used as a case study in support of the science of astrology itself! The natal chart of Ramachandra indicates a yogic Rajayoga, a rare planetary pattern, wherein the native rises to be a King in the materialistic sense even while renouncing all worldly pleasures. It is an established fact that Rama during his reign over the kingdom of Ayodhya lived a simple hermit's life. Mars being exalted in the 7th house of marriage indicates a bold and courageous spouse, but at the same time this made her sharp-tongued. It is this latter maleficent effect to Mars that led Lakshmana to leave Sita alone in the cottage in search of Rama. Venus' exalted position in the 9th house of travel and destiny gives a public life with spouse. Sita followed Rama during His exile, while in contrast, Lakshmana left his consort behind in Ayodhya. The Jupiter-Moon conjunction in Cancer forms the well-known Gajakesari yoga; it blesses the native with simplicity, honesty and religiosity and confers fame due to these qualities. Sun, the significator of soul in deep exaltation (in Aries) in the house of karma suggests that Rama was a higher, perhaps a dual soul; he was the King of Ayodhya, and the Divine Incarnate of Lord Vishnu simultaneously.

Although miracles shown by Rama are not too many, yet Rama demonstrated the peak of high moral character which has given sustenance to the Indian culture. Rama's profile has given a direction to the human life-force towards its ultimate goal – the realization of Truth. Sri Rama, the central character of Ramayana, epitomizes all that is noble and ethical on this earth. He is the embodiment of Truth and Righteousness. Indeed, Rama is Truth and Righteousness personified. Thus, His story and noble character has all along been one of the most reverential themes of Indian culture. People, not only of India but also of several other countries, have derived inspiration from the life and character of Rama as depicted in the Ramayana.

The word 'Rama' is in-built and inherent in the Hindu culture. No prayer is possible without the use of this word. Infact, Rama figures daily in millions of prayers. Hindus, in general, greet each other with the expressions like "Ram Ram" or "Jai Ram Ji". This is very common in the rural areas where villagers meet and greet each other. Millions of Hindus use this word in their names either in the beginning or in the middle or in the end. Politicians and traders organize special "Rama Puja" or "Rama Katha" and programmes of devotional songs sung in praise of "Rama". In Sanskrit, the word 'Ram' is written with a symbol resembling the colon which signifies the "ah" attached at the end of the word "Ram" with the correct Sanskrit pronunciation as "Ram-ah". Rama is the name of the venerated hero of the epic 'Ramayana'. It is because of this reason that the name "Rama" is held sacred and in the highest esteem by the Hindus. Indeed, the sound vibrations of the word "Rama" are greatly symbolic and deeply considered to have spiritual sensation.

According to the Hindu spiritualists, the 'R' sound connotes power and masculinity. The words 'Ra' and 'm' represents respectively the male and female principles which are complement to each other. Together, they constitute the word "Ram", symbolizing the **One Supreme Reality** – the Ultimate Truth. This unification of the male and female principles as the Supreme Reality is seen in the image of Shiva and Shakti. The name Ram-ah comprises of three constituents – the first two being 'Ra' and 'M' while the third word 'ah' is the sound which stands for the divine energy. The word 'M' indicates 'Ma', 'Maman', 'Mother', 'Madre', and 'Matter' which has healing and comforting connotations. Thus 'mmmm' vibration is considered sacred which occurs in the most auspicious and pious word "Aum" pronounced "Auummmmm——". Indeed when the third part of the name (mantra) Ramah, is the sound 'ah'. This is identified with energy. Thus, when the three constituents 'Ra', 'M', 'ah' are put together, the combination takes the shape of a powerful mantra in the form "Ram-ah" – combination of male and female principles, energized by the 'ah' ending. Together, these three constituents in the combined form symbolize the One and only one Supreme Reality – called the Brahmn.

The sound vibrations produced by the recitation of the mantra "Ram-ah" are considered by the Hindus to be highly beneficial for the spiritual progress. Continuous repetition of the phrase "Ram-ah" and meditating on it is generally recommended for the Hindus. Continuous recitation of this mantra and deep meditation on it converted a robber Ratnakar into a great sage Valmiki who, being the contemporary of Lord Rama, gave an eye witness account of His profile which came to be known as 'Ramayana' – the most sacred epic of the Hindus, but equally relevant to other communities and races of the world. In the Bible – the holy book of the Christians, there are a number of people named 'Ram' just as "Hezron begat Ram" and "Ram begat Amminadab", one of them being an ancestor of King David. In Hebrew of the Jews, the word Ram means, high, tall, handsome and supreme. According to some Hindu spiritualists and preachers, Rama was, indeed very tall and handsome about 10 feet tall since during that time people were generally taller than the people of Dwapur Yuga or of the present Yuga. Even in Islam, the word 'Rama-dan' has been rephrased as 'Ramzan' – the holy days of festival by the muslims.

Eulogies to Rama, the epitome of highest human ideal conduct (Maryada Purushottam) have been sung, written and spoken of for millennia. Mohammed Iqbal, the famous Urdu poet of India (who later migrated to Pakistan after partition of United India) popularly known for his song of India (Tarana-e-Hind) "Sare Jahan Se Achchha Hindustan Hamara", penned down the following profound lines for Rama: "**Hai Ram ke wajood pe Hindustan ko naaz, Ahl-e-nazar samajhte hain inko Imam-e-Hind**". Iqbal goes to say in the same poem titled simply 'Ram'. The miracle of this luminescent truth brightens the dust of India like the dawn of an era. Iqbal's analysis of Rama's persona paints the total spectrum of His multifaceted personality and also His impact on India's psyche over the ages. Lord Rama the eternal universal hero lives in the hearts of billions irrespective of race, belief, cult or geography. Being a person of high moral standards (Maryada Purushotam), Rama was strong in human values. He was such an expert warrior that He could vanquish demons and enemies almost effortlessly. Yet despite being an incarnation of God (Avtaar), He conducted Himself wholly as a human being in thought, word and action.

Ramayana is one of the most inspirational epics adored and venerated almost everywhere in the world, *viz.* America, Cambodia, Argentina, Bali, Russia, China, Thailand, Indonesia, Burma among others. Indeed, one finds Rama – the Universal Hero, a vibrant living legend in the consciousness of people across the globe and perhaps beyond. There are several versions of Ramayana which mirror the philosophy and values held dear by the followers of various religions, including their subtle theological differences. These versions also reflect attributes, though different from their depictions in the older narratives given by Vedic sages, yet exhibit the richness and beauty of the epic giving new insights into one of the world's best classics.

The Mahabharata is considered to be the greatest epic in its content, philosophy and form, not only in India but in the whole history of human civilization. It epitomizes the ethical excellence of the ancient Hindu society, believed to be penned down about 5000 years before the beginning of the Christian era. The world known Bhagvat Gita which is undoubtedly the protein philosophy of Hinduism is only a fraction of the hundred thousand verses which constitute its original format. Depicting a self destroying rivalry between the two royal families of cousins, the Kauravas and the Pandavas, generated by the unethical greed, jealousy and lust for power on the part of the Kauravas, unleashed the inevitable and most destructive war ever fought, resulting ultimately in the triumph of the righteousness (Dharma) championed by the Pandavas duly guided and spearheaded by Lord Krishna – the embodiment of righteousness, bravery and political sagacity. In fact, the epic throws up a rich plethora of characters which pointedly reflect different temperaments and persona. It is prudently declared that there is nothing in the world, which is not given in the epic of Mahabharata.

Elaborating the divine personality of Krishna, the modern spiritual Guru Sri Sri Ravi Shankarji interprets Krishna's birth on the night of half-moon, on the eighth day of the first sight of the moon in the first fortnight of the month, as the moment symbolizing the two aspects of the supreme reality – the seen and unseen, the visible material world and the invisible spiritual realm. Krishna's birth also signifies His complete mastery of both material and spiritual aspects of the human life. All the teachings imparted by Krishna are most relevant to the present times in the sense neither one is required to get absorbed in the material world nor one needs to get renunciated from it. His teachings include both compatible and incompatible qualities which get manifested in one's life. The word Krishna means the most attractive – the Self or the being. Indeed it means the Self of every being which shines through one's personality, dexterity and divinity. The whole essence of His teachings is to maintain the perfect equilibrium between joys and sorrows, pleasures and pains, prosperity and adversity. The reason that so many people are not able to realize this reality is that they are constantly stuck in the mud of cravings and aversions because of their sinful deeds sunk in ignorance and delusion. There are, however, pious people who have faith in the Divine and realize the distinction between the light of spirituality and darkness of ignorance. Krishna is, thus, the symbol of all that is the total blossoming of all aspects of human life and the Divine enlivened with His cosmic nature in one's consciousness.

Krishna's cosmic form and His supreme divinity reveals the characteristic features of His incarnation demonstrated through miracles beginning with the time of His birth and repeatedly afterwards to the pious and deserving souls. His composed equilibrium was always in absolute consciousness with endless mystery created by Him. He was the centre of everything as the cosmic cause and effect. Throughout even during the Mahabharata War, Krishna remained an observer allowing the drama of cosmic principles of Karmas (Actions) taking its own course according to the dictates of the divine constitution of Dharma and Justice. Nevertheless at times, He would guide Arjuna and intervene only when He would find Dharma in danger, deviating even at the cost of His own prescribed cosmic principles. But otherwise He would allow things to happen in their own way and would observe the happenings with absolute detachment. Krishna was indeed both a play-writer and a player of the game. He is remembered as a fine example of non-detachment while living in the world of attachment. He advocated the realization of the Supreme Reality with total attitudinal transformation of the inner self. He always allowed the cosmic principles of Karma philosophy to prevail over the divine intervention. He could avoid the Mahabharata War since He could wipe out the evil and demonic powers in no time but He allowed the war while Himself being just a charioteer in the battle and a detached observer. Even at the time of leaving His physical body, He desired His own departure from the world through the arrow of an erring hunter. The unique aspect of Krishna's divinity is that His Omni-presence, Omni-potence and Omni-science never get obliterated.

The philosophical aspects of the two great epics 'Ramayana' and 'Mahabharata' are depicted as embodiment of almost everything that provides deeper knowledge and learning of the ancient India polity. These epics, among other several Hindu scriptures, simplify the knowledge contained in the Vedas that would stand the test of all times to come on one hand, and on the other, educate and guide people about the spiritual ideals in a simple way. These epics have been equipped with powerful dialogues to invoke and reinforce reverence (Shraddha) for God and strengthen faith in this Supreme Divine Power. Both Ramayana and Mahabharata are considered to be essential instruments to convey the doctrines of Hindu philosophy rooted in spiritual experience. The characters of Rama and Krishna as well as their messages are real embodiments of deep philosophical knowledge of spirituality. Even the characters of Ravana and Kumbhkaran in Ramayana, and those of Kansa and Duryodhana in Mahabharata portrayed as the evils give a clear warning to the people to refrain from the demonic tendencies. The ten heads of Ravana symbolize the ten evils that an average human being suffers from namely: desire (Abhilasha), lust (Kama), anger (Krodha), greed (Lobha), attachment (Moha), arrogance (Mada), hatred (Ghrina), envy (Irshya), jealousy or malice (Dwesh) and fear (Bhay). Killing of Ravana symbolizes the overcoming of those negative tendencies.

Since from time immemorial, Hindus have been having faith in the existence of the divine beings Rama and Krishna, and adoring them, there must be some truth behind it. Therefore, one must have faith in the faith of millions and billions of people. Rules of Dharma have to be made applicable to life situations, demonstrated through the two great epics of **Ramayana** and **Mahabharata**. Ramayana is the Ganga and Mahabharata is the Yamuna of the Hindu cultural rivers. They are the source and sustenance to the moral and spiritual values. Whatever is found in these epics in respect of Truth (Satya) and Righteousness (Dharma), may be found elsewhere too, but what is not in these epics, cannot be found elsewhere. While Ramayana is the elixir of the human life, Mahabharata is a cultural encyclopaedia. Ramayana excels in demonstrating the love and unity of various personalities, depiction of the divine majesty and superb power of Rama for Truth and Dharma, the indomitable strength and courage of Lakshamna, the heart-rending devotion and sacrifice of Bharata, the astounding energy and invincibility of Hanuman, the touching humility and dedication of Sita, loyalty and obedience of Shatrughana. Ramayana teaches the love and respect of a son to his parents, a friend to a friend, of a student (disciple) to a teacher (Guru), and a father to his children or of a devotee to God, and of an emperor to his peoples. The Mahabharata authored by the

Sage Ved Vyas portrays Krishna as the protector using Pandavas as the symbols for fighting for the cause of righteousness. Indeed, Mahabharata is the grand tale of the rise and fall of the human empire with Gita providing the real and ultimate knowledge of the spiritual philosophy.

While Valmik's Ramayana and Tulsidas's Sri Ramcharitra Manas together depict the character of Rama both as a man of history and God-incarnate respectively. Valmiki's Ramayana is greater of the two as it is the original source of immortal history of Rama where as Tulsi's Sri Ramcharitra Manas entrails sentiments of devotion towards Rama as God. Likewise both the great epic Mahabharata and its subsequent poetic version as Bhagvat, authored by the same author namely the sage Ved Vyasa who was contemporary of Krishna, projects Krishna as a human being and also as the God-incarnate on the earth. The miracles shown by both Rama and Krishna are very aptly depicted in both the epics of Ramayana and Mahabharata. Indeed, Mahabharata is full of Krishna's miracles termed as Krishna sports (Leela) which generate a devotional feeling towards Krishna as God-incarnate.

Infinite is God and infinite are His stories. Each saint sings and hears these stories in divergent ways. In every cycle of creation, God manifests and incarnates Himself to protect and uphold righteousness and destroy evil and wickedness, and to enact lovely sports and show miracles of various types. The great sages, on each such occasion have sung His stories and described His miracles while relating wonderful anecdotes of several kinds. Hearing these sacred stories and seeing these divine miracles, the sages have rooted among the devotees a deep faith in God – the almighty. There is no limit to the stories of God's manifested form of Hari Vishnu and Maheshwar Shiva as well as of God's incarnated form of Sri Rama and Sri Krishna. The sages and devotees are fully aware of these stories and miracles of Rama and Krishna. The special feature of these stories and miracles is that they all characterize the parameters of faith in God and Dharma (Righteousness) as the central theme. The precise role of both Ramayana and Mahabharata is to explain and expatiate the Vedic teachings. Both provide sustenance and support to the moral and spiritual ideas as well as the ideals. An epic is considered to be a superb form of spiritual contribution to the philosophical and religious literature. In its purest form, an epic is loftiest art of a civilization.

The two great epics Ramayana and Mahabharata are considered to be fifth and sixth Vedas while Sri Ram Charit Manas and Gita are regarded as their corresponding Upanishads. Gita occupies a special place in the school of Vedanta representing one of the three authoritative works on Vedanta, according to the Vedantic sage, Adi-Sankaracharya. The Bhagvat Gita literary means 'Song of God'. It begins with the word 'Dharma' and ends with 'Mana'. Dharam means 'essential Being' while 'Mana' means 'My'. Together they mean 'My essential Being' which is the theme of Gita. The aim of life should be to realize one's essential Being; to discover the Supreme Self within and to attain spiritual enlightenment. The Gita forms the philosophical aspect of the epic of Mahabharata – the great work of the great sage Vyasa. Its 701 verses are spread over 18 chapters which in turn may be divided into three parts each comprising of six chapters, explaining Vedic aphorisms in the following way: **Tat Twamam Asi or That Thou Art. The first six chapters describe Tat or That. The middle six chapters pertain to Twam or Thou. The last six chapters refer to Asi or Art. It all means that Tat is the Self within, Twam stands for the Supreme God. Finally Asi indicates that the Self in everybody**. Thus Self in a being and God are one. The Gita leads one to the ultimate state of spiritual enlightenment. Moreover, it offers to the real philosophy of life which can be translated in everybody's life. Gita makes a thorough analysis of the human personality which is made up of matter and spirit. Gita helps in refining and sieving out matter. What remains is spirit. Matter comprises of three distinct attributes or characteristics namely purity (Sattva), passion (Rajas) and ignorance (Tamas) called the 'Gunas'. These traits are like the generic codes in a human personality since they determine the quality of thoughts, emotions and actions in a person. Together they bind a person to the world. Tamas is a state of inertia and indifference due to ignorance. In this state, the good qualities get shrouded and one's inherent talent is prevented from its manifestation. Rajas is a state of discontent and stress striven with turbulence in the mind. Sattva is the tranquility of mind, calmness and contemplativeness. This is the state of spiritual excellence.

A lot has been written on the teachings of the Gita. Bhagvat Gita is often called the essence of all the four Vedas, since it highlights the basic concepts and enunciations of the Vedanta philosophy. It elaborates the notion of God and His transcendental omni-presence, omni-potence and omni-scient, embodied souls as constituents of God and their involvement in the cycle of birth and death based on the actions performed by them. It elaborates the nature of the Atman or soul and the process of its transmigration, renunciation of the materialistic attachments, with action (Karma), devotional love (Bhakti) and divine knowledge (Brahmn Jnana) as the main spiritual pursuits for realization of God. Indeed, the Holy Gita presents some of the most important truths about divinity in a language that is clear, memorable and charged with sentiments. It is an anthology of poetic verses and a prose manual. Its method is linear but circular and descriptive. It returns to its own central point of Karma philosophy. Gita's passages are charged with special impact, as they are the spoken words of God himself. Spiritual aspirants through the ages have been inspired to memorize Sri Krishna's teaching and thereby soak their minds with the revelations of God incarnate. Gita stresses the philosophy of detachment and dedication through action and service (Karma Yoga and Seva); of the sense of discrimination and dispassion through knowledge and meditation (Gyan and Dhyan); and through total faith and devotion (Shraddha and Bhakti). However, the Karma Yoga is thought to be Sri Krishna's special message and the very heart of the Gita's teachings.

Gita is aptly held as the most sacred scripture of Hinduism. As briefly mentioned earlier, the 'Bhagvat Gita' constitutes the central component of the epic of Mahabharata. It is a dialogue between Krishna the Lord and Arjuna, His devotee and friend. Gita is even sometimes considered to be a Veda in itself since it is the voice of God Himself incarnated as Krishna, while some treat it as the essence of all the Upanishads. It offers a teaching on the proper relationship that exists among God, the universe and the living-beings *i.e.* among the creator, creation and creatures. The Gita provides an invigorating blend of the call of duty for adhering to the path of truth (Satya) and righteousness (Dharma). It offers a way out for harmonious human relationship, for realization of a higher being operating between an individual and the human society, for inter-relatedness of all the beings in the universe both animated and inanimated, and demonstrates the Supremacy of Godhead above everything and every being.

Sri Krishna maintains throughout the Gita that the true renunciation means the renunciation of the lower self, the ego, desires, attachments and aversions. Gita endorses the broader concept of Yajna as a sacrifice in a larger sense by emphasizing any action as an offering to God, and that every action, including even inhalation and exhalation, is to be performed as Yajna. Another most important teaching of the Gita, namely the Bhakti – Yoga, the path of devotion to God, heralds the very beginning of the theory of the divine incarnation which finds many elaborations in all the Holy Scriptures. Indeed, Gita offers a real philosophy of harmony in which all paths and attitudes are recommended for leading to the highest goal – the Brahmn, with Karma Yoga, Jnana Yoga, Dhyana Yoga and Bhakti Yoga as the most unifying elements. Gita has the immense power to elevate and broaden the level of consciousness of a spiritual aspirant to the grandeur of the universal consciousness, that is, the Brahmn. Gita represents the sum and substance of the essential teachings of the Upanishads. While Adi-Sankaracharya calls Gita as the summary of the basic ideas of all the Vedas, the Gita itself is an Upanishad of Mahabharata which is considered as the sixth Veda, the fifth Veda being the Valmiki's Ramayana. Another way of God realization, as prescribed in the Gita, is the concept of Yajna or sacrifice. Generally, the Yajnas are performed for the fulfillment of the performer's desire, but Gita, utilizes the notion of Yajna as a significance step for sacrifice in the larger sense, and provides an entire ethical paradigm centered around the social and cosmic good. Sri Krishna gave the final word on Yajna when He said that Sakshat Brahmn can be realized by seeing in all elements of the act of offering, including the offerer himself or herself as nothing but Brahmn.

As stated earlier the Vedas and the Upanishads are generally called the Srutis. One of the chief goals of these srutis is to glorify the divine love and create a sense of deep devotion for God, as a friend, as a philosopher, as a guide to humanity in all matters of living, and as a loving father and mother. God is always considered to be inseparable from the human beings in the conceptual framework of 'Narayana' and 'Nara', coming to their help even unasked for and unsolicited. Infact, the human beings themselves do not know that they need God's help. But God knows it even beforehand. This is the divine love characterized in the Epics and Puranas. God's friendship with human beings is the special touching and distinguished feature of his transcendental love adored in the srutis. Love between God and His devotees is the true representation of their sentiments and feelings for each other. While Krishna-Arjuna love is that of depth and dignity, Prahlad-Vishnu love is that of adoration and devotion, but love of the Gopis for Krishna seems to be the romance of the soul in its ecstasy of God-vision reaching the highest peak of devotion. The total surrender to God which one experiences in this ecstasy of God-love is a state of entire merger which one experiences in God-union. The instances of Yashoda's motherly love (Vatsallya) or Radha's love for Krishna or for that matter that of Draupadi's love for Krishna or Mira's love for Krishna or Prahlad's love for Vishnu are some of the illustrations of the super-individual and super-social nature of the soul's love for God. Equally and more importantly on the other hand is the way of the love from God in which He breaks all rules and codes, and runs to His devotees personally without hesitation even for a moment. Krishna, in Bhagvat Gita, has clearly and emphatically declared that He shall personally take care of His devotees when they are individually and undividedly united with

Him. Rasa-Lila of Krishna with Gopis in Vrindavan is the height of the ecstasy of God's love whose devotion reaches the point of melting into the spiritual bliss – a penultimate stage of actual union with God. This is the state where not only the devotees run after God tearing down all the empirical shackles of personality-consciousness, but God Himself comes running to the devotees, God wanting devotees is much more than the devotees wanting God. It is not enough if the devotees seek God, but the highest devotion is where God seeks the devotees. The devotional love of the Gopis of Vrindavan in Dwapur Yuga for Krishna and that of several saints in Treta Yuga craving for Rama's love are examples of that highest devotion and love for God.

Love for God, mostly keeps the devotees in a state of reverence and devotion. This is termed as love and adoration of God (Ishwar-Pradhan Bhakti) as the Creator, Father, Mother and Sovereign Supreme. Love as an internal contact which a devotee develops with God is deeply intimate. Such a love goes by the name of affection and affirmation (Madhurya-Bhakti) in which intellectualism, rationalism and analysis cease to operate and the soul speaks to God in the language of heart. It is a stage of love with God which needs neither any philosophy nor any mode of devotion. Saints Narada travelling to all the realms of the Cosmos, and contacting God on one side and meeting men, gods, angles and even demons on the other, is a representation of the significance of divine devotion. The stories and analysis portrayed in the epics and various holy scriptures make the relevance of God's love more interesting, thrilling and vibrating to the soul. While listening to the stimulating glories of God, these epics and scriptures emphasize that God can hear and speak to the devotees, even the devotees can speak to God. The paradigms that these scriptures employ for describing God's relation with human beings and *vice-versa,* signify that God is nearer to His devotees than perhaps it is imagined. God's relation with His devotees is neither a commercial bargain nor a compromise nor even a give and take settlement. God in the scriptures is not merely portrayed as Father or Mother but equally as a Friend, a Saviour and a Protector. Human relations may help each other when maintained at a requisite level but the relationship with God is not conditioned in any manner. It is based on Pure love, where God loves His devotees more than the devotees seem to love Him.

3.3 Hindu Philosophy

Hindu philosophy – the ancient science of India, is consistent with the theology and metaphysics of the Vedas – the most holy scriptures of the Hindus. It is based on certain fundamental precepts which together provide a rational and foundational basis for an highly exalted way of both spirituality and religion while opening new vistas to the conception of creation, and perception of the existence of the universe. Its principal importance lies in its proclamation of the Vedic philosophy of the Universal (Cosmic) Self (Soul). Indeed, its philosophical system unfolds in several stages of enlightenment some of which are related to following aspects among others:

- The intense desire for realization and/or visualization of God.
- The discrimination of the reality of the appearance of truth from the illusion (Maya).
- The tendency of mental consciousness heading towards self introspection, and quenching thirst for spiritual knowledge and supreme wisdom.
- The attainment of complete identity with the Brahmn and its Existence leading to tranquility and peace with concentration upon Atman.
- Renunciation from all attachments and desires leading to complete absorption in the Supreme Consciousness or the Brahmn – the final stage of consummation.
- Attainment of liberation of the soul from the cycle of birth and death of the body.

An individual who is able to achieve the aforesaid stages of enlightenment and realize the unity, of the individual self with the Cosmic Self, and who can feel himself illuminated, detached from body feelings, pains and pleasure, only he becomes then purified and liberated from sins. Such an individual gets trans-visioned and becomes a real spiritualist with realization of his own self as prevailing in all directions. He, then, feels himself as his own creator or inventor of God and knows all the facts in their true form, for all times to come.

Some of the important characteristics of the Hindu philosophy are as under:—

- The Hindu philosophy constitutes the most magnificent and imposing system for leading a purposeful life.
- The Hindu philosophy has been offering the most fundamental and pristine revelation to the humanity for the hundreds of thousands of years.
- The Hindu philosophy speaks of eternal truths which guide the human evolution in conformity with 'Atman' or the divine scheme of Nature.

- It has been claimed by some spiritual scholars that all existing monolithic religions of the world are off-shoots of this ancient science of the Hindu philosophy. In this sense, each monolithic religion of the world is regarded as a ray emanating from this unique system of Hindu philosophy.
- Hindu philosophical system is an unchangeable and sparkling source of Truth that the scientists and spiritual scholars pursue in order to give a fresh impetus to the modern scientific culture and to arrive at the complete solution of the crucial problem agitating the humankind of today.

The Hindu philosophy is generally classified into six metaphysical systems namely the following:

- The Vaisesika – the science of Matter given by the sage Kanada.
- The Nyaya – the science of Reason or logic enunciated by the sage Gautama.
- The Purva Mimamsa – the science of Action and Meditation given by the sage Jaimini.
- The Samkhya (Numerology) – the science of evolution founded by the sage Kapila.
- The Yoga (Union with God) – The science of Intellect propounded by the Sage Patanjali.
- The Uttara Mimamsa also called the Vedanta – the complete science of God and Soul of the Abstract, theorized by the sage Vyasa of the Mahabharata fame.

These six philosophical systems enunciate that each is independent and sufficient in itself as a guiding path to final liberation. Each of the systems, indeed, teaches a particular philosophy, where everything is independent of other systems. A human being can certainly progress in his spiritual evolution along the path towards the final goal of 'liberation' by following the principles of any one of these systems. However, at the same time, the totality of wisdom is more amply unveiled by the knowledge of all the six systems, each of them constituting itself a link in a harmonious garland, a facet of the whole truth, the highest expression of which is to be found in the last philosophical school – that of Vedanta.

The mastering of matter, the evolution of spirit, and the knowledge of the Divine in the abstract sense, are the three objectives for which the study of the six philosophical thoughts are generally recategorized by spiritual scholars into four systems namely: Nyaya – Vaiseska, Samkhya-

Yoga, Mimamsa and Vedanta. Even each of the six philosophical thoughts developed its own system built on its distinct content and methodology, yet Vaisheshika, propounded by sage Kanada, provides theoretical bases for Nyaya due to sage Gautama which excels in providing rules and conditions of arriving at valid knowledge. Similarly, the Samkhya provides the metaphysical postulations whereas Yoga provides the necessary regularity discipline for achieving the ultimate goal of life, that is, the liberation (Moksha). In fact various philosophers and scholars find all the systems culminating in the Vedanta which constitutes a grand scheme for realizing the essence of human life. The salient features of these four philosophical systems are briefly summarized as follows:

(i) **Nyaya – Vaiseska** essentially considers the entire universe as comprising of six components: Substance, Attribute, Activity, Generality, Individuality and Inherence. Nine type of substances are enumerated out of which the first seven namely earth, water, fire, air, ether, time and space serve as the material cause of Nature, and the remaining two have been identified with soul (Atman) and mind (Manas) which are identified with the existence of living beings. The word 'Nyaya' denotes the science of reasoning which means logic while 'Vaiseska' stands for metaphysics (beyond matter or science) and Ontology means the theory or science of existence. Nyaya holds Atman as a unique, ubiquitous substance to which all cognitions, feelings and connotations belong. It leads the mind to a conclusion based on logic and epistemology (the theory of knowledge). Thus, **Nyaya and Vaiseska together represent the Nyaya-Vaiseska which means logical knowledge of the theory and philosophy of existence**.

According to Nyaya-Vaiseska, an individual self like a human being comprises of three basic constituents namely soul (Atman), mind (Manas) and body (Sarira) augmented with five senses of knowledge (Jnanendriyas) and the five senses of action (Karmendriyas). Self is the essence of human personality. It is eternal, indestructible and infinite. Indeed, it is Atmic. It knows all and enjoys all. Mind, body, senses and consciousness are distinguishable adjuncts of the embodied self – the human being. Consciousness emerges in the waking state when the self is in contact with the external world through the agencies of body, mind and senses. Consciousness is an attribute of the soul and mind. The philosophy of Nyaya-Vaiseska requires the cultivation of knowledge that the self (Atman) is central to human existence. Atman is neither body nor mind nor senses, but what controls them and synthesizes their operations. It acts as a unifying factor of all types of cognition and action. It is the foundation of human life. It also cultivates awareness that mental development is accidental. It requires development of an understanding so as to empower human life to achieve the highest good namely liberation of the soul *i.e.* cessation from the cycle of births and rebirths. The way out to achieve this goal is to overcome selfish desires and impulses, cultivation of right attitude which vanishes ignorance, infatuation, bondage, pain and pleasure. This school of thought prescribes the pursuit of a discipline which is ethical, intellectual and spiritual on the lines of the path of action (Karma), path of knowledge (Jnana) and the path of devotion (Bhakti) for God-realization.

(ii) Samkhya-Yoga is a blend of two doctrines, viz., the Samkhya and Yoga (like the system of Nyaya-Vaiseska), of which the sages Kapila and Patanjali respectively are considered to be the two chief exponents. Samkhya is one of the oldest systems of philosophy. Combined with Yoga, its main axioms and principles have been referred in Rig Veda and in various related Upanishads. Sankhya-Yoga finds a prominent place in the Bhagvat Gita. Sankhya means the philosophy of right knowledge which is predominantly intellectual and theoretical whereas Yoga is a practical discipline leading to the realization of the reality visualized in Sankhya. The philosophical system of Samkya-Yoga is known for its theory of evolution as well as for reducing the numerous categories enunciated in the Nyaya-Viseaska to the two fundamental aspects namely 'Purusha' and 'Prakriti' *i.e.* the subject and the object. Indeed, Samkhya explains reality with the help of two metaphysical spiritual entities Purush and Prakriti where Purush is all consciousness, but without any action, while Prakriti is assumed to be primordial matter suffused with activity. Creation is viewed as the outcome of the interaction between the two eternal ontological axioms of Purusha and Prakriti. Prakriti in its original basic attributes – Sattva, Rajas and Tamas, remains in a state of equilibrium. When this equilibrium gets disturbed by its proximity of Purusha, the evolutionary process of the universe starts taking shape. The Cosmic Self referred to as the subject, though passive by itself, excites Prakriti, the object, upsetting the equipoise of the three attributes

Sattva, Rajas and Tamas and unleashes the process of evolution and dissolution. This process of interaction between Purusha and Prakriti gives birth to the profile of human personality along with other beings both animate and inanimate, sentient and insentient.

According to Samkhya, there are three constituents of the human personality *viz.* the soul (Atman), the subtle body (the Linga Sarir) and the gross physical body (the Sthula Sarir). It is equipped with an inner apparatus (Antahkarana) comprising of intellect, the ego-sense and mind which account for various types of subjective, and psychic experiences including perception, discernment and volition. The human personality is autonomous in existence. It enjoys reality at the phenomenal level, its ultimate sources being the unconscious Prakriti and conscious Purusha. Samkhya accounts for the evolution of the universe from the subtle to the gross elements, human personality being one of the evolutes having both the elements. Yoga prescribes an elaborate psycho-physical course of action which brings in the desired ethical and spiritual development of human personality. However, the development of human personality in yoga is visualized as a process of involution, a journey back home to the metaphysical matrix. The True Self *i.e.* The Cosmic Self (Purusha) is eternally free. However, the empirical self (Human Being) or individual self suffers from bondage, a release from which is obtained through the paths of Knowledge and Yoga.

(iii) **Mimamsa** is a system of philosophy that stands for the reality of everything that exists. Universe is real, eternal and uncreated. It rejects theory of efficient cause (God). It accepts the existence of Soul, entirely distinct from body, mind and sense. It admits plurality of souls. Self (Atman) is the essence of human personality. It is conceived as both subject (the knower) and the object (the known). It energises body, mind and senses, though different from them. Human personality in Mimamsa is taken to be a living relationship between the self (Atman) and its adjuncts mind, body and senses. The soul is self-luminous, all pervasive and is known as the doer in the 'I-sense'. It is the true experience of things in life. Knowledge is a property of the soul. Mind (Manas) in the Mimamsa philosophy holds the status and role assigned to Antakaran as in the case of Samkhya-Yoga. The physical body and the senses are also treated as real entities so far as the embodied self is concerned.

Mimamsa stands for the study of the interpretation of the Vedic rituals and ceremonies also. It tries to justify the Vedic sacrifices (Yajnas). The ethic of the Vedas is obligatory. Dharma in Mimamsa is action based. Human beings are obliged to pursue Dharma which requires the performance of actions (Karma), some leading to worldly gain and others to liberation (Moksha). In line with most of systems of Indian philosophy, Mimamsa holds liberation (Moksha) as the highest ideal of human existence. As in the case of Nyaya-Vaiseska, reality in Mimamsa is classified under categories of substance, quality, action, universe and non-existence, rejecting inherence of God and replacing it by soul. Mimamsa adds 'darkness' and eternal 'sound' to the nine types of substance presumed by Nyaya-Vaiseska. Mimamsa insists on adherence to Dharma, transcribed into a code of conduct laid down in accordance with the Vedic-Principles. Like Nyaya-Vaiseska, Mimamsa also maintains that after liberation, soul exists only as 'Sat', devoid of consciousness and totally insensitive in the absence of its habitat, the body.

(iv) **Vedanta** stands for the 'end of the Vedas' both in the sense of constituting the concluding portion (called Jnanakanda) of Vedas, and containing the essence of the Vedic philosophy with Upanishads providing the metaphysical meaning. Vedanta has numerous variations on the metaphysical issues concerning the individual self, the universe, the Absolute reality and their mutual relationship. Vedanta philosophy acknowledges individual self as the centre of divinity and its development in realizing the divine which culminates in transcending the 'world of appearance' marking the pilgrims progress from That, Thou, Art to Soham (So Aham). As said by Bhagwan Sri Sathya Sai Baba, the divine beings, who from the moment of birth realize their divinity, utter "Soham Soham"! (that I am) from the time of birth. But ordinary mortals ask "Koham Koham"?" ("Who am I?"). They do not realize that the answer is: "I am God". A few earnest seekers start with "Koham" and end with the discovery "Soham". The conception of individual self is true to its metaphysical mainstay: that is, individual self has only empirical (Worldly) existence. A remarkable feature of Vedanta is its ontology of individual self that reduces all dualistic and pluralistic entities to one ground source, the Brahmn. The highest ideal for Vedanta is the self-realization which can be attained by the removal of the veil of Maya which can be attained by gaining the divine knowledge (Brahmn Vidya).

Generally a comparative view of the philosophies of Nyaya-Vaiseska, Samkhya-Yoga, Mimamsa and Vedanta is made on the following lines:

- Nyaya-Vaiseska looks at the divine phenomenon as the 'intelligised self'. However, its theory of creation in terms of atoms and unseen potency is untenable as it fails to convince how a non-intelligent can provide drive to another non-intelligent (atom).
- Samkhya-Yoga, conceives of individual self as a 'spirit in solitary splendour' and also propounds that Prakriti (Primal matter) is the prious of the evolution. It is also not tenable because it is not in accordance with the teachings of the Upanishads, being based on inferences only. Prakriti is non-Intelligent and the world cause, according to the scriptures, has to be intelligent. Hence, Prakriti cannot be the cause of the universe. Moreover, in the process of realization, the cause, referred to as the self, has to be gained whereas the Prakriti is to be abandoned. Also, the views ascribing causality of the world to what is other than Brahmn, have not been found in order.
- Mimamsa philosophy views individual self as engaged in 'sculpting in its own image'. It stands for reality of everything that exists and rejects the theory of 'Efficient Cause' of the Universe. Moreover, it believes in plurality of souls.
- Vedanta believes in two basic aspects of spirituality. First, the philosophical thoughts and their concept of the Self. Secondly, the theological aspects namely Advaita (Non-duality), Visisthadvaita (Qualified non-duality) and Dvaitva duality do not match their metaphysical enunciations. Both aspects characterize an analytic philosophy, phenomenology and theology.

Modern effort is focused on bringing the rich spiritual thought of ancient India to the Western audience that understands the need for transcultural study in a globalized world. It also tries to contribute to the re-establishment of Hindu philosophical thought in original and non-traditional ways. The classical Indian Systems (Hinduism together with Buddhism, Jainism and Sikhism) believe that consciousness should be understood as a unique phenomenon that contrasts the Western view of materialism. The debate, however, centres around whether the Indian spiritual phenomenon, described metaphorically as the enlightenment or luminosity, depends on a relationship with materialism or reflexivity with itself. What is striking is that consciousness is at the centre of understanding? Thus, Indian philosophy of spiritualism is different from the Western logic of Aristotle which seeks to express functional and materialistic relationships as the features of reality devoid of their awareness.

Western logic has led to vast advances in computation. However, it is now being recognized everywhere that there are certain basic features of human personality that the computation does not capture. The computational logic can only perform simple human forms of reasoning through complicated algorithms. It cannot, however, comprehend accurately the human consciousness and its functions while being consistent with the modern neuroscience. The Indian classical thought is analytico-synthetic, pluralistic and often concerned with abstract theories of reality.

The Indian philosophy of Hinduism believes in the axiom of "Aham Brahmasmi" and "Tat Tvam Asi" which means "I am Brahmn" and "You too are That". Brahmn is the eternal, unchanging, infinite, immanent and transcendental reality. Indeed, Brahmn is the Absolute Reality. Everything springs from Brahmn: "I am the manifestation of that Brahmn and so are you". This concept of oneness, makes a person realize the power of the phrase, "Aham Brahmasmi". It wipes out the distinction between individual self and the Divine self.

In ancient India during the period of seventh and sixth century B.C., a classical philosopher Charvaka is believed to have introduced a philosophical system based on materialism. The chief doctrine of this philosophy was that body was everything and the real purpose of human life was to enjoy the world by any means, as death was the ultimate end. It was focused on the principle of "eat, drink and be merry", as this is indeed the way of life of some of the communities of the world dominated by the Western/European culture. However, many Hindu scholars do not treat Charvaka as a philosophy which never got evolved, and hence remained frozen in time.

Viewing or reviewing these philosophical systems somewhat critically, it is realized that each system highlights certain aspects of Reality. It is only when someone puts them together that they reveal a whole scheme of the creation and its prious. According to the philosophy of the atoms named as Vaishaeshika, also called Atmic Pluralism, death is not the end of life and there is after life *i.e.* life after death. The believers in this philosophy scientifically analysed and divided everything to its smallest component called atom (anu). They considered the atom to be the foundation of everything, and that nothing like God or Soul is true. "Only fate is acceptable." They declared. Then came the philosophy of Logic called Nyaya which believed that the body (materialism) and the atom were insentient. It believed in both body and soul, the conception of soul, however, being elementary. According to this philosophy, everything depended on logical deductions – the "smoke indicates fire" type of logic. However, it had no answer to the questions like "can one overcome sufferings and sorrows through logic?" It is based on the belief in attaining liberation through complete knowledge.

The next philosophical system called 'Sankhyas' (Numerology) which is considered to be a speculative philosophy. Its propounders and believers went beyond the atom and the soul. They proclaimed that the idea of sentient and insentient realities as they appear is acceptable. What is called matter is Prakriti which is a combination of three qualities namely equilibrium (Sattva), dynamism (Rajas) and inertia (Tamas). It is a dualistic philosophy based on the belief in Self (Purusha) and Matter or Nature (Prakriti), that creation is due to proximity of Purusha and Prakriti, and that realization of the distinction between Purusha and Prakriti leads to liberation. It is closely linked to Raja Yoga *i.e.* the theoretical basis of practical Yoga – the philosophical system, which believes in the techniques of meditation to achieve transcendence. The believers in this philosophy, called the Yogis, are of the opinion that people suffer because countless thought waves rise in their minds which force them to act and their actions are recorded inside the unconscious part of their minds. Until mind is cleared of these thoughts and actions, one cannot be free and liberated. Every thought or action produces a chain of thoughts and actions. Yoga, therefore, propounds thought control as the way to attain ultimate peace.

The philosophy of Purva-Mimamsa is based on belief in the Supremacy of Vedas with a focus on their ritualistic aspect. According to this belief, a brain-dead man too has a body and mind, but he is like a vegetable. This philosophy stands for the Vedic rituals, ceremonies and sacrifices (Yajnas). It is action-based and believes in performance of actions, in line with the Karma Theory, based on the Vedic-Principles.

Finally comes the Uttara Mimamsa – which is also known as the Vedanta. This school of philosophy is based on a metaphysical (philosophical or ontological) aspect or interpretation of the Vedas contrasting their ritualistic aspect believed by Purva Mimamsa. Owing to ignorance, a person thinks that he/she is a body and mind, and hence he/she suffers. Behind both body and mind, a person is a soul, the Self Realization of this Self will lead to the Ultimate Truth – the Supreme Reality *i.e.* Sat-Chit-Anand (Truth-Awareness-Bliss). Various interpretations of Uttar Mimamsa, called the Vedantic Philosophy led to the emergence of a large number of sub-schools of this philosophy of which three are most important and influential. Discovered in greater detail in Chapter 4, first is Advaita (Monism) originally propounded by Gaurdapuda and established and propagated more convincingly by Adi Shankaracharya as the doctrine of non-dualistic reality based on belief in the Supreme Being (Brahmn), with no attributes. Second is Vishistadvaita (Theistic Monism) also called qualified non-dualism which believes in plurality within unity. According to this philosophical thought, while the Supreme Being (Brahmn) is different from the soul (cit) and matter (acit), both soul and body (matter) are dependent on the Supreme Being (Spirit). The third principal interpretation upholds duality or dualism (Dvaita) which stresses on the idea of God totally separate from souls and matter.

The Charavak philosophy called also the Lokayata School of thought believes that life by itself is neither blissful nor full of sorrow. It is how a person makes it. This philosophy firmly believes in living joyfully, the concept of joy being totally mundane, earthly and materialistic. It corresponds with the idea of physical pleasure minus spiritual bliss. Indeed, Charavak philosophy negates Vedas, existence of God and the idea of rebirth. It actually believes in hedonism and making living physically blissful ignoring its spiritual aspect.

The premise that God or Supreme Being is Truth-Awareness-Bliss (Sat-Chit-Anand) has been accepted by almost all the philosophies of Hinduism. But it would be over simplication of the Vedic system, to negate the world altogether. In fact, some Upanishads consider the phenomenal reality of human existence with its physicality as an instrument of realizing the Noumenal that is the ultimate reality – the Brahmn. Vedic philosophies, however, proclaim that life is full of both bliss and sorrow or pleasure and pain which are tide and ebb in the ocean of life, while the latest Indian philosophies of both Buddhism and Jainism are diagonally opposite to the Charavak philosophy and believe that life is full of sorrows and sufferings – a dismal view of life. The Vedic philosophy, as revealed in Gita, believes that existence of joy and sorrow is a reality which is related to the Karma Theory and which, if treated with equanimity and meditation, will lead to liberation, and oneness with the Supreme Reality – the Brahmn.

- Hinduism is a great reconciler of ideas, and provides a link between spirituality and science, tradition and modernity, material prosperity and spiritual ascension, and the spirit of enquiry and faith.

- Hinduism combines equanimity (sambahavs) with social work, devotion (bhakti) with conviction (Shraddha) or devotion with strength, and patriotism with an universal brotherhood. Besides, it reconciles the three different schools of Hindu philosophy – Dvaita, Vishihstadvaita and Advaita, describing them as different stages in one's spiritual development.
- Hinduism wants intellect to be balanced with love, mystical nature with reason, and practice with method. Its words soothe and inspire, inform and educate, jolt complacency and deep-seated notions, and act, like the surgeon's knife to dissect fears, prejudices or complexes from the subconscious mind.

Much can be learnt from it in different spheres of life: psychologists can grasp that mind is a refined matter, and the body a concretized mind, and that the way to control the mind is to attain a higher state of consciousness. Physicists can learn that consciousness is a fundamental reality; that there is no such thing as strict causality, and that what we call matter, is in fact, potential energy. Mathematicians can understand the vedantic view that space and time are a continuum. Chemists can know that the ultimate aim is to discover one element, from which all others have been derived. Neurobiologists can benefit from the dynamics of higher consciousness, provided by them. Management-experts can realize that the management of the Self must precede everything else, and that true motivation comes from within. Educationists can grasp that they cannot educate, but only help children to grow in terms of their nature. Students of yoga can understand that this ancient science is not for building up a 'muscular body', but for Self-realization. Besides, they need to remember that 'violent exercises are positively harmful'. Occultists can know that the display or misuse of extrasensory powers, deviates one from the spiritual path. Religious leaders can realize that nobody is less divine, and that if a religion cannot help one to find out God, it is useless. Humanists may assert that 'no books, no scriptures and no science can imagine the glory of the self that appears as human'. Rationalists can feel happy that Advaita Vedanta is a practical, scientific, secular, spiritual, and an all-encompassing way of life, which can help one to achieve higher goals.

Hinduism believes that each human being is like a bubble on the cosmic ocean, though a small one, in comparison with prophets or saints, who are bigger bubbles. But someday, all will merge into One, followed by the new creation which 'will bring new water to go through the process all over again', meaning that puissant souls will keep coming. Its observation that it is good to be born in a Church but bad to die there, was not sectarian, but a pointer to the fact that human beings normally adhere to forms and ceremonies throughout life, and fail to rise up in spirituality. They do not understand that Christ and Buddha are not names, but denote the Supreme state which they need to attain.

The ideas of Hinduism are so prolific that one can get tips on cooking, grinding spices, travel, music, fine arts, or the use of incense and flowers for good feeling. Despite material advancement, man is restless, tense and worried. Always in a hurry, in fulfillment of his worldly pursuits, he has forgotten his real Self, and become a victim of negative perceptions. It is in this context that the ideas of Hinduism become relevant.

Chapter 4
Supreme Reality and Its Manifestations

Spirituality is considered to be the foundational base of human philosophy. Its role **is considered to be fundamental to the human evolution. The spiritual ideals, principles** and pursuits all are related to the philosophy of life. The complex issues of material prosperity and social living will remain as crucial as ever much along with the concerns of the human aspects of culture and morality. But there is an agenda of spiritual ideology – signaling something beyond all that is necessary for body and mind. It is the soul voicing truth, raising the core issue of existence, its very purpose and meaning, and its ultimate goal.

From time immemorial, the human mind has been engaged in exploring the meaning of life. In its long, arduous and sustained pursuits, it has been conjecturing that there is an abiding reality behind life which makes it meaningful and sustainable. This reality is designated as the Supreme Reality, also known as the Universal or Cosmic Soul or the Universal Consciousness or Cosmic Consciousness or the Brahmn. Supreme Reality means the eternal truth. Reality cannot be something which exists today and is gone thereafter as if it were not there before. Reality overpasses the periphery of time in the sense that it is eternal and has always been in existence. The universe looks to be a reality, whether partly visible or partly perceptible, whether be called matter or spirit, but seems to be having an everlasting existence. For, if that were not the case, or whatsoever had even once been the case, the universe could never have arisen. Even the common intelligence demands some basis to account for the existence of the universe. Thus, the original 'something' must have always existed, must still exist to-date and is bound to exist in the future. This is generally termed as the Supreme Reality or Absolute Reality or Ultimate Reality which is considered as beginningless and endless, that which is eternal.

In this context, a number of questions arise such as the following among others: **What are the basic principles and aims of human life? How can a human society afford to generate a system that does not include the fundamental spiritual values in its evolution? What is the real purpose of life? What is the calendar of the soul? What is the divine power called God? Who is God? Where does He live? What does He do? Where is the beginning and end of the Universe? What is life after death? What is the Supreme Truth or Reality of the whole phenomenon?**

Such philosophical questions demand clear and concise answers. Human life will remain devoid of its true meaning unless it seriously engages itself in finding answers of such questions to elevate its level of spiritual consciousness. This chapter deals with the above questions in relation to the Supreme Reality and its manifestations in its following three sections with a focus on Brahmn and the Universe in section 4.1, the Divine Power and its Trinity Principles in section 4.2 while the section 4.3 revolves around the Divine incarnations and Human beings.

4.1 Brahmn and the Universe

Vedanta is considered to be the protein philosophy of Hinduism. The Vedantic assertion seems to be more convincing. It states that Brahmn alone is the Supreme Reality. The so-called creative activity ascribed to Brahmn may be interpreted as its sport. The Universe is not separate from Brahmn. The non-evolution and evolution of the Universe are like the folded and spread out conditions, respectively of a piece of cloth. The individual soul is related to Brahmn as reflection to prototype. It is the individual soul which acts, enjoys, transmigrates and strives for a rebase, and regains it. It remains entangled in the cycle of 'birth and death', and keeps on migrating through different states of consciousness waking, dream and deep-sleep. This migratory process comes to an end when the soul realizes the non-dual Brahmn, which is attributeless and formless. The attributes ascribed to Sagun Brahmn are for the sake of meditation (Upasna or Sadhana). The Brahmn appears to acquire form because of its adjuncts like the reflection of one sun in several pots/reservoirs of water. The one who realizes the Nirguna Brahmn attains Brahmn itself.

The Brahmn, according to Vedanta, is the Supreme Reality. All other beings, animate or inanimate, sentient or insentient, visible or invisible, are unreal. Sometimes, Upanishad is quoted to have described Brahmn in negative terms – not this, not that (neti, neti). Swami Sivanand disagrees with any negative description of the Brahmn. According to him, though it is not possible to conceive of Absolute Reality, yet Brahmn is neither void nor emptiness (Shunayata). On the contrary, Brahmn is supremely complete (Paripoorna). The Brahmn, according to Swami Sivanand, is eternal, infinite and the Supreme Bliss. He describes Brahmn in terms of positive attributes such as divine wisdom, dispassion, power, strength, prosperity and eminence among others. Brahmn is all pervasive which surrounds everybody from all sides, inside, outside, above and below. Every being is in it and it is in every being. Brahmn is the support of all phenomenal world. It is unchanging amidst changing, permanent amidst impermanent, and imperishable amidst the perishables. Brahmn according to Swami Sivanand, is beyond the reach of common human mind and senses, and hence, its existence cannot be proved by experimentation. Nevertheless, its existence can be realized through experience. Swami Sivanand further asserts and confronts the atheists, who want the conclusive proof of the existence of the Brahmn, by telling them that nobody can equally give the conclusive proof of the non-existence of the Brahmn.

It needs to be realized here that 'Neti, Neti', the so-called negative description ascribed to the Brahmn is only in the epistemological (providing proof of God) sense, as ascribing any qualification to Brahmn would be going against the very concept of Brahmn enunciated by the Advait School of Vedantic thought because any attempt to describe any 'attributeless' Brahmn is notional and it reveals the limitations of human sensibilities to even conceptualize anything which defies any human experience.

Brahmn in the Vedantic school of philosophy is perceived into three levels of abstraction. The Supreme Reality, known as pure consciousness, the Absolute, the one without attributes and forms is **Nirguna, Nirakar Brahmn** who is infinite. Next stage is that of **Sagun Nirakara Brahmn** – the One who is equipped with attributes but is formless. The third stage is that of **Saguna Saakar Brahmn** having both form and attributes. The three stages may be related to the three corresponding philosophical perceptions of non-duality, qualified non-duality, and duality. Understandably the devotees find it easier to comprehend and worship the Brahmn called God with both form and attributes.

The Upanishads or Vedantic genres coming at the end of the Vedas, as commentaries and interpretations, contain a unified exposition of the Vedantic concepts of the Hindu philosophy. Their philosophical optimisms have been systematized into 'Brahmn Sutras' or the 'Vedanta Sutras', and later expanded and explained by many sages and spiritual philosophers. Three leading Hindu philosophers, Adi Shankaracharya, Sri Ramanucharya and Sri Madhavacharya gave their philosophical perceptions. Accordingly the three schools of philosophy are called Advaita (Monism or non-dualism), Visishadavaita (Theistic or qualified monism or non-dualism) and Dvaita (Dualism) are identified with these three spiritual philosophers namely, Shankaracharya, Ramanucharya and Madhavacharya respectively. Though differing in terms of their metaphysical aspects, the underlying principle in all the three philosophical thoughts is one and the same: that, the phenomenal universe is the eternal reality that cannot be perceived by the human senses or cognized by the human mind; that Brahmn exists within and beyond everything, while the easiest place to find it is within oneself; that the individual self is one with the Universal Self; and that Brahmn is the cause of the Universe. In other words, the same principle of Atman is present in all beings and it is called Divinity. The Divine incarnations such as Rama, Krishna and Sri Sathya Sai can be recognized by their divine human forms.

According to Adi Shankaracharya, existence of the individual soul has no meaning. Only Brahmn exists since Brahmn as space in a pot is identical with the infinite space outside it. When the pot is broken, the inner space within the pot is same as the space outside the pot. Thus an individual soul is same as the Universal Soul called the Brahmn. According to the non-dualism (Advaita) view advocated by Adi Shankaracharya, Brahmn is the ground source of the universe. Everything emerges from it and merges back in it. It is existence-consciousness-bliss (Satcchidanand). It is the greatest goal realized by the realized souls. The self is not different from the Brahmn. The Brahmn is attributeless and formless (Nirguna Brahmn).

According to the other spiritual philosopher Sri Ramanujam known for qualified non-dualism, Isvara, the Sagun Brahmn (Brahmn with attributes) is the ultimate reality of Nirguna Brahmn as the latter cannot be known by any means, be it, perception, inference or scripture. Sagun Brahmn is called the God: the Truth (Satyam), the Consciousness (Jnanam) and the Infinite (Anantham). There are three realities *viz.* God or Isvara, (The Sagun Brahmn), the individual soul and the material world *i.e.* Paramatman, Praani and Prakriti (creator, creatures and creation). The individual soul and the material world constitute the body of Ishvara. Consciousness, according to Ramanujam, is an act of cognizing the object by the subject. It is neither a subject itself nor an object itself. It is not even a witness. It is an inseparable quality and not a substance. Consciousness is not created. It is continuous and eternal. It is inseparable from the subject in all its cognitive activities. Knowledge of the self is a stepping stone for reaching the final unification of Atman and Parmatman. According to Sri Ramanujacharya, an individual soul exists eternally as a spark of Brahmn and it is a part of the Brahmn. At the time of creation, the individual soul emerges from the Brahmn and at the end of the cycle of births and deaths, it merges back into Brahmn. This union does not seem to be same as the complete resemblance of the individual soul with the Universal Soul as in the case of monism. Since the emphasis is on the union of individual soul with the universal soul, therefore, some degree of individuality remains before the unison.

Sri Madhavacharya, another evolved philosopher and commentator of the Vedanta, believes in the dualism in the sense that he treats Brahmn as separate from the individual souls as independent entities existing as such. There is no mergence or union of the individual soul with the Brahmn. According to him, Brahmn is the ruler of the individual souls as He is the divine power who creates, sustains, and dissolves, then creates again, periodically through eternity. Thus, whatever be the truth about these differing philosophical thoughts, the basic essence of the Vedanta is that Brahmn, the sole Supreme Reality, exists eternally – without beginning and end. The Universe, irrespective of the level of degree of its reality, has been caused by Brahmn. It is the vesture of the Brahmn. A comprehensive enunciation of the Supreme Reality or the Brahmn and its manifestation, namely the Universe is the purpose of discussion in this section.

Sri Adi Shankaracharya – known for revival of Vedantic philosophy, brought into it a more rationalistic and logical approach. He extracted the truths of Vedas and put them in a systematic and systemic form. By unifying the numerous descriptions of Brahmn, Shankaracharya showed that there is one and only one Supreme, Noumenal Absolute Reality who, with His supreme divine and phenomenal power called Maya as the instrument, created the whole universe suffused with its entities that are both in animated and inanimated forms and which are its evolutes like the components and parts of a body. Maya is the innate, eternal and un-definable universe-manifesting power of the Supreme Brahmn which works spontaneously through its twin aspects, namely the projecting and veiling aspects. It is the Maya that evolves the universe within the framework of Space-Time-Causation through its projective aspect leading to the creation of the Universe – called the visible phenomenon of God while its veiling aspect represents the invisible power of God. Brahmn is the ultimate being, which is neither male nor female, neither good nor bad, nor gold nor silver but the moment it takes the form, this form is Maya or Illusion or the feminine aspect of Brahmn. Whole creations including all the suns, planets and universes, all the five elements earth, water, fire, air and ether have emerged from the Golden Womb or Hiranyagarbha – the first eternal womb form which is self-pervading and engulfing everything.

Shankaracharya's philosophical view is based on three levels of Reality or Truth: the **Highest Truth** as it is in itself what he termed as the **Absolute Reality** – the Brahmn, the Noumenal Supreme; the **Manifested Reality (Truth)** in the form of the phenomenal universe – the foundation of all material/worldly relations, thoughts and activities; and the **Empirical Realty,** the entity which represents the substratum of the phenomenal universe. The three levels of Reality are true at the same time in their own spheres without contradicting each other. Shankaracharya further postulates that the Supreme Reality – the impersonal Brahmn appears as the personal God (Ishwara), the Creator and Lord of the Universe. Rather it is the same Reality which is manifesting as God – the creator, living beings – the creatures and universe – the creation. The only difference is that the Brahmn is the Absolute, Supreme and Noumenal Reality, whereas the other two entities namely the universe and the beings are relative and phenomenal realities.

Thus, the first level of Reality is the absolute unchanging Reality, unaffected by the three divisions of time – past, present and future – and always the same. An entity according to the spiritualists is said to be Absolute Reality if it is not subject to any change. Even if an entity undergoes a conditional change, it cannot be termed as absolutely real. An unchanging reality is what is called an Absolute Reality or Absolute Existence. Such a reality is designated in the Upanishads as the **Supreme Reality** – The **Brahmn**. It is realized as the pure self within every being – the unchanging witness of all changes, and is experienced at Noumenal level.

Second level is the continuously changing dynamic reality which is termed as the **Universe** and which is experienced at the phenomenal level. It is this reality, also called 'Relative Reality', in which the empirical persons live and act, philosophize and realize values. Such a reality has only conditioned phenomenon or empirical reality or phenomenal reality of day and night on the earth. The individual souls – the living beings which, like the reflections of the sun in water, are reflections of the Supreme Reality (Brahmn) as embodiments of the psycho-physical organisms. These individual and embodied souls have bondage and liberation from the phenomenal point of view but the real Inner Self (Inner Dweller) in all beings, being Brahmn itself, is the foundation of the universe, is even pure, free, perfect and eternal, like the sun, which is ever luminous and has no day or night for itself, though it is the cause of day and night on the earth.

The third reality, according to Shankaracharya, is the apparent reality like the mirage which is experienced and is mistaken for water, but is not amenable to activity as water. Such apparent objects do not have even the empirical reality but can cause fear and trouble due to delusion or mistaken notions. However, according to some spiritualists, the universe, being an ever changing flow as the function of time, cannot be dismissed as unreal like the mirage, because living beings exist, act and move in their empirical personalities. They experience and conduct all their activities.

All entities in the universe are related to each other as conditioned realities and have their mutual relative validity as long as they last. Change is the very essence of the universe. It is dynamic and continuously moving and changing. The changing universe of names, forms and perceptions draws its reality from the unchanging Absolute or Brahmn. It owes its existence to the Supreme Reality – Brahmn, who transcendents time, space and causation which are the aspects of Maya-power – the instrument of the manifestation of the universe. It is in this sense that the universe is the Relative or Phenomenal Reality when compared to Brahmn – the Absolute Reality. Thus, the Ultimate/ Supreme Reality is the non-dual indivisible and invisible Brahmn, and from that whole, the universe has emerged through its inscrutable power called Maya – the twin principle of projection and veiling. In relation to the universe and the living beings, Brahmn associated with its Maya-Power is God (Ishwara), the Creator and Lord of the Universe. Thus, infact this Brahmn, seen from the phenomenal point of view is the triad of God-Soul-Universe (Ishwara (Jagdish)–Jeev–Jagat) and will always appear to be so.

Postulating the above as the fundamental axiom, Shankaracharya conceptualized that the **Absolute Reality,** being non-dual and the origin of everything, is pure and beyond the reach of the words and thoughts. It is attributeless ('Nirguna'). It is, indeed, the Inner-Self ('Pratayksh – Atman') of all, the eternal being. It is self-cognized within phenomena;

it is intuitively cognized directly and intimately as the Pure Witness-Self ('Sakshi') within, by all beings. It is the origin and source of all objective experiences, internal or external, on the phenomenal plane, just as one is aware of one's eyes without seeing them, for they enable one to see all things and beings but one's own eyes. This is what is known as the noumenal point of view. All the phenomenal attributes are the products of **Relative Reality** or **Nature** ('Prakriti') or **Maya** which comprises of three Attributes (Trigunatimika – Satva, Rajas, Tamas). Since Brahmn is the absolute Reality, it remains untouched and unaffected by the attributes (gunas) of Maya and their products. It is Nirguna, in this sense. Related to Brahmn – the Absolute Reality, the Absolute Infinite Truth – Consciousness – Bliss (Sachitanand), arises this mysterious and variegated universe of time-space-causation which is known as the **Relative Reality** and is postulated as Maya – the power of Brahmn or the Universe. **Since the universe, its entities and its beings (psycho-physical organisms) are within the framework of time, space and causation, therefore they are all finite as compared to the Brahmn who is infinite, limitless and boundless**. Hence, they are all only relative and derive their features and characteristics from Brahmn – their foundation and source. They all together constitute what is termed as Maya. In short, **Brahmn is the absolute reality** and its **Maya is the relative reality**.

The Absolute Brahmn, thus causally associated with the totality of the relative universe (Maya) is known as the **'Isvara'**, the God – the ruler of the universe and its beings. The variegated universe is diversified by time, space and causation perfected by Maya – the Relative Reality or Phenomenal Reality. Maya is conceptualized as having two aspects namely veiling power ('Avarana-Shakti') and projecting or manifolding power (Vikshepa Shakti). Such a perception of Maya has been enunciated in the Vedas. Maya, according to Adi Shankaracharya, is the innate or natural, eternal and inseparable power of Brahmn, while Brahmn remains unaffected by its own power of Maya and its manifestated universe, just as fire is not affected by its own innate burning power and its radiation. The universe was not created at any particular time. It is beginning-less and is eternally manifesting itself to external observers, who are themselves part of the universe, just as there is no beginning for the burning power of fire and the shining characteristic of light which are cognized only by experiences external to them. The burning power of the fire, the shinning characteristic of light, and the projection of the Universe by Maya are designed activities but look to be spontaneous, innate and natural acts.

The universe, being within time-space-causation phenomenon, is witnessed by the unchanging Self as continuously changing, like a flow or process of time, subject to modification, permutation and combination, and activity. The phenomenal universe (Maya) consists of the permutations and combinations of five basic elements (air, fire, water, ether, earth), organic structures or bodies, life, senses, mind etc. The living beings (creatures) are endowed with all evolutionary manifestations of the Maya-power who derive their consciousness and revealing power from the Self (Atman). A human being who appears as the empirical soul (living being – Jiva) equipped with psycho-physical feature called intelligence identified by body, senses, mind, desire etc. is called the empirical person (human being) – the thinker, experiencer and doer in the universe. This empirical person – called a human being, undertakes various types of activities to satisfy his desires and goes through joys and sorrows, knowledge and ignorance, birth and rebirth etc. according to his deeds. This eventually becomes his bondage ('bandhan 'or 'sanskar'). In due course of time, this empirical/bodied person becomes aware of the Supreme Self (Atman) within him. Gradually, through sadhana, good deeds, purification of his intellect, sense-control and various other ways, he is able to feel the grace of God from within since 'Isvara' – the Paramatman (Supreme Self) is the Atman (Self) WITHIN HIM AND WITHIN ALL. The person gives up desires, attachment, ego etc., and the Supreme Self reveals itself to him. It is only then, this empirical/embodied person realizes that the Self is the Source of his very existence, life and experience. With this realization and identification with the Self, the empirical human personality dissolves and the soul (jiva), which was only the reflection of the Supreme Self (Atman) encased in the limited frame, disappears and merges into the Supreme Self. This is termed as liberation (Mukti), realizing the identity of the Self with the Absolute, while the game of the Universe continues for other living beings (jives).

A few relevant questions arise in this context: **What is this divine phenomenon? Why does the universe arise and Brahmn appears as God ('Ishwara')?** Both the questions are related to Brahmn, which is beyond words and thought, beyond time, space and causation, and which is Absolute and infinite. The existence of Brahmn as the Absolute Reality has to be believed and accepted as an axiom so that the relative reality – an infinite power of Brahmn known as Maya can be understood. It is this postulated principle which by nature is relative, that is to say that Maya is a fact from empirical (observation) point of view, which is experienced and seen in effect. Maya, however, is not Maya for Brahmn, just as fire is not hot to itself. Maya is an off-shot of

Brahmn and not vice-versa. Maya is a creation of Brahmn and not the other way *i.e.* Brahmn is not the creation of Maya. Maya really does not exist as an independent entity. Its existence is relative to the existence of Brahmn. One may, therefore, assume the existence of Brahmn, as the Absolute Reality and describe Maya, the Relative Reality, as Brahmn's innate, natural, inseparable and spontaneous power of appearing as many, appearing as the universe with its beings. Just as waves are integral to ocean though one may speak of the ocean and its waves as if both are separate and independent of each other. Waves are due to the ocean, and not that ocean is due to the waves. Waves are a relative reality whereas ocean is an absolute reality. Thus, **Brahmn is Absolute Infinite, Truth-Consciousness-Bliss (Sat-Chit-Anand) from the noumenal point of view, whereas Maya is the Relative Reality conceived from phenomenal point of view comprising of Sattva – Rajas – Tamas.**

It is impossible to investigate the nature of the whole universe in detail though the astro-physicists have been busy in theorizing it in their own way. It is, however, a well-known and realized fact that the **universe is an experiential object** (Maya) **distinct from experiencing the subject** (Brahmn) **and can have its meaning only in relation to Brahmn**. Spiritualists realize that behind all what is happening in the universe including the universe itself is the same Brahmn, philosophically designated as the Pure Self (Atman). The trigunatmika Maya has two fundamental aspects namely the **Veiling Power** and the **Projecting Power**. In other words, Maya projects the universe and its components by covering up the Absolute Reality (Brahmn) by the veil of the three traits (gunas); Sattva – Rajas – Tamas. Accordingly, the phenomenal universe as a whole is supposed to have emerged from the Absolute Brahmn effortlessly and spontaneously. Brahmn, being the Supreme Reality and Truth, nothing that emerges from it can be obnoxious, haphazard, or irrational. When Brahmn is looked upon as God (Ishwara), the projection of the Universe is His sportive play (Lila) being played through His power of Maya. As said earlier, Maya is the eternal inseparable power of Brahmn. The issue, however, is not the establishment of the reality of the Universe but to find out its true nature, the nature of Reality, and the real nature of the Brahmn – designated as the Pure Self.

According to the Upanishads, 'Brahmn' and individual soul (Atma) are same. What is true of 'Brahmn' is also true of 'Atma'. The Upanishads further declare that the knower of 'Brahmn' becomes 'Brahmn' Himself, that everything and everywhere is all 'Brahmn', and that the realization of the Atma (Atma-Vidya) is Brahmn. This is the central theme of the Upanishads. According to the spiritual scholars, everything revolves around this theme. Brahmn or Atman is considered to be the Absolute, Existence (Truth) – Knowledge – Infinite (Satyam – Gyanam – Anatham Brahmn). Being infinite, it is the nature of Absolute Bliss (Anandam) as well. Often Consciousness ('Chit') is used in place of knowledge (Gyanam) and thus 'Brahmn' is generally referred to as Sat-Chit-Ananda or "**Satchidanand**'. Thus, transcendentally Brahmn and Atma are identical. But empirically, Brahmn using Maya as His power, is viewed as God (Ishwara) while Atma is conceived of as the 'living being' (jiva), the individual soul associated with the body and is the actor as well as the experiencer in the universe. God (Ishwar) is the inner controller of the universe and is looked upon as the Super-Soul (Parmatman) with the individual soul (Jivatmna) as its part. The Infinite Absolute Brahmn is always the substratum of all names and forms, giving them substance and reality. The names and forms of the living beings are only appearances of the Reality without any independent existential reality. Further, Maya is experienced only just like a dream. The Infinite or the Absolute Reality does not feel the absence of finite or the relative reality; it is the finite and the relative reality which experiences the presence of the Infinite and the Absolute Reality. Thus, from transcendental point of view, Maya ceases to exist for the realized while from the empirical point of view, it is experienced.

Faith and logic are the two options for accepting the existence of reality at different levels. Faith leaves aside logic. It does not bother about rationality and scientific evidence. It simply accepts as the ultimate truth that there is an eternal 'real entity' the 'Brahmn' the Absolute Reality – the infinite unchanging God which manifests as the universe and the beings either as His real eternal parts or as separate entities. Such an assumption or faith makes the things easier and more beautiful. But, then there is a community of people, which includes rationalists and scientists among others, for whom it is not a philosophy of truth but popular theology. In several respectable and rational philosophies like Marxism, even a personal God is not acceptable and several types of arguments are emphasized against the existence of such a God. Even where God is accepted, the perceptions of God and His relationship with the universe and its beings are found debatable. Faith, however, is a sentimental preference while some have a conditional belief in the objective vision of God. Brahmn, however, as the Self, is within the constant infinitive experience of all, and, therefore, cannot be philosophically denied. Faith, however, generates an irrefutable place for God, since God is nothing but Brahmn glued with Maya as viewed from the empirical plane.

Is it, then, justified to deny the reality of God and only accept the universe as 'Real'? It simply means accepting the Relative Reality while rejecting the Absolute Reality. It would amount to accepting the relative reality of day and night while denying absolute reality of the existence of the sun. The experience of day and night, winter and summer, cold and heat is true for all. If one rises high up in the sky just as space travellers do, one shall realize that day and night are experiences conditioned by the movement of the earth. The sun neither rises nor sets; the sun is neither hidden nor loses its brilliance. These are relative views from the earth, and yet the sun is absolutely necessary for all the phenomenon to occur. It is actually conditioning of the earth that makes days and nights for the world. Similarly, it is conditioning of Maya that makes the Absolute Reality (Brahmn) appear as creator – creatures – creation to the people as empirical being. But, then again a doubt may arise: **Is not the absolute reality of oneness of Brahmn vitiated by positioning another entity called Maya**? No, it is not since Maya itself is an inseparable power of Brahmn. It is not different from Brahmn but a part of it.

The Absolute Brahmn in the transcendental sense is called 'Nirguna' Brahmn *i.e.* the Brahmn as it is, without the phenomenal adjuncts and attributes. Nirguna Brahmn is also designated as Para-Brahmn while Sagun Brahmn is designated as Apara-Brahmn which does not signify higher or lower, as is mistakenly viewed by some, for they are not different, neither they are two separate realities but the same reality – viewed in its transcendental and empirical aspects respectively. It is not that Brahmn has been diluted to become God. The distinction lies in the perception. The Absolute Infinite Brahmn is beyond the reach of any thought or conceptualization, while God, the Sagun Brahmn, is the supreme or highest concept, the phenomenon aspect of the Absolute Reality (Nirgun Brahmn). Such a conceptualization makes Brahmn appears comprehensible just as the sun.

From the relative point of view, Brahmn is conceptualized as personal God who possesses Maya as His active Power (Shakti), under His control, and is, therefore, sometimes referred to as 'Mayadhish'. With Maya as His power, the Brahmn projects the universe through its (Maya). It is immanent (inherent) in the universe as God (Ishwara), and transcendent. God creates and controls the universe from within (Antaryamin) as its Soul. As long as one has attachment to one's personality as body, the Relative Reality as God (Ishwara) is more relevant to him than the Absolute Reality as Brahmn. One can approach God (Ishwara) through various ways *viz.*, Love, Service etc. and receive His grace. Absolute Brahmn can be realized through the grace of God since Brahmn alone appears as God. Hence devotion to God is advocated even for those who wish to realize the Absolute Brahmn. **"God in His absolute state, says Swami Chidbhavananda, is beyond the ken of mind and speech. He is indefinable. But when He is immanent in the universe, He is depicted as Sat – Chit – Aanandam (Existence – Knowledge – Bliss). There is no other connotation which is as appropriate as this".**

God (Ishwar) as Sagun Brahmn with the whole universe projected by its Maya power, and the creatures (Jivas) as individualized psycho-physical organisms (living beings) as parts of the universe, are inter-related phenomenally as whole and part. The basis and substance of the universe is also nothing but Brahmn. The pure Absolute Brahmn appears as this triad of **Creator – Creatures – Creation** (Ishwar or Jagdish – Jiva – Jagat) or (Parmatman – Praani – Prakriti) in the phenomenal state, while remaining as Absolute Reality in the noumenal sense. It is this triad, which appears as the three sides of the triangle of empirical existence – the Relative Reality – that are interlinked and always go together. According to Adi Shankaracharya, it is immaterial whether Ishwara (God) is interpreted as Brahmn or Brahmn is considered as God. In the Upanishadic sense, the terms Brahmn and God are not two separate entities (Realities) and are used interchangeably, just Brahmn and Atma are used interchangeably in various holy scriptures. One is neither superior or inferior nor higher or lower than the other. Both are same beyond Maya and beyond time, space and causation. They are the transcendental (para) and relative (apara) views of the same Reality. From the transcendent point of view, the Absolute Reality (Brahmn) appears as the Creator (Paramatman), the self of the universe, and as the Atman, the self of the creatures (living beings – praani) who are a part of the universe. From the relative point of view, this Absolute Reality is considered as the Lord and Soul of the Universe (God-Ishwara), and the living beings as the lord and soul of the material body (jiva – praani). **The living being stripped of its individual conditioning, and the God (Ishwara) stripped of the cosmic conditioning, do not differ from each other as regards their essence.**

If Maya is the source of all manifested existence, Ishwara is the universal witness who assists in unfolding of the Cosmos. Maya is the power (Shakti) inherent in God (Ishwara), and it is by virtue of this power that this objective and material world exists with variety of names and forms. The two powers that characterize Maya, the power of concealing (Avarana Shakti) and the power of projection (Vikshepa Shakti), are with respect to the jiva, fully active, whereas with respect to the Ishwara, who is free from all tamas (darkness), only the power of projection is being exercised. Ishwara remains beyond the influence of Maya while jiva believes in the multiplicity of Maya and remains wrapped in it. The jiva takes the material world as real while Ishwara, on the other hand, identifies Himself with the Totality of the Universe.

Madhavacharya – the chief exponent of the duality school of Vedanta had a firm conviction in the basic distinction between God and the individual soul. He glorified this distinction not only between God and Soul, but also differentiated between soul and soul, between soul and matter, between God and matter and even between matter and matter. He strongly believed in the distinction between Infinite – the Brahmn, and the finite, with Brahmn being the source of all reality, consciousness and activity. Existence, according to Madhavacharya, is a test of reality. It is a way of realizing the distinction between the real and unreal. Bondage in the world and liberation from it is also real. It is only through devotion to God that can help the individual to find the way to liberation since the divine grace is one fundamental requirement for salvation. Madhavacharya also believed that evil is also creation of God just as virtue is a boon of God. **God is eternally separate from nature, eternally separate from the human soul. God is eternal; nature is eternal; so are the souls. Nature and the souls manifest and change, but God remains the same.** According to the dualists, again this God is personal, in the sense that He has qualities. He has human attributes. He is merciful, He is just, He is powerful, He is almighty, He can be approached, He can be prayed to, He can be loved, He loves in return, and so forth. In one word, **He is a human God, only infinitely greater than others**; He has none of the evil tendencies which a human being has. Nature is the material out of which God creates the whole world.

All the codified religions of the world are dualistic. They have to be so because the ordinary man cannot think of anything which is abstract. Human beings naturally like to cling to that which their intellect can grasp. They believe in a God who is entirely separate from them, a great king, high, mighty monarch as it were. At the same time they consider Him purer than the monarchs of the earth; they attribute to Him all good qualities and remove the evil qualities from Him – as if it were ever possible for good to exist without evil; as if there could be any conception of light without a conception of darkness!

With all dualistic theories the first difficulty is: **How is it possible that, under the rule of a just and merciful God, there can be so many evils and sins in this world**? This question arises in all dualistic religions; but the Hindus never invented a Satan as an answer to it. Sri Madhavacharya, for example, conceives Ishwara as the Supreme Being (Person), 'Purushottama' with the whole universe as His body, made of pure subtle substance, the individual souls (jives) as His inseparable components, like rays of the sun. For Him, God is the Supreme Soul (Parmatmana) of the entire universe, and its beings – the central sun immanent in the universe-body. For the embodied person, the Supreme Soul may appear transcendent. This version of the dualist view is considered to be valid empirically for the purpose of love and worship, as it is the relative view of the same Absolute Brahmn.

Generally, the Vedanta philosophy begins with the views of those who are known as the qualified non-dualists, Ramanuja being their chief exponent. They make the statement that the effect is never different from the cause; the effect is but the cause reproduced in another form. If the universe is the effect and God the cause, it must be God himself – it cannot be anything but that. They start with the assertion that God is both the efficient effect and the material cause of the universe; that He Himself is the Creator, and He Himself is the Creation. The word 'creation' in the West, is regarded as something coming out of nothing. What is meant by creation in the Hindu philosophy, is projection of that which already exists. The whole universe, according to this view, is God himself. He is the material of the universe. 'As the spider spins the thread out of its own body, likewise the whole universe has come out of that Being'. If the effect is the cause reproduced, the question is: **How is it that this material universe, which is not fully intelligent and perfect, is produced from God, who is not material, but who is considered to be totally perfect, who is eternal intelligence? How, if the cause is pure and perfect, can the effect be quite different? What do these qualified non-dualists say**? They say that the triad – God, nature, and the soul are one. God is, as it were, the super soul, and nature and souls are the body of God. Just as a human being has a body and has a soul, so the whole universe and all individual souls are the body of God, and God is the Soul of all individual souls. Thus, God is the material cause of the universe. The body may be changed – may be young or old, strong or weak – but that does not affect the soul at all. It is the same eternal existence, manifesting through the body. Bodies come and go, but the soul does not change. Even so, the whole universe is the body of God, and in that sense it is God. But the changes in the universe does not affect God.

Both dualists and qualified non-dualists admit that the soul is by its nature pure, but through its own deeds it becomes impure. The qualified non-dualists express it more beautifully than the dualists, by saying that the soul's purity and perfection become contracted and again become manifest, and that what they are now trying to do is to remanifest the intelligence, the purity, the power which is natural to the soul. Every wicked deed contracts the nature of the soul, and every good deed expands it; and these souls are all parts of God. 'As from a blazing fire fly millions of sparks of the same nature, even so from this infinite being, God, these souls have come'. Each has the same goal. The God of the qualified non-dualists is also a personal God, only He is interpenetrating everything in the universe. God is immanent in everything and is everywhere, and when the scriptures say that God is everything, it means that God is interpenetrating everything. There is not a particle, not even an atom in the universe, where He is not. Souls are all limited; they are not omnipresent. When they get expansion of their powers and become perfect, there is no more birth and death for them; they live with God for ever.

Non-duality, the Advaitism, is considered to be the fairest flower of philosophy, where human thought attains its highest expression, and even goes beyond the mystery which seems to be impenetrable. However, the non-dualistic Vedanta is too abstruse and too elevated to be the religion of the masses. Even in India, its birth-place, where it has been reigning supreme for millions of years, it has not been able to permeate the masses. Indeed it is difficult for even the most spiritually evolved persons to understand Advaitism. According to the non-dualist, if there is a God, that God must be both the material and the efficient cause of the universe. Not only is He the Creator, but He is also the created. He Himself is this universe. The non-dualists believe that there is but one Existence, the infinite, the Absolute One. In that Existence people dream all the various dreams. It is the Atman beyond all, the infinite, beyond the known, beyond the knowable; in and through that they see the universe. It is the only reality. The Vedantist does not call it either he or she – these are fictions, delusions of the human brain. Everyone and everything is the Atman, the Self-formless, pure and ever graceful. It is the name, the form, the body, which are material, and they make all this difference. If these two differences of name and form are taken away, the whole universe looks to be same and one; there are not two, but one everywhere. There is neither nature nor the universe – only that one Infinite Existence which is the Supreme Reality – the Brahmn.

Reality is also described by various other forms and names: physical, mental, psychological, socialistic and scientific realities. But all these realities are changeable, relative, bound by time and space. What is that reality, which is Absolute or Ultimate or Supreme? This question is essentially concerned with the Spiritual Reality or the Supreme Truth in the sense of spirituality. Vedas call it Brahmn. Can Brahmn be ever defined, known or understood or realized? The central focus of all the six Hindu philosophical systems, described in Chapter 3 of this book, is to answer this fundamental question and explore the nature of creatures, creation and the creator (Praani, Prakriti and Parmatma).

Brahmn, as described in the Vedas, as the one and only one that presents itself as the Absolute Reality or the Supreme Reality – one who without a second, is eternal, omni-present, omni-potent and omni-scient, one who is described as pure Truth-Intelligence-Bliss or Truth-Awareness (Consciousness)-Bliss (Sat-Chit-Anand *i.e.* Satchitanand), who is all pervasive, who is the basis of the whole universe, its all forms and names, all beings both sentient and non-sentient, and who is infinite and pure. Although He is considered to be unknowable in general, yet can become knowable when ignorance is dispelled and illumined by the knowledge of Vedic dictum such as "I myself am Brahmn" (Aham Brahmasmi). In this way, Absolute Reality Brahmn presents itself as one's pure and infinite self. Thus, just as the lamp illumines the objects surrounding it, it is through certain pursuits described in the Vedas such as pure action (Punya-Karma), spiritual wisdom (Brahmn Gyan) and true devotion (Sat-Bhakti) and others, one can realize and hence know this Supreme Reality (Brahmn). Such a process of knowledge of the Brahmn that 'I myself am the Absolute Reality' ("Aham Brahmnsmi") removes the veil of darkness or ignorance or what is termed as nescience or illusion or delusion ('Maya') is called enlightenment. Indeed, a pure mind and an abiding quest for knowing this Absolute Reality is needed and this Absolute Reality presents itself as seeker's own pure and infinite Self. This Vedic method of knowing Brahmn or God is neither a privilege of any particular community nor is bound by any boundary nor even limited to a particular place of worship, temple, church or mosque nor hidden in the sky, beyond earth, mountains or deep below the oceans. The Hindu sages and seers have declared that even the knower of the Brahmn becomes Brahmn himself. The ultimate aim of divine knowledge is experience of the realization of the supreme truth, infinite consciousness and highest bliss. This knowledge leads to God-realization; hence each living soul is qualified or entitled to achieve the absolute truth *i.e.* invent Godhood or God for himself or herself.

The essence of Shankaracharya's philosophical perception of monism or non-dualism is that Brahmn – the Absolute Reality is the one and only one Reality. The universe and individual souls are manifestations of that Unique Reality. This philosophy of monism or non-duality (Advaita) enunciates the unity of the whole existence *i.e.* God, universe and the individual souls.

One afternoon at Varanasi – a sacred city in North India, Adi Shankaracharya, after taking a bath in the Ganga was proceeding towards the temple for his routine prayers when he saw a man approaching him from the opposite side while brooming the street. In accordance with the then prevalent social practice, although evil and totally irrational, Shankara who preached oneness in all living beings, told the man to get aside and move away so that he (Shankara) could pass though the passage. The man asked Shankara, "**By asking me to move away, are you trying to separate matter from matter or soul from the soul? You have enunciated the philosophy of monism by saying that the absolute Brahmn is everywhere and in everything – in you and in me, and yet you want me to get away from you as if I were different from you. Is it this body not built up of matter that you want to separate from that body of yours which is also built up of matter? Or do you wish to separate pure awareness *i.e.* the soul which is present here in my body from the same awareness *i.e.* the soul present there in your body? Moreover, does it make any difference to the sun that is reflected in the pure waters of the Ganga or in the impure waters of this drain of the street? Is there any difference in the space as such, be it in golden pot or in a mud pot? In the self-existing ocean of blissful consciousness, in the inner-self, where there are no waves of agitating thoughts, how can there be this great delusionary distinction – men and men**?" Struck by these words of the man, Shankaracharya got awakened and realized that the man had taught him, his own philosophy of the non-duality of the One Infinite Self, who exists everywhere and in everything. Shankara got fully convinced that the man (incarnation of Shiva) was his real Guru (Preceptor) who made him see the one and the same Infinite Consciousness which illumines all experiences during the waking, dream and deep-sleep states, that is the sole witness of the entire existence and activity of the Universe and which is the very life-spark in all life forms.

Brahmn is where the mind dissolves. He is the one. He is Virupaksha – one who is formless yet He sees all. Just as people know that there is air all around them; they can feel it. But what if the air also starts feeling the people? Space is around everybody. Everyone feels and identifies space. But what if space also identifies and has feel of everybody? Scientists call this phenomenon as theory of relativity. The one who sees and that which is seen are both affected when mutually seen. The formless Divine – Brahmn is all around and is seeing everything. He is the seer, the object of sight and the scene. The one without beginning and end is Brahmn. He is present everywhere, always. He is eternal. He is the fourth state of consciousness, the Turiya state, the state of deep meditation, that is beyond the waking, deep sleep and dream states.

According to another school of thought, everything in the universe is a manifestation of some cause behind it. Cosmic evolution is also a manifestation caused by the existence of the Cosmic God who Himself is not caused by anything prior to Him because God is timeless eternity. The precision and methodology, with which the Universe is seen to be working with its solar systems and galaxies, can only be the work of a Grand Architect who designs and shapes this perfectly ordered system of working of the Universe. His existence should, therefore, be also seen like His artistic workings of Nature as a whole. Such an Architect is named as God. Plato's foundational thought, centred around a Universal Idea, directly corresponds to the Vedantic view of the Brahmn with its urge as the Creative Hiranyagarbha, and its Universal-Soul as the Virat depicted as in the Upanishads. Plato's realism is the same as the all pervading God (Ishwara) standing above the created beings. Same analogy applies to Aristotle's doctrine of the evolution of the soul of the matter into its Perfect Form. This is somewhat not dissimilar to Shankaracharya's concept of Absolute Reality and Relative Reality. It further characterizes the interconnectedness of the Noumenon as the Phenomenon in Kant's view from which Hegel raises his structure of the Absolute and the Relative.

Descriptions and explanations given in the scriptures of every religion speak of God creating the universe out of His own Will not because He developed a desire but because of His instinctive Nature automatically operating, as the sun shedding light without any desire to do the work of shining. God creating the Universe does not imply an action or work done by some human being. It is wrong to personify God and assume God as one large human being thinking and working literary like human beings. God is believed to be timeless being, and no action is conceivable where time is absent. The scriptures simply clarify the philosophical descriptions of the origin of the creation of the universe which arises due to an inborn belief that the creation must have an origin, and hence must have a creator. This is a hypothesis which cannot itself be explained by any rational process of investigation. Indeed, any question regarding the creation by God would fundamentally lack scientific basis. The infinity and the omni-presence of God, which is accepted by everyone, precludes the possibility of a Universe without God.

Not long ago, science used to claim that the universe consisted of distinct and different elements of matter. But later, it proved that they were not really different from each other and were infact, characterized by the underlying same energy or 'Shakti'. Earlier, science enunciated that matter could be converted into energy and energy into matter. Latest scientific view is that matter and energy are no longer different from each other. Shankaracharya's monism proclaims the same view but put in the philosophical language, it says that Brahmn is the only Absolute true source of all beings whether matter or energy while the universe being its relative reality. The scientists (Astrophysicists) also maintain that there is nothing absolute in the characteristics of the universe. It is all relative. Spiritual scholars of the theory of non-duality, however, strongly believe that Brahmn is perfect, complete and absolute. Despite the vast physical universe has been formed from the Brahmn, yet the Brahmn continues to be the same infinite and absolute. How is this possible? How can an entity remain same even when a part of it has been taken out of it or subtracted from it? The reason being that when a finite is taken out of an infinity, then the remainder is always an infinite entity. For example, consider the counting numbers 1, 2, 3, 4, 5, 6, ..., which are obviously infinite. When a finite number of elements say 1, 2, 3 are taken out, the remainders are the natural numbers 4, 5, 6, ...which remain as infinite entity.

Also in the philosophical context, the infinite looking Universe has not come out of the infinite Brahmn. It is simply a case of the infinite Brahmn appearing to the senses as the Universe. The Brahmn did not create the Universe, neither did it transform itself into the Universe. It just looks like the Universe due to the illusion (Maya) – "**What appears to be what is not**". In other words, the infinite looking Universe is the appearance of the infinite Brahmn. In the mathematical language, it can be interpreted by saying that the infinite looking Universe is the image of the infinite Brahmn under the rule of some abstract mapping. As said earlier, Dualism (Dvaita), the philosophical system evolved by Sri Madhavacharya, however, makes a distinction between the Brahmn and the Universe by treating them as separate entities, the independent real and the dependent real respectively. Sri Madhavacharya strongly believes that the formless aspect of the Brahmn is different from the

Universe – its manifested form. The formless aspect or the unmanifested aspect of the Brahmn is beyond the human comprehension. It is only the realization or experiential aspect of the Brahmn which is possible to attain, (though that too is not easy), by means of the paradigms of meditation, action, knowledge and devotion, as prescribed in the Vedas, the Upanishads, which together constitute the summary conclusion at the end of Vedas, and hence also called the 'Vedantas', and later repostulated in the Geeta. Vedic philosophers indeed arrived at this truth of a unitary and monistic conception of the Brahmn.

The Hindu scriptures say that the Supreme Reality is eternal and unchangeable. It is no distortion of any kind. The Supreme Reality is beyond the distinctions of time, space and individuality. The Hiranyagarbha or primordial seed of life that self-emanated with the help of five basic elements of ether, air, fire, water and the earth, took the form of the vast Universe. To understand this phenomenon, it is necessary to comprehend the process of transformation of the matter since only matter can be transformed. Consciousness is non-transformable. Anything which is lifeless is called the matter and hence can be transformed. The body in any form, human or animal or plant, has consciousness whether less or more, low or high, till the life breath is present in it. Hence, it will get transformed once the consciousness is lost. The body without consciousness will get mixed up with soil and could give Consciousness – the Soul, the shape of a plant one day. Here this soil and the plant are one and the same but in different forms and names.

According to some spiritual philosophers, Reality can be viewed at three levels: the **Absolute Reality** (Supreme Reality), the **Relative Reality** and the **Illusory Reality**. Reality of the non-dual which is the infinite non-dual consciousness of being (existence) is what is termed as the Absolute or the Supreme Reality. This is called the Brahmn, the primordial, and that which has no distortion in relation to time, space and individuality. Thus, Vedanta philosophy proclaims that all that is present is Brahmn and that Brahmn is the Absolute or the Supreme Reality. While the empirical world is projected in all its diversity. This gives an impression about the existence of the Relative Reality in relation to the Absolute Reality. Anything that is relatively real appears to be real at certain times and under certain conditions. Since it is not real at all times, it is not real even when it appears to be real. An erroneous imagination of something which does not exist is called an illusion of Reality called the Illusory Reality. Illusion and hallucinations have no existence apart from the mind that imagines them in Illusory Reality.

Consider for example clay which may be assumed as Brahmn. A potter makes a pot out of this clay. The pot becomes the relative reality. Even though it is still clay, yet it is visible in the form of a pot. Once the pot is broken, it will go back to its original form, clay. An individual who purchases the pot can think that he can make use of it by cooking rice in it. This is illusory reality. This is one's pure imagination since one can cook rice or boil water or make tea but the pot may even crack while on the fire or even before it is put on the fire. In Vedanta, the oft-repeated analogy is that of the rope and snake. Due to its appearance in the form of a rope, it is called a rope. This is the relative reality. If someone, in darkness, mistakes the rope to be a snake, then this is illusory reality. One can even imagine a rope to be a coiled snake, piece of stick or a crack in the ground. All this is left to the individual's imagination.

The illusory reality is generally termed as 'Maya' in Hinduism, which is a process of unsubstantiated illusion. Delusion, the other name of 'Maya' means the failure to perceive the divine essence of nature while treating it as a mere mechanical process unrelated to Brahmn. The fact is that Maya is inherent in the attitude of those who perceive, not in that which is perceived. So long as the individual considers himself/herself as the main or chief actor on the stage of the world play, he or she is in the world of Maya. But as soon as he or she recognizes the essence of finite to be in the infinite and realizes that he or she is just an instrument of a hidden purpose, he/she will try to get out of this world of Maya for a continuous inner search and spiritual enlightenment. Even divine souls in their state of incarnations had their moments of the impact of Maya lurking over their minds and making them to live a life of form, while forgetting its essence. The Lord Vishnu, who incarnated as 'Varaha' to destroy evil and reassign to Earth her rightful place, is believed to enjoy the pleasure of the senses, even forgetting the bliss of Vaikuntha under the spell of Maya until He was awakened by the sage Narada and made conscious of His real divinity. Same is believed to be the case of Rama, the incarnations of Vishnu as the normal human being who had to be reminded to come out of the worldly affairs and return to Vaikuntha.

The pure Absolute Brahmn appears as the triad of God-Living Beings-Universe (Jagdish – jiva-jagat) in the phenomenal state while remaining noumenally in its own Absolute nature. It is Brahmn, the Reality itself, which appears as all the three – God – Living Beings – Universe. They are the constituents, the three sides of the triangle of empirical existence, which are interlinked and always go together.

Brahmn, with its power of Maya, projects this universe and assumes the role of God and living beings to play the game of the universe, just as in the dream, the dreamer's mind itself assumes the roles of the doer, the dream-ego-that is, the subject – and all the objects and being within the dream. If a particular living being gets out of the game by giving up its living-hood, the game comes to an end for that living-being but it will continue for other innumerable living beings as long as they live. The game is ever there as one of the aspects of Maya.

Swami Vivekananda presents the ultimate non-dualistic philosophic view. Brahmn alone is the Truth or Existence – Consciousness-Bliss (Sat-Chit-Anand). The philosophization, however, is possible only in the realm of the living beings. The appearance of the universe as a whole including the perceiver's individuality, disappears only in the state of realization of the Brahmn. This is because, in the non-dualistic view, everything that exists is the Infinite Brahmn alone, and the appearances derive their validity from Brahmn in all states. This is due to Brahmn's imponderable power called Maya, giving rise phenomenally to appearances. They all derive their validity from the Absolute Reality – the Brahmn – their common substratum. The validity of the universe refers to its phenomenal validity in the dualistic state.

The whole idea of the Brahmn and the Universe is also sometimes, interpreted in another way. There is only one Absolute Spiritual Reality (Brahmn) which is apparently dichotomized or polarized into Subject and Object, within the framework of time, space, and causation, amenable to change and activity, by its inscrutable Maya-power. Since the Subject and Object are the same on Reality – apparently polarized, which continue as the substratum of both as the unchanging source and the witness of all experience, they are of the same substance and have the same status and validity, though they apparently differ diametrically. Whether the Universe is perceived or not, whether it is valid or not, whether it is independent of one's consciousness or not, depends upon one's own condition of personality and the state of one's realization. In each stage, the universe is of the same substance and has as much validity as the perceiving individual subject. Thus, the empirical universe can be characterized from the point of view of the individual consciousness, from the point of view of Universal Consciousness, God (Sagun Brahmn), and from the point of view of Absolute Reality (Transcendent or Nirgun Brahmn).

The phenomenal God is verily the Supreme Brahmn personified (Sagun Brahmn) as much as the universe and the individual souls are phenomenal. He is co-existent with the universe and the souls. His incarnations as Rama, Krishna, 'Sai Baba' among others are also phenomenal whom the human beings love and worship as God. Indeed, God, Universe and individual souls are co-related. Empirically, there are different grades of reality and unreality; While Brahmn alone is Absolute and always Real, all its manifestations through Maya within the framework of time-space-causation have relative or phenomenal reality, derived from Brahmn, their substratum. However, what is to be remembered is that, whether these assumed forms of Brahmn – the correlatives God-Soul-Universe, bondage and freedom etc. are considered real or unreal from the transcendental plane, their mutual relationships remain the same as the empirical plane, as they have the same empirical status and reality, with their respective roles to play in the game of the Universe.

Brahmn is not a Person, in the phenomenal sense, it is the source and substance of all personalities through its power of Maya. Of the three phenomenal aspects of Brahmn, Sat, Chit and Anand, the Sat (Existence) aspect is manifest in all beings – sentient and insentient; the chit aspect is Manifest in minds, and the Anand (Bliss) aspect is manifest in pure modes of mind. In its fourth dimension (Turiya), the source of the other three aspects, Brahmn is infinite (Anantha), beyond all phenomenal descriptions. It is beyond all phenomenal attributes and forms which can be conceived of. It is Satyam-Jhanam-Anantham (Absolute Existence – Knowledge/Consciousness – Infinity) and hence of the nature of Absolute Bliss (Ananda) as well.

Pure Sat or Existence (Truth) is beyond all such characterizations, just as knowledge cannot be characterized as 'He' or 'She' or as a person, though the Hindus do personify Saraswati as the goddess of knowledge. What is really meant by Nirguna (Attribute less) is that no attributes, which are experienced and conceived objectively by the human beings, can be applied to the Brahmn. It, being, the Non-dual Infinite, the distinction between quality and substance, that is generally made in normal usage, is not valid in the case of Brahmn. These attributes or qualities are the products of the three gunas of Maya, which remain in Brahmn (like heat in fire without affecting it), being its very nature. Similarly, Brahmn, though attributeless (Nirguna) itself, is the source of all the attributes (guna) which are produced by its Maya in the dualistic phenomenal existence and superimposed on Brahmn called 'Saguna Brahmn' or Brahmn with attributes or God (Ishwar). Even God (Ishwar), being infinite, has no definite form. It is not possible to say that God (Ishwar) is male or female or what else, although religionists have differently conceived 'Him' since nobody knows or can know objectively exactly what God is. Again, when God acts, He (She) has to act through His powers. Then actually, it is His powers that act spontaneously. Since He and His powers are identical, His activities take place spontaneously since He is not deliberately using His powers for deliberation. His Will is again an act which must arise itself. Suppose the personal God is the Soul and the Universe is His body. Then, the powers are vested in God – the Soul of the Universe. He acts through the body. In this case also, the powers within must be first motivated by the Soul, which in itself is formless, and the Soul is not apart from the body. If the soul has to motivate the powers, it has to think or will, and the will or thought has to arise spontaneously. If the thought or will has to be produced by an act, then that act again has to be willed which lead to a circular movement. Thus, the spontaneous origination has to be accepted. In other words, whether God acts through some form or without it, with organs or without organs, all that happens occurs spontaneously by His mere presence. This is described as the 'Lila' or Sport of God or Maya of the Brahmn, both having the same significance.

Indeed, the Maya-power also arises spontaneously from Brahmn projects the Universe and its beings, and makes all life's activities possible, just as fire radiates heat and light spontaneously, and not as an act of its will. Hence, Brahmn, conceived as, God, acts spontaneously. In fact, they are not two different entities. It is because of the fact that Brahmn is infinite and perfect, and of the nature of Sat-Chit-Anand, whatever spontaneously emerges from God, is termed Satyam-Shivam-Sundaram. When Brahmn is considered as God, the Lord of the Universe, He controls it but is not cognized by all since He envelops Himself with creative Maya (Yoga-Maya). It is, in fact, Brahmn as God (Ishwar), who makes things possible, enables activities to happen and conceptualizes ideals for perfection. Thus, Brahmn as God exercises all the divine powers of Universal Lordship as long as the universe and individual souls exist. What is really meant by superimposition on Brahmn is that those who find themselves within the universe projected by Maya endowed with a personality, superimpose their perceptions and conceptions of the triad of individual Soul, Universe and God on Brahmn. That is why so many conceptualizations of God, the Soul and the Universe are projected by different religions, philosophies and sciences. Some perceive God as 'He', some as 'SHE', some as 'Ardhanarishvar', some with form, some without form, some as Trinity, some as Unity; and so on and so forth, according to different points of view while there are some who deny a creator-God altogether. Similarly different people hold different views with regard to the Soul and the Universe. Some theologians consider the person God as the Supreme.

According to Shankaracharya, it is immaterial whether God is Brahmn or Brahmn is God, both in the Upanishadic sense, are the same reality. Both Brahmn and God or Brahmn and Atman are used interchangeably in the commentaries on Gita, Upanishads and Braham Sutras. There is neither superior and inferior, nor higher and lower, in the non-dual Infinite, beyond Maya, beyond time, space and causation. They are the transcendental (Para) and relative (Apara) views of the same Reality. From the transcendent point of view, the Supreme Reality Brahmn appears as the Parmatman – the Supreme Self of the Universe, and as the Atman – the individual self of the living being, who constitutes a component of the Universe. From the phenomenal point of view, God is considered as the Lord of the Soul, of the Universe and of the living beings as the lords of the respective individual souls. Thus, the great Brahmn is the irrefutable, infinite Absolute Reality while God is none other than Brahmn relatively viewed. Since Brahmn cannot be characterized as male or female or as a combination of both and since these are only phenomenal concepts, therefore Brahmn is called 'It'. What is really meant by 'Nirguna' or 'Nirakar' means that Brahmn has no attributes or forms. Brahmn is non-dual infinite. This makes Vedanta philosophy fully scientific, practical and universal.

Maya is the power (Shakti) inherent in Ishwara (God). It is by virtue of this power that the objective world with its amazing and enormous variety of forms and shapes is revealed. If Maya is the source of all manifested Existence, God (Ishwara) is the Universal Witness who assists in unfolding of the cosmos. A living being (Jiva) is an empirical individuality – a spiritual element or an individual soul enveloped in psycho-physical structure associated with multiple conditionings such as gross manifestation, subtle manifestation and causal manifestation. The living being (Jiva) and God (Ishwara), stripped respectively of their individual and cosmic conditionings, do not differ from one another as regards their essence. In everyday language, the living being is but the empirical ego, and its particularization is due to the causal limitations such as the physical body or the senses. Thus, the living being is the causal aspect of the manifested physical body or senses, whereas God is the causal aspect of the manifested universe. The reason being that the living being is bound by the limits of Maya whereas God is beyond the influence of Maya. The living being under the impact of Maya, believes multiplicity to be the ultimate truth, and all the afflictions around it whereas Brahmn is above the realms of Maya. Normally, the living being identifies itself with the physical organism with which it is associated, which is why it looks upon everything, that does not belong to its body, as being outside of itself. The living being, therefore, considers the objective world as real, it entertains preferences and indifferences, likes and dislikes towards others. God, on the other hand, is identified with the Totality of the Universe. Thus, each of the triad namely, the being, both animate and inanimate, Maya-power and God, together constitute as the three entities of Relative Reality from an empirical or phenomenal point of view while all the three are in one and only one – Brahmn, the Absolute and Supreme Reality in noumenal sense.

The great scientist Albert Einstein is given the credit for his revolutionary theory of Relativity, whereas the fact is that it was great Indian Vedantic philosopher Shankaracharya who, more than twelve centuries prior to Einstein, discovered Maya as a Relativity Principle endowed with infinite spiritual potentiality and projection of the soul as Atman. It is even sometimes doubted whether Einstein was a relativist in the real sense. Indeed, he established that space, time, matter and energy are not real in themselves but are only phenomenal observations made in relation to some super-natural entity. In fact, **Einstein went to the extent of raising a question himself by asking: "If all observations of the world are relative, then what isn't?"** According to Einstein theory of relativity, matter and energy are treated as a single entity – just the manifestation of a single continuity that extends through all events, past, present and future constituting what is called space-time-continuum (causation).

It has always been fascinating to study the way the idea of God figured in the lives of astrophysicists and metaphysicists including even the mathematicians. They often have mystical beliefs while observing the laws of nature in relation to a divine phenomenon. Some have even tried to prove the existence of God through rigorous mathematical postulations. Notable among such mathematicians, as mentioned earlier, has been Pascal – the inventor of Probability Theory, who while supporting the existence of God, postulated that even if one did not know that God existed, the benefits of believing in God far outweighed the drawbacks of such a belief. The well-known Swiss mathematician Euler proved the existence of God by calculating the value of the famous transcendental number 'e' in the court of Catherine the Great, to dispute the atheist Denis Diderot. Newton, in his old age, gave his mind increasingly over to speculations about the unfathomable mysteries of God. Mathematicians generally play with infinity and are often found to have remarked the idea of God (as an infinity that is more numerous than any other entity). Given infinity, there is always a greater infinity leading to the infinite phenomenon called God. The natural numbers 1, 2, 3, ... are generally known as the divine numbers which a German mathematician L. Kronecher to announce "God made the natural numbers; all else is the work of man".

Mathematicians are also comfortable with the idea of nothingness or 'shunya' (zero) – an important concept in the spiritual philosophical thought related to Metaphysics. The number zero, invented by the Hindus, denotes the presence of absence – a paradox. The great Indian mathematician S. Ramanujam, with minimal educational background and with no appropriate mathematical foundation, contributed enormous mathematical results and theories which to-date are the prominent areas of research and which, as he believed, were gifted to him by the goddess who would appear in his dreams. God is a mysterious entity before which the intellectual arrogance stands tamed and exposed.

4.2 Divine Power and the Trinity Principle

The three philosophical perceptions of the Absolute Reality namely non-duality by Sri Shankaracharya, qualified non-duality by Sri Ramanujacharya and duality by Sri Madhavacharya are sometimes interpreted in the following way:

- God in the formless stage of non-duality and His realization as Brahmn through the path of meditation (Sadhana) and divine knowledge (Brahmn Jnana).
- God's manifestations as the trinity of Brahma – the creator, Vishnu – the sustainer and Mahesh (Shiva) – the dissoluter, representing the stage of qualified non-duality attainable through the path of 'action (karma) and service (sewa); and
- God's incarnations in the form of Rama, Krishna and Sai represent duality, as the first stage of experiencing God in the human form through the path of faith and devotion (Shraddha and Bhakti).

According to Sri Ramakrishna Paramhans, Brahmn and Shakti are one and the same in complete harmony with each other that is hidden in the three apparent different philosophies of duality, qualified non-duality and non-duality to be experienced through the three corresponding paradigms of devotion (Bhakti), action (Karma) and knowledge (Gyan) respectively.

The Upanishads elaborate the Supreme Reality in terms of its three aspects: **Viraat**, **Hiranyagarbha** and **Avyaakruta**. **Viraat** manifests the external, gross and visible world – the entire visible universe including the five basic elements namely, ether (space), air, fire, water and earth. Viraat is that form of the Atma that dons a physical body. Viraat is also known by two other names: Vaishvanara and Vairaajasuta. Vaishvanara appears as the 'I' consciousness in each individual while Vairaajasuta exists in the mysterious form, in everyone but unseen, performs all actions but behaves as if it does not, experience everything but does not reveal it, and exists in everyone but remains undetected.

Hiranyagarbha is that aspect of the supreme reality which is the basis and source of all wisdom manifesting all knowledge: worldly, ethical, religious, spiritual and scientific. 'Hirnay' (Gold), as a symbol of life (Praana), and 'garbha' (matter), a body of lifeless mass, indeed, Hiranyagarbha is known as the sun of knowledge (Jnana Bhaskara). It appears as golden (Hiranya) as the Sun rises and makes the world appear in golden colour. Hiranyagarbha looks like a golden egg (an elliptic form in the geometrical terms). The Hindu scriptures believe that the whole creation manifested from the Hiranyagarbha aspect of the Supreme Reality. Indeed, it is the origin of all living beings including their human form vested with Vijnana, Sujnana and Prajana in order to enable them to discriminate between the temporary and permanent, between the truth and falsehood, between the good and bad, between the virtues and vices, etc.

Hiranyagarbha, like the Viraat aspect of the supreme reality is also known by two other names: **Sutraatmaka and Praana.** Sutraatmaka links all livings and bestows bliss to them. This is like a thread (Sutra) which passes through a necklace of gems or a garland of flowers. This is the unifying thread, also called the **Brahmn Sutra.** The thread is interpreted as God existing in equal measure in all living beings without any distinctions while inculcating unity in them. Praana is the life-force of all living beings. Thus, the Hiranyagarbha is considered to be the substratum or aggregate of all the living beings. While Hiranyagarbha is the macro cosmic feature of the Brahmn, a living being (an individual) is a microcosmic feature of the Brahmn. In some way, Hiranyagarbha and the individual living being (called Jiva) are considered to be the two distinguished features of Brahmn. Hiranyagarbha abides in the body as its praana (the life-force) at the heart of every living being.

Avyaakruta, the third aspect of the Brahmn, is absolutely formless-unmanifested. It exists in the causal body having no limbs but does all actions. It has no ears but listens to everything and performs every act in creation, but possesses no form. Avyaakruta is also known by two more names Inner Soul {**Antaratma and God (Easwara)**}. Antaratma motivates, inspires, urges and influences everything. This is inner voice which produces every sound. Easwara is embodiment of all forms of prosperity, power of action and represents all types of actions. The divinity, which fills the entire cosmos, exists in all living beings and is named as Atma by the Vedas. According to the Upanishads, Brahmn is not merely what is seen outside as the universe but also the self inside each and every being. At the transcendental level Brahmn and Self are same and equal. In other words, the foundations of the Universe and of the individual are one and the same. This means Universal Consciousness is same as the individual consciousness. But at the physical and mental level, the individual is micro (small) while the universe is macro (infinity). Therefore according to Bhagwan Sri Sathya Sai Baba, the physical form of God is same as the Universe or the Cosmic form which is equal to individual's body multiplied by infinity. The Cosmic form is referred to as Virat Swarup while the cosmic mind is called Hiranyagarbha.

In its 'Hiranyagarbha' theory, the Rig Veda contends that initially cosmos was a single entity consisting of life (Praana) and matter (body or 'bhuta'). The great ancient scriptures call it Hiranyagarbha. According to Rig Veda, existence is a two-aspected reality comprising of the pairs of entities namely life and matter, light and darkness, male and female, Purush and Prakriti, and so on. This reality apparently looks to be in conflict but deeper inside it reveals its inherent oneness or unity. Its Ardhanarishwar form is eternal, an incessant and infinitely recurring process of manifestation. It is the symbol of the unity of outer duality with inner absolute oneness reconciling the ever conflicting male and female aspects of the same supreme reality. Ardhanarishwara is the visual manifestation of Shiva's wish of becoming many from being one, the combination of three words: Half (ARDHA), Female (Nari) and God (Ishwara). Shiva and Shakti or Shiva and Parvati are known as 'Purusha' and 'Prakriti'. The word 'Purusha' is commonly understood as the 'Male Aspect' which is the source of existence or creation while 'Prakriti' is the 'Female Aspect' which is the process of creation or nature or existence. The source of creation or existence is eternal while the happening of creation is consequential. Considering the source (of creation or existence) as the part of the process of creation would not be appropriate.

Shiva is always in the ecstatic state of mind and Shakti gets drawn to Him. This is the state when everyone is within oneself. This was the state of ecstasy when Parvati (incarnation of Shakti) found Shiva, within Himself, and felt the desire of experiencing this ecstasy. Shiva smiled and invited Parvati to come and get merged into Him. When she entered Shiva's state of ecstasy or world of ecstasy, she merged into Shiva and became half of Him, while Shiva had to shed half of Himself to accommodate Parvati. This metaphysically means that the inner male and the outer female meet in a perpetual state of ecstasy, that is to say, that outer duality uniting with inner absolute oneness, the Supreme Reality. It, however, does not mean that two persons are longing to meet physically. It essentially means two dimensions of life longing to meet – outside as well as inside. This reality is being expressed in a beautiful dialectal form that Shiva with Parvati as a part of Himself became Half-Male and Half-Female.

Shiva is the symbolism of ultimate masculinity even when He is half-female. Indeed, it does not mean that Shiva became half of Parvati because that is how nature happened to manifest. First was Purusha, and then Prakriti manifested. This manifestation has three basic aspects: creation, maintenance and dissolution; the three fundamental forces playing a huge game. In Hinduism, these three forces are respectively called Brahma, Vishnu and Mahesh. These are not three persons or people floating on the clouds or resting or reclining on the lap of a big serpent-shaped being called Sheshnaag or sitting on the top of a hill. These are essentially three basic dimensions without which nothing can happen in existence. Brahma is about genesis, it is one of the manifestations of the Brahmn. Vishnu is about the organization of existence and Shiva is oblivion. Going deep down, these three forces get merged into one. The trident (trishul) constantly indicating that though there are three on the surface, deep down, they are one and the same Purusha also called the Brahmn. These three forces, when function as one, are also called Mahadeva. Generally, the sages call the destroyer Mahadeva. It is because of this reason that creation and maintenance only exist in the lap of oblivion. It is the empty space which is the most expansive, boundless and it is in the lap of empty space that the existence conducts itself, splits apart and reunites. To-date scientists have not been able to specify the energy which they call dark. They don't yet know its nature. They call it dark energy because they are not able to perceive it or see it. Vedas called Shiva, 'the Dark One', His night, called Shivratri, is the darkest night of the month. Thus, Shiva is the largest manifestation of existence. The largest thing out there is empty darkness which is referred to as Shiva. Maha Shiva Ratri, the Great Night of Shiva, is the meditative and transformational aspect of nature. Shiva is the pure consciousness.

In the beginning there was nothing but the Great Void, the True Absolute wherein all was still, empty and silent. There was total vacuum and eternal darkness. The silence of the Absolute was disturbed by the thought (sankalpa) in the cosmic mind, the mind of God. This thought was followed by the creation of the Universe. Sri Sathya Sai Baba often says that the Universe is a reflection of God – The cause is God and the effect is the Universe. The individual mind is an element of Hiranyagarbha. The Hiranyagarbha is a subtle entity. The Universe emerged from Hiranyagarbha. Sai Baba has been materializing Hiranyagarbha on various occasions particularly on the occasion of Hindu's holy festival 'Shivratri'. Holding it before a dazed and spell-bound crowd of devotees, Sai Baba, once, said "**God (Ishwara) is the aggregate of all individual souls (Jivas); Virataswaroopa (Cosmic Form), that of all individual bodies and Hiranyagarbha (Cosmic Mind), that is, of all individual minds.**"

The word Paramatman – The Universal Soul or the Universal Self is used for God – The ultimate source of cosmic energy or divine energy, which animates the Universe. The vital forces, which animate the individual body, derive their energy from Jivatma which is an element of Paramatman or God or Brahmn. The individual self is the Jivatma and the Universal self is the Parmatman. The same relation exists between an individual conscience and the Universal conscience. This implies that the individual conscience is the voice of Parmatman, the voice of God, the voice of Brahmn. The mind originates from Atma and the speech originates from the mind. Thus, Shiva is Atma-Swarupa, Vishnu is Manoswarupa and Brahma is Vakswarupa and in this way the three manifestations of God namely the Brahma, Vishnu and Maheshwara are intimately inter-related.

There are eight-appellations of God (Paramatman or Parmeshwara) demonstrating His divinity namely: manifesting as all-pervading cosmic sound, pervading all moving and unmoving objects, all-pervading effulgence, sacred speech, eternal bliss, manifestation of Maya and the embodiment of all prosperity. Brahmn is, therefore, described as attributeless, pure, all-pervading eternal, unsullied, consciousness, free and embodiment of sacredness. When the unmodifiable transcendent and immanent Brahmn – the supreme reality or the Universal Soul, instead of being just 'being', decides of 'becoming', then it is designated as God or 'Eshwara' (Almighty). Nirakara and Saakara are just two attributes of God. According to ancient Hindu scriptures (Puranas), divinity functions in the cosmos in five names: Para-naamam, Vyuha-naamam, Vibhava-naamam, Antaratma – naamam and Archana-naamam.

Para-Naamam refers to the abode of the Supreme namely Vaikuntha where the Supreme Lord dwells under the name of Para-naamam, as an effulgence and oversees everything but he is not visible to anyone and no one can see his form.

Vyuha-Naamam refers to the supreme Lord who reclines on a serpent on the ocean of milk, can be seen only by the Gods (Devas) and fulfils their desires. Ordinary beings cannot see Him.

Vibhava-Naamam refers to various forms in which the supreme being (Lord) incarnates on earth as Avatars like Rama, Krishna and Sai Baba.

Antaraatma-Naamam refers to the divine as an indwelling spirit who resides in the inner self of a living being.

Archana-Naamam refers to the form in which the divine can be worshipped and adored for securing His grace.

A reference is always made of Shakti or Bhagawati the united form of Saraswati, Lakshmi and Durga (Parvati). The trinity of Brahma, Vishnu and Maheshwar are always accompanied by these goddesses their respective consorts namely Saraswati, Lakshmi and Shakti (Parvati or Durga). Saraswati the consort of Brahma, is the goddess of speech, learning, science, arts and music. The Goddess Saraswati is always depicted, often with a veena and a book in her hand while riding a swan. She is always worshipped by students, writers and musicians. She is considered to be the Goddess of harmony, wisdom and knowledge. Lakshmi, the Goddess of fortune in Hindu mythology, is the consort of Lord Vishnu. According to legends, she sprang from the froth due to churning of the ocean in full beauty with a lotus in her hand. She is usually portrayed as a woman of nature, beauty, seated on a lotus and often with a lotus in her hand. The Goddess, Shakti, is energy. She connotes feminine creative energy. She is considered as an energizing phenomenon which finds its manifestations in all natural forces. Durga represents her dominating principle who crushes the demonic forces against which even Gods were powerless. Goddess Kali, born from Durga's brow represents the power of annihilation. Shakti is worshipped in many different forms. Shakti is energy while Shiva is matter. Their combination creates synergy. Matter and energy are embedded in nature (Prakriti). Metaphorically both Shiva and Shakti are depicted as Ardhanareeshwar, explained earlier.

While describing the beauty and vastness of Shiva, Sadguru Jaggi Vasudev, an eminent spiritual scholar of India, said in one of his interviews published in the Speaking Tree column of the Times of India dated March 7, 2013, "**This vast emptiness referred to as Shiva, is a boundless non-entity that is eternal. Since human perception is**

limited to form, many wonderful forms for Shiva have been visualized: The enigmatic non-perceivable God (Ishwara); the auspicious Shambho; the disarmingly naïve Bhole Nath; Dakshinamurthy, the great master and teacher of the Vedas and other ancient holy scriptures; the easily forgiving Ashuthosh; Achaleshwara, the absolute stillness; Nataraja, the most dynamic of dancers. As many aspects as there are to life and many more can be ascribed to Shiva. All types of aspects, including even the mutually contradictory and undigestable amalgamation of qualities of existence have been ascribed to the personality of Shiva". Several Shiva Purana stories related to the modern scientific concepts such as the Theory of Relativity and Quantum Mechanics, have been beautifully linked. Indeed, the Shiva Purana is considered to be the highest science of elevating human nature to the highest peak of consciousness. Even yoga has been expressed in the form of a science without stories attached to it in a deeper sense. Infact yoga and Shiv Purana are inseparable, since the fundamentals of both are the same.

'Shiva Tattva' can be experienced through the knowledge of the Vedas. The state of Shivoham (I am Shiva), Shiva Kevaloham (there is only one Shiva) is attained. Shiva can't be experienced without yoga. Here yoga doesn't mean only physical postures (asanas) but the experience of 'Shiva Tattva' is possible through meditation and pranayam. Panchmukha or Panchtattva means five faces of Shiva: water, air, fire, earth and space. Understanding these five elements is knowledge of the five elements (tattva gyan). Worshipping Shiva is dissolving in 'Shiva Tattva'. Shiva is the cause of all causes. "**Shiva is the refuge of everybody**: **He who grants freedom from the cycle of birth and death**; **He who gave the sacred scriptures at the dawn of time**; **He who is the source of purity and perfection**; **He who is the bridge from death to immortality**; **He whose grace has made everybody to long for His lotus feet**", **says, Shvetashvatara Upanishad**.

Next to the symbol of OM, referred earlier, the Shivling is arguably the most powerful and popular symbol in Hinduism. The Shivling, which is worshipped across India, is a phallic symbol representing the creative power of Shiva. It is held in a circular base, both together symbolizing a state of conjugal bliss, a perfect union of the mind and body or the coming together of Purusha and Prakriti. Shiva lives with his wife Parvati and their two sons. His form as Ardhnariswara means half female and half male. Shiva's vahan or vehicle is Nandi, the bull who is knowledged personified and is said to have taught Hanuman of the Ramayana fame, the secrets of the Vedas.

In the holy Trinity, Shiva is coloured white for purity and for his association with the snowy mountain ranges where He lives. His three eyes represent the three worlds. The third eye is also symbolic of his wisdom and ability to see the "beyond". The moon that adorns his head represents the movement of time. And through its waxing and waning, Shiva creates the different seasons and rejuvenates life. It is also in the moon that people get an idea of the contrast between Shiva and Vishnu who is associated with the Sun.

Normally seated in a meditative (yogic) pose, people often come across Shiva as Nataraja. This is his dance posture. With his hair flying around in all directions and his hands and feet in dynamic motion, Shiva as Nataraja is symbolic of the dance of creation: a guided dance of which He, the Master, is in complete control. The source of all movement within the cosmos is represented by the flames that surround him. Nataraja wears a cobra coiled around his upper arms and neck symbolizing the power over one of the most feared creatures. The snake also represents reincarnation as it sheds or molts its skin symbolizing the transmigration of bodies from one life to another. His uplifted left foot grants eternal bliss to those who approach him. The other foot treads firmly upon the dwarf of ignorance, allowing the birth of knowledge. And as Nataraj dances away the illusory world of Maya, it is transformed into one of power and enlightenment.

Maha Shivratri, the holy festival of Hindus, is considered to be an auspicious night of the spiritual union of the seeker with Shiva – the God. As stated earlier, it is the merger of duality into absolute monism. This occasion, therefore, needs to be observed as an endeavour to realize the Ultimate Truth, the Supreme Reality by controlling the passion and dispelling ignorance. Sri Sathya Sai Baba says, "**Vigilance this night is to be secured by Sadhana, that is, by means of devotional songs (Bhajan) or the reading of sacred texts or listening to the reading of such texts; not by attending film shows or gambling or playing cards. Be engaged in seeing good, listening good, speaking good, thinking good, doing good; that is the programme for the vigil tonight. Make it also the programme for your entire life**". Chanting "OM Namah Shivaya" throughout the night increases the luminosity component in a human being and takes him/her closer to Divinity.

'OM' represents the unmanifest state and the word "Namah" means bowing. Thus 'OM Namah Shivaya' means bowing to Shiva the source of OM. The word 'Shiva' literary means enlightenment. It simply means three principles: **Absolute Purity, Absolute Knowledge** and **Absolute Spiritual Practice**. Shiva always in a state of meditative ecstasy. If His meditation is disturbed, it generates radiance which is suddenly released. Whosoever or whatsoever comes in the line of this radiance, gets burnt to ashes, within no time by the opening of the third eye of Shiva, who otherwise remains cool. Shiva is always willing to undergo any pain for the sake of others. He drank poison generated during the churning of the ocean (Samudramanthan) to save the world from destruction. His two headed drum (Damru) represents, the Brahmn in the form of word (Shabda Brahmn). Shiva carries a trident (Trishul) which is interpreted in two ways: One it represents, as stated earlier, three forces of creation, maintenance and dissolution and the other being as the symbol of three traits/characteristics of nature (Prakriti): Sattva, Rajas and Tamas.

The 'Shivlingam' is the representation of Shiva principle and energy, it is the very source of life energy, created by the resolve of Shiva, has the capacity to attract and emit the three attributes (gunnas) of Sattva, Rajas and Tamas. The energy of the Shivlingam is unbearable at times, therefore it is located on the ground firmly fixed with half-part under the ground. The mythological story tells that Shiva lives in the Himalayas, the coolest place on earth where everything is cool. To provide a feeling of coolness, a pot is held above a 'Shivlingam', from which drops of water fall one by one on the Shivlingam. In Kashmir, a natural snow 'Shivlingam' occasionally arises automatically in a snowy cave called Amarnath Cave. Shivlingam is a symbol for meditation to give a glimpse of innerself – the consciousness. The 'Jyotilingams' (flame lingas) emit radiance of the Shiva principle and energy. Both 'Shivlinga' and 'Jyotilinga' emit knowledge (Jnana), devotion (Bhakti) and detachment (Vairagya). Hence chanting 'OM NAMAH SHIVAY' brings closer to Divinity.

A Distinction is generally made in Hinduism in respect of the trinity principles namely the philosophical trinity and the religious trinity. The philosophical trinity pertains to the Sagun Brahmn in the form of three principles namely the Universe, Paramatman (Universal Soul, the Energy or Life principle also called the Spirit) and Matter. The religious trinity refers to Supreme Lord (Isvara) manifested in the forms of Brahma (Creator), Vishnu (Preserver/Protector) and Shiva (Dissoluter or Liberator). The Brahma (Creator) of the religious trinity must not be confused with the Brahmn – the Supreme Reality. In fact, Brahma, Vishnu and Mahesh (Shiva) correspond to the three functions of the One Divinity (Iswara – the religious form of the Brahmn) namely creation, preservation and dissolution or Generation, Organization, Dissolution abbreviated as GOD. Indeed, these three entities are the three manifestations of the same Brahmn. One manifestation is symbolized with Lord Vishnu, and His various incarnations including those of Rama in the Treta Yuga and Krishna in the Dwapur Yuga. Another manifestation is identified with the Sai Trinity believed to be the divine incarnations of Shiva, Shiva-Shakti and Shakti in the respective forms of Shirdi Sai Baba, Sri Sathya Sai Baba and awaited Prema Sai Baba.

In the word "God", there are three letters: G, O, D. The letter G refers to "Generation" (Creation) that is Brahma, the letter "O" stands for "Organization" (protection and maintenance), that is Vishnu and the letter 'D' refers to "Destruction" or "Dissolution" which means "Shiva" (Maheshwara). Thus the word GOD combines the manifestations namely. Generation, Organization and Destruction (Dissolution). These three deities presiding over Creation (Brahma), Protection (Vishnu) and Dissolution (Shiva) are the three manifestations of God. Therefore, God has the divine prerogative. He can create anything, protect anything and dissolves anything. God is considered to be having control over Generation, Organization and Dissolution. Devotees and believers have been having their individual opinions with regard to forms of God. As a result, a whole range of God's formations termed as gods and goddesses is adored to suit their different beliefs, needs and occasions. Several non-Hindus, even some Hindus also, scoff at the notion of so many gods and goddesses. Just as god of the gods, Lord Indra also known as the god of space (Aakash Dev), god of air (Pawan Deva), god of fire (Agni Dev), god of water (Varuna Deva). Even the Earth is adored as a goddess 'Mother Earth'. This is because the Vedantic philosophy permits a wider choice of conceptualizing and comprehending the Absolute Brahmn.

God at the abstract level is termed as AUM possessing six qualities namely Omni-present, Omni-scient, Omni-potent, Non-attachment, Grace and Glory, as full-manifestations of the Supreme and Absolute Reality; the Nirguna Brahmn. Thus, all shapes of God including His manifestations and incarnations are just various forms of the same supreme Nirgun Niraakar Brahmn, which shines as Sagun Brahmn or Sagun Saakar Brahmn. To clarify the confusion about God and His manifestations, Sri Sathya Sai Baba has said that God really has no form but the Supreme Being who, through its divine powers projects Himself in its various forms (as well as the vast and mysterious Universe) like Brahma, Vishnu, Mahesh as well as their further incarnations Rama and Krishna including various divine personalities like Buddha, Mahavir among several others. All that is required is intense love for God. When that love is expressed, then God responds and obliges the devotees by appearing in that glorified form since the devotees tend to view God essentially in their envisioned forms. Such devotees perceive God as clearly as they perceive the external bodies. God or the Ishwara, though said to be formless, can assume or adopt any form. He has endless forms each being an embodiment of God and God manifests in the form that a devotee yearns for it because it is the form or embodiment or personification of God which grants him the greatest satisfaction and fullest sense of God-Realization.

The Rig Veda on mystery of the divine power says, "In the beginning, there was neither nought nor ought. Then there was neither sky nor space atmosphere above. What then enshrouded all this Universe? In the receptacle of what was it contained? Then there was neither death nor immortality. Then there was neither day, nor night, nor light, nor darkness. Only the Existent One breathed calmly self contained". The Atharva Ved says, "The whole of this Universe is stationed in the Omni-present and the Omni-potent God ....Him they call the Kala, Infinite, Pervading the infinite space".

The divine power according to some spiritual scholars, is indeed a reality since it has an apparent appearance in the form of the universe and whole creation. It is a self-evident truth. The terms like the '**inner-reality**' and '**outer-appearance**'; '**inner-self**' and '**external force**'; '**inner-most essence**' and '**manifested form**' are some of the all metaphysical thoughts which respectively constitute what is termed as "being" and "becoming". According to some philosophical views, the metaphysical separation into **Reality** and **Appearance**, into **Being** and **Becoming**, into **Spirit** and **Matter**, into **God** and **Illusion** (Maya) must be recognized. Spirit and Matter are considered to be the two fundamental features of the divine entity with all kinds of variations and modifications. But there is another philosophic view which presents the divinity in terms of consciousness. The spiritualists of this view paint this apparent and self-evident divinity which is beyond the vision of some philosophers.

Some spiritual scholars believe that the Supreme Reality and its expression through its manifestations as the Universe as such, are not separate things but one and the same thing – an unbroken unity. What is illusory is the materiality of divinity and not its existence. This according to them, is the ultimate reality which they have spoken of Spirit and Divinity. While everything else exists relatively, this alone is the Absolute Reality which is called the Brahmn, because Brahmn is ultimately believed to be everything and everywhere.

The divinity, which fills the entire cosmos, exists in every living being as Soul (Atma) and Atma is non-perishable. This soul is universal because of its Universal Existence. The human body, the family, the community, the province, the nation or the world as a whole are examples of the universal existence in different degrees of particularity. The divinity exists even if none of its individuals/particulars exists. This is so because the divinity acts as an integrating cohesive force among the associated particulars. It does not need its particulars/individuals for its existence. The divinity can exist even without the existence of its particulars. This eventually leads to the analogy that the Absolute Brahmn exists irrespective of the existence of its relative aspect which means the Brahmn exists even if His world of creation does not exist. However, it is believed that the Brahmn with the Universe exists just like a family. No doubt, it is often found to be difficult to visualize the existence of community or for that matter the divine power independent of the particulars.

The divine power, designated as the Brahmn – the Supreme Reality, has been grandly magnified in the Bhagvat Gita in a superb way having hands and feet everywhere; innumerable number of eyes, faces and heads everywhere; and merging into and emerging from everything. It is depicted as the illuminator of all the sense-organs, but in itself, it is none of them. It is described as the support behind all diversity but is not identified with anyone of these. It is the reality behind appearances. Being above substances and qualities, relations and modifications, it is painted as attributeless although being the substratum of all. It is inside and outside, below and above everything, but it has itself neither any inside and outside nor any below and above. Being the foundation of all movement and activity, it is not characterized by any movement or activity. Being the very Seer and Knower, as the basic subject, it cannot be seen, heard or even thought/perceived by the mind. Being endless and infinite, it is everywhere like a limitless expansion, but as the self of everything and everybody. Nothing can be nearer nor farther from its presence. Among the beings that are divided, it may look divided as their substratum, but by itself, it is not divided as it is the very awareness behind all possible divisions. Everything is absorbed into it, everything is consumed into it, as it were, and it stands unparalleled as a blend of eternity and infinity, as the light of all lights, glorifying in its radiance beyond the darkness of ignorance. Eight types of potencies have been attributed to this Divine Power called Brahmn in the sense that it is the source of **all sounds**, **all motions**, **all lights**, **all speeches**, **all blessings**, **all excellences**, **all illusions** (Maya) and **all propensities**.

According to another spiritual interpretation, AUM is composed of four elements namely three vocal sounds A, U, M and the fourth sound, that is not heard, the silent which is known as Anahata Nada. It stands for the Divine Power called the Infinite Brahmn – the Supreme Being, while the three syllables with vocal strands represent its manifestation as the trinity of Brahma (A for Creation), Vishnu (U stands for Preservation) and Mahesh (M stands for Dissolution). The power of AUM is vital in revealing the Brahmn, the supreme Being, the whole Universe and the Absolute Truth. AUM is the word that all Vedas glorify; all sacred studies and all-existence seek. It is the supreme means of salvation. The three sounds, A, U, and M represent the three states of Consciousness: A as the first state of waking consciousness (Viswa); U is the state of dreaming consciousness (Taijasa); and M is the deep-sleeping consciousness (Prajna). The sound of the word 'AUM' or 'OM', as the fourth state (Turia) of Supreme or Super Consciousness, is beyond the sensory experience and the end of evolution. It represents the inevitable pause of silence between two successive chants of AUM. It is marked by a condition of absolute bliss and is a gateway to Brahmn for the seeker. According to a further elaboration, the first letter A refers to "Viswa" which experiences the world of objects, Dream refers to a reflection of the impressions gathered during the waking state and is typified by the second letter "U" which comes next to "A", sound-wise, and is between "A" and "M". The dream state is indeed an intermediate state between waking and deep sleep. The state of Deep-Sleep marks the last aspect of a resting mind, and this is typified by "M".

According to some spiritual scholars, the divine power always has two urges: Evolution and Involution. To merge into the Absolute Brahmn, is the goal of Advaitic Spiritual practice. With the aim of obtaining this unity, spiritual seekers use various methods of spiritual practice to identify themselves through spiritual meditation/sadhana of the Brahmn or its particular manifestation and worship with full concentration on some appropriate symbol. The Upanishadic prescription of OM as the mystic syllable proves more effective because its continuous recitation has the effect of bringing about concentration of thought. OM is identified with Brahmn. The sound OM, the Pranav, represents the entire Brahmn. The whole cosmos gets permeated with Pranava. OM is regarded as the most natural expression of Brahmn. The form of OM has a point above its crescent. This symbolizes the immensity of the Brahmn. The crescent symbolizes air while the circles denote sound. The semicircle below the circle symbolizes the first wave of energy. The wave lines at the bottom represent the primordial waters. In the word OM, the letter 'O' dedicates the origin, as well as the 'point of singularity or 'Shunya' (vacuum) from which the Universe is believed to have emerged. The letter 'M' represents the 'matter; that emerged from this point O. It is also a simultaneous representation of particle and wave, indicating an underlying unity. It appears to have a mystic power and to be worthy of the deepest meditation. OM is the Original Mantra which contains life's tantra. OM is the Original Mystery which contains life's history. OM is the Original Moment which witnessed the 'Big Bang' event. OM is the Original Matter which is widely scattered. OM is the Original Music which disseminates Cosmic vibrations. OM is the Omni-potent Mother representing all goddesses together. OM is the original Manas into which one can see self-reflection and measure the degree of one's distortion. OM is the peace and peace is OM. The three syllables A, U, M respectively represents Atma, Mind and Body. The word 'Parmanu' (atom) seems to have been originated from the world 'Pranav' – pervasive all over the universe.

Several versions of the divine power called Brahmn along with its symbolic representation AUM, are given as the following among others:

1. A, U, M (OM) – Sound Form
2. Brahma, Vishnu, Mahesh – Trinity Form
3. Generation, Organization, Destruction – GOD Form
4. Atma, Body, Mind – Spiritual Form
5. Waking, Dream, Deep-Sleep – Consciousness Form
6. Lakshmi (Wealth), Saraswati (Wisdom) Durga (Power) or Parvati – Shakti (Goddess) Form or Maya
7. Space, Time, Continuum – Cosmic Form
8. Sat (Truth), Chit (Consciousness) Ananda (Bliss) – Divine Form
9. Satyam, Shivam, Sundaram – Transcendent Form
10. Bhuh (Earth), Bhuwah (Air), Svah (Sky) – Three Dimensional Form
11. Past, Present, Future – Time Form
12. Birth, Life, Death – Worldly (Samsaara) Form
13. Fire, Wind, Sun – Light Form
14. Sattwa, Rajas, Tamas – Guna Form (Attribute Form)

The aphorism, "I am Brahmn" (Aham Brahmasmi), is an eloquent version of the idea of "AUM": Atma and Brahmn are synonymous. A still further expression is – "I am He" (Soham). Thus, AUM is the distilled essence of "Soham". According to Sri Ramakrishna Paramahamsa, AUM, the Pranava, loses itself in 'Samadhi' – the super consciousness, during contemplation. Pranava is that which pervades creation or runs through Praana (breath). The underlying idea is that AUM represents both manifest world and the unmanifest – what is beyond. Brahmn is the fundamental, ultimate, imperishable changeless sub-stratum because of which the multifarious changes take place in the multitudinous names and forms in creation. Brahmn is the noumenon transcending all phenomena. AUM as Atman, the indweller, is a silent witness to all worldly experiences in the different state of consciousness, but remaining unaffected by any. Indeed, the central principle of non-duality in Advaita philosophy helps in the realization of God: that the macrocosm and microcosm are not two but one and only one. The chanting of AUM is helpful for controlling the mind – fundamental to the path of spiritual evolution. Indeed, AUM signifies both God with form (Sagun Brahmn) for the ordinary seeker – every common human being, and God without form (Nirgun Brahmn) for the advanced aspirant – evolved being. In the initial stage, AUM serves as a preliminary support, and then inspires later to proceed further into the lofty realms of the formless God – the Nirguna-Nirakar Brahmn. The seers and sages, from time immemorium, have been establishing an innate and intimate relation between mind and breathing. When breathing is smooth and rhythmic, the mind is calm and stable. According to the Geeta, whoever chants AUM at the time of death gets liberated, which is possible only when a constant and continuous habit of pranyama is done throughout life. Pranayama is a yogic exercise to regulate the mind. It offers a simple procedure of inhaling slowly through the left nostril for one unit of time, retaining for four units and exhaling though the right nostril in two units, in the ratio of one – four – two. The cycle can be repeated alternatively with the left and right nostrils.

There was nothing in the beginning except That One existing with self-impulse (Svadhaya), AUM the eternal sound manifesting as the immutable syllable (Akshara) which when joined became the immutable work (Shabda). Sequentially arranged, it became the sentence (Vac) and Grammar (Vyakarana) became the sole instrument for explaining the mystery. It was followed by speech which was used for communication and referred to as language (Bhasha), the natural spoken form with Sanskrit as its refined form. The Vedas concealed mystical (spiritual) essence in the form alone. Though syllables (Akhshara) and word (Shabda) are immutable in essence, they change their forms suggesting new meanings through a process of conventional understanding as to what words shall stand for things according to time, place, people and context. This is how the Divine Power transformed eternal sound of AUM into syllables, words and sentences, enabling creation of a vast knowledge and wisdom consolidated in the form of four Vedas. It is generally believed that the contemporary societies changed the meaning of the original words '**Satya**' – the essence of existence to truth; '**Dharma**' – the perennial foundational principles of creation to performance of duty based on righteousness or having attribute or following particular belief or religious creed; **Shradha** – receptive resonance of AUM to a faith or a belief or creed or cult or words of preceptor (Guru); and **Darshana** – the philosophical awareness of the divine existence, energy, power or person to merely the physical act of seeing.

In reality, **there is no substantial difference between Brahmn and God. If at all a distinction is made, it is very thin and that too in terms of the perception. As stated quite after earlier Brahmn is a transcendental view of the Absolute or the Supreme Reality while God is its phenomenal view termed or Relative Reality**. It is like seeing the light through a prism or without it. The reality is one and the same. Brahmn spontaneously appears as God when looked from within the Universe. All names, forms and attributes arise spontaneously though the Maya-power which the human beings, as empirical persons, experience as if they are other than Brahmn. But in fact, they are not different from Brahmn.

The manifestation of God (Ishwara) in the names of Brahma, Vishnu and Maheshwara is nothing but forms of the trinity. It is not a physical form, but the form of consciousness. Brahma, Vishnu and Maheshwara are limitless, infinite and all-pervasive. This trinity of Brahma, Vishnu and Maheshwara permeates the entire cosmos in the macroscopic form. The trinity is also present in its microscopic form in the living beings. They exist in the smallest of the small and also in the vastness of the vast. Although, it is not possible for anyone to see the infinite cosmos and the trinity that pervades it, yet it is possible to realize their existence since they reside in every being. Lord Vishnu is the preserver or conserver of the Universe. In preservation or conservation, nothing is created or destroyed. The soul is neither created nor destroyed. Thus, it is eternal. Conservation also results from simultaneous creation and destruction. According to the Bhagvat Gita, the body is created and then gets destroyed. It is destroyed and then created. Either process contributes to a transient conservation. In other words, conservation is intimately linked to both creation and destruction. According to various holy scriptures, the Brahmn exists within and without all living entities. It is stationary as well as dynamic. It is subtle and gross, near and far.

The five basic elements namely space (Sky or Aakash), air, fire, water and earth are the main ingredients of life. Their related properties are sound, touch, colour, taste and smell. Space, air, fire, water and earth are assigned the respective number of sub-properties one, two, three, four and five. Their combination is determined by a mathematical formula called factorial five *i.e.* 5! = 5x4x3x2x1 = 120 *i.e.* one hundred and twenty. For example, fire is hot and red in colour, water makes a characteristic rippling sound, it is cold to touch, its colour is white and it is sweet to taste. The earth makes a characteristic rattling sound, it is hard to the touch, its various colours are blue, red and green, its soil is sweet, sour and so forth in taste; it smells, both pleasant and unpleasant. The five senses which perceive them are hearing, touch. sight, taste and smell. Space-Time phenomenon is the fundamental base of divine creation. Unless there is space for creation, and unless there is time to create, there cannot be creation. The origin of creation, therefore, implies the projection of space and time in a blend of instantaneous co-eval (of the same age or epoch) and co-eternal participation. Like the 'Big-Bang' theory attributed to the cause of creation, the holy scriptures of the Vedanta philosophy delineate the process of creation as having been evolved as a consequence of the cosmic act of Brahmn – the Supreme Being whose will of deciding to be differentiated from its own pure being became an intensely powerful vibration leading to the manifestation of the space-time continuum.

This space-time continuum is causing an unending sea of omni-present vibration giving rise to a pattern manifesting into the governing principles **sound** ('Sabda'), **touch** ('Sparsa'), **colour** (Rupa), **taste** ('Rasa') and **smell** ('Gandha'). The potential force of this five sense-data concretizes itself into the form of a gross-visible universe of gases, liquids and solids on one hand; and of space, air, fire, water and earth, on the other. These potentials and forms together constitute what is termed as the physical universe. This physical universe/cosmos further undergoes an intense gyrational motion due to which it organizes itself into the logical order of both ascent and descent, called as the fourteen realms of being or fourteen worlds, seven upper realms emerging from the earth, and the seven lower realms going deep down the earth. The upper seven realms constitute a more and more liberating tendency and expansion of dimension, while the seven lower realms follow a sequential order of descent into greater and greater negativity of perception. Both characterize more and more distance from earth – the centre of upper seven realms as the degree of ascending towards heaven while the lower seven forming the opposite counterpart as the descending regions of depth interpreted as hell.

The divine power has three features namely **the perceiver, the perceived** and **an intermediary link connecting the perceiver and the perceived**. The perceived remains the external world of earth, water, air, fire and sky, that is, the obvious material components of the universe, which is just matter, nothing more and nothing less. The perceivers, who are able to perceive this external form of the universe are known as materialists metaphysically, and realists epistemologically. However, the perceivers have to be endowed with a consciousness of something being perceived by them without which there would be no perception *i.e.* there would be none to know that the universe exists at all. Even to assume that the universe can exist without there being any perceiver of it is just another way of acknowledgement of the process of consciousness of the independent existence of the universe without a perceiver. Yet, the individual perceiver is not totally an independent and isolated perceiver of the perceived – the universe. There has to be a connecting link between the perceiver and the perceived. This link cannot be a part of the material universe since matter cannot evoke a consciousness of perception. Also, it cannot entirely belong to the individual perceiver, for, otherwise, it would be restricted to the location of the individual, and then there could be no linkage between the perceiver and the perceived. This link, therefore, has to be transcendent both to the perceiver and the perceived, and yet ranging above both as belonging to neither of them, though immanently (inherently) present in each of them. This invisible link is known as 'Adhidaiva'(consciousness), while the perceiver is called 'Adhyatma' (subject) and the perceived, the 'Adhibhuta' (object). This transcendent/ invisible link is the divine power operating in, and through everything, and existing as a hierarchy of linkages between the subject-object relationship in the evolutionary process of the universe in varying degrees in the ascending and descending orders religiously termed as gods or angels, and demons respectively.

Based on the hymn of Cosmic Creation in The Rig Veda, the Hindu religious system, as stated earlier, recognizes and adores gods such as Sri Ganesha, Surya (Sun), Skanda (Kartikeya) and others identified with five basic constituents of life namely, the space, water, air, fire and earth. The greatest gods, however, are considered to be the trinity of

Lords: Brahma, Vishnu and Mahesh associated with their respective consorts (divine powers) namely the goddesses Saraswati, Lakshmi and Durga (Parvati) along with their various incarnations elaborately eulogized in the eighteen Puranas (highest/ancient religious books). A set of six specified books out of the eighteen cosmic histories are diverted to the glorification of these gods and goddesses. The basic Hindu religious system is founded on the hymns of the Veda-Samhitas, the Upanishads, and the Bhagvat Gita. Nevertheless, the postulations and enunciations of gods and their respective divine powers (goddesses), is a common phenomenon with a few other civilizations also of the world in line with their system of religious ideology and worship. Only the designations and visualizations differ in accordance with the ethnic, geographical and cultural environment of the people. The concept of a 'higher than one-self' is an imperative need of everybody to survive in a state of assured and secured protection, and fulfillment of one's eternal aspirations and hopes. Thus, the tripartite system of the Universal Being into the subjective (Adhyatma), objective (Adhibhuta) and an intermediary link namely consciousness (Adhidaiva), raises the question of the whole range of theological enunciations. Consciousness (Adhidaiva) is the divine power that controls the subjective and objective sides of the Universe.

The Hinduism traces the origin of all things to God – the Absolute, the Universal Being (Brahmn) manifested in three divine forms namely Brahma, Vishnu and Mahesh. It is believed that Brahma is the inexhaustible source from which emanated the first four divine creations known as '**Sanata**', '**Sarandon**', '**Sanatana**' and '**Sanatkumara**'. They are believed to have declined to accept the offer of the Brahma for helping Him in the process of creation since they opted to get immersed in the Supreme Reality – the Brahmn. It may be noted that Brahma – the creator is one of the manifestations of the Absolute-Brahmn, the other two being Vishnu (the protector) and Shiva (the Dissolution). Eventually, the refusal of the four divines to help Brahma to carry out the process of creation led him to generate ten subsidiary divine beings or the creative powers known as '**Marichi**', '**Atri**', '**Anginas**', '**Pulastya**', '**Pulaha**', '**Kratu**', '**Bhrigu**', '**Vasishtha**', '**Daksha**' and '**Narada** as mentioned in Chapter 3. These names correspond also to the great sages (Rishis) endowed with cosmic capacity. Also arose from Brahma, the first man called the Manu – considered to be the father of humanity. This inclusive person is, then, separated into the first male and the first female, called Manu and Satarupa respectively. According to Srimada Bhagvat, this couple had two sons and three daughters whose relationship with the first progeny of Brahma mentioned earlier became the cause of the further diversification of the creative forces. According to another version stated in the ninth book of the Bhagvat, creation arose from the sun, on one hand, with whom began the Solar Dynasty and from the Moon, on the other, who became the source of the Lunar Dynasty. These two lineages are said to reach up to the latest personages in recorded human history.

The Vedic philosophy has evolved, not as a linear, but as a cyclic theory of time comprising of yugas (aeons or epochs), manvantaras and kalpas. The universe is without any beginning and without end. It is continuous process of recurrent phases of manifestation and dissolution. Four yugas (epochs) of the world have been described as Krita Yug, Treta Yug, Dwapara Yug and Kali Yuga. In the first yuga *i.e.* Krita (Satya) Yuga, whose duration is computed to be 4800 god-years, each god-year being equal to 360 man-years, there is perfect and eternal righteousness (Dharma). In the next three yugas, namely Treta, Dwapar and Kali, consisting of respectively 3600, 2400 and 1200 god-years. Righteousness (Dharma) gradually declines by one-fourth in every yuga, remaining to the extent of one-fourth only in the Kali Yuga. At the end of each Manavantara (the series comprised of the four yugas), there is Pralay, complete destruction. Thereafter, the golden age reappears. This cycle of creation, destruction and recreation of the Universe continues eternally.

Thus, Krita or Satya Yuga means perfect Dharam Yuga during which the moral order is firmly established. During the second yuga *i.e.* Treta Yuga means three quarters of Krita Yuga, the world is sustained by only three fourths of its total virtue or Dharma. During the Dwapar Yuga, only two of the four quarters *i.e.* half of Dharma are effective. Finally in the Kali-yuga, the present dark age, which began in the year 3102 B.C., the world subsists on only one-fourth (25%) of the full strength of Dharma. During this age, human beings and their world are at their worst with complete moral degradation.

Kali-yuga is often described as Kalaha Yuga (the epoch of discord) in which there is total chaos such as, misunderstanding between parents and children, quarrel between husband and wife, disharmony between the educators and the learners, and so on. People are indulged in cruel deeds worse than the beasts. They are devoid of compassion and sympathy. They neglect the path of morality and righteousness. People are reluctant to make efforts to follow the path of truth, righteousness, love, peace and non-violence. They fail to understand and believe that in the changing state of material body, there exists a changeless and eternal Atma. In the Krita (Satya) Yuga, longevity of life was much more. The physical structure of the living beings was gigantic. For example, human beings used to live for thousands of years. Life in the Krita Yuga, remained in the body as long as bones were intact. In Treta Yuga, the physical structure was slightly smaller than that of the people in Krita Yuga. Life remained as long as muscles and flesh remained in the body. In Dwapara Yuga, life remained as long as blood circulated in the body. In the present Kali Yuga, life remains as long as there is food in the body. Without food, the Kali Yuga living being cannot survive. In Krita and Treta Yugas, human being were very close to the human form of God. In these two Yugas, Atma (Soul) was more important whereas in the Dwapar Yuga, Mind became more relevant. The decline actually started towards the end of Dwapar Yuga since body became more important. In the current Kali Yuga, neither Dharma nor Satya nor Prema is important because mind is uncontrollable. The demonic values like ego, anger, desire, greed, jealousy, lust and hatred are dominating the human life because of lack of control on mind and senses. According to the Hindu tradition, a world or a Loka is a part of the Universe. The Universe is divided into three parts each part is called a world or a 'Loka'. Three parts or three worlds (lokas) are heaven, earth and nether world (Paataal).

Affirmation of One God as the transcendent and immanent creator of the Universe is called **Theism**. This Supreme God is proclaimed and adored in ecstatic language in several epics of the Hindu religion. The Rig Veda is reported to have affirmed such an absolute Brahmn – the Supreme reality in which every individual soul, be it god, human being or any other species, has to find itself wholly and completely. The system which overcomes the limitations involved in the concept of God as the Supreme Being and which provides the way of Theism defining God, is known as Monism. As stated earlier also, Monism is the form of the philosophical axiom which means affirmation of the absolute – above the concept of individual personality which is bound by limitations in the huge Universe of space and time. Vedas expound the vastness and beauty of this universe as an embodiment of the Supreme Being who is transcendent, immanent and omni-present. This ultimate reality is the all encompassing 'Purusha' (person) who is portrayed as all heads, all eyes and all limbs, who envelopes and permeates creation from all sides, and who stands above everything as the glorious immortal. The Vedas proclaim once and for all, the oneness of God, the universality of religion, the inseparability of the constituents of the social structure and utter imperativity of it for everyone to realize the Supreme Being – the infinite power in an act of inner awakening.

The Vedas further say that there was neither death nor immortality, for there was no differentiation whatsoever. Naturally, there was neither day nor night. There was only that one present, throbbing in all splendour and was glory but appearing as darkness to the eye that would like to behold it. There was nothing second to it. It alone was. From it arose the creation. How it all happened, no one can claim to say anything, for everyone came after the creation. This is the central point of the Vedantic tradition. Existence is one. Its various epithets like Maya, Sun, Indra, Varuna, Agni, Yama and many more unify in the unique singleness of the Supreme Being. A hymn of the Yajurveda gives a thrilling invocation of the Supreme being as Rudra – Siva, wherein He is addressed in all the visible and conceivable forms of creation. The Almighty God is the big and the small, the gross and the subtle, the low and the high, the distant and the near, the visible and the invisible, what is and what is not. Every type of individuality, form and action, every category of living species, everything that is animate or inanimate, all that is gracious and all that is frightening, and every deed that a human being is capable of doing, all things through which Nature works and is revealed, are adored as the forms of Shiva presenting a paradigmatic approach to the Supreme Reality. This Supreme Reality which transcends the three states of waking, dream and deep-sleep, is the non-dual Infinite Brahmn, who alone is Truth-Consciousness-Bliss (Sachidanand). Where there is duality, there one sees the other, smells the other, speaks to the other, understands the other. But, where the One above is (where there is non-duality), who can see what and by what, who can hear, smell, speak, touch, think and understand what by what. Whosoever has the self awakening within one-self, he is equivalent to the Brahmn, he becomes the doer of all things and he himself becomes the Brahmn – The Absolute.

Throughout the ages, the existence of God has been the most intriguing theme that occupied the minds of the philosophers, thinkers and scientists. Indeed, God, Universe and the living beings are considered to be three fundamental aspects of Metaphysics, of which existence of God is the most profound mysterious phenomenon. Lack of faith in God, and the urge for direct insight in this mystery surrounding God is leading humanity towards a greater dependence on reason and logical enquiry. Spiritual philosophers expound validity of the holy scriptures directed towards acceptance of God as a matter of faith and conviction. However, the major focus of all philosophical expositions has been all along the line of a common goal of exploring such a reality which is transcedenting the universe and whose nature requires to be established on firm grounds. The focus of science on the other hand, has been not only on the philosophical exposition about reality, but also exploring the fundamental basis of creation.

According to Sage Kanada regarding the creation of the Universe, earlier nothing existed. There were no sun nor planets nor earth nor sky, etc. There was only pitch darkness around. The combination of atoms resulted in the formation of hard matter of very high density. Consequently, a lot of heat got generated and all of a sudden, this hard matter exploded with a big bang scattering into pieces and spread all over. This became the basic cause of creation. Indeed, this is also the view of the modern scientists. The sound that emanated with the big bang is termed as "Pranav"' Omkara, the primordial sound by the spiritual philosophers. Thus, the atom is, in a way, their fundamental basis of creation. It was again Sage Kanada who recognized, many thousand years ago, the principles of Hydrogen and Oxygen. The scientists observed that hydrogen represented the water principles while oxygen represented the fire principle. Atom is not visible to the physical eye but it is present everywhere. The atomic process is highly mysterious. By conducting proper investigation in it, one can understand divinity through it.

The entire universe has been created by the Divine Will. It is a consequence of Bhagavat Sankalpa – the Will of God, which is the cause of creation. As discussed elsewhere also the cause has two aspects – the material cause and the efficient cause. The material cause resulted into Cosmos while the efficient cause is both transcendental and phenomenal, both being and becoming. With the emergence of the Divine Will, Brahmn became Easwara or God and by that will alone, God created the Cosmos manifesting Himself as all this. Maya, also as the divine will, inaugurated the manifestation of the Cosmos. Maya exists in every being and every activity. It has three characteristics: Satwic, Rajasic and Tamasic. The facets of that Divine Will are called power of Knowledge (Jnana Shakti), power of the Desire (Iccha-Shakti) and power of the Action (Kriya-Shakti). Srishti (creation), Sthithi (sustenance) and Laya (dissolution).

As said earlier, the whole cosmos is made up of five basic elements: Space, Air, Fire, Eater and Earth. Their subtle qualities are represented by sound, touch, form, taste and smell. All these have emerged from Sat-Chit-Anand (Truth – Consciousness – Bliss), the Primal Source. Besides these five basic elements, there are other four essential elements. These are the mind, the intellect, the will and the ego. Nature (Prakriti) consists of all these nine elements. Beyond this Prakriti; there is another higher realm known as Para-Prakriti. It is through Para-Prakriti, a human can become a Divine. Prakriti binds a human being, where as Para-Prakriti divinizes him/her. Prakriti is concrete, corporeal and intangible. It subsists beyond mind, space and time. Prakriti is the material cause for the Universe and Brahmn is its efficient cause. The Universe is the body of God. Either for the creation or for the existence of the world, Maya and Para Brahmn remain as the bases. Para Brahmn alone cannot be responsible for creation. Creation is possible only when Para Brahma and Para Shakti or Maya come together. Para Shakti and Para Brahmn are interdependent and are both needed for creation. In a way, Maya is the mother and Para Brahmn is the father of the Universe. Maya is the form of God whereas Para Brahmn is the name of God Himself. Thus creation and God are not distinct. Without God, there cannot be any creation. According to the Vedas and Upanishads, nothing is unintelligent or unconsciousness. It is only a matter of degree or gradation. Consciousness alone exists. Therefore, there is nothing like unconsciousness, inert or dead matter anywhere. Praana is the force from which generates forces.

While the Samkya doctrine of dualism of '**Purusha** and **Prakriti**' leaves an unbridged gulf between consciousness and matter, the Vedanta philosophy, on the other hand, postulates that matter is also a phase of consciousness. Vedanta affirms the indivisibility of consciousness which is the Absolute Brahmn. Vedanta, therefore, affirms the absolute reality of the Brahmn as the very source of the origin and final destination for the merger of everything. The existence of pure consciousness cannot be denied or even doubted since no one can deny one's own existence. Even denial of the existence of the self would indirectly admit the existence of consciousness of having denied it. The pure consciousness is the self of everyone which asserts itself always as the 'I' in every form of experience. Even the phenomenon of birth and death, the coming and going of things, creation and dissolution of the universe, are the processes involved in consciousness itself related to this 'I' principle. While time destroys everything, it cannot destroy consciousness because even the process of destruction also has meaning only when it is in the context of consciousness. Thus consciousness can have neither birth nor death. It is beyond the concepts of Space and Time. Being above Time, it is eternal *i.e.* timeless (Kalatita). Being beyond Space, it is infinite. This is the true self whose essence is consciousness. It is absolute truth-awareness-bliss (Sat-Chit-Ananda). Though the three states of consciousness namely working, dream and sleep are of daily experience, yet there is the fourth state (Turiya) of consciousness called the '**Atman**'. Its further evolution to the State of 'Samadhi' makes it dimensionless. Consequently, the 'Atma' gets identified with the Universal Brahmn since consciousness is the nature of Brahmn which exists in every individual as the **'Atman'**.

Through the path of unselfish action (Karma) in the service of others, through the deepest devotion to God (Bhakti), and through the knowledge of the Absolute Brahmn as the sole reality (Gyaan), the soul attains salvation. The holy scriptures declare that the Will of God (Ishwara) is the source of all creation. But subsequently, the created individuals assume in themselves a sense of autonomy and independence from God's universal creation and behold it as an object of sense-perception. When this isolation of the individual from cosmic realm takes place, the individualized consciousness falls headlong, as it were, into the empirical states of sleep, dream and waking leading to the compulsive urges of desires and ego. Freedom from this turmoil of individual existence attained through various modes of salvation brings back its merger in the Brahmn. This is basically the philosophy of Monism propounded by Adi-Shankaracharya in his interpretation of the Vedanta. This, however, is differed by other spiritual philosophers like Ramanuja and Madhavacharya. According to Ramanujachaarya, the relation between the individual and the Brahmn is not that of complete identity or merger but it is that of relatedness, as the body is related to the soul, but is not identical with soul. The Universe is the body of God. The way to God is devotion and not knowledge in the sense Shankara has defined it. While Shankara's thesis is called Absolute Monism (Non-Dualism) holding Brahmn as the Supreme and the only Reality, second to which there can be nothing while that of Ramanuja known as **Qualified Monism** holds that Brahmn is qualified by the realities of the world and individuals.

Madhavacharaya's enunciation, however, is radically different from both of those of Shankara and Ramanuja. His doctrine is that **Vishnu** is the ultimate reality, the world is real, the individuals are real but differ from one-another in the various scales of bondage and freedom. The individuals are servants of God as totally different from God, and also from the world of matter. He believes in the reality of triology namely: God, Universe and the individuals (living beings). According to him, Veda is the final authority through which alone **Vishnu** or **Narayana** can be attained through devotion. In Salvation, the individual does not merge itself with God in an intrinsic manner as Ramanuja holds. Madhavacharya has postulated five kinds of differences namely that (i) between God and the individual, (ii) between God and the Universe, (iii) between the Universe and the individual, (iv) between one individual and the other, and (v) between one part of the world and

Universe. Spiritual philosophers hold that liberation according to Shankaracharya is like water mixing with water or milk mixing with milk; according to Ramanuja, it is like water mixing with milk; and according to Madhavacharya, it is like rice particles mixing with sesame. However in this presentation, apart from the Vedantic School of Thought the term Vedanta, however, is a name given to any system of thought that recognizes the attainment or realization of God as the Supreme aim of life, in one way or the other.

4.3 Divine Incarnations and Human Beings

A number of questions are generally raised in respect of the divine power particularly in relation to God and His incarnations namely: **What is the process of incarnation and re-incarnation? How is it that people are able to identify a divine incarnation? Why does God incarnate in the form of a human being? What is the great purpose of divine incarnation?** The answers to such questions among others have two aspects namely: a deep faith in the holy scriptures which narrate the stories of divine incarnations, and a necessity felt by the scientific temper of probing that every visible thing must have its origin somewhere, and that all things must have been made by someone as a cause preceding an effect.

The concept of rebirth, incarnation and re-incarnation has found its acceptance by almost all the races and communities all over the world. Not only Hindus but also various other religious faiths have been believing in this notion such as Christianity and Islam while the Nile valley civilizations of Egypt had such a profound faith in this theory that they built stupendous pyramids to preserve the bodies of their pharaohs for their lives to return. In the Vedic philosophy of the Hindus, faith in the eternity of soul is a divine principle. This is equally true of other religions namely Buddhism and Jainism. The doctrine of rebirth is considered as the only logical explanation of the karmic philosophy of life. In the Hindu scriptures, however, there have been a few but rare and exceptional cases of immortality and non-rebirth. At least seven such immortals are quoted namely: Aswathama, son of Guru Dronacharya of the Mahabharata fame, who could invoke the Brahmastra – the ultimate weapon of destruction; the demon King Bali, the grandson of Prahlad – one of the greatest devotees of Lord Vishnu; the Sage Ved Vyasa, the great Spiritual Scholar author of Mahabharata and Srimad Bhagvatam and compiler of all Vedic knowledge summed up in the form of four well-known Vedas; Hanuman – the legend of Ramayana and the greatest devotee of Lord Rama; Vibhisana – the youngest brother of the demon King Ravana of Ramayana fame but having unshakable faith in Rama as God; Parashuram – one of the incarnations of Lord Vishnu who liberated the people from the torture of the then warriors community known as Khyatryas and Guru Kripacharya – an extraordinary teacher of both Pandavas and Kouravas of the Mahabharat.

In the Bhagvat Gita, Lord Krishna says to Arjun, "**Both you and I have passed though many births; you know them not, I know them all.**" These words provide a clear proof of the process of rebirth and reincarnation of living beings. In ancient Iran, called Persia, reincarnation was believed as the fundamental aspect of its religious faith. The learned philosopher of earlier civilizations including the leading minds of various religions always believed in the possibilities of the occurrence of the reincarnation. The famous Greek philosopher Plato, for instance, believing in the theory of incarnation and re-incarnation, used to say, "Soul is older than body, and the souls continually come from the abode of the dead into new life." He considered knowledge as sacrosanct. He further said, "To search and to learn is simply to revive the images of what soul saw in its pre-existent state in the world of realities." The ancient Romans too, accepted this doctrine. According to an eminent Roman philosopher A.D. Seneca, the mother's womb holds a life for nine months in order to make it ready for another birth, which is not the end of the process but is the continuity of eternity. Christians, Jews, and Muslims also have tremendous faith in the transmigration of souls which, in other words, means reincarnation. Even German philosophers like Manuel Kant and Leibnitz (also a mathematician) were most prominent among several others who have accepted reincarnation in explaining human existence. Some of the top scientists used their probing minds to understand the phenomenon of incarnation and reincarnation, and admitted it as a compulsive acceptance in the absence of any alternative explanation.

The theory of incarnation and reincarnation is one of the main features of Hindu metaphysics which has been beautifully summed up by Swami Vivekananda who said, **"Of all the theories that have been held by man about himself, that of a soul entity, separate from the body and immortal, has been the most wide spread; and among those that held in belief in such a soul, the majority of the thoughtful had always believed also in its pre-existence. At present, the greater portion of the human race, having organized religion believe in it; and many of the best thinkers in the most favoured lands, though nurtured in religions avowedly hostile to every idea of the pre-existence of the soul, have endorsed it."**

The believers in the theory of rebirth and reincarnation hold the view the soul represents the eternity of the immortal spirit and therefore it takes the form of existence. This process, according to them, of transformation of soul continues indefinitely in pursuits of higher and nobler stage leading towards the ultimate goal of salvation. According to the sages, seers and spiritual scholars, this concept of reincarnation has been prevailing from the dawn of human history with an unshaken intensity of conviction. Modern minds, however, demand concrete visible proofs to believe such a perception of the phenomenon of incarnation in the same way as they demand a physical proof of the existence of God. Nevertheless, neither existence of God nor reincarnation of soul can be denied just because of the absence of visible or physical proofs of the either entity.

Hinduism believes that the difference between a human being and a divine incarnation (Avtaar) is that a human being experiences fifteen attributes (five working organs, five sense organs and five basic elements of creation), but he is not their master. The five working organs of talking, walking, rejecting (excretion) and eating; the five sense organs of hearing, touch, sight, taste, smell; the five elements: earth, water, fire, air and space together constitute the said fifteen attributes. The 16th as the divine attribute is identified with the all knowing Paramatman. An Avtaar is beyond the five elements. A human being has two eyes. He can recall only past and see present. The divine incarnation is supposed to have many eyes which are spiritual eyes. He is able to see in front, behind, above, below. The divine incarnation is believed to be omni-present, omni-potent and omni-scient. A divine incarnation, like Rama, Krishna or Sri Sathya Sai Baba, by looking at people could see the past, present and future of the people, and everywhere and in every direction.

Hindus believe that the divine incarnation takes place whenever there is a decline of Dharma (righteousness), rise of demonic tendencies (forces), and there is yet a remnant of virtues, yet a trace of righteousness, for otherwise of what use of doctor is when the patient is already dead. When virtue and righteousness are afflicted with fear for their survival, then God incarnates to uplift drooping spirits, to revive faith and to protect all those who are virtuous. He guards and guides everyone to promote faith, virtue and righteousness. Granting fulfillment of realization of the goal to the seekers is also one of the missions of the divine incarnation. To achieve this goal, God appears in various forms of which human form is the most prominent. God becomes human so that human can become at least a real human if not God.

God adopts various forms (not necessarily the human form) according to the need of the situation. For example, Matsya Avtaar or **'Fish incarnation'** refers to the ancient legend of the fish and the deluge wherein Manu embarked on a ship with the sages and the seeds of all existing plants and trees of great medicinal values. Kurma-Avtaar or the **'Tortoise incarnation'** arrived to support the mount Mandara that had started sinking during the Samudra-Manthan or churning of the ocean. Varah-Avtaar or the **'Boar incarnation'** came to kill the demon Hiranyaksa and lifted the earth out of the deep waters in which it has been submerged. It is also a symbolic representation of saving the world from the deluge of sin.' The Narasimha-Avtaar or the **'Man-Lion'** incarnation is a combination of man (the best of higher creatures) and the lion (the best of lower creatures) representing the embodiment of valour. He saved Prahlad, His great child devotee from the oppression and torture by the father, the demon Hiranyakashpa. Vaaman-Avtaara or the **'Dwarf incarnation'** the first incarnation in human form, is connected to the legend of then demon but noble king Bali. God, in this Avtaar, approached the king Bali for a small gift of land to cover only three steps but covered the three worlds with three steps, liberating thereby the humanity from the demonic rule.

The next five incarnations are in the proper human form. Parasurama Avtaara exterminated the tyrannical among the Kshatryas (a warrior race) who were oppressing the people. The story of Rama-Avtaar has now become an immortal epic – Ramayana, while Krishna-Avtaar, is considered to be the first Poorna-Avtaar (incarnation complete in respects), the incarnation in total as Krishna, as the supreme statesman, warrior, hero, philosopher and teacher. God, Himself as Krishna, is the expounder of the Bhagvat Gita. Buddha-Avtaar or the incarnation of God as Buddha, though earlier not included in the cycle of the Avtaar, was however, incorporated as the ninth Avtaar as Buddha representing the enlightenment of the humans. The tenth Avtaar – The Kaliyug Avtaar, later in the form of Sai Trinity earlier as 'Shirdi Sai, later as Sathya Sai and the future Prema Sai with a mission to establish Sanatan Dharma and to inculcate a reign of Satya (Truth), Dharma (Righteousness), Shanti (Peace), Prema (Love) and Ahimsa (Non-Violence).

The word Kalki, according to Sai Baba, refers to the Avtaar of the Kali Yuga. The horse (Ashwa) of Kalki Avtaar signifies the mind which is perpetually restless. It is never steady. A horse is always moving its tail or leg or ear. Likewise mind is always jumping this way or that way. Only God, incarnated as a human being, can fully control the mind and hence, this Avtaar symbolically is always shown sitting on a horse. When God incarnates in the human form, it is very difficult to see the divinity hidden in his human body. People see His body and then draw parallels with their own bodies; they cannot distinguish the two human personalities. In case God does not incarnate in the human form, then people will have no opportunity to know and love God, nor they can afford to stand God in the super human form. For example, Arjuna could not bear the Viratswarup of Lord Krishna for a long-time and prayed Him to come back in His human form.

In the present world of science and technology, God is incomprehensible to the human beings because a divine can be understood only by the divine. A human being has to merge in God or to become God to comprehend God while an Avtaar provides a way out for the human beings to seek direct experience of Divinity. This is possible only through human form. Indeed, Avtaar is the starting point to invent God because Avtaar is God in the human form. An Avtaar provides an opportunity to human beings not only to begin their exploratory journey from known to the unknown but also shows the way to reach the goal of realizing the Supreme Reality – the Brahmn. An Avtaar offers a step by step guidance on how to achieve the ultimate aim of inventing God.

Krishna assures in the Bhagvat Gita: "**For the protection of the good, for the destruction of evil forces, and for the firm establishment of Dharma, I am born in every age**". It is commonly believed that God manifests periodically in every age as an Avtaar. Though Gurus and saints are many, an Avtaar is a separate and singular phenomenon comparable to none other. The Guru is a realized soul while an Avtaar is an evolved soul who takes human form for the welfare of mankind. When an Avtaar takes birth, it is a case of Avtaaran or descent of divinity, in order to facilitate man's ascent to divinity. An Avtaar's birth is voluntary through Vidya Maya or Yoga Maya whereas man is born under the spell of Avidya Maya or ignorance. Man's body is 'mrinmayam', made up of natural elements and his birth is karma janam or due to his actions of the past life, good or bad. The Avtaar's body is 'chinmayam', embodiment of Chit or pure consciousness and His birth is either 'prem janam' (embodiment of love) or 'leela janam' (embodiment of sport) brought about by prayers.

God's descent on earth in human form can only be an act of supreme compassion and love, to give people the key to Ananda or bliss. He comes for the spiritual regeneration of humanity through truth and love. Sri Sathya Sai Baba says, "**The Avtaar comes to reveal man to**

himself, to restore to him his birthright of inner bliss. He comes to awaken humanity to its spiritual reality and inform that every human being is actually an Avtaar or incarnation of the Divine".

The Avtaar behaves in a human way, so that mankind can feel kinship with Him and emulate the ideal behaviours and exemplary patterns set by Him. As narrated earlier in Treta Yuga, Rama took birth in Ayodhya, as much to vanquish evil represented by Ravana as to demonstrate the ideal of the perfect man (Maryada Purushottam). In Dwapara Yuga, Krishna came to quell the unrighteous (adharmic) forces represented by His uncle Kansa and the Kauravas, and to enlighten seekers about the three paths to salvation – karma, jnana and bhakti. When an Avtaar takes birth, Maya walks with Him. It is difficult to pierce the thick veil of Maya that surrounds Him and cover His reality. "**Thickly veiled by My Divine Power (Yoga Maya) I am not revealed to all. The deluded world knows Me not as the unborn and eternal**" (Bhagvat Gita). Thus, though the Avtaar may be in the midst of people, many may mistake Him at the most a realized soul or a god-man or a holy man. Others may doubt his divinity or disbelieve him entirely. Skeptics are part of the drama that surrounds the Avtaar. For every believer there is a non-believer. The doubt (kshobana) factor is whereby an Avtaar sometimes willfully confuse his followers. The Avtaar creates confusion in the mind of the devotees by some word or action, which clouds rather than reveals His omni-science. This is considered as a test of the faith and devotion of the devotees in God. The Kaliyuga Avtaar has to reveal His glory and heal the world with Satya, Dharma, Shanti, Prema and Ahimsa.

A complete Avtaar or an Avtaar complete in all respects has sixteen divine attributes (Kalas). In the Tretha Yuga, Lord Rama originally had twelve attributes. Parsurama, another Avtaar had three attributes. When Parsurama surrendered to Rama and embraced Him the three more divine attributes passed on to Rama. That made fifteen attributes to Rama. The remaining one attribute was represented by the three younger brothers of Rama jointly namely Lakshmana, Bharatha and Shatrughana. Another view is that Rama was equipped with twelve attributes and four more attributes were augmented by the three younger brothers and His most ardent devotee Hanuman. The Avtaar of Dwapar Yuga, Lord Krishna was born with all the sixteen attributes. The present Avtaar Sri Sathya Sai Baba also is believed to have been born with sixteen attributes. This is self-explanatory from Sai Baba's own loud and clear declaration when He said, **"In each Yuga, you have the Avtaar of the Lord come to redeem, revive and rebuild. At the**

present time, Maha Sakti (Super Power), Maya Sakti (Power of Illusion) and Yoga Sakti (Power of Vision with God) have come, all together, in one human form. Your endeavor should be to draw near and earn grace therefore."

In a subsequent declaration, Sri Sathya Sai Baba said: **"This is a human form in which every divine entity, every divine principle, that is to say, all the names and forms ascribed by man to God, are manifest. Do not allow doubt to distract you. If you only install, in the alter of your heart, steady with faith in my divinity, you can win a vision of my reality. Instead, if you swing like a pendulum of a clock, you can never succeed in comprehending the Truth and win that Bliss. You are very fortunate that you have a chance to experience the bliss of the vision of Sarvadaivatwa Swarupam (The form which is all forms of all Gods) now, in this life itself."**

At times, Sri Sathya Sai Baba told His devotees. **"The whole universe is in the palm of my hands".** The sixteen attributes in an Avtaar may be divided into three groups of five divine powers (Sakthi) each. The first group consists of the five powers (Saktis) are:—Creation, Preservation, Dissolution, Possessing the account of all the previous existences or Tirodhyak, and Dispensing Special Grace or Anugraha. The middle groups of the five powers (Saktis) are applicable to the present. Then the same group of five powers (Saktis) for the future. These two additional groups before and after the central group, are applicable to all the past incarnations and future incarnations respectively. The fifteen powers (Saktis) are put together to His Omnipresence through Time, that is to say that He is always present and beyond Time or His all pervading Awareness has instant knowledge of all things, at all times. Thus, by means of these fifteen attributes, the Avtaar creates, sustains, dissolves, assesses and modifies though the time, that is, from past to present to future with reference to the body, mind and soul. The sixteenth attribute is that of Being. This is how it makes sixteen attributes in an Avtaar.

The divine incarnations in human forms have special powers and strengths but they use these powers according to the need of the situation and in a discreet manner. Although, each of the Avtaar has human body, yet He is free from the human attachment. The divine incarnations live like other human beings. They eat, talk and sing like other human beings. They behave like all human beings and speak the same language, but their nature and actions are beyond the comprehension of the human beings.

The divine incarnations occasionally reveal their divinity through various types of miracles called the "Chamatkars" for the welfare of the human beings. These miracles attract the people to them. This attribute of attraction is another characteristic of divine incarnations. It is not possible to understand the nature and actions of the Avtaar. Saints or messengers come in the human form with a specific purpose to help some divinely inspired and restore the reign of righteousness. Such divine incarnations are regarded as Ansha Avtaar – partial manifestations of aspects of the Divine. Some of them are known as messengers of God. For example, Zoroaster first declared, "I am in the light." Then he said, "The light is in me." Finally, he declared, "I am the light". These declarations can be compared to three forms of Hindu philosophy of God, enunciated earlier as duality, qualified non-quality and non-quality. Likewise Jesus recognized his own divinity and declared, "I am the son of God". This is the stage of duality. Later on when he acquired some qualities of the Divine, he announced, "I and my Father are one". This was the stage of qualified duality or qualified non-duality. Finally, when Jesus achieved all the qualities of divinity, he declared, "I am myself God". This is the final stage of non-duality.

Sri Shankaracharya, a divine personality in his own way, considered himself a servant of God and preached the non-dual doctrine. He said, "**The bodies are different, the forms are different, but the inner self is one alone**". Hence, God is one and the goal is one. Enabling human being to have faith in God is one of the major objectives of divine incarnations. Divine incarnations, divine messengers, divine personalities and holy men of the highest order, all over the world and all through the times, have been known for their miraculous powers. Mankind's greatest saviors have been supposed to be endowed with divine attributes which the ordinary human being do not possess. There are numerous examples of the divine miracles performed by the holy men, saints and divine personalities in the Krita (Satya) Yuga, Treta Yuga and Dwapar Yuga. Even in the current Kaliyuga, miracles have been performed by the divine beings such as Zoroaster, Christ, Buddha, Mohammed, Nanak, Shirdi Sai and Sathya Sai Baba, some of which have been described in chapter 5 and 6.

A miracle is a manifestation of divinity in a human being. To a scientist, a miracle is something that happens contrary to the nature. When people think of miracles in the context of scientific possibility or impossibility, they have to go beyond the frontiers of man-made knowledge. The marvelous inventions contributed by modern science have given hope that impossible phenomenon may seem to be attainable.

The miracles of the divine souls, which are termed as impossible today, may be possible tomorrow with the advancement of science and technology. The hidden, mysterious and supernatural phenomenon of miracles, which transcends the frontiers of human knowledge, calls for newer visions and attempts to understand these miracles. To reject them outrightly, does not seem to be proper, just because they are beyond the scope of human comprehension or outside the dimensions of science. Just as science has no limitations, new challenges have to be met coming from both natural science and supernatural phenomenon.

Bhagwan Sri Sathya Sai Baba has been openly and candidly demonstrating these miracles since His birth in 1926 which have been inviting the attention of the scientists, parapsychologists, philosophers, rationalists, atheists of all shades. from all countries and continents of the world including the religious believers of all faiths, different communities from various casts, colours and creeds who have been seeing these miracles with their own eyes, days after days, months after months, years after years. This is a clear proof of the existence of the divine power of Sai Baba. **Can such miracles be shown by scientists, rationalists, intellectuals, parapsychologists? Can they create matter out of Vacuum?** It is an open challenge for the scientists and non-believers among others. Sri Sathya Sai Baba has been vindicating the divine power of the divine messenger of the past *viz.* Zoroastera, Buddha, Jesus, Mohammed and Guru Nanak as described in Chapter 5.

The divine power of Sai Baba equally demonstrates ample proof of the divinity of the incarnations Rama and Krishna whose miracles are well-known and scripted in the epics like Ramayana and Mahabharata. Rama, with his divine power of the toe of his feet, could lift and give life back to Ahalaya who was converted into a rock by the curse of her husband (another example of a manifestation of the divine power of a saint) or with his superhuman archery could fell down seven trees simultaneously (in a row) with one arrow, speaks of the divine power in the human form. Even His ardent devotee Hanuman did several divine miracles actions such as flying in the sky, increasing or decreasing his body-size to search for Sita or lifting the hill containing the life giving plant to cure Lakshmana who become unconscious due to the impact of the powerful weapon used by Ravana's son Meghnath. The way in which the great Incarnation of God as Krishna who demonstrated the divine powers through divine miracles shown right from His birth and later by furnishing divine robes to Draupadi to protect the honour and dignity of a woman or the way in which the invisibly satiated the appetite the Sage Durvasa and His thousands of disciples, showing His huge and stunning form (Viraat Swarup) while being as a messenger of peace to the court of the Kauravas on behalf of the Pandavas, His revelation of divine power to Arjuna (while giving through him, the divine message of Gita), against the mighty and power of the great warriors like Bhishma, Dronacharya and Karna in the Mahabharata, are all some of grand and glorious divine miracles which can be worded in any appropriate language.

The point is that such miraculous divine occurrences are the subtle workings of a divine power beyond the comprehension of the human mind to bring out the fact that the Supreme Power – called God exists and can be visualized or realized only by love and devotion, and not by modern scientific theories or rational analysis. The tales about the miracles of these divine incarnations, the divine messengers and various other divine personalities may contain some exaggeration. Even after allowing sufficient margin for exaggeration and distortion in the origin of several stories of their miracles, validity of the essential aspects of the past miracles cannot be denied especially after viewing the astounding miracles of the divine power of the Sai phenomenon. According to Sri Sathya Sai Baba, the miracles are the divine manifestations. Every devotee should try to understand the significance and purpose of those miracles. The main purpose of these miracles is to lead the human beings to the Ultimate Reality called the Brahmn. Thus, the miracles are not for exhibition but a divine manifestation with a divine purpose, and which cause no harm to anyone.

God, according to Sri Ramakrishna, sometimes works through His Divine Incarnation in human forms who can be worshipped and loved as intensely and as effectively as God Himself. God can be worshipped as male or female, there is no end to God's manifestations. God cannot be confined to one particular opinion. Direct or indirect experience (Anubhuti) of the Nirgun (attributeless) form of God is beyond all words and thoughts. Such an experience can surpass all that is mentioned in the Vedas, Upanishads and other holy scriptures. When the direct experience of the Highest Brahmn comes, said Ramakrishna, then Vedas and Vedantas look like straw or dry grass. Ramkrishna, generally, used to speak passionately about God – the great purpose of human life and the way to attain it as earnestly as possible. "**Cry to the Lord with an intensely yearning heart and you will certainly see Him.** People shed a whole jug of tears for wife and children. But who weeps for God? If they cry to Him with a real cry, they will realize Him", said Ramakrishna. He further assured that discrimination (Viveka), reflection and analysis (Vichara), detachment (Vairagya), loving devotion (Prem

Bhakti) and worship (Puja) are some of the ways which lead to the goal of God realization.

Sri Ramakrishna also spoke of qualified monism (Vishisht advaite) of Ramanuja with great fervor. The Universe, according to Sri Ramakrishna, with its various components has to be included in the totality of Brahmn. The consciousness (Chit) has to be qualified with matter (achit). The followers of non-quality would disagree with his views on qualified monism. But for Ramakrishna, monism is as valid as qualified dualism. For him each seer's opinion deserves due respect. Ramakrishna, however, never spoke of compromising monism. He held the view that the true self of man is one with Brahmn and non-duality or monism is the ultimate reality but the knowledge and experience of monism cannot be attained so easily. Indeed, it is not meant for the common people or an average spiritual seeker. For the common people ordinary spiritual aspirants and householders, complete devotion (Bhakti) wedded with knowledge (Gyan) and selfless action (Karma) in the form of service to others constitute the most feasible way.

Sri Ramakrishna often spoke of the identity of Brahmn and Shakti, the goddess of divine power, whom he would call Kali. He held the view that the Nirguna Brahmn is eternally free from the process of creation, preservation and dissolution, while Sagun Brahmn is Kali – the Mother responsible for the three cosmic activities. Indeed, for him, Brahmn and Kali are same He used to tell the ardent believers in formless God to accept the form of Kali as Brahmn. However, if they thought of God as Mother, they would feel an intimate closeness to Him. Thus, Kali, to Sri Ramakrishna, was Saguna Brahmn with Nirguna Brahmn in the background. So too were the other forms of the Mother, like the goddess Durga seated on a lion (the Simhavahini). Also for Ramakrishna, the divine incarnations like Rama and Krishna fall in the category of Sagun-Brahmn. Sri Ramakrishna was equally devoted to these incarnations or manifestations of the Sagun-Brahmn. Finally, Sri Ramakrishna remarked about the appearance of various religious sects and creeds and said that such sects or creeds will come and go but Sanatana Dharma will stay for all times, all ages and aeons to come.

Spirituality is a philosophy and religion is a system to follow the path of spirituality linked with God. Generally religion revolves around some divine personality who receives in some way a divine revelation or an illumination from God. Thereafter he either reveals this revelation in writing or tells it to the people by word of mouth. Being aware of his mission as a prophet or as a divine messenger, he tries to reach as many people as possible who develop an understanding of his proclamations and become his disciples or followers. Being commanded by God, when such a divine soul descends into the public view, he/she brings a new spiritual pulse to the world. He is fully aware that she is an instrument through which the Higher Power – the Supreme Reality can be realized. Jesus became God's messenger to mankind. Knowing this he likewise said, "It is not I, But my Father who has sent me." Mohammed became the prophet because he used to receive the divine instructions and communicate those instructions to the people. Same is the case with other prophets like Zoroastra and Guru Nanak Dev among others. The job of a divine messenger is to deliver the divine message to the people. It is up to the people whether to accept or not to accept, to follow or not to follow, to obey or not to obey. A prophet's or a messenger's responsibility is to sow the seeds of divinity among the people, the sprouting of which will be seen by the later generations. When a prophet has accomplished his task, he disappears and then the beginning of an organized religion is seen. The prophets do not come to establish any organized religion. They come to give not any material thing but the divine teachings which remains for centuries in the hearts of their followers and disciples.

The followers of divine prophets and messengers get together after the disappearance of their prophets and form a brotherhood or something to keep them together which leads to an outward expression to the Inner teachings of their prophets culminating in the form of an organized religious system. Such a system, initially, is pure and its teachings are closer to the preaching of the prophets. It is later that such teachings degenerate and often become rituals wedded with superstitions. The pure divine message of the divine messengers begins to lose the real essence and takes the form of a regimented system mutilated by their ignorant followers or narrowed by the bigoted zealots. But then this is inevitable. The original visions and divine revelations rise, grow and then fade. Consequently, the orthodox religions begin to follow and flourish in the name of God. The only way in which a religion, in its pure and divine form, can be established is by devotion to and proper worship of God, and not by arguments or discussions. The followers of a messenger or a prophet must follow the path of sincere devotion through worship embedded with four fold ways: Child like attitude of humility, forgetfulness of self, stilling of mind and connection with some human intermediary who is competent to lead the devotee to God-realization.

Religion is supposed to loosen human beings from their material desires, to get rid of their respective egos, and to motivate them to follow the true essence of worship to God. The basic feature of human personality is that an individual operates through the body at the gross physical level, through the mind at the intellectual level and through the soul at the spiritual level. What distinguishes human beings from other living beings is that human beings are gifted with a higher level of consciousness. They are equipped with an ability to exercise power of discrimination and decision. Amongst all of God's creations, only human beings can intellectually analyze, determine their respective value systems, and decide for themselves their way of action. They have the option to enhance the power of their analytical abilities by gaining knowledge and skill in the least management techniques on one hand, and imbibe the basic characteristics of the value system as the foundation of total quality management, on the other. Value-based Human Management means fusing the three fundamental axioms of Spirituality namely: Truth (Satya), Love (Prema), Righteousness (Dharma), among others – in conduct and in life as a whole. Spirituality harbours all faiths, emphasizes the unity of all religious experience and the oneness of divinity. Spirituality makes human beings completely committed to the service of mankind. It inspires them from within and directs them from without. It illuminates the heart and transforms (Consciousness); that resides in every being whether animate or inanimate.

According to evolutionary process propounded in the Hindu religion, there are 8.4 million species of living being on the earth of which human beings are said to occupy the top and rare position. This evolutionary process which involves births, deaths and rebirths, is considered to be a gradual ascent from soil to plants, from plants to insects and animals, and then to human beings and further to the divine beings. There is a countless variety of the sub-species even among these broad categories of soil (mineral), plants, insects, animals and human beings. The number 8.4 millions of species gives a scientific picture of unthinkable specifications in the structure of the living beings. However, from soil to the Absolute is indeed a huge sequential procedure of gradual ascent involving millions of mutations, transformations, births and deaths through numberless ages, till the divinity is reached in actual experience. It is believed in the Vedantic tradition that upto the level of the animal, penultimate to the human stage, the process of ascending series of evolution is spontaneous, without the lower species having to struggle to evolve into the higher level. This is termed as natural evolution. The logic advanced in this case is that Nature works automatically of its own accord in the case of these species in which the egoism of self-consciousness has not adequately manifested itself. But from human-beings onwards, a consciousness of the struggle on their part appears to be inseparable from the natural evolution although even then the universal working of the Nature cannot be claimed to have ceased its functions. Indeed, Nature's task remains incomplete until the Absolute Divinity is realized.

Based on Shankaracharya's philosophy of non-duality (monism) and a deep analysis of the subtle potentials of human nature and human history would, however, reveal that human autonomy, though not devoid of the ego's boast, is more or less a spontaneous activity and there is no such thing as an individual doing anything by itself. This also looks to be true because of the inter-connected and inter-dependent phenomenon of things in the universe, one thing depending on another thing or related to it even for its very existence and survival. The epic illustration of Krishna in Mahabharata, being at the back of every action, brings out the truth of the Divine Power of the Absolute Brahmn being there at all times as the directing power behind every event in creation, protection and dissolution, and behind every function being performed by various species of living beings. The evolution of consciousness, however, does not end with the human-beings since a human being may be described as the image of God only figuratively but not truly, for there has to be a further ascent in the process of evolution from human to divine. This is the stage which acts as a link between the human-beings and the ultimate Brahmn. Higher levels of life, beyond the human state, as propounded in the Upanishads, are in the form of great seers, gods of heavens, and divine incarnations, almost converging to the realms of God (Ishwara) and Brahmn. A human being, vested with the compulsions of being born and dying, is far from attainment of the aspired perfection in the spiritual scheme of evolution, and there is a long way higher up from human to divine and from the divine to the Brahmn. Sri Aurobindo has also given a vivid description of the stages of evolution from human consciousness to superhuman consciousness.

Consciousness, in its purest form, cannot be differentiated. It abides in eternity. Pure consciousness, when it enters the human body, get suffused with materialistic desires and becomes polluted. Thus descending from divinity, the pure consciousness constantly flows downward. It flows from inner-net to outward and drifting farther and farther from the Divine Soul. Thus, those who flow along the downward current towards the material world, remain ruled by the material consciousness, while those who move upward the stream flow towards the Divine Source, are supposed to have achieved spiritual consciousness or what is termed as the eternal consciousness, and which is also termed as the 'Self'. The 'Self' or the eternal consciousness or also called the Super-Consciousness exists eternally. The 'Self' in both present and transcends the three states of consciousness namely waking, dreaming and deep-sleep states, remains unchanged while progressing towards the Supra-Causal state in deep meditation, called Turiya. At this state of consciousness, the ego and duality both get obliterated and the seeker attains the highest state of spiritual consciousness – the seat of the Supreme Being – the abode of the Brahmn.

Human nature seems to be made in such a way that it feels that there must be some cause behind everything that happens. Change of weather/seasons, rising of the sun and moon, appearance of stars in the sky at night, blowing of winds and falling of rains, and such other several occurrences which generate a curiosity to know as to how and why this whole phenomenon is working. Seeking of the causes of observed effects is ingrained in the very constitution of human mind. All this is related to the fundamental **law of cause – effect** which states: **"Effects follow causes, even as causes precede effects. While the effects are important enough to require necessary consideration, the causes have precedence and, determine all such considerations. The effects are often the visible and tangible things; the causes are not always direct objects of perception**." It is this phenomenon of cause – effect that brings a sense of a 'higher than oneself' which is incessantly operative in the human beings making them to seek and discover ways and means of delving into the realm of the unseen. The primary impulse in the human mind takes the shape of evoking the perception of some superior power or an invisible force behind these occurrences and phenomena. This is generally known as the stage of spiritual awakening popularly named as **Animism** which regards Nature as inwardly filled with certain intelligent spirits or embodied souls. This is the stage which is also known as **spiritism** accepting the existence of gods and angles in the heavenly world, a stage which religious historians call **polytheism** – adoration of many gods directly controlling and monitoring the phenomena of all creation. The multitude of various gods and their many-fold functions and performances become the sources of mythology and epics with an important goal of developing religious consciousness. Human world has been involved in this stage. As a result, every religion has been glorifying vigorously its power and knowledge through the stories of its mythology and epics. Indeed, mythology is the preceding stage of **Theology** which deals with the study of a system of religious thoughts. Some religious historians describe this stage by naming it as **Henotheism** which means a particular god is considered as the highest god, raised above all other gods in the hierarchical echelons. There is also a grouping of gods into a single body of divine power.

Every material object in the world is filled with spirit (Atma). Though matter and spirit appear to be different, yet matter and spirit are intertwined and inter-related. Matter is gross and derives its energy and sustenance from spirit. This spirit has been highlighted in Brahmasutra. The invisible vital force (Praana) is the basis of all living beings which include plants, animals, insects, birds, reptiles, and human beings among others. Praana (life-force) has no form, while the body has a form. There is, however, the Atmic principle which confers all the potencies for the Praana (life-force). It is because of the power imported by the Atman that living beings are able to activate their bodies. The body inherently is inert. It is made up of different kinds of material substances. The Vedas declare that it is the presence of 'praan' (life force) which animates the body. The body itself represents inert matter. The life force operates in the body as a vibration and vibration derives its power from Praana. In human beings, there is an inner psychic system (Antakaran) which is made up of mind, the intellect, the will and the ego. The ego is linked to the Praana (life force). It is encased in the sheath of integrated awareness. The mind is linked to the will and is encased in the mental sheath. It functions between the soul and the vital life force. The life force functions between the mind and the body. The intellect (buddhi) functions above the level of mind, while the vital life force functions below the mind. Human beings and the Divine are integrally related to each other like the object and the image. Creation comes into existence only when God (Parmatma) – the Super Universal Soul and the living being (Jivatma) – the individual soul, come together. Human being is the most refined of all living beings that exist in the infinite cosmos and at the very apex of God's creation.

Some of the profound researches regarding Human Personality in Indian Philosophical Thought suggest various aspects of human personality as held in different classical schools of Hindu philosophy. While Nyaya Vaishishika holds human personality as the combine of matter and mind powered by spirit (the intelligent self), the Sankhya Yoga views it as spirit in solitary splendour evolving from matter, mind, universe intelligence and after mitigation of three attributes (gunas) resting as self (kevalya-state). Similarly for Mimimansa, human personality and its evolution is based on Karma/Dharma, enabling one to sculpt one's own destiny. The Vedanta, as the culmination of all Hindu traditions, highlights that Thou Art (Tattvan Asi) through meditation (Sadhana or Dhyan) and divine knowledge (Gyana). In fact all schools of thought represent a spectrum of various elements of one reality – the divine human.

According to the Vedas and Upanishads, nothing is unintelligent or unconsciousness. It is only a matter of degree or gradation. Consciousness alone exists. Therefore, there is nothing like unconsciousness, inert or dead matter anywhere. Praana is the force from which other forces of nature – gravity, electricity and magnetism evolve. It was always assumed that these forces are not intelligent. Now even the scientists are discovering that this is not true. These forces are also intelligent. The most important system of all these is the one which is inside the body named as the vital system which deals with the operations of the life force 'Praana' – an energy quantum distributed equally throughout the body, giving it strength like the flow of electric current through every pore and cell of the body system. Infact, 'Praana' is the life line of the body. It means energy combined with consciousness – the force with self-regulated motion or movement and not governed by anything else, vibrates, throbs and animates in a particular manner or pattern. Any part of the body gets paralyzed if it is not touched by this life principle called the 'Praana'. The physical body as such has no life without 'Praana'. The life principle 'Praana' is said to function in five ways namely **Praana** itself, **Apana**, **Vyana**, **Samana** and **Udana**. Praana is that vital force which ejects the breath out in exhalation. Apana is what pulls the breath within inhalation. Vyana is the circulatory force which causes the equidistribution of blood through the blood vessels spread throughout the body. Samana is the energy of heat that digests the food in the stomach. Udana is the state of deep sleep and also is said to cause for the separation of the true person from the body at the time of death.

As regards **human personality**, it is a composite structure of the physical, vital, sensory, mental, intellectual, causal and spiritual layers. The physical layer is the outermost crust called the human body of a person. It is composed of the same stuff as the earth, water, fire, air and ether called the basic elements of the physical world. The chemical components of this body comprise of various elements. This human body is just a leather bag full of the elements of solid matter, liquid including blood and water, gas, brain and heart, with space providing its volume. Food intake maintains the body, energize it with subtle forces generated through the digestion of food which permeate the entire body in its various systems like the circulatory, respiratory, alimentary and so on.

The questions, however, arise: **Why does Praana act in this manner? What causes the Praana to function like this**? The answer to both the question is the same. As said earlier, it is the mind which makes the Praana to perform the aforesaid five-fold functions. It is, infact, the mind which works through the sense-organs namely, seeing, hearing, touching, tasting and smiling. Mind performs four functions: as '**Manas**' (indeterminate thinking); '**Budhi**' (determinate or discriminative thinking); '**Chitta**' (memory or remembrance); and '**Ahankara**' (the ego principle). The ego-principle asserts and arrogates to itself, the self-identity of human individuality through its layers right from the physical to the casual. The 'Praana' is a sort of link between the physical body and the internal organ, the psyche closely related to the mind. The faculties of feeling pleasure and pain, the sentiments and emotions of all variety, are the characteristics of the mind-stuff, the psychic organ. Rationalization, discrimination, decision-making and logical judging faculty all together constitute the phenomenon which is generally termed as '**Budhi**' or the pure wisdom. It is this function of the mind which draws conclusions based on the pros and cons of a situation, either by deductive or by inductive inferences. A detailed treatment of these aspects of mind constitute what is known as human psychology which is beyond the scope of this work.

Hinduism believes in the mantra of **Gayatri** the protector of Praana and the goddess of wisdom and pure intelligence, and Yajna, a noble act. Gayatri protects 'Praana', the source of liveliness, consciousness and vitality. It grants the ability to move, work, think and possess wisdom. Indeed, life itself is called Praana. It is the presence of Praana that keeps alive the body. Praana is the soul residing in body. Due to the presence of Praana, living organisms are called Praani. A person who is full of Praana lives in a different world. He is enthusiastic, determined, courageous, patient, hopeful and active. Human strength is derived from Praana, not from bones and muscles. A person whose Praana is strong becomes powerful and hard-working and achieves happiness in the external world – materialistic happiness and spiritual happiness of the inner-self. The essence of life is Praana because it controls physical capabilities. God has provided this Praana in plenty to the living beings. It is present all around and can be stored by invoking the grace of Gayatri. Indeed, Gayatri inspires the brain to remain saturated with divine, virtuous qualities, which in turn inspire people onto the path of true well-being. Cultivating noble thoughts, and practicing righteous deeds increase their strength. With every act, they become stronger. On the other hand, thoughts and actions inspired by impure intelligence decrease the power of Praana day by day. True wisdom keeps lifestyle luminous (satvika) – pure and austere – by maintaining control over the senses like willful avoidance of lusty food, practicing celibacy, simple or natural daily routine and hard-working attitude. These qualities keep life energy, preserve strength and increase lifespan. Normally an individual is trapped in Maya due to which he remains attached to constricting elements in life. He experiences pain and suffering, and ends up having led a purposeless life. This happens because of the lack of righteous knowledge. Gayatri Hymn (Mantra) acts as a bright, divine light, a message of hope for people caught in the darkness of ignorance. It opens up the door to material, spiritual and mental bliss. It grants a third eye; the eye of wisdom through which one can look at the world prudently and attain the aim of life, self-awakening. This is the philosophy of the Gayatri Hymn. It is considered to be unique in the whole of Vedic literature because it enables the practitioner to worship (Upasna), propitiate (Stuti) and pray (Prarthana) – the three modes of praying to identify with the divinity.

Human beings feel vulnerable. They are always fighting a war against circumstances and struggling for financial, emotional and social security. They have the ability to choose from a variety of options available to them. They miss the past, remain worried in their present and keep on planning for the future. Looking around the nature, it seems that the birds, reptiles and animals live with scarce planning, less manipulation and no worrying about the future. They remain contented in the present with whatever little, need-based, they obtain. Human beings are equipped with the sense of imagination, conceptualization and manipulation. However, the fear of destiny, unknown fears, suspicion, anxiety and abstract intuitions, continuously dominate their personalities. Because of their mental and intellectual capacities, the human beings are able to invent tools and technologies to transform the external world for self-comfort and security. Abstraction and imagination are the natural gifts granted to the human beings that they can comprehend the 'inner world'. They are the rare species who can raise the **questions such as, Why this creation? Who has created this Universe? How it has been created**? Thus, this type of heightened ability of thinking and comprehension is bestowed only on the human beings. It is, therefore, destined for the human beings only to realize and understand the 'self' leading them to gain self-knowledge and spiritual wisdom. According to the ancient scriptures of Hinduism and reiterated by Bhagwan Sri Sathya Sai Baba, the human form is unique in the sense that a human being is equipped with 80 per cent divinity while an animal has only 15 percent divinity. Therefore, a human being can raise himself to union with God, whereas the animal can never be free of its natural state. The human being serves to reveal the indwelling unseen divinity. The expression of life is upward through the human to the Divine. By virtue of human birth, the next step is the realization of the Divine. Human life is sacred and must be appreciated as having the highest value. Human birth is a special opportunity to get freedom from the cycle of birth and death. It is one-time chance for God-realization because God can be realized only through human birth.

It is generally believed that a human birth is very rare. Once an individual soul attains the human form, then he is no longer under the control of nature. He or she, then, has the unique capacity of free will, with an opportunity for further evolution from human to divine. While enjoying the faculty of free will, every human being is focused on achieving four objectives: security, pleasure, righteousness and liberation. What provides him/her security – emotional, economical/ financial, and social, is called 'Artha'. Seeking pleasure is another objective of a human life. This is called 'Kama' in Sanskrit. This include sensuous pleasures, intellectual pleasures. Anything that satisfies the senses, that gives mental pleasure *i.e.* pleasure to the mind, and that gives body pleasure is 'Kama'. This also includes the aesthetic pleasures. The third objective namely 'Dharma' means harmony in the human conduct, behaviour and social service. 'Moksha' is the last and lasting objective of a human being. This means liberation from body pleasures (Artha), sensual or even sensuous pleasures, and detachment from the worldly matters.

Philosophy and culture are some of the qualities that the human brain can delve deep into while invention, discoveries and pursuits are some other faculties that make the human beings more creative than other species of nature. "**He who knows the first vital thread, binding all the things formed in the shape, colour and words, knows only the physical form of the Universe, and knows very little. But he who goes deeper and perceives the string inside the string, the thin web binding separate life-forces with cords of unity, knows the real entity. Only he knows truly the mighty omni-potent, omni-scient and omni-present God, who is within and beyond all formulated entities of the vast Universe. Penetrate deeper to know the ultimate truth**", says Atharva Veda.

To the Greek philosopher Aristotle, God is the unmoved mover towards whom everything gravitates as if pulled by a powerful magnet. All the variety and material shapes of things tend gradually to unfold an essential form which expands itself in an ascending sequence of evolution leading towards a Pure Form, which is God. Immanuel Kant, a German Philosopher rejected the possibility of knowing God through understanding and logical reasoning, holding thereby the conviction that the Supreme Reality cannot be expected through the rational faculties of a human being which are limited in their operation in relation to the phenomenon of Space and Time. Thus, Kant, inadvertently or otherwise, seemed to have acknowledged the existence of a super-phenomenal reality called God. Hegel, another German philosopher, followed the path of logic and propounded God as a universally pervasive phenomenon which, by positive, negative and synthesizing processes, rises gradually to higher and higher forms of knowledge until the Ultimate, the Absolute is reached.

Some other scholars relate the concept of God to the mathematical notion of infinity. Such a concept, according to them, is beyond the comprehension of the human mind unless the infinity is shown to exist in reality. Indeed, infinity cannot have a fixed location. Its realm is infinitude. What is infinity? That which is not finite. That exactly is the description of God. Moreover, the dispenser of justice behind good and bad deeds has to be someone beyond the world of good and bad. Such an entity obviously has to be an infinite being. Infinitude is the true nature of the existence of God. Furthermore, even in the context of the object-subject relationship, there cannot be consciousness of the object by the subject unless there is a transcendental conscious principle linking the object and subject which would be the Veritable Infinite termed as God.

Religious mythology has a special significance. It raises the human imagination and feeling into the visualization of a blend of glory and power. It brings an idealization of human instinctive aspirations and perception of things in direct contact with a kingdom of human values, spiritual beings and divine personalities. It stimulates human perception to a stage of profundity and perfection through the grand and glorious descriptions of spiritualists and divine personalities. Mythology so portrayed lifts the human thought from the frailties and limitations of earthly possibilities and enables the human mind to roam freely in that envisioned world of aspired achievement. According to an eminent philosopher poet Dante, all illustrative depictions of the epics rising above the historical grounds to the regions of the ruling gods, do not constitute mythology in the sense of substanceless conceptualizations, but are the portrayals of the deep possibilities, profundities of which the human soul is capable, and which height of the divine power, the soul is able to envision between the lowest earth and the highest heaven. Ideas move the world. Action follows thoughts. Events take place first in the world of the physical phenomenon and gradually move through the layers of space-time to the heavenly realm of spirituality.

Religious mythology provides a comprehensive grasp of all reality in its forms, degrees and states which effectively bridge the gulf between human beings and nature, and between nature and God. The myths of religion, therefore, constitute active meditations of the spiritual consciousness on the higher realities of life. The fables and fairy tales which are enjoyed in leisurely readings cannot be termed as vacuous ideas from the human mind because all ideas are rooted in a vivid expression of same level of reality. That is why, the stories with super-physical and superhuman depiction of gods charge the human feelings and pull them out from the enclosure of their hibernation. Their repeated narratives reinforce the love of their culture, as if epic history and drama are the very essence of their religious foundation.

The existence of God can be realized only through the path of devotion to Him. Love and adoration of God as the Sovereign Supreme or as the Ishwara or as the Master of Creation is the way in which His existence can be realized. Intellectuality, rationalism and scientific or analytical approach cease to help in the invention of God. It is because of this love and adoration of God that seers like Narada can travel to all the heavenly worlds penetrating through the Cosmos for contacting God. It is a representation of the significance of the divine devotion that it can have an impact on everyone and everything portrayed in the vibrating and thrilling legends of various Epics and Puranas. God's creation is said to be constituted of different realms or 'Lokas' as they are called to realize the relevance of God to creation. Notable holy scriptures employ various techniques of presenting God as a Personality and glorifying Him as if God lives in a realm as a human being does. The special emphasis of these Epics is that God can act, hear and speak like the human beings. The stories, analogies and legends that these scriptures employ for describing God's relation with living beings, signify that God is around them. He is portrayed as Father, Mother, Guru, Friend, Supporter and Saviour. Lord Krishna has proclaimed in the Bhagvat Gita that He is the Creator, Protector, Dissolutor, Saviour, Sustainer, Onlooker and the Supervisor and with many more such characteristics which make out that God is all and is everything.

All living creatures, human beings, animals, insects or crawling reptiles, as well as nature and its plants have sprung from the common origin. All are the divine sparks of God – the absolute Brahmn. Therefore, all should treat each other with love and reverence. The only way for them to understand each other is through good will and tolerance. Nature has tremendous patience. It waited for millions of years to bring out the human beings. It is willing to wait for millions of years more to make the human beings as spiritually perfect beings. Nature itself is an expression of God. Human beings should follow the path of nature which is full of good will, patience or tolerance. Apart from the two parameters of good will and tolerance, there is another essential trait and that is hope or optimism which indeed means faith in the divine planning. There should be an eternal faith that whatever happens is for the ultimate evolution of mankind. If there is a faith in a divine plan of all beings, even the hardest sufferings can bring a positive and constructive outcome. Faith in God, as the third parameter, helps everything and everybody. The fourth and the last mode is the attitude of worship to God and service to the living beings. Service means an inner dedication, a desire to be constructive in life and to do something positive for the humanity, no matter how small the service is, how limited is its scope. An inner attitude of service is the real dedication to the humanity and devotion of God. Good will, tolerance, faith and service together should determine the four paths of true religion.

Chapter 5
Divine Messengers and Their Doctrines

Spiritual Universality means profound respect for all religious philosophies and faiths. The concept of religious secularism has been vibrant in the Indic region with the realization of not only of one supreme divine power called God but of the essential oneness of all existence. Hinduism proclaims that all paths of religious faiths and worship reach the same destination as different rivers merge in the same ocean. The Ultimate Truth of the Supreme Reality is one and the same although it appears differently to different people of different religions. Every form of prayer and worship is a valid way to reach the same Supreme Self. The vision of Spiritual Universality believes in equal respect for the Vedas, Ramayana, Gita, Bible, Quran, Guru Granth Sahib and all other holy scriptures. The religions and spiritual paths proclaimed in all such sacred scriptures get harmonized into one Universal Spiritualism envisioned by Swaami Vivekananda.

The modern materialistic concept of secularism permeates disbelief in all religions since it is confined to the political philosophies wedded with vested interests. Secularism, in the present age of advanced science and technology, has to be based on the science of every religion and its spiritual philosophy equipped with axiology so as to lead the humanity to a state of peaceful and harmonious coexistence. Spiritual universality must have the propensity to absorb a multitude of thoughts including even atheism in the sense that there should be no place for excommunication. Indeed, there seems to be common acceptance among all major faiths in their refined outlook that there is only one and the same source of human evolution: Hindus call it Brahmn – the Supreme Reality, Christians call it Abraham, and the Muslims call it Ibrahim. The difference, if any, among Brahmn, Abraham, and Ibrahim is that of semantics.

All religions and spiritual philosophies of the world speak of one God as Supreme Being. But whom do they refer to? Does God have a specific name and form? If so, then how is that God considered to be universally supreme yet hidden from everyone's eyes? All faiths believe that God is not a person. It is the most subtle phenomenon or an entity called the Supreme Reality or Supreme Power which is omni-present, omni-potent and omni-scient. God is considered to be that divine quality which is present in every particle of matter, which fills the atmosphere and galaxies which is everywhere. Sri Ramakrishna said, **"God with form is just as true as God without form"**. According to him, an individual cannot realize or experience God even if he or she has the slightest doubt of His existence and the trace of worldliness. One can be directly aware of the Brahmn in one's innermost consciousness only when one renounces all sense of form, taste, smell, touch and sound, and only when one's mind is completely under control or still. This means leading the mind to a Supreme Being that rules the Universe. How to know this top most being on the ladder of evolution? Is God a person – a he or a she or an it? It is said that God is nameless and formless. Yet, various names are given to God who is worshiped in several forms.

Presence of God is claimed to be felt through many ways such as prayers, chants, offerings, meditation and devotional songs that invoke the divine presence and connect to God within one's innerself, keeping body in poised postures with folded hands, kneeling on the floor of the place of worship or squatting on the ground, raising arms over one's head and in various other ways. All religions preach some such ways which derive their strengths from the spiritual truths envisaged by prophets, divine messengers, divine personalities and sages. Various rituals and practices have been prescribed by them for disciplining the mind and developing love for God. Every religion has certain symbol which is like a rallying point e.g. for Hinduism (Sanatan Dharma) the symbol is the omni-present 'OM'; for Christianity, it is the Cross, the test of everything which deserves to be called Christian; for Islam it is the Crescent, for Buddhism, it is the wheel, for Zoroasterism, the symbol is 'fire'; 'Shalom' of the Jews in Hebrew means peace and wholeness.

Throughout the human history, God has revealed Himself to humanity through a series of divine Messengers and Prophets, each of whom founded a great religion. These divine personalities appeared for the purpose of educating humanity about the Creator and for cultivating the spiritual, intellectual and moral capabilities of the human race. The relationship between God and human beings is fostered through prayer, knowledge of the scriptures revealed by these personalities, loving devotion to God, moral self-discipline, and service to humanity. The most important aspect of cultivating a spiritual life is that an individual increasingly develops those innate qualities that lie at the foundation of human happiness and social harmony. The coming of each new Prophet marks a fresh spiritual impulse, stimulating spiritual enlightenment, and hence spiritual advancement. The purpose of the advent of these divine personalities is to make humanity understand the nature of God, which is limitless, infinite and all-pervading. It is impossible for the mortals human beings with limited intellects and finite capacities, to directly comprehend the reality of God. It is through these Prophets and Messengers that God's divinity and His attributes can be realized providing a pure channel for the communication of God's will to humanity. God's messengers and prophets have a two-fold aim; one they are divine beings reflecting God's will, the other, they are also human beings, subject to birth, disease, suffering and death. They have distinct physical identities and they appear at periodic stages. These variances give rise to cultural distinctions between religions that sometimes conceal their inherent unity. Fundamentally, however, their message has been the same. Each has stressed the importance of faith and devotion for God, obedience to His will and love for humanity. Although the divine messages have been varying in formats, yet each has taught that individuals should treat others as they would like to be treated themselves by others.

God is infinite. He has neither a beginning nor an end. Those who have complete faith in God and who love Him unconditionally do realize a Divine Power they cannot see. God, who is both manifest and unmanifest, appears in the physical form of a Prophet. For, people only follow someone whom they can see and hear. Only with God's blessings, grace and mercy, a person begins to realize God. Only then the divine power starts operating through him. God chooses prophets, and when the right time comes, gives them knowledge. The chosen ones become receivers of divine revelations. After God begins using a person as His Messenger, that person no longer works from his own mind or his own heart. It is all God's work. All prophets come from the same light. They all give the same basic message. None comes to change this message. They come to remind people of the earlier divine messages which the people may have forgotten. The followers, however, separate various religions into fortresses, each claiming one of the religions as their own. God is neither a Hindu nor a Muslim, nor a Christian. He is indeed always One. Light of God cannot be confined to man-made enclosures. It radiates throughout all Creation. No prophet belongs to just one caste, creed or community. Jesus is not confined only to Christianity; Moses is not only a Jew; Prophet Mohammed is not only a Muslim; and Guru Nanak Dev is not only a Sikh. They came not to establish institutionalized or sectarian religions. These divisions are created by human beings and reflect their own attitudes. By contrast, prophets come into world with a message from God. They come to remind people of divine teachings, making them fresh and new again. They come to teach love, motivate sense of service to humanity, and remove ignorance by enlightening people with the knowledge of God. They come to transform the human society and show how to live a life based on spiritual and moral values. Human beings have spiritual wisdom deep within them. The One who creates the world is already present in them. But it is only when a prophet appears and starts speaking to them with divine wisdom and awakens this knowledge in them.

According to Swami Ramakrishna Paramhans, the essence of all religions is God-Realization. He was guided by two preceptors (Gurus) namely Bhairavi Brahmni and Tota Puri who seemed to have inculcated in him the teachings of all religions including Christianity and Islam. As a result, Ramakrishna found common emotional similarity in all religions leading to God-Realization. Eventually he declared, "As many faiths, so many paths", in line with the basic maxims of the Universal Religion (Sanathan Dharma) propounded by Hinduism. Ramakrishna left his physical body during the early hours of 16 August 1886 with his last message that God-Realization was the supreme goal of all living beings for which control over lust, greed and attachment was essential. While breathing his last he said to his disciples, **"I have not passed away, I have gone from one room to another"**.

The divine personalities, all over the world and through all times have been known for their divine powers manifested through several types of miracles which remain unexplained in terms of logic or rationality. They include Zoroaster, Buddha, Jesus, Mohammed and Nanak, among others who have been known to be endowed with divine attributes that are not possessed by the ordinary human beings. Some critical rational minds, at the same time, have also been doubting the divine powers of these divine personalities generally known as prophets or messengers. Along with the demonstration of their miraculous powers, these divine beings have been preaching moral and spiritual values through their discourses and doctrines which took the shape of some kind of a religion believed in and followed by millions and millions of people. The believers and followers always have been developing faith in the miraculous divine powers of the divine beings who have been preaching their doctrines in the form of religious principles.

With elements of Nature and all its aspects sufficiently explored, science, while trying its best to find answers to this phenomenon of divine miracles or divine power vested in some divine personalities, ultimately reached a conclusion where supernatural phenomenon did not appear to be unreal. With this compulsive submission of appreciating the supernatural or superhuman powers manifested by rarest of the rare human beings and looking at the creation, one finds an unexplained power even in the smallest of the living creatures some of which cannot be performed even by those who are vested with superior intelligence and ability. An ant can ascend any height to trace a sweet candy travelling any distance. A bird can fly high in the sky while defying the laws of gravitation which is beyond the capacity of a human being. It is equally true of man's inexhaustible power of mind in inventing miraculous things. This is all true. **Then why can't the superhuman powers be possessed by certain human beings**? What is happening in nature is certainly a miracle some of which is explainable by the human mind but not all and indeed some remains unexplainable. Ramanujam, a young Indian mathematician is one such example among several others, whose contributions to mathematics are uncomparable and exemplary. **Why are there galaxies, stars, planets and satellites, and why are they moving in a perfect and harmonious order**?

A miracle is undoubtedly a manifestation of divinity in a human being. Rules of nature are the laws of the creator. A perfect soul or a divine soul can itself become Nature, and then can do what Nature does. What a perfect soul in the human form does is termed as a miracle. It is same what nature does which is equally a miracle. "**A miracle**", says Sri Sathya Sai Baba, "**is only an evidence, not an exhibition of the spiritual power which mankind needs to realize. It is a sign which helps to turn into faith, devotion, inquiry** and **realization of man's own atma**". A miracle is shown only to sense the purpose of providing evidence that divine power does exist. When Sai Baba materializes a golden chain or a piece of sugar candy or when He heals a sick person, His purpose is to create faith of the observer in the divine power and to give him an elementary lesson to strengthen his belief in the existence of an ultimate power called God. Miracle is a message by which the divine beings, both divine incarnations and divine personalities, want to raise the level of consciousness of human beings to a state of spiritual awareness and make them realize that human destiny is guided under spiritual conditioning. It is one of the ways of transformation to lead humanity to divinity. Divine discourses and messages are some of the other ways which help the process of transformation. Indeed, there are some divine personalities who do not use the method of divine miracles to achieve this purpose of human transformation. They are confident that they can succeed in this mission through divine discourses and preachings. Mahavir, the last 'tirathankara' of the Jains, is considered to be one such divine beings among others.

Modern historians search for biographical and eventful details of eminent persons which should be acceptable as actual in the historical terms. Their problem is to determine how much of the material available can be accepted as historical. A substantial part of the historical material is generally a legend much of which cannot be summarily dismissed just because its authenticity is open to suspicion on technical grounds. In many cases, there is an evident possibility that some historical authenticity may remain suppressed beneath a super structure of the associated legend. Not all of such possibilities can be satisfactorily tested. It is, therefore, desirable to structurize all such material and wherever possible to affirm or reject it. Since most of the biographic profiles of various divine personalities, sages and saints are given in the religious books, it does not mean that their biographical sketches in human terms are inadequate and unauthenticated. The historians should not forget that lives of the divine personalities belong to a different category. The super natural events linked with these divine personalities cannot and should not be considered as irrelevant. These events are generally written by the faithful, for the faithful and of the faithful, and are accepted by those who have witnessed with their own eyes such divine or superhuman or supernatural powers. Sri Sathya Sai Baba has been the living example of that faith which is a self-evident truth since it has been seen every day and witnessed by millions and millions of people including the modern historians and scientists. The miracles demonstrated openly by Sri Sathya Sai Baba should be treated as an ample proof of the miraculous powers of the earlier divine personalities or incarnations like Rama, Krishna, Zoroaster, Buddha, Christ, Mohammed and Nanak among several others some of which remain unknown and undiscovered. Just because the historians are not able to discover or explore the truth of the divine powers of the divine incarnations or divine personalities, it does not mean that such divine beings never existed or the miracles associated with them are not to be treated as authentic. In this chapter, besides the miracles of divine messengers, the divine messages of a few divine personalities like Buddha and Mahavir; Zoroaster and Christ; and Mohammed and Nanak are briefly stated along with their spiritual doctrines in line with the respective holy scriptures associated or identified with them.

A religious scripture, as described in Chapter 3, is generally considered to be an authoritative work which helps in regulating the human behaviour and modifying it for leading a religious life. The axioms and doctrines prescribed in a religious scripture teach not only eternal values but also preach the temporal values suitable to persons of all ages, communities and all creeds. The eternal values are universal in character where as the temporal values are secular in context. Both are important and beneficial to the human beings. Moreover, a religious scripture may contain some divine revelations of a prophet or an incarnation of God. A scripture's value also lies in its revelations of super sensory knowledge which is obtained only from divine sources. An authoritative scripture is usually the sum total of the utterances or discourses of a prophet who is eventually recognized as the founder of the religious principles based on his utterances or doctrines. His doctrines, principles, discourses together constitute what is termed as a religion. Further, a scripture translates the ancient teachings in a modern context. Teachings in Upanishads, in the Gita, in the Zenda Avesta, in the Dhammapada, in the New Testament, in the Quran or in the Guru Granth Sahib are valid when reiterated and interpreted in the modern context and will remain valid even in the future contexts. Any religious idea, which does not show the way to a healthy evolution of the human society and does not touch upon spiritual values of life, becomes irrelevant over the time. All the great scriptures of the world preach religious ideals to embrace all that exist in the world, and all that is good and great. A number of scriptures ordained by various divine personalities through their preachings and utterances have been highlighted in this chapter along with their profiles.

5.1 Buddha and Mahavir

Even since the dawn of the Universe, the human race has been feeling uncomfortable and unsettled in the vast ocean of things around. It has been exploring in the quest for something firm, supreme and eternal. Possessed with a desperate urge for something like eternal peace, its underlying philosophy has been to grope in the governing principles of nature which eventually led it to reach the zenith of scientific knowledge and advancement. Its longing for the ineffable feeling of relief beneath the violent turbulence of the mind, led it only to outer revolutions of various types such as the political, economical, industrial and scientific. However, its fundamental, foundational and innermost evolution of spiritual quest remained unquenched till the advent of Buddha which brought the much needed spirituality-based human inner evolution in the early phase of the present aeon – called the Kaliyuga in the language of Hinduism.

The word 'Budh' means an awakening. Therefore, 'Buddha' means one who is awake. When Gautam Buddha was once asked whether he was god, angel or saint, he replied, "I am awake". These three words transformed the Prince Siddhartha to Tathagata Buddha, and Buddhism came to be identified with a renunciate who woke up to awaken the whole humanity. The well-known Buddha Purnima is considered to be the most sacred day in the Buddhist calendar, celebrated all over the world. It is the full moon day (Purnima) of the month of "Vaishakha" in the Vikrami Calendar of Hinduism. This holy day is connected with four most important events of Buddha's life – his birth, renunciation, enlightenment and complete liberation.

According to Buddhism, the universe is a creation of collective actions (karmas). Buddhist cosmology believes that an individual knows his/her future by his/her actions. An individual is born a million times and has a lot of chances to improve himself or herself. In Buddhism, there is a relationship between the concept of interdependence and emptiness. When one looks at the mirror, one thinks that it exists by itself. But when analyzed properly, one thinks about the people who made that mirror and all those who helped in its manufacturing transportation, distribution and sale. Once one realizes that there are so many persons involved in procuring the mirror, only then one understands the concept of true existence. In Buddhism, the emphasis is on being good to others. When one learns to cherish oneself, one extends the feeling to others as everybody has a Buddhist nature.

Lord Buddha, the founder of a great religion, was a divine incarnation. Buddha, according to Hinduism, is considered as the ninth incarnation of God, after Krishna, the eighth incarnation since He is considered to be a fully enlightened divine (human) being superior even to the gods. Buddha's supernatural or divine powers were in the nature of what only the Supreme Power could will and act. Buddha believed in the divine powers which according to Him, were within the control of man and which were achievable by constant and deep meditation. Buddha, however, cautioned His disciples and followers neither to demonstrate these powers nor to misuse those powers but use them only for the welfare of the people. Buddha believed in preaching doctrines by the miracle of persuasive power and warned His disciples not to perform the miracles before the common people for the sake of any worldly gain for themselves. In this sense, Buddha is also considered as a divine messenger and a prophet.

The Indian as well as Asian literature is full of knowledge about Buddha's remarkable and unique way of preaching. According to the Sinhalese tradition, Buddha was born in 623 B.C. and died in 543 B.C. While according to another calculation, derived from established dates of the life of the great Hindu Emperor Ashoka, Buddha was born in 563 B.C. and died in 483 B.C. Nevertheless, both calculations obviously show that Buddha lived for eighty years. Whatever be the time of the emergence of the biographies of Buddha, his profile cannot be separated from his divine miracles as mentioned in the Buddhist sacred texts. Indeed, in that ancient time of faith, a divine saviour could not have appeared just as an ordinary person and work as a deliverer of the mankind. However, whether Buddha's miracles were real manifestation of his divine power or not, is a mystery. Nevertheless, it is desirable to look into the miraculous occurrences linked with the life of Buddha. Buddha was not born in an ordinary way as other mortals are born. Infact, he was born like some other divine being *viz.*, incarnated or divine personalities.

Buddha was born in a royal family with Suddhodana, the king of Kapil Vastu, as his father and the queen Maya as his mother. The mother Maya, in a mid-summer full night, saw in her dream that she was lifted up away to the Himalayas where she was bathed in a lake and laid down to rest on a heavenly couch with a golden mansion on a silver hill. She saw the Bodhisattva in the form of a little white elephant with six tusks, beautiful feet, a splendid trunk and teeth like a line of gold, with a graceful gait and firm joints who walked around her couch three times, and came near to touch her right side in order to enter into her womb. As soon as the elephant, as the future Buddha, entered the womb, gods appeared to sing praises in her favour and the dream came to an end. With that dream, the queen Maya came to carry her child in her womb and thus, the conception was divinely mysterious. Indeed, it was not a conception under the normal human conditions. It was a divine phenomenon as true of various divine incarnations or divine messengers like Rama, Krishna, Zoroaster and Shirdi Sai among several others including the latest divine incarnation in the form of Sri Sathya Sai Baba. Several miracles are associated with the birth of Buddha. It is said that as soon as Buddha was born, the world was filled with light, the blind could see, the deaf could hear, the dumb could speak, and the lame could walk. The nature also showed amazing signs of vigour. The Brahmins and astrologers predicted that queen Maya was carrying a son who was destined to be a monarch but will decide to become a renunciate to remove the veils of ignorance from the world.

While being in the womb of His mother, the baby Buddha was seen sitting cross legged in a dignified squatting posture. The mother felt no pain while the baby would stretch his hand for preaching. During the tenth month of pregnancy, the queen Maya expressed her desire of going to her parents for delivery. The king made all arrangements for her safe journey. On her way when the queen reached the garden of Lumbini-Van, a resort which was full of fragrance of the flowers of plants and trees, where she wanted to stay for rest. This place is near the ancient Kapil Vastu identified as Rummindevi near village Nigliva, district Bhairava in Nepalese Terai, region. The queen was taken to a beautiful spot under a grove of sala trees to take rest. Whenever in need of support she thought of holding a branch of the tree, the branches of the big tree would come bending down to enable the queen to catch hold of a branch. While doing so, still standing and holding a branch, the queen gave birth to her baby son, and thus Buddha was born on the full moon day of Vaisakha. Even after so many years of this auspicious event, the place still retains its historical character. At the birth site, a pillar is engraved with an inscription, "Here the Buddha was born", erected by Ashoka. To the amazement of her attendants, the baby, immediately after birth, stood up and looked eastward. Soon was heard the voice of the gods from above announcing the arrival of the divine being. Thereafter, the baby Buddha walked seven steps. At each step, a lotus would spring up beneath his holy foot. **While looking towards the East, the baby Buddha declared, "I will reach the highest Nirvana"; turning towards South, he exclaimed, "I will be the first of all creatures, pointing towards the West, the baby declared," "This will be my last birth"; and finally looking towards North, he said, "I will cross the ocean of existence"**. This was the first supernatural phenomenon witnessed by all these who were present there at the birth place of Buddha.

Queen Maya and her new born baby were carried back to the capital of Kapil Vastu. Unfortunately just after seven days of child's birth, the queen mother Maya died. The child was, therefore, nursed and looked after by His aunty Gautami, the sister of the queen Maya. It was after her name, the baby Buddha was called as Gautam, also because the king's gotra was Gautam, while the baby was named as Siddhartha. Once during an annual ceremony of ploughing fields by the king, the child Gautam was left alone under a tree since his attendants went to see the festive ceremony. Left alone and finding no one around him, the child Gautam sat on the couch cross legged in the squatting posture and went into his first meditation. The tree, under which sat Gautam, did not turn his shadow off him, instead continued covering the child with its shadow irrespective of the movement of the sun rays. This was another supernatural phenomenon which was seen by the father who felt moved out of reverence for his son Gautam Buddha. This event is generally attributed to the deeper sense of suffering and pain caused to young Gautam on seeing the small worms and insects being killed during the ploughing of the fields.

At the school-going age, the King Suddhodana took young Siddhartha in a royal way for his admission to a school. On reaching the school, young Siddhartha took out a slate and started writing a long list of sixty-four alphabets which included even the alphabets of the Chinese language, reciting, at the same time, a piece of moral lesson beginning with each letter. This miracle convinced the teacher Visvamitra that the young prince was not an ordinary pupil but an embodiment of all knowledge, and hence he did not require any schooling.

Prince Siddhartha was married to Yashodhara at the young of sixteen. However, the prince was getting more and more detached from the worldly life. Being distressed due to the thoughts and sights of people's sufferings, and witnessing on three occasions, the frailties of old age, sickness and the inevitability of death, the young Siddhartha planned to leave home in search of the Truth. At the age of twenty-nine, he was blessed with a son, yet another bond of attachment to take him to the worldly life. Thus, without talking to any one, he finally decided to renunciate the luxury and comfort of the royal life and left the palace in the late hours of a dark night, and disappeared. Thereafter, Gautam's great search for the Truth began. Subjecting himself to extreme physical hardships, practicing penance in dense forests, roaming from place to place and seeking guidance from the learned scholars and sages, Siddhartha finely reached Gaya (Bihar, India) where he reduced his body almost to bones while doing penance. At last one day, after taking a bath in the nearby river, he sat down under a peepal tree with his supreme resolve that he would not get up till he achieved his goal. Sitting in deep meditation, finally the light of wisdom and great knowledge of the truth, descended to his mind and eventually, Gautam, the prince Siddhartha became Buddha – the Enlightened one. That time he was only thirty-five years old. For the next forty-five years till his death, Buddha travelled from one place to another to preach his doctrines.

Many people including even the sages and kings came to Buddha's fold. He showed several miracles besides his preachings. Providing food to thousands of Bhikshus (the name given to Buddha's disciples), curing a sick and weak boy who was not able to walk, removing thereby the agony of the boy's parents, bringing showers of rain for a caravan of thirsty travellers travelling through a desert and saving people from the epidemics, while preaching against the then bad practice of sacrificing animals for pleasing the gods and converting the vulgar behaviour of young boys into singing of melodious hymns in praise of Buddha. Seeing such several miracles and having been convinced by the preachings of Buddha, the kings, the courtiers, the seers and the general public came to Buddha for peace and tranquility. They started following the doctrines of Buddha. Thus, in this way the process of Buddha's miracles and preachings continued, and people from various places continued following his doctrines till Buddha reached the age of eighty. By now he was weak and fragile.

When Buddha reached a place called Kushinagar identified with Kasia, district Deorya, in the present Indian State of Uttar Pradesh, and came to a grove of sala trees after crossing the river Hirannawati, and lied down. Fragrant flowers started falling down on the body of dying Buddha along with the sandalwood powder from the sky enjoined by the divine music and singing through the air paying their tributes to Buddha. While breathing his last, Buddha gave his disciple Ananda his last instruction: "**Therefore, O, Ananda, be ye lamps unto yourself Betake yourselves to no external refuge. Hold fast to the Truth as a lamp. Hold fast as a refuge to the Truth. Look not for refuge to anyone besides yourself**". Buddha breathed his last and miracles also followed. His body could not be moved until heavenly wishes indicated the directions in which it was to be carried. The body would not burn until the monks walked around the funeral pyre three times and stood in front of the feet of the dead body. As soon as the monks did so and bent their heads before the dead body, the pyre caught fire by itself. Prior to touching of the body by the fire, one of the monks standing and mediating near the covered feet of Buddha, got a strong urge to see the holy feet of Buddha once again. The holy feet bearing thirty two signs of greatness emerged from inside the coverings of the pyre like a full bloom moon emerging out of the dark clouds. The assembled devotees burst into tears on seeing this miracle and the holy feet merged back to the coverings after the monks had placed their heads beneath the feet. Finally, when the body of the Enlightened One – Buddha was consumed by the flames, there came down suddenly the showers from the sky to extinguish the fire. The bones remain untouched by the flames which later became the holy relics to serve the great purpose.

Buddha, the Enlightened One, prior to his achieving the Supreme Knowledge – the knowledge of the Ultimate Truth, had manifested his superhuman powers by overcoming the attacks on him from the evil spirits, or from Nature such as storms, extreme cold and hot weather and deep darkness around him till he achieved the desired goal. Buddha gave to the mankind, "**four Noble Truths: Life is full of suffering; Desire is the cause of suffering; Suffering ends at the destruction of desire; and Desire is destroyed by Right Living. He advised people to follow the Noble Eight fold path**. **The Right Vision, Right Aims, Right Speech, Right Action, Right Livelihood, Right Effort, Right Mindfulness, and Right Meditation**. Each Path when explained carries the lessons of perfection in life.

According to Buddhism, wheel is one of the greatest achievements of mankind. The wheel is useful to the people in many ways. It represents a whole corpus of teachings and is far above all other wheels of teachings. This wheel has eight spokes which stand for the eight-fold noble path. It is the wheel of righteousness (Dharma) called the 'Dharmachakra'. The rim, which holds the spokes of the wheel, represents mindfulness and perfect **'samadhi'**, the centre of the hub of the wheel is 'shila' or moral discipline. The whole wheel, therefore, represents the three major teachings (sikshas): discipline (shila), wisdom (prajna) and mindfulness (samadhi). The turning of the wheel or 'Dharamachakra Pravartana' is the phrase which refers to the Buddhist teachings. The three turnings of the wheel gives three main messages: the first turning teaches true existence, the second non-true existence and the third that some phenomena exist truly whereas others do not.

A treatise compiled on the teachings of Lord Buddha through his poetic utterances on various occasions is what constitutes 'Dhammapada' the holy scripture of the Buddhists. Dhammapada means the way of Dhamma *i.e.* the way of righteousness (Dharma). This is an important religious book – a component of the epic 'Tipitaka' (Three Baskets) containing all teachings of Buddha. The three baskets are known as **Vinaya Pitaka**, **Abhidhamma Pitaka** and **Subta Pitaka**. Just as the Bhagvat Gita is the handbook of the Hindus, so is the Dhammapada of the Buddhists. The followers of Buddha are expected to memorize the Dhammapada and recite at least a few verses from any part of the book at the oral test held just before they are given higher ordination. Dhammapada has been written and translated in many languages. It presents the essence of the teachings of Buddha in 423 melodious verses grouped in 26 chapters. Lord Buddha preached Dhamma to the people for forty-five years, moving from place to place. His teachings are interspersed with similes. For instance, the very first verse, the simile of a wheel following the hoof of the draught-ox is given to point out how the bad 'Karma' follows its performer. Similarly, the simile of the shadow of a person is given in the second verse to show how the result of good 'Karma' follows its doer. Indeed, the Dhammapada is based on the Karma philosophy as expounded in the Bhagvat Gita of the Hindus.

Buddha's teaching are related to human sufferings. These are focused to find a solution to the problem of suffering that he renounced the luxurious worldly life. After the attainment of Enlightenment ('**Nirvana**') and emancipation from suffering, Buddha devised a path to the supreme bliss and taught people that morality brings happiness and peace. One becomes happy or sad depending upon one's deeds, intentional or volitional. Buddha advised the people to follow five precepts that would bring happiness here and hereafter: "**Do not kill, Do not lie, Do not have illegal sex, Do not steal and Do not take intoxicating drinks**". Buddha advised His disciples, '**mind control**' and '**sense control**': The controlled mind generates ten values such as: **generosity, morality, meditation, reverence, service, merit-transference, rejoicing in others' meritorious deeds, hearing the Dhamma, expounding the Dhamma and straightening one's views**. This **Noble eight-fold** path, advocated by Buddha, has been regrouped into three-fold categories namely: Morality, Concentration and Wisdom. The Bhikkhu's (Buddhist follower/disciple) aim should be to practice and develop these three traits. People should abandon evil deeds and cultivate good deeds. They should develop detachment and control desires. Renouncing sensual pleasures with no impediments like senseless desires, ill-will, sloth, restlessness, brooding, and indecision. people should cleanse themselves of the impurities of the mind. Meditation is the only way to remove these impurities and attainhood of Arhantahood (the state of Jivanmukti) namely: Satapatti (Stream-Entering), Sakadagami (Once-Returner), Anagami (Non-Returner), and Arhanta (Realized).

Buddha used the term 'Brahmin' to mean 'Realized'. Thus, the two terms 'Arhanta' and 'Brahmin' seem to have been used to indicate the same attainment. According to Buddha, "**No one becomes a Brahmin by birth. He, who is free from impediments; free from clinging; who has cut off all fetters, who trembles not, who has gone beyond ties and who is unbound, is the real Brahmin**". Wherever there is a Realized one, Brahmin or Arhanta, whether in a village or in a forest, in a valley or on a hill, there is peace and serenity. In this sense, Buddha was also an Arhant but with a difference. Buddha was Supremely Enlightened. He rediscovered the path of emancipation – the Noble eight-fold path. The disciples who follow this path devised by Buddha, become Arhantas. There can be many Arhantas at a time, but there cannot be many Buddhas at a time. The advent of a Buddha is a rare phenomenon which happens once in an epoch.

Vivekananda regarded Buddha as the greatest seeker ever. **"He never bowed down to anything.—neither Veda nor caste, nor priest nor custom. He fearlessly reached as far as reason could take him, such a fearless search for truth the world has never seen"**. Buddha's rationality was ironically accompanied by His infinite compassion and love as He reached out to all irrespective of status or creed. He advised people to get rid of all delusions, myths and superstitions. Buddha would often say, "**Be A Lamp Unto Yourself**". His other teachings include the four Divine Abidings (doctrines) namely: Loving-kindness (metta), compassion (karuna), sympathetic joy (mudita) and equanimity (upeksha). According to Buddhist scholars, Buddhist principles lead to dispassion and not to passion; to detachment and not to bondage; to diminution and not to accumulations; to having a few wishes and not to many desires; to contentment and not to discontent; to seclusion and not to gregariousness; to the arousing of energy and not to indolence; to frugality and not to luxurious living.

According to the Buddhist view renunciation means renouncing of sufferings that come from afflictive emotions which in turn arise from a deluded view of the nature of the Ultimate Reality. Renunciation does not mean that the seeker has to leave the material world to go in the wilderness of forests or in the chill of the mountain caves. The practice of renunciation can be done while living the humdrum existence of daily life for which it is essential to control anger, hatred, frustration, and despair while cultivating the motivation to get rid of the sufferings and their causes. Meditation is another middle way. It means to meditate on all sentient beings and their well-being and liberation from sorrows and sufferings.

The Buddhist view does not accept the concept of God, Atman, prophet, miracles, mantras, pilgrimages or rituals. People could attain Nirvana through their resolve, motivation and effort. Buddha's doctrine states that phenomena of the Universe arise together in a mutually interdependent web of cause and effect, somewhat similar to what has been proclaimed in the Geeta. From the Buddhist perspective, nothing arises independently. Everything arises from a complex net of inter-related causes. While this complex web may not be easily comprehensible, it indicates that each action has an effect on the larger world.

The Buddhist philosophy recognizes the importance of the concept of emptiness and interdependence. Emptiness or Vacuum or Shunyata is a key concept in Buddhist philosophy. Vacuum or emptiness does not mean nothingness. It is not non-reality. Emptiness is form and form is emptiness. This is a paradox of the concept of emptiness. It should not be confused with nothingness. Indeed, emptiness means that an object, animate or inanimate, does not have its own existence independently. It has its meaning and existence only when all its elements or components come into play leading to the understanding and perception of its existence in a clear way. For example, consider an empty cup or a glass or a utensil or a pot or any other container. One can easily observe that it does not contain any liquid or water or any other material thing in it. Is it really empty? No, it is not. It is full of air. Even if a container is in a state of vacuum, it is not empty. Indeed, it contains space, radiation and may be lighter darkness. Thus, the container is always full of something or the other which is not visible to the naked eye of a human being. Yet, it is its inherent containment but it has come into existence because of several of these intricacies that the Buddhist concept of emptiness is often interpreted as nihilism.

Nihilism as a concept means that reality is unknown and unknowable that nothing exists. Whereas the Buddhist concept of emptiness says the ultimate reality is knowable and that in no case should the concept of emptiness be taken to mean nothingness. According to the well-known Buddhist scholar, the Dalai Lama, "**As your insight into the ultimate nature is deepened and enhanced, you will develop a perception of reality from which you will perceive phenomena and events as sort of illusory. And that mode of perceiving reality will permeate all your interactions with reality. Even emptiness itself which is seen as the ultimate nature of reality, it is not absolute, nor does it exist independently. We cannot conceive of emptiness as independent of a basis of phenomenon, because when we examine the nature of reality, we find that emptiness itself is an object. Look for its essence and it will be found that it is empty of inherent existence. Therefore, the Buddha taught "the emptiness of emptiness**". Some philosophers hold the view that there is an essence in everything that is around, whether animate or inanimate. After all, the essence of the container ultimately exists in the realm of the mind. The Dalai Lama says that shunyata is the absence of an absolute essence or independent existence. If something that exists, it is because of several other factors. Some thinkers believe that there can be no phenomenon without its constituents.

Every phenomenon in the Universe, according to Buddhism, has to have parts or constituents or components to come into being. This leads to the concept of interdependence which states that nothing is completely independent in an inter-connected world. One of the Buddhist doctrines states that phenomena arise together in a mutually interdependent web of cause and effect. Thus, from Buddhist point of view, nothing exists or arises independently. Everything exists or rises from a complex set of inter-related causes and effects. This view is in line with the Vedic Principle of the world as one family (Vasudhaiva Kutumbakam) in the sense that all animate and inanimate are inter-connected. Indeed, Buddhism originated the concepts of emptiness and interdependence which are closer to Hindu philosophy of cause and effect. This brings nearness to the notion of relative reality propounded by Adi Shankaracharya later enunciated by Albert Einstein in modern theory of science. There are Buddhist traditions closer to Hinduism that refer to the collection of scriptures preserved in Sanskrit at the renowned University of Nalanda (Bihar, India), where the literature and understanding of philosophy and logic were profoundly refined by the Buddhist scholars of the time. Sanskrit is a crucial part of Buddhist heritage, says the Dalai Lama. India, according to him, is regarded as the Holy Land (Punya Bhumi) by the Buddhists monk and scholars.

Another divine soul, born in the year 599 B.C. as a prince, lived in the palace as an ascetic for thirty years. Thereafter, renouncing everything and everybody including his parents and family, took to penance as a wandering monk in search of truth. After twelve years of severe penance, he gained enlightenment – the true knowledge and subsequently devoted his remaining life in preaching the paths of righteousness (Dharma) and liberation (Moksha) to the people. He is known as Lord Mahavir believed to be the last and twenty-fourth 'Tirathankar' (a divine messenger), who revived the spiritual principles, enunciated by the earlier twenty-three tirathankars which are eternal. Prince Vardhaman could recall each detail of his previous births; he was a blessed child. According to Jainism, Lord Mahavir, an angel in the heavens, and the twenty-fourth tirathankar, was conceived by a Brahmin lady called Devananda. However, in accordance with the Jaina traditions, no tirathankar had ever been born in a Brahmin family. Thus, to maintain the tradition, Devananda's fetus was swapped with that of a Kshatrya who happened to be the queen Trishala wife of the then king

Siddharth. This is how Lord Mahavir had two mothers and a half-brother. Lord Mahavir left his family at an early age and dedicated his life to meditation. His philosophical principles bring happiness and peace to anyone who assimilated their essence and followed them. His long years of penance were so hard that it is a miracle he survived them, and because of this, he came to be known as Vardhaman Mahashraman Mahavir. He died in the year 527 B.C. at the age of 72 years.

He had conquered sleep and hunger and had no need of spoken words. It was 12 years later that his speech flowered into spoken words. He observed for the first time that nothing was static. Everything is forever on the move; there is nothing but flow and flux. Each being, however, loved or cherished, will inevitably and surely perish one day. In the flow of time, there is no refuge for the living. Mahavir deduced seven basic tenets from the phenomenon pertaining to living, non-living, temptation, bondage, contentment, restraint and salvation. The non-living is also known as matter, the manifest form; the abstract is the conceptual or the felt. The living is bonded to karma or action. The living entity might not be under the guidance of balanced philosophy, but because it is conscious, it moves towards realization.

Space is the foundational concept of Jaina philosophy. It has a number of atoms which revolve unobstructed in it. Whatever allows life to permeate it, is known as space. The question is, what is Dharma? To Mahavir, the Dharma of the Sun is to burn and give heat. The Dharma of earth is to accept and sustain, whereas the Dharma of the physical body is to decay and degenerate. There is an eternally revolving wheel on the screen of day and night. One can see the wheel and the circumference of the wheel, but not the axis. The day human vision crosses the limits or circumference of the wheel and fixes itself on its centre, it can will the axis and that will be the beginning of Dharma in life. Therefore, Mahavir says: **"The nature of things is Dharma."** The ultimate Dharma, however, is non-violence, truth, integrity, celibacy and non-hoarding. These five basic tenets constitute what is known as the Jain Religion.

The core of Jaina Philosophy revolves around the doctrine of non-violence (Ahimsa), that is, non-injury to any living being. It does not accept the concept of God. However, it believes in two independent and separate eternal entities: life (soul) and non-life (matter). While soul is the essential characteristic of life, non-life comprises of five basic factors namely: motion (Dharma), rest (Adharma), space (Akasa), gross-matter (Pudgala) and time (Kaal). The soul is considered to be formless – the consciousness (Chetna) which assume forms and get involved in the worldly activities.

It is in this sense that Jainism is considered to be dualistic but unlike the philosophy of duality enunciated in Hinduism by the eminent philosopher Sri Madhavacharya. The Jainism believes that soul is pure. It is equipped with unlimited knowledge, infinite bliss, and unbounded power. As in Hinduism, Karma (Action) in Jainism is the cause of life and death. Freedom from the shackles of karma is by stopping the influx of new karmas and eliminating the acquired karmas. The acquired karmas can be eliminated through a process of fasting, not eating a certain kind of food, control over taste, living in solitude, atonement, expiation of sins, modesty, service to the needy, study of pious literature, meditation and renunciation of ego. The new karmas can be avoided by following the three golden codes of Jainism: **Right Path**, **Right Knowledge**, and **Right Conduct**, all within the strict doctrine of Non-violence (Ahimsa) leading to atonement of final 'Nirvan'.

The true meaning of non-violence, according to the Jain Religion, is that one practices it at all levels of consciousness. In practical living, there are 108 types of violence. Enacted violence is that for which the individual is responsible. Then there is violence which people bring about through others or forces others to do for them; also, there is violence which people witness, and for which they do nothing to stop. The third type of violence is all pervading. Each one, during a life time, is witness to varied acts of violence on other people. Women are burnt, children tortured and people stand by and watch it all happening. They are surrounded by evil, but they look the other way. Thus, such people individually and collectively become responsible for distortions in society. Each one is a participant, as well as a victim of these acts of violence. This is the pattern forever being repeated over hundreds of thousands of years. All are responsible for the misery that surrounds them. Being born itself involves a kind of violence. The very breath that people inhale causes the death of an infinite number of invisible life forms. The seed, that is put into earth, also exploits the earth for its own growth. If the seed is destroyed, then, instead of becoming the exploited or the exploiter, it will break free of the cycle of being or becoming.

According to Jainism, there are five vices namely lust, anger, greed, attachment and ego which generate violence of all types. Lust destroys purity and power of the soul. Anger is a fire that burns the self and others. Greed keeps one in a state of continuous seeking and chasing desires. Attachment is the root of all sufferings and creates a sense of illusion. Finally, ego is the greatest enemy of the soul and it generates delusion. The culture of violence can be eliminated by following the spiritual principles leading to an intellectual communication with the soul – the Supreme entity enunciated by Jainism. Lord Mahavir advised a socio-cultural tradition and non-violence. He discarded superstitions, caste-system, blind-faith and gender-inequality. He advocated equity and scientific attitude. He evolved a radical movement of economic equality and social justice. The five-fold Mantra, that is, recited in Jainism offers obeisance to the Arihants or perfected beings, siddhas or the liberated souls, acharayas or upadhayas or teachers, sadhus or renunciates and not to any divine power called God, which is non-existent. Jainism lays great emphasis on rational, scientific, compassionate and ethical way of life based on complete equanimity and tranquility. The first tirathankar Rishabhdev, preached six precepts: Asi (Sword of defence); Masi (Art, Culture, Literature and Education); Krishi (The Agriculture); Vidya (Schooling, Knowledge and Training); Vanjiya (Trade and Commerce); and Shilpkala (Architecture, Handicrafts and Skills).

Mahavir valued truth after non-violence. Truth, too, has various shades and meanings. Energy is needed to experience religion. When young, most people spend their energy on unethical things and activities. The energy could, however, be used to free oneself from ageing and ailment. Desire leads man through many a dance, and in the end, becomes a source of torture. Forever one covets what the other has, thus indulging in one or the other form of stealing or theft. The tenet of the Jain discipline is hardest, that is, to overcome covetousness. Mahavir says that by the mere act of feeling the need for what is not one's own, they commit a sin.

Mahavir's philosophy is known as 'Anekantvada', the end of all division; but behind this is intense multiplicity and unity of meaning and understanding. A human being is an amalgam of body and soul just as a lamp is both the clay saucer and the oil. The oil permeates the clay saucer and dust settles on it. This is comparable to the materialistic invasion of the human state. There are 42 types of matter consciousness.

If the pressure and attack of outside influence can be stopped, it is known as 'Samvar'. There are 62 ways to stop the invasion of Karma and these are known as 'Samitiyan' and 'Guptian'. Vardhaman says that any creature that can stay free of violence, falsehood, sins, covetousness and avarice can become blameless. People carry the burden of many births. If they were to be rid of these accumulated layers, what would be left? The untouched core of being is to know and confront immortality.

The term 'philosophy' has been differently defined by different philosophers and savants down the ages. Aristotle, for example, defined it as the 'science of principles' or 'first beginnings'. The dictionary says it is the "seeking of wisdom or knowledge, especially that which deals with the Supreme Truth or the ultimate reality, or with the most general causes and principles of things and ideas, and human perception and knowledge of them; physical phenomena or natural philosophy, and ethics or moral philosophy." Philosophy is also defined as a system of principles of conduct of life. According to the Jain philosophy, the word 'jain' is derived from the term 'jina' which means one who conquers oneself. Anybody can become a jina. Jainism rejects the idea of creation or a creator – God. As stated earlier, non-violence (Ahimsa) is of paramount importance. It advocates, respect for the rights of individuals and peaceful co-existence for all. It believes that grass and rocks, too, have consciousness. They are beings with one and the same sense of consciousness like the other living beings insects, reptiles, animals and human beings among others. Multiple view points (Anekantavada) constitute an important concept of Jainism. Truth and Reality are perceived differently by different people. Jainism believes that the soul is bound by action or deeds (Karmas) and rebirth depends on the individual's Karma. Establishing of Karmas in the domain of the soul is called 'Asravas' and an attempt to stop these Karmas is known as 'Samwara'. While removing Karmas from the domain of the soul is 'Nirjara' and in the end is salvation (Moksha). Spirituality is all about overcoming one's own imperfections and that is when one reaches the state of bliss, where nothing really affects the individual. In that state of calm, one finds ultimate knowledge.

Jain philosophy consists in the voluntary but consistent intellectual and moral striving for the removal of obstacles on the way to right vision leading to right knowledge of the world as a whole, and to right conduct with the explicit object of ultimately realizing the free and happy state of being. That is the true purpose of life and actions, after all. Jainism says there are two fundamental factors of the world: Jiva, the cogitative substance or the soul, which is further analyzed into various gradations of being, and Ajiva, the non-cogitative substance, the non-living or the non-soul, involving objective things and processes. These are the basic factors that Jain philosophy very minutely examines in order to attain the end freedom or moksha of the soul. In the trinity of right vision, right knowledge and right conduct, the word 'knowledge' becomes quite dialectical in its exploration. These three principles are the main subject matter of Jaina philosophical speculation. Jainism upholds this standpoint along with other Indian branches of philosophy such as the Charvaka, Nyaya, Vaisesika, Sankhya and Buddhist. Some Jain philosophers maintain that the "dialectic method of reasoning identifying logic with metaphysics was originated with the Jaina sages, and has been prevalent in the field of philosophy in India much before the West knew it. For Jainism, the world-process is without beginning and end. Also, right knowledge begins from right vision by a coherence of right thought and reasoning. It can only lead to right conduct. It is the knowledge which embraces the constituent factors of the world in the dialectic movement of thought and being.

"Have compassion towards all living beings. Hatred leads to destruction. Respect for all living beings is non-violence... Real enemies live inside yourself, they are anger, pride, greed, attachments and hate...It is better to win over self than to win over a million enemies," said Mahavir. Nirvan or liberation from human bondage in Jain thought is achievable through a detailed analysis of the nature of reality and the notion of karma. In its unique assertion that the soul itself is a material cause of drawing a veil over its real nature, the Jaina tradition shifts the onus from external causes and influences to pinning responsibility on oneself for one's salvation – the soul itself has the capability to become free also. The interplay between the structure of the soul and the processes of 'Karma' is itself rooted in the dynamics of 'Anekantavada', a metaphysical dissection of the empirical world. The many-sidedness (Anekanta) of reality implies that no single point of view can be construed as the whole truth since empirical knowledge is limited according to relative perspectives.

This idea is elaborated in the abstruse logic of the doctrine of seven conditioned predications, wherein each statement is expressed from seven different relative points of view, and each view is prefixes by a "maybe" or "relatively". Maybe something is real and may be it isn't. Perhaps it is both real and unreal, or it could defy description. Such a dialectic of the relativity of knowledge rules out any categorical or absolutist pronouncements. It shows how each judgment can effectively be only relative and conditional. It examines the empirical world psychologically, and in doing so, seeks to reveal the relativity of the mind itself. Jaina philosophical view lies somewhere between the Vedantic assertion of Brahmn as Absolute and the Buddhist postulation of 'change as permanent' and throws up a pragmatic blueprint for a more peaceful co-existence, where all views are accommodated out of the belief that all minds are relatively conditioned, and are actually interdependent. 'Anekantavada' respects each opinion or view in knowledge in the sense that all perspectives of reality are uniquely true from the knower's own view of reality; yet no single view can be construed as complete or perfect.

The principle of Non-Violence (Ahimsa) is the philosophical basis of ethical living in Jainism. Its metaphysics lays the ground for acceptance and respect for opposing views. The Jaina sees this as possible only in the realization of interdependence, that all life and beings are inextricably bound with each other. Ahimsa thereby becomes a natural empathy for another being, rather than just an outer sympathy. The metaphysics of 'Anekantavada' provides the key to an understanding of the world of Mahavir – the multiplicity of the world is to be resolved through emphasis on an ethical way of living, of **compassion** and **forgiveness** through the five 'Anuvratas' laid down for 'Shraviks' for laypersons: Ahimsa, Satya, Asteya or Non-stealing, Celibacy (Brahmacharya) and Non-possession (Aparigraha). It then provides in rare cases, the trigger to pursue the Jaina renunciate ideal of Kaivalya Jnana, just as Mahavir ventured forth in search of the real nature of reality, beyond the contours of the conditioned mind. Such a way out is open only for those who have first understood the nature of reality. Since, Jainism studies nature in its two essential aspects: living and non-living, it is therefore universal in nature, having the vital property of 'Chetna' or consciousness, perception and knowledge. This living matter, commonly known as 'soul' in the worldly language, is subjected to the process of transmigration that is continuously perpetuating the cycle of birth and death through eternity. The soul's manifestation each time in a new body is called birth. Correspondingly, exit of that soul from the body is known as death. This process has been going on since eternity and will continue to do so till the soul is liberated from its own implicating Karmas, and is thereby free to obtain salvation or moksha.

Jainism believes that there are innumerable forms of life which synthesize the soul and body in different permutations and combinations. Human life is considered to be pre-eminent since it possesses the capacity to embody a separate sense called 'mind' along with the five other senses, and through this composite medium of cognition, it can perceive the truth of nature. From the ordinary point of view, the soul in the body is alive with four pranaas, the five senses, energy in the body, age and vital respiration. But from a realistic point of view, the soul is alive due to its chetna shakti or consciousness which is its main characteristics and cannot be separated from its core being.

According to Jainism, the universe is existing since eternity and will last till infinity, and it is based on the scientific premise of 'cause and effect'. With every cause there is an effect. With action in nature there is a reaction. Potential energy is transformed to kinetic energy and in this process of transformation nothing is lost or gained. Modern science also states that vital matter can neither be created nor destroyed. This universe has always existed. Jainism is based on this theory that the universe was not created by anyone and no one can destroy it. Thus, the Universe is eternal, according to the Jain philosophy.

In Jainism, the cause of a soul's embodiment is related to the karmic activities it has accumulated in its karmic form from innumerable lives in the past. These karmas produce resulting consequences and soul experiences comprising happiness as well as sorrow in the present life. Because of karmas the soul is subjected to 'attachment', anger, greed etc. which pollute and burden its real nature. These karmas can be dispensed with in human life and the soul can emerge triumphantly into the illuminated realm of salvation. The process of shedding karmas is directed through the act of meditation.

According to Hinduism, there exists the polarity of purusha, the male principle and prakriti, the female principle. Jainism is of the view that in human life, the two biological forms, male and female and in the present worldly society the two kinds of lifestyles, .the householder's and the monk's – each of these dimensions can benefit from the practice of meditation. In the new age this process of meditation and learning about the concept of the universe is extremely important. If this concept becomes clear one can approach salvation without doubt. The way to salvation through these two kind of lifestyles, can be culled from Jainism. It states that the householder should know what is soul and what is body, what is birth and what is death, what are the properties of soul and what are the properties of non-living matter. He should know about karma in the light of cause and effect theory; how does one get rid of karmas which are accumulated in the soul through eternity. The time will come when householders will attain right perception which is the basis of the achievement of moksha. After achieving the objective of right perception one can adopt the lifestyle of monks and nuns for the practice of meditation. A monk's life demands renunciation of worldly involvements; that is, family life, business life or any sort of commercial occupation. He or she could glean a lot from a study of the literature of Jainism or concentrate or meditation. It is up to the seeker to find out the best way to achieve self-awareness and salvation. Although in the present age, salvation is a rare achievement, one can always try to get closer to the eternal Truth.

Jainism says that in the path of religion, one wins over one's vanity, one's imperfections and frees oneself from the clutches of karma. In war one fights for worldly and physical gains which are temporary and mortal whereas in the battle of Dharma one aims to achieve infinite peace and eternal bliss. The intrinsic nature of an object of living being is known as its dharma. Tirathankars knew the nature and dharma of the entire universe and would explain it to the people. Tirathankars remained detached and were above various ragas or passions and dwesha or malice. They, thus would become vitrag. Vitrag Tirathankars would engage in the spiritual renaissance of the world and through their preaching would show the path of enlightenment.

Jainism observes that the modern style of living and rapidly growing materialism has led to the erosion in the moral fabric of the society. As a result falsehoods, dishonesty, corruption and immorality have penetrated deep into human psyche. Shady deals, profiteering, adulteration and tax-evasion have become the order of the day in business and industry. Inefficiency, negligence, nepotism, bribery and shirking responsibility are conspicuous in the government at all levels. Good conduct, fellow feeling, morality and humanity are becoming a thing of the past. Society has degenerated to an all time low and, if left unchecked, will head towards abysmal decay.

Jainism places great emphasis on right conduct, Samyak-Charitra, in daily life. Right conduct aided by right knowledge, Samyak-Jnana, in the light of right faith, Samyak-darshan, is the gateway for salvation. Moral and spiritual elevation of the society shall occur when the individuals raise their conduct and character to greater heights. Lord Mahavir defined the right conduct as observing these five virtues – ahimsa or non-violence, satya or truth, asteya (falsehood) or non-stealing, brahmacharya or celibacy and aparigraha or non-possessiveness. Other religions also describe these five virtues but ahimsa finds a place of pride in Jainism.

Ahimsa and anekant (unity in diversity) have provided a firm base to Lord Mahavir's spiritual heritage. Ahimsa is essential for peaceful coexistence while anekant facilitates better understanding and assimilation of divergent ideologies and thus helps promote tolerance. Ahimsa implies a love of life in all living beings and a firm belief in the principle of "live and let live". Thoughts of attachment and aversion, raga and dwesha and any action done under their spell constitute violence. Lord Mahavir propounded that violence results from the attachment with worldly possessions and vanity. He preached that complete detachment from this world is a prerequisite for the practice of non-violence. All other ways to non-violence are superficial and imperfect.

Anekant means understanding an object from all points of view or in other words giving due consideration to all shades of opinions without any dogma. It trains the mind to give due respect to the feelings and ways of life of other persons and communities. It makes one tolerant towards others' point of view thereby promoting interpersonal and communal harmony. Within the society Anekant is a powerful tool to end intolerance, dissension and conflicts. Anekant, if practiced truly by all communities, will mean the end of the scourge of inter-caste strife and communal violence. Anekant is thus the foundation pillar of religious harmony and the sheet-anchor of secularism, in the Jain philosophy.

The message of Lord Mahavir is valid for all castes, creeds and communities and is relevant in every era. Ahimsa and anekant are conducive in inculcating virtues such as kindness, fraternity and benevolence. Anekant can help to cultivate tolerance, respect and fraternity amongst the nations, whereas ahimsa is the key to world peace and stability. Spreading the message of Lord Mahavir shall diminish the hostilities in the world. Consequently it could lead to demilitarization of all nations and put an end to the unending arms race in the world. Resources thus spared could then be utilized for developmental projects for the welfare of the people. Jainism believes that one should not injure, subjugate, enslave, torture or kill living being, organism, or sentient being. This doctrine of non-violence is immaculate, immutable, and eternal. Just as suffering is painful, in the same way disquieting, and terrifying all living beings including animals, organisms, and sentient beings, is painful.

'**Acaranga**' is a holy Jain scripture of a very high order. It reveals the transcendental truth and eternal universal laws. It comprises of 12 principal scriptures of Jainism called Angas. It contains three-fold fundamental message: **"Everything takes birth; everything perishes; nothing is permanent"**. The Angas are generally in the form of sermons which embody the teachings imparted by Tirathankar Mahavir to his first apostles, the Gandharas. Besides the Angas, Uttaradhyayana (believed to be the last sermon of Lord Mahavir), and Dasavarkalika are widely studied by all Jain monks. Kalpa Sutra, the life history of Lord Mahavir, is highly rated. But the Acaranga is considered to be most important of the Angas since it is believed to be the first book which contains authentic teachings of Lord Mahavir. From the language, contents and their presentation style, the holy scripture of Jainism namely the Acaranga appears to be a work of 3rd or 4th century B.C. It is interesting to note that a number of Hindu divine beings like

Uddalka, Angirasa, Narayan, Vidhura, Narada and Dvaipayana Vyas are respectfully mentioned. This scripture may help one to get a glimpse of the purest and the earliest form of Jainism, and its relation with Upanishadic thought. It has eight chapters and lays down the philosophical precepts and psychological reasons for moral conduct of an ascetic.

The Acaranga emphasizes the knowledge and renunciation of weapons of violence with a difference – the weapon both physical and mental which can hurt the living beings. It is focused on the conquest of the world – both external and internal. Parents, wife, children, relations etc. wealth constitute the external world while the internal world comprises of attachment, aversion, love, hatred, desires anger, greed, deceit and ego. The book urges an aspirant to forebear with patience and equanimity all obstacles which inevitably come in the spiritual path in the form of favourable and unfavourable circumstances. It advocates **righteousness** with non-violence as its essence. Faith, knowledge and conduct leading to non-violence constitute the true path to righteousness, and leads further to freedom from the bondage of Karma. Self-control and Abstinence from indulgence in sense-pleasure together form the essence of the teachings of this book. The principle of removal of the impurities caused by the past Karmas forms the subject-matter of the book which means detachment from friends and relatives, from the physical body and belongings, name and fame, luxury and prosperity. **'Mahaparijna'** (Super Knowledge) and **'Vimoksa'**, (Liberation) from the bondage, lays down rules of conduct for monks with regard to food, clothing, treatment during illness, protection from heat, cold and rain, as also the way in which they should conduct themselves. The book also advises monks, weakened by old age and unable to bear the rigours of monastic life, to reduce their food-intake and finally give up the body while fasting with courage and equanimity.

The Jain philosophy of the Acaranga is essentially focused on **Self-Control** with Non-violence (Ahimsa as the eternal law), **Self Conquest, Need for Vigilance** and the **Nature of the Free Soul**. Self-Enquiry begins with the fundamental questions such as: who one is and where one comes from. Whether the Soul takes birth again and again or not, nor it is known what were the persons before the present life, and what will they be after death. Such an enquiry into the nature of the self is stressed as the basis of all knowledge in Acaranga. The subtle spiritual truths regarding one's soul, its past and future lives, cannot be known by ordinary means. The quest for such a knowledge makes one, a believer in soul, believer in the world, believer in the karma and believer in self-effort and leads to a fourfold faith which becomes the basis of the principle of 'Ahimsa' (Non-violence) – the eternal axiom of Jainism.

The Acaranga forcefully advocates the principle of Non-violence (Ahimsa) and attempts to deepen the sensitivity of individuals towards the sufferings of others so that a harmonious social order free from violence gets prevailed. It further stresses the fact that the existence of a creature cannot and should not be denied just because it is low or weak or small in size in the scale of evolution. Acaranga recognizes six classes of living being with numberless lives or Jivas, not only embodied in animals, human beings, gods, insects, reptiles and plants but also in the four basic elements of survival namely earth, water, fire and wind. The lives in these four elements, though unable to express themselves, do feel pain, as somebody may cut or hit a blind-man. No suffering should be inflicted on any of these living beings whether in an animate or inanimate form. Everyone should follow the path of **Ahimsa** (Non-violence). All breathing, existing, living, sentient creatures should not be slain, nor abused, nor tormented, nor driven away.

Self-Conquest is the philosophical aspect of Jainism as emphasized in the Acaranga as the path of righteousness in terms of right conduct. For this, it calls for the conquest of mind before physical restraint or austerity can be adopted. True renunciation lies in giving up attachment and the notion of 'owning'. Relinquishing possessiveness generates relinquishing of possessions. Thus the scripture urges the aspirants to purge their mind full of all desires and attachments. Running after pleasures would cause more pain and sufferings not only to the self but to others also. It, therefore, exhorts an aspirant the need for vigilance and cautiousness. An aspirant or a sage who follows the right path as emphasized in the Acaranga, becomes liberated from the cycles of birth and death. He/she, then becomes a free soul.

Paryushana is a major 10-day Jain festival celebrated during the month of Bhadrapada. In this period, participants practice self-purification, self-criticism and self-control in order to achieve self-improvement. Devotees during these days partake of simple and frugal meals once daily and abstain from worldly vices and addictions. They rededicate themselves to practice dharma as the scriptures define it. Jain scriptures speak loftily of the human form of the Atman. The human incarnation of the Atman is a rare privilege and should not be frittered away in the pursuit of physical pleasures and material gains. Human beings are seen as the best and the most perfect creations of the living beings and this incarnation must be utilized by the Atman to rid itself of worldly bondage. Dharma and Viveka or discrimination differentiates human beings from other life forms. Viveka helps realize the true Self or the Dharma of the Atman.

The Dharma of the Atman – Dasha Lakhsyana in Jainism – is considered to be a prelude to attain Nirvana or eternal bliss. It comprises of 10 traits such as: Shedding Pride and Ego; Honest and Righteousness; Truthfulness and Ethics; Cleanliness and Freedom from vices; Self Control and Abstinence; Tapa or Devotional Penance and Meditation; Tyaga (Sacrifice) and Charity; Control of Desire and Greed; Celibacy and Character; and Peace and Non-violence.

Non-violence, however, occupies the top position in the code of conduct – Anuvrata, propounded by Lord Mahavir. Non-violence is to be treated as the ideal of righteousness (Dharma). As an ethical principle, non-violence is rooted in the Jaina-metaphysics of Anekantavada of reality in the abstruse of logic of different relative opinions. Discrimination on the basis of caste, creed and colour constitutes violence because it harms and hurts the sentiments of those who are discriminated on account of such factors. Killing another sentient being whether plant or animal or human being is violence. It is unethical. Violence does not mean merely man killing a living being but quarrelling, fighting, offensiveness and aggressiveness are also considered to be acts of violence. Even criticizing, backbiting and ridiculing others are also forms of violence. Dishonesty and betrayal in financial and commercial matters also constitute willful violence because such acts hurt deeply the persons who are cheated of their money.

Non-violence (Ahimsa) is an important spiritual ideal along with other ideals namely truth (Satya), righteousness (Dharma), peace (Shanti) and love (Prema). It is highly essential for awakening the spiritual consciousness. Indeed, non-violence implies fearlessness and non-aggression. It is the necessary condition for building a healthy and moral social order in the human society. It cannot be a choice. The non-violence code as the basic vow (Anuvrat) is a very comprehensive mode of spirituality propounded by Lord Mahavir. Non-violence leads to love which brings peace as a path of righteousness to realize the ultimate truth. It is a state of consciousness. Removal of ignorance and true knowledge are essential for self-realization, self-control and social harmony. Non-violence (Ahimsa) brings to an end of the inter-play of the opposites like pain-pleasure, sorrow-happiness, aversion-attraction, hatred-love, loss-profit, failure-success, insult-respect, denigration-appreciation, conflict-harmony, aggression-gentleness, vice-virtue, evil-good and bondage-freedom. In short, non-violence is a Nirvana which lies in the right faith, right knowledge and right conduct.

5.2 Zoroaster and Christ

The historical records suggest that three great religions of the world namely Buddhism, Jainism and Zoroastrianism were born within one hundred years of one another in the sixth and the seventh centuries B.C. It was Zarathustra or Zoroaster who founded Zoroastrianism in Persia, now Iran. In India, this religion is popularly known as the religion of the Parsis. Zoroastra is revered as one of the greatest prophets of all time. He is believed to have given to the Parsi community an evolved and ethical religion. The Parsis worshipped different deities that they believed dwelt in the different objects of nature, like the sun, the moon, the stars, fire, wind and water. Temples were built for each deity, and idols were worshipped. Zoroaster denounced all this and founded a 'pure' religion, free from idolatry. He was distraught by the problem of evil and brooded over it with intense solemnity when, all of a sudden, enlightenment came to him as it happened to Buddha. Thereupon, Zoroastra's soul was imbued with God's revelation. He set out to spread the message to the world, for what use was it if God's word lay inside him unshared? He looked at the sun and said: "**Thou great star: what could be thy happiness if thou hadst not those for whom thou shinest**".

The Zoroastrians' philosophy is proclaimed in their Holy Book Zend-Avesta. Two-thirds of the original scripture which consisted of 350,000 words was destroyed during the external invasions; the one-third that remains contains the liturgical collection called Yasna, including the five most sacred books known as Gathas. It was written in an ancient dialect which closely resembles Vedic Sanskrit and holds the same status for Zoroastrians as the Bhagvat Gita does for the Hindus, the Quran for the Muslims, the Old Testament for the Jews, and the New Testament for the Christians. The essential wisdom that flows from the Zend-Avesta is this: **The entire universe is ruled by two primeval powers of Good and Evil. The good power is represented by Ahura Mazda** or Ormuzd and the evil by **Angra Mainyu** or **Ahriman**. Ormuzd is supported by six deified virtues of good thought, right law, noble government, holy character, health, and immortality. Ahriman is helped by most of the old nature-deities of the popular faith. Somewhere between the two powers stands the human being. He has to choose between good and evil. If he chooses good, he goes to paradise; if he chooses evil, he goes to hell. The underlying faith is that goodwill triumph in the end and that evil will be extirpated. But what is new and interesting here is that choosing good does not imply praying, but working. The best work or action lies in fighting invaders, destroying wild things, clearing fields, building bridges, irrigating barren land, and in the performance of good deeds – in promoting civilization. In Zoroastrianism, the supreme God is Ahura Mazda, the Lord of Wisdom. As a Buddhist scholar Lewis Brown writes, "**Ahura Mazda is, in essence, the spirit of civilization, and the only worship acceptable to him is the spreading of order and stability**". Another interesting thing is that in this creed no mercy is shown to evil. Ahura Mazda stands for justice, not mercy. Emotion has no place in it. One has to be a man of unbending good thought, word and deed. The abiding principle is that good has to be promoted and evil routed mercilessly. Even good animals like the cow and sheep have to be nursed and looked after well, while dangerous, and obnoxious creatures like rodents or snakes, killed.

The Zoroastrian philosophy is pragmatic; its chief instrument is hard work. Zoroastrians also put a great premium on learning. It is through wisdom and the good mind that knowledge emerges about the material world and its environment. Knowledge is the key to good living. Clearly, technology and the understanding of the workings of the material world are central to an understanding of Zoroastrianism. A spiritual Zoroastrian then, is the one who enjoins leading a full life in the material world, but always in accordance with the natural environment or what is today loosely referred to as ecology. The approach to community problems may be better resolved by recognizing ecological importance of a living planet, and by analogy, the ecological balance that must be maintained within the human community, if it is to survive. At the level of principle and on closer examination there are great similarities between the ecology of the planet and between the socio-religious balance of the Zoroastrians. In the past, this realization brought the community to staggering heights of prominence and excellence. In Zoroastrianism, the notions of wealth and well being are seen as positive attributes. Sharing of wealth is doctrinally considered to be imperative.

Divine occurrences seem to have several common features prior to the advent of the divine incarnations, messengers and prophets. The advent of Zoroaster, the prophet of Persia was predicted much before his actual arrival on the earth. Zoroaster is worshipped as a divine prophet in Iran who brought to the mortal world the light of knowledge. The persisting doubt of controversy about the antiquity of the Gatha (the Gita of the Parsis) provides a scanty biographical sketch of Zoroaster. It indicates the era when Iran was passing through a critical time and the mother earth was wailing with pain by undergoing terrible tribulations and sufferings due to the wrath and cruelty inflicted by the demonic and evil forces. To soothe anguish and pain of the Mother Earth, the Lord Almighty, Ahura Mazda (God of Persia) sent his messenger Zoroaster to free the people from the evil forces and bring in them the faith in God.

The advent of Zoroaster as a divine prophet is loaded with mythological stories and miracles. Description of several incidents related to his early childhood seems to give an impression of his superhuman being. Zoroaster began his life on earth with a royal miracle. Born of the parents Dughdas (mother) and Porushaspa (father), as a newly born baby, Zoroaster laughed loudly instead of crying aloud as every child does at the time of birth. It was equally a strange sight when the baby after having laughed loudly, sat up and made some sacred utterances. Even his brain also started throbbing violently that no hand could touch his head. The father Porushaspa brought some wizard named Durassobo to see the strange baby. But when the wizard, because of his evil designs of killing the baby, tried to crush the baby's head between his hands, the baby's head throbbed violently that the wizard fell back. Thus, by showing the miraculous power right at the time of his birth, Zoroaster invited the wrath of the king Duransarun of that territory. Apprehensive of the unforeseen dangers from such a new born baby, the king, who patronized sorcerers and magicians, came to the house of Porushaspa to see the infant himself. He saw the baby lying in peace in the cradle. Being overcome by his evil designs, the king decided to kill the child to ward off any danger to his kingdom. As soon as he drew his dagger to stab the baby, the king's hand suddenly got paralyzed. The king got scared in frustration and realized the power of the baby. The king's failure to kill the child did not put an end to the dangers to the baby's life. The local wizard Durasrobo successfully convinced the child's father Porushaspa a simple minded person, that his son was possessed by evil spirits or the devils and hence, the child's life was a potential danger to the whole community. Hence, the only option left for the child's father was to give his consent for killing the child in the interest of his community. A helpless father gave his unwilling consent and the wizard Durasrobo took the child to the desert, kept it inside a bundle of firewood and put it to fire. Assured of success, the wizard left. But firewood did not burn the child. Early morning, the mother Dughdao, frantically searching child, found the infant sitting quietly on the scattered firewood. Thus, Zoroaster remained safe and sound inspite of the murderous attempts made on him by the evil forces.

The evil wizard along with sorcerers took permission from the king Duransarun to take all possible steps to eliminate the miraculous child

Zoroaster. A herd of oxen was driven towards the child to trample him to death under the feet of the animals. The child remained safe since a big bull covered the body of the child under its four feet as other animals ran across the path. Again the child was taken to a drinking-pool for the horses, and was placed there to be crushed under the feet of the rampaging horses. But in this case also, a big horse covered the body under his four legs and saved him. The evil forces again put the little Zoroaster in a den of wolves when the beasts were away. Inside they killed all the young wolves and placed the baby among the dead bodies of the young wolves with the expectation that when the mother wolves would, on return, find their dead off-springs, they would tear the baby Zoroaster to pieces in anger. However, it was amazing to find that the divine played its role. The furious wolves calmed down on seeing the child, obediently kept quiet and paid no attention to the child. It is said that two celestial cows entered the den of the wolves and fed their milk to the child prophet Zoroaster. A few more attempts were made on the child Zoroaster like poisoning him and putting horrifying witchcrafts on him. This is somewhat similar to what was done to Prahlaad, an ardent devotee of Lord Vishnu whom Prahlaad's father, the powerful demon King Hirenkhshayap, considered his sworn enemy and inflicted a number of cruelties to dissuade him from worshiping Vishnu as God, in a story of His incarnation as Half-Lion and Half-Man (Narsingh), related in Srimad Bhagvat Puran of the Hindus.

Being amazed at the survival of the child Zoroaster despite several attempts on his life, father Purushaspa realized that Zoroaster was not an ordinary child and hence deserved an extraordinary care. He took Zoroaster to a safer place for his education and placed him under the care of a pious teacher. Zoroaster grew up to boyhood, and when he was twenty years old, he decided to seek the truth in his own way. He left home without telling his parents and made a secluded cave on Mount Ushidarena as his abode, where he devoted himself to deep meditation for ten years. Wandering herdsmen passing through that mountain cave used to give him food. Also, some neighbouring villagers used to bring food for him. During these years Zoroaster established communion with the divine beings and God. Divine power was waiting for him when he came out of the cave. Zoroaster saw a glorious vision of the Archangel of Love who asked him about his wish. Zoroaster replied by saying that he wanted only to know God's will and work for Him. Being pleased by his reply, the angel asked him to keep aside his material body and follow him to see God, Ahura Mazda. The Zoroaster asked God, "**Which of God's creature is the best on earth**?" came the God's answer, "**He is the best of all men who is pure of heart**." God

Almighty, then put Zoroaster to certain tests. After Zoroaster passed those tests, God, in His great grace, gave him the Avesta and declared him the Prophet of God. The Prophet Zoroaster was then commanded to go and preach his doctrine: "**Destroy the evil and teach the path of Righteousness**" became the mission of the Prophet Zoroaster.

Thus, carrying the sacred Avesta in hand, Zoroaster proceeded with the divine mission to lead mankind to the path of righteousness. The evil forces vanished and sorcerers fled as soon as Zoroaster started reciting Avesta. His prophetic utterances converted many persons into his disciples and followers. Zoroaster and his followers went place to place to spread the Divine message of Avasta. One day, they came across a lake which was necessary to cross, but there was no boat. Zoroaster stretched forth his hands in prayer and the water divided of itself, and the faithful marched through the dry-shod of the lake. Zoroaster found his mission a difficult task because of the strong opposition from his rivals which included among others, the wealthy and powerful, arrogant and evil-doers. In frustration, Zoroaster prayed to God for inspiration, help and advice. God appeared before him and blessed him with six more Revelations to help him in the successful accomplishment of the divine mission. The fundamentals of these revelations appeared before Zoroaster in the form of six angels of knowledge: Archangel Vohumanah – the angel of Love and Wisdom; Archangel Asha Vahishta – the angel of Righteousness from whom the prophet learnt the symbolic value of Fire representing the light of God and Purity of Soul who also taught him the mysteries of the Eternal law of Truth; Archangel Khshathra who taught Zoroaster about the Omnipotence and the Sovereignty of God Almighty who also told him that wealth is sacred only when it used for the service of the poor; Archangel Spentar-Maiti – the mother of all creatures who told him the value of reverence to the mother Earth; Arachangel of Perfection named Hourvatat who represented God's grace upon the faithful to be perfect; and finally Archangel Ameretat, representing immortality who also was known as the queen of vegetation. Armed with reassurance and emboldened by the divine knowledge from the six revelations or visions, Zoroaster marched forward to show the path of light to his fellowmen.

Eventually, Zoroaster reached the territory of Balk ruled by a powerful emperor named Vishtaspa whose court was a stronghold of wizards and sorcerers. The common people of this kingdom were simple but highly superstitious. The only way to bring these people out of their superstitions deeply rooted by wizards and sorcerers was to transform the emperor. As desired by God Himself, Zoroaster went to the court of the emperor Vishtaspa with Avesta in his hand and challenged the king's learned men for a debate. The king's men did their best to denounce the Zoroaster's doctrines but were defeated in argument in the very presence of the king. The king expressed his willingness in the Prophet's doctrines and allowed him to stay in the kingdom till further decision. This gave an ample chance to emperor's wise men to discredit Zoroaster through dirty tactics. One day when Zoroaster was away from his shelter, these wicked men bribed the servant to silence and filled the Zoroaster's room with several heads of dogs, cats and other animals. The emperor was duly informed that how dangerous was Zoroaster who practiced sorcery of the worst type even while enjoying emperor's hospitality as a guest. This sight enraged the emperor who ordered Zoroaster to be thrown in a prison.

Zoroaster realized that his mission seemed to be failing unless a great miracle was shown to the emperor to change his mind, and also to establish his faith in the existence of the Divine Power, called the God Almighty. Indeed, an opportunity came for this purpose. While Zoroaster was in prison, the emperor's favourite horse, named Bahzad, was struck with an undiagnosed and unnatural disease. As a result of which, the four feet of the horse got entered into its body causing it thereby tremendous pain. Even the emperor on seeing the horse wreathing with this terrible pain became very sad and full of sorrow because he loved the horse very much. The wizards and sorcerers in the emperor's court tried all methods but failed to cure the horse. When Zoroaster came to know of this problem, he offered to the king emperor to cure the horse, provided he accepted four conditions which the king readily agreed.

The first condition was that the emperor should accept Zoroaster's faith as Divine Faith and Zoroaster as the Prophet. As soon as the king accepted this condition, the first foot of the horse came out of its body. The second condition was that the emperor's son should work to defend this faith with full devotion. The moment, the prince agreed to do so, at once came out the horse's second foot from its body. The third condition was that the queen should accept the Zoroastrian Faith and work for it. The queen readily agreed and the third foot of the horse also came out. Finally, the last and the fourth condition was that the emperor should hold an enquiry as to who was responsible for filling his dwelling place with animal's heads and punish the guilty forthwith. The emperor conducted an immediate enquiry and the servant of the house disclosed the plot of the emperor's wizards and sorcerers, to defame

Zoroaster. The moment the guilty persons were caught and punished, the fourth foot of the horse came out and the horse was back to its normal shape. This miracle convinced the emperor and his people that Zoroaster was, indeed, a real prophet who possessed the divine powers and hence, deserved veneration. What the preaching of the divine doctrines could not achieve, the divine miracles did it. Zoroaster showed the emperor many more divine miracles in order to establish his faith firmly in the divine power called Ahur Mazda. Later on Zoroaster did many more miracles as the Prophet of Iran while preaching the divine doctrines.

Eventually, the Prophet Zoroaster established a number of Fire Temples, while carrying on his mission of educating the people and converting them to have faith in God. Zoroaster left his mortal body at the age of 77. According to an Iranian legend, Zoroaster consumed himself in a supernatural fire (Agni-Smadhi) and reached back the heavenly abode. The last of miracles of Zoroaster happened at the time of his death. When from among the enemy forces, some warrior struck the prophet with a naked sword, the prophet threw a rose at the slayer. The holy rose at once turned into fire and burnt alive the slayer in no time. Zoroaster died but the Zoroasterian Faith remains alive till date.

As in most of the religious faiths, a great book – called **Zend Avesta** – is still preserving the Zoroastrian community. It is often remarked that Zend is the language in which Avesta is written while it also means commentary. Thus Zend Avesta means the Avesta along with its commentary. The **Yasna**, **Vispered**, **Vedidad** and **Yashts** are the four parts of the Zend Avesta somewhat parallel to the four Vedas of the Hindus. Gathas, the Cream of the Avesta, are the outpouring of the God-intoxicated Prophet Zoroaster, in an extremely archaic language. The close affinity between the Vedas and the Avesta, both in language and contents, to some extent, suggest that they were intimately related to each other. The striking similarity between the two indicates that the two languages could not have been separated before they were transformed to their present status. The scanty autobiographical elements in the Gathas and other scriptures like the Vedas, and various legends provide sufficient material for drawing up a life sketch of the Prophet identified with this holy scripture. Iran (Persia) was passing through a critical period, and the Mother Earth was wailing. To soothe her anguish, the Lord Almighty '**Ahur Mazda**' sent down His messenger Zoroaster [Zoro (golden) Aster (Light)] which means the '**Golden Light**'. Its etymological meaning, however, is 'the possessor of old or yellow camels'. Zoroaster preached a new religion and urged the nomadic people to cultivate land. Zoroaster's radical reform was to rid humanity completely from all allegiance to deities implicated in magic.

Five Gathas of Zoroaster are the compositions which look like a mass of prayers, songs, legends, prescriptions, rituals and morals, full of fervent devotion, ethical elevation and lyric piety. The Gathas are the song-offerings with a fine ethereal fragrance coming from the lips of Zoroaster – a poet, a philosopher and a prophet, all rolled into one. Flashes of Prophet's communion with God, as revealed in the Gathas, are invaluable. The message highlights the tranquility in thought, the harmony in expression, and the graceful blending of music generate feeling in the Gathas that leave deep impression on those who explores them in depth. More than their poetic excellence, their vigour and drive provided by the Prophet has kept the lamp of this religion burning through millennia.

In the monotheistic theory of creation, Ahura Mazda is the one and only creator of the universe. At the same time, the prophet proclaimed, there is some force in the Universe, which obstructs the work of Ahura Mazda. The Gathas, thus visualize twin spirits, which came together at creation's early dawn, one for protection and the other for annihilation. These two spirits are known as Mainyus: Spenta Mainyu (the good spirit) and Angra Mainyu (the evil spirit). Some hold the view that Spenta Mainyu and Angra Mainu, though subordinate to Ahura Mazda, are His creations. Thus, in the ladder of life, a step can take a human being either upwards to Ahura Mazda through Spenta Mainyu or downwards through Angra Mainyu. Philosophically, evil is just the negation of virtue, and when this negation gets personified, it becomes Angra Mainyu. The prophet wages unflinching battle against Angra Mainyu and inspires all mankind to this fight, while assuring that the spirit of evil will ultimately get vanquished and Spenta Mainyu will be victorious. Man is the creator of his own destiny. In the battlefield of the world, being a true soldier of Ahura Mazda, he must hold on to the path of righteousness. The main constituents of the path of righteousness are **humta** (good thought), **hukta** (good word) and **huvarshta** (good deed). Repeated references to fire in the Gathas abundantly show that Zoroaster himself held fire in high esteem, and preached worship of Ahura Mazda through the symbol of 'fire'. **Atar** (fire) is, thus, considered to be the purest and holiest of Mazda's creation.

Though controversy persists about the metaphysical dualism in the prophet's teachings, yet a few scholars have taken a monistic aspect of Ahura Mazda for He is like Nirguna Brahmn the Supreme Reality in Hinduism. Zoroaster preached spiritual monotheism with an illusion of metaphysical dualism to intimate morality by drawing a sharp contrast between what is good and what is bad, between what is virtue and what is evil. Zoroaster used to pray to God and say, "**Reveal yourself within me O Ahura, and through divine wisdom grant me the desire for perfection through your devotion, O Mazda, grant us goodness as reward for prayers, through righteousness, the full vigour of soul and all embracing love through good thoughts**."

Finally, Zoroastrianism forecasts the advent of the '**Saoshyant**' who will consummate the work of regenerating the world by completely eradicating evil. The souls of the wicked will get purified. The souls of righteous will arise. Free from evil and misery, the world will enter upon a new age. The Saoshyant in the form of Sri Sathya Sai Baba has already appeared and He has been doing His work as planned and predicted by Zoroaster.

Moses, Jesus and Mohammed are considered to be the three unique divine personalities who founded the three monotheistic religions of Judaism, Christianity and Islam in order of succession. It is interesting to note that all the three religions originated from the same place, the holy city of Jerusalem, a three thousand years old metropolis – the capital of modern Israel. The city is sacred to millions of Jews, Christians and Muslims all the world over. The holiness and sanctity of the land of Jerusalem is linked to the traditions and faith originated by their three respective divine messengers. While the atmosphere is changed with the ringing of bells from churches, sounds of prayer calls from the mosques and chanting from Jewish synagogues, the aura that surrounds this place is an indicator of the strong faith of the devotees that the land is blessed with God's physical presence. Indeed, Jerusalem symbolizes the confluence of three religious faiths, which are considered to be monotheistic Dotted with synagogues, churches and mosques, Jerusalem looks like a big pilgrimage centre, it is the heart of the three faiths of Judaism, Christianity and Islam. While the Jews feel the divine presence, here, the Muslims believe it to be their third holy shrine after Mecca and Medina since prophet Mohammed believed to have visited this site. It was here that Jesus made his painful walk while carrying the cross from the point of trial to his place of execution where now stands the Church of Holy Sepulcher.

Long long ago, the Jews (also called Hebrews) came to Egypt in search of food due to a famine which affected their motherland Jerusalem. Egypt was prosperous and fertile due to the magnificent river Nile. Initially, these migrant Jews were perceived as a threat to Egypt and hence were enslaved. The Jews suffered at the hands of Egyptians.

However, they had a ray of hope and believed that one day a messenger of God would come who will get them freedom from the slavery of the Egyptians, and lead them back to their promised land. Indeed, the Deliverer – the messenger of God who came to set the Jews free from slavery and lead them to their land was none other than Moses. Moses was chosen instrument of God for the deliverance of the Jews from slavery at the hands of the Egyptian Pharaohs. Moses was the first born in a Hebrew household. Egypt's Pharaoh Rameses-I ordered all Hebrew first born to be killed. To save Moses, his mother set him adrift on River Nile in a basket. The baby Moses was discovered by the Pharaoh's daughter. Moses was brought up in the palace of Pharaoh Seti. He grew up to become Seti's favourite, much to the jealousy of his own son Rameses. Later, Moses was thrown out of Egypt when it was found that he was a Hebrew. Moses's miracles include among others the turning of his rod into a cobra, his touching of Nile waters converting into blood, covering of Egypt with darkness for three days, emerging of fire from the floor of Pharaoh's palace and Moses's making a way though the sea by bifurcation of its waters to lead his Hebrew people on to the mountain safely where God gave him the well-known ten commandments for the Jews to follow.

The principal doctrines were adherence to the truth, an upright character and unity of thought, word and deed. He had a great sense of justice and had the ability to be equanimous both in glory and in fall. Moses was the rarest combination of self-confidence and humility which means transcendence of the Self. He lived with slaves and worked with them. Moses was exhorted by God to ascend Mount-Sinai and receive Ten commandments. As directed by God, he climbed the Mount-Sinai to receive God's Ten Commandments which together constitute what is called 'Tohra' or the Old Testament.

Torah like Veda is considered to be the holy scripture of the Jews which provides inspirational guidance for spiritual living. It represents the type of religious literature which directs human life towards God. Torah guidance is conveyed to the people essentially on the lines of three fundamental teachings: **Eternal Truth**, **Spiritual Practice,** and **Universal Love and Peace** which together constitute the three pillars of the Decalogue (The Ten Commandments) that comprises Torah. This great prophet was deeply concerned with the Absolute Truth or the Ultimate Reality – the God. He had three great visions – each of which revealed to him the Divine attributes namely: **spirituality, universality** and **eternity**. This is indeed religious realism which contrasts between what is real and what is unreal, between the reliable and the fallible, between substance and shadow. The ultimate contrast is brought out between God and the world, between spirit and matter, and between soul and body. The message comes forcefully at the end: "**yea, the dust doth return to the earth as it was, but the spirit return the unto God who gave it**". The sum total of the matter, after all has been considered is: '**Revere God, and keep this precepts, for that is the whole of man**' – That is the essence of life. Various people face difficulty in deciphering Torah's message, largely because they fail to discern the different levels through which it communicates. Words or verbal images are by their very nature body-and-mind centered. One of the commentaries puts in this way: "**The Torah speaks in the language of humans**". That is a perfectly understandable observation with respect to the linguistics of the matter. But, obviously also, the message pertains to the '**truth of God**'. Torah contains an anthology of great Jew biographers like Abraham, Josephur, Isaiah and of the prophet Moses.

Both Zoroaster and Buddha generated lot of hostilities because of the demonstration of their divine miracles. Zoroaster, infact created enemies because of his miracles, but also overcame them by the same weapon. Similarly, there were people who doubted Buddha's divinity and criticized his doctrines. However, Buddha also triumphed over them by with his miracles and messages. The case of Jesus is difficult. It was perhaps more because of his miracles and less for his doctrines that he was subjected to painful crucification. According to some believers, it was his own desire that by suffering crucification, he would provoke people to rise and revolt against the tyranny and injustice. People did rise with the cross held aloft and thus Christianity spread from continent to continent embracing a large number of human beings. The cruelty and pain of crucification that Jesus suffered came to him as a punishment for his miracles at the hands of the then rulers.

Although Jesus's life span was too short, yet his preachings spread far and wide even among the common folks of the remote and neglected places. Jesus's circle of activity was limited and his miracles were seen and experienced by his nearest disciples, and by the poor, the sick and the helpless. The miracles and doctrines of Jesus came to limelight in much later times to follow since some of the contemporary historians and writers were not aware of existence of Jesus and his miracles. One of the historians Tacitus of the time of the New Testament made a mention of Christ in reference to the Christians and their new faith. It was, in fact, in the Jewish history of that time that a direct reference to Jesus is found. Josephus, a Hebrew historian, who was born in Jerusalem in 37 A.D. and who became an officer in the Jewish administration, wrote that Jesus was the Christ and therefore, was superhuman, but despite his own saying so, he (Jesus) was crucified. However, according to some historians, Josephus could not have written so in praise of Jesus for fear of punishment at the hands of the then rulers. Thus, as in the case of Zoroaster and Buddha, so also in the days of Jesus, there were biographers to sketch his life's profile. Like in the case of both Zoroaster and Buddha, the later biographers or historians found many fragmented information from the gospels on the doctrines of Jesus's disciples like Mark, Mathew and John among others contributed to the biographic profile of Jesus full of his miracles and messages. However, some historians to-date are not prepared to believe Jesus's miracles of healing since according to them, these miracles were not sufficient proofs of Jesus's divinity. In any case, the purpose here in this book is not to go into the controversies over the personality of Jesus, whether historical or mythical. The real purpose here is to present a brief account of some Jesus's profile and his famous miracles as known from the gospels, and his divine messages given in some of the published works on him because of which he is believed to be divine.

The blinds received their sight, the lame could walk, lepers were cleaned and cured, the deaf could hear, the dead rose up and the sinners were purified. All this could be possible only by the divine power in Jesus, which emerged from God. Nearly forty miracles of Jesus have been found in the gospels which are generally classified into six different categories such as the **Miracles of Divine Personality**, **Miracles of Divine Compassion**, **Miracles of Divine Understanding**, **Miracles of Resurrection**, **Miracles of Refreshment**, and **Miracles of Teaching**.

Palestine, the land of the Hebrews, was a part of the vast kingdom of Rome. A part of Palestine was known as Judaea where Harod, at that time, was the native king serving under the Roman Governor of that region. In that province of Judaea, there was a small and quiet village name Bethlehem situated near the ancient city of Jerusalem. Jesus was born here inside a stable of an inn. Like the predestined arrivals of divine personalities/incarnations pronounced before their actual birth, such as Rama, Krishna, Zoroaster and Buddha, Jesus's birth was also pronounced by the divine Angel Gabriel who came from God to earth to meet a virgin named Mary, living at a place named Nazarath in Galilee, a small neighbouring town outside the domain of Judaea. The Virgin, Mary, espoused to a man named Joseph, heard from the Angel Gabriel. "**Fear not Mary, for thou hast found favour with God. And behold thou shall conceive in the Womb, and bring forth a son, and shall call his name Jesus, who shall be great and shall be called the**

Son of the Highest". Thus, by the Will of God, His Son was destined to come through Mary's womb because she was pure. It was unlike the conception of other mortals. It was divine and similar to the births of several earlier divines like Rama, Krishna, Zoroaster and Buddha, the latest being that of Sri Sathya Sai Baba.

Thus in a cold night of December, to their utter amazement, some shepherds resting near a camp fire in their fields to keep themselves warm, saw a glowing light which almost blinded them, and heard a voice from above: **"Fear not, For, behold, I am the Angel of the Lord and bring you a news of great joy in the world which will make all the people of the earth happy. Fear Not, for unto you born this day a Saviour, in the city of David, who is Christ of the Lord. And this shall be a sign to you that you may find Him. The baby is wrapped in swaddling clothes and lying now in a manger**". Hearing this mysterious voice, the puzzled shepherds ran towards the town of Bethlehem, they searched for the announced place and reached the spot where the holy child was lying in a manger inside a stable behind an inn. Yet another miracle happened that very night. Three wise men of the East, who were not inhabitants of Israel, but were on their journey towards that land, while observing the stars in the sky, got astonished to see a new bright star pointing its brilliant light downward to the stable of the inn and saw the child. There they bowed down to offer homage to the infant. Before leaving the place, they utter a few words of prediction that the Jews had at last got their Lord Saviour who would dethrone King Harod and would lead them to salvation. Thereafter, the Angel of the Lord appeared in the dream of Joseph who was asleep at that time and directed him to arise and take the child along with the mother Mary, and flee with them to Egypt, for the safety of the child and remain there till it was safe for them to return to Bethlehem. Joseph got up and taking the dream as the God's desire, he took the baby and the mother by night, and fled to Egypt, resembling the event associated with Lord Krishna's birth in the prison, and then carried by his father Vasudev to a safer place at Nandgaon, also called 'Gokul'.

Herod, the then native king of Judaea, came to know of the miraculous birth of the baby, Jesus. According to the prediction of the wise-men of East, that this newborn baby would dethrone him, the king Herod ordered his soldiers to capture that baby. Having failed to distinguish the holy baby from others, while the baby was already missing, the king's men killed all the babies, born in Bethlehem that night. Thus, Herod was satisfied that the baby Jesus had been killed. This episode related to Jesus's birth is more or less similar to the birth of Krishna in the Dwapar Yuga. After the death of king Herod, Joseph along with Mary and young Jesus came back to the village Nazareth in Gelilee where they lived peacefully. Jesus grew up as a young man and came to be known as Nazarene, meaning a man from Nazareth. As a young man, Jesus became aware of his superhuman powers. It was the right time for him to begin his missionary work. Having found five men to believe in his holy words and to accompany him, in his journey, Jesus reached a small town Cana to participate in the marriage ceremony in a family related to Mary. However, it was found that the quantity of wine to be served was not enough for the member of guests who arrived for the wedding. There a beam of light suddenly showed Jesus the way out to solve this problem of the hosts and gave him an opportunity to show his divine power. Jesus looked around and found big jars of stone, empty or semi-empty. He ordered the attendants to fill the jar with water and in a moment, he transformed water into wine at his will. Thereafter, he instructed the attendants to pour water-turned wine into the pots of the guests including the governor of Cana. This was the first miracle which Jesus demonstrated publically. The persons who saw this miracle were completely astonished and equally amazed were Jesus's five disciples named: Simon Peter, Andrew, John, Philip and Bartholomew, who then became his faithful followers.

Eventually, Jesus showed many more miracles just as enabling his disciples in catching plentiful of fishes when they were disappointed on not being able to catch fish despite several prior attempts. On another occasion, Jesus saved his disciples and others in the boat, which was caught in furious tempest while crossing the lake Gennasaret, surrounded by hills, by making the storm to be still. The fame of Jesus moved like a strong wave throughout the people living around Galilee particularly the poor, sick and the needy. Jesus paid his most attention to the most wretched among who were suffering from various incurable diseases and used his divine power to treat them such as converting an abnormal person to become normal through his soothing words, saving the dying son of a father, saving the life of a trusted attendant of an army officer, curing a person suffering from paralysis by making the paralytic patient to stand up and walk, cleaning a leper suffering from the terrible disease of leprosy and turning him into a perfectly healthy man; making a motionless person to walk, touching the eyes of a blind man and restoring his eye sight, and curing a deaf and dumb person by putting his fingers into men's ears and touching his tongue where voice and hearing became normal, among several such miracles.

The news about Jesus's miracles spread far and wide. Wherever Jesus, along with his disciples, went, people in large numbers came following him. Jesus started giving sermons to the people about the kingdom of Heaven. Sometimes huge crowds would assemble to hear Jesus's sermons. At one such occasion, people came from long distances, listened to Jesus's speech and they stayed. They did not go back. They were all hungry. Jesus asked his disciples to arrange food for them. The disciples told Jesus that they had no food except five loaves of bread. Jesus asked the disciples to bring those five loaves and told them to divide the crowd of hungry people in lines and make them sealed on the ground. When counted, the number of persons was counted to be five thousand – men, women and children. Jesus, then, raised his eyes upward towards heaven, took to the five loaves and broke the breads into pieces and handed over to the disciples to distribute as meals to the people. Jesus continued breaking bread loaves into pieces, and the disciples continued distributing to the people sitting in lines until all the people enjoyed the food like heavy meals. The food got multiplied and the people collected it and filled their baskets with the surplus food. This amazing miracle was seen by the five thousand people who came to know that the food for them came out of only five loaves of bread. This miracle made them believe that Jesus was not an ordinary human being, that he must be some divine-being.

At another occasion, late in the night, soon dark clouds covered the sky and a heavy storm came. Jesus at that time realized that his disciples on the sea were in danger. High waves could overturn their boat. Jesus came to the sea shore and continued walking. When the land ended, he still continued walking on the surface of the sea water. The disciples were amazed to see that Jesus's feet were not going into the water. He was walking on the sea water as if he was walking on the land. He walked straight towards the boat over the rising waves. The disciples on the boat observed a while glow of light encircling his head, his robes became brighter under that light, Jesus saved his disciples on the boat and brought them to the shore. Infact, he made his disciple Peter also walk on the water, though for a few moments.

At some other time, Jesus showed his divine form to his disciples who saw that the face of Jesus was glowing bright like the sun, his robes looked white like the snow, emitting bright rays, the place around Jesus was covered with a glow of lightening and Jesus stood transfigured as a Divine Being, possessing the divine brilliance of God with four divine figures talking to Jesus. Then came a heavenly voice from God which said, **"This is my beloved son. I am well-pleased with him. Listen to**

his words". Suddenly after a deep silence, the disciples saw Jesus back into the human form. The two divine figures, recognized by the disciples as the two prophets Moses and Elias, told Jesus that suffering and tortured death awaited him on earth, he must rise to the occasion and make his body strong to bear that suffering and torture. Thereafter, Jesus hold his disciples not to reveal to anyone the divine phenomenon they had witnessed.

Apart from this divine phenomenon, Jesus showed many more miracles related to resurrection – giving life to the dead. Once, Jesus saw a burial procession approaching a graveyard. He came near to the bier and asked the bearers to halt. Next he touched the bier and directed the dead to rise. The dead-man at-once stood up as if from deep sleep. Jesus also saved the life of the daughters of the head of the synagogue. Perhaps the most amazing miracle of resurrection was shown by Jesus in a small town of Bethany near the city of Jerusalem. There lived Lazarus along with two sisters Martha and Mary. They were intimately known to Jesus. Jesus got the message that Lazarus was dead for four days. Accompanied by the two wailing sisters Martha and Mary, Jesus reached the hill side on a rock where lied the cut out tomb of Lazarus, covered with a slab of stone. A large number of mourners also joined them. Jesus asked the mourners to remove the stone and looked upwards towards the heaven to offer silent prayers. Thereafter, Jesus turned his eyes down towards the tomb of Lazarus and commanded him to come forward. Thus, from inside the dark grave, the dead Lazarus came out to open day light, still covered with the burial clothes. A sudden silence overtook the people of which many turned believers and hence followers of Jesus, while to some of them, this miracle looked like an evil omen. Then on-believers saw in Jesus a threat to their traditional and ancient beliefs.

Soon the news of this extra-ordinary miracle of resurrection became the talk of the town of Jerusalem. Jesus's enemies and opponents promptly prepared the charge sheet against him that he was working against the established Jewish law as well as against the authority of the Roman Emperor. Consequently, in Jerusalem, the soldiers came to arrest Jesus. At that time, the disciple Peter got enraged and in order to have his Jesus took out a knife and attached a soldier cutting down his ear. Thereupon, Jesus intervened, stopped Peter. He came to the bleeding soldier and touched his injured ear. Immediately, the deep wound of the soldier got healed by the very touch of Jesus's hand. Eventually, Jesus was taken for trial. Rome was being ruled at that time by the Emperor Tiberius Caesar. The governor at Jerusalem, Pontius Pilate, passed death sentence on Jesus on the charges of his activities against the Jewish faith and for trying to establish a new kingdom – the kingdom of Heaven as against the kingdom of Rome.

Thus, outside the City of Jerusalem, on the Calvary Hill, Jesus was crucified in a most painful and brutual way by piercing nails through his palms and feet, he offered his last prayer to God and said, "**Father, Forgive them, for they know not what they do**". The soul of Jesus left his body on the cross. There too, a miracle happened. This was the miracle of the Resurrection of Jesus. It is said that the dead body of Jesus was carried to a cave where it was kept hidden. The formal burial, which was supposed to take place on the following day, was postponed since it happened to be the day of solemn Sabbath – the day of no work by the law. A group of mourners, who followed the bearers of the dead body, saw from a distance how the body was kept inside the cave and the entry point closed. They returned the following day with the hope of seeing the body of Jesus once more. To their utter dismay and shock, they saw that the stone that covered the entry to the cave was not there, and the body of Jesus was no longer to be seen inside the cave. The disciples with Mary came weeping, bent down and peeped into the cave but saw inside that two angles in white, one sitting, at the head, and the other at the feet, of the lain body. The angles told the women not to weep and see behind. They turned their face back and saw Jesus standing.

Divine miracles constitute an integral part of every divine incarnation and divine personality whether a prophet or a messenger. Divine miracles, therefore, are indispensable with any faith and Christian faith is not an exception. But the divine miracles do not form the only way towards faith. Coupled with preachings and above all, doctrines of a divine personality, they are the real effective ways of bringing human beings to have faith in God. These miracles for Jesus were the manifestations of the divine power and signs of salvation. He wanted people to understand the significance of his miracles and messages which needed to be understood like lessons in action.

Jesus presented to humanity a vision of the kingdom of God on the earth – a kingdom that depended neither on wealth nor on power, but on virtues. Such a kingdom, also called the kingdom of Heaven, had no place for the demonic vices like ego, desire, greed, jealousy and hatred; no exploitation of the weak by the strong and no distinction among the human beings. It is indeed a kingdom of love, where the love of God is followed by the love of humanity. That domain of love had no room for anger, malice, greed and lust. "**Love your enemy**", Jesus said, "**bless**

them that curse you, do good to them that hate you, and pray for them that despitefully use you and prosecute you". Jesus advised people to hate sin, but not the sinner. He said, "**Forgiveness is divine, Do not retaliate** or **pay evil with evil**. Jesus believed in change of heart not change of faith or religion. He was a Messiah of love, kindness and forgiveness and always preferred the merits of humanity, modesty and purity. He used to say," **Blessed are those who have not seen and yet believe. Blessed are those who feel the spiritual need. Blessed are those who have endured persecution for their uprightness**".

The Word of God inspired by the Holy Spirit is what is known as the New Testament. Such a Word of God simply requires spiritual awakening to be understood. The depths of God can only be realized by the Spirit of God. The New Testament was not offered as a book for the first 15 centuries but given as an oral recitation of the doings and sayings of Jesus Christ, proclaimed by Him. God spoke or thought Himself in Jesus, as God's logos (word, thought, consciousness) made into a human being. God is the Holy One (Sat-Truth) beyond all names and comprehension, who has made Himself available for union in intimacy (as father) with Jesus, as the image of the unseen God. Jesus made God comprehensible to humanity, he made God trustworthy for the people so that they could bond with God and could realize the external humanity to internal divinity in Jesus through his Death and Resurrection, and finally ascend with him to share divinity in him. The humanity in Jesus was the incandescent in God, enjoying the perfect union with the Father.

The New Testament is the book of revelation – an epic drama presented in four independent gospels – each one compiled by St. Mathew, St. Mark, St. Luke and St. John. The Gospel of St. Mark is considered to be the most fundamental treatise on Jesus with its central focus on three major features of Jesus's public life namely: His Baptism; His Transfiguration; and His Death, and Resurrection. One of the best ways to realize these three manifestations of Jesus is to visualize them in the light of the philosophy of spiritualism.

(a) Jesus's Baptism is his experience of spiritual awakening in his humanity to clarify about his union with God. In the ecstasy of the Holy Spirit, Jesus's previously dark, deep, intuitive knowledge of his union with God got lifted into a new knowledge of himself (self-realization): God, who is ineffable and beyond all, by that very transcendence can also be intimate, and is freely so is 'Father' to Jesus, and Jesus's own being drawn from the Father in his own depths, Jesus is His Son. Jesus's famous declarations "**God is my father, my father and I are same, and I am myself God**". This is clearly a transition from duality to non-duality through qualified non-duality in line with the spiritual philosophy of Hinduism.

(b) At his transformation, Jesus prayed again in the ecstasy of the Holy Spirit. He received the divine message to bring the humanity out of the slavery of worldly values and lead it to the spiritual values. Jesus went down into the depths of human suffering, and took on the full psychic burden of sin, its illusions and its bitter end in death. Jesus did it by loving human beings even their sins, giving himself away to them even in death, and by love he drew all people and the whole cosmos into his intimacy with God. In that intimacy with the Father, who created the world, Jesus identified love into a new creativity, morally and spiritually recreating it, and moving it along to share God's union with himself.

(c) The experience of merger in God that Jesus had in his dying state is the true realization of that to which he got awakened at his Baptism: a complex non-dual from duality that he himself was God. In his Resurrection, the father awakened Jesus from death into a new advaita (non-duality) raising him to the status of Lord Jesus drawing humanity into his union with God. Eventually a new bliss of union got manifested into his glorification in the Father. Together with the Father, Jesus poured out into the world the very 'bond' of his union in the Trinity – the outpouring of the Holy Spirit.

Bhagwan Sri Sathya Baba in some of his discourses told that Jesus was a grand Master with a purpose – the mission of restoring love, charity and compassion in the heart of man. He had no attachment to the self, nor paid any heed to joy or sorrow, loss or gain. Like most divine seekers, Jesus searched for the Divine in the objective world. He sought to find God within himself. From the attitude of his spiritual enquiry and asceticism being a Messenger of God, he could now declare himself the son of God. Later, as the God-consciousness within him got established, Jesus could declare, "**My Father and I are one**" Jesus realized in the twenty-fifth year that he was Christ. Early in His life He announced, "**I am God's messenger. I have come as a servant to all God's children**". Later Jesus retired from the world to be alone and contemplated over the nature of God. It is believed that Jesus was totally immersed in God. Craving for God still more, it is reported that Jesus dwelt even more deeply and constantly in God's love. He continued this practice for several years and practiced a number of intense spiritual disciplines. He realized that the embracing love of the Father was his own basic nature. He declared, "**My Father and I are one**". After obtaining Divine Unity with God, and realizing that He and the Holy God were one and inseparable, He made the famous declaration "**I am myself God**".

The New Testament is a verbal icon of Jesus living in complete union with God – the Father. Here the Risen (Awakened) Lord Jesus is not simply presenting, shimmering in the oral recitation in liturgy of his doings and sayings, not simply representing all this to morally improve the believer, he is showing himself (darshana) to transform the humanity. Thus, **The New Testament is an exposition of the divine experience which lies beyond words, and guides humanity into the world of the Holy Mystery**. The primordial events of human life are consecrated in the sacraments, human life is sanctified in the divine framework, the innermost depths of the human soul and transformed in solitary contemplative prayer.

The New Testament, like all other holy scriptures, expounds the nature of self-hood as the Ultimate Reality (Brahmn and Atman), and a self which is a person who can act, make love and enjoy communion with God. Such a self can spiritually unfold to the point in which it knows all other things as fundamentally spiritual and all other persons as subjects. Jesus was never felt any separation from the Father God. Jesus said, "**I am the Resurrection and the Life. He that believes in me, though he shall die, yet shall live. He that lives and believes in me shall never die**".

Jesus Christ sacrificed his human form on the Cross on a Friday which is known as the Good Friday as the annual commemoration of the event. The symbol of the Cross for the Christians in Christian Churches is considered to be a symbol of glory and reverence, of redemption and liberation, of ego-lessness and God's unending love for humanity. Indeed, It stands for Jesus's compassion – a suffering with or an enduring with all those who suffer and endure pain and sorrow in the world. Pain and sorrow are inevitable elements of human life. Nobody can escape these inescapable components of living. The Cross is venerated by the Christians in solemn way, particularly on a Good Friday it is celebrated as the climax of Jesus's unconditional love for humanity. It gives a direct message that God Himself is the unconditional and unending love. God suffers and allows Himself to be crucified on the Cross of life. Thus, Good Friday is not only a day of passive suffering but rather an active suffering. Jesus died on the Cross because he preached eternity of the kingdom of God and challenged the authority of the then high priests, religious leaders and their interpretation of the law. His death brought an end and non-acceptance of the false charge against him that he was plotting to subvert the then Roman rule over Palestine. Indeed, the Cross symbolically stands for all those who suffer for the cause of justice, who work for the upliftment and liberation of others, and who put themselves on the path of righteousness and service to society.

Christmas and Easter are the two high-point customs in Christianity. Easter is the day of the resurrection of Jesus or his victorious rising from the dead, three days after he died on the Cross. Jesus was on the cross for three hours. The Christian devotees all over the world spend an equal amount of time listening and meditating on the seven messages that Jesus gave them from cross as well as reflecting on the spiritual force his sacrifice had on the humankind. Forty days prior to this, through intense prayer and fasting, the devotees contemplate and pray for divine mercy to overcome the human weakness. This is identified with the decision that took Jesus forty days of fasting, praying and meditating followed by his feet washing of his disciples as an act of spiritual depth, symbol of ego-shedding, a sharing with people and a sharing with God. The previous evening is known as Maundy Thursday, Jesus ate his last meal with his twelve disciples as an event associated with deliverance from generations of bondage. To-date, this event is remembered as the Passover meal – passing from bondage to liberation. During meal-time on this particular Thursday evening, an extraordinary event took place when Jesus suddenly got up, while everybody was engaged in eating, and started washing the disciples' feet and wiping them dry with a towel in his own hand. This caught the disciples by surprise and shock, and dumbfounded. This, he gave, as the message of a profound mystery of love and service to humanity, as an act of spiritual awareness.

The forty days of fasting and praying is considered to be the Lenten season which begins on Ash Wednesday on the arrival of the spring season when the priests perform the ceremony of applying ash on the forehead of the believers and say, "**Remember, these are dust and unto dust thou shall return**". This is the time to forgive enemies as Jesus forgave his persecutors before his life ended by saying, "**Father forgive them, for they do not know what they do**". The last week of Lent is known as "The Holy Week" – the week immediately preceding Easter or resurgence Sunday following the Good Friday. The relevance of the figure '40' is given in different ways in different situations by different scholars on Christianity. An equal important relevant of 40 days is given in the Holy Bible in relation to the Old Testament by Exodus that Moses prayed to God while staying on Mount Sinai for 40 days. After getting freedom from the Pharaoh of Egypt, the Jews travelled for 40 years to reach their native land, Israel.

Another interpretation is that not only Jesus fasted and prayed for 40 days before his crucification, he was laid in the tomb for 40 hours after his death and before he was taken up into the heaven. Jesus Christ is revered as one of the most important spiritual leaders of the world. His profile and his teachings are of immense significance to the humankind. While reading the holy Bible, one finds that the Old Testament clashes with the New Testament, in the sense that former says, "An eye for an eye and a tooth for a tooth", whereas the later preaches, "If your enemy strikes you on one cheek, offer him your other cheek". Indeed, Jesus single-handedly brought a deep impact on the lives of people all around the world. Jesus is reported to have travelled to India and gained a deep spiritual insight, by visiting various spiritual centres of India.

Crucifixion and resurrection are fundamental to Christianity. It is believed that Christ's death on the cross was not accidental; it was ordained even before his death. His resurrection also was according to the divine plan. Christ used to speak of his body being destroyed and about raising it again in three days. He is reported to have said that he had the power to lay down his life and bring it up again. His death was necessary for the salvation of humanity in line with the saying, "there is no remission of sins without the shedding of blood: Resurrection, indeed, proved to be a proof of the immortality of the soul. It is also an indication of the Day of Judgement when everyone has to give an account of his life, according to the Bible. All sufferings should be considered as temporary misfortunes. In the Christian tradition, the sacrament of confession is also of paramount importance because according to its belief, the act of repentance and retrieving one's spirit from negative places is essential in order to enter the heaven.

Christianity offers the best hope of eternity in heaven in a body similar to the one the person now inhabits. According to some spiritual scholars, title, "the Christ" means the "anointed of God". Christianity is not only a religion for congregational worship alone. It is also an expression of the highest, universal and most sublime truths for those who desire to commune directly with God. This is what Jesus meant when he declared, "God is my father", then after a pause, he said, "My father and I are same", and a little later, he said, "I am myself God.

Many Christians visualize God as the venerable old man depicted in a painting at the Vatican and they commonly think of God as the heavenly Father. They are not able to bridge the gap between the impersonal Creator of this Universe and an anthropomorphic being. They try to come up with the notion of God manifesting the existence of Adam, the first man and Eve as the first woman, along with a forbidden fruit for both. However, a lot more spirituality minded Christians, do try to come up with the philosophical concepts and refer to God as the 'Cosmic' Foundation of Being. Divine Consciousness is described by Swami Yogananda as '"the centre everywhere circumference nowhere". This indeed is what Jesus meant also when he said, **"Neither, shall they say here nor to there, for, behold the Kingdom of God is within you"**.

5.3 Mohammed and Nanak

It is generally believed that prophets and other divine messengers appear on the earth with the major objective of transforming the human society so that the world of human beings become the land of God where darkness becomes light, wickedness takes the form of virtues, and love becomes the norm of human race. These prophets and messengers are generally believed to be equipped with some super-human powers, generally called the divine powers. These divine powers as such make them distinct from the ordinary human beings. Because of these divine powers vested in them, these super-human beings called the divine personalities perform some unbelievable miracles for the welfare of the human society and for generating faith in the existence of the Ultimate Divine Power – called God, Ishwar and Allah among others. Some people, however, do not believe in this phenomenon of divine power, even though this divine power has been continuously manifesting in various visible forms. A description of this divine power vested with Buddha, Zoroaster and Jesus Christ has been given in sections 5.1 and 5.2 of this chapter. Sri Sathya Sai Baba is one of the latest glaring proof of this divine power who has been showing miracles of all kinds to the bewilderment and amazement of the people all over the world belonging to all types of categories including scientists, rationalists and even the non-believers. Such miracles were also demonstrated by Shirdi Sai Baba, the earlier incarnation of Sri Sathya Sai Baba. A brief account of the profiles of both great divine beings along with their miracles is given in Chapter 6 of this book. Here in this section we give a brief description of Hazrat Mohammed the prophet of the Muslims and Sri Guru Nanak Dev the first Guru of the Sikhs, a brave and bold community of India known for their valour and sacrifice.

In the third month of the lunar calendar, Mohammed, the Prophet of Islam was born in the city of Mecca in Arabia in 570 A.D. According to some Islamic scholars, Mohammed never claimed any divinity for himself. They claim that Koran (also written as Quran) declared him a messenger of God (Allah). All his sayings and doings as well as his approval of actions done in his presence, are all recorded in the Islamic literature. The miracles reportedly related to Mohammed are vividly reported to be mentioned in the holy Koran and several other texts and biographies. Many miracles are related to Mohammed's life since his birth. It is said that when Mohammed was born, a glorious light radiated from his mother Ameena that its brightness spread far and wide; and the stars came down close to the earth.

Mohammed's father Abdullah received divine indicators at the time of the arrival of the prophet. One such divine indicator in the form of a white light between his eyes was observed by a woman who was an expert in the scriptures. That night a mysterious voice announced the arrival of the lord of people who would be born as the child of Ameena, the wife of Abdullah and would be named as Mohammed. Ameena also saw the indicators of divinity when she saw a light coming out of her body by which she could see the castles of Syria. Unfortunately, soon after, her husband Abdullah passed away, without having the good fortune of seeing the birth of his child – the future Prophet Mohammed was, thus, born post-humously from the mother Ameena, but was brought up by the foster mother Halima, sister of Ameena. The physical growth of the child Mohammed was unusual and unlike other children. He was a perfect child at the early age of two. When Mohammed was merely six years old, a miracle happened to him. While away with his foster-mother to look after the lambs at some distance from their home, Mohammed saw two men in white clothes came to him with a gold basin full of snow. They seized him and washed his heart, his belly with that snow and thoroughly cleaned him. Then they weighed him against ten of his people and found that Mohammed outweighed them. Then, they weighed him against a hundred, and then a thousand, and found that Mohammed had overweighed them too. They felt that if the child is weighed against all his people, he would overweighed them too.

Mother Ameena passed away when young Mohammed was six years old. Thereafter, he was looked after by his grandfather Abdul Motalib. After the death of the grandfather, the young Mohammed came under the care and guardianship of his uncle Abu Talib. Quite often, young Mohammed used to accompany his uncle to distant places for trade. Once they went to the town of Busra (Iraq) which was an important trade center and also a centre of Christian pilgrimage where Christian preachers and holy monks lived. One of these holy men named Bahira, who lived in a Monastry, used to study a holy book which was preserved to be read by the monks. The book contained some unknown secrets about the supernatural phenomenon. The monk Bahira saw from his cell that among the travellers, there was one above whom floated a dark patch of cloud in the sky to provide shade. When this caravan of travellers stopped under the shadow of a big tree to avoid the scorching rays of the sun, the branches of the tree bent down upon that particular young traveler to protect his body which till then was being protected by the cloud. The monk saw that this traveller was a young boy and felt that the boy possessed divinity in him because of the miraculous shade provided to him by the cloud and the bent branches of the tree. The monk approached the boy's uncle and told him that the boy was an extraordinary being and he should protect him from the Jews. To do so, he should go back to his own land and keep the boy safe from the Jews. Mohammed felt depressed by the ignorance and superstitious beliefs of the Arabs around him. They were far away from the reality of spirituality. The influences of teachings of Zoroaster and Christ had no effect on them. Young Mohammed's mind used to revolt against the prevailing conditions of his time.

Sadia Dehlvi, a prominent Islamic Scholar writes in one of the 'Speaking Tree Columns' of the *'Times of India'* that just at the young age of 23, prophet Mohammed brought together under one umbrella, the scattered nomadic warring Arab tribes and united them into submission to one God. This could be made possible because of the strong appeal of Mohammed's nobility and character. After fighting several battles with rough Arabs for 10 years, Mohammed was recognized and accepted as a prophet because of his qualities of honesty, humility, justice, compassion, forgiveness and generosity. Like several other divine messengers, Prophet Mohammed cultivated moral excellence among his followers. He taught that the path leading to God-realization consisted of kindness, righteousness, patience, forgiveness and moderation. Mohammad said, "**Adorn yourself with the attributes of God**". He, presented a model for making progress from self-centredness to move towards God-centredness.

At the age of 25, Mohammed got married with a relative Khadija, who was a widow older to him by 15 years and a rich and prosperous lady. Both lived together happily for 25 years and had two sons and four daughters. By that time, Mohammed had become popular because of his exceptional talent, worldly wisdom and spiritual knowledge.

People used to come to him for his wise consultation and advice, on various issues related to their personal and social problems. One night when Mohammed was asleep, a divine messenger appeared in his dream and told him to read the writings on a fabric woven with patterns. When Mohammed awoke from his sleep, remembered those writings seen by him in the dream. But, Mohammed could not understand these writings and consulted an old learned man who had deep knowledge of various scriptures of Jewish and Christian faith. The learned man told Mohammed that the writings indicated a message for him from God to get ready for a divine mission. The next vision followed as expected. One day Mohammed was midway on a mountain when he heard a voice from Heaven telling him that he was a prophet of God and that he had the divine mission before him. That time Mohammed was forty years old. From then onward Mohammed continued receiving divine messages and revelations. Thereafter, Mohammed became the Prophet of God.

As willed by God, every prophet must be convinced of the Almighty's divine power. As stated in a Muslim scripture, a miraculous night journey was ordained for Mohammed accompanied by Archangel Gabriel. One night, when Mohammed was in deep sleep next to Kabah, the Archangel Gabriel (Jibril) woke him up and took him on a strange white-winged animal, called lightening (Buraq) from the Mecca to Al-Aqsa – a place of prayers in faraway city of Jerusalem, The Angel then took Mohammed through the Seven Heavens, one by one where Mohammed saw countless angels everywhere. Beyond the Seventh Heaven, passing through veils, he reached the divine Light of Allah's presence. Mohammed realized that what eye cannot see, mind cannot visualize, where time, thought and feelings disappear, there was only complete calm and the brilliance of the Divine Light – the Creator of the Universe. It is believed that he found Abraham, the friend of God, Moses (the divine messenger of the Jews) and Jesus Christ offering their prayers along with some other prophets. After the prayers were over, three vessels were brought before Mohammed, containing milk, wine and water. Thereafter Mohammed heard a voice from above that "if he takes water, he and his people will be drowned in water; if he takes wine, he and his people will go astray; but if he takes milk, he along with his people will be rightly guided. Mohammed, there upon took the vessel of milk and drank it. Gabriel, then told him that he and his people will be rightly guided. Mohammed returned to his house in Mecca and related the experience of his night's journey to the people in the morning. But no one was willing to believe such a story. However, Mohammed gave the correct description of Jerusalem which convinced the people about the truth of his experience of journey during the previous night. Thus, people started believing the words of Mohammed.

Some of the most miracles are related to his ascent to Heaven; making the moon move sometimes around the Kaaba and splitting of moon into two halves; creation of water for the congregation of the believers to perform their usual pre-prayer ceremonial washing; creation of food at the house of a man named Abu Talha for his companions, arranging food in the form of dates for the soldiers digging trenches for the army; and for the guests of his adopted son Ali. Several more miracles are described in many texts.

As the last days of his earthly life approached, Mohammed described to his disciples about the paradise (heaven). The day when the Prophet Mohammed breathed his last, his dead body did not look like the dead body of other mortals. When the disciples and followers gathered to perform the last rites, a dispute arose on how the body was to be washed before burial. Then a divine miracle occurred. All the disciples and followers felt sleepy and all went to deep sleep. During the sleep, they all saw that everybody was sinking in water up to the chest and they heard a heavenly voice directing them to wash the dead body of the prophet with clothes on. The disciples got up from the sleep and washed the dead body with clothes on by pouring water on it. Thereafter another dispute came up. The prophet's body laid upon his bed inside the house. The dispute started over the place of the burial as to whether to bury the body inside the mosque of the Prophet or at the place where some of his departed companions were buried. But the heavenly voice declared that no prophet dies but he is buried where he died. Accordingly, Mohammed's dead body was buried beneath his bed in a grave on which he left his mortal body at midnight and no Imam or Cleric was called to perform the last prayers over the Prophet's dead body. This is reported to have happened on 8th of June 632 A.D. Mohammed breathed his last and departed from the world on his birthday. It is because of this reason that his birthday, 'Id-e-Milad-un-Nabi', is not celebrated as a festive occasion like the other two 'Eids".

The period before the arrival of the Holy Prophet in Arabia was one of ignorance. Wars were fought for petty matters, superstitions were rift and respect for women at its lowest. The social fabric of the Arabs veered more towards vices and debauchery than religion. Principles like justice and righteousness, which are taken for granted in the human society, were thrown to the winds. It was in such difficult circumstances that the Holy Prophet announced his message – one that would change the face and social fabric of the Arabs, and perhaps the world forever. Within a period of 23 years, with extreme patience and with the odds of success staked against him, the Prophet attracted people towards Allah's message. Enmity was replaced by brotherhood and superstitions traded with firm beliefs and reliance upon Allah. It is a divine phenomenon that either God or His messenger – a divine being appears on the earth as and when it is in deep chaos and conflict. This is a historical supernatural truth which is true of all religions. Mohammed was also born in the turbulent times. The jungle rule of 'the might is right', prevailed in the then human society. Selfishness and arrogance were considered as the pride values. People used to take pleasure in plunder and rejection of human values. They used to make fun of morality and justice. Mohammed created a unique culture of Islam though sermons and discourses based on the principles of truth, honesty, justice, love and brotherhood declared as proclamations of Allah – the God. Mohammed not only spoke of such human values among several others but himself practiced these values by living them in the real sense. He led a very simple life like an ordinary poor person and would do every task himself rather than expecting his wife and others to do for him. He would prefer to suffer the pain by leading a life of piety rather than bothering about worldly enjoyments.

Prophet Mohammed always emphasized on purity and righteousness based on the teaching of the Holy Koran which says, "**All praise is due to Allah the Creator and the Sustainer of all the worlds. Since God has created all things, all the things naturally depend on Him for their sustenance and existence**". God is the Master of all knowledge about everything, hidden or manifest. He knows of a human's heart as well as the secrets of his nature. Those alone are believers whose hearts are full of God's love, whenever God's name is mentioned and when the word of God is recited to them, their hearts are filled with faith in God and love for God, for it is only God who can put them on the path of righteousness.

The Holy Koran comprises of 6616 verses spread over 114 chapters (surahs) based on the divine revelations received by Prophet Mohammed from time to time over a long span of 23 years during his meditation sessions in the desert cave hill called Hira. It deals with various phases of the Eternal Truth such as the creation of the Universe on one hand, while on the other it expounds religious, spiritual and moral teachings or pronouncements known as 'Hadith'. While the anthology of divine revelations – the Holy Koran occupies the first place of authority in Islam, the Hadith is recognized as the second most important authority. Both together, in their order of priority constitute and regulate the religious system and personal code of conduct governing the lives of the believers/followers known as the Muslims. **The Holy Koran is known as the Book of Wisdom, Light, Mercy and Guidance on humanity**. The book is also called **'Al-Furquan'** – the criterion to judge the right and wrong, and distinguish between truth and falsehood. The Arabic word 'Allah; (or Al-llah-'All High') – the Supreme Being is used for God. The Koran lays the greatest emphasis on the uniqueness of 'Allah' which is the foundational basis of the Islam.

Final accountability on the Day of Reckoning, for every noble or evil act done in the worldly life, is the most sublime and cardinal principle of Islam. Faith in Allah – the Supreme Being, the prophets and the scriptures; Regular prayers five times daily; Fasting in the month of Ramadan; Payment of the purification tax (Zakat) to the poor and needy; and Performance of the Haj pilgrimage by those who can afford it are the **five fundamental principles of Islam**.

Duties and obligations towards the creator; and Duties and Obligations towards the fellow human beings are considered to be the two categories emphasized in Islam. Service to **God through Service to human** (similar to "Manav Seva is Madhav Seva: Said by Sri Sathya Sai Baba) is the underlying basis of both aspects of Islam exhorting believers to be compassionate, truthful, just, kind, charitable and generous to the orphans, widows, old, sick, destitute, neighbours, relatives, parents, children and thus please Allah – the Merciful. At the same time, husbands and wives, and parents and children are exhorted to mutually perform their duties and obligations with moral uprighteousness. The Holy Koran has also laid down norms of social and economical dealings. It has stipulated a noble code of social conduct for the followers to do service both in the time of war and peace. Righteous conduct and morality together constitute the basic norms of the social living in Islam.

Islam literary means 'Peace and Stability' which is achievable through submission to the will of Allah – the Merciful who is Omni-Scient, Omni-Potent and Omni-Present. The entire humanity, accordingly to the Holy Koran, constitutes one family of God. The Prophet Mohammed gave to mankind Islam, the faith of the personal surrender to God – The One and the Only Absolute Almighty, Allah, is all powerful and all merciful. God is eternal and changeless, the Supreme Being to source of the endless universe in its manifold manifestations. Life is only a manifestation of that fathomless creative force. A human being, mortal possessing immortal soul, needs to understand the purpose of the soul by realizing the importance of having absolute faith in God. Islam, therefore, advocates complete surrender to God, while for human beings, it is love of God which establishes their relation with God. Islam is a religion, as explicitly stated by Mohammed himself, that gives equal respect to all other religions of the world, recognizes their existence, their legitimacy and their message. It emphasizes on the social welfare of the people irrespective of their caste, creed or colour. Islam recognizes the spiritual values that are inherent to human understanding, ethics of life and social concerns for progress and perfection. It clearly distinguishes between a common human being called a 'Bashar' equipped with common physical, biological and psychological characteristics and a person who is recognized with respect by philosophers, poets and religious leaders, called an 'Insaan' possessing exceptional traits of humanity, love and brotherhood. Some of the salient features of Islam are: both Muslims and non-Muslims are equal in the eyes of the Islamic law; Non-Muslims have the same right to life-protection; no tax imposed, but proportionate liability is shared by non-Muslims citizen of an Islamic nation bearing the war expenses; guarantee of freedom of religion for both the Muslims and non-Muslims ensured; and equal constitutional status for all members, Namaz or the five times daily prayers is one of the five pillars of Islam which is prescribed for every Muslim and centred around ten points namely: **closeness to God; prevention from indecent and shameful things/ doings; purification of heart; development of mind and comforting the soul; remembering Allah and His greatness; developing discipline and will power; guidance on the upright path of life; showing equality; unity and brotherhood; and showing obedience and gratitude to God**.

Sufism is a unique mode of Islam for God-realization. It enables human beings to carry on this supreme mission of oneness with God. Sufism is, in essence, a concept of divine unity which generates consciousness within the bounds of one's own spiritual and earthly life. It is antidote against all kinds of impure and unholy tendencies related to the mind. Soul and heart of a human body. It is described as the renunciation of all pleasures of the transitory world. The follower of Sufism is the one who seeks to reach the rank of being lead to self and alive to truth by means of a struggle. A Sufi sees the world as an experiment; a system of symbols continually unfolding. Profound meditation on the nature of reality – metaphysics and cosmology is also a mode of intellectual knowledge for a Sufi. The two widely debated concepts are called the unity of being, and the unity of vision. Once a human being recognizes the blended spiritual and social bonds of his soul, heart and mind, then for him God is eternal light of heaven and earth. Islam and Sufism are two pacific forces. During the time of the

Caliphs, Islam was known for its tolerance and freedom of scientific inquiry. This incidentally was when Europe was still languishing in the dark ages. Unlike the present times, most of Europe used to look to the Arabs – who were then the torch bearers of Islam – as a course of knowledge. This was the period of consolidation for rationalist thinking and propagation of natural sciences and mathematics, both fields in which the Arabs made great contributions. Some new contributions to mathematics were made by both Hindus and Arabs. They discovered numeral system and trigonometry. Algebra was discovered by the Arabs. The very word al-jabr is Arabic, which, like so many other things, founds its way into Europe from Spain from where it spread to whole of Europe and the world.

Although prophets and divine messengers are considered to be various manifestations of one and the same Supreme Reality called the Brahmn or God, yet their followers try to differentiate them in accordance with their notions and beliefs. However, all are accepted as the divine beings whether Rama, Krishna, Buddha, Mahavir, Zoroaster, Jesus, Mohammed and Nanak with their divine revelations as sacred as their religious preaching and doctrines in the form of the Holy Scriptures. The divinity which existed in these prophets and messengers is the same everywhere in every living being including their followers. This divine principle, therefore, does not find favour with any such distinction among various divine beings whether preachers or followers. Followers can verify the validity of the divine revelation of each prophet of their own accord and accept the faith on the basis of their own conviction and experience, if any. All religions which aim to bring about individual and social transformation are mostly based on theism except Buddhism and Jainism which are considered to be non-theistic religions established respectively by Buddha and Mahavir based on moral excellence and non-violence. Yet, one of the latest religions of the world namely Sikhism is based on theism which began with the advent of Guru Nanak Dev – a staunch believer in the divine principle of God, and the first Guru of the Sikhs and Hindus together.

Of all the profiles and biographical sketches, Nanak's divine personality is revealed as a life of miraculous and marvelous manifestations of the divine power. Nanak's biography is full of the events connected with his divine miracles. His own hymns, numbering about one thousand, have found a respectable place in the holy scripture of Shri Guru Grant Sahib. Although these hymns do not show enough of his actual life profile, yet the earliest accounts about his biography can be seen in his birth stories published in Gurmukhi script of Punjabi language in the form of '**Janamsakhis**'. These texts, however, do not mention the names of their authors. Nevertheless, these texts speak of Guru Nanak Dev, the first Guru of the Sikh faith. Unfortunately, these texts do not give a chronological order of events associated with the life of Nanak. It is believed that the holy books containing Nanak's biographical sketch was compiled after his death or possibly some of the events were composed well within his life-time. The works of the First Guru himself were collected and compiled during the time period of the Third Guru, Amar Das and later by Guru Arjun Dev who compiled in 1603-04 the Holy Scripture well-known as the Adi Granth or the Guru Granth Sahib, which includes a glimpse of Nanak's life.

Sh. Guru Nanak Dev, the first Guru of the Sikh faith was born in a small village Talwandi in the Punjab State of undivided India (which now forms a part of Pakistan) in the early hours of the morning of 15th April 1469. When grown as a young man, Nanak lived in the town of Sultanpur from where he began his travels and finally settled in a village named Kartarpur on the bank of the river Ravi where he breathed his last on 6 September 1539. When Nanak's mother Tripta gave birth to her child who was named Nanak, divine indications appeared to mark the advent of a divine personality in the form of the child's cry resounding like the laughter of a grown up person.

The Japuji are the very first words uttered by Nanak after self-realization: Nanak sat on the bank of river in total darkness with his friend and follower; Mardana. Suddenly, he removed his clothes and walked into the river. Mardana called after him, "Where are you going? The night is so dark and cold!" Nanak went further and further; he plunged into the depths of the river: Mardana waited....but Nanak did not return. Mardana ran back to the village and woke up everyone. It was midnight, but a crowd collected at the riverside because everyone loved Nanak. They ran back and forth the whole length of the river bank but of no avail. Three days passed. By now it was certain that Nanak had drowned. The people imagined that his body must have been carried away by the swift current and perhaps eaten by wild animals. The village was in mourning. On the third night Nanak appeared from the river. The first words he spoke become the Japuji.

When Nanak disappeared in the river; the story goes that he stood before the gate of God. He experienced God... God spoke to him, "**Now go back and give unto others what I have given unto you**". The Japuji is Nanak's first offering after his God-experience. Unless one drowns oneself completely in God, one cannot hope to invent God. This is the symbolic and spiritual meaning of drowning in the river. One will have to lose oneself, one will have to drown. Death is completed only after three days, because the ego does not give up easily. The three days in Nanak's story represents the time required for his ego to dissolve completely. Since the people could only see the ego and not the soul, they thought Nanak was dead.

The one who is lost invariably returns, but he returns as new. He who treads the path most certainly returns. While he is on the path he is thirsty, but when he returns he is a benefactor. He left as a beggar, he returned as a king. Whoever follows the path carries his begging bowl; when he comes back he possesses infinite treasures. To appear before God, to attain the beloved, are purely symbolic terms and not to be taken literally. There is no God sitting somewhere on high before whom you appear. But to speak of it, how else can it be expressed? When the ego is eradicated, when one disappears, whatever is before one's eyes, is God oneself. God is not a person – God is an energy beyond form. To stand before this formless energy means to see Him wherever one looks, whatever one sees. When the eyes open, everything is He. Ego is like the mote in one's eye; the minute it is removed, God stands revealed before him. And no sooner does God manifest, than one also becomes God, because there is nothing besides Him.

Nanak returned, but the Nanak who returned was also God himself. Then each word uttered became so invaluable as to be beyond price, each word equal to the words of the Vedas. Nanak's father Kalyan Chand, popularly addressed as Kalu, brought a learned scholar named Hardayal who observed the child after birth and became aware of his future. Hardayal paid homage with folded hands to the newly born baby and told the father Kalu that both Hindus and Muslims would revere the child who was bound to become known both on the earth and in heaven and whom the ocean, earth, sky etc. would give him the way wherever he would go. Nanak would worship and acknowledge One Formless God and will preach others to have such a faith. The divine attributes of the infant were noticed at an early age. In the seventh month, Nanak could sit like a yogi with legs underneath in a squatting posture.

People living around Nanak's house were surprised to see his spiritual inclination at the little age of five. Nanak was admitted to a school when he was seven years old. One day in his class, Nanak wrote on both sides of his slate, a composition of his own when he did not know even the alphabet of any language. This composition was a poem in Punjabi written in some strange script which had raised a few questions along with their answers: "**Who is truly learned? He who**

unravels divine knowledge is the real scholar (Pandit). **The one who created the world is the God of all existence. Fortunate is their advent into world who love and serve Him".**

Nanak had reached a stage where the true knowledge was within his control and therefore learning of alphabet was not required by him. Some of Nanak's miracles of boyhood, as believed by disciples and devotees are: restoration of the damaged crops; shadow of a tree remaining fixed over his body when he slept to save himself from the scorching heat of the sun in a forest where he had gone along with the herd of the cows and buffaloes while the shadow of all other trees had moved accordingly to movement of the sun rays; and yet on another day, a big cobra covered Nanak's body and protected his face from the sun rays while Nanak was asleep.

Worried over the astonishing events happening with Nanak, his father got him married at the young age of twelve. Although Nanak got occupied with his family work, yet he used to spend most of his time in visiting temples and mosques. At the age of sixteen, Nanak realized his total transformation from the worldly world to a world of renunciation. Most often he used to be in a state of meditation and in quest for something higher. Being in this state of mind, Nanak took neither food nor water for three months continuously. The worried father Kalu consulted a local physician Haridas whom Nanak himself told in a poetic manner that there was nothing wrong with his body and that his mind was searching something else. The physician assured his father and others that Nanak needed no treatment since there was no disease that required a cure. Giving up his miraculous fast after three months, Nanak pondered over the real sickness that had afflicted the whole mankind which needed a spiritual healing.

Nanak realized oneness of all and saw no difference between men and religions. He proclaimed that there is neither a Hindu nor a Muslim because all belonged to the same category of men. This infuriated a Muslim Quazi who complained to the Nawab Daulat Khan of Sultanpur. While the arguments were in full swing in the court of the Nawab, it was time for the afternoon prayers. Everybody went for the prayers (Namaz) in the nearby Mosque. Nanak also went along but did not kneel down for prayers which was noticed by the Quazi who then brought to the notice of the Nawab by saying that Nanak had not joined the Muslim prayers although he claimed to feel no difference between Muslims and Hindus. Therefore, Nanak looked to the Nawab and said, "What prayer was I expected to join? The Quazi's mind was not in his words. He was conscious about me that I did not kneel down for prayers. Moreover, Quazi's mind wondered to his new-born foal (young one of a horse or a mare) he had left loose in his yard before coming to the mosque, and that he feared that the foal may not have fallen in the neighbouring well". The Quazi immediately realized that the Guru possessed the supernatural powers of knowing his thoughts and bowed before Nanak. Not only the Quazi but also others who were present there at that time paid their obeisance to the Guru, while the Nawab himself expressed his desire to give up his authority and give all his property to Guru Nanak Dev. With a changed heart the Nawab saw yet another miracle that this treasury got completely filled with riches which had appeared from an unknown source. Indeed, the Guru was not hankering after power or wealth. He left Sultanpur with Mardana on his divine mission of bringing spiritual awareness to the people.

Guru Nanak Dev travelled far and wide. He visited several places not only in India but also many other countries of the Indian subcontinent. He traveled extensively and continuously for about 23 years. During these travels, Guru Nanak Dev performed several more miracles when and wherever necessary such as the following among others:

- Converting an immense tree into foliage giving warmth while resting during a shivering winter night in a remote place named Gorakmata situated in the ranges of Himalaya near the abode of some Hindu ascetics known as Nath Yogis, who bowed down at the feet of Guru Nanak after realizing divinity in him.
- On his way to Tibet, Guru Nanak halted at a village Chunthang in Sikkim and gave some rice as food and some banana leafs to use as plates to the hill people of that area to eat, who had never seen these things before. But instead of eating the rice, those people sprinkled rice over a field and buried the banana leaf. After Guru Nanak Dev had left the place, plants came up in large numbers to produce rice and banana.
- Once in Delhi, while passing through a road, Guru Nanak Dev came across a dead elephant surrounded by the weeping mahouts over their loss. Taking pity on them, the Guru asked them to utter the name of God over the face of the dead elephant. As soon as they did so, the elephant came back to life. On hearing this miraculous news, the Sultan of Delhi reached the spot and in disbelief, he challenged the Guru to repeat the miracle. With this, the elephant fell dead. However, the Guru did not revive the elephant just to please a sultan, who later understood the feeling a spiritual Guru who used his divine

power out of compassion and not because of threats or doubts, and realized the divine power of Guru Nanak Dev.

- During the rule of the first Mughal emperor of India, Babar, Guru Nanak and his disciple Mardana were captured by the soldiers of the local Mughal commander, Mir Khan at a place named Sayedpur and were sent to prison where they were made to do the work of carrying a load from one place to another. To his utter disbelief, Mir Khan saw that the load on Nanak's head was being carried without resting on his head, and the horse was following Mardana without its reins in his hands. Mir Khan informed the emperor Babar about this who was greatly astonished. In the meantime, Nanak was taken to a camp where women were being forced to grind corn. The Guru was also given hand mill to do the same work. But the wheel of the hand mill, when touched by Guru Nanak, started moving of its own. By then Babar reached the place and saw by himself that miraculous activity. Seeing Babar, Nanak recited a hymn which moved Babar. The emperor, therefore, touched the feet of Guru and apologize for what had been done to him. He offered to Guru take something from him. Guru told the emperor that he would take nothing except that he should release all the prisoners of Sayedpur and return their properties which Babar readily did.
- During the journey through Kashmir, Guru Nanak Dev came to the mountain ranges to see Lord Shiva and other divinities on that sacred and selected place. There he met some Siddhas who possessed some superhuman powers. They had also heard about such powers of Guru Nanak Dev. In order to test the divine powers of Nanak, they offered him a pot and asked him to fill it with water by his divine powers. Before Guru Nanak could do, the Siddhas used their super human powers and filled the pot with jewels. Knowing their motive behind all this, Guru Nanak broke the pot, reconstructed it, uttered hymns on it and then filled it with water by using his divine power. Siddhas were not yet convinced of Guru's divine power. They decided to put Guru through further test. They persuaded the Guru to attend the special occasion of the congregation of several Siddhas being hold at a place named Achal. While assuming that Nanak would not venture such a ardous journey through the mountain ranges, they informed him that they themselves could reach the place in three days. After saying this, they left for Achal. On reaching

there, to their utter shock, they found Nanak already at the congregation and realized the divinity in him.

- During his journey to Mecca, the holy place of the Muslims, Guru Nanak was accompanied by a Haji who observed that a small cloud floating along in the sky over Nanak's head protecting him from the hot sunrays. The Haji told Nanak that no Hindu had ever gone to Mecca. Therefore, he should walk along with him. Having said that, the Haji went ahead of Nanak. After some time Haji looked back to see Nanak and found to his surprise that Nanak was not to be seen. The Haji regretted and repented for his discrimination of a Hindu. Nanak, however, reached Mecca crossing through the rocky paths and entered the holy precinct. Having been exhausted, the Guru lied down in the colonnade and felt asleep with his feet towards the holy Kaaba. Nanak was still in deep sleep. It was now time for the evening prayers (namaz). When the Quazi saw Nanak sleeping in the irreligious posture with feet towards Kaaba, he felt annoyed and told Nanak it was unholy to stretch feet towards Kaaba, the house of God. Opening his eyes, Nanak told the Quazi to turn his feet to that direction where there was no house of God. Enraged by this statement, the Quazi along with some devotees turned Nanak's feet. But whatever direction, they turned Nanak's feet, they found to their utter amazement, Kaaba also moved along with movement of Nanak's feet. Realizing this miracle that Guru Nanak must be some divine being, the Quasi realized his mistake and kissed Nanak's feet and felt that he had met a divine fakir of God. This miracle of the Guru in Mecca was not the last. In the old scriptures of the Arabs, there were some writings predicting that someday a 'dervish' (divine messenger) named Nanak would come to Mecca and then water would rise in the wells. Having read those writings, the Quazi invited other clerics (Pir) to have some conversation with the dervish Nanak. There during the discussion Nanak finished his saying by uttering the word 'Vahiguru' and forthwith, water started rising in the wells, thus fulfilling the prophecy mentioned in the holy scriptures of the Arabs.

Nanak left Mecca for Medina from where he went to Baghdad, the capital of Iraq. Outside the city, he sat near a tomb and started singing melodious hymns in praise of God. The orthodox Muslims felt enraged as the songs of a stranger seemed irreligious as music was not permitted near that tomb. A large number of people gathered there to punish

Nanak for his non-religious action near the tomb. The Guru, however, greeted them with a divine invocation in the style of Muslim's call for prayer. Hearing this, the entire crowd got immobilized and realized that Nanak was a divine messenger, a Dervesh (Messiah).

Continuing their travels far and wide, once Guru Nanak and Mardana reached a place called Hasan Abdal – near the ancient city of Texila, now in Pakistan. At the peak of a neighbouring hill, there lived, a Muslim saint Baba Wali of Kandhar. Feeling thirsty and finding no water around, Mardana climbed to the top of the hill and reached Baba Wali. After having introduced himself to Baba Wali and disciple of Guru Nanak as a great spiritual being with divine powers, Mardana requested Baba Wali for some water. On hearing this, Baba Wali became furious and said to Mardana, "If Guru was such a divine being, why can't he create water for himself and you". When Mardana returned having failed in his efforts, Guru asked him to lift a small piece of stone at a place near the hillside. As Mardana did so, came gushing out water like a fountain. Mardana drank water to quench his thirst to his full satisfaction. The moment water started gushing out of the spring, at the same time Baba Wali's water-reservoir on the hill starting ebbing rapidly and dried up. Due to this, Baba Wali got furious and out of anger, he rolled down a huge boulder in the direction of the Guru and Mardana sitting below. As the heavy stone came rushing downhill, Guru Nanak raised his arm with his palm open. The stone rock stopped midway. Having seen this amazing miracle, Baba Wali came down and fell at the feet of Guru Nanak. Till this day, Guru's palm-print or 'Panja' stands on the site of the actual occurrence. The spring of water also remains to-date. A Gurudwara built at that spot is one of the most sacred shrines of the Sikhs, and is known as Gurudwara Panja Sahib.

While travelling through Orissa, Guru Nanak and his two disciples Bala and Mardana reached Puri where the famous temple of Jagannath (the Lord of the Universe) is situated on the seashore. They selected a secluded place on the sea-beach for rest. Immediately on arrival, Guru Nanak Dev went into deep meditation. Both Bala and Mardana felt hungry. They went here and there to find some place with facility for their night food. But the place was so isolated and there was no person visible to them to help them in getting some food for them. They got frustrated and felt distressed that they perhaps selected a wrong place for their night's rest. Immediately then, somebody emerged from darkness with food and water in gold utensils. The stranger left leaving behind what he had brought for them. In the early dawn of the following morning, it was found in the temple that the utensils of gold, in which food used to be served for Lord Jagannath, were missing. The king of that region was immediately informed and was requested for enquiry. However, the king who on the same night had seen a dream in which Lord Jagannath told him about the presence of the Guru on the sea beach, was himself preparing to go to the place in a procession to pay homage to the Guru. When the priests told the king about the theft, he just smiled and proceeded towards the place on the sea-beach where he found Guru Nanak still in meditation and the utensils were lying near the two disciples sleeping nearby.

Guru Nanak Dev realized that the time had come for leaving his earthly body. He decided to select one of his disciples to be his successor who would continue imparting his message to the world. For this, the Guru devised a test. He started walking on a road. A crowd of his disciples also followed him. At some point, out of nothing, there appeared on the road plenty of copper coins. Some of the disciples and followers collected the coins and went back home. After some time, there appeared silver coins on the road which many of the remaining followers collected and went back to their homes. Next, appeared the gold coins on the road. All the remaining followers except two collected the gold coins and left for their respective homes. Nanak was still walking ahead followed by only two persons. Finally, he came to a cremation ground where cremation of dead body was about to start. The dead body was stinking lying beneath a sheet covering the body. Guru asked the two followers as to who of them would eat the flesh of the dead body. Terrified by this question, one of the two followers left the place. The remaining person requested the Guru to tell him from which end of the dead body he should start eating. The Guru directed him to start from the feet of the corpse. As soon as, this last man, named Lahina, bent-down to reach the feel of the corpse and lifted the sheet, he saw to his utter surprise, not the dead body, but Guru himself was lying under the sheet. Lahina passed the test successfully and hence was nominated as the successor of the next Guru and named as Guru Angad.

Guru Nanak Dev, after selecting one of the disciples Lahina, through a gruesome procedure devised by the Guru himself, as his successor and nominated him as the next guru named as Guru Angad, he got ready for his last journey to depart from the world. Both Hindus and Muslims gathered to pay him their last tributes. They saw Guru sitting under a tree. He heard the whispering of both Hindus and Muslims on the last rites to be performed. The debate resulted into a dispute. Thereupon, Guru Nanak solved the problem by telling Hindus to put flowers on the right side and Muslims to put flowers on the left side of his body. Guru asked them to leave for the night and to check in the morning whose flowers remained fresh, would have the choice. Soon after, he asked them to recite the holy hymns in praise of God. As the disciples started singing, the Guru pulled the sheet over him and covered his body completely from toe to head. When in the morning the sheet was lifted, there was nothing but the flowers of both Hindus and Muslims remained fresh. The whole congregation fell on their knees. Guru Nanak Dev left the world on September 1539. It is believed that, the monuments which were raised for the Guru, were swept away by the river water in accordance with Guru's last wish.

Guru Nanak Dev appeared as a divine soul with a mission of bringing purity in the heart of the people so that the world could become an appropriate place for the mankind. To the human society suffused with desire, greed, and forgetfulness of the soul, Guru Nanak showed the way to move from the material world to the spiritual one, from illusion towards God realization. Although God in His absolute form is unknowable and is far beyond the human comprehension, yet God endowed with attributes appear to come within the human perceptions, Nanak emphasized the unreality and impermanency of all beings, of the world and of the universe. It is only the Brahmn who is eternally true, for unlike His creation, He does not pass way. He is immortal, absolute and formless. Nanak said that God is the absolute Brahmn who has thousands of forms and yet has no form. Such being the attribute of the Omni-present, Omni-scient and Omni-potent God, Guru Nanak Dev desired to bring His realization and presence to the hearts of the short-lived mortals.

Guru Nanak came during the age of Bhakti (Devotion). The devotion (Bhakti) for God was a matter of human heart and not of rituals while pilgrimages as ceremonial performances. "**If the name of God is printed in the heart, the heart is open to devotion and devotion opens the path to God realization**," said Guru Nanak Dev, "**all men are the same, religious-pride**, and **caste-discrimination are notions of impurity. Such impurities must be discarded**." Guru Nanak asked the people to believe in the fatherhood of God and the brotherhood of men. The ultimate purpose of life, according to Nanak, was to work for a union of heart with God through His Name recitation or chanting which imparts the eternal bliss.

The Guru Granth Sahib is held sacred by all who believe in its teachings. Sikhism is for universal brotherhood, founded by Guru Nanak Dev and nurtured by the next nine Gurus. The word Guru is used for one who can take one from Gu or darkness to Ru or light, to the light of knowledge to eliminate the darkness of ignorance. **"If one is lucky, one finds the true Guru. Without good luck he is not to be found. Meeting the true Guru, one becomes gold, But only if God so desires, O man! Remember God with devotion. God is found through the true Guru. And one remains merged in God. The true Guru helps one gain knowledge. And the doubts are removed. The true Guru makes one realize God. And frees from the cycle of birth and death. With Guru's grace, the dead become alive. And the reborn devote themselves to God. He alone attains salvation. He gets rid of his ego, He controls the uncontrollable, Gains the knowledge of good and evil. And merges into the ultimate, said Guru Nanak Dev".**

To emphasis the concept of universal brotherhood, Guru Nanak Dev portrayed himself as "neither a Hindu nor a Mussalmaan". The word Sikh in Punjabi is from the verb 'sikhana', which means 'to teach'. In a sense, everyone is a learner throughout life. The Guru Granth Sahib essentially and mostly contains messages of the Gurus available directly in their own verses.

The fifth Guru Arjan Dev collected and systematically organized the 'baani' (poetic saying) composed by the first five Gurus, 15 saints or devotees (Bhagtas), 11 learned scholars and others in 31 different ragas and compiled them into the Granth Sahib. Guru Arjan Dev dictated the text of the holy Granth to Bhai Gurdas to prepare the first master copy. This Granth is also called as 'Pothi Sahib'. He organized its first 'prakaash' in the Harimandar Sahib at the Golden Temple in Amritsar on August 16, 1604, and nominated an old Sikh from Guru Nanak's time, Bhai Buddhaji, as the first Granthi. The final version of the Granth Sahib was prepared by the tenth Guru Gobind Singh at Damdama Sahib and this was transcribed by Bhai Mani Singh. It included the 'baani' composed by the ninth Guru Tegh Bahadur. Bowing before this holy Granth at Nanded, Guru Gobind Singh exhorted all Sikhs on October 6, 1708 to accept Guru Granth Sahib as the last Guru henceforth.

Guru Granth Sahib is a precious gift of India to the whole of mankind. It is an embodiment of love and brotherhood of human beings with a universal appeal. This holy scripture provides an inspirational religious and spiritual guidance to the people. According to the tradition established by the first Guru, Sh. Guru Nanak Dev Ji, of transmitting the spiritual power to the successor nominated by him, the final act of succession by Guru Govind Singh was done by his declaration that Granth Sahib would, henceforth be the tenth and last Guru of the followers, who would be known as the Sikhs. Guru Arjan Dev not only included the hymns of his predecessors, but also of the other Indian saints imbued with divine love which included the compositions of the first four Gurus – Guru Nanak Dev, Guru Angad Dev, Guru Amar Dass, Guru Ram Das, along with those of Sant Kabir, Sant Namdev, Sant Ravidas and Baba Farid among others.

Guru Granth Sahib starts with Japji - the morning prayer, followed by (Rahiras), the evening prayer and concludes with (Kirtan Sohila), the night prayer. Precision and beauty of its presentation in 33 sections is a unique feature of this scripture. Cast in the traditional verse forms (Slokas and Pandis), it contains several well-known classical ragas, several hymns and songs making use of popular folklore while maintaining the inner and integral linkage of music and verse. The first section comprises the inspiring song of the first Guru, Shri Guru Nanak Dev Ji called Japji, the final section is a collection of assorted verses while the remaining 31 sections are named after the well-known classical ragas of various types which are recited individually as well as in congregation by the followers both as morning and evening prayers. The recitation of these ragas and hymns give a soothing and ambrosial solace to the hearts of millions who listen to them with full concentration. **The Sikh philosophy embodied in the Guru Granth Sahib is basically a philosophy of action, community living and service to humanity**.

According to Guru Granth Sahib, God is Omni-present, Omni-potent and Omni-scient. Everything is created by God and He lives in His own creation. The living beings (Jivas) and the world are the creations of God. God is one and His name is Truth (Satnam). Guru Arjan Devji writes, "**Unity becomes plurality and plurality ultimately becomes Unity**". God is deathless and birthless. He is self-existent and can be realized by the grace of the Guru. God is the only eternal entity which has created Purusa and Prakriti. He is the Parmatma from whom all other Atmas emerge and after doing their duty, converge back to Him. God is Adi, Paramadi and Anadi. He is the creator of three Gunas: Rajas, Tamas and Sattva. These Gunas are created through His Maya with two characteristics: God is immanent in the world and transcendent dissociated from Maya. God manifests into His Sagun form to satisfy His devotees according to their desires and entreaties.

The philosophy of Sh. Guru Granth Sahib dwells also on the microcosm. Human body is itself a small word wherein God lives. The whole universe is epitomized in the human body. The true seekers explore the body and discover the divine treasures hidden in it. God can be realized by the grace of a true Guru – the Divine Teacher. God Himself is Jagat-Guru (World-Teacher) – an ocean of truth, knowledge and compassion. The name of the God is God Himself. The word of the Guru is the Guru himself. The God and Guru are one but the disciple bows first before the Guru even in the presence of God because it is through the grace of the Guru that the disciple is able to realize God. **"Guru and God are present together, whom should I bow first. My Gratitude to the Guru who introduced me to the God" (Guru Govind Dono Kharey, Kis Key Lagoon Paye, Balihari Guru Aap Ke Jo Govind Diyo Batae**). Divine Grace has a very significant place in the philosophy of the Guru Granth Sahib. God controls Karmas of the human beings. God gives sense of free will to the human beings to act and realize the State of Bliss. Karma is the cause of birth and death, and the beatitude can be attained only by His grace.

Five stages of spiritual development have been prescribed according to the philosophy of Shri Guru Granth Sahib as epitomized in Japji Sahib of Guru Nanak Dev Ji. These self-explanatory stages are named as Dharam Khand (Sphere of Duty), Gian Khand (Sphere of Knowledge or Comprehension), Saram Khand (Sphere of Endeavour), Karam Khand (Sphere of Action) and Sach Khand (Sphere of Ultimate Truth) which respectively mean Righteousness, Knowledge, Effort, Action and Truth. Ego and desire are the two main demonic tendencies which block the way to God-realization since both these tendencies are not compatible with the path of devotion to God. What is the way out, then? How to get rid of ego? How to overcome the desire? The first step is to develop faith in God and realize that He is omni-present, omni-potent and omni-science. The second step is to realize that a human being is a tiny speck on the creation canvas in comparison to the domain of God. While realizing Nature as the manifestation and abode of God, one should feel the presence of the Supreme Being in every object of Nature – hills, mountains, valleys, oceans, beings both animated and inanimated. Nature is His creation and cosmic play. Nature is the source of joy and peace. Sri Guru Nanak Dev Ji says, **"In Nature we see the Lord, in Nature we hear His speech, Nature inspires the divine awe, Nature is the essence of joy and peace.**"

Guru Nanak Dev Ji asserts that every being is an embodiment of the divine light and human being is a part of Nature and God, therefore, his goal should be to merge in God. While meditating upon God in the form of Kirtan (devotion song or Bhakti), a human being should live life as a householder, while earning as an honest livelihood and doing community service which is the core of Sikhism. While elaborating Nature as an attribute of God (Vaheguru), the fifth Guru Sh. Arjan Dev Ji said, **"The Supreme being is Karta Purakh, the Creator, transcendent**

and All pervasive. Creation is His manifestation. True is He and true is His creation. All has emanated from God Himself. He is the Data (Giver) as well as the Karta (Doer)". Nature teaches humility which is regarded as the first step towards self-realization. Lack of humility leads to ego and desire – the root causes of all evil impulses. **"When the True Lord Himself grants forgiveness, then one does not have to enter the cycle of reincarnation again,"** said, Guru Nanak.

Lovingly called 'Baba' and 'Sachche Padshah', the true king, the founder-guru of the Sikh faith proclaims the world to be the creation of God. The Almighty reveals Himself through His creation only. Nanak propounded simple monotheism. In his hymns, he emphasizes the unity and uniqueness of the Supreme Being. The one God is Omni-potent and Omni-scient, is both 'Sat' (truth) and 'Nirankar' (formless). God is also Omni-present. By meditating on His Creation and through devotion, one could attain Self-realization and experience mystical union with the Divine. While describing the pleasure of knowing God, Nanak assets that He is to be found in one's own heart. God is everywhere. Nanak sees the hand of God in everything. He sees Him even in objects like numbers. When he was employed as a shopkeeper, while weighing objects, on reaching the number 13 (tera, a word that denotes the numeral as well as meaning 'yours') Nanak would slip into a trance and repeatedly chant: "Tera, tera, tera"...............everything is yours, everything is yours, O God, ...

Guru Nanak's spirituality was based on work ethics: kirt karo (work hard), vand chhako (share the reward), and naam japo (recite the Name). He emphasized the virtues of simple living and high thinking. He preferred staying at the house of a poor carpenter, Lalo, rather than accept the hospitality of a rich man, Malik Bhago: **"The bread served by Lalo, earned by the sweat of his brow, is like sweet milk but what you offer me is the blood of the poor,"** he said to Bhago. Nanak institutionalized the tradition of sangat – (spiritual congregation) of followers – and pangat or guru-ka-langar, the community kitchen where all were welcomed with open arms. Nanak's poetry appeals as it reveals spiritual truths in simple language. He did not dismiss mundane duties as being inconsequential; rather, he taught how to infuse spirituality in everyday chores. To a farmer, Nanak said: **"The body is a field, let the mind be the plough of thy good deeds, let thane honest stirring be the channels that irrigate the field, sow the seed of the Holy name, make the clods of the field level with contentment and wear as a farmer the pleasant grab of humility."** Every act of sustenance and every thought, word and deed can be transformed to a higher plane with the spiritual insight. In the words of Bhai Gurdas: "**By manifesting the Eternal Name, the Guru redeemed all the four corners and all the nine realms of the earth**."

Going by the Bible, in the beginning there was light. But going by the Rig Veda, in the beginning there was sound. Naad Brahma or sound is the Supreme Being. Sikh theology enshrines the concept in Shabad, the Divine Word of the Guru, and accords their singing the honour of the sole mode of worship. Shabad, the very words of the Guru, is the Guru incarnate. And the Guru is the Enlightener, the Instructor who shows the path leading to the Divine, and puts the mortal in direct communion with the Supreme Being. This is why the Shabad is so important. The praises of the Lord are to be sung only in the words, Shabad, embodies in the scripture Bani, revealed by the founding Gurus. In short, the Divine Word is the Shabad, the singing of His glories is the right speech: one should listen to it and recite it always, and the Perfect Guru will take care of the rest. The Shabad, the words of the Granth, is the Guru. The Granth is divided into 31 chapters which are named after the ragas in which the hymns are sung. Literally 98 per cent of the Granth is in musical composition. The discourses with the Siddhas living in the mountain are set in raga Ramkali. Those with the Muslim savants are in raga Tilang. The idea was to talk in a natural language.

There are five milestones on the path of spiritual awareness leading to peace, and this is expressed beautifully in the Gurbani: The foremost step is to develop faith in the existence and benevolence of God. Off and on, mysterious coincidences and sudden happenings occur which bring about the fulfillment of desires and give a new direction to human lives. Blessed are those who recognize these small miracles as the voice of God. Awareness of such esoteric incidents fortifies one's faith in Him. When faith is anchored, one completely surrenders oneself to His will. Having developed faith in God the next step is to rein in the turbulence within. The surging ocean of passion and emotions must be stilled and inner quietness achieved. God can be felt and experienced only in the deepest of silence.

In one of his compositions Guru Nanak said, "**As long as we are in this world, we should listen to others and say something to them**." This is the basic principle of dialogue, of exchange of opinions or ideas. During his four lengthy journeys to the east, south, north and west, he opened a dialogue with all the existing faiths, not in today's empirical or utilitarian language, but in ethical and spiritual language capable of expressing human realities and spiritual values. He filled the inter-religious space with love, ethical humanism and spirituality. He approached every religion as his own and presented his own faith and philosophy as everyone's religion, in the crucible of eternal Truth. He travelled to various centres of religious pilgrimage. His dialogue with scholars (pundits), sages (sadhus) and ascetics yogis of every sect, as with mullas, pirs and kazis continued throughout his life. He visited the places of pilgrimage of Kurukshretra, Mathura, Haridwar, Banaras, Gaya as well as those in Bengal, Assam and Sri Lanka. He visited the sufi establishments at what is now known as Pakistan and shrine sites along the west coast of India. He travelled beyond India in the west to Mecca, Medina and Baghdad. There are accounts of still farther travels to the east to Tibet and China. He reached mount Sumer and had a long dialogue with siddhas (hermits). He recorded his discourse with siddhas in his famous composition, Siddha Goshti (Dialogue with siddhas).

Guru Nanak won overall by the power of loving devotion. He was not a sectarian reformer attached to one community of faith or part of the world. He was a preacher of the divine Reality, transcending all particularities of the race or clan. In his encounters with the Hindu sages and renunciates of all types (yogis, siddhas, vedantists, vaishnavas, shaivas), Buddhists, Jains, and different sects of Muslims, Guru Nanak told them that religion is without its moorings till it joins the main life current of humanity and socially and spiritually insinuates itself into them. While Guru Nanak changed old beliefs into new ones by the infusion of values, he projected his perennial wisdom into the stream of consciousness of other faiths by telling them how they could become true Muslims, good Hindus or enlightened yogis. Every religion at its ethical and spiritual best mingled with the religion of Guru Nanak which appealed to the people of every faith as their own at its best.

Guru Nanak Dev did not ask people to deny the temporal existence but urged them not to succumb to the fascination of the visible and the exterior, but to turn towards the inner light and music that could be received from God, and move towards a more and more complete interiority which would lead him to the vision of Supreme Reality – Brahmn.

Nanak's non-sectarian creed arose from the depth of his Divine Realization. For him, "No one is Hindu, no one is Muslim". He stood for the essential divinity expressed through humanity. According to Nanak, sectarian beliefs and rituals generate man-made barriers and unending hypocracy. Nanak spread the message of divine-humanism with all embracing love. He believed in Nirgun Brahmn – the invisible (Alakh Niranjan), without form and attributes, the one without a second beyond all dualities of delusion, shaped his ideals and percepts. The ultimate reality, according to him, revealed as Sagun Brahmn through shaked or cosmic vibration, the Omkar is the divine expression to which the ephemeral world owes its existence. His perfect synthesis of dualism of Bhakti (Devotional Music) with absolute non-dualism reflects the essential singularity of the ultimate being – the Nirgun Brahmn. His inborn simplicity and contentment characterize the central theme of his teachings. Nanak advised everybody to recite the name of the Eternal One (Akal Purukh) repeatedly with utmost devotion and lead a life of simplicity while doing service to humanity and sacrifice for the cause of humanity with full humility. As stated earlier, Nanak used to advise his disciples to grow in meditation with recitation ('Jap') involving purity, silence, concentration, patience, faith and satsang (good company) on a daily basis. He said, **"I belong to no sect and adore but one God. I see Him in earth below and heavens above, and in all directions"**.

Every divine prophet or messenger brings with him the latest word of God – the divine message to the humanity as soon as it enters a new phase of its existence. Every divine messenger is a torch bearer of a long-promised Divine revelation destined to transform and lead the human race to spiritual life. His declaration is the hope of spiritual revival and human development based on spiritual ideals and paradigms. Baha'u'llah, yet another divine messenger affirmed three fundamental unities at different levels. First, the absolute unity of the divine reality which is the foundation and ultimate goal of all beings. The being of humans is nothing but a manifestation or a reflection of that divine reality with a keen longing for God-realization. This is the supreme manifestation of God through whom the invisible becomes visible. Appearance of prophets in each age is in accordance with the stages of human evolution with a focus on the highest human perfection – an actualization of the Divine Being, which is latest in all beings. The second level of Unity is related to the realm of divine manifestations. According to Baha'u'llah, all divine messengers and prophets are, in fact, one and the same essence of the Ultimate Truth with same purpose and goal of spiritual transformation of human kind. The divine messengers are spiritual physicians who prescribe different medicines depending upon the type of illness and disease with the sole goal of treatment and cure of human patients. Baha'u'llah talked about "progressive revelation" as the third level of unity, while emphasizing unity of the sun and horizons as a metaphor to convey his idea. What differentiates Buddha and Mahavir; Zoroaster and Jesus; and Mohammed and Nanak is not their existential reality but only their human appearance. They are different horizons from which the same divine reality is shinning brilliantly. Baha'u'llaha spoke of human unity as a metaphysical or essential reality. The human soul is a mirror of divine attributes and hence every human soul is a mirror of divine unity and sacred reality. The human realization of the Divine is possible not only by avoidance of human advancement in the field of materialism but also its sacred unification with the realm of spiritualism. This fusion is possible through the harmony of the socio-political realm; the harmony of thought, word and action; harmony in the religious faiths; harmony of the nations; harmony of races; and harmony of languages. It is through the fusion of these various levels of harmony that the power and splendor of God get revealed, which can be experienced by one and all, and which assist the process of God-realization.

Whether it is Buddha or Mahavir, Zoroaster and Jesus, or Mohammed and Nanak, all such divine personalities among several others and various streams of Vedic philosophy of Hinduism, have separately or singly or jointly tried to show the way to the realization of the existence of a divine power called the Supreme Reality, the Brahmn or God. Their major concerns have been to express and explain various ways such as their miracles or preachings or both to show humanity the path of God-realization. They have all stressed, time and again, the God-realization is a State of Unity or Oneness of the microcosm with macrocosm, a complete fusion of the individual self (being) with the Universal Self (Being). This is also termed as a state of liberation or salvation characterized by freedom from all types of attributes where contradictions and inconsistencies of various forms and diversities of various kinds disappear or merge in the vast ocean of absolute-state of oneness. Duality gets transformed to qualified non-duality which ultimately end in the complete non-duality, giving a candid message that the manifest universe of beings, both sentient and insentient, matter and energy, prophets and followers is one of the mysterious ways of demonstrating the existence of a Supreme Divine Power, generally called God.

Chapter 6

The Sai Phenomenon and Its Mission

According to Hinduism, God is the embodiment of Omkara – the manifested form (Saakar) of the formless (Niraakar) who is Attributeless, Eternal, Omni-present, Omni-potent and Omni-scient. He shines as Truth-Consciousness-Bliss (Satchinanand), incarnates in various forms to restore Truth (Sathya) and Righteousness (Dharma) as and when necessary. In the greatest epic Mahabharata, Lord Krishna says to Arjuna (Bhagvat Gita Chapter IV, 7-8).

"Yada Yada Hi Dharmasya, Glanirbhavati Bharata

Abhyudanam Adharmasya, Tadatmanam Srujamayaham"

"Whenever there is a decay of Dharma (righteousness) and an ascendancy of unrighteousness, I manifest Myself in age after age for the protection of the virtuous, the destruction of the vicious and for the establishment of righteousness".

This is the mission of incarnation or advent of God in the human form. Various other divine personalities, sages and saints also appeared in their own way at proper times to fulfill the above mission. God appeared several times in several forms in the Satya Yuga but every time for a limited purpose. In the Treta Yuga, God incarnated in the complete human form as Rama to protect the sages and renunciates from the onslaughts of the demons led by the King Ravana in order to restore truth and righteousness. In Dwapar Yuga, God incarnated again in the human form to protect people from the cruelties of the demonic forces represented by Kansa, and to wipe out the evil forces like Duryodhana in order to re-establish truth, righteousness and peace.

The current aeon of Kali Yuga, according to Hinduism, is marked by the appearance of various divine messengers, prophets and personalities notably like Lord Buddha, Vardhaman Mahavir, Zoroaster, Jesus Christ, Prophet Mohammed and Guru Nanak Dev among several others. The advent of Kalki Avtaar (divine incarnation in the current Kali Yuga) is identified with the beginning of a reign of Universal goodness, peace and prosperity. It is predicted that at the end of Kali Yuga, the divine incarnation bearing the name of Kalki will emerge to put an end to wickedness. This Avtaar is expected to wipe out the suppression, oppression and evil tendencies, and establish the kingdom of Truth, Righteousness, Peace, Love and Non-Violence. It is believed that the process of Kalki Avtaar started with Shirdi Sai, which continued with the divine incarnation of Sri Sathya Sai Baba, to accomplish the Sai mission with the future advent of Prema Sai. On being asked about relevance of the Kalki Avtaar, Sri Sathya Sai Baba said, "**The word Kalki refers to the Avtaar of the Kali Yuga. The horse (Ashwa) signifies the mind which is perpetually restless. A horse is never steady. It is always moving its tail or leg or ear. The restlessness mind is compared with this horse. Only God can fully control mind and therefore, Kalki Avtaar is always shown riding a horse. The Kalki Avtaar has already appeared on the earth, first as Shirdi Sail Baba, at-present as Sri Sathya Sai Avtaar who is controller of horse-like mind of a human being**".

Bhrigu Samhita or Bhrigu Naadi is a collection of ancient scriptures written on palm leaves. It is considered to be a very respected spiritual manuscript written by Sage Bhrigu about 7000 years ago. It supposedly contains everybody's profile. The manuscript is known all over the world for its reputation of giving accurate predictions which came to be true over the time. Gifted with divine intelligence, Sage Bhrigu made innumerable predictions which people came to know through Bhrigu Samhita. The copies of this manuscript and the corresponding translated predictions are available in a few places in India which includes Hoshiarpur, Mumbai and Pune among others as well as in Nepal.

As described in Bhrigu Naadi (Samhita), the great sage Bhardwaj, after the study of all the available Vedas, wanted to perform a yagna, as advised by Lord Indra. He desired to have Goddess Shakti (the consort of Lord Shiva) to preside over the yagna. Thus, Bhardwaj reached Kailash – the holy abode of Lord Shiva and Goddess Shakti to invite them. On reaching Kailash, he found Shiva and Shakti lost in the cosmic dance. Bhardwaj waited for eight days – while being ignored by the Goddess Shakti who kept on smiling at him while dancing with Lord

Shiva. Completely disheartened and disappointed, the sage Bhardwaj decided to return out of frustration. As soon as he started descending, he suffered a serious stroke which paralyzed the left side of his body. Lord Shiva, noting this, approached Sage Bhardwaj, cured him completely by sprinkling water on him from His vessel (Kamandala) and consoled him. Thereafter the Mother Shakti, happily accepted the sage's invitation for the proposed yagna. Lord Shiva gave the sage three boons that both He and Shakti will be born as human beings thrice in the Bhardwaj lineage or gothra: Lord Shiva shall first come alone as Shirdi Sai Baba, then both Shiva and Shakti will appear together as Sathya Sai Baba, and finally Shakti alone will come as Prema Sai Baba.

The first incarnation, as Shirdi Sai Baba, of Lord Shiva alone happened during the period between 19th and 20th century while the second incarnation, as Sri Sathya Sai Baba of Puttaparthy, of both 'Shiva and Shakti', occurred during the period between 20th and 21st century, described respectively in the first and second sections of this chapter. The third incarnation – the incarnation of Goddess Shakti; as announced by Sri Sathya Sai Baba, will be known as Prema Sai, who will be born in a village Gunaparthi in the Mandaya district of Karnataka State of India. Saying this to Hislop – a great devotee of Sai Baba in an interview in January 1969, Swami asked him for the ring which He had materialized for him the day before. Enclosing the ring in His palm, Swami blew the creative breath three times through His thumb and forefinger, opened His hand and there was the portrait of Prema Sai. From this portrait, picture has been produced which is now easily available. In this picture, Prema Sai has been shown a tall, thin, peaceful young man with a calm face and a beard with shoulder-lengthy hair, dark colour. Swami said to Hislop, "**Prema Sai is only in the process of birth so I cannot show more of him. This is the first time He is shown to the world**".

Hislop reported to have told his devotee friends that the portrait of Prema Sai on the ring has been changing gradually. Baba further said, "Prema Sai, **the third Sai Avtaar, will promote the gospel that not only does God reside in everybody, but everybody is God. That will be the final wisdom that will allow every man and woman to go to God**".

The meditation (Sadhana) in the Krita Yuga was through tranquility of mind and body, in the Treta Yuga, it could be accompanied in terms of Yaganas (Sacrifices), in the Dwapara Yuga, it was feasible through meditation, prayer and yoga, and in the Kali Yuga, it is achievable through just singing with complete devotion the name and glory of God. The methods like Yoga, Dhyana and the Sadhana are very difficult to practice in the Kali Yuga, but the singing and hearing the stories and glories of God is very easy. Reciting and singing of the stories of God will remove the attachment to bodies and senses, and will make the devotees dispassionate and will ultimately lead them to self-realization culminating into the desired realization of God.

The concept of 'Avtaar' (divine incarnation) is an integral part of Hinduism, "Sambhavami Yuge Yuge" is the eternal promise given by Vishnu to despairing humanity of God's descent on earth as divine incarnation in human form or Avtaar at periodic intervals. This, however, is neither easily understood nor accepted by many. When an individual transcends duality of illusion to become One with divinity, he achieves God-realization. When such a God-realized person is able to retain human consciousness while continuously enjoying God-hood, he is called the sadhguru or perfect preceptor. An Avtaar is love personified, the divine glory and energy concentrated in a human frame.

Avtaaric periods are like the spring tides of creation, bringing in a new release of power, a new awakening of consciousness, a new experience of life. Characteristics of energy and awareness, are limited to a few advanced souls. They are vested with a higher level of consciousness and are geared to divine energy. The Avtaar appear in different forms, under different names, at different times, in different parts of the world. Their arrival coincides with the timing when humanity suffers from injustice, impropriety and untruth. When things get so bad that human beings seem enslaved by desire, driven by greed, held by fear, and when the strong exploit the weak, when the rich oppress the poor, the time is ripe for the appearance of an Avtaar. When an individual finds no peace, immorality increases, crime flourishes, religion is ridiculed, corruption spreads throughout, the social order gets disoriented, and human beings become desperate, then this is the moment for Avtaar's appearance who uses all circumstances as means to lead people towards God-realization through the stimulating power of a divinely human example and of a life supremely lived.

The Sai Phenomenon is a divine process of incarnation (Avtaarhood) and re-incarnation which transcends the barriers of time and space. It can neither be explained nor comprehended by the scientific methodology or modern technology which are themselves constrained by the limitations of time and space. As said earlier, the Sai Phenomenon is identified with its three phases of divine manifestation: first phase identified with the earlier manifestation in the form of Shirdi Sai Baba; the second phase associated with the manifestation as Sri Sathya Sai Baba of Puttaparthy in the district Ananthpur of the Andhra

Pradesh State of India; and the third and final phase of the divine power is in the future manifestation as Prema Sai in the Karnataka State previously known as the princely state of Mysore. Sri Sathya Sai Baba – the second manifestation of the Divine Power, in His Guru Poornima discourse on 6 July 1963 at 6.30 A.M. in the Prayer Hall of Prasanthi Nilayam, openly declared as under:

> **"I have been keeping back from you all these years one secret about me. The time has come when I can reveal it to you for this is a sacred day. I am Siva-Sakthi, born in the gothra of Rishi Bhardwaj according to the boon won by that sage from Siva and Sakhti. Siva Himself was born in the gothra of that sage as Sai Baba of Shirdi. Siva and Sakthi have incarned as Myself in his gothra now. Sakhti alone will incarnate as the third Sai to the same gothra in Mysore state".**

The first two sections of this chapter deals with the brief profiles of Shirdi Sai Baba and Shri Sathya Sai Baba along with their miracles and divine messages. The third section is identified with the Sai Mission with an implicit reference of the third Avtaar in the form of Prema Sai.

6.1 Shirdi Sai Baba

The fact that Sai Baba of Shirdi was the incarnation of Lord Shiva is obvious not only from the above announcement made by Sri Sathya Sai Baba but also from Shirdi Baba's declaration in His own words: Baba said, **"He was Omni present, occupying land, air, country, world, light and heaven, and that He was not localized. To remove the misunderstanding of those, who thought that Baba was only His body three cubits and a half in size, He incarnated Himself in this form and if any devotee meditate on Him, day and night, with complete Self-surrender, he will experience complete union (without any difference) with Him like sweetness and sugar, waves and sea, eye and its lusture"**. The profile of Shirdi Sai Baba is as wide and deep as the infinite ocean. One can dive deep into it and bring out precious gems of knowledge (Gyan) and devotion (Bhakti). The tales and teachings of Shirdi Sai are so amazing that they provide mental relief and peace to the people afflicted with sorrows and miseries of worldly life. The teachings of Shirdi Sai are loaded with Vedic knowledge and wisdom which the devotees and the sages try to seek through meditation and yoga.

Doubts, speculations and conjectures are made about the exact date and year of the existence of Sai Baba of Shirdi. The second God-incarnate, Shri Sathya Sai Baba of Puttaparthy, has set at rest all the speculations and conjectures about His earlier incarnation as Shirdi Sai. In His Dussehra discourse of the year 1992, He revealed the exact profile of His own incarnation as Shirdi Sai Baba, which is described as follows:

> Pathri, a remote village in district Manmad of Maharashtra state of India, became the first holy center for the Sai incarnation of God in the Kaliyuga. In the early times, Pathri was known as Parthpur named after Partha or Arjuna, the hero of the Mahabharata, and the third of Pandava brothers. In this village, situated on the banks of the beautiful river Godavari, lived a man named Ganga Bhavadya along with his wife Devagiri Amma. While Ganga Bhavadya worshiped Lord Shiva, his wife used to adore the mother Parvati. Both of them belonged to the Brahmin cast with Bhardwaj gotra. Although the couple was financially self-sufficient but deficient in one respect. They were childless. Both were pious and would always pray to God. Ganga Bhavadya used to earn his livelihood by plying boats across the river. One night it rained heavily. The river Godavari started getting flooded. After taking his food, Ganga Bhavadya went towards his boat to anchor it at a safe place lest it would be washed away with the strong flow of the river water. In the meantime, the wife Devagiri Amma closed the door from inside since she did not know when her husband would return. However, she kept the oil lamp lit and sat for prayers to her favourite deity Mother Parvati.

Late in the night, someone knocked at the door. Devagiri Amma, thinking that the person knocking the door must be her husband – Ganga Bhavadya, hurriedly opened the door. To her surprise, she found an old man standing at the door and shivering with cold. The old man came in and asked permission from Devagiri Amma to allow him to stay for the night because of the heavy rain outside. Since Devagiri Amma liked to honour guests, she permitted the old man to stay for the night in the verandah of her house, thinking that the old man must be from a neighbouring village. She arranged bed for the old man to sleep in the verandah while she herself remained inside and bolted the inner door. After some time, there was again a knock on the inner door. When Devagiri Amma opened the inner door and found the same old men asking for some food since he was hungry, although there was a divine glow on his face. Thereafter, Devagiri Amma mixed some flour with curd and gave it to the old man since food could not be cooked so late at night. The old men ate the food and tried to sleep but could not due to pain in his legs. He knocked the door once again and asked Devagiri

Amma if any woman could massage and kneed his legs without which he could not sleep since he was in the habit of a massage by his wife. Devagiri Amma was stunned at such an awkward request from a stranger unknown, especially when she was alone in the house. However, she did not want to disappoint the old man. Thus, she went out of the house from the back door to look for some professional lady who could do the job of massaging and might help her out of this critical situation. But unfortunately she could not find such a lady. Being disappointed she returned to her house and went straight to her prayer (puja) room, the only way out to rescue from this peculiar dilemma. Indeed, Devagiri Amma was completely confused and upset. In such a situation, she cried before the idol of the Mother Parvati and prayed for help to be rescued from such a humiliating situation in the absence of her husband. Right at that very moment, she heard a knock at the back door of her house. Hurriedly wiping out her tears, she opened the door and found a lady standing there. The lady told Devagiri Amma that she was from one of those houses of professional ladies which she visited earlier. The woman further told her if she could offer her services. Devagiri Amma somewhat felt a sigh of relief and expressed her gratefulness to the lady for this offer of help, and took her straight to the old man in the verandah. Thereafter she bolted the door from inside. She thanked the Mother Parvati to save her from a strange predicament. As soon as she settled down on her bed, there was yet another knock on the front door. Devagiri Amma, thinking that her husband Ganga Bhavadya must have returned, opened the door. When she opened the door, she was absolutely stunned by the vision. She was confronted with the Divine couple Shiva and Parvati.

Devagiri Amma became totally speechless and in that puzzling state of mind she bowed down at the lotus feet of Shiva and Parvati. Indeed, God has manifested before Devagiri Amma in the form of Shiva and Parvati, to bless her. Thereafter Parvati suggested to Shiva that they should bless her together. Shiva, however, replied that he had actually come to test her devotion and therefore He would bless her separately. Since Devagiri Amma had called Mother Parvati for help, therefore she should bless her first. Thereafter, Mother Parvati blessed Devagiri Amma with two children – a son and a daughter, while Shiva gave her the boon that He himself will be born to her as her second son. With her eyes full of tears of gratitude and joy, Devagiri Amma closed her eyes. The divine couple vanished as soon as she opened her eyes. Thrilled with excitement of joy, she eagerly waited the arrival of her husband to share with him the joy of divine experience.

As soon as the storm settled down, Ganga Bhavadya returned early morning. The wife Devagiri related the divine experience she had that night. However, Ganga Bhavadya did not believe her and attributed it to some hysterical utterances of a woman left alone on a dark and stormy night. He did not take her experience seriously. However, subsequently he proved to be wrong. The couple was eventually blessed first with a son, and after one year, they had a daughter. After a few years, the advent of the third child became apparent. In the meantime, Ganga Bhavadya started losing interest in his professional and domestic work. Instead, he developed a strong desire to have face-to-face Darshan of Lord Shiva. His yearning for Lord Shiva became so intense that he decided to leave his family and home. He prepared to go in search of Lord Shiva. Devagiri Amma tried to persuade him not to leave the family and home. Moreover, since the boons given by Mother Parvati had been fulfilled, Lord Shiva was about to take birth as their third child. As such, it was not desirable to desert the family and leave home in search of Lord Shiva. Ganga Bhavadya, however, was not satisfied with these persuasions. He would not be contented with the vision of Lord Shiva through the human body of a boy. He wanted to have the darshan of the pure splendour of Divinity in the form of Lord Shiva without the mask of a human body. Thereafter, Devagiri Amma also decided to go along with her husband as dutiful wife. The two children were sent to her mother's house. Devagiri Amma followed her husband while carrying the child expected to be born soon.

After travelling into the wilderness for some days following her husband, Devagiri Amma felt the symptoms of her expected delivery and asked her husband to wait for her. But Ganga Bhavadya just continued his expedition. Devagiri Amma halted under the shadow of a big banyan tree where she gave birth to the expected child in fulfillment of the boon given by Lord Shiva. That was 27 September 1836. It is a coincident that Rani Laxmi Bai of Jhansi, a great Indian freedom fighter was born in the same year. Devagiri Amma arranged a bed of leaves, placed the newly born child on this bed of leaves. She covered the child with more leaves and left the child in order to follow her husband. She did not even wipe the bloodstains off the body of the new born child. This happened on the Vijay Dashmi (Dussehra) day, 27 September 1836, as declared by Sri Sathya Sai Baba, the incarnation of God and re-incarnation of Shirdi Sai Baba in his Vijay Dashmi discourse from 4.30 – 6.15 PM on 27 September 1992, where the author of this book was present.

Incidently on that very day and that very moment, Mr. Patil a Muslim Sufi was returning to his village in a tonga with his wife. As soon as the tonga approached the banyan tree, Mrs. Patil felt the need to answer a call of the nature. The tonga was stopped and Mrs. Patil alighted from the tonga and went in the direction of the banyan tree. On reaching near the banyan tree, she heard screams of a newly born baby and found a child under the leaves with bloodstains on his body. Mrs. Patil understood that the baby must have been born only a few minutes ago and has been abandoned by his unwedded mother to avoid social embarrassment. She immediately called her husband and showed him the baby. Both Mrs. and Mr. Patil looked around for the mother of the baby. However, their efforts failed to search the mother of the baby and guessed that the mother seemed to have left the baby because of some compelling reasons. Eventually, they decided to take the child to their house. The Patils had no children of their own. Thus, they decided to adopt this child as a gift from God and brought him up as their own son and named him as Babu.

When young Babu attained the boyhood, the foster father Mr. Patil died leaving behind Mrs. Patil to look after the boy. Indeed, Babu was not an ordinary boy. He used to play with other boys of his age. His activities used to cause Mrs. Patil several type of problems due to his mischiefs. One day, Babu, while playing a game of marbles with his friend – the son of a neighbouring wealthy man, won all marbles. The son of the wealthy man wanted to win back his marbles which he had lost to Babu. To do so, the boy must continue playing the game which was not possible without marbles. He went to his house and brought the golden saligram (globular stoned) used for worship in his mother's prayer room. Thus, in this way he decided to continue the game till he was able to win back the marbles but the boy lost even this Saligram also to Babu. On losing even the Saligram, the boy felt that Babu had cheated him and he demanded his marbles and Saligram back from Babu. But Babu refused to return it. Then the wealthy man's son got frightened and confessed his mistake before his mother by telling her everything that had happened in the game of marbles. A horrified mother (wife of the wealthy man) came running to Babu and asked him to return the Saligram. But Babu refused to return the marble. No amount of persuation, argument and pleading worked with Babu. Finally, the rich man's wife decided to force him to return the marble. Instead, Babu suddenly put the Saligram in his mouth. The lady compelled Babu to open his mouth. As soon as Babu opened his mouth the lady saw a cosmic vision of the Divine in place of Saligram, the whole cosmos which Yashoda had seen in the mouth of young Krishna in the Dwapar Yuga.

The rich man's wife – the mother of the boy got stunned on the sight of the cosmos. Babu laughed and told her to go to her prayer's room and look for the Saligram there. To her utter amazement, the mother of the boy found that Saligram had miraculously arrived back to its proper place in the prayer's room. Realizing the importance of such a cosmic vision, the rich man's wife prostrated herself at the lotus feet of Babu – The Sai Baba of Shirdi. From then onwards, the rich man's wife started visiting Babu's house everyday and touching Babu's feet, till the ignored villagers forced her to stop this outward act of homage to Babu. When she made sure that no one was around, she would call Babu and offer Him food and sweets. She could not express her love openly due to communal problems because Baba was considered to be a Muslim by everyone being brought up by a Muslim couple. She had developed great affection for the child. Babu was behaving in a troublesome manner. In those days religious intolerance between Hindus and Muslims in that region was growing rapidly. There was a considerable bitterness between members of the two communities.

Babu used to visit Hindu temples and sing praises of Allah – "Mien Allah Hoon!, Allah Malik Hai! He would declare this and recite the Quran and perform prayer (namaaz) in the Hindu temples. That was not all over. He would enter a mosque and declare 'Rama is God'. 'Shiva is Allah'. He would recite Vedas and Bhagvat Gita in the Mosques. His behavior became a puzzle to the public. Seeing this, Hindus used to chide Babu thinking that this Muslim boy was scoffing at them. Muslims abused Him because he, being a Muslim, practiced the path of Hindus. Gradually this problem became even more serious. Members belonging to both the communities went to Mrs. Patil and complained about Babu's behavior. She could not tolerate Him anymore as she was getting old. Noticing that Baba was interested in the Hindu traditions, she wanted to send Him to an Ashram. Babu stayed for six years in the Patil's house *i.e.* from 1836 to 1842.

Unable to deal with this situation, Mrs. Patil handed Babu over to a pious scholar and sage named Venkusadas of Selu village. In those days communal bitterness was at a peak. Therefore, Venkusa did not like to accept Babu, who was assumed to be a Muslim. That night a divine person appeared in Venkusa's dream and said. "That Child is Parmatma. It is your good fortune to accept Him as your disciple". Venkusa immediately accepted the child. Venkusa was extremely fond of the Boy. He loved Him lot and used to say, 'All this is Yours'. In every matter, he used to give priority to Babu's view. He also came to know that Babu was only brought up by the Muslim sufi named Patil and that

He was not his own son. He even realized that the boy was an incarnation of God through his divine dream. Considering all these facts, he concluded that Babu was a Hindu and got His ears pierced according to the Hindu custom.

In view of this, the other boys in the Ashram became jealous of Babu. They began to dislike Babu. The climax come when one day Venkusa sent Babu to the forest to fetch some bilva leaves for worship, a group of boys followed Babu. At the appropriate time, the boys overpowered Babu and gave him a merciless beating. One of the boys hit Babu with a brick which caused a deep injury on his forehead. Babu bled profusely all the way back to the Ashram. He did not utter a single word of complaint against the boys except that he showed the brick to Venkusa. Seeing babu in this condition, Venkusa was deeply grieved and was moved to tears. He quickly tore a part of his own dress and bandaged Babu's wound. When Babu left Ashram, the same brick with babu's blood stains was given to him as Guru-Diksha. The young Babu received the brick stained with the own blood as a token of the love and reverence towards him from Venkusa. The brick became dear to Babu. Babu left the ashram where he stayed from 1842 to 1851, *i.e.,* for nine years.

He left Venkusa's *ashram* and reached Shirdi, a very small village at that time. He stayed there for about three years and then went about wandering from place to place. After wandering for many years, he reached a place called Dhoopkheda. It so happened that a well-to-do Muslim gentleman by the name of Chand Patil lost his mare while on his way to Aurangabad. He kept on searching his mare but there was no trace of the mare. Disappointed, he started walking back to his home. On the way, he saw a queer looking man sitting under a mango tree. He had cap on his head and he wore a long rope (kafni). Under his arm pit was a satka and he was preparing to smoke a clay pipe (Chilm). Seeing Chand Patil, the man called him in a friendly manner and offered him to share his chilm. The strange man also asked Patil why he was carrying a saddle. Patil told the man that he had lost his mare. The man asked Patil whether he had looked in the stream nearby. Intrigued, Patil went to the stream and to his utter surprise, the mare was standing there eating the grass. Patil returned to the place where the odd man was getting the chilm ready for smoking. But two things were needed, fire to light the pipe and water to wet the Chhapi (a piece of cloth through which the smoke is inhaled). Chand Patil watched with great amazement that the man thrust his tongs into the earth and outcome a burning amber. Then the man hit the ground with his satka whereupon water began to ooze out. The chilm was, thereafter, lit and the chhapi wetted. Chand Patil was bewildered on this rare miracle and requested the odd man to accompany him to his home and accept his hospitality to which the odd man agreed. Chand Patil's brother's son's marriage was to be celebrated there. Chand Patil invited the odd man and requested him to accompany the barat which was scheduled to go to Shirdi. The man joined the marriage party where other looked at Him and asked. 'where have You came from? He replied, 'From Kailash'. They said, 'There is no such village around'. He said, 'It is not visible to you'. He ate whatever was offered and reached Shirdi once again along with the marriage party. That was in 1858. From that day till 1918 *i.e.* for sixty years. He did not leave Shirdi till he attained Samadhi in 1918. During that time Sri Ramakrishna Paramhansa (1836-66) iniated Swami Vivekananda (1863-1902) into realization of God. Thus, Sri Ramakrishna Paramhansa was an early and Swami Vivekananda a later contemporary of Shirdi Sai who outlived both.

Baba came to Shirdi along with the marriage party and stopped at Khandoba's temple (Vishnu's temple). Malasapati was the priest of that temple. He was a great devotee with a pure heart. He had high regard for saints and sages. He has just finished worshipping when he came out and saw Baba at the entrance door. Being pure hearted devotee of God, Malasapati immediately developed a liking for Baba. Baba's attire looked like that of a Muslim fakir. Baba appealed as a great soul. He greeted Him saying, 'Avo Sai'. Sai means Lord, God and Master. Because of his pure heart, Mahalsapati realized Him as God (Ishwar).

Hearing this address filled with devotion, Baba stood there, smiling. Malasapatli offered 'Prasad' to Baba. Baba refused to take it and said, "I just had it". Then the priest thought he had offered to God, how did He eat? He asked himself, "This is a small temple and I had been watching. How did He eat in the meanwhile" and further asked. "This is a small temple and I had been watching. I did not notice You eat". Baba said, "Just now, you have offered it to Me. You can't see Me eat". Baba's amazing words and the radiance on His face confirmed that He was some divine soul, Malasapati saluted to Him.

Adjacent to the temple was a room where idols meant for the procession were kept. Since that room was vacant, Malasapati prompted Baba to stay there. Baba stayed there. Malalsapati would give Prasad once in a while and Baba went begging for food every day. To Malalsapati and others who joined him, Baba would preach Vedanta. Baba told the people that he had the mastery over all subjects. He had not studied anything but knew everything. Everything is contained in

Him. He never served any guru. God is everybody's guru. He even showed some evidence of this. Baba wore a saffron cloth on his head. He wore a long robe and a lungi. He would not talk much and lived by begging from four houses daily. He always sat under a neem tree. Sometimes, he used to talk to himself. No one could understand the significance of his activities.

The people of the village began to discuss Him amongst themselves, "Who is this young man who doesn't talk to anyone, who lives on alms and sits under a neem tree? One day the people of Shirdi asked him, 'Who are you sitting under this neem tree? Give us some information about yourself". Baba asked them to bring a pickaxe (hoe) and dig a hole at a particular spot. When it was dug, at first, brick were found and underneath was found a flat stone. When the stone was removed, a corridor was seen. Some courageous men went through it. The corridor led to a cellar where cow-mouth shaped structure, wooden boards and japamalas were seen. The most astonishing thing was that four earthen lamps (Diyyas) were burning there steadily as if someone had lit them just then. They were surprised and thought, 'Who lit these lamps and when? How are they burning in this place where there is no air?' When people began to question Baba about them, he put them off by telling them, "It is My guru's place, his holy residence". The corridor was closed as before. From then on that place came to be known as "Gurusthan" (the place of Guru) and people prostrated there. While glorifying the greatness of Gurusthan, Baba said, "Those who clean the place, make rangoli design, offer incense and light lamps in the Gurusthan on Thursday and Fridays, shall derive all benefits and attain bliss".

Baba always sat on one particular side of the neem tree. After some days the leaves on that particular side gave up their natural bitterness and became tasteless. The leaves on the other side remained bitter. Somehow devotees came to know about this and concluded that Baba must be a great soul. Once there was a heavy down pour in Shirdi. All the streets of Shirdi were flooded. On the request of the people Baba shifted to a mosque and remained there from that day onwards.

Malasapati had realized that Baba was a great soul. Every day he used to pay a visit to Baba and have conversations with Him. Through conversations, his feeling of Baba being a great soul grew stronger. After developing complete faith in what he believed, Malasapati introduced Baba to his friends, Appa Jogle and Kashinath. They too realized Baba as a great soul. They began to look after Baba's requirements. Through them another person called Appa Kote Patil came to visit Baba along with his wife Baijabai. On seeing her Baba said, "She is My mother" and smiled lovingly. Just by having a glimpse of Baba, Baijabai developed immense love for Baba. From that day onwards she ate only after she had fed Baba. Even if Baba went to the hills or outskirts of the village, she would search for Him and offer Him food. Baba too loved her family. They had a son named Tatya. Baba had a very loving relationship with Tatya.

Baba used to beg oil from the shopkeepers and light lamps in the mosque. Once all the shopkeepers decided not give oil to Baba since they felt that it was wasted practice. When, as usual, Baba went to ask for oil, they all gave a distinct 'No'. Unperturbed, Baba returned to the Masjid. Baba put water into a tin pot, and filled all the earthen lamps with it and lighted them. The wicks began to burn and kept burning the whole night, more radiantly than ever. Seeing this the villagers realized that Baba was a divine soul. The shopkeepers who watched this with surprise and dismay fell at Baba's feel and pleaded with Him to forgive them. Baba told them, "**Children, if you like to give, you may give it. But possessing a thing, never say that you do not have it. This is a lie and a great sin. It is fine if you say that you cannot give it. Practise *dharama* and obtain salvation**". From the day this miracle took place, Baba's fame spread throughout Shirdi and everyone began to adore Him.

Baba always sat in the northeast direction in the mosque. In the southeast direction, a dhuni (fire place) was kept burning. Next to it were water pots. In the noches on the walls, hookah pipes were preserved. Next to Him was a sack full of wheat grain. Next to it was a quern. He would beg for wheat grain and then would put them in the quern and grind them. In this way he washed away all the sins of the devotees. Hemand Pant, a name given to Mr. Dabholkar, the original author of Sri Satcharita in Marathi, has related an eye witness account of a miracle performed by Baba. This is reproduced here in his own words, as under:

> "It was sometimes in 1910 A.D. that I went one fine morning to the Masjid in Shirdi for having a darshan of Sai Baba. I was wonder struck to see the following phenomenon. After washing his mouth and face, Sai Baba began to make preparations for grinding wheat. He spread a sack on the floor and thereon set a hand-mill. He took some quantity of wheat in a winnowing fan, and then drawing up the sleeves of His Kafni (robe); and taking hold of the peg of the hand-mill, started grinding the wheat by putting a few handfuls of wheat in the upper opening

of the mill and rotated it. I thought what business Baba had with the grinding of wheat, when he possessed nothing and stored nothing, and as he lived on alms". Some people, who had come there thought likewise, but none had the courage to ask Baba, what he was doing. Immediately, this news of Baba's grinding wheat spread into the village, and at once men and women ran to the Masjid and flocked there to see Baba's act. Four bold women, from the crowd, forced their way and pushing Baba aside, took forcibly the peg or handle into their hands, and singing Baba's Leelas, started grinding. At first Baba was enraged, but on seeing women's love and devotion, He was much pleased and began to smile. While they were gridding, they began to think that Baba had no house, no property, no children, none to look after, and therefore He did not require any wheat-floor for making bread or roti, what will He do with this big quantity of floor? Perhaps as Baba is very kind, He will distribute the flour amongst us. Thinking in this way and while singing, they finished grinding and after putting the hand-mill aside, they divided the flour into four portions and began to remove them one per head. Baba, who was calm and quiet till now, got wild and started abusing them saying, "Ladies are you gone mad? Whose father's property are you looking away? Had I borrowed any wheat from you, so that you can safely take the flour? Now please do this. Take the flour and throw it on the village border limits". On hearing this, the women felt abashed and whispering amongst themselves, went away to the outskirts of the village and spread the flour as directed by Baba.

Some passersby saw this and asked the Shirdi people, "What was this that Baba did?" They replied that as the cholera epidemic was spreading in the village and this was Baba's remedy against the same; it was not wheat that was ground but cholera epidemic subsided and the people of the village were happy. I was much pleased to know all this; but at the same time my curiosity was also aroused. I began to ask myself. What earthly connection was there between wheat flour and cholera? What was the casual relation between the two? And how to reconcile them? Apart from the meaning which people of Shirdi put on this incident of grinding wheat, there is a philosophical significance too. Sai Baba lived in Shirdi for almost sixty years and during this long period, He did the work of grinding almost every day – not, however, the wheat alone; but the sins, the mental and physical afflictions and miseries of His innumerable devotees. The two stones of His mill consisted of Karma and Bhakti, the former being the lower and the latter the upper one. The handle with which Baba worked the mill consisted of Jnana (Knowledge). It was the firm conviction of Baba that knowledge or self-realization is not possible, unless there is the prior act of grinding of all our impulses, desires, sins; and of the three gunas *viz.* Sattva, Rajas and Tamas; and the Ahankara (Ego), which is so subtle and therefore so difficult to be got rid of".

Baba named this Masjid 'Dwarakamayi'. It is mentioned in the Skanda Purana that scholars and wise ones called a place as 'Dwaravati' which was open to people of all the **four castes** at all times. Since Baba was omniscient He called it 'Dwarakamayi'. As mentioned in the scriptures, not only people of the four castes, but also people belonging to all communities and even birds and animals were given equal privilege in the Masjid. Baba's Masjid had no open doors because it had no doors at all. It was always open. It was succour to many. Scholars and wise men called it a sacred place. One can observe this in Baba's Leelas (sports). Thus Baba gave equal importance to all religions. In the presence of Sai, all men behaved with a feeling of brotherhood and equanimity.

Once a Muslim called Javahar Ali came to Shirdi. He could recite the whole Quran and had a silver tongue. With this he attracted people. By that time Baba had become very popular in Shirdi. Recognizing this he began telling that Baba was his disciple. Though he told everyone about this, Baba remained silent and never objected. Javahar Ali actually was a resident of Rahata, a village near Shirdi. He planned to build an 'Idgah' near the Veerabhadra temple at Rahata. Hindus became angry with this. Quarrels arose on account of this, and because of this, Javahar Ali had to leave Rahata. He ran away to Shirdi and began being theatrical.

Javahar Ali considered Baba naive. Since Baba possessed a lot of powers, he wanted to attract people by saying that Baba was his disciple. He took Baba and went to Rahata. Baba too acted like a true disciple. That fool did not recognize Baba's omniscience, but Baba being omniscient, recognized his foolishness. The devotees of Shirdi who loved Baba, did not like Baba to stay away from them in Rahata. So they went in a deputation to bring Baba back to Shirdi. When they met Baba near Idgah and told Him the purpose for which they came, Baba said, 'Why did you take the risk of coming here? He is very ill tempered. Better return to Shirdi before he comes and quarrels with you'. While they were negotiating thus, Javahar Ali returned. He was very angry with the people for trying to take away his disciple. There was some discussion and it was finally decided the both should return to Shirdi.

Before Baba reached Shirdi, a saint named Devidas came to Shirdi. He lived in the Maruti Temple. He was a scholar who knew the religions **(dharmas)** of all communities. Once, people of Shirdi organized spiritual competition between Javahar Ali (who thought that he was a great scholar) and Devidas. Both had a discussion. Javahar was defeated and unable to bear the defeat and insult he fled from Shirdi without telling anyone. People were happy at this. He returned after many years. But this time, as soon as he came, he prostrated at Baba's feet and left silently. **Through this leela, Baba showed by actual conduct how one should behave with patience and tolerance, devoid of ego and how one should perform the duties assigned to a disciple. He practiced what He preached**.

Sometimes Baba practiced extraordinary yoga. No one could do it. As one of the yogic practices, it is said that once Baba took a piece of clean white cloth, 3 inches broad and 22.5, feet long and gulped down his throat, thereafter he removed it slowly by pulling out with one end. With this the digestive system is cleaned. But what Baba used to do was quite different from this. He would vomit out His intestines, wash them clean near the well, and place them on the branches of a tree for drying. Later He would gulp them down. People used to become astonished seeing this. Apart from this, Baba used to perform another yoga practice when no one was present in the Masjid during the nights, Baba would sever all the limbs of His body and strew them separately at different places and remained in yoga Samadhi. In the morning he would assemble them again. Once a devotee saw Baba doing this yogic practice. Having been terrified with the thought that Baba was hacked to pieces and murdered, he ran to his house. He did not inform anybody lest he would be held responsible for the murder since he was the first to see the so-called murder and was the first informant, and therefore knew something in this matter. So he kept quiet and was awake the whole night. In the morning he saw some devotees returning after Baba's darshan with Vibhuthi Prasad. He was surprised and slowly went to the Masjid. Baba smiled at him and asked, 'Were you afraid last night?' He was all the more shocked and thought, "Sai is not an ordinary person, he is Sarveshwara" and prostrated at Baba's feet. He later explained the whole story to everyone around. Everyone was surprised and also happy to know that Sai is omnipotent. This incident deepened their devotion to Baba.

A devotee named Abdullah used to come to Baba. He used to do a lot of service for Baba. Initially, he served a fakir called Amiruddin on the banks of river Tapati. Once, Baba appeared in Amiruddin's dream, gave him two mangoes and told him to give mangoes to Abdullah. When Amiruddin woke up, he found two mangoes lying on his bed. He gave the mangoes to Abdullah and said. "Child, in Shirdi there is a great soul called Sai Baba. Go to Him, serve Him, and become liberated"'. Abdullah reached Shirdi and visited Baba. Baba was extremely happy and said, 'Look! My crow has come'. Later he was asked to serve Baba. Abdullah remained there and served Baba all through his life.

Gradually Baba's fame spread all over the country. Hundreds and thousands of people began coming to the Baba. Though many people offered many things to Baba, Baba continued to lead a fakir's life. He ate only what He would obtain by begging. Many devotees used to bring various dishes that they would prepare to offer to Baba. Baba used to touch them, sanctify them, and returned it to them as Prasad. Later, after everyone left for their meal, He would have His meal in the Masjid, along with Abdullah, Shyama, the local school teacher, and other devotees. At such times curtains were drawn in the Masjid. Once the curtains were drawn, no one would go inside.

Baba personally planted some trees and watered them. He called the place 'Lendibagh'. In the evening Baba would stand in front of the Masjid. He would walk up and down or lean against the wall and converse with people walking on the street. In the evenings, Baba would go to the Lendibagh. After His return, devotees would offer Him 'Arati'. Every evening Baba used to distribute the money that was collected from the devotees during the day. By that time, many beggars would gather in front of the Masjid. However much came into the hand was given away. He would put His hand in the pocket and pull out the money. Depending on the person, however much was given to that person every day, only that much money came into His hand. Everyone was surprised at this miracle. Baba never expected anything in return from these people. There was no limit to Baba's distribution of money. If any newly married couple came to Him, He would give them a rupee each. This tradition continued till the end. Like money, even food was distributed to fakirs, beggars and also to birds and animals that were around.

Usually Baba would sit on a sack and keep the brick under the hand for support. This was the same brick which Baba had received as a 'guru diksha' from His Guru Venkusa. While sleeping, this brick would serve as pillow for Baba. Baba's nature was childlike. No one knew when He would laugh, when He would get angry and when He would become serious. Baba would not talk much. He would smile but not laugh loudly. Laughter was very rare occurrence. Baba was very fond of children. He used to play with them. Baba was an embodiment of compassion. His compassion was not limited to humans alone, it even extended to birds and animals. His compassion flowed on trees too. Once a neem and peepul tree grew next to each other in the Lendibagh. They were not strong enough and began to shrink. Being omniscient and omnipotent, Baba protected them in a strange way. Every day he would come to these plants, wrap them on either sides and shake them vigorously. After a few days these plants grew and became huge. These trees are present even today in the Lendibagh. Between these trees Baba lit the Akhanda jyoti (eternal light), which, according to some people, is still burning.

Baba's compassion flowed on inert stones. Abdullah and Madhav, another devotee of Baba, used to wash their clothes on a big stone. Once they saw Baba sitting on it. From then onwards they began worshipping it and avoided washing clothes on it. Baba often sat on that stone. Once a devotee took a photograph of Baba while sitting on that stone. This photograph is now commonly available at all Shirdi temples. The stone is still preserved in Dwarkamayi for the sake of viewers. By sitting on it out of compassion, Baba turned an ordinary stone into a divine stone, worthy of worship. One could not comprehend the nature of Baba's compassion. He had equal vision on all-movable and immovable. He was never perturbed by worldly things.

Baba was 5.5, feet tall and His body was radiant with a golden complexion. His eyes shone bright even in the dark. Devotees used to talk about this strange feature. They felt that Baba was subtly proclaiming that – "Though you are in the darkness of ignorance, I, being self-illumined, *can see you*". With big nostrils, cute lips, white moustache and beard, His head covered with a cloth, He appeared like Lord Shiva and conferred bliss to the devotees. Not merely did He appear as Lord Shiva and please His devotees, He even declared once that he Himself was Shiva.

One day, Baba summoned Dada Kelkar, one of His close devotees, and told him, 'Today is **Guru Pournima** "perform **Guru Pooja**". None of the devotees present there, knew the meaning of Guru Pooja. Kelkar asked Baba what Guru Pooja meant. Baba used to tell his devotees that a Guru was necessary for self-realization, for attaining patience and for developing faith in God. He further told them that even the great Avtaars like Rama and Krishan also had their Gurus, like Vashishtha and Sandipani respectively. Baba asked Kelkar, "Who do you think is a Guru? God alone is the Guru. 'GURUR BRAHMA, GURUR VISHNU, GURUR DEVO MAHESHWARA'. He is **Brahma**, He is **Vishnu**, He is

Maheshwara, and He is the Supreme Absolute. The true Guru is one who combines the three forms of the Trinity, the God who preside over creation, protection and dissolution. Thus God alone is the real Guru, declared Baba.

On hearing this, Kelkar asked Baba, 'Should I worship Brahma, Vishnu or Rudra?' Baba declared in a voice of assumed anger: 'Eh saitan! Here I am! Offer worship to me!' Thereby Baba made it known that He was Brahma, Vishnu and Rudra. Later, He said, 'Worship the nature that exists as I and I alone'. All those present there understood that Baba was the divine incarnate. One day after the Arti, Baba made the following divine revelation; "**Be wherever you like; do whatever you choose, remember this well that all what you do is known to Me. I am the Inner Ruler of all and seated in hearts. I envelop all the creatures, the movable and immovable world. I am the Controller – the wire puller of the show of this Universe. I am the mother-origin of all beings – the Harmony of three Gunas, the propeller of all senses, the Creator, Preserver and Destroyer. Nothing will harm him, who turns his attention towards Me, but Maya will lash or whip him who forgets Me. All the insects, ants, the visible, movable and immovable world, is my Body or Form**".

Several miracles related to the Omni-presence, Omni-potence and Omni-scient of Shirdi Sai Baba as a divine have been given in various books published in this context. Various peculiar actions of Sai Baba attracted millions and millions of people from far and wide places. Protection of devotees from death, averting their ailments, helping them to desist from evil tendencies, providing solutions to their personal and professional problems, removing their doubts and suspicious about this divine power, disclosing some events of their past lives, denial of superstitious beliefs in them and controlling desires were some of the miraculous happenings attributed to Sai Baba. Spiritual upliftment of His devotees, equipping them with spiritual knowledge, bestowing love and blessings on their off-springs and giving them several types of dreams and visions to help them minimize their difficulties of life were some of the remarkable features of Sai Baba. Testing devotees' faith in God, bestowing salvation on them, and refusing any kind of Dakhshina from them were some of the other special traits of the personality of Sai Baba. A large number of examples of the above assertions can be seen in the literature on Sai Baba of Shirdi such as the following among others:

- Transforming hot weather into cool atmosphere to enable the devotees experience the bliss of cool breeze; halting heavy rain to enable them to reach their homes safely; extinguishing fire to save the haystacks of farmers; stopping hurricanes to save the houses of villages; saving children from being snatched by devilish forces; giving eye sight to blinds; and accepting food from the houses of devotees far away from Dwarka Dwehakamai – His abode to make the people realize that Sai Baba is Omni-present as God.

- Appearing in the forms of several creatures like dogs, cats, ants, among others to eat food at devotees' houses; saving animals from being slaughtered; curing patients of their diseases like asthma, plague, convulsion etc. giving darshans in the form of the deities they worshipped; giving dreams to the devotees to solve their problems; materializing visions of rivers like Godawari, Ganga, Yamuna and showing Prayag through these visions; communicating with devotees through telepathy and blessing padukas to make the devotees realize his embodiment of all creatures, all deities, all sages, all animals and inanimate beings, that Baba was not bound by time and space, and that He cannot be judged by body consciousness and enlighten them that Sai Baba is Omni-potent as God.
- Communicating messages to the devotees in order to save them from various types of dangers to their lives; forewarning them of the inevitable misfortunes they might come across; delaying them from undertaking journeys and travels to protect them from the possible mishaps; cautioning them from being cheated or robbed; exposing the hypocracies of their insincere prayers; making the skeptics to realize the existence of God; strengthening their faith in God and reading the minds of various categories of persons are some of the instances which amply justify the Omni-scient of Shirdi Sai as God .
- There was a Mamlatdar (collector) named Nana Saheb Chanderkar posted at Jamner in district Khandesh – about 160 kilometers away from Shirdi. He was a great devotee of Shirdi Sai. His daughter Maina Tai was on the family way at the advanced stage and the delivery could take place any moment. But she was unable to bear the labour pain. Nana Saheb thought that Baba's 'udi' (Vibhuti) was the only way out to help the process of delivery. However, udi had just finished and thus, he was very much upset. In the meantime in Shirdi, one devotee of Baba named Ramgir was preparing to travel to Jalgaon. He was summoned by Baba to carry vibhuti (udi) in order to deliver it to Nana Saheb at Jamner about fifty kilometers away from

Jalgaon. Ramgir did not have enough money to travel from Jalgaon to Jamner. He had money sufficient for travel up to Jalgaon. Walking on foot such a long distance was utmost difficult. However, Baba, being Omni-scient, understood Ramgir's dilemma and told Ramgir not to worry about anything. All arrangements for his travel from Jalgaon to Jamner will be made. Ramgir went up to Jalgaon with whatever money he had. As soon as Ramgir reached Jalgaon, he started getting worried on how to proceed to Jamner. Exactly at that very moment, a horse-cart driver (Tongawala) approached Ramgir and offered the ride upto Jamner by saying that Nana Saheb had sent the horse-cart for some Babugirbuva, a name given to Ramgir by Baba. Thus, Ramgir reached Jamner and gave udi to Nana Saheb. On drinking the mixture of udi with water, Naina Tai had a safe delivery. Nana Saheb was happy and thanked Ramgir for bringing the udi in time. Ramgir, on the contrary, told Nana Saheb that it was his greatness to arrange a horse-cart for him at Jalgaon without which it would have been impossible for him to reach Jalgaon in time. Nana Saheb got surprised and said that he had not sent any horse-cart for Ramgir. He got puzzled and came out to see if the horse-cart driver was still there. To their utter surprise, neither the driver nor the cart were seen anywhere. Both Nana Saheb and Ramgir realized that the cart-driver was Baba himself because only Baba used to address Ramgir as Babugirbuva. This is one of the several instances of Sai Baba's Omni-presence.

- Another miracle is cited by Arthur Osborn of England (London) in his book – "The incredible Sai Baba" (Kamath & Kher), which is as under:

  Osborn lived in Calcutta for four years. He was deeply interested in spirituality. He had an old lady Miss Dunton as his neighbour. Miss Dunton had been a nun in her young age but was given absolution of her vows by the Pope because she was not able to observe the rigorous code of a convent. While her application for release from her vows was still pending, she was in great distress and also almost penniless. One day, while sitting in her cell lost in her deepest gloom, she suddenly felt the presence of a man in front of her. He was barefooted and looked like a holy man. She was surprised since there was no way for anyone to enter her cell. However, the man did not look to be a holy man of the West. The holy man asked her for a gift. Miss told him she had no money. The holy man told her that she had thirty five rupees in a box in the cupboard up there, which she had forgotten completely. Miss Dunton was taken aback about by the holy man's prescience. She at once opened the cupboard and found the box containing exactly thirty-five rupees. As soon as she turned around, the holy man had disappeared. She left the convent and went to stay with her nephew who turned out to be a kind and loving person. Thus, her worries about her future were over. Osborn also wondered who this holy man could be but the description given by Miss Dunton about the holy man matched Sai Baba of Shirdi. To confirm his conjecture, he showed a picture of Sai Baba who took a good look at the picture and exclaimed with amazement: "Yes, that is He! He had even the same white kerchief on his head!" Orborn writes that Miss Dunton had never heard of Sai Baba before. Thus, this is one of several examples of Baba's Omni-science.

- On Deepawali day in 1910, Shirdi Baba, while sitting near the dhuni arranging the sticks, suddenly thrust His both hands into the burning fire of the dhuni. Seeing this, Shyama, His ardent devotee and others immediately pulled Baba away from the fire. They all were shocked and asked Baba why he had done that. Baba told them that there was nothing except that the child was safe. No one understood what Baba meant. All pleaded with Baba to explain to them in detail what had happened. Baba, thereafter, told them that in a village, a blacksmith had fallen ill and therefore, his wife was working the bellows of their furnace. Her husband called her for some help. Forgetting that her child was on her chest, she suddenly stood up and the child slipped into the furnace whom Baba had saved by thrusting his both hands into the fire. Every one became sentimental and tears rolled down from their eyes. In the meantime, Nana Saheb, who was also there, summoned a doctor to treat Baba's burnt hands. But Baba refused any medication, instead allowed Bhagoji – a devotee to apply ghee (butter oil) on the wounds and continued doing so till the wounds got healed. A similar incident is mentioned about one of His opponents and staunch critics whom Baba saved from death as a result of a snake bite. There are several other instances of Baba's Omni-potence.
- Hemand Pant once had a dream wherein Baba appeared in the form of a sanyasi (sage or a renunciate) and told him that He would come to his house for a meal during the day on the

occasion of Holi. This was in 1917. Hemand Pant woke up and related the whole dream to his wife. Both were surprised as how Baba could come to their residence at Bandra from Shirdi so far off. However, being devotees, they had total faith in Baba even if it was a dream. Thus, Mrs. Pant worked delicious food and more than usual. By noon all preparations were made but no one came. Several other guests were also invited. Therefore, serving of food was commenced after oblation was made to God. As everyone was about to start eating, there was a knock on the door. Hemand Pant opened the door and found two persons named Ali Mohammed and Moulana Ismu Mujavar standing in front of him. They gave Hemand Pant a photograph of Baba wrapped in a newspaper. Hemand Pant felt very happy that Baba had come in the form of his beautiful photograph.

- The story behind the Sai Baba's photograph is quite revealing. Ali Mohammed was a Sai devotee. He used to keep Baba's photograph along with several other pictures including an enlarged photograph of his teacher Abdul Rahman. However, Noor Mohammed, brother-in-law of Ali Mohammed came to visit him when he was sick in the hospital and saw those pictures and photographs. Noor Mohammed pressurized him to throw the pictures and photographs into the sea since idol worship was against the principles of Islam. Ali Mohammed sent someone to go to Bandra and throw all the photographs and pictures into the sea. After a few days, when Ali Mohammed returned from the hospital to his house, he was surprised to find Baba's photo in its usual place beautifully smiling. When all photos and pictures were thrown into the sea, how could this photo of Baba escape? He thought that the person whom he had entrusted this task might have forgotten to carry this photograph to throw it in the sea. However, he thought surprisingly: how could a person forget this one photo of Baba only while taking all the pictures and photographs to the sea. Ali Mohammed feared that his relative would destroy it if he would see it. To avoid that situation, Moulana Ismu Mujavar advised him to give this photograph to his friend Hemand Pant who happened to be an ardent devotee of Baba as indicated by Baba in the dream of Hemand pant. Indeed, Baba in physical form is not different from his portrait form.

One night Baba was alone in the Mosque. A Muslim devotee was sleeping a short distance away from the mosque. At midnight he woke up for some reason. To his utter surprise, he saw a huge ball of light entering the mosque from the sky. The following day Baba told him that a few guests had come. He had food prepared for them and kept it aside in the mosque. No one could know about the secret of behind all this enactment. Perhaps the gods from the heavens might have come to pay their obeisance to the Almighty divine incarnate.

Mohan Shyama was a school teacher in Shirdi. Baba used to call him Shyama out of love. Once Shyama asked Baba, "Are Vaikunth, Sathyalok (Brahmlok) and Kailash really present? Do Brahma, Vishnu and Maheswara really exist? If so, kindly show them to me". Baba told Shyama to close his eyes. As soon Shyama closed his eyes, he saw Brahma in Sathyalok (Brahma Lok), Vishnu in Vaikunth and Maheswara at Kailash. Later Baba told Shyama that the Puranas, Shastras, Upanishads and Vedas are all true. All these have been written by the sages. People should have faith in these holy scriptures. To several devotees, Baba is an embodiment of all deities. He is Para Brahmn. He is indeed, Brahma, Vishnu and Shiva who generate, organize and dissolve the whole creation. All deities obey His command. Even death follows His orders. Concentrate and meditate any form of chosen deity or this Sai form. Have **faith** and **patience** as the spiritual goal of life.

Apart from showing miracles, Baba used to transform people and prepare them for spiritual upliftment. He would choose a method suitable for a person. For example, He identified Dasganu for singing devotional songs because he was fond of music and dramas. Dasganu was a police constable. In order to save him from the likely dangers to his life and possible punishment at the hands of government, he started living in Nanded where some devotees of Baba gave him fertile agriculture land at cheap rates which became the course of his livelihood. Dasganu was a good writer and a singer also. He used to compose and sing devotional songs, and people used to come in large numbers to listen to his melodious bhajans because of which he became famous. Dasganu dedicated his life in spreading the message of Baba through these devotional songs. Eventually, by Baba's grace, he came to be known as a Sant Dasganu. Thus, Dasganu was spiritually uplifted by Baba. Later Baba entrusted the responsibility of organizing devotional songs (Kirtans and Bhajans) to Dasganu Maharaj. Likewise, Abdullah, Shyama, Kashinath, Kulkarni, Hari Sitaram Dixit (later known as Kaka Sahab Dixit) and H.V. Sathe, a deputy collector in Bombay were among several others who were uplifted spiritually. Baba used to advise His devotees to develop detachment for the 'Deha' (Body). Baba also used to disclose the past lives of some devotees and bestow salvation on them.

Turning to Shyama, Sai Baba said, "**If a man utters my name with love, I shall fulfill all his wishes, increase his devotion, and if he sings earnestly My life and My deeds, him I shall be set in front and back and on all sides. Those devotees, who are attached to Me, heart and soul, will naturally feel happiness, when they hear my stories. Believe Me that if anybody sings my Leelas, I will give him infinite joy and ever-lasting contentment. It is My special characteristic to bless any person who surrenders completely to Me, and who does worship Me faithfully, and who remembers Me, and meditates on Me constantly. How can they be conscious of worldly objects and sensations, who utter My name, who worship Me, who think of My stories and My life and who thus always remember Me? I shall draw out My devotees from the jaws of death. If My stories are listened to, all the diseases will be got rid of. So, hear My stories; and think and meditate on them, assimilate them. This is the way of happiness and contentment. The pride and egoism of My devotees will vanish, the mind of the hearers will be set at rest and if it has whole-hearted and complete faith, it will be one with Supreme Consciousness. The simple remembrance of My name as 'Sai Sai' will do away with sins of speech and hearing**".

Baba used to teach His devotees the secular values of life. He used to educate the people that all religions are good. Many Muslims used to object to the Hindu way of worship in the mosque, while many Hindus would feel unhappy when Baba used to pronounce "Allah Malik' in the temples. But Baba's teachings enlightened all of them. Baba was equally against the conversion of one's religion into another, because He used to tell the converts that body and mind were meant for salvation and not for conversion. Baba's grace offered 'Sadgati' not only for men whether Hindus or Muslims but even for animals also. Once a tiger imprisoned in cage was brought before Baba, who was suffering from some serious disease. Baba gave orders for opening the door of the cage. With faith in Baba's word and divine power, the door of the cage was opened. The tiger came out of the cage, slowly approached Baba and began to stare at Baba. Baba also stared at the tiger for a long time but an eye of compassion. Within a few moments, the tiger put his head down at the feet of Baba and prostrated. Soon, the tiger fell down and died. The tiger passed away in the divine presence of God. He was actually a great soul. The tiger represented the ego which fell before the divine power of Baba.

No doubt, Nana Saheb Chanderkar, Kaka Saheb Dixit, Shyama, Mahalasapati, Tatya and Abdullah were among some of the close devotees of Baba. However, there were few other persons who would always criticize what Baba used to say and do. These rivals were in the habit of talking ill of Baba merely out of jealousy. They used to spread all sort of false rumours about Baba. In 1886, Baba fell ill due to severe attack of asthama. The devotees around Baba could not bear Baba's suffering and pain but were helpless as they could not do anything although they were willing to do anything. Realizing their sufferings due to this ill health, Baba called Mahalasapati and told him that he was about to go to God but would return after three days. In case, He did not return in three days, His body should be buried here in His place of living and the flags of both Hindus and Muslims should be fixed on it. Thereafter, Baba immediately fell in the lap of Mahalasapati who cried at this heartbreaking situation. Devotees all-around were weeping. The news of this incident spread all over Shirdi and in the other nearby areas.

Baba's rivals found an opportunity and demanded the burial of the corpse. They pleaded that keeping the corpse for three days was not advisable because of fear of spreading of some disease emitting from the corpse. However, Mahalasapati firmly disallowed the burial because Baba, as said by Himself, would come back after three days. Thus, for three days continuously, all devotees and villagers, offered prayers while facing opposition from the rivals. After three days, Baba returned to His body in the early morning. Devotees felt a sigh of relief on seeing Baba again in the live form. Baba, by enacting this play, showed to the world that He was not body as the devotees believed but He as a divine soul. As a result of this incident, whenever Baba fell ill, the devotees would think that Baba might give up the body and return to it. As foretold, Baba would recover soon.

Earlier also such a phenomenon had occurred in 1912 when Baba fell ill in a similar manner. The disease started worsening day by day. Devotees started weeping while thinking that Baba would give up His body. All devotees started performing Rudra Abhishekam reciting Vishnu Sahastranama and Anusthan. They started doing prayers and singing devotional songs, in Baba's name. At the same time, the close devotees started talking about the burial or cremation of the dead body which they wanted to ask Baba and which they could earlier never ask Baba since no one could had the courage to do so. Baba, being Omniscient, realized this and came back to life. He summoned Nana Saheb and told him that He was not leaving this world. However, He would indicate when the time was due. Everyone was thrilled to listen this from Baba Himself. Such an incident was repeated in 1915 also.

Tatya son of Baija Bai fell ill in 1918. His health deteriorated. He was bedridden and could not come even for Baba's Darshan. Baba Himself was not keeping good health. He also became weak and fragile. Madhav used to clean the mosque. As usual, while he was sweeping the floor, he found Baba's brick there. He lifted it and held it in one hand while sweeping by his other hand. Unfortunately, the brick fell from his hand and broke into two pieces. Madhav suffered terrible agony on seeing this. He was even scared that Baba would feel annoyed with him for breaking this brick which Baba used to keep it under his head as a pillow. In the meantime, Baba came in and took the two pieces of the brick in His hands. Baba neither got angry with Madhav nor said anything to him. However, He held the pieces in His hands and said, "Child, this brick was my companion. Its breaking indicates that My 'Karma' has come to an end".

As Vijay Dashmi approached in the same year 1918, not only Tatya's health got deteriorated further but also Baba Himself had a high temperature. As desired by Tatya, he was brought near to Baba. Baba got some pudding and helped drink it, even though Baba Himself was in a worse condition. Crying out Baba, Baba, Tatya fell in Baba's lap. While smiling in despair, Baba applied udi on Tatya's forehead and sent him back to his home, whereas Baba's own condition started getting worse day by day. Several devotees started coming to Him on hearing the news of His serious illness. Baba said to His devotees, "**Not only Me, from now onwards, My Samadhi, too will speak. My bones too will speak. My nerve too will respond**". The news that Baba was about to leave His body spread far and wide. The devotees were weeping at the thought of their separation from Baba. On seeing the condition of the devotees, Baba said to all of them, "I am not dying. Truly speaking. I have no birth or death. I only wear and give up bodies. Eight years after giving up this body, I shall take up a new one. Eight years after Samadhi, I will incarnate again in a southern region to distribute what is cooked now". Even in His last moments Baba said, "**Call me Sai, from the depth of your heart and I shall respond saying 'oye'**.

Saying these words, Baba forced Dixit, Shyama and others to go for lunch, although they were not willing to leave Baba in that condition, they did not like to disobey Him and they left. A few devotees including Lakshmi, however, remained with Baba. Baba called Lakshmi and gave her first five rupees and then four rupees billing her thereof that these nine rupees were symbol of the nine types of devotion (Nevdha Bhakti). Receiving these nine rupees, Lakshmi wept and everybody began to cry. Baba breathed his last at 2.30 p.m. on October

15, 1918, the Vijay Dashmi Day, while Ekadashi had just started. Baba's body was laid to rest in the place reserved for installing the idol of Lord Krishna. That place, eventually, became the Samadhi Mandir of Baba. It is now considered a divine and holy shrine. At that time Dasganu was performing Sai kirtan in a village. That night Baba appeared in his dream and told him that the mosque had been demolished and he had left. Baba furthered asked him to go to Shirdi along with his co-singers, cover His Samadhi with a shawl and perform the Nama Saptaham (Name Rememberance Week). Saying this Baba vanished and the dream ended. Dasganu got up shocked and told everybody about this dream. He immediately rushed to Shirdi along with his companions. He reached Shirdi crying for Baba. As commanded by Baba, he performed puja and conducted Nama Saptaham at Baba's Samadhi. All the devotees were in grief. Baba's closest 'sevak' Abdullah, being completely grief stricken, started spending whole time near the Samadhi. One day Baba physically appeared before Abdullah and said "Abdullah, **Samadhi is for the body, but who can actually burry Me? I am eternal. I will incarnate in Andhra after eight years**". So, saying this Baba vanished into the air. These words of Baba consoled Abdullah.

Baba invariably used to utter "Allah Malik" which means "God is Lord". He would lovingly sing of Rama and sometimes other forms of God. The mosque (masjid) he stayed in he used to call it as "Dwarakamayi" – abode of Krishna. On one side of Dwarakamayi was a 'tulsi vrindaven' basil orchard and on the other, was a holy fire and its ashes or what was called "udhi" which Baba used to distribute with His grace and blessings. Devotees would often surround Baba, seeking His love and mercy by offering "arati". Baba said in so many words, "**If anyone utters my name with love, I shall fulfill all his wishes and increase his devotion**".

Sai Baba of Shirdi had a very deep knowledge of Gita and Koran. There are several stories in the literature published on Sai Baba of Shirdi. Baba was equally a spiritual philosopher having profound knowledge of the Hindu philosophy and Vedas on one hand while being well-versed in Islamic religion and Sufism. Indeed, Sufism is the bridge between Islam and Hinduism. Baba respected every religion and exhorted people by precepts and examples to be tolerant and charitable to each others' religious sentiments. He never liked conversion of one faith into another. Once a Hindu, who converted to Islam, came to Baba, but Baba is reported to have slapped him and told him, "Aren't you ashamed to change your father?" Baba was equally against the conversion of a Muslim into a Hindu. Indeed, He was against change of one's religion. Baba was a unique blend of all faiths and observed no barriers of religion, faith, race, creed, region, language or nation. He used to confirm each devotee in his/her own faith and spiritual practice. Lokmanya Bal Gangadhar Tilak met Sai Baba on 19 May 1917 when Baba told Tilak, "You have done a lot for the people, but now devote yourself to your own welfare".

Baba used to tell His devotees that God exists and there is nothing higher than God. God is infinite, eternal and complete in all respects. God is Omni-present, Omni-potent and Omni-scient. He is the creator, sustainer and destroyer. All should have faith in God and surrender to Him voluntarily to His will. Not a leaf of tree or a blade of grass can move without the will of God. The devotees should perform their duties properly with detachment as instruments of God. They should follow the path of truth and righteousness and do their actions (karma) without expectation of any reward.

Baba used to tell His devotees that whatever he did was an attempt to offer them Brahmajana (spiritual knowledge) for which one has to give up the five life forces, five senses, the mind, the intellect and the ego. For this, one has to follow the paths of truth and righteousness. Baba used to tell the devotees to concentrate and meditate in their minds, the form of their chosen deities with faith and perseverance – the only way to achieve the spiritual goal of life merging with the Para Brahmn. Baba prescribed Karm Yoga, Bhakti Yoga and Gyan Yoga as the three ways to achieve the spiritual goal. One can follow either or all of the three ways only by the grace of God. For achieving grace of God, one must rise above the stage of Tamoguna (delusion) and Rajoguna (passion), and inculcate the attribute of Satoguna (purity) by doing good to everyone as an offering to God. He told the devotees not to think that Baba is dead and gone. They will hear Him even from His Samadhi. He will communicate with His devotees. Baba's life continues to be His message and His teachings unrestricted by any barriers, as an active ocean of love and compassion.

The teachings of Sai Baba of Shirdi may be summed up as under:

> 'Shraddha' (faith) and 'Saburi' (preservance) together constitute what may be termed as the divine message of Shirdi Sai Baba. Indeed, 'Shraddha' means deep conviction and absolute faith in God and Guru (preceptor) who is embodiment of God, an incarnation of God manifested as Brahma, Vishnu and Mahesh. Baba often used to tell His devotees that they should not only listen to the discourses from their preceptors but also have total faith and confidence in them. Saburi, according to

Baba, means patience and perseverance. He used to tell His devotees that 'Saburi' generates virtue and pious thoughts, eliminates all sins and afflictions, and removes fear and ignorance. It leads to complete success and total perfection. He would motivate people to participate in the process of life and do the prescribed duty with a feeling of surrendering heart and soul to God. He would urge them to overcome lethargy and laziness, and strive for self-realization leading to God-realization. He would ask them to study holy books and sacred scriptures, feed the hungry, meditate in God or chant His name, and work in a detached way. Meditation could be done in any form of God or His own form who could be seen in the physical form. This will help in the concentration in God, and remove the mental distinction among the meditation, act of meditation and the object being meditated upon. He would often say, "**Do not go anywhere in search of God, that is me. Barring your name and form there exists in you, as well as in all beings, a sense of Being or Consciousness of existence. That is Myself. I have no Form. I always live everywhere. I carry on as a wirepuller of all actions of the those who trust me and merge in me. Do not entertain the sense of doership in doing service to the people. Be entirely egoless in all things, and thus your spiritual progress will be rapid**". Baba often used to say,

"**God exists, He is eternal and very compassionate. Never shake faith in God. He is the protector of all. His ways are unique, inscrutable and mysterious. He is Lord and Master of the Universe. There is no truth other than Him. This Universe is a Sport (Leela) for Him. Surrender the fruit of action to God. Let your love and compassion flow to all creatures of the world. God is always in your heart. You can see both animate and inanimate. Do good and offer it to God. God pervades the whole Universe. He is unborn, eternal and everlasting. Earn His grace by service to the needy. If you do good, good will follow. You cannot escape what is ordained for you. You have to face it. Face it either with groan or with smile. Earth will return to earth and the soul will fly away. Give water to the thirsty, food to the hungry, clothing to the naked and shelter to the homeless and God will bless you**". Once, while addressing His devotees, Baba said,

"**Control your mind and desires. Destroy ego and anger. Develop love for everyone. You will attain peace of mind. Know that Sai's Spirit is immortal. You are being etched by this immortal spirit.**

Whatever you do, whatever you think, bear this in mind that Sai is always aware of everything. Those, who meditate on Sai, repeat Sai name and sing about Sai, get transformed. Sai loves devotion, Make Sai as the sole object of your thoughts and actions. Have faith in Sai. Sai will always protect you and guide you towards the right path. Always feel that Sai is with you and you are with Sai. Sai is around you. Repeat Sai's name and no trouble will come to you. Surrender to Sai and Sai will never let you down".

While giving permission to Hemand Pant for writing of the Sai Charita. Baba said, "I fully agree with you regarding the writing of Sai Charita. You do your duty, don't be afraid, steady your mind and have faith in My words".

6.2 Sri Sathya Sai Baba

In the fulfillment of the second boon promised by Lord Shiva to the sage Bhardwaj, and also, as foretold in 1918 by Shirdi Sai Baba that after eight years of His attaining Samadhi, both Shiva and Shakti incarnated in the human form of Sathya Narayan Raju in a remote village Puttaparthy of Ananthpur a southern district of India. Born as a child of the pious parents Eshwaramma (mother) and Pedda Venkama Raju (father) of Bhardwaj lineage (gothra) belonging to the Ratnakar family of the solar dynasty, the present incarnation of God in the name of Sri Sathya Sai Baba has been demonstrating His divinity in various ways to the whole world since His birth on 23 November 1926. The advent of this latest incarnation of God as Sathya Sai Baba had been predicted in various ways by various sages and divine prophets. For instance, the sages like Bhrigu, Mahrishi Shuk Dev (son of great sage Ved Vyas – author of the epic of Mahabharata who also compiled the four Vedas in their present form) and sage Agastya had prophesied thousands of years ago about the advent and mission of Sri Sathya Sai Baba.

According to Shuka Nadi, written by the sage Shuka Dev, Sri Sathya Sai Baba – God incarnate, will be equipped with all divine powers and attributes. He will be a 'Sankalpa' 'Siddha' (Proven Resolute) (whatever He wills, is bound to happen), will be in Nirvikalpa (non-vacillating) state of mind and His mission will be to restore Dharma (Righteousness), to do everything for the welfare of the people and to preach the spiritual and moral values. He will have the divine power to appear in different forms and show His omni-presence even in the far off places. He will establish various centers and institutions like hospitals and educational institutions and undertake various other activities for the benefit of the needy. He will move among the people like an affectionate mother to all. He will be an embodiment of love

(Premaswaroopa), bliss (Anandswaroopa), truth (Sathya Swaroopa), and knowledge (Gyanswaroopa). Also, predicted thousands of years ago in the Upanishads, the coming of Sai Avtaar includes three incarnations namely Shirdi Sai, Sathya Sai and Prema Sai. People born in the present generation should consider themselves quite fortunate that they got the chance of seeing the Poorna Avtaar of Kaliyug during their life time. This has been revealed by Baba Himself in conversation with Hislop in his book on 'Conversation With Sathya Sai Baba'.

Zoroaster had mentioned in the holy scripture of the Parsis 'Zenda Avesta' about the full incarnation of God with the name 'Rasthi' which means Truth or Sathya. Jesus also foretold about God's incarnation as Sathya Sai Baba in the holy Bible in 9th chapter versus 11 through 15. In one of His divine discourses. Sri Sathya Sai Baba, revealed the simple statement of Jesus Christ in his own words, "**He who sent me among you will come**", and he pointed to a lamb. A lamb is merely a symbol, a sign. It stands for the Voice – Ba – Ba; the announcement was the Advent of Baba. "**His name will be Truth**". Christ declared, Sathya means Truth. "**He will wear a robe of red, a blood-red robe**:" (Here Baba pointed to the robe He was wearing). "**He will be short, with crown of hair**. The lamb is the sign and symbol of Love. Christ did not declare that he will come again. He said, "**He who sent me will come**". That Ba-ba is this Baba and Sai; the short curly-hair-crowned red-robed Baba, has come. He is not only in this Form, but, He is in every one, as the dweller in the Heart. He is there, short with a robe of the colour of the blood that fills it.

Even prophet Mohammed had declared the advent of God in the human form who would be identified by a few glaring marks on his body such as a mole on the left cheek, thick black hair on His head, a broad puffed up forehead, a small nose bulging in the centre, slightly short in height, His face will change colours and His feet will resemble like those of a lady among several other marks of identification. This human form of God will know the teachings of all religions right from his birth. He will have the knowledge of the world right from when it came into being. Ask Him for anything, He will promptly materialize and give it. He will move among His devotees and bless them with His own Hands. Every heart that sees Him will have a feeling of bliss. His devotees will crave to see Him time and again. During the last twenty years of His life, He will become the emperor of the world. By that time more than 60% of the world population will believe Him. Muslims will be the last to accept Him as God. He will materialize things from His hand and mouth (lingams). He, being the Lord of Universe, will teach truth, righteousness, peace, love and non-violence.

According to Swami Vivekananda, if there is even going to be a Universal faith in the world, it must be the one which will be infinite, it will believe in God whose sun will shine upon its followers and non-believers, on saints and sinners alike, and which will be the sum total of all the religious faiths, and will have infinite space to accommodate more and more. Such a faith will have no place or scope for persecution or intolerance in its approach while its philosophy will recognize divinity in every being, whose focus will be centered around every place aiding humanity to realize its own true divine nature, and where divinity in every human being will allow no emotional or physical or material coercion of any kind.

Maharshi Aurobindo with his infinite yogic powers entered into absolute solitude and did severe meditation for three years continuously from 1923 to 1926 praying to God to incarnate for the welfare of the world. On November 24, 1926, Aurobindo came out of his penance and told the people that Lord Krishna had descended on the earth yesterday *i.e.* on November 23, 1926. Later he said, "My penance has borne fruit. In order to fulfil my desire, God has descended. Now I have nothing else to do. "After saying these last words, the Maharshi handed overall the responsibilities of the 'ashram' to a western lady later named, 'Mother', and took up the vow of silence.

Nostradamus, an eminent French astrologer gave the following predictions which are very closely relevant to the advent of an incarnated divine like Sri Sathya Sai Baba: **"He who has been awaited for such a long time, will never appear in Europe. He will appear in Asia. One from the league issued from the Great Hermes. His power will rise over all other Kings in Eastern countries", (X-75)**. Here reference to the Great Hermes means the Greek Messengers of God *i.e.* the advent of the Divine Principle or Power. Nostradamus further wrote, "**The triplicity of waters will give birth to a Man who will choose Thursday as His Holy Day. His voice, reign and power will rise across land and sea, amidst storms in the West" (1.50)**. Here the triplicity of waters means a place surrounded by waters (seas) on three sides. Puttaparthy, the place of Birth of Sathya Sai Baba and His abode Prasanthi Nilayam are both surrounded by three oceans namely, the Arabian Sea, the Indian Ocean and the Bay of Bengal. Also, Thursday is considered as the holy day by the Sai devotees all over the world. Still further, Nostradamus said, "**An occult mystic who will not be clergy but body, soul and spirit having all powers, everything under His feet, just as in His seat in the Heaven" (11.2)**. Nostradamus, finally declared, "**The earth and air will freeze so much water; when all will**

come to worship Him on Thursdays. What will be, was much so beautiful before. From all parts of the world they will come to honour Him. (X.71) "The sacred pomp will come to lower its wings because of the coming of the Great Law Giver. He will raise the humble and plaque the rebels. No one like Him will ever be born on Earth." Concluded Nostradamus.

According to the holy scriptures of the Hindus, human beings and other living beings take births or rebirths in accordance with the law of Karma (actions or deeds). However, the Avtaar (God's incarnations) do not take place like the human beings. Same is true of the divine messengers or prophets like Zoroaster, Jesus or Mohammed among others. Avtaar in all the previous aeons had chosen women of very high virtues to be their privileged mothers. In the Treth Yuga, Lord Vishnu took birth as Rama after identifying Koushalya – the first queen of King Dasseratha of Ayodhya, who took sweet pudding (payasam) which emerged out of the yagna fire performed by King Dasseratha. Likewise in the Dwapar Yuga, Lord Vishnu took prior permission from Devaki and Vasudev when they both were in Kansa's prison to be born from Devaki. In the Kaliyuga, Lord Shiva chose Devigiri Amma as His mother in His incarnation as Sai Baba of Shirdi. In the same way, both Lord Shiva and the Goddess Shakti selected Eswaramma as their noble mother to be born as Sathya Sai Baba. On being asked by the editor of a newspaper named Nav Kal published from Mumbai in 1970, from Sri Sathya Sai Baba, "**Since when are the Divine Powers being manifested in you? Instantaneously came the reply from Sai Baba, "From birth, in fact much before that. Before taking birth in Raju family in Puttaparthy, I was in Shirdi as Sai Baba and prior to that I was Krishna**". Likewise Baba was asked by a devotee – a scholar well-versed in the holy scriptures like Vedas and Upanishads; "Swami, Did you incarnate by entering the world directly (Pravesa) or through human conception (Prasava)?" Baba instead of answering the question Himself, requested His mother Eswaramma to answer the question herself. The mother Eswaramma said, "I had a dream in which an angel of God (Sathyanarayana Deva) told me not to be afraid if something should happen to me which depended on the will of God. That morning, while I was at the well to draw water, a great ball of blue light came rolling towards me. I lost consciousness and fell towards the ground, and thereafter I felt it entered my body". Baba smiled and told the scholar that He was not born through conception but through an entry – through a descent and not through contact.

In the twilight of the dawn of 23 November 1926, inside a mud house with a thatched roof in a remote village Puttaparthy near the banks of the rainy river Chitravati was born a child who came to be known as Sri Sathya Sai Baba. The name of the child at birth was Sathyanarayan Raju while Raju being his family surname. A wonder preceded this birth. As the mother Eswaramma was on the advanced stage of family way, she heard melodious sounds from the musical instruments kept in her house specially when there was nobody to play the instruments. Being surprised on these sounds, father Venkappa Raju consulted a local learned Brahmin scholar who interpreted these sounds as the indication of some auspicious signs for the future of the awaited child.

Mother Eswaramma started her puja of God Sathyanarayana on the night prior to the predicted day of the birth of the child and continued till late hours in the next morning when she felt the delivery pangs. At the same time, Eswaramma's mother-in-law was performing the same puja in a neighbour's house which she continued inspite of being informed about Eswaramma's critical condition. Having completed her puja, when the mother-in-law returned to her house and offered Prasad to Eswaramma who on eating the Prasad gave birth to a son. The child was named after the diety Sathyanarayana for the simple reason that the child was born at the end of prayers offered to Lord Sathyanarayana and that too when the mother had just finished eating the Prasad, Another miracle followed the birth of the baby. The women in the house were alarmed to see some movement under the cloth on which the baby was kept. As soon as they lifted the sheet, they found a deadly cobra beneath the baby which slipped away as quickly as it had come unseen without harming anybody. Yet another miraculous event happened. As mentioned earlier, in a faraway place called Pondicherry, now Pudducherry, that day after prolonged meditation, Maharishi Aurobindo surprised his devotees by announcing that God has descended on the earth. This was on 24 November 1926.

Sathyanarayana Raju, the child popularly addressed as Sathya, became popular with the villagers of Puttaparthy because of the special features of birth and subsequent events that took place after His birth. At the tender age of four or five years, the child Sathya used to feed the hungry even at the cost of He Himself remaining hungry. He used to live without meals for several days because he would distribute his own share of food to the needy and beggars. On being asked by the anxious mother as to why He was not eating food at home. Young Sathya would give vague answers by saying that He was taking food from an old generous man by whom He was invited for eating food with him. However, no such old man lived in the village. The mother, therefore, insisted on knowing the truth. Sathya promptly raised his tiny right hand palm and brought near the mother's nose to make her to smell the flavour of a just-eaten food. The palm did produce an excellent fragrance of ghee and milk which satisfied the mother and make her believe in what Sathya told her.

Soon after happened yet another incident of miracle. Once a few beggars were brought by Sathya to His house. He persuaded His sisters to distribute rice to them. When a last beggar received his share of rice, the family bowl of rice became almost empty. However, the sisters noticed that the bowl, instead of getting empty, was getting filled up mysteriously with the same quantity of rice as there was before. Sisters were confused to see this and were unable to realize the leela of young Sathya Sai. Indeed, Sathya's grandfather Kondama Raju was perhaps the first to realize the divinity in his grandson young Sathya Sai since the boy used to narrate various stories from the holy scriptures which were even beyond the capacity of the learned scholars, what to say of a young boy of Sathya's age. Sathya never liked the non-vegetarian food occasionally cooked at home. He, therefore, invariably stayed with his grandfather and cook vegetarian food for him since the death of his grandmother.

It was common phenomenon with young Sathya to materialize candy, toys, pencils, chalks and such other things for his young playmates while telling them that these articles were coming to him from some goddess. Nevertheless the boys used to believe him and adopted him as their 'Guru'. Sathya was admitted to an upper primary school at Bukkapatnam, about 5 kilometers away from Puttaparthy where he attracted the attention of several teachers because of his hidden divine powers, and also because of his devotional activities such as devotional songs (Bhajans), worshipping ways (Pujas) and Aarthis, before or after school hours. Sathya was considered as a mysterious boy vested with some divine powers. Once in his class, a teacher kept on giving dictation on a lesson which every student was taking down but Sathya was not writing anything. On being asked by the teacher why He was not taking down the dictation, Sathya replied that whatever the teacher was giving as dictation to the students, was already known to Him, and hence He did not feel the need of writing all that was being dictated. The teacher, however, did not like such a true answer and being provoked, he asked Sathya to stand on the bench as a punishment for not obeying his instructions. Very obediently, Sathya stood on the bench and remained standing on the bench till the ringing of the bell for the next period. At the end of the period, as soon as the teacher tried to get up from the chair, he was shocked to see that he was unable to get up as if his body got glued with the chair. Since the next period had begun, the next teacher entered the class. His name was Mehboob Khan. Coming closer to his colleague, he heard from him that he was not able to come out of the chair. Mehboob Khan saw Sathya standing on the bench and understood the whole thing. He told his teacher colleague to order Sathya to get down. As soon as the teacher did so and Sathya got down, the teacher was able to come out of the chair. This is an example of divine power of young Sathya.

Sathya continued to be incomprehensible and mysterious to the people including even his own family members. Singing verses from Sanskrit books, talking about moral values and giving lecturers on spirituality were some such activities among several others which convinced his father that the boy Sathya was under the influence of some supernatural forces. Once in the morning of May 23, 1940 when his father was out of house, young Sathya summoned all the inmates of his house. Waving his hand in air, he materialized sweets and flowers for them. Soon, villagers heard about this miracle and gathered around Sathya's house to watch His miracles. Out of nothing, He materialized bowls of rice cooked in milk. On hearing all this, Sathya's father returned. Reaching his house with a stick in his hand and unable to control his temper, the father shouted at the son Sathya; "What are you doing? Who are you? – a ghost or a god?" I am Sai Baba, replied Sathya, while maintaining his cool. People gathered there had never heard such a name like "Sai Baba". On being asked by a family member about Sai Baba, young Sathya said, "**Your Venkavadhoota prayed that I be born in your family**: **So I have come**". Venkavadhoota was a sage and believed to be a distant ancestor of the Raju family. This further added to the shrouded mystery about young Sathya. His father thought that since the name Sai Baba sounded like a Muslim name, the son Sathya was perhaps under the impact of a ghost of a Muslim Faqir called Sai Baba. Two opinions arose among the villagers that either Sathya was possessed by the spirit of some unknown dead Muslim by the name of Sai Baba or Sathya was an incarnation of a great Holy Man of that name. To clear the confusion, Sathya threw a handful of jasmine flowers to the ground. The flowers fell scattered but incredibly soon formed a shape of the letters 'SAI BABA' in Telungu. The villagers began to ponder whether young Sathya was the reincarnation of the Sai Baba of Shirdi – a name some of them had heard from somewhere.

Family members of Sathyanarayana Raju did not take seriously His declaration that He was reincarnation of Shirdi Sai Baba. Eventually,

Sathya was sent to a town Uravakonda in June 1940 to restart his studies in a high school under the guardianship of His elder brother Sheshma Raju. In Uravakonda, Sathya began a weekly 'Bhajan' session where he would sing bhajans (devotional songs) in praise of Shirdi Sai. Several persons including even the teachers of the school used to join these Bhajan sessions, even though they were not fully aware of the personality of Shirdi Sai. The brother Sheshma Raju, however, did not take it seriously what Sathya used to do or sing bhajans. In October 1940, He took Sathya along with others to a place Hospet to enjoy Dussehra festival where there was a temple of Virupaksha which was famous because of its architectural beauty and its history related to the Vijay Nagar empire of medieval Deccan known as Hampe. Seshma Raju and others went inside the temple but Sathya remained outside. A priest lighted a lamp so that the visitors could have darshan of the idol inside the sanctum sanctorum. There in place of the idol, they saw an image of Sathya standing with a smiling face. Puzzled and confused, they all came out of the temple where outside, they saw Sathya standing alone in a pensive mood. Thus, after seeing the mysterious image of Sathya in place of the idol inside the temple and Sathya himself standing outside the temple, the visitors were overcome by the feeling that perhaps Sathya was indeed a divine being in the human form as claimed by Him that He was reincarnation of Shirdi Sai Baba. The news of this incident spread far and wide. People started believing in what Sathya had been saying and they started gathering to offer prayers to Him not only in Hospet but also back in Urvakonda.

On 20 October 1940, the Wednesday, Sathya went to the school as usual, attended the morning prayers and thereafter He left the class. From school, He went straight to his brother Seshma Raju's residence where, after leaving His bag of books before His brother's wife declared to her, "**I am no longer your Sathya, I am Sai. I do not belong to you henceforth. I belong to my devotees.**" Thus, detached in this manner of the renunciates, Sathya walked fast towards a place outside the town, selected a secluded spot and sat there in a calm and meditative posture. He started singing a bhajan with first two lines

"Maanas Bhajre Guru Charnam,

Dooster Bhava Sagar Tarnam"

People who followed Him from the town gathered around Him and joined Him in singing the bhajan in chorus. Brother Seshma went running to the place. Sathya said to him, "Give up all your efforts to cure me. I am Sai. I do not consider myself related to you". People started pouring in and offered puja and prayers to Sathya thinking that He is now a renunciate. Sathya's shocked parents came from Puttaparthy to plead with Him to return home. "Who belongs to whom?" consoling his mother, Sathya left that place after three days. On 23 October 1940, the young boy Sathyanarayana Raju, at the age of 14 years, declared his reincarnation of Sai Baba of Shirdi who had left his earthly body in 1918 approximately eight years before the birth of Sathyanarayan on 23 November 1926. A remarkable incident took place on this momentous occasion. A photographer, after having heard Sathya's declaration, reached the place where Sathya was sitting. He wanted to take photograph of young Sathya Sai. While adjusting the focus of the camera, the photographer saw a big stone obstructing his focus and requested Sathya to move a little away from the stone. But his request went unheeded and thus having left with no choice, he clicked the camera to capture Sathya's face along with the stone. When the film was developed and printed, the photographer was amazed to see the picture of Shirdi Sai imprinted in front of Sathya Sai.

Sathya Sai left His home and started living at a small shelter in Puttaparthy. His divine declaration spread far and wide. People from various places started coming to Sathya Sai to have a glimpse (Darshan) of reincarnation of Shirdi Sai Baba. Some old and aged persons, who were devotees of Shirdi Sai Baba during His life time, starting coming to Sathya Sai – a fourteen year old boy who proclaimed Himself as the reincarnation of Shirdi Sai. Some of them believed while a few others were still skeptical. One such person was the then queen of a small princely state of Chincholi. Her husband, the late king of that state was a close devotee of Shirdi Sai. He used to go to Shirdi Sai frequently and on some occasions, even Shirdi Sai also visited the place of Chincholi. The queen, therefore, thought of going to Puttaparthy and see for herself the reincarnation of Shirdi Sai to discover the truth about the proclamation of young Sathya Sai. After reaching Puttaparthy, she invited Sathya Sai to her palace. After reaching the palace, Sathya Sai described the structure of the old palace and pointed out the changes made in it. Sathya Sai then enquired about a tree and a well which existed during the period of Shirdi Sai. An old employee of the palace confirmed existence of the tree and the well at the spot indicated by Sathya Sai. Both tree and well were destroyed during the renovation of the old palace. Subsequently Sathya Sai enquired about a small stone statue presented by Him as Shirdi Sai to the then king of the state. A thorough research of the stores of the palace brought out the statue. All this convinced the queen about the truth of the claim of Sathya Sai that He was indeed the reincarnation of Shirdi Sai. Not only this but also

Sathya's stories of the past lives of some other persons convinced the people about the divinity of Sathya Sai.

The open and candid declaration by young Sathya Sai about His previous incarnation as Shirdi Sai caused a sensation in the whole village of Puttaparthy and its surrounding areas. Baba in his previous incarnation as Shirdi Sai, had told Kaka Saheb Dixit in 1918 that he would re-appear after 8 years. When the nephew of Kaka Saheb came to Prasanthi Nilayam for the holy Darshans, Baba at once recognized him as he was a frequent visitor of Dwarakamayi at Shirdi accompanying his uncle Kake Saheb. Baba called him to His side and told him that He had come exactly as He had assured his uncle 8 years after His taking samadhi there at Shirdi. Baba further told him that He is the continuation of the same Sai of Shirdi. Baba also told many other facts of the life of the previous Sai. He described Shirdi and the surrounding areas as well as the devotees who used to come to Shirdi not only Dwarakamayi but also the Margosa tree, the Puti mandir etc.

Thus, young Sathya Sai came to be acknowledged as the divine being, the expedient of all knowledge, the self-enlightened, self-inspired, a supreme one who was born divine and who appeared as incarnation of God endowed with absolute infinite powers. The faith in Sathya Sai as incarnation of God continued growing gradually. His miracles started attracting the people from far off areas of the country. As a result, this Sai phenomenon spread even outside India and the devotees from the whole world started coming to Puttaparthy for Sai Darshan. The news media such as the newspapers, magazines and several other publications published the stories of the miracles of Sathya Sai Baba. Popularity of young Sathya Sai generated a lot of jealousy in the minds of some malicious persons who tried to make attempts on his life in various ways including mixing of poison in his food. This alarmed his older brother Seshma Raju who wrote young Sathya Sai to give up his miracles and return to school to continue his studies. By that time Sathya Sai was twenty one years old and he wrote back to Seshma Raju the following letter:

> "My dear one! I received the communication that your wrote and sent; I found in it the surging floods of your devotion and affection, with the undercurrents of doubts and anxiety. Let Me tell you that it is impossible to plum the hearts and discover the natures of Jananis, Yogis, ascetics, saints, sages and the like. People are endowed with a variety of characteristics and mental attitudes; so, each one judges according to his own angle, talks and argues in the light of his own nature. But we have to stick

to our own right path, our own wisdom, our own resolution without getting affected by popular appraisal. As the proverb says, it is only the fruit-laden tree that receives the shower of stones from passers by. The good always provoke the bad into calumny; the bad always provoke the good into derision. This is the nature of this world. One must be surprised if such things do not happen.

The people too have to be pitied, rather than condemned. They do not know. They have no patience to judge a right. They are too full of lust, anger and conceit to see clearly and know fully. So, they write all manner of things. If they only know, they would not talk or write like that. We, too, should not attach any value to such comments and take them to heart, as you seem to do. Truth will certainly triumph some day. Untruth can never win. Untruth might appear to overpower Truth, but its victory will fade away and Truth will establish itself.

It is not the way of the great to swell when people offer worship, and shrink when people scoff. As a matter of fact, no sacred text lays down rules to regulate the lives of the great, prescribing the habits and attitudes that they must adopt. They themselves know the path they must tread; their wisdom regulates and makes their acts holy. Self-reliance, beneficial activities – these two are their special marks. They may also be engaged in the promotion of the welfare of devotees and in allotting them the fruits of their actions. Why should you be affected by tangle and worry, so long as I am adhering to these two? After all, the praise and blame of the populace do not touch the *Atma*, the reality: they can touch only the outer physical frame.

I have a 'Task': To foster all mankind and ensure all of them live full of *Ananda*. I have a 'Vow': To lead all who stay away from the straight path, again into goodness and save them. I am attached to a 'Work' that I love: To remove the sufferings of the poor and grant them what they lack. I have a 'reason to be proud', for, I rescue all who worship and adore Me, I have My definition of the 'Devotion" I expect: Those devoted to Me have to treat joy and grief, gain and loss, with equal fortitude. This means that I will never give up those who attach themselves to Me. When I am thus engaged in My beneficial task, how can My Name be ever tarnished, as you apprehend?.

I will not give up My mission, nor My determination. I know I will carry them out; I treat the honour and dishonour, the fame and blame that may be the consequence with equal equanimity. Internally, I am unconcerned. I act but in the outer world; I talk and move about, for the sake of the outer world and for announcing My coming to the people; else, I have no concern even with these.

I do not belong to any place; I am not attached to any name. I have no 'mine' or 'thine'. I answer whatever the name you use. I go, wherever I am taken. This is my Very First Vow. I have not disclosed this to anyone so far. For me the world is something afar, apart. I act and move only for the sake of mankind. **None one can comprehend My Glory, whoever he is, whatever his method of enquiry, however long his attempt**.

"You can yourself see the full Glory in the coming years. Devotees must have patience and forbearance..."

The letter speaks for itself. The saviours before Sathya Sai had all suffered denunciation from beginning to end of their lives. Attempts were made on the lives of Zoroaster and Buddha. Jesus suffered crucifixion. Yet, to the end, they stood firm on their respective grounds. Ultimately they did triumph and the Truth prevailed.

Soon the Sathya Sai phenomenon came to the knowledge of the countries outside India. The Sai phenomenon thereafter got transformed into a global debate. Observers, inquirers and skeptics from the continents of Europe and America made their way to remote Puttaparthy for a direct experience of the phenomenon. Soon there arrived scientists of all disciplines, researchers, fellows of learning bodies, and members of university faculties. These men and women were no devotees, they were analysers. Surprisingly enough, many of them who came to scoff, stayed on to pray. The results of their findings surprised their countrymen. Thousands upon thousands from across countries and continents made pilgrimage to Puttaparthy round the year.

Miracles did not cease. The message of Sathya Sai reached hundreds of thousands. Year after year and decade after decade, the abode of Sathya Sai looked like a spiritual centre of the whole world. To myriads of men, He was the Revealed One, the Incarnation, the God in human form. By the last decade of the twentieth century the Sai message reached millions and millions of people consisting of Hindus, Buddhists, Jains, Zoroastrians and Christians who stood together to represent a single fraternity of His. What the young Sathya Sai predicted to his brother Seshma many years ago – "You can yourself see the full Glory in the coming years" – proved true.

Sathya Sai Baba have been showing miracles every day since His birth but more openly after declaration of His incarnation. His miracles have been seen by millions and millions of people from all countries, all races and all religions. This phenomenon continued till date. His miracles have been elaborately documented in several books written about Him. There has been an avalanche of literature of the authors' experiences (including the author of this book) with Baba which invariably include a series of miracles related to their personal lives. These miracles are sufficient to convince the devotees about the Omni-presence, Omni-potence and Omni-scient of Sri Sathya Sai Baba. No doubt, miracles have been shown by many other divine personalities and divine beings, like Zoroaster, Budha, Jesus, Mohammed and Nanak among several others (also stated in Chapter 5 of this sequel), but all those divine beings never claimed themselves as God. They have always been claiming to receive their divine powers from some supreme power called God. However, in the case of the Sai phenomenon, whether in the form of earlier Shirdi Sai Baba or the later Sri Sathya Sai Baba, a clear proclamation has been invariably made that they are incarnations of God Themselves like the earlier incarnations of Rama or Krishna. In a sense, the experience has been as if God Himself has been moving among the people and talking with them whether as Shirdi Sai or Sathya Sai. Indeed, rightly, Sri Sathya Sai Baba's divine power demonstrated by Him through miracles and in various other ways have been natural in as much as a sufficient proof of His Omni-presence, Omni-potence and Omni scient.

What Sri Sathya Sai Baba did is quite a different act of creation which is neither magic nor siddhi power either. He did so not because of any desire of demonstration or exhibition of His powers but in His case it has been a kind of communication with people to convince them of a divine power's love and care for them. Sathya Sai Baba would give, through these miracles, people a sense of security and protection they needed in time of distress. The miracles would create a symbolic link of the devotees with their Sai God covering long distance between them. As and when the devotees needed Sai Baba, these objects would get materialized by Baba for them, flash the message as if by wireless or by SMS and He instantly would come to their rescue. There have been several such instances about which hundreds of books have been published.

Sri Sathya Sai Baba would create some objects in just the same way as He created the Universe while several other objects are brought from their places where they were. There were no visible messengers to carry out His orders to bring things but it is because of His divine will (Sankalpa) that would create or bring the objects in a moment. Indeed,

Sri Sathya Sai Baba has been the Omni-present, Omni-potent and Omni-scient phenomenon. Various miracles shown by Him have been nicely and rightly classified under the categories of materialization, transformation, healing, rescuing and helping devotees in danger or trouble, revelation of other bodily forms as divine or ordinary human beings, and appearing in devotees' dreams. This book is a testimony of one such dream given to the author.

Materialization of the objects like vibhuti (holy ash), nectar (honey) on the photographs of Sai Baba and various other deities in the far distant worship places in the houses of thousands and thousands of devotees has been a common sight. Various objects like sugar candy, fruits, watches, rings (a diamond-studded ring for the author also), necklaces, portraits, photographs, precious stones, gold chains, gold or diamonds ear tops, lockets, pendants, lingams, crucifixes, cameras, metal containers full of vibhuti, religious relics, and recovery of (gifts presented by Baba earlier) lost by the devotees and several other objects have been materialized by Baba by waving His right hand in a circular motion in the clock-wise direction. Materialization of vibhuti for Abhishekam, creation of lingam from His mouth on the festival day of Shivaratri, resurrection of persons supposed to be clinically dead and healing of patients suffering from the dreaded disease such as cancer have been some of the most prominent miracles among several others shown by Sri Sathya Sai Baba.

Vibhuti, the term used for the sacred ash materialized by Baba and given to the devotees is a sign of His grace. It heals and purifies the devotees. The ego of a devotee gets burnt by the fire of divine illumination. It equally conveys the basis spiritual message that everything is bound to get reduced to ashes. Vibhuti, according to Baba, burns the desire and lust. It is symbolic of the life-death cycle in which everything ultimately reduces to ash. Baba once said, "**After Shiva had burnt the god of desire, Kama, into a heap of ashes, He adorned Himself with the ash to shine as the conqueror of desire**". Appearance of Vibhuti on the photographs or pictures placed in the devotee's homes at far off places is still a common phenomenon.

Long back, Vibhuti Abhisheka was an annual feature on the morning of the auspicious day of Shivaratri, to honour Shirdi Sai Baba. A silver statue of Shirdi Baba used to be placed on the platform. First, Sri Sathya Sai Baba would materialize precious stones and grains of rice, and pour them into a sacred fire burning in a container kept nearby for the purpose. Then Baba would bless a vessel containing water and then used its water to give a bath to the statue of Shirdi Baba. Next, He would take a long whisk, dip it into the water and sprinkle it on the heads of the devotees gathered around. Baba would walk out to sprinkle the showers of this water on all the devotees. Thereafter, a person would hold an empty urn inverted over the statue of Shirdi Baba. Baba would roll up the sleeve from the right arm and thrust it into the upturned urn and start moving His hand in a churning motion. Immediately, vibhuti would start showering on the statue of Shirdi Baba from all sides. It would stop the moment Baba would bring His arm out of the urn, but would start showering again, the moment He would thrust His left arm and restart the churning process. This process used to continue till the status of Shirdi Baba would get completely covered with vibhuti. This ceremony sometimes used to take place even on the occasion of Dussehra festival. This annual feature was stopped long before.

Another spectacular miracle of Sri Sathya Sai Baba is related to the annual production of an oval/ellipsoid shape **'Shiva Lingam'** on the occasion of **Mahashivratri**: The lingam is the symbolic representation of Shiva-Shakti. Worship of lingam is considered to be the highest form of prayer. In every Shiva temple, a Lingam is always placed in the inner sanctum. The Lingam signifies the Omni-presence, Omni-potence and Omni-scient of God. This is the symbol of the beginning as well as the end of everything since everything emerges from it and gets subsumed in it. The Lingam that emerges from the Para-Brahmn – the Universal Absolute, is the whole cosmos first conceived as a wish, later taking the shape of an idea and eventually it is adopted as a will. The cosmos is the concretized Will of Shiva. The Lingam is ellipsoid in shape with two centers, emerging out from one and merging in the other. This is the symbol of duality – one coming out and the other going back into the one being the source, sustenance – the basis of the two. That is why the Linga is considered as the Universal Symbol of God which is the Form emanating from the Formless. The Lingam creates itself in God and God creates Himself in the Lingam. The Lingam, therefore, the basis of all creation as "OM", is the basic sound. Thus, the Lingam is considered to be highest object of worship. It brings the worshippers in rapport with the Supreme Reality. How it does, remains a mystery which can be explored through one's inner realization.

Sri Sathya Sai Baba has been materializing Lingams of stone, gold and crystal. Quite often there has been an inner light in some Lingams that would glow and change colours. It is generally around Shivratri, the Lingam would start its formation in the stomach of Baba during the week preceding the holy day. A broad aura of dazzling white border would envelop Him wherever He is and Swami even sometimes would indicate the formation of Lingam. Baba has said on certain occasions that He finds it difficult to postpone or prevent the formation of Lingams within His body. After making a round of giving 'Darshans' to devotees, as soon as Baba would give His discourse, and just after the discourse or sometimes during the discourse, some physical changes would become visible on Baba's face.

After taking a few glasses of water, the Lingam would come out of His mouth. Sometimes more than one Lingam is formed. It is mentioned in the relevant literature that sometimes, there have been two or three or more Lingams. In 1970, Baba stopped the public viewing of the materialization of Lingam and in fact, up to 1973, the viewing of Lingam materialization was confined to some limited number of close devotees. In 1974, Baba resumed the public viewing of the Lingam materialization but in 1977, this practice was stopped again. However, after 22 years, in 1999, Lingam materialization again started which has been finally stopped since 2007. After the Lingam materialization in 1999, Baba made a historic declaration during His discourse. **"You have had the good fortune of looking at the Divine Vision. You have also seen the Divine significance of the Lingam, and that will grant you complete salvation. So far as you are concerned, you have attained complete salvation and there are no more rebirths for you – ... What you have really seen is the secret of creation.—Having witnessed the secret of creation, do not spend your time in an unsacred manner; do not do work that will be called unsacred; do not promote ideas that will be called unsacred and do not look at things which will be called unsacred vision"**. In 1999, on Mahashivratri Day, when Baba materialized a Shiva Lingam, He announced that all those who witnessed the event would be granted the boon of Moksha (liberation). The author himself witnessed this event on two occasions. This Lingam, as told by Baba Himself, is the Cosmic Egg symbol, the ellipsoid which the breath of God inflates and deflates. Baba has been materializing this Lingam with a view to enable the devotees to visualize the power that projected the Universe and to raise thereby their conscience level.

The literature on Sri Sathya Sai Baba is full of such miracles and many more described in an innumerable number of books and articles. The healing miracles performed by Baba are well-known in curing people, including even the non-devotees, of several dreaded diseases like cancer, heart disease, Parkinson, ulcer, epilepsy; gifting eyesight to the blind, making the lame to walk; taking upon Himself the illness of His devotees; and resurrecting the dead. Several examples in this context may be seen in various books on Sai literature. The author himself has been kept alive by the grace of Bhagwan Sri Sathya Sai Baba through various ways such as materialization of vibhuti postponing his angiography for a long time at one occasion, materializing of vibhuti tin full of vibhuti and refilling it by a puff from His divine mouth at another occasion and finally putting His divine hand on his heart. It is not possible to illustrate all the examples in this book for the obvious reasons that the book has a specific theme. Yet a few examples are highlighted which are most relevant to the theme of this book: one is about Baba's taking over a paralytic attack of a devotee on His own body while declaring, thereby, His real form as Shiv-Shakti Swarupa; and the others related to the resurrection of persons who were clinically declared dead by the doctors or saving the lives of persons who were unaware of Sai Baba.

On one Friday, 28 June 1963, Baba asked Prof. Kasturi, His close devotee and secretary, in the afternoon Darshan to announce that from tomorrow onwards, there would be no darshan and interviews for a week. Neither Prof. Kasturi nor anyone else understood or conjectured the reason for this sudden announcement. Neither anybody could gather the courage to ask Baba the reason of this announcement. Next day on 29 June 1963, at 6.30 in the morning, Baba suddenly fell unconscious. The devotees around Him, initially thought that perhaps Baba had gone into a trance while travelling in His subtle body to give the badly needed relief to some far distant devotees. The devotees were used to this kind of miracle Baba had been doing in the past. These trances known to some devotees had been over after a few hours during which Baba would remain unconscious. But after some time (a few hours say) Baba would come back to his real form. This time, however, it did not happen so and the devotees got apprehensive and started arranging some medical aid for Baba. To a doctor, it appeared to be an attack of tuberculosis meningitis, with possible tuberculoma while according to some other doctor, it could be a cerebral thrombosis or stroke. When efforts were made to give some treatment through an injection, Baba gained some consciousness and refused any treatment by saying that the trouble would pass off during the period of next five days. Four severe heart attacks occurred during these five days. Baba's left side got paralysed and became stiff and insensitive. The sight of His left eye and speech got also badly affected.

Exactly after five days of the attack on 4 July 1963, Baba's condition improved sufficiently so that he could announce that the clot in His brain had been dissolved and that there would be no more attacks. Yet, the left side of His body was still paralysed and also His voice was feeble. Baba, however, during those five horrible days had indicated that one of His devotees at a far off place was about to be attacked by a stroke and heart attack so severely that he would not survive. Thus, Baba had taken the disease of His devotee on Himself with all the symptoms of paralysis, heart attack, partial loss of eyesight of the left eye, numbness etc. The devotees understood the whole thing and felt a sigh of relief. Subsequently, in the evening of Guru Poornima Day, 6 July 1963, Baba was virtually carried by the devotees from His bedroom to the crowded prayer hall. The left side of His body was still in the paralytic condition. His speech was still feeble. For a few minutes, Baba sat in the chair on the dais of the prayer hall occupied by more than five thousand people. Slowly Baba gestured for water, drank a few drops and then dipping His right hand in the water. Sprinkled a few drops on His left side and leg. Next He stroke His left hand with His right hand and same with His left leg. In a few seconds, Baba's leg, eye and whole the left side of His body started getting normal. Within a few more seconds, Baba rose from His chair and began His Guru Poornima discourse in the same normal melodious voice. People felt cheerful and got excited with happiness. Baba was on His feet for an hour and gave the Guru Poornima discourse as if nothing had happened before.

During this discourse (Kasturi), after describing the origin and reason of His ailment, Baba disclosed the most awe-inspiring and amazing secret about His incarnation as Shiva-Shakti Swarupa described earlier in the beginning of this chapter. Baba told that many centuries ago, there was a sage named Bhardwaj who was a diligent scholar of Vedas seeking to have a mastery of all the Vedas for which he was given extension of life by Lord Indra several times so as to enable him to complete the study of Vedas. Eventually, Lord Indra had to tell him that the Vedas were countless and their study could never be completed. Thus, Lord Indra initiated the sage to perform a Yagna which would give him the realization and satisfaction that he expected from Vedic studies. Indra pointed out to three mountain peaks to the sage and asked him to take handfuls of earth from each as a vast accomplishment of the study of Vedas. At the same time the sage Bhardwaj decided to perform the Savithra Yagna, as advised by Lord Indra. He went to Kailash to pray to Sakthi for Her presence at Yagamantapa, for She is the Diety of Spiritual Sakthi. Here Baba interpreted the Yuga as the state of individual spiritual purity in the sense that one can be in Kaliyuga even while being in the previous Yugas of time. What Baba meant was that Kailash is a point in spiritual Sadhana, the moment of Supreme Bliss. Thus, Bharadwaj, by his Dhayana and Dharana entered the state of

Samadhi where he tried to contact the Prakriti aspect of the Universe, the Sakthi aspect, the Core of the Energy – the secret of the Atom, of the sun and of the entire Universe.

For full eight days, the sage Bhardwaj continued visualizing only Siva – not Sakthi, the Prakrithi Principle, though both Siva and Sakthi are inseparable. He saw Siva in the Thandava dance immersed in the thrill of creation, preservation and dissolution, the dance with one step as evolution and the next step as involution. Indeed, Siva and Sakthi were both doing Thandava Dance, although Sakthi was not visible to the Sage Bhardwaj. Thus Bhardwaj got disappointed and depressed Siva warned Sakthi about the consequences of her disregarding the yearning of the sage, for even She had a responsibility to fulfil. Thereafter, Sakthi appeared and became visible to the Sage Bhardwaj. But She just smiled and continued with the Cosmic dance. The sage became utterly desperate and turned to descend to his normal abode. But since, he had turned away from the smile of Sakthi, he got cursed due to which his limbs would not move, he lost his voice and half his vision. Seeing this, Siva took pity on the Sage and revived him by sprinkling water from His Kamandalu because of which the Sage became normal and was able to ascend again towards the Kailasa Stage of Samadhi. Eventually, then both Siva and Sakthi gave him their Beatific Vision and assured the sage that they both would be present at the time of sacrifice *i.e.* completion of the Yagna. Thus, when the Yagna was over, both Siva and Sakthi appeared before Sage Bhardwaj and blessed him by telling him that they would both take human form and come on the earth, three times, all in the lineage of Bhardwaj Gothra. Siva alone will be born first as Shirdi Sai Baba, the Siva-Sakthi together as Sri Sathya Sai Baba and later, Sakthi alone will take the human form as Prema Sai Baba. Thus, Sri Sathya Sai Baba is Siva-Sakthi Swarupam. Siva said to the Sage, **"Sakthi made you suffer for eight days, she gave you Darshan and even then, you suffered so much disappointment that your limbs were benumbed and your voice failed and your vision – half of it – was lost. When both of us take human birth in your lineage, as Siva-Sakthi, this Sakthi will suffer for eight days, as you suffered now and at the end of the period, I will sprinkle water and revive her as I did to you"**.

Thus, Baba said to His devotees that the destined event had to happen and to save also a good person's life. Indeed, this miracle had to wait until a good person was to receive the stroke. Thus Siva had to revive Sakthi and put an end to the suffering. It is because of this background that Baba sprinkled water with His right hand (Right Half representing Siva) and stroked the left hand and leg (The Left Half representing Sakthi). Baba revealed that Sakthi had to undergo the penance and pains for eight days and that period ended only at 6.30 A.M. July 6, 1963 counting from Saturday, 29th June 1963. Thereafter Baba became normal as before.

A number of cases of resurrections has been documented again to date in which Sri Sathya Sai Baba brought the dead persons to life namely: Mr. V. Radhakrishna, Walter Cowen, Mr. Charles Penn, an unnamed lady and Brigadier Bose, among others. Three most prominent cases are described here as follows:

- One Mr. Radhakrishna of Kuppam was in Puttaparthy in 1953 for the Dussehra festival. He was suffering from severe gastric ulcers. While in Puttaparthy, the disease became acute, he went into coma. Baba was informed about it. However, Baba told his wife not to worry. On the following day, pulse of Radhakrishna stopped and his body became cold blue and stiff. He was clinically dead. The body remained unchanged even till third day morning and began to smell. When Mrs. Radhakrishna went to see Baba, she was told not to worry. After some time, Baba came to the room where dead body of Radhakrishna was placed. Baba stayed alone with the dead body of Radhakrishna for a few minutes. Thereafter, when Baba opened the door, Mrs. Radhakrishna found her husband looking up and smiling. Not only Radhakrishna got new life but his gastric ulcer also got vanished. After seven years of his resurrection by Baba, Mr. Radhakrishna was again in pain. He was given morphine because of which the pain subsided but he developed sleep-walking. Consequently he sleep-walked and fell twenty feet down a well which had water up to thirty feet. During that night, the family came out looking for him and pulled him out. Next day, he reached Puttaparthy where Baba called him and told him, "My shoulders are aching with holding you up so long last night".
- The case of an American devotee, Walter Cowen happened on the Christmas Day December 25, 1971. While staying with his wife in a hotel named Connemara Hotel in Chennai (then called Madras), Mr. Cowen collapsed due to a heart attack. He was taken to a nearby hospital, where he was examined and declared brought dead. At that time Baba was also in Chennai where Cowen and Hislop families had come for participation in the All India Conference of Sai Organizations. Mrs. Cowen went to see Baba who told her that he would come to the hospital. When next morning Mrs. Cowen reached the hospital, she was told that

Baba had come, seen Cowen and gone back. To her amazement and equally with great happiness, She saw her husband alive and being looked after by the hospital staff. Moreover to her utter surprise, the ailments Cowen had been suffering, also had vanished. After a few days later, Cowen was reported to have told about his experience with death. Shortly after his death, Cowen remained in the subtle form near his physical body in the ambulance. At that time Swami came and took him to a large room, somewhere in the heavenly world before a panel of judges. There Cowen was shown many of his past lives. He was shown a great person of high importance and he had always been working for the welfare of humankind. Thereafter, Swami told the panel of judges that He was taking Cowen back to the Earth because some work was yet to be done by him. Cowen died after eighteen months at his home. Later Swami told Mrs. Cowen that He wanted to save her from the pain and botheration of taking the dead body of Cowen to her hometown for it was better for him to die in his own country.

- The third case is related to Brigadier S.K. Bose with whom the author had good rapport as a verandah friend (sitting in the verandah of the Prasanthi Mandir). Prior to his acquaintance with Brig. Bose, the author had heard the resurrection story of Bose. It happened on 20 October 1988 – the Vijaydashmi (Dussehra) day at ten in the morning in the Poornachandra Auditorium at Prashanthi Nilayam, when the poornahuti, the final offering was performed by Baba. Soon after this, Baba started His discourse. Brig. Bose was sitting in a chair where several other elderly devotees were sitting in a row of chairs. Prior to coming to the Poornachandra Auditorium, Brig. Bose had been suffering from high fever but he became alright on that day. While Baba's discourse was going on, a sudden commotion took place on the right side of the stage. Brig. Bose had trapped onto the floor and two devotees were making him lie down comfortably. Two doctors rushed to this place and examined Brig. Bose. In the meantime, Swami stopped His discourse abruptly and came towards Brig. Bose. Swami made some gestures with His both hands as if He was driving away something hovering around the body of Brig. Bose. The doctors attending Brig. Bose indicated to Swami signaling the death of Brig. Bose. Swami bent down, lifted the shoulder of Brig. Bose and gave a pat on the back of his right shoulder with His right hand saying, "Bose, get up", who at once opened his eyes. As soon as Brig. Bose saw Swami, he folded his hands and sat up. The two doctors were amazed to see this. Swami again patted Brig. Bose on his left shoulder and directed him to stand up and said to him, "Go up the steps of the stage and sit near the window; you will get some fresh air". Brig. Bose gently climbed up the steps and sat near the window. Later Brig. Bose reported to have told what he saw in the subtle form. He said, "I saw my lifeless body lying on the ground. Sai Baba came and looked at my dead body. He made some gestures in the air with His both hands as if He was driving away something hovering over my head. When I looked up, I saw a huge bird, a few feet above. The majestic bird was golden brown in colour with streak of white at its neck. It was looking at me kindly. Suddenly the bird disappeared as Bhagwan (Sai Baba) approached my body. I could clearly see Dr. Chari and Dr. Patel rushing to the body and examining it meticulously. An American devotee Mr. Richards was also near the body. I saw Dr. Patel signalling to Swami that there was no trace of life in the body. Next, I heard Swami's commanding voice, "Bose get up". I at once opened my eyes and sat up with folded hands. His pat on my right shoulder instilled great energy in me. He commanded me, "stand up, go up the steps of the stage and sit near the window". I obeyed Him and went to the stage. Bhagwan walked back to the stage and resumed his discourse. I had felt no agony or pain while dying; it was very peaceful! Swami brought me back to life!" Brigadier Bose lived for another twelve years after his resurrection and did lot of construction work in Prashanti Nilayam including building of the Sarva-Dharm Samaikya Stupa, the pillar symbolizing the unity of all religions of the world, in the commemoration of the 50th birth day celebrations of Bhagwan Sri Sathya Sai Baba.

A very large number of devotees have had experience of being helped, rescued or saved from some serious trouble or dangerous incident or in some other personal situation. Baba has Himself declared more than once that He will help or rescue a devotee as well as others including even the non-devotees as soon as they call me or call God by any other name. There have been several such instances of resurrections and experiences of persons being rescued from death by Baba, both devotees and those who had never heard of Baba. When rescued those persons who were not aware of Baba, the purpose seemed to be to summon their spiritual upliftment or spiritual guidance.

Once, flying a small plane over the mountains of Sierra Nevada, one Mr. Al. Drucker was caught in a violent storm. Continuously struggling for two hours, he tried to save the plane. His companion had become unconscious and was lying in that state in the plane. Having failed in all his rescue attempts, Drucker called out to God for help, while surrendering Himself to His will. Immediately, a voice over his radio came and guided him to a nearby airport named Reno Airport while at the same time the plane was running out of fuel. In the meantime, his companion regained the consciousness. Both Drucker and his companion landed safely at the Reno Airport. Thereafter the control tower incharge asked Drucker how he was able to get there. Drucker replied that a ground controller guided me to the airport who saw me in trouble through a radar. The tower man was surprised and told Drucker that the area he was flying over was a reserved area for American Indians (Red Indians) – a wilderness area and there was nothing up to 200 miles from the airport with no ground stations, no controllers, no radars whatsoever. Both Drucker and his companions were equally surprised. Soon after, they travelled towards Mexico and went to a yoga centre run by one Indira Devi. Sai Bhajans were being sung there. There he saw the picture of Sri Sathya Sai Baba. Drucker become emotional on looking at the picture of Sai Baba and somehow felt from inside the heart that He was the person who guided him to airport on that night when he was caught in the storm while flying his plane.

On receiving full information about Sathya Sai Baba, Drucker straightaway flew to India and reached Prashanthi Nilayam. At the Ashram he was made to share a room with an elderly Indian who told him his own miraculous rescue story. The man was a State Government official, a friend and follower of Mahatma Gandhi. He told Drucker that once while driving along a narrow hilly road with his wife, he had to swerve to avoid another car. While doing so, his own car got off the track and fell into a several hundred feet deep ditch. Before losing consciousness, he heard his wife calling out 'Rama', 'Rama'. When they regained consciousness, they were both unhurt but the car was a complete wreckage. A few months later, by chance, the officer came across a crowd gathered somewhere to see Baba. A devotee approached him and told him to sit in the front row as directed by Sai Baba. When Baba appeared for Darshan, He came up straight to the man. "Ah! You have come. You must thank your wife for your life. If she hadn't called me, you would now be dead. I pulled you both out of that car and made you sit on the ground unharmed, even though you did not think of me once. But I have saved your life many times before without you even knowing it. Do you remember the Air Raid Warden?" This man, as a student in London in 1940, had been ordered by an air-raid warden to leave his room so as to get into a shelter before the house, where he was living, had a direct hit. He assumed the warden might have been killed.

Once Phyllis Krystal – an ardent devotee of Baba, was flying to London along with her husband after their second visit to see Baba. The place stopped at Beirut and soon afterwards, the plane was hijacked by some Arab terrorists on a suicide mission. Phyllis silently called Swami for help, with Baba's gifts in her lap. She received a clear message from Baba to send love to the ferocious terrorists. She was unable to do it and requested Baba to do it through her. Immediately, the hijacker became nervous and suddenly their mind changed. Finally, they directed the plane to reach Amsterdam Airport. The passengers were allowed to disembark the plane. Soon after the plane went into flames but Phyllis and her husband were safe although badly hurt due to the stampede caused by rushing out of the passengers.

Revelation of divine forms as other body forms is yet another miracle which Swami showed to several devotees, particularly those who have been very close to Him. In some cases, such a divine revelation has been captured in a camera also. Sai Baba chooses a particular form suitable to the '"Isht Dev" or particular divine form in a diety is worshiped by a devotee to demonstrate to the devotee that God can take any form, yet it is the one and only one God. Once, a devotee clicked his camera to capture Swami's real form. When the Polaroid photograph was taken out, everyone present there was astonished to see on the photograph, the form of Lord Dattatraya – the Trinity, the composite divine form of Brahma, Vishnu and Mahesh. Thereafter, Baba told the devotees, **"Because I am with you in this human form, I move about among you as one of you. You, therefore, do not understand Me nor do you realize that I am Dattatriya amidst you"**. The same Dattatriya form was shown to late Col. Jagarao and his wife once at a picnic stop. Further for the understanding of Mrs. Jogarao, Swami waved his hand and produced a photograph of Himself in the chariot of Lord Subramanian with a cobra circled around Him.

Once, when Baba and Mr. Kasturi were alone in a room and talking about Shiva Shakti aspect, Baba said, "Kasturi look at me" Kasturi related that as he looked up, what he saw was startling and deeply moving. Instead of Swami's familiar appearance, he saw Nandi the bull (Shiva's vehicle), upon which sat Shiva on one side and Shakti on the other in a characteristic pose. The vision remained before his eyes for a few seconds and then melted back into Baba in his usual form. Late Prof.

S.N. Saraf, the second vice-chancellor of Sri Sathya Sai University (then known as Sri Sathya Sai Institute of Higher Learning) related to the author, his personal experience of Swami's divinity. It was the day of the annual function of sports being held at the University's stadium. Like every year, 'Prasad' was distributed to all present there and everybody was eating Prasad of dry fruits. Sawmi, as usual, was not eating anything. Prof. Saraf offered some dry fruits to Swami but Swami ignored it. After some time, as it was getting hot, Prof. Saraf requested Swami to take at least a few sips of water. As soon as Prof. Saraf offered water, Swami turned his eyes towards him. Prof. Saraf was startled to have a glimpse of several rivers and oceans in Sawmi's eyes. Once Swami, while talking to His students, revealed a divine secret and said, **"Lord Sriman Narayan has come down to this earth in human form as Sathya Sai. Understand and accept this fact. Like Lord Rama's and Lord Krishna's, this too is a Poorna Avathar. Great sages and spiritual preceptors were sent here from time to time by the divine power. But here you see the very incarnation of the Universal Absolute on earth"**.

Prof. Erlendur Haraldsson, an eminent scholar and a great psycho-scientist in the field of Medical Science, came to Prasanthi Nilayam, not as a spiritual seeker but as a hard-core scientist to explore the physio-pscho phenomenon identified with Sri Sathya Sai Baba. He also brought with him a team of other scientists to conduct a thorough research of the Sai Phenomenon. The central aim of this team was to prepare an investigative report on the Sathya Sai Phenomenon. Prof. Haraldsson had earlier heard about the miracles of Shri Sathya Sai Baba in 1972 and therefore, the investigative curiosity brought him to India earlier several times *viz.* in 1975, 1976 and 1983 with a project to study the Sai phenomenon. At the end of his long research pursuits, Haraldsson published his famous book "Miracles Are My visiting Cards". Being a research monograph, this book goes a long way to meet the need of spiritual seekers who are particularly interested in the Sai phenomenon of Sri Sathya Sai Baba. In an interview with Haraldsson and his colleague Karlis Osis, Baba, by waving his hand, as usual, materialized a shining golden ring (which He put on Osis' finger and which fitted well) with a big coloured picture of Baba on a stone. While praising the achievements of science, Baba told them that methods of science could never explain the mystery of the Sai Phenomenon. Baba, explained the need of both the mundane and the spiritual life going together in a harmonious way like a 'double Rudraksha' materialized by Baba which looked like a twin orange or a twin apple. Baba gave that Rudraksha to Haraldsson. Both the scientists were stunned into silence. In another interview, sitting closer to Baba, both the scientists saw most attentively.

Baba, as usual, waved His hand, closed His fist and opened it. This time it was a big necklace, 32 inches long, 16 inches each side, studded with nine types of stones, arranged in nine groups, each interspaced by a gold bead, and with a picture of Sai Baba set in a golden rosette frame an inch and half in diameter. The necklace was given to a lady devotee. The two scientists concluded that the necklace was too big to be hidden in a man's fist, and that it came from nowhere in a material sense. Both the scientists came again and again, and every time they were puzzled to see the strange phenomenon of Sri Sathya Sai. They asked Baba how was He able to produce such objects. Baba told them "The ability comes from the superconscious". Studying the phenomenon in all logical ways, the two scientists felt convinced that the Sai Phenomenon, as demonstrated by Sathya Sai, was beyond the range of scientific comprehension. No amount of investigative efforts could lead them to anywhere near the Sai Phenomenon, as demonstrated by Sai Baba, through His divine power.

Appearance of Swami in devotees' dreams is a common phenomenon. Swami says, "**Whenever I appear in a dream, it is to communicate something to the individual; it is not a mere dream, as is generally known. It is a real appearance**". The author himself has sufficient experience of Swami's dreams. Once, the author was staying in Bangalore at some relative's house. Swami, at that time, was in Brindavan, Whitefield. After lunch, he had a little snap. During this short period of sleep, Swami appeared in dream and did Vibhuti 'Abhishekam' on him. On some other occasion, the author was surrounded by flood waters and rivers on all sides in a dream when Swami came and caught hold of him by His hand and took him out of the surrounding water. Likewise, Swami appeared in the author's dreams several times to solve his personal problems like selection of a site for housing, matters related to his health and family. Even this book as mentioned in the 'tribute' is an outcome of the Swami's command given to the author in his dream.

A brief account of the important landmarks of the profiles of Bhagwan Sri Sathya Sai Baba with regard to His miraculous work, has been published in 'The Universal Sai' issue of *The Times of India* presentation dated 22 November 2010 and released on the occasion of His 85th Holy Birthday celebration. Sri Sathya Sai Baba is one of the most popular spiritual leaders of contemporary India. He has attracted a following which runs into billion cutting across barriers of caste, language, region and nation. He shot into fame because of the miracles performed by Him, specifically his ability to materialize the holy ash and other material things from out of thin air but also because of His spiritual divine message to the world through His discourses demonstrating His command over the knowledge contained in various religious scriptures and through His social welfare schemes such as free medical treatment including even heart surgeries, etc. water projects, and free education from KG to PhD among several other programmes. The rationalists consistently targeted Him. But, Baba, as He is referred to out of reverence and affection by his devotees, only emerged stronger from these controversies.

Sri Sathya Sai Baba is known for working out miracles of a different kind. Miracles in the form of super speciality hospitals where free treatment is given or a massive drinking water schemes in the parched hinterland of Andhra Pradesh and Chennai or a free educational system.

The high and the mighty of the land would touch his feet and seek his blessings. Baba would give them all, the same message of love. Baba said, "**Human beings are increasingly turning to godmen and godwomen. This is basically a search for God. The divine is there within each person. The search is for this divinity. God realization cannot be seen as a sign of insecurity. It is a positive aspiration to be one with God**". Even as mankind is relentlessly searching for God, it finds itself engulfed by more and more misery. The reason for this state of affair is attachment to materialism which is the root cause of all sufferings and sorrows. Once this attachment ends, then one can experience divine bliss. There is no doubt about that. Since God does not have any material attachment. He does not attach any importance to the suffering of His own body. Baba further says, "**The best way to serve God is to serve the poor, the weak, the downtrodden and the underprivileged. There is divinity in each human being hence one should love and serve fellow human beings selflessly**".

Religion can be best pursued through the axiom postulated by Sri Sathya Sai Baba who says, "**There is only one religion – the religion of love; one caste – the caste of humanity; one language – the language of heart and there is only one God – He is omnipresent. There is no escape from human misery because it is all due to karma. The need is to adopt the path of righteousness. One should surrender oneself to the Almighty**". Chamatkaar or miracles have been His visiting cards, as evidence that divinity can transform earth into the sky and vice versa. To doubt this is to betray an inability to grasp the grandeur of the universe. He used to get lot of satisfaction while gifting these talismans to the devotees. The suffering millions would flock to Him. He has been only performing a divine mission.

One of His major tasks was to clean up His own country first, then go to other countries. He wielded enormous influence over the top politicians of the country to impress on them the need to inculcate values in public life so that India would be much better place. Baba used to tell the politicians they had a choice to pursue good or bad governance; that politics without principles, science without humanity, education without character and commerce without morality are not only useless but can prove to be negatively dangerous and harm people at large. Baba never read newspapers. Even though He never read any newspaper, yet He was aware about everything that was happening round the globe. What is necessary today is that the newspapers should be more careful and responsible in their reporting. Publishing of sensational and baseless news must be avoided. No negative and baseless reporting, specially of those at the helm of affairs of the country, should be done since it has lot of repercussions abroad. If there are any doubts, then they should be cleared after free and frank discussions with the persons concerned. Truth should not be compromised under any circumstances. He would attach tremendous importance to education because that education had been divorced from values. Education bereft of values is meaningless. The need is to restore values to education.

6.3 Sai Mission

Faith in God is one of the strongest pillars of Sanathana Dharma. The holy messages and teachings of divine incarnations, prophets and divine messengers have always inspired the spiritual aspirants. The phenomenon of divine incarnations is unique to the spiritual philosophy of India that is Bharat. The believers look upon God as the saviour of humanity. God, therefore, must manifest Himself. The advent of an incarnation (Avtaar) is, thus, acclaimed as the greatest event that can happen to humanity. God as the abstract entity, eludes the human imagination. God's incarnation in the human form is easy to understand. This is perhaps the most satisfying way of knowing God. The Divine incarnation in the human form becomes the inspiration for spiritual search. Although, every human being is potentially divine, yet grace, protection and blessings of incarnated God is required.

An incarnation embodies the Sagun characteristics of the Supreme Being *i.e.* the Nirgun Brahmn. The incarnated God is accessible and approachable to the needs and aspirations of human beings. Its grace, however, falls on all especially on those who are ripe for it and deserve it. Almost from the dawn of the Universe and humanity, it has been the privilege of India where divine incarnations have been taking place. Indeed, India has been bestowed the honour of many divine incarnations, divine messengers, several spiritual scholars, sages and seers who have been the leading lights on the path of spiritual wisdom. Sai Trinity, after God's incarnations as Rama and Krishna, is the most remarkable and amazing phenomenon of the present epoch namely Shirdi Sai Baba as the first Avtaar, Sri Sathya Sai Baba as the second Avtaar and Prema Sai as the future Avtaar.

Spirituality has been the central characteristics of the Hindu culture which has contributed to the greatness of India that is Bharat, and is perhaps the basic cause of its survival despite several onslaughts on its very existence. The descent of God as a Divine incarnation in the human form and the ascent of a human being to Divine perfection are the two inevitable aspects of Hindu's faith and philosophy. Its spiritual philosophy provides a super-structure on which basic human values are based, with faith in God and profound love for Him as the deep foundations. Shirdi Sai Baba used to advise the people to make a beginning for exploration of spiritual wisdom by accepting God as the first and foremost spiritual axiom. This is what God in His incarnation of Sri Sathya Sai Baba has been asserting that firm faith in God and deep love for Him together constitute the starting point for any spiritual attempt. This is indeed true because when the aspiring soul takes the first step towards God based on love and faith, then God hastens to take it under His eternal care and protection.

The underlying message of all spiritual philosophers is that paths are many but the destination as the goal is one. Various philosophical thoughts prescribe various ways to suit the temperament and inclination of the spiritual seekers who are preparing to embark upon a journey of spiritual enquiry. The path of Karma or selfless service is an action-oriented paradigm. The path of Bhakti or devotion suits one who is inclined to engage in devotional songs or prayers accompanied by the constant remembrance of the Supreme God. The path of Jnana or self-knowledge and spiritual wisdom befits the seeker who is introspective and reflective by temperament. Sri Ramakrishna Paramhansa and Surdas among several others chose the path of devotion while Ramana Maharshi advocated the path of spiritual knowledge. Lord Krishna has emphasized the path of Karma as one of the most essential and unavoidable paradigms of Self-realization or God-realization. The teachings of the Sai Mission provide simple and effective ways to achieve the goal of God-realization.

The Sai phenomenon is a glorious trinity which transcends the limitations of time and space to become one with all-absorbing and all-loving Divine. Once in reply to a query about His birth and His parents,

Shirdi Sai Baba said, "**I have no residence, I am the attributeless Absolute. My name is embodied 'Dehi'. The world is my abode. Those who think I reside at Shirdi do not know the real Sai for I am formless and everywhere.**" The dynamics of the personality of Shirdi Sai, the versatility of His accomplishments, the miracles He showed and the peculiar mysticism attached to His profile are sufficient to convince the people that He was God-Incarnate. Shirdi Sai Baba used to assert by saying that so long as the six elemental passions of lust (Kama), anger (Krodh), greed (Lobha), attachment (Moha), and jealously (Matsaya) are not sublimated, so long as the mind continues mongering and chattering, so long will it be futile for the seekers to seek God. The most amazing miracle of Shirdi Sai has been his very being and existence on earth. The recognition of this reality leads to a close analysis of the distinction between sainthood and Avtaarhood, which eventually leads to the truth that Shirdi Sai Baba was an Avtaar.

Avtaarhood is a concept grounded deeply into the pedantic concept of the Brahmn. While other religions have talked of God sending prophets and divine messengers to redeem the human society, the Hindu scriptures have gone beyond this, exclaiming that God Himself comes to the earth from time to time in the human form to act like a human being so that He can accomplish His self-assigned mission within some particular self-allotted time-frame. Whenever, there is the fading of righteousness (Dharma) and the uprising of the evil, then the Divine takes birth as a human being. Though the Divine does limit itself, yet it does not, at the same time, get entangled in the inevitable mechanism of the laws of action (Karmic laws) known to the ordinary human beings. The very word 'Avtaar' means a descent, a coming of the Divine power into the human world. The mission of such a descent is not only to take birth in the human form to hold the ideal of righteousness (Dharma) but also to make the human beings conscious of their divinity to ascend to Godhood.

Shirdi Sai Baba often used to identify Himself with Vithoba, with Dattatreya, with Narayan, with Krishna, and with many others such divine beings mentioned in the Hindu scriptures. He sometimes used to declare that He, in His visible human form and the supreme invisible God, were one and the same and that He was another revelation of the same Divine Personality (Purushottama). All His declarations were proofs enough that Shirdi Sai was no ordinary divine messenger or prophet, but the Divinity which manifested itself in order to mould the thoughts, feelings and senses of human beings to bring in them the divine perfection. All His miracles should, therefore, be regarded as the signs of God's omni-presence, omni-potence and omni-scient, a proof of His divine ascent and a proper understanding of His divine nature and message. It will be better to substitute the word miracles by the more comprehensive term sports (Leelas). The Divine Leela is one of the most aesthetic aspects of religious philosophy. It lies in the nature of the Supreme God to reveal Himself and His Divinity. His Leelas are His manifestations not the miracles performed by a magician but to sport with His devotees. Indeed, these miracles include among others making the lames walk, the blinds to have recovered their sight, and the deaf to hear, healing and curing the sick from a dreaded disease like cancer. Both Shirdi Sai and Sri Sathya Sai Baba very often used to give vibhuti to the devotees which is considered to be the sacred ash. Many Hindus apply a vibhooti (holy ash) mark on their foreheads before prayers. The importance given to holy ash makes it evident that the religious practices prescribed by the great tradition focuses on maintaining a system that safeguards both physical and spiritual wellness.

Besides the miracles and sports, mastery on the knowledge of the Shastras, the Puranas and holy books of various religions has been phenomenal reality of both Shirdi Sai and Sathya Sai. Their interpretations and elucidations of the difficult passages were extremely revealing and inspiring. The declaration of their divinity and their true being have been self-revealing.

"I am God – I am Mahalaxmi. I speak the truth sitting as I do in the mosque. I am Vithoba. I am Ganapathy. All offerings made to Ganpathy reach me. I am Dattatreya. I am Laxmi Narayan. Why go for Ganga elsewhere. Hold you palm at my feet – here flows Ganga. I am Maruti. I am the attributeless absolute Nirguna. I have no name and have no residence. I embroiled myself in Karma and got this body. I am formless and in everything. I fill all space and am Omni-present. I am in water, in dry places, in crowds and solitary wilderness. I am in the fire and in ether. I am the Progenitor of God. Meditate on me as pure Anand Nirakar, but if you cannot do this, then meditate on this Body exactly as you see it. I am not the body or the senses. I am the eternal Sakshi (witness)," said Shirdi Sai.

From the dawn of civilization, all spiritual scholars, intellectuals, sages, saints and even scientists have been engaged in the search of the Supreme Reality. Most of them came to the conclusion that there is some divine entity which is invisible, intangible, unrelated, colourless, who has neither eyes nor ears, neither hands nor feet like the human beings but, who is eternal, all-pervading, undecaying and the source of everything, every-being, animate or inanimate, sentient or insentient.

This is indeed Brahmn, the so-called Absolute of the Vedanta. This is the only reality called God and there is nothing outside God, yet within God, there are many other realities. Within Him, there exist as components different material objects and many conscious souls. Indeed, God is omni-present, omni-potent and omni-scient. God created the Universe full of material objects out of matter which also eternally exists in Him. The souls are conceived as infinitely small substances which also exist eternally in Him.

Confused believers and even staunch non-believers are found to be going to a place of worship. They leave their rational selves at the door, and for the duration of their worship, suspend their logical faculties and believe in what they otherwise think is irrational. Scientists are often found to be praying with deep faith, believing in the theory of Creation even as their minds acknowledge the theory of evolution. Their minds also struggle a tug of war in which they battle the demands of their rational thoughts, which at the same time dictates clear and precise steps unfettered by religious platitudes. This is a common phenomenon observed during early mornings that the call of the muezzin brings both believers and non-believers to a mosque for prayers. After some time, the church bell rings, signaling both the faithful (Angelus) and agnostics to their worship time. Much earlier say at 4 a.m. onwards, the devotees are found to be thronging the doors of temples which include not only the believers, even the non-believers, stopping there briefly to pay obeisance, while making their peace with God. Nevertheless, on every religious occasion, whether Shivratri or Janamashtami or Ramanavami or every Christmas or Easter or on every Eid, both believers and non-believers are found to be participating in all rituals and ceremonies.

They are by their very nature conscious and self-luminous. Every soul is endowed with a material body in accordance with its Karma (Deeds). Bondage of soul means its confinement to its body. Liberation is the complete freedom of soul from body. Soul identifies itself with body by ignorance of its real nature and functions as if it were body and becomes attached to the world. The force of this attachment causes its rebirth in accordance with its deeds (Karma). Freedom from this bondage of attachment can be attained by self-realization. By the study of Vedanta, a human being realizes that his soul is distinct from his body. His soul is tiny component of the Brahmn. Spiritual paradigms are some of the important ways to get freedom from this bondage and feel God-realization.

There is almost complete unanimity among the spiritualists and scientists, believers and non-believers that there are certain fixed and fundamental laws which govern this Universe. To insist on the element of difference between the finite self and the infinite self or the individual self and the Universal Self is not metaphysically sound. The axiom of identity asserts oneness of existence with the Absolute, and not the synthesis of the two. Knowledge relating to God keeps face with faith. **In whom is the Universe, who is in the Universe, in whom is the Soul, who is in the Soul, who is the Soul of a living being**? Knowing Him *i.e.* God and therefore, the Universe along extinguishes ignorance and fears, and brings an end to misery and leads to the enlightenment and realization of God. It is only through the perception, and realization of the Eternal Truth – the Oneness of All Beings that the God-realization is attained. The spiritual paradigms of Karma Yog (the path of Action), Jnana Yog (the path of knowledge) and Bhakti Yog (the path of devotion) among several others lead to the path of God-realization and hence God-visualization. God-realization means some experience with the help of all the five senses which leaves a lasting impression on the mind. When a human being look inwards to realize his true self, then God becomes manifest to him. In a simple language, God realization means self-realization. It is the realization in a person that he is not just a body and mind with the physical organs, but there is something within his self – the Atman that is God, distinct from the perishable things. The comprehension of this truth puts him on the right path to God-realization.

The phenomenon of incarnations of God in various forms is common to all religions. But in Hinduism, this phenomenon is unique in the sense that God Himself appears in various forms according to the specific purpose and time. Earlier incarnations of God in the human form with complete divine powers as Rama and Krishna are most remarkable in the sense that till date they are adored and worshipped as God by the Hindus. The two complete incarnations as Rama and Krishna took place prior to the advent of the later two complete incarnations of God namely Shirdi Sai and Sri Sathya Sai Baba in the Kali Yuga. The believers believe that Rama came about ten thousand years ago, while Krishna appeared about six thousand years ago. Rama Avtaar was for the mission of restoring Truth (Sathya) and Righteousness (Dharma), while Krishna had the additional mission of peace (Shanti) where as the present Sai Avtaar had the mission of restoring all the three spiritual ideals along with the missions of love (Prem) and non-violence (Ahimsa). One of the common characteristics in the Sai Avtaar is that they have no affinity or attachment to the members of the family to which they belong to. The earlier incarnations of God as Rama and Krishna had primarily the role limited to family and kinsman also with whom they chiefly lived, while the later Sai incarnations have been entirely for the devotees and spiritual aspirants.

It is believed in Hinduism that there are in all sixteen characteristics in a full (Poorna) Avtaar: Five pertains to the possession of five senses which are true of both animals and human beings. The Avtaar shares the four attributions of mind, reason, emotion and ego with the human beings. But there are seven more characteristics which are unique to Avtaar only. Of these four are **Srishti** – the power of creation or materialization; **Sthithi** – the power of fostering, guarding and protecting; **Laya** – the power of dissolution or destruction; **Thirodhana** – the power of making things disappear, while the remaining three characteristics are true of a complete Avtaar namely: **Anugraha** – Grace which may be of two kinds, grace for the deserving and grace conferred irrespective of the recipients deserving like an unexpected shower. The final characteristic or attribute *i.e.* the 16th characteristic of a complete Avtaar is His Omni aspects namely Omni-presence, Omni-potence and Omni-scient. Sri Sathya Sai Baba has openly declared that He is full Avtaar (Poorna Avtaar) of God, that He is Sarvadevaswaroopam (All Gods and Goddess combined into one), that He is Saakar (God in Form) of the Niraakar (Formless Brahmn), whose form is recognizable. On His 39th birthday in 1964, Baba openly and categorically declared, "**This is the man-Form in which every divine entity, every divine principle, that is to say, all the names and forms ascribed by man to God are manifest**". "**I am Sainath, Lokanath and Anaathnath, the same God who saved Gajendra—, the saintly boy Dhruva, poor Kuchela (Lord Krishna's classmate, Sudama), and the helpless Prahlad, son of demon king Hiranyakshap**".

Avtaar are born with divine powers while saints and holyman have to work hard to acquire some of these powers. Shri Sathya Sai Baba says, "**My miracles are part of the unlimited power of God and are in no sense product of yogic powers which are acquired. They are natural, uncontrived. There are no invisible beings helping me. My divinity will bring the object in a moment. I am everywhere**".

An Avtaar has a 'Samku Chakram' on the soles of His feet. It is a circular mark. The physical body of an Avtaar is always born with certain distinguishing marks on its left side, in the form of birth mark and moles. A mark on the chest is indeed a Hallmark of Avtaar-hood. All Avtaars have it. Sai Baba has showed this mark to some devotees. It resembles an Eagle which Baba explained as the sign of the Garuda (eagle), a symbol of action (Karma) and its two wings represent faith

(Shradha) and devotion (Bhakti). A few special characteristics of Sri Sathya Baba have been described in various books in the following way:

Sai Baba's every moment has been full of grace. His very presence has been creating a feeling of bliss in the hearts of those who would come for His Darshan. His eyes has a rare calmness and electrifying effect. He has been always full of love. He never lost His temper. His face kept on changing colours. He has been an ocean of compassion. A mere glimpse of Sathya Sai Baba would provide a sense of tranquil. He used to take no breakfast. He would take a spoon of Raagi as a brunch. He would sip a few drops of water. Yet, this body weight remained constant. He never slept because according to Him, He had no need of sleep. Baba used to be accompanied by a scent like that of jasmine. Although Baba never read books, yet He quoted widely from many scriptures. He knew the whole of spiritual philosophy and every religion. His native language has been Telungu but He could speak any language He wished to speak. Baba's sense of humour has been having a universal appeal. He has been very strict disciplinarian. There are several other mysterious characteristics of Sri Sathya Sai Baba which cannot be comprehended which have been most frequently observed such as hand gestures. At times, He used to move His hand, palm up, in a slow circular motion and would brake a strange movement of fingers as if writing in the air. These gestures have been interpreted differently by devotees. Occasionally, if a devotee happens to talk to Him about his problem, His answers used to be His saying "He knows and helps the devotee not to worry, He will take care of it". Baba has vast knowledge of any spiritual subject without having apparently read or studied the huge literature required for such knowledge. He spoke on any subject including medical science with miraculous clarity and authenticity. He has declared, and demonstrated in several cases that He fully knew the past, present and future of everybody, living or dead. Quite often, He would disclose the inner most thoughts of devotees. **"It is not"**, Baba used to say, **"that I first enter your mind, probe it, then come out and tell you what you are thinking or feeling. Actually, I am always residing in your mind so I am fully aware of all that goes on therein at all times. There is nothing hidden from me"**.

Sai Mission is primarily focused on restoring the **spiritual values, secular values** and **social values** throughout the world. A spiritual aspirant or a devotee of God is a person who accepts the five axioms of spirituality as enunciated by Sri Sathya Sai Baba namely: Truth (Sathya), Righteousness (Dharma), Peace (Shanthi), Love (Prem) and Non-violence (Ahimsa) and tries not only to follow these values but also adopt them in his/her life. Ahimsa or non-violence, according to Sai Baba, does not mean merely non-killing but it includes even injuring feelings of others by harping on their misfortunes or by hurting the sentiments of others or by causing harm to them in any way. Every human being must try his or her best to purify the quality of life with a goal to lead a perfect life – which should set an example for others. It requires a steady faith continuous meditation, and deep devotion to God. God is moved by devotion. Devotion means renunciation of the two black-god parents namely ego and desire. It means dedication of all actions and thoughts to God. If every action and thought is offered to God, then it takes the form of real worship *i.e.* Devotion with every action and thought in God is a worship to God in the real sense.

Meditation, Yoga, Prayer, Contemplation, Chanting and Singing devotional songs – all are ways of adopting spiritual values in life. Developing love and reverence for everyone, speaking the truth and acting virtuously, Repeating the name of God in any form, Avoiding indulgence of talking ill of others and finding faults of others, and Refraining from causing pain to others are some of other essential spiritual values of life. To know 'Atma' within self is the most essential mode of spirituality. This is possible through 'Ekaant Bhakti' which is possible only through continuous '**Sadhana**' (meditation) and removal of impurities and waves of likes and dislikes hovering around the mind. Ekaant Bhakti helps in the effective control of mind and experiencing one's self. Control of mind does not mean holding it steady without wandering around. Its correct way is to clean the mind of impure thoughts. Mind control leads to self-control which leads to self-realization – means God's realization. Meditation means rising above desires. Meditation is described by Baba as the royal road, the easy path to self-realization *i.e.* God-realization.

According to Bhagwan Sri Sathya Sai Baba (discourse on July 20, 1996; Sanatham Sarathi – June 2012), since ancient times, many people have been making efforts to experience God by practising four types of worship (Aradhana) as prescribed by the culture of Bharat: Satyavati Aradhana, Angavati Aradhana, Anyavati Aradhana and Nidanavati Aradhana. In Satyavati Aradhana, the devotee worships God with faith that He is immanent in every particle of the Universe just as butter is present in every drop of milk. Like oil in the sesame (til) seeds and fire in wood, God pervades the entire manifest creation. The devotee worships God with the awareness that He pervades the entire universe and believes that the universe is the effect and God is the cause. In the Angavati Aradhana, devotees consider each of the five basic elements namely ether, air, fire, water and earth as the manifestation of God and worship them. In the Anyavati Aradhana, people ascribe to God various names and forms with specific attributes namely Shiva as Gangadhara, Vishnu as the one who holds conch, disc, mace and lotus in His four hands, Krishna as the one who sports a peacock feature on His head and plays on His divine flute, Rama as the one who wields the bow in His right hand, and Saraswati, the goddess of harmony and music, with veena in her hands. Thus, in this form of worship, people adore God by attributing various forms and names to Him. In the fourth type of worship namely Nidanvati, people perform nine forms of devotion (Noudha Bhakti) namely listening (Sravanam), singing (Kirtanam), contemplating (Smaranam), serving (Sevanam), salutation (Vandanam), worshipping (Archanam), servitude (Dasyam), friendship (Sneham) and surrendering (Nivedanam). By following these nine paths of devotion, people contemplate on God and attain the goal of inventing God.

Sai Baba's miracles and messages have been well-documented by several devotees including even the scientists and educationists all over the world. He has been the living proof of the existence of a divine power called the God. It also shows that divine power is unlimited, infinite and beyond the bounds of time and space. Sri Sathya Sai Baba has been an embodiment of that divine power. A detailed view of Sai Baba's profiles and His mission have been very well documented in the exemplary works namely the four-volumes of '**Sathyam, Shivam, Sundaram**' by late professor N. Kasturi. Indeed, Sri Sathya Sai Baba is Sathyam, Sivam, Sundaram. In his discourse on 7th July 1961, Baba spoke on these three words. He said, "**Sathyam is the function of the Intellect, Sivam of the Consciousness** and **Sundaram of the heart; Sathyam is splendour, and Sivam the recognition of the Truth inside it and Sundaram, the nature of that Truth. Sathyam is Jnana, Sivam is Karma and Sundaram is Bhakthi"**. He further said that He is the syntheses of all antitheses, the harmony behind all apparent discordances, the melody that pacifies all distractions. He is inner Principle as well as the outer Force. **He used to say, "I am in you, with you, near you, behind you, beside you"**.

Sai mission has rapidly and amazingly spread not only in India but in various other countries also, covering almost all the continents of the world without any publicity or propagation of any sort. It seeks to train the passions and the emotions of the people to educate their impulses, and directs their faculties of reason to paths that are beneficial to the individual in particular and the human society in general. The Sai phenomenon cleans and purifies the mind which is the breeding ground of desire and attachment, ego and anger, expectations and aspirations, and of greed and lust. The Sai mission considers the spiritual values of Truth (Sathya), Righteousness (Dharma), Peace (Shanti), Love (Prem) and Non-violence (Ahimsa) as more essential than the blind faith in the rigid doctrines of various religious practices. Earlier, Shirdi Sai said, "**I do not belong to any religion. God accepts everyone and every religion belongs to Him. So I also accept all religions and all people. If there is no humanity, then there is no God". The same message is echoed by Sathya Sai Baba, who said, "Let the different faiths exist, let them flourish and let the glory of God be sung in all the languages and in a variety of tunes. That should be the ideal. Respect the differences and recognize them as valid as long as they do not extinguish the flame of unity**".

As early as in 1950, Sri Sathya Sai Baba declared the plan of His divine mission: "**The first sixteen years of this Body's earthly career have been spent in Leela (play and pranks), the next sixteen is being spent in Mahima (Manifestation of Power and Glory**). After the thirty second year **Sri Sathya Sai Baba said, "You will see me active more and more in the task of Updesa, teaching the erring humanity and directing the world along the path of Sathya, Dharma, Shanti and Prema. Not that I have decided to exclude Leela and Mahima from the thirty second year. I only mean re-establishing Dharma, correcting the crookedness of the human mind and guiding mankind back into the Sanathana Dharma will be my main task thereafter**".

Puttaparthy – the birth place of Sri Sathya Sai Baba, was a remote and small village when His mission began. During the early period, devotees from outside Puttaparthy used to come by bullock carts and some even on foot because there was no paved road. After a few years, the road to Puttaparthy was made useable for vehicles like cars and buses. Later in view of the need and growing size of Puttaparthy due to the establishment of Prasanthi Nilayam, and also in view of the coming up of newly built Super Speciality Hospital, not only the road has widened and made completely motorable but an airport has been also constructed for the use of VVIP like ministers and governors. The Railway line has been branched from Dharmavaram to Bangalore through Prashanti Nilayam Railway Station for the convenience of the devotees coming from far off places like Hyderabad and beyond from North India. This developmental aspect of Puttaparthy, lately being titled as Global City, related to the spiritual and social transformation that has been brought by the Sai mission is remarkable particularly for the benefit of innumerable number of people coming from various parts of India and other countries of the world. All this happened during first seventy years of the Avtaaric mission of Sri Sathya Sai Baba.

The major obstacle for the Sai Mission, however, has been the widespread skepticism over Sathya Sai's amazing declaration about Himself in the early years, particularly with regard to His declaration of the reincarnation of Shirdi Sai Baba, that too in a country like India well-known for the presence of an enormous number of godmen, saints and gurus who would hesitate to accept the supremacy of divinity in some one other than themselves. Nevertheless, with many astonishing demonstrations of His miracles and His revelations of the life of Shirdi Sai to His devotees with whom He came into contact, Sri Sathya Sai Baba gradually removed the veil of skepticism and convinced many of the skeptics about His divinity. Several non-believers and skeptics got convinced about Sai Baba's divine power due to visions, miracles and His knowledge of the Vedas and Upanishads, revealed through His discourses. Sri Sathya Sai also made clear, right in His early age that He is God in human form who has come amongst the people to re-establish the values of Sathya, Dharma, Shanti and Prem. Baba said, **"Whenever there is a languishing of dharma or righteousness and an upheaval of unrighteousness, I create myself, for it is part of the primal resolution or sankalpa, to protect, the spiritual structure of the universe. I lay aside my formless essence and assume a name and a form suited to the purpose for which I come. Whenever evil threatens to vanquish good, I have to come and save it from decline".**

The beginning of the Sai Mission and its preaching may be traced to Swami's total command at the scriptural knowledge demonstrated through His lecture at the All India Divine Life Society Vedic Conference in 1957 where He established His acceptance by leading Spiritual Scholars and Vedic Pandits including even Swami Shivanand of North India. This was followed by his recognition in 1962 when Sri Sathya Sai Baba inaugurated the annual week-long Veda Purusha Saptah Yagna at Prashanti Nilayam. It was here that eminent Vedic scholars and pandits of acknowledged Sai Baba's Vedic knowledge and accepted Him as their Guru. Soon after Baba's recognition got confirmed on a firm basis when literature on Baba's profile and mission got published which included the prominent authors like Howard Murphet, Dr. Hislop among several others both from India and overseas. Gradually, there appeared ever growing publications of a large number of books written on personal experiences, analyses and impressions of Sai Baba, while his inexhaustible and ineffable love for all attracted a stream of visitors both from India and abroad. Visitors from the countries of USA, Canada,

Australia, South America, Africa, Europe and South East continue growing in large numbers along with vast flood of devotees from several parts of India. The emphasis of the Sai Mission, included, **'Love All'**; **'Serve All'**; **"Service to Humanity is Service to God"; and 'Education in Human Values'** for the all-round personality development of the young children through its 'Bal Vikas Programmes" and 'Sai Centres' all over the world. The pace of this development of Baba's world-wide mission greatly increased during nineteen eighties and nineteen nineties. The establishment of the Super Speciality Hospital (now known as Sri Sathya Sai Institute of Medical Sciences) in 1991 gave rise to an avalanche of international media's interest in Baba and His Mission which impressed many foreign professionals, not only for its original architectural design and structure but also its ambitious free medical treatment to all irrespective of caste, creed and religion.

The earlier Avtaar, Shirdi Sai Baba, laid the foundation of Sai Mission with a noble system of universalism with His message of unity of all faiths. The mission of the later Avtaar, Sri Sathya Sai Baba, has been to strengthen the secular integration in order to make everybody realize that the same God or Divinity exists in everyone and to respect every religion. Finally, the next Avtaar, Prema Sai, is destined to promote a set of principles that will convince humanity that not only God lives in everybody but everybody is God. The Sathya Sai Avtaar has been saying, **"For the protection of the virtuous, for the destruction of evildoers and for establishing righteousness on a firm footing, I incarnate in human form from age to age"**. When disharmony overwhelms the world, the Lord will incarnate in human form to establish the modes of harmony and peace, and to re-educate the human community in the path of peace. Every step in the life of the Avtaar is pre-determined. Rama came to feed the roots of truth and right conduct. Krishna came to foster righteousness and peace and love. Now, all the four are in danger of being dried up. That is why the Sai Mission has come. It has come to repair the ancient highway to God. It does not represent any particular sect or creed or religion. Sai Mission has come to light the lamp of love in the hearts of the whole humanity. The Sai Avtaar have been armed with the fullness of the power of the formless God to correct mankind, raise human consciousness and put people back on the right path of truth, righteousness, peace and love to divinity. The major task of the Sai Mission is to transform every heart, to make everybody realize that the same God resides in everyone and to inculcate spiritual and moral values in everyone. The Sai mission is to achieve the supreme task of uniting as one family the whole humanity through the bond of brotherhood, of affirming the faith of every religion, of illumining the divine reality of each human being and of instructing all communities to recognize the common divine heritage that binds human to human so that humanity can rise into divinity which is expected to be the supreme goal of human endeavour.

Sai Mission is the essence of all religious faiths including those of Islam, Christianity and Zoroastrianism with the founders and preachers of all religions and with the sole ideal of bringing unity and harmony of different faiths. The Sai Mission emphasizes real secularism – love for all religions of the world. It preaches universal religion called 'Sanathan Dharma'. Sai Baba has been teaching this Universal Religion as Sanathana Dharma in thought, action and word. The word Sanathan means eternal beyond measure, and the word 'Dharma' means a code of thought, word and deed based on Truth. Thus, Sai mission like Sanathana Dharma is the essence of all religions and all religions have their roots in Sanathan Dharma because it teaches the values and ideals of all religions differing only in their modes and paradigms. It is based on the knowledge of our Universal self – the Atma pervading all beings. To equate it with one specific religion is equivalent to limiting it with a name and a form focused on the limited precepts of that religion. Baba says, "**My object is to preach the unity of mankind, and make you realize the connection which exists between man and man. God is beyond the 'gunas' (attributes) so it is not possible to say that God is this or that, and has such and such attributes**". No religion can put any limitations on God. **How can infinite and boundless God be bounded by limitations**? Thus the Sai mission like the Universal religion is one where love, the essence of all religions, flows through it. The term Sai mission has acquires several interpretations: relating to time, relating to the world, relating to the heart, relation to a sect, and so on, which come into use in the modern times. The Sai Mission in its form and essence together constitute what is termed as the Universal religion (Sanatana Dharma). Baba has exalted Truth, Righteousness', Peace and Love as the four pillars of Sanatana Dharma. Truth (Sathya) is that which is changeless and is the reality underlying all that exists. Righteousness (Dharma) ordains observance of certain proprieties of conduct for social and spiritual development. Peace (Shanthi) means eternal bliss and Love (Prema) can be an experiential feeling of oneness. Thus, the Sanathan Dharma – the Universal Religion is the essence of the Sai Mission.

Sai Mission means harmony of all religious faiths and cults. It interconnects the basis of all organized and founded religions of the world. The aims and objectives of various systems, faiths and religions, as stated in Chapters 3 and 5 are same. Their goals, targets and purposes are all the same. No religion teaches hatred. Their focus is to educate the people to follow the path which is beneficial to the individual in particular for spiritual growth, and the society, in general for universal harmony. Sai Mission considers the philosophies and precepts of all the different faiths and religions more essential than the blind faith in their commandments and ritual theories. Baba says, "**All of you who have entered the Sathya Sai Organization, if anyone asks what is the religion of Sathya Sai and of Sathya Sai Organization, you must have the courage and determination to say with one voice, that the essence of all religions is the religion of the Sathya Sai Organization**". God is one, in many names, people see it's manifestations. Baba is the unique human embodiment of the Cosmic Consciousness – Brahmn. Sai Baba says, "**If you are a Hindu, be a good Hindu, if you are Muslim, be a good Muslim; and if you are a Christian, be a good Christian, because God is Omni-present.**" Echoing the same view, Shirdi Sai Baba said, "**I do not belong to any religion. God accepts everything, and every religion belongs to Him. So I also accept all religions and all people. If there is no humanity, then there is no God.**"

The fifty feet high pillar called 'Aikya Stambha' or 'Column of Concord' situated inside Prasanthi Nilayam depicts the symbols of major religions of the world on the Sai Insignia or Sai Emblem or Logo of Sarva Dharma (all religions). It consists of a circle with a lotus at its centre and, in circles around the edges, the symbols of five religions: Hinduism (OM), Buddhism (Wheel), Zoroastrianism (FIRE), Islam (CRESCENT & STAR), and Christianity (CROSS). The Sarva Dharma emblem was designed by Sri Sathya Sai Baba Himself. The Hinduism 'OM is a mystic monosyllable representing Brahmn; the sound of the Universe, the sound of Creation; the manifested universe and the Unmanifested Absolute. Baba says, "AUM (OM) is a name of God which can find universal acceptance. The Christians say 'Amen' in their prayer which is a slightly different from of 'AUM'. Indeed, 'AUM' has the universal relevance and applicability. It cuts across the bounds of time, space, religion and culture. It can be pronounced by all people irrespective of their cast, creed or religion. 'OM' is the divine sound; the sound of the Universe; the sound of creation; indestructible sound. Written as 'OM', its pronouncement is made up of three characters forming a composite syllable A-U-M, with A representing Brahma (the Lord of Creation), U for Vishnu (the Lord of Protection) and M for Shiva, the Lord of dissolution *i.e.* birth, life and death. The pronunciation of AUM resounds in one's heart as well as in the heart of the universe. The symbol 'OM' of Hinduism summarizes within itself the process of Being and Becoming. It is a way out for spiritual success.

The symbolism of Hinduism (OM) describes all the varying forms of religious beliefs as well as social and religious practices taking their source from the Vedas. Hinduism is considered to be a major religion of India although it is without any individual founder. Indeed, it is Sanathana Dharma which comprises all beliefs from atheism through animism and polytheism to absolute monism. Baba says, "**The Hindu religion has divine roots which gave it the inherent strength to withstand several onslaughts on it in the past**." India is a land of the Hindus. The word 'Hin' means 'hinsa' (violence), Du means Duur (far away from). Thus Hindu means a person free from any desire to be violent to cause injury or harm to anyone. Hindu Dharma is religion which has faith in the doctrines of Karma, of rebirth and of the advent of divine incarnations. Hindu Dharma alone accepts these three doctrines.

The Buddhist wheel reminds the wheel of cause and consequence of deed and destiny. It is the wheel of righteousness (Dharma) that rectifies all. The sacred fire of the Zoroastrians symbolizes the offering of all bitterness in the sacred fire to emerge Grand, Great and Godly. The message of the crescent and star of Islam is that be like the star which never wavers from the crescent but is fixed and steady in faith. The Christian's cross signifies: cut the 'I' feeling (ego) clean across and let the ego die on the cross to endow eternity. The Sai Emblem or logo, having the symbols of five major religions has an open lotus on a raised pedestal, in a circle, bordered by five petals and five small leaves. Each petal contains a symbol of each of the five religions. In the centre is the stem, with traditional lamp on the top, which stands for the spinal corn channelizing the fire of Yoga, that purges man to Godhood. Its lotus shaped top symbolizes the growth of human nature into divine. From the core of the lotus leaps the glowing flame that denotes the supreme effulgence. The outer circle signifies all – comprehensiveness and the periphery inscribes the five symbols of the above said five religions.

One of the beliefs maintained by Islam is that there should be no use of a form or an image in the worship of the formless God. The great divine personalities like the poets Kabir and Rahim visualized a bridge between Hindus (who believe in both formed and formless God) and Muslims (who believe only in the formless God). Although born of Hindu parents, Shirdi Sai had a Hindu and Muslim teacher. He wore Muslim dress, spoke Urdu, Muslim language, and often referred to God as Allah, the Master, He has many Muslim followers. Sathya Sai stresses that His teachings and message are for people of all religious faiths and the Muslim symbol (Star and Crescent) is one of the symbols on the Sai Emblem.

All religions are the different forms of expressing love for the same God. Not only different modes of worship have the same purpose but also their basic doctrines are somewhat similar. Whatever be their outward rituals and formulated creeds, the inner purpose of every religion is love for the same and one God. The Sai Mission is constantly focused on preaching the great inner unity of all religions. "**There is only one religion**"' says Baba, "**the religion of heart – the religion of love**". The aim of His preaching is not founding a separate religion or sect of 'Saism' or 'Sai Religion' but promoting every religious faith for the universal harmony. Baba says: "**He has not come to propagate a new religion but to liberate man from creeds, rituals, and exploitive superstitions. He is God come down to raise man to God. This transformation has to begin with the individual**". The core of Sai Mission is to give one supreme message – the message of love based on faith in God. The essence of all religions is love for God. Baba says: "**So none has to give up his religion or deity, but through them worship the one God in all. I have come not to disturb or to destroy but to confirm and vindicate everyone in his faith**".

India's ancient name is Bharat. It is the land of the Vedas. It is the land where God has been appearing in various forms. There is no other country of the world where God has ever incarnated or reincarnated. It is the land of sages and seers. No other country can claim to have so many divine personalities. India is a land of spirituality with emphasis on the 'Atma' which is the core of Indian philosophy. Baba says: "**Bharatha means the land of those who have rathi (attachment) towards 'Bha' or Bhagwan, that is to say, the God**." Bharat is considered to be the Guru of Humanity. Baba further says: "**What a great fortune to be born in Bharath, which is redolent with the fragrance of God, echoing through ages the voices calling humanity to proceed along the path of God. The saints and seers from this land have been teaching the people of East and West manifold ways to lift the veil of ignorance that hides God from Man**." India is considered to be leader of the world in the field of spiritual philosophy. Its exalted metaphysics; the daring discoveries of philosophical concepts like the doctrines of 'Karma'; 'Incarnation' and 'Rebirth'; the concepts of 'Prakriti' and 'Parusha'; its spiritual paradigms whereby the spiritual seekers can seek unity with the divine.

India's gifts of Vedas and Upanishads; the significance of the Creator and His manifestations; and above all, the assertion of human's supreme destiny of attaining his potential divinity through effort and grace coupled with many other sublime axioms of Truth (Sathya), Righteousness (Dharma), Peace (Shanti), Love (Prem) and Non-violence

(Ahimsa) are some of its special glorious features among several others. Vedas represent the Bharatiya culture. Vedas are without a beginning or end. In other words, Vedas are timeless. A Vedic mantra related to God works as a magnetic field of the magnetism of God. Vedas came from certain fundamental divine sounds and their variations. Vedas are God's breaths and can be transmitted from person to person only by voice. Baba said that the Vedas cannot be translated because its slightest modification of the sound changes the meaning of what is said and no written language is able to represent all of the Vedic sounds.

Baba has assured the people in one of his discourses that there is no reason for mankind to be extremely worried about the future, for the Golden Age of humanity is soon drawing near. Sai Baba has declared, **"I have not come to set a foot a new cult; I do not want people to be misled on this point. I affirm that this Sai form is the form of all the various names that man uses for adoration of the Divine. So, I am teaching that no distinction should be made between the names Rama, Krishna, Ishwara, Sai – for they are all My names"**. He has assured them that Sai Yoga which started form 1999, will flourish in 2030 and onwards during the days of His next incarnation as Prema Sai. He has further assured the people that He will use His powers and influence as Avtaar to prevent nuclear war. He has said to His devotees in great earnestness not to leave His Organizational fold, not to try to get out of the umbrella of His divine protective grace lest they should be subjected to any harm at the hands of nature's fury. Everyone has opportunity to enter the new Golden Age. But each one has a choice to decide his own future whether he wishes to continue living in the wilderness, a life of illusion, or move forward along the spiritual path and enter the new Golden age.

The teachings of the Sai Mission are fully documented in literature published by Sri Sathya Sai Sadhana Trust (Publication) and in several other publications emanating from the devotees. Based on first four volumes of Sathyam, Shivam, Sundaram by late Prof. N. Kasturi, a very close devotee and secretary of Sri Sathya Sai Baba; Sathya Sai Speaks Series, Summer Shower series, Vahinis Series and Baba's discourses published in the monthly magazine Sanathana Sarathi, a few brief idea of the basic teachings of Sri Sathya Sai Baba along with several interpretations published in other books have been summed as under. However, this is not the exhaustive summary of the Sai Mission which is indeed beyond the capability and capacity of the author.

- The three chief principles of the Sai Mission are: the universality of all religions; the 'Atma' as divine spark, is the indweller of all beings which is the basis of all brotherhood of human beings and the fatherhood of God *i.e.* Universal Consciousness; and God is love – the quickest and most direct way to Him through love in action (Karma) or self-less service. Baba says, "**You yourself are three persons, not one: the one you think you are, the one others think you are, and the one you really are. The one you really are is God. God is in you, with you, above you, around you, behind you. All of you are Divine reality**".

- Sai Mission enunciate five axioms for spiritual developments. These are Truth (Sathya), Righteousness (Dharma), Peace (Shanti), Love (Prem) and Non-Violence (Ahimsa). Baba says, "**Follow the path of truth and Dharma**"; "**Love all, serve all**"; "**See good, hear good, speak good and do good**"; "**Practice Sadhana (meditation) – Dhayan, Tapa, Namasimaran (Recitation of the name of God)**"; **and** "**Manav-Seva (Service of humanity)**", **is Madhav Seva (Service of God)**.
- The central point of Sai Mission with regard to leading a quality life is to see that divine quality in every being and to love that divine quality and not be bothered by all other actions and characteristics of that being. A human being can achieve spiritual attainment, happiness and hence liberation.
- All are children of God and hence Divine in their own way and equal before God. One should, therefore, try to live in unity and harmony with all irrespective of their creed, colour or other qualities. People should not live in ignorance of their true nature and purpose of existence. The spirit has evolved from mineral existence to vegetable, animal, birds, reptiles and finally to human beings. The purpose of human existence is to realize its divinity. It is because of sinful impurities and demonic tendencies that people get separated from God. Until these tendencies are removed by the people, they are deemed to repeat birth on Earth. By turning their lives to God, they can purify their lives and help themselves to manifest divine qualities. When divinity manifest in human beings, they are saved from the need for further birth.
- All religions are paths to the same goal. They all teach the same basic morality and all people adore the same God – for there is only one God and He is Omni-present.

Following teachings may be summed up as Sai's Gospels as the core of the Sai Mission:

- Practice three things: Non-Violence (Ahimsa), Truth (Sathyam) and Celibacy (Brahmacharya).
- Remember three things: Death, Pains of Samsara (life on earth) and God.
- Remove three things: Egoism, Desire and Attachment.
- Cultivate three things: Humility, Fearlessness, Patience.
- Eradicate three things: Lust, Anger, Greed.
- Like three things: The Wise, Liberation, Self-less Service.
- Admire three things: Generosity, Courage, Nobility.
- Hate three things: Jealousy, Falsehood, Backbiting.
- Revere three things: Guru, Renunciation, Discrimination.
- Control three things: Tongue, Temper, Tossing of Mind.
- Avoid three things: Harsh Words, Ill-will, Negative Thoughts.

Baba advises the devotees to control Rajas and Tamas aspect and cultrate the Satvic quality. He says, "**If there is righteousness in the heart, there will be beauty in the character. If there is beauty in the character, there will be harmony in the house. If there is harmony in the house, there will be order in the nation. If there is order in the nation, there will be peace in the world**".

Every divine incarnation is full and complete in relation to the time, environment and purpose. God incarnated as Rama to re-establish the ideals of Truth and Righteousness. The divine incarnation of Krishna followed to foster the values of Love and Peace. In the present Yuga, these sacred principles are in danger because of the dominance of evil forces. The Sai Mission is vested with cosmic power to eradicate evil and demonic tendencies among the people and to re-establish the spiritual ideals of Truth, Righteousness, Peace and Love. Indeed, whenever discord, disharmony and strife overwhelm the world, God incarnates from time to time, age to age, in order to protect the spiritual ideals and show the humanity the way to love, harmony and peace. This happens because divine incarnation is the only way out for the said purpose. God takes the human form and conducts Himself in a human way so that the human beings can feel kinship with Divinity. The divine incarnation rises to the godly heights so as to inspire human beings to reach God and make them feel the realization of the indwelling God within them. The earlier incarnations like Rama and Krishna had to annihilate some identified individuals as enemies of the virtues, and thus to restore the path of spiritual values. Presently, wickedness has tainted the human society so much that it stands under the threat of total destruction. It is because of this reason primarily that the Sai Mission has been evolved armed with the full divine power to save humanity, raise human consciousness and lead people back on the right path of Truth, Righteousness, Peace and Love to Divinity.

The holy Sai Mission has the Divine purpose of generating through the maxim of pure love, an environment of brotherhood of mankind to save the world from a possible nuclear holocaust. The purpose of God's triple incarnation, earlier as Shirdi Sai Baba, then as Sri Sathya Sai Baba and later as Prema Sai Baba, is to re-establish the spiritual ideals of Truth, Righteousness, Love, Peace and Non-violence and the unity of mankind. This may look to be a controversial proclamation to those who are not aware of the depth of the Hindu philosophy which believes in the system of divine incarnations and their missions. The trinity of Shirdi Sai Baba, Sathya Sai Baba and Prema Sai personifies the Divine Power. Sri Sathya Baba said, "**God is man and man is God. All of us have something of God, the Divine spark, within us. All men are Divine like myself with the spirit embodies in human flesh and bone. The only difference is that they are unaware of this Godhood.**" For the doubtful and confused, Sai message is that those who want to secure pearls from the sea have to dive deep to fetch them. It does not help them to dabble among shallow waves near the shore and say that the sea has no pearls and all stories about them are false. Likewise, if a person wants to secure the love and grace of God, he must also dive deep and get submerged in Sai's grace. Then and only then will he become one with God and invent God.

The three divine incarnations of the Sai phenomenon occurring at three different timings and at three different places are not separate in the sense that there is complete Oneness of all the three with the sole mission of the re-establishment of the spiritual values. The first incarnation as Shirdi Sai Baba laid the foundation of these values for unity and integration of all and gave mankind the message of Duty, that is Work. Shirdi, Sai Baba emphasized two virtues for well-being: faith or '**shraddha**' and patience or '**saburi**'. The two virtues are complementary. Each is both, the cause as well as the effect of the other; and both are the means as well as the end of the other. Between them they contain a complete code of conduct for life. Shraddha is deep faith that helps one accept all happenings – the good and bad - with equanimity. Faith is what makes a disciple trust his Guru. Saburi or patience is not just the ability to overcome the urge for instant gratification. Patience is not the art of *ad-hoc* management of mental restlessness. Patience is the intuition that inspires one to just be and wait for the Will of God to unfold and work itself out. Patience is what enables a tree to let all its leaves fall without demur. The tree stands denuded, without a sense of shame, despondency or heartbreak. It stands as comfortably as ever. It lets the sun, the air, the rain and the season to work their magic. They denude it; they later laden it. The tree surrenders to them, not out of helplessness but out of natural design. When the season turns, tender new leaves dress it with flowers and fruits in due course. Patience is not to stoically brave winter in the hope of spring; rather, it is to accept spring and winter alike. It is to surrender with a joyous heart to the will of God as represented by the current moment and condition.

Faith is the insight that tells one that patience and surrender to the will of God is the best course of life. Wisdom is in understanding and valuing both faith and patience. Patience is born of faith and in due course it serves to strengthen faith. If patience and faith are so intricately woven, why did Shirdi Sai emphasize these as two virtues? Why did he not advocate either this one or that? If faith is exclusively emphasized, it can promote blind belief. On the other hand, if patience is singularly emphasized, it can lead to the shirking of responsibility and indolence. Patience without faith can become sloth. Faith minus patience can turn banal. Either way, the result will be counter-productive. In tandem, the two virtues uplift. If both patience and faith are required, which among these comes first? Where does one begin? Asking which should come first, patience or faith. It perhaps depends on an individuals's spiritual configuration as to which path suits his psyche best: faith or patience. Whichever route one may begin with, the two paths keep twinning and finally the two converge towards a common goal.

The mission of the second incarnation as Sri Sathya Sai Baba has been to make everybody realize that the same God or Divinity prevails everywhere, resides in everybody and therefore, people should love and help each other irrespective of caste, colour or creed. Thus, every work becomes an act of Worship. Later, Prema Sai, the third divine incarnation will have the task of promoting the feeling that not only God lives in everybody, but also everybody is God. That will be the light of Ultimate Wisdom which will enable every person to develop that feeling of being God. Thus Work, Worship and Wisdom are considered to be three respective holy missions of the trinity of the Sai Phenomenon. The three missions together constitute one common aim of God-realization. The set of spiritual values of truth, righteousness, peace, love and non-violence forms the common basis of cementing, unifying, integrating the human attitudes so as to generate the Oneness which lead to God realization.

In the present scenario, the evil is so widespread that humanity cannot afford the impact of a nuclear holocaust in the event of world war. It is for the prevention of such a nuclear disaster and to raise the human consciousness above the evil forces like anger, hate, violence, and re-establishment of spiritual values is essential. For this, God's realization through brotherhood of mankind is the only way out. Everybody has sense of God, the Divine spark within himself or herself. Awareness of that God within needs to be generated. Human beings are bound by the nature and type of their past deeds (Karma). A divine incarnation like Rama, Krishna or Sai Baba is not bound to the body but free of this bondage. The difference is that a human being is filled with ego and desire whereas, a divine incarnation though in the human form, is much above and away from ego and desire. Bound by ego and desire the individual self degenerates into arrogance and selfishness. Self-realization is the way to cleanse the Self of ego and desire. Then one can reach a state of consciousness revealing the true Self that is God. This is what Vedanta means when it says that one must get rid of ego and desire to realize Oneself *i.e.* Self-realization. One has, therefore, to rise to a level of consciousness to achieve Self-realization, and to become one with the cosmic self. "**Self-realization is God-realization. Thus, man reaches God**," says Sri Sathya Sai Baba.

The Sai Mission is showing the mankind the way to inculcate spiritual values of love, devotion, detachment, desirelessness and egolessness so as evolve it to a higher level of enlightenment. It is leading the people to a higher level of consciousness to enable them to understand the deep meaning and purpose of spiritual values in order to turn their tendencies to the path of truth, righteousness, peace, love and non-violence. Various educational institutions and social service organizations founded by Sri Sathya Sai Baba are designed on the spiritual basis so as to reform the socio-economic system of the human society. For this, the educational institutions present a model of quality and value based educational system where education is free from primary level up to the post-graduate level. A number of hospitals including the super-speciality facilities presents a model of social service where the medical treatment including surgeries is free of cost. Hundreds of thousands of organization are doing this type of noble service all over the world where education and health facilities are provided free of cost with the sole aim of generating the spiritual values of truth, righteousness, peace, love and non-violence. Sai Mission has started several other welfare projects like water supply, village (Gram) service and free medical camps among others. The whole purpose behind all these social service and welfare activities is to convince the people that the only way to evolve the latent Divinity in them is to control ego and desire.

Millions and millions of people in India and abroad, are willing to accept this message of the Sai Mission for the simple reason that there is no test, nor there can be any for such a Sai phenomenon except the faith in God. The way the educational and social services are being given to the people all over the world totally free of cost is not possible for a human being or a group of human beings. All this is possible because of divine Will and Power. Only the Divine like Sathya Sai Baba can do it and hence in that sense Sai Baba is God. Indeed, His mission is to help mankind dissolve the barriers of ego and desire. This will enable the individual self to merge with the Cosmic Self, that is, Parmataman. Indeed, Sai Baba's plan is to bring the human society into the spiritual domain of the five pillars of truth, righteousness, peace, love and non-violence with an obvious objective of enabling a human being to overcome the body-mind frontiers so that his embodied soul *i.e.* Jeevatman can merge with Paramatman, that is his individual self can merge with the Cosmic-self. This merger is God-realization. Sri Sathya Sai Baba says, "**God is within you, seek Him, feel Him, embrace Him. He is there deep inside you, the self. What matters is not the body, nor the mind, nor the brain. It is not the desire of the desiring, nor is it the object of desire, that matters. All these are simply outer manifestations of the indwelling God. It is you who appear as the smiling flower or the twinkling star. You have everything within you. Find it. Discover it. Know it. Realize it.**"

Sages and seers have been teaching the human society to realize the Truth about the creation, creatures and the creator. They have been impressing upon the people to adore the creator that is God and follow the path of spirituality so that the God enshrined within them reveals His full glory to them. Spirituality sharpens the inner vision of a human being so that he can visualize his Atmic Reality. Indeed, spirituality can transform the human society so as to enable a human being to flow smoothly towards the limitless ocean of Divinity. Spirituality teaches the ideals of truth, righteousness, peace, love and non-violence, and shows the path of Unity, Oneness and tolerance. It awakens the moral values all over the world and inspires the human society to do service to the needy through which it reveals Divinity. It shows the way for liberation of mankind from its ignorance. Bhagwan Sri Sathya Sai Baba has been exhorting the youth to participate in various forms of service to the poor and disabled. He has been insisting on the students to progress not only in their academic studies, but also equally in social service and in developing skills which will make them useful in the society. All religious sects have a common goal of God-realization although they may differ in their approaches and follow different paths to achieve that common goal. God is one and only one without an equal but known differently to different people in various names and forms. The eternal truth, however, continues to hold their devotion to God because only faith in God can help them in shedding ego and controlling desire so that they are able to do selfless service to humanity. Bhagwan Sri Sathya Sai Baba say, **"Service to man is service to God, and it is the noblest form of worship to God."**

It is not possible to analyze the Sai phenomenon on the scientific lines because it is a divine phenomenon. Nobody has the capacity and technology for such an analysis. It is equally impossible to explain the mystery of Sai miracles, actions and doings. Although Sai's teachings and preachings fit not only into the Indian philosophy but for that matter into every human tradition and philosophy. He is unique and extra-ordinary. Several ordinary and extraordinary people used to flock to Him for solace. His physical presence has been a great relief to His followers. Everyone, who went to Him for His Darshan, felt an experience which was unique in its own way and started loving Him. Everyone has a feeling of Him of being some Divine power. All eyes in the Darshan Hall used to be focused on Him for a view of Him. His grace and love flew equally on everyone, everywhere and at all times.

This is something beyond the capacity of human comprehension because it is an attribute of Divinity of Sai Baba. His message exhorts people to love God, serve humanity and earn God's grace. Baba did not preach any singular form of religion but only spoke of the cardinal principles of Truth, Righteousness, Peace, Love and Non-violence which cut across every religion, faith and creed. Divinity and faith in God are not commodities which can be purchased from any consumer store. Neither they are the chemicals which can be tested and analyzed in a laboratory. A great amount of effort is required by everyone whosoever wants to see God in Him and received His grace. Divine grace cannot be taken from an ATM machine installed in a small corner of a Bank. It is only through the paths of right actions (Karma), spiritual knowledge (Jnana) and the devotional love (Bhakti), one can have an access to the Divine realization.

The sacred book of Bhagvat Gita speaks of the desire to seek God and realize Him through these three paths mainly among several others. In Gita, Krishna discloses His real identity as an incarnation of God to Arjuna with the sole purpose of showing His Divinity simply to re-establish Righteousness (Dharma). Likewise Sri Sathya Sai Baba has been demonstrating the Divinity in Him and preaching the spiritual values to humanity. To see that Divinity and realize Sai Baba as the incarnation of God, an aspiring devotee will have to become Arjuna to have a vision of Sai Krishna.

On November 23, 1976, Baba's 51st birthday, while giving His birthday discourse, Swami said, **"My powers are not acquired. They are Divine and beyond the comprehension of scientists. Science has limitations like a wooden ladder which cannot be used to reach the skies above. An Avtaar comes armed with the four powers of Chamatkar (Miracles), Sanskar (Tributes), Paropakar (Welfare or Service) and Sakshatkar (God-visualization). He attracts people by His Divine qualities, transforms their character, exhorts them to serve mankind and grants Him God-realization."**

Bhagwan Sri Sathya Sai Baba's open and bold declaration about His own divinity echoes the minds of His devotees till date in explicit words, "**I willed for My own pleasure to create this vast universe. Before that, there was none to understand me. I merely willed. That is all. Mountains rose, rivers flowed; the earth below and sky above took form; oceans rolled; the Sun, the Moon, deserts, everything took shape to demonstrate My existence. Humans, animals. birds – all living beings began to speak, to hear and to move about; Man was accorded primacy. I equipped the human brain with My discriminitative wisdom**". His divine message to the whole humanity given in His discourse dated 23 November 1979 is reproduced here in His own words on a separate page.

Divine Message

Bhagwan Sri Sathya Sai Baba in His Divine Birth Day Discourse dated 23 November 1979 gave the following missionary message to all His devotees:

To all Active Devotees,

Your Mission Has Begun

"Your mission has begun. Those are My words to you, My devotees. Each of you has a unique and valuable part to pay in this life time. Only those whom I have called can serve Me.

My Mission has now reached that point in time when each of you now has work to do. This planet has a purpose in the great galaxy in which it is held. That purpose is now unfolding before our eyes. I call upon you to radiate the Bhakti (devotion) with you so that its unseen power will envelop all who come into your orbit. To successfully perform your part, always remain centered upon Me. Allow yourself to impart that purity of heart within you towards all human beings and all living creatures and do not reach for the fruits of your work.

This part of My mission is performed in absolute silence. You are My instruments from whom My love will pour. Be always aware that the moment you let your ego descend upon you. My work ceases. When you have overcome your negative unmindfulness, you will again become My Source.

The multiplication of My Love will be felt throughout the world. I have prepared you for this work over many incarnations. I have drawn you to Me. I have made great steps in My Mission over these past incarnations. My work is ceaseless and so your work, too is without end.

Know that I am within your and without you. There is no difference. Rid yourselves of petty matters forevermore. You are now

ME and I am now THEE. There is no difference. My Darshan (Spiritual Blessings) will pour forth from Me to and through you. You may be unaware of this constant action. Be ever pure of heart and soul and mankind in your lifetime will benefit from your unique qualities.

Others, too will join Me in this Mission when I draw them to Me. The time is approaching when all humanity will live in harmony. That time will be here sooner than one expects. Before it arrives be prepared for whatever is needed to reveal to every living thing the true purpose of existence. It is not what anyone alive can imagine. It is not something that one can try to aspire to. It is beyond all comprehension. I can say that its beauty is magnificent beyond all dreams. And as each of you perform your silent work, I embrace you to My Heart and henceforth your souls shall be lifted up and your eyes will reveal My Presence within.

This I say to all My Devotees from the Lord's Mountain Top where all the Universes become one.

By about My Work, My beloved Bhakthas. Your breath will carry the scent of the Blossoms of Heaven. Your example will be that of Angels. Your joy will be My Joy".

Bhagwan Sri Sathya Sai Baba

(Excerpts from Divine Discourse – November 23, 1979)

Epilogue

Various philosophical enunciations are offered regarding the perception of God such as ontological, cosmological and teleological among others. The ontological reasoning affirms that existence is the very essence of the idea of God. "**Where has this name God come from? If there is no God, how can the name God come into existence? Without the existence of God, the word God would not have originated**", says Sri Sathya Sai Baba. Indeed, the very God-idea, according to the famous Greek philosopher Plato, leads to the faith in the existence of God. While supporting the ontological enunciation of God, the cosmological view holds that the Universe is contingent, and this contingency implies the necessity for the existence of a Supreme Divine Power. By the same logic, the teleological enunciation argues that the complexity and variety in nature needs harmony which feels the necessity of a designer, and this necessitates the existence of such a Grand Designer. All the three arguments rest their case on the truth of the existence of God.

All human visualizations are rooted in some sort of human experience, which cannot transcend spiritual dimensions. Indeed, these human visualizations are nothing but reflections of human perceptions. Then **how do people justify human faith in God, who is believed to be attributeless Brahmn – the Supreme Divine Power beyond time and space, and hence beyond human visualization or imagination**? The answer lies in the very question itself in the sense that an individual's perception of any entity enable him/her to include or logically infer reality that transcends experience. However, human minds are so focused that they can affect abstractions and then experience those abstractions by objectifying or personifying any idea or a principle. The idea of the infinite God, that is Brahmn, is arrived at only through inferences but is understood only through concretization or personification. Incarnation of God, the Highest Principle and the

First Cause is thus, arrived at not only through inferences but also through experiences.

According to Bhriguvalli, also called the Taittriya Upanishad, Sage Bhrigu asks his father Varuna, "Who or what is Brahmn or the Ultimate God?" Varuna replies, "That from which all beings originate; emerge; That in which all beings rest; and that in which all beings merge; that is Brahmn". To find the inner meaning of all this, Sage Bhrigu did a long meditation and came to realize that all beings consisted of several layers, and discovered Brahmn as the foundation of all layers, and that a human being is Brahmn himself. He concluded that Brahmn is the Ultimate Truth. Bhrigu in the first stage of meditation thought of Brahmn as physical 'Annamaya' (made up of 'Anna' *i.e.* food) for it is in the matter that is present everywhere and it is the physical universe perceived through the sense organs of human beings. He was then advised to proceed further. After meditating more. Bhrigu thought of Brahmn as the life force *i.e.* (made up of 'Pranamaya' or vital life sustaining energy). But soon he realized that the reality cannot be just vital energy, since the whole universe is vibrating, being animated with the universal energy. At the third stage of his meditation, Bhrigu comprehended Brahmn as 'Manomaya' (made up of 'Mana' or mind) and he felt that the Universe is nothing but the thought process ('Bhavamaya'). All the objects that are seen and felt are nothing but the consequences of human thoughts. At the fourth stage, Bhrigu went further down into the profound depths of meditation and realized the Truth as 'Vijnanamaya' (made up of Vijnana, intellect). But by now while reaching the fourth stage, Bhrigu's ego also started melting which is a common phenomenon with the spiritual seekers and aspirants. Intense meditation, on reaching the fourth stage, had freed Bhrigu of his ego as well as purified his heart from all the blemishes of worldliness and made him ready to have the perception of the Supreme Reality or the Ultimate Truth. Finally, when sage Bhrigu meditated further, he perceived the Supreme Reality, the Ultimate Truth as 'Ananandamaya' (full of Anand or Bliss) the Supreme Bliss. He felt as if the whole universe was pervaded by bliss and bliss alone – closest to the Ultimate Truth. When Bhrigu reached this stage, he just had no capability to describe it for that Reality is indescribable. He invented or visualized the Brahmn – The Supreme Reality. This is what Vedanta describes – Truth (Sat), Consciousness – (Chit) and Bliss – (Anand) *i.e.* Sat-Chit Anand which is all-pervading.

The Brahmn, according to Vedanta, is the Supreme Reality. All other beings, animate or inanimate, sentient or insentient, visible or invisible, are unreal. Sometimes, Upanishad is quoted to have described Brahmn in negative terms – not this, not that (neti, neti). Swami Sivanand disagrees with any negative ascription of the Brahmn. According to him, it is not possible to conceive of Absolute Reality as nothing. Brahmn is neither void nor emptiness (Shunyata). On the contrary, Brahmn is supremely complete (Paripoorna). The Brahmn, according to Swami Sivanand, is eternal, infinite and the Supreme Bliss. He describes Brahmn in terms of positive attributes such as divine wisdom, dispassion, power, strength, prosperity and eminence among others. Brahmn is pervasive which surrounds everybody around from all sides, inside, outside, above and below. Every being is in it and it is in every being. Brahmn is the support of all phenomenal world. It is unchanging amidst changing; permanent amidst impermanent, and imperishable amidst perishables.

It is the human sense of separation, created by limited perception by its intellect that makes one Truth-Consciousness-Bliss (Satchit-Anand) appear as many diverse units – like the reflection of moon in many pots full of water which gives the impression that there are many moons each shining in a separate pot of water. It is the same light, the light of the same Brahmn, which lights up all beings, whether animate or inanimate. Bhagwan Sri Sathya Sai Baba says, "**After long searches here and there, in temples and in churches, in earths and in heavens, at last you course back. Completing the circle from where you started, to your own soul and find that He for whom you have been seeking all over the world, for whom you have been weeping, and praying in churches, and temples, on whom you were looking as the mystery of all mysteries shrouded in the clouds in nearest of the near, is your own self, the reality of your life, body and soul. That is your own nature. Assert it, manifest it. It is truth and truth alone, that is one's real friend, relative. Abide by truth, tread the path of religious enquiry**".

The atheists, while denying the existence of God, vehemently claim that the believers in God have been committing horrible acts of sins and crimes in the name of the religious creeds ascribed to God whereas the so-called Omni-present, Omni-scient and Omni-potent entity called God has been remaining inactive and silent. Thus, they interpret God's inaction and silence as God's non-existence, and in this way, they conclude the non-existence of any Supreme Divine Power called God. Infact, they challenge and protest the very idea or essence of God. They strongly feel that if the so-called God created the Universe and put it in motion, why then He became silent, aloof and indifferent to what has been happening everywhere? According to their views, if God, at-all, creates the individual souls, off and on, then why there is the existence of the evil that manifests in the form of crimes, sins and cruelties leading to sorrows and sufferings, injustices and exploitations, and birth-based deformities and inequalities that make some people more privileged than others. Nevertheless, such depressing, disturbing and disgusting views give an impression that somehow there is some iota of feeling of God in the inner minds of such aggressive atheists which include among others some of the greatest minds such as scientists and intellectuals. Indeed, they realize that the visible amazing structure of the universe, things and beings so meticulously organized, seem to suggest the existence of a Grand Design or a Great Mind or a Supreme power which however, needs to be explored. In pursuits of such divine evolutions, both scientists and philosophers devise what they term as Cosmic Evolution, Biological or Creative Evolution and Spiritual Evolution.

The believers firmly believe that there is only one divine force in the Universe. It bifurcates itself, and then bifurcates itself again, and still again, and so on, until it shows itself in the form of many apparently different forces but trace them back to their original source and then finally found to be one. This divine power is named as God who dwells hidden in all other forces. A living being is an instrument of this force – the Supreme Power. A human being cannot use the divine power but the divine power can use a human being or a living being as its instrument. This divine power is able to manifest in every possible form and on every possible plane. Working through the living beings, this power plays the real role in the creation of Nature and its dissolution. In the sequence, miracles happen whether material or mental or spiritual because that divine power has no limitations. This is precisely the purpose of evolution, and the purpose of incarnation.

In the present age of Internet, technology and information explosion, it is interesting to know that there is even more information on the topic of God which reigns supreme, whether or not one believes in His existence. The atheists endorse it by not believing and the believers by surrendering to God. The former do it by disproving His existence and the latter by trying to establish it. The question therefore arises is, "**Does God really exist**?" Believers take the knowledge in the Vedas or the scriptures of other religions, as their base, whereas the non-believers have the force of their own logic. But logic is a peculiar thing – it can be used both ways to support and nullify and is, in the end, inconclusive. Even in a court of law, mere arguments are never entertained without supporting evidence. People generally have a concept or idea of God, which may or may not be commonly found acceptable. It is the firm conviction in the existence of God which refutes all arguments against the faith in God. Bhagwan Sri Sathya Sai Baba says, **"First of all have faith in yourself. If you do not have faith in yourself, you cannot have faith in God. Therefore, one who denies God, denies oneself. One who has faith in oneself will have faith in God"**. A systematic and systemic approach would be to refer to the scriptures or books that refer to the word 'God', check its use and find out how it has been defined.

The Vedas describe God as the most subtle entity with three cardinal characteristics: an inanimate material of perishable nature (matter) composed of five basic elements namely earth, water, fire, air and ether; countless individual souls existing as animate mortal finite entities; and one eternal animate infinite divine entity (power). The individual soul is subtler than matter and the divine entity (called the Supreme Soul) is subtler than the individual soul. Matter comprises of particles – electrons, protons, neutrons and positrons. The individual soul being subtler than matter can reshape, relocate and work upon finite portions of matter, which God as the most subtle divine power and the Supreme soul holds complete control over matter and individual souls. This control operates through centrifugal force which is directed from within to outwards. God regulates the existence of individual souls and enables them to refine, retune and evolve through the process of enlightenment culminating in their salvation. This process of refinement and evolution involves association of individual souls with physical bodies through the phenomenon of birth, growth, ageing and decay which repeats itself in a cyclic way. An individual soul is endowed with limited knowledge, understanding and intellectual capacity, while God, the supreme Soul, on the other hand is omni-potent, omni-present and omni-scient and equipped with multifarious traits such as creation, protection and dissolution among others. It is just out of deep faith, an individual soul tries to view the formless God with visions, images and forms of various types which lead to the evolution of several cults and religions. If only these individual souls as human beings realize this simple metaphysical truth expounded in Vedas, they can converge to a common and shared understanding of God, and hence can attain God-realization. Brahmn or God, according to Vedas, is the only reality beyond limits of space and time. The three schools of the philosophy namely dualism (Dvaita), qualified monism or non-dualism (Vishisht – Advaita) and monism or non-duality (Advaita) are the three complementary stages of reaching the same goal of God-realization. All faiths and religions are different ways to realize the same Godhead, while the Bhagvat Gita proclaims three major faiths to obtain this stage of God-realization namely the path of Karma and Service, the path of Meditation and Divine Knowledge, and the path of Love and Devotion among others.

The believers refer to God as Ishwara, Bhagwan, Brahmn and so on. It is only after studying several scriptures and books, they find faith in God acceptable. Both believers and non-believers need to have clarity of the concept. If there is a creation, a product or effect, the effect must have a cause. Everyone, has to accept this. There may be a dispute about the nature of the cause. Something cannot come out of nothing. So if the whole creation is the effect, there has to be something in the origin, a cause. Something exists and that self-evident being has to be accepted. It is this existence or pure being which is accepted as God. Without taking recourse to the Upanishads, take the example of government officers, ministers or secretaries. Each officer has the power to do so many things. They are all part of the collective government power. The government exists but not seen while it is experienced as realized through its laws, orders and its decisions that are carried out by its functionaries, who operate because of the power of the government. Even a peon in the office, wielding this power allocated to him, proves the existence of the government.

Although human mind is capable of comprehending a lot of this whole phenomenon, yet it is not able to understand a lot more, and this lot more needs to be understood which requires axiomatic faith as the foundational base in the existence of some Supreme Being, often called the Universal Consciousness or Cosmic Intelligence or God as such. Indeed, this requires more faith, less logic. After all, the concept of God is not a utopian idea. The Universe created by God is a reality. Its solar system is, indeed, friendly to the creation. There are believers who express their deep gratitude to the sun in the form of the recitation of the 'mantra': "Om Bhaskaraye Namah", while offering water to it.

It is not possible to see with the human eyes the electrons, neutrons and protons without the help of instruments, yet their effect can be felt. The spiritualists say the same thing: God is not visible to the human eyes, but one can feel the effect of His presence. One can see and feel that the Universe is working so intelligently while permeating tremendous wisdom. It is not only the spiritualists and theists who say that the Universe is full of intelligence. Even the great scientists like Einstein have acknowledged this truth, who said, **"It is not a dead universe, it is not a 'stupid' universe, it is an intelligent universe"**. According to the biologists, the human body is a leather bag full of trillions of cells. Each cell contains within itself a nucleus which further contains in itself DNA while inside the DNA, there exists the chromosomes. Further, inside the chromosomes, there exists the protons inside of which are located strings of energy which exists eternally, which can neither be created nor destroyed. This is termed as the energy consciousness by the biologists. This energy consciousness contains information of every second of human existence on the earth. When the physical body of a human being dies, its energy consciousness floats in different dimensions. It keeps on taking different forms till it becomes neutral. In the spiritual language, this energy consciousness keeps on incarnating and re-incarnating. The process continues till this energy consciousness recognizes the Divinity within itself in the language of spirituality while the biologists would talk about the free will of this energy consciousness. Einstein said no event could be postulated without the presence of a witness, an observer. What exactly is the purpose of this intelligent universe? Another eminent scientist David Foster answers, "**To become more intelligent**". This is precisely what the spiritualists have been propounding. From unawareness to awareness – from unintelligence to intelligence – there is a way and there is the goal. The Upanishads say; "**Tamsoma Jyotirgamaye", 'O' God take me from darkness to light**".

The non-dual monistic (Advaita) philosophy, propounded by Adi Shankaracharya, seems to be the point where Astrophysics intersect with Metaphysics as described in Chapter 2. The Astrophysicists see the linkage between 20th century physics (mass, frequency, wave and energy) and the monistic unity of the Universe as the common meeting place. They feel that this linkage formalized by Albert Einstein and other scientists suggest that the whole mesh of the Universe blend into 'One that exhibits itself as Many'. This supports the monistic view that everything is but the manifestation of One – called God. The meaning of the terms space and time take on different dimensions when Astrophysics come out with new discoveries and theories such as the one proposed by Einstein where one is taken to the lofty state of spacelessness and timelessness. This gives the most propound sensation of the most mystical God as the source of all as creation.

Existence of God cannot be proved in a scientific manner. Nobody even can prove it. Infact, if God is proved, He will no longer be God. Then He will become a thing and then God existence can be tested or analysed in a laboratory. "**Who knows this truly, and who will declare it, what paths lead together to God**? Only **His manifested aspects are seen which exist on supreme mystical planes**?," says Rig Veda.

According to one belief, creation is the creator and hence Universe is the God, that there is no distinction between God and the universe. There is no separation between God and the Universe. They are two aspects of the same One Energy. Creation is the manifestation of the Creator. God's existence can be realized through His manifestation which is the visible universe. In view of this, Osho, a great spiritualist philosopher of India, calls God "Creativity". According to him, it is an on-going process which is unstoppable. Not that one day God created the world, and stopped thereafter. Creation continues. It is moment to moment moving. It is a dynamic process and God is not separate from it. It is through meditation that one can reach to one's inner-most core of intelligence. Then one can become so silent that one's own intelligence is revealed and in that very revelation, God is revealed. Supporting this view, the Holy Bible says, "**For what can be known about God is plain to all, because God has shown it to them. Ever since creation of the world nature, His invisible namely His eternal power has been clearly perceived in the things that have been made". According to a Japanese proverb, "Do you need proof of God? Does one light a torch to see the Sun**?".

The question "Does God really exist?" needs to be answered convincingly. The great Indian sage Raman Maharishi said, "**I am is the name of God while God is none other than the Sel**f". Adi Shankaracharya, who revitalized Hinduism, said of his enlightenment, "**I am Brahmn….I dwell within all beings as the soul, the pure consciousness, the ground of all phenomena**". Jesus Christ proclaimed by saying, "**God and I are one**". People, in general strongly believe that God does exist. They have been always in search of Him because of the persistent feeling that there is some power behind the whole creation. It is that power that has caused the persistent feeling, people call God. To the question "**Where is God**?" the answer given is: "**God is everywhere. God is in everything. There is no place where God is not**". To the question "**Who is God**?" the answer is: "**God is supernatural, immortal entity, having special powers over the lives and affairs of the living beings and the course of nature". What is His shape and structure**?" The answer is "**His shape and structure is the whole universe – totality of all the things that exist, considered as an orderly and harmonious system**. The Universe is eternal, immortal, limitless, endless and dimensionless from within which emanate billions and billions of galaxies, planets, asteroids, meteors, comets, blackholes and everything else including elements and matter. The Universe is the continuous expanse extending indiscriminately in all directions, boundless, without beginning and end. People cannot visualize the

Universe as it is far beyond their perception. The Universe has been there; it is there; it will be there, eternal, forever the same, unchanged. It is evident that every happening is brought about unexpectedly by some eternal divine power that is continuously creating and controlling everything. Every living being is only an instrument of that divine power and as a part of what is happening in the world. As the planets rotate and revolve in their orbits as the divine power ordains, human beings carry out what God ordains to cause action, reaction and chain reactions.

In his exposition on the Brahmn Sutras, Swami Sivananda says that the scriptures are the true source of knowledge about the Brahmn since Brahmn alone is the source of the scriptures. Brahmn is the source of the universe. In other words, the Brahmn is omniscient. The scriptures are the key to acquiring knowledge about the Brahmn. As Swami Sivananda further puts it, "**Brahmn is not merely the creator, the sustainer and the destroyer of the world. He is the source or womb of scriptures and is revealed by (the study of) scriptures**." The underlying point being that the Brahmn is beyond comprehension in the physical and the intellectual sense. The descriptions given in the Srutis (literally translated, 'As it is said') is based on the experiences of seers and sages, which can be infallible. According to the Srutis, the Brahmn is itself supposed to have breathed forth the (knowledge contained in the) Vedas. The Brahmn is formless, colourless, and without attributeless. So it cannot be comprehended by the human senses through direct perception. One can infer the existence of fire by the accompanying smoke, but the Brahmn cannot be established even by inference or analogy because there is nothing with which it can be compared.

Can God be seen and experienced? This is a question that has confounded humanity since the beginning of time and creation. Swami Vivekananda used to say, "**If there is God, I must see Him**." This strong urge and intense pursuit for the Divine set him on his search for a preceptor or Guru who could show him the true path to God. Before meeting Swami Ramakrishna Paramhansa and accepting him as his spiritual Guru, he met several saints who obviously could not show him God and quench his thirst. He insisted that if he did not see God, he would not accept their claims about the existence of God. Seeing is believing. One will have to become Vivekananda to search for a Ramakrishna to see God.

What is the origin of the universe? Where did it come from? Ancient Sankhya philosophy provides a possible explanation, which comes quite close to the accepted scientific explanation of the day.

Sankhya philosophy says that the interaction of Purusha and Prakriti is responsible for creation of matter and the universe. Purusha is an omniscient, omnipresent, indivisible entity. Interaction of Prakriti, another invisible entity also called Energy of Nature, with Purusha is responsible for the creation of the universe. While, Purusha is sometimes considered as multidimensional space and Prakriti as the time. Sankhya also states that in the beginning, three forces – golden (Satvic) rule, silver (Rajas) rule and iron (Tamasic) rule were in equilibrium. When that equilibrium was disturbed because of interaction of Prakriti with the Purush, the creation took place to form the universe. But Sankhya is silent on what caused the disturbance. This is similar to what some scientists today say about the birth of the universe, that in the beginning, time and multidimensional space were in equilibrium. The universe came into being when that equilibrium was disturbed. Why the equilibrium got disturbed, scientists are unable to explain. Various theories abound, like the Big bang, but now it is said that nobody knows for sure. A possible answer according to Sankhya could be that multidimensional space wanted to "become" many or to experience more. This space, sometimes called Purusha in Sankhya philosophy, Akash or God space, as enunciated by Adi Shankaracharya, just wanted to experience more and many. After the spacetime equilibrium was disturbed, multidimensional space started flowing. This flow produced gravity and mist which became the cause of visible matter and galaxies. The mist apparently gave rise to matter which formed the visible world. This is what scientists call production of matter from vacuum. Interplay of time and multidimensional space giving rise to the visible world is similar to the interaction of Prakriti and Purusha as propounded in Sankhya philosophy. Mist formation is a continuous process. With time, more and more space seems to have been used for it to form the visible universe. The rest of space still remains invisible and could be the basis of dark matter and dark energy Astrophysics talks about.

The Holy Vedas say, "**The non-existent was not then, Nor was the existent, The Earth was not, nor the firmament, Nor that which is beyond. (When there was nothing then), what could cover what, And where and in whose care did the waters and the bottomless depths then exist? There was no death nor immortality then; There was no sign of night, nor of day. That one breathed without extraneous breath with His own nature. Other than Him there was nothing beyond. In the beginning there was darkness, Intensified darkness, indistinguishable darkness, All this visible universe was reduced to its primordial nature. This primordial universe which was enveloped by the All-pervading power of One, before whom the universe of**

matter is a trifle became One (that is, came into existence) through the force of His intense activity and spiritual fervour. In the beginning the Divine Will arose. This was the first seed of the mind of the Creator. Those who can see beyond by putting their mind and heart together, found the binding link of the existent in the non-existent. The non-existent existing in the existent. The rays of the Divine Will spread across the whole world. They spread below and above and the result was that small and big organisms bearing seeds were born. As the existence of Earth was dependent on the Divine Will of the Creator, the position of matter was lower than that of the spirit which acted with the Divine Will."

There are several high-profile philosophers and intellectuals who have churned out many ready-reckoners and voluminous treatises on ways and means to God-realization and emergence of the universe. The clan of clerics and pseudo saints have played havoc with the lives of many believers. These self-declared god-men virtually sell religion and spirituality. They have devised queer ways of earning faith and loyalty from their followers. Some of them unhesitatingly declare from their podiums, if they ever changed their guru, they would earn the wrath of God. Their interest lies in perpetuation of ignorance of the masses for obvious reasons. Do they have any answer as to why Swami Vivekananda went on changing his gurus till he was shown God by Swami Ramakrishna Paramhansa who was the last Guru he went to and, who then piloted his life. The rest is history.

Sri Adi Shankaracharya said: "**Three things are difficult to obtain, and if obtained, may be due to the grace of the Divine – human birth, desire for liberation, and guidance of a spiritually enlightened person**". Most people believe in the existence of God, and also in the presence of a soul (Atman) in every living entity. Yet not many consider it necessary to inquire into and understand the nature of God or of the soul. They pay perfunctory obeisances to God and occasionally seek mundane (material) favours from Him. They are quite contented to go through life, on the lines of Charvak philosophy mentioned in Chapter 3, with its fleeting pleasures and not so with fleeting miseries, simply fulfilling the four activities common to all species of life – eating, sleeping, mating and defending. Finally time (kala) overtakes them and they succumb to death, without having realized the true essence of human life.

There are three aspects of human life: the material, which concerns body, mind and its thought process; the spiritual aspect, which concerns the soul and God; and the relationship among them. A majority of people spend their entire lives catering only to the needs of the body and mind. The most compelling of these needs is to please the senses (kama), for which they need wealth (artha). To acquire wealth, they adopt any means, fair or foul. Vedanta does not deny the people the enjoyment of sense pleasures or the necessity of earning money. In fact Vedanta accepts humankind's requirement for both and has prescribed for it the four pursuits or objectives (purusharthas): code of values (dharma), wealth (artha), sensuous pleasure (kama) and liberation (moksha). Vedanta, however, cautions not to chase only sensuous pleasure (kama) and wealth (artha) indiscriminately and recommends that these two pursuits are regulated by code of values (Dharma). Thus, value (Dharma) is placed before sensual pleasure (kama) and wealth (artha) as it regulates the two. These three purusharthas are called trilogy (trivarga) and they serve humankind's material quests. Liberation (Moksha), the fourth pursuit, is separate from the trilogy (trivarga), because it is a spiritual quest. For liberation (moksha), knowledge and realization of the soul is a prerequisite. Sadly, however, people mostly neglect the obligation to understood the soul. Although several questions plague their minds, they do not try and search for answers. What is the nature of God? And of the soul? What is the relationship between the two? What happens after death? How does the soul trans-migrate from one body to another? Are there heaven and hell? What is the purpose of life?

Vedanta holds that human birth is very rare and, therefore, very precious and it should not be wasted. The Srimad Bhagavatam states, "**Having obtained, after many births and deaths, this rare human body, though ephemeral, offers an opportunity to attain the highest perfection (liberation from the perennial cycle of birth and death)**". A human being is graced with a unique nature. He is distinct from and far superior to all other life forms. He is endowed with a highly developed consciousness and abundant intelligence coupled with the ability to discriminate. Vedanta considers this faculty in the human being, when not under the sway of his sensory instincts, urges to be truly unique. But he fails to manifest his unique nature because the animal tendencies in him are overpowering. If he can subjugate or sublimate these tendencies, his real nature, humanness, will come forth and his spiritual awareness will start growing. He should, therefore, not waste this precious human body, which is the highest form of life among the 8.4 million life species, and instead use its unique nature to inquire into and discover the higher spiritual dimensions of life. The rarity and usefulness of the human body is once again highlighted, also by Lord Krishna Himself, during His last discourse to His friend and devotee, Udhava, in the Srimad Bhagavatam says, "**The human body is very rare and attainable only by one's good fortune. It is a most suitably built ship, which, when captained by a competent preceptor (guru) and favoured by the wind of God's grace can be used to cross the ocean of material world (samsara). If a man fails to utilize all these favourable conditions, then he should be called a suicider, a killer of his own spiritual self**".

Since time immemorial, efforts have been made to give a concrete, concise and conceptualized description of God. The process of assailing philosophical factors in shaping religion led it to a superstition-ridden system which has deprived people of experiencing God as the Supreme Reality called the Brahmn. Adi, Shankaracharya says: "**Brahmn is the only truth; the world is a dream or a delusion; and the individual; soul is not different from the eternal Divinity**". According to the Hindu scriptures, God is the Sagun Form (Brahmn with attributes) of its Nirgun form (Brahmn without attributes). The visible trilogy of Creation (Brahma), Preservation (Vishnu) and Dissolution (Mahesha) is the manifestation of the Sagun Brahmn (God) and their incarnations of various forms. It is also generally believed that the Universe is an energetic phenomenon. As scientists go deeper and deeper into the subject, they observe that matter is essentially a mass of energy, that it is energy which is manifested in myriad form of matter throughout the Universe. It also realized that universe is an expanding phenomenon, and that there is an uninterrupted process of creation, preservation and dissolution. In this unending process, God energetic presence works. His very presence activates this process. Inventing God means realizing His supreme splendor and beatitude through His process of creation, preservation and dissolution.

What is, then, the reality of God? Indeed, His reality is mysterious. Neither logic nor any exploration can unravel His mystery. Human beings are incapable of grasping this reality because of their limited intellect and limited power of comprehension. Absolute Reality can neither be intellectually concocted nor physically manufactured by the human beings who are conditioned by the limitations of their existence. The Supreme Reality always exists since it is eternal. The emergence of the universe is spiritually explained as the dynamic aspect of Pure Consciousness appearing as vibrations somewhat akin to the ocean waves. The entire phenomenon of creation, preservation and dissolution is termed as a vibration on the canvas of Pure Consciousness. There is a boundless space with neither inside nor outside in which the universe takes birth, develops and perishes. This phenomenon remains intact in a perfect state of equilibrium. The moment this phenomenon of cosmic evolution is set in motion, the equilibrium gets disturbed resulting in the appearance of duality of consciousness in the form of the subject and the object. The subject and object are so intimately inter-related that one cannot be separated from the other just as the darkness cannot be separated from night, and light cannot be separated from the day. The two aspects namely subject and object are interpreted as the perceiver and the perceived, also named as Shiva and Shakti, the principle of existence (being), the passive or static aspect of Pure Consciousness, while the latter stands for the primordial creative energy – the power of consciousness, its dynamic aspect. The Shiva aspect is everlasting, eternal and supremely pure Brahmn. It appears as space, time and universe, but it does not undergo any transformation. It maintains its immaculate purity while providing support to all things. The Shakti aspect represents the object in dual relationship with the subject. It is considered to be the cause of cosmic evolution that generates all vibratory motions and changes that occur in the universe. It generates the entire cosmic drama (play) with the Eternal Being at the centre of the cycle of time-space phenomenon. Shakti represents the creative power in the kinetic aspect of Pure Consciousness – the Divine Mother of the Universe.

Sri Ramakrishna calls this Shakti as the personal aspect of the impersonal. Both personal and impersonal, according to him, are the twin aspects of the same reality – the Eternal Brahmn – the Supreme Purusha while the Shakti is named as Prakriti (Nature). The most amazing phenomenon of this Supreme Reality is that its both aspects namely Shiva and Shakti or Purusha and Prakriti are inseparable in the sense that one is unconceivable without the other. Thus, the Supreme Reality is a mysterious phenomenon wherein the seemingly contradictions are harmoniously blended, and wherein, the Being and the Becoming, Consciousness and Matter, Absolute and Relative, Impersonal and Personal, Purusha and Prakriti, Subject and Object, Shiva and Shakti, Brahmn and Maya, and Unmanifest and Manifest, all different expressions of the same Supreme Reality, are held together in one embrace. Purusha is the seer while Prakriti is the object of sight. Purush stands for consciousness or life whereas Prakriti represents nature which is responsible for bringing into existence the creation and its constuents such as the five basic elements namely earth, water, fire, air and ether; their five attributes – touch, taste, sight, smell and sound; five organs of perception (Gyan Indriyas); five organs of action (Karm Indriyas); the mind; the sense of discrimination and ego which all together constitute thirteen instruments. Prakriti or Shakti is energy while Shiva is the energizer, the Shaktiman, since the cause pervades its effects, therefore Prakriti pervades all the objective world and its constuents. But Purusha's pervasiveness is even greater than that of Prakriti in the sense that Purusha – the God pervades both Prakriti and its evolutes, the objective world and its elements. Prakriti carries out the process of creation with Purusha as Her Lord and under His supervision. Virtual creation is thus Purusha Himself while Prakriti is His agent to carry out the process of creation, preservation and dissolution. The Purusha has two other distinct features namely that of the individual (Jeev Atman) and the Supreme Soul (Paramatman). Besides, the two distinct features, the Supreme Soul has further three aspects namely Nirgun Brahmn, (without form, attributes), Sagun Brahmn as God with His manifestation as the trinity of Brahma (creator), Vishnu (preservator) and Mahesh (Dissolutor); and various divine incarnations of which most prominent being in the human forms with attributes and divine powers.

As said earlier, Prakriti is constituted of the three attributes (Gunas) and the Paramatman is supremely above the Prakrati. Although, Paramatman is beyond the Prakriti, yet it is the origin of Prakriti. The eternal process of the appearance and disappearance of Prakriti does not in any way affect the Supreme Paramatman. The symbol of the Cosmic (Divine) Mother expounds this fact in terms of three attributes (Gunnas) in the process of the evolution of life. It is an indication of the sentient emerging from the insentient. Philosophically, 'Rajas' gets the upper hand over 'Tamas'. The golden colour of the Mother Durga with her red cloth symbolizes 'Rajas' with its capacity to enrich the phenomenal life. Sarasvati, the goddess of learning, Lakshmi, the goddess of wealth, Subrmanya, the god of valour and Ganesha, the god of wisdom, all attending on the Cosmic Mother indicate the ways and means for enriching the earthly life. Just above the head of Durga. The Snowhite Lord Siva is seated absorbed in deep meditation. This is the symbol of 'Sattva', which transforms all earthly activities into spiritual activities. Ultimately, the three Gunas of Sattva, Rajas and Tamas get transcended and the Absolute is attained. All the three attributes are glued with the physical life. But as one progresses towards the Atman, life gets refined. Ultimately life in the Prakriti is transcended and Godhood is reached. The meaning of the individual soul from the Prakriti takes place when it is free from the pride and delusion, with the evil of attachment conquered, ever dwelling in the Self, the desires completely stilled and freezed, and liberated from pleasure and pain. Then the undeluded individual soul (Jeevatma) reaches that Great Eternal – the Supreme Soul (Paramatman).

What is the Soul (Atman)? What is the Individual Soul (Jeevatman)? How is it related to the Supreme Soul (Paramatman)? Atman is the source and sustenance for the body, mind, intellect and consciousness (chitta). It helps in discrimination (Viveka) between what is right and wrong, what is proper and improper, and what is truth and untruth. It is the higher wisdom (vijnana) and the science of consciousness (sujnana). All human beings assume a particular form at a particular time, like an infant, a child, a boy, a young man and an old person. These different forms at different stages have no independent existence. It is transition from one stage to the other. However, the Atman is the source and sustenance for all these entities. It is the fundamental principle. This fundamental principle itself originated from the Parmatma – the Maya veiled Sagun Brahmn. The individual soul (Jeevatman) is never separate or independent of the Supreme Soul (Paramatman). As a wave is a part of the sea likewise the individual soul is eternally a component of Supreme Soul (Paramatman). The relationship between the individual soul and the Supreme Soul (Paramatman) is analogous to the relationship between the space in pot and outside. Because of ignorance, the individual soul gets identified with the Prakriti and evolves the senses and the mind. As a result, the individual soul becomes indulgent (Bhogi) in the external world through senses and enjoys the sense-pleasures. But it becomes a renunciate (yogi), the moment individual soul choses to refrain from the activities of the senses. Its level of identification with Paramatman is in direct proportion to the level of its sense-control. Sense control is a broad term which includes mind (manas), intellect (Buddhi), consciousness (Chitta) and egoism (Ahamkara). Mind is constantly wavering unsure of whether something should be done or not. Intellect is the faculty of determination that sheds doubt and takes a firm decision. Consciousness concentrates and enquires into the nature of things which includes also the memory. Egoism is self-arrogance which is the root cause of suffering. The consummation of the individual soul (Jivatman) with the Supreme Soul (Paramatman) has been construed in the Upanishads in a logical manner. In order to understand this fundamental principle, people ascribed different names to it. Some call it AUM, the primordial sound. Others call it Tat Tvam Asi – That Thou Art. Yet others call it Brahmn. Some other give it some names like Rama, Krishna, Allah, Easwara and Jesus. These different names and forms are given for the purpose of identification only. Divinity, however, has no name and form. The names and forms ascribed to the Supreme Soul – God are based upon one's liking for a particular name or form. God is One without a second. Yet, different people at different times are deluded by different names and forms. One can say it is all their imagination. Though names and forms are different, God is only One.

When an individual being gets engaged in the welfare of others, his duties are viewed as service to God and his surrender to the Will of God. He gets merged with God and becomes one with God at the time of leaving his earthly body. The individual being is the individualized consciousness. Since there is a beginning and an end to the process of individualization, it is classified as perishable. While God is the Lord of delusion (Maya), He is imperishable. Being the Lord of Maya, God assumes various forms and assumes various names such as Siva, Narayana and Bhagwan. The cosmic power, God, has been assuming various forms and names such as Sri Rama, Sri Krishna and Shirdi Sai the latest to date as Sri Sathya Sai. In view of this, God is also called Saguna Brahmn. Even while being in the human body, God remains untouched and unaffected by it. As Nirguna Brahmn, It is Pure Consciousness – an Indeterminate and Intense Consciousness. Limitations of time, space and causation gain no access to it. That is why some theological names such as Sadasiva, Adinarayana, Parasakti are attributed to it. The phenomenon of Divine Incarnation is eternal and uniform. It is not selective and solitary as some people would believe it. It happens whenever and wherever a necessity arises. The entire universe, sentient and insentient, is a manifestation of God. An Incarnation is a special manifestation of God. He embodies Himself as a human being in this mundane world in order to establish the highest of the spiritual and moral ideals governing life.

God is supremely above virtues and vices. There is no need for Him to entangle Himself in action of any kind, good or bad. He is merely the changeless Witness. In His presence, activities take place in nature. Though Himself actionless, His Grace is ever in favour of the virtues. Sri Krishna's agreeing to be an unarmed charioteer of Arjuna signifies this great truth. Further, God is ever the Great Charioteer residing in the hearts of all. His presence as Conscience within the embodied beings is perceptible to the virtuous, but to the wicked His inner presence remains clouded. One of the renowned spiritual leaders, Sri Ravi Shankar says, "**Since ages, sages have been striving to reduce the gap between God and ourselves. There are two ways to do this: one is to elevate humankind towards Divinity – this is called Siddha, and the person who achieves this state is believed to have attained perfection. The second way is to bring God to human level in the form of an Avtaar. Here, Divinity manifests itself for the sake of humankind. So, man rising up to God Siddha; God coming down is Avtaar because He cares for you and wants to communicate directly with you.**" One of the greatest wielders of all actions in the on-going Kali Yuga has been Shirdi Sai followed by Bhagwan Sri Sathya Sai Baba

– the latest incarnation of God. In the midst of intense activity, He remained supremely serene and unaffected. The events, great and small left no more impression in His mind than a reflection does in a mirror. Nothing in the universe could distract Him from His wonted poise. The gist of His teaching is: "**Fight the battle of life. Let the virtue in you vanquish the vice. Any useful work that falls to your lot gives you enough of opportunity for self-discipline, emulation and emancipation. The Divinity within you is your ever available guide. Attuning yourself to It, do your job as splendidly as you can. Every hero is obliged to wage the Mahabharata war in and through his own life.**"

Incarnations of God appear to wipe off wicked people from the face of the earth. That has been an extraordinary work under extraordinary circumstances. Among the saviors of mankind there is an exemplary trait which is common to all. Their profiles give a message to the mankind. Their ideals primarily are sieved through their personal conduct. What they practice in varying situations count for everything. Rama's profile in the great epic Ramayana, presents the highest standard of truth and righteousness while performing His duty as an obedient son, a devoted husband, an ideal brother, a sincere friend and a loving father. He also proved to be a great warrior who fought against the demonic forces led by the demon king Ravana and eliminated them, while establishing thereby the ideals of truth and righteousness. There is a mistaken belief that Sri Krishna's case does not come under this rule. The sponsors of this view contend that humanity will do well to emulate Sri Rama and Sri Krishna in two different ways. Imitate the life of the former but imbibe the instructions of the latter, dare not imitate the actions of Sri Krishna. This, in short, is their mistaken contention since this idea is born of an imperfect understanding. Sometimes, a question is raised as to what particular aspect of Sri Krishna's character defies imitation. Many puerile moralists hold that Sri Krishna's relationship with innumerable milkmaids (gopis) stands on an exclusive footing, and that no mortal dare copy it. In other words, they maintain that some actions of this kind are undesirable for being like Sri Krishna. But this position of the pseudo-moralist arises from an imperfect understanding. Sri Krishna, the enchanter of the gopis was hardly twelve years old, when He concluded His sports with the milkmaids of Brindavan. Is it ever possible for a boy of under twelve to have any kind of conjugal relationship with hundreds of women? Does the biological plan of nature admit of such a possibility? Moreover it must be noted that those milk-maids proved themselves faithful to the core to their husbands. Those gopis used to invite the entire lot in the township to come and join them in their mirth with the divine lad. This communion of the gopis with Krishna was just spiritual ecstasy of pure and pious love which need to be emulated with God as the young boy Krishna, and the billions of people and beings in the universe, as the gopis of Vrindavan – the Universe.

Hinduism believes in portraying the divine characters from their original puranic and mythological contexts and putting them into their creative incarnations. Buddhism and Jainism are basically atheistic religions although Hindus treat both Buddha and Mahavir as divine beings. Jews and Christians are strongly monotheistic. While Jews do not believe in the concept of incarnation, in Christianity Christ is God's son, but not an incarnation of God. In Islam, God is formless, but His attributes are known in the sense that He is compassionate and merciful. In the language of Hinduism, God is with attributes (Saguna Brahmn) but also He is without form (Nirguna Brahmn), and rightly God is called Ishwar by the Hindus.

Whenever a Divine being incarnates with a supreme mission in life, a talented sage also appears on the earth with a holy mission. His sacred duty is to make a faithful record of the great events associated with the Divine Incarnation. It is only through the explanation given by the sage that the Divine Descent and Divine Sport become somewhat discernible to the man of ordinary understanding. Sage Valmiki came along with Sri Rama and expounded His profile. Similarly Sage Vyasa accompanied Sri Krishna and drew a genuine pen picture of His earthly sojourn, thrilling as it was with miraculous events. Space was no barrier between him and Sri Krishna. Likewise, the huge Sai literature including the regular periodicals Sanathan Sarathi, Vahini Series, four volumes of Satyam Shivam and Sundaram, Sathya Sai Speaks Series, Summer Showers and several books authored by His devotees reveals the divine potentiality to reflect the mind and spiritual message of Sri Sathya Sai Baba – the Kali Yuga Avtaar of God.

In an incarnation of God in the human form, and in that humanness, one can get a glimpse of divinity. Incarnations of God and divine messengers have made their teachings simple for the welfare of the people, so that both Illiterate and literate, children and grown-ups, young and old are able to grasp the spiritual teachings with ease. Abstract principles and abstruse ideas are brought by the divine incarnations and messengers within the bounds of the knowledge of common man. Any commentary on their teachings is stupendously full of idealism. On the other hand there have been commentators who as a class have tried to lead their own cults and creeds through the inspired utterances of the divine personalities. These divine personalities have given their spiritual food to humanity with natural ease and simplicity. Their message to the aspiring souls is what the mother's milk is to the hungry baby. The utterances of Sri Rama, Sri Krishna, Buddha, Jesus, Mohammed, Nanak, Shirdi Sai and Sri Sathya Sai among several other divine beings require no clarification or elucidation. They directly appeal to the heart and head of the common men and women.

What is the primary function of God? What exactly is God's work? What does He do? The answers to such questions are given by great spiritual scholars in the following way: God does everything in the world. He uses several beings as His instruments to carry out all activities related to the mission of His incarnations which occur from time to time from aeon to aeon or from epoch to epoch. God creates, sustains and dissolves through His manifested Trinity forms named as the Creator (Brahmn), Sustainer (Vishnu) and Dissoluter (Mahesh). God does everything through His various representatives and missionaries. As a preacher, He preaches; as a teacher, He teaches; as an administrator (ruler), He leads the way how to administer (rule), as a soldier, He fights; as a trader, He trades; as a doctor, He treats and cures; and several many such activities of the worldly life. He is in the creation and the creation is in Him. He pushes down the haughty and egoists. He destroys the evil while protecting the virtuous. He pushes up the humble and pious. He generates the feeling of love. God is everything and everything is God. God is in every being and every being represents God. God permeates all creation.

Gita offers a clear and exhaustive exposition of God as Existence – Knowledge – Bliss or Sat – Chit – Ananda. The profile of each of the divine incarnations viz. Sri Rama or Sri Krishna or Shirdi Sai or Sri Sathya Sai is the most sublime embodiment of Vedantic principles. The greatest contribution that an incarnation of God makes to the world is His personal profile and His divine message. He is necessarily a divine being in human form with a message. His actions and conduct, even more than His utterances deliver that message in unmistakable terms. Through the force of His character, He exerts an abiding influence on those who come in contact with Him. His demeanour under varying circumstances teaches humanity more eloquently than His declamation. The life of each divine incarnation has been the message for the humanity.

The core of the Dvaita, Visishtadvaita and Advaita needs to be known in terms of the three categories of Supreme Reality: Jagat or the universe is one category, Jivas or the individual souls that live in the universe form the second category and the Substratum behind the universe and the innumerable souls is the third category generally named as Jagdish. This third one is the repository of all knowledge and power. Not only does it sustain, but also governs and controls the destiny of the Jagat and the Jivas. Enshrouded as the Jivas are in the Jagat, they subject themselves to countless births and transmigrations. Through transmigration they either evolve to higher orders of life or involve in the lower ones. Virtues and righteous acts help them go upwards. Vices and sinful acts drag them downwards. Mukti or emancipation is effected by giving oneself away in toto to God and complete disentanglement from the meshes of the world is thereby obtained. Liberation (Mukti) is the goal of all living beings (Jivas).

According to Dvaita, the universe, the individual souls and God are three separate entities. God rules over the universe and the souls. Souls in their ignorance are entangled in the universe. Through devotion to God and through His mercy obtained thereby, the souls have to free themselves from the bondage of the world and attain the realm of God. This state of living with God in Heaven is termed liberation (Mukti). There the living beings (Jivas) are eternally in the presence of their Lord. Their individuality is not lost because of liberation (Mukti).

Visishtadvaita literally means 'qualified non-dualism'. God alone exists, according to it. The cosmos is His body. The living beings (Jivas) exist as innumerable life-cells in that cosmic body. As the rays of the sun are inseparable from it, the individual souls cannot be separated from God. With the dawn of intuitive knowledge, it has been realized that Paramatman (God) – the Supreme Soul is the whole and an infinitesimal part of it. The attainment of this knowledge leads to emancipation. Complete self-surrender is the means to the attainment of this goal. In the state of liberation (Mukti), the individual soul (Jiva) is ever aware that it is a limb of the Lord.

Advaita literally means non-dualism. What are termed as Jagat and Jiva and Brahmn are not really separate entities. Reality is one without a second. It is Existence-Knowledge-Bliss Infinite. It has intrinsic power to manifest itself as the Jagat and the Jiva. This inherent power goes by the name of Maya. This is the implication of the word Advaita. It is because of his ignorance that the living being (Jiva) fancies that he is separate from the universe and the Substratum behind it. With the dawn of knowledge this feeling of difference vanishes. The Reality alone exists. Because of its Mayasakti It manifests Itself as the Jiva and the Jagat. Resolving this Sakti into Itself, It also remains unmanifest. In Its kinetic state it is Saguna Brahmn (Conditioned Reality), in the static Nirguna Brahmn (Absolute Reality). As the wave subsides into the ocean the individual soul dissolves into the Absolute. This is emancipation according to the Advaita system of philosophy. Bhagwan Sri Sathya Sai Baba says, "**One should have a mental image of a form of God, fully developed mind poured into that form. When the image of God is seen outside, it is qualified dualism. When seen in the mind, it is qualified monism. When form is absorbed into the Atman, that is Advaita, non-dualism. The two preliminary steps are not separate stages: they are contained in Advaita as buttermilk and butter are contained in milk. The image of God seen outside should be taken into the mind and then into the soul.**"

According to the scriptures, human life itself is a composite of these three systems of Vedantic philosophy. In the wakeful state, a human being moves about and does various activities of life. The world he lives in and the persons he contacts are all entities independent of him. He is then in the domain of Dvaita. Then comes the next state. The experience of this world of multiplicity goes to sleep. The world of variety vanishes. The dream-world comes into being. The same plurality is experienced again. But the men and world found in dreams are different from those found in the waking state. One has external reality while the other is a phantom of the mind. The dream world of plurality exists nowhere except in the mind of the experiencing individual. Here there is a perception of dualism while actually it is all monism. This is the position of the Visishtadvaita. Finally there is the coveted dreamless sleep in which contentless unconsciousness alone persists. The self that is in the waking and dream states continues to be in the dreamless slumber as well. This is the position of Advaita – one without a second. Mutually exclusive though these are, these three experiences, wakefulness, dream and dreamless sleep are indispensable to a human being entangled in the meshes of the world.

Bhagvat Gita does not exhort anyone to be a dualist, a qualified monist or a monist. Sri Krishna said, "**Wake up your supreme consciousness. Be established in your divine nature. You are omnipotent in your sphere. Perform your duty with ease and spontaneity. You have not come into this world to drag on a wretched existence. There is an inviolable and holy relationship between you and this world. It is yoga to make this relationship operative. Do achieve this in a magnanimous manner. Through effective functioning let all of your faculties pay homage to your ever-expanding consciousness. As the blossom sends forth its fragrance, let your love become all embracing and inspiring. Like the blazing sun, may your intellect throw lusture on all that you contact. When you wake up to**

this spiritual eminence Duality (Dvaita), Qualified Non-duality (Visishtadvaita) and Non-duality (Advaita) take their respective places and function in the hierarchy of your enlightened personality".

It is remarkable that Sri Sathya Sai Baba has also neither been concerned with the relative merits or demerits of religions nor did He ever took a serious view of the subtle differences among the multifarious system of Advaita, Visishtadvaita and Dvaita. His entire attention has been focused on transforming human life into a spiritual dynamo. His every effort has been for the benefit and enlightenment of His devotees. Nothing in the world has been alien to His all-embracing divine love. His divine grace has been the greatest fortune that His devotees receive in superabundance. With characteristics such as these, Bhagwan Sri Sathya Sai Baba has been the embodiment of all the traits of perfection mentioned in Gita or Ramayana or in various other ancient religious scriptures. The teachings of Bhagwan Sri Sathya Sai Baba are in tune with those of Gita or Ramayana. Pondering over the utterances, actions, and teachings of the divine incarnations of Sri Rama, Sri Krishna, Shirdi Sai and Sri Sathya Sai, one feels that there is endless scope for striking parallels between them, while keeping out creeds, cults, dogmas and philosophical disputations.

The individual souls are the manifestations of the Supreme Reality, the Brahmn. These individualized souls are subjected to ceaseless activity. Karma is concomitant with service to humanity. As light and heat happen to be part and parcel of the blazing sun, Karma and Seva are inherent in an individual. Between an individual and his Karma, the enunciation of one necessarily contains the enunciation of the other. Karma Yogi, therefore, is the most important of the individual souls. Indeed, each activity is actuated by Will. There is no Karma independent of the Will. Man wills to walk, to eat, to sleep, to wake up and so on. The gross manifestation of the Will is action. The entire creation is the manifestation of the cosmic Will. All forms of Will resolve themselves ultimately into the innate desire to preserve life that transforms itself into innumerable activities. Existence, not extinction is the essential nature of the soul. Individual souls have emanated from the Supreme Soul – God. Preserving life in the face of death and seeking permanence in the midst of perdition, are the workings of the Divine Will to assert existence. The assertion of existence of Karma Yoga is called **Sat** or the **Truth** aspect of the Supreme Reality, the Brahmn.

Inert matter exists and a living being also exists. The only difference between the existences of these two has to be taken note of. A living being is aware of its own existence while the other is not.

Awareness is born of cognition and it is self-evident. A living being knows that it exists. The act of knowing is cognition. There is a variation in the intensity of cognition. Highly evolved beings have more of cognition while those in the early stages have it enshrouded in inertia. The difference between one life and another is in the degree of cognition. This difference is that of degree, not of kind. Intelligence, awareness, cognition, consciousness, conscience – these are terms indicating the same faculty. Path of Knowledge (Jnana Yoga) wedded with the path of Meditation (Dhyan or Sadhana) delineate the path of becoming brighter and brighter like a burning lamp reveals itself and its surroundings in an increasing measure. It also begins to throw increasing light on the objects brought to its presence. Suppose that the lamp is placed in a glass case, coated with dirt, bright though the flame is, its brilliance is seemingly tarnished. To the extent the glass undergoes cleansing, brilliance becomes patent. The divine lamp of Intelligence is enshrined in the temple of the human frame. As the faculty of understanding undergoes purification, the inner Light begins to shine with greater glory. The processes of cleansing the faculty of understanding deal with the path of knowledge and meditation. God as Light is ultimately realized by the seeker that what shines through the human flame is none other than the inextinguishable Cosmic Light. The path of Knowledge (Jnana Yoga) coupled with the path of Meditation (Dhyan Yoga) contributes towards the purification of the faculty of understanding until it reaches its culmination in Awareness or **Consciousness – 'Chit'**, aspect of the Supreme Reality, the Brahmn.

The Divine Consciousness pervading all living beings is none other than the Brahmn, itself. This Brahmnattwa permeates not only human beings, but also plants, reptiles, birds, beasts and animals and whole creation. Brahmn-consciousness cannot be limited to a particular being, time and place; it permeates the entire creation. The nameless, formless Brahmn is omnipresent and all-pervading. He is indescribable, incomprehensible and immeasurable. There is only one sign for Divinity, that is, Consciousness. In whichever form this Divine Consciousness permeates, it will assume that form – it may be the form of a plant, bird, an animal or a human being. Ishwarattwa, therefore, can be described as Divine Consciousness which pervades all human beings and all creation. "Sarvam Shivamayam" – all that you witness in this objective world is a manifestation of Brahmn. It pervades all the three worlds: Earth, space and nether regions. It exists in all the three periods of time: past, present and future. Divine Consciousness does not differentiate between people or species. It is only the people who make distinctions between themselves as father, mother, brother and sister, based on their earthly relationships with each other. In reality, every living being is an embodiment of Divinity. God assumes all names and forms. Once Parvati, the consort of Lord Shiva enquired of Him, "How can people recognize Divine Consciousness which is said to be all-pervasive?" Shiva replied that the same consciousness that is imminent in Him is permeating all living beings. He also explained that it was permeating every cell of her body as well. One cannot explain this; it can only be experienced or inferred.

God is attributeless. It is the devotees who ascribe different names, forms and attributes to God. Based on their imagination, they picturise God in different forms. People describe the form of God as Rudra and Shantiswarupa. But, God is always an embodiment of Bliss. He is always pleasing and smiling. To imagine such an Embodiment of Bliss in a different form is only the making of the devotee. If at all there are any such illusions, one has to get rid of them. One has to realize Divinity by cultivating faith in God and love for Him. It is only love that can bind God. Through such divine love, the oneness of God has to be realized. The best sadhana would be to realize unity in Divinity and worship God as such.

Seeking knowledge of God leads to devotional Love for Him. The more one understands God, the more one loves Him. Logic and Love are the obverse and the reverse of the same fact of Godhood. The inter-relation between cognition and emotion is indeed patent in all stages and phases of life. To sublimate emotion to the highest pitch is the summum bonum of life. The feeling of love leads to the cultivation of devotion to God. Purified emotion is Bhakti or devotion. Even impure emotions become pure when directed towards God. Man's love of God increases in direct proportion to his being soaked in His glory. As iron is attracted towards a magnet, a man of devotion is attracted towards God. It is in search of this Bliss that individual souls struggle and hug life. But for its bliss, life would not be tolerable even for a moment. Out of the fully blossomed flower of emotion, flows the nector of Anandam. The path of faith and devotion (Shraddha Aur Bhakti Yoga) exhorts man to feast on it. This Love is God and God is Love. Pure Love generates sweetness. It also expresses itself as bliss. Supreme bliss is divinity itself. Anandam Brahmn – Bliss is Reality. Sat-Chit-Anandam or Life, Light and Love are the three inseparable phases of the same Supreme Reality, the Brahmn.

Thus, Path of Action and Service (Karma Yoga Aur Seva) postulates Sat. Meditation and Divine Knowledge (Dhyana Aur Divya Jnan) postulates Chit, and Devotion of faith in God and Love for God

(Shraddha and Bhakti) generate Bliss. All the three paths or pursuits culminate in Yogeswara. The aspirant is expected to follow all the three paths simultaneously until he reaches a state of realization of Sat-Chit-Anand, the Brahmn. Performance of action with sense of service is considered to be superior to the renunciation of action and without expectation of fruits of action. Karma Yoga, Jnana Yoga and Bhakti Yoga are not mutually exclusive. They are complementary to each other. With the mind purified by Karma Yoga, and with the senses subdued, one realizes oneself as the Self of all beings, With the self detached from the external contacts, one realizes the bliss in the Self, one whose happiness is within, whose delight is within, whose illumination is within, only that person or yogi gains the beautitude of Brahmn. With sins destroyed, doubts (dualities) demolished, minds disciplined, heart delighted in the welfare of all beings, and the one who discharges his duties without expectations attains the beautitude of Brahmn. Such a person does not get attached to sense objects and actions. Gita proclaims that those who are free from passion, fear and anger can comprehend God and get purified. He who is devoid of ego and desire is called a spiritually evolved person. He, who abandons attachment to the fruits of action, is always contented. He who engages himself in action (Karma) and service (Seva) is an evolved soul. He whose body, mind and senses get purified because of desirelessness, remains balanced in success and failure, in happiness and sorrow, and engages himself in singing the glory of God, gets spiritual enlightenment, and hence God-realization. Receiving the grace of God is conducive to action (Karma), Knowledge (Jnana) and devotion (Bhakti). God provides the ways and means for the aspirants to evolve stage by stage in their paths of Karma, Janana and Bhakti. Endowed with faith in God, whatever form of God, as aspirant or a devotee worships, God makes that faith steady and strong. A devotee and believer in God, who constantly adores God, can understand Him to some extent. He who takes refuge in Him, only he realizes in full his individual self and hence the Cosmic Self.

Adi Shankaracharya, Swami Vivekananda and Chaitanya revived the three Yogic paths in the present aeon (yuga) called the Kali Yuga namely path of meditation and divine knowledge (Dhyan Aur Gyaan), path of Karma and Service (Karma Aur Seva) and the path of faith and devotion (Shraddha Aur Bhakti) corresponding to three fundamental aspects of human life namely philosophical, pragmatic (functional) and psychological (sentimental). Shankara's path of knowledge not only brought a deep influence on the post-Buddhist philosophy, the idea of vacuum (shunyata) but also taught the path of acquiring spiritual (divine) knowledge, discriminating between the real and unreal as the road to liberation and realization of God. The material or secular knowledge also called the lower knowledge enable the people to lead a financially progressive life while the acquisition of spiritual or higher knowledge or the knowledge of metaphysics helps a person to inquire and seek God, His Cosmic Mind, manifestation of the Universe. Vivekananda stressed on the path of Action (Karam Yoga) and Service (Seva) by making work/activity (Karma) not only a spiritual path for individual progress but also a means for social progress while by asserting service to humanity as service to God as a rule of life. Maha Prabhu Chaitanya came and gave the wonderful and simple path of developing faith in God and devotion (Bhakti). Without compromising the other paths, the path of devotion, according to Chaitanya, seeks nothing but deep love of God by cultivating faith in Him and singing devotional songs of God's glories, while the mind becomes pure and loving vibration for God sprouts in the heart. Indeed, devotion, which is possible only with faith in God, is both the path and the goal. The present world of Kaliyuga is complex. Therefore, Vivekananda talked of harmony and went a step further by suggesting a combination of all the three paths. He said, "**Each soul is potentially divine. The goal is to manifest this divinity within by controlling nature, external and internal. Do this by work and service; psychic control (meditation) and philosophy; and devotion and worship**." This combination of three paths is the only way to God-realization, to grasp Him. He is one and alone. He is formless existence. He is what baffles every terminology. There is no word to comprehend Him. Nobody can find out the depth of God, the limit of God for He is higher than heavens, deeper than the depths of oceans. His measure is longer than the space and broader than the universe.

Brahmn is the Absolute Reality. It is supremely beyond time, space and causation which are the characteristics of the Universe. That is why, it is called the Supreme or Absolute Reality. Brahmn is the substratum, basis and background of the panorama of the universe. The changes that take place in the universe do not affect the Brahmn. It is even Itself, the Being behind the Becoming of the Universe. It is the nature of the Brahmn to appear as multitudinous conscious beings called the individual souls (Jeevatman). The five basic elements – either (space), air, fire, water and earth are perishable in contrast to the Brahmn who is Imperishable. He is the Cosmic Soul – the Hiranyagarbha whose rays are the individual souls. All the beings in the Universe are controlled by Hiranyagarbha. He is Omni-scient, the Ruler, the Subtlest, the Support of all, Incomprehensible to the unrefined mind, the Effulgent like the sun and Beyond all darkness of ignorance. A human being endowed with spiritual strength equipped with three divine gifts namely the physical body occupied in work and service to humanity, unwavering mind in seeking divine knowledge and heart absorbed in full devotion and love of God with all the doors of body closed and uttering the one-syllabled 'Om', thinking of Brahmn, attains the Supreme Goal, a human being or an individual consciousness merging in the Cosmic Consciousness.

Sagun Brahmn or God as the manifestation of the Supreme Brahmn in the form of the trinity principles of Creation (Brahma), Preservation (Vishnu) and Dissolution (Mahesh) incarnates as Sri Rama, Sri Krishna and Sri Sathya Sai and assumes a human form just as the bounded souls (Jeevatmans) do. But an Avtaar is bounded in the manifested body no more than the sky (space) seen through a window that is bounded within the limited frame of that window. The manifested body of an Avtaar is mutable; but in reality He is immutable and unsurpassed by the ordinary human beings. Indeed, His Supreme State remains unknown to those who do not have faith in God. The real nature of an Avtaar remains hidden because of the veiling capacity of delusion (Maya). God (Ishwara) seems to be concealed by His own Yoga Maya while actually He remains unaffected by it. Ishwara is the Lord of Maya, having complete control on it while an ordinary human being is under the impact of Maya. The appearance, stay and dissolution of the beings are all acts of Maya. Time also exists in Maya. The beings that were in the past, that are in the present and that are to be in the future are all known to God. The individual souls, however, do not remember their past lives, nor can they know their future. How, then, can they know about God – the Cosmic Soul?

Divine Knowledge (Brahmn-Jnana) cleanses the individual soul (Jeevatman) of its fallen state and reinstates its divinity (Brahmnhood). The knower of Brahmn becomes Brahmn. Spiritual Wisdom (Brahmn-Vidya) is, therefore, a superb purifier. Self-knowledge is the home-coming of the Jivatman. The whole universe is pervaded by Brahmn in its unmanifested form. All beings exist in it. Brahmn has the divine power to bring forth the universe. But Brahmn itself remains unattached, unmanifested and unaffected by its phenomenon of creation, preservation and dissolution. Brahmn in the veil of God is the backbone of the activities of Prakriti. It assumes occasionally, a perfect human form with the purpose of saving humanity and bringing it on the right path. Venturing in the divine pursuit, the human beings imbibe the divinity increasingly. The Rig Veda, The Sama Veda and the Yajurveda deal respectively with the origin, sustenance and the end of Prakriti. Vedas are the sacred books which proclaim that sound emerged from the space and became itself the seed from which the elements fire, air and water emerged in succession. Sound is, therefore, treated as Nada-Brahmn which persists eternally the syllable 'OM'. The aspirant, who gets fixed in the chanting of OM, evolves in Divinity.

The goals of human life should be striving for a spiritual life while seeking wider knowledge and searching for more happiness. All these three categories are nothing but the modification of Sat-Chit-Ananda (– Truth – Awareness – Bliss) which means life, light and love. This is a comprehensive description of God, and God is the direct or indirect goal of all being. God is the supporter of all beings since all sustenance comes from Him. As the sea is the owner of waves, Cosmic Life is the owner of individual lives. God is, therefore, the Lord of the Universe. The Universe and the beings emerge from God and merge back into God, while God is the Witness being the Cosmic Consciousness. God is the only lasting shelter to those who want to be freed from the cycle of births, deaths and rebirths. God is the one sincere friend residing in the hearts of the people in the form of Consciousness and directing them to the path of righteousness. What is ocean to the wave, God is to the entire Creation. He is, therefore, the Foundation, the Protection and Dissolution. As the Immanent Reality, the working of God in and through the Cosmos has its glory. God as sun, gives heat and sunrays. He is the cause of rain providing water through streams, rivers, wells and lakes. In His manifested form, God is the becoming of the Cosmos and in His unmanifested form He is the being. The Individual Souls (Jivatman) and God (the Paramatman) separated by the time, get united for eternity. Brahmn is the source and witness of the Universe that emerges from it, and merges back into Him. This Eternal Brahmn is cognized to some extent by the perfected beings like the great sages. But His glory in its entirety can never be known even by the highly evolved saints and sages. He only remains partially revealed even when He embodies as an Incarnation like Sri Rama or Sri Krishna or Shirdi Sai or Sri Sathya Sai.

In His Absolute State, Brahmn remains unknown and even unknowable. But in His Transcendent State, a glimpse of Its Reality is intuited by the incarnations of its manifestation – God and by the perfected souls like the divine messengers or prophets, the great rishis and divine personalities like Adi Shankaracharya (who propounded the non-duality principle), Ramana Rishi, Swami Ramkrishan Paramhans and Swami Vivekananda among several others. Brahmn is unborn, beginningless and endless. It is the Supreme Sovereign of the Universe. Even Its Transcendent Reality is visible only to the enlightened ones. But

Brahmn filters Itself down further so as to be available even to the ordinary aspirants. According to their attainments acquired through their Karmas in the present and past lives, they become the instruments for the expression of the Sat-Chit-Ananda. Such enlightened souls include among others the great Rishis and Sages like Bhrigu, Marichi, Atri, Pulah, Pulastya, Kratu, Angiras, and others. Electricity manifests itself in various forms in the instruments suited to those forms. In whatever form this energy expresses (manifests) itself, the power is the same. Likewise, the primordial power of God is evolving itself into the glorious varieties of sentient and insentient, abounding in Nature.

Brahmn is the origin of everything and everything evolves from Brahmn. Para Brahmn is the Supreme Brahmn, Nirguna Brahmn who is Pure Consciousness. Apar Brahmn is Ishwara, Saguna Brahmn, the Reality with all attributes and glory. Param Dhama – the Supreme Abode is the substratum of everything manifest and unmanifest. God (Bhagwan) is He who fully manifests six divine qualities which are Omni-potence, Omni-present, Omni-scient, and who knows past, present and future of all beings. Generation (Creation), Organization (Preservation or Protection) and Dissolution (Annihilation) are its manifestations. From time to time, He incarnates in the human form. His glory in its entirety is known to Him alone and to none else. The individual souls in the human forms are sometimes called as Purushas and God being the eternal Presiding Diety over the Prakriti, is aptly eulogized as Purushottma. He is addressed as Jagatpati – Protector of the Universe. The relationship between Iswara and Jivatman is like that between magnet and iron. The Jivatman (Individual Soul) grows increasingly in divinity as it dwells on the divine attributes of the Paramatman or Purushatman (the Supreme soul). God is the innermost Self in all beings which are all His gross manifestations. Sri Ramakrishna said, "**Know the One that is the root of everything. Then truth becomes self-evident to you. Put the number one first and then adjoin the zeros to it; this done, the zeros have their value. Without the number one, they are valueless. The many get their values from the original number one. Ishwara is the number one, and universe and the beings zeros appended to it**". It is almost impossible to describe the manifestations of God. These are infinite. All the splendours in the Nature are the attributes of God.

"**God is the innermost Self in all beings, which are all His gross manifestations. He is the Science of the Self which is Divine Knowledge (Atma Vidya or Brahmn Vidya or Brahmn Gyan). He is the beginning, the middle and also the end of all beings. He is the**

material as well as the efficient cause of the Universe. God is with form, without form and also transcending all these. He alone knows who and what He is", said Sri Ramakrishna. God is the seed of all beings whether moving or unmoving. There is no end of God's manifestations. Whatever is visible, glorious, prosperous or powerful, has sprung from a spark of His splendour. The sum total of God and His manifested universe is one and only one Brahmn. God is Rama, Krishna and Sai Baba:—the wielders of weapons used for the good of the people, for annihilation of the evils and demonic tendencies prevalent in the world, and for re-establishment of the values of truth (Satya), righteousness (Dharma), peace (Shanti), love (Prem) and non-violence (Ahimsa).

Existence of the individual souls, visible to the naked eye, in the form of physical bodies: human beings, animals, reptiles, plants, rocks is a sufficient evidence to show the existence of the Universal Soul – called the God who is ever-existent, eternal, infinite and endless. This Universal Self or Soul gives birth to the individual souls and in return, all the individual souls together constitute what may be termed as the totality of all beings of all forms – the Universal Soul, the God. Indeed, existence of individual souls in various forms gives an enough proof of the existence of the Universal Soul – the God. This is a fact which is self-evident, which cannot be denied even by the so-called staunch atheists, scientists and rationalists. The body, adopted by an individual soul, comprises of the five basic elements of fire, air, water, ether (sky) and soil (earth). A day comes when the individual soul leaves the body. While the individual soul gets back to its source, the Universal Soul, to merge into it, the body gets perished and merge back into the five basic elements of fire, air, water, ether and earth. The Upanishad's maxim says, "Aham Brahmmasmi; Tat Twam Asi" *i.e.* I am Brahmn, so are you". The Hindu philosophy holds that this Brahmn is Truth-Consciousness-Bliss *i.e.* "Sat-Chit-Anand," which means Pure-Being (Existence or Truth), Pure Consciousness, and Bliss. A human being, as an individual soul – a spark or a component or an element of the Universal Soul, therefore is an eternally pure awakened and free self.

The Absolute Brahmn is the central theme of the subject-matter of all religious scriptures. The key to comprehend this unknown Supreme Reality is by accepting principles of divine existence, consciousness and bliss. This is quite logical because a spiritual seeker can be expected to evolve only gradually and has to start with what is already known or familiar to him. This is a pedagogical way of inventing the Absolute Brahmn or its form as God manifested as the trinity of Creation

(Brahma), Preservation (Vishnu) and Dissolution (Mahesh). Indeed, the eternal Brahmn cannot be described in the way the material objects are perceived by the human senses. His hands and feet are everywhere. His eyes, ears and mouth grasp everything. His face is in all directions. He is Omni-present, Omni-potent and Omni-scient. He is visible everywhere, in everything and in everybody. He is transcendent Being enveloping all that exist. Perception of an object, of a living being and of a functioning process, leads to the perception of the entire universe which eventually reveals the existence of its Creator – the Absolute Reality. Existence of visible objects in creation and creatures indicate the existence of their creator. This can be easily understood by an example or a simile. A building structure is visible to the human eye and therefore, its existence is believable in the human perception. It is equally perceivable to the residents of that building. The builder of that structure exists which is a fact that cannot be denied, though he may not be visible to the residents. Indeed, the existence of the building and its occupants visible. The existence of its builder is an undeniable truth but the builder may or may not be visible to the occupants. Likewise, the creation and its creatures are visible to the human eye but the creator is not visible in the same way. He is visible through the objects of creation and creatures. Every form and name of an object and a creature is the name and form of their creator. Thus, the Absolute Brahmn or God is knowable as existence which is an undeniable truth. Adi Shankaracharya perceived this Absolute Reality essentially as figureless, featureless, attributeless Nirguna Brahmn, but manifesting itself with personal attributes as Saguna Brahmn, and ultimately wrapped in Maya, as God with attributes of creation, preservation and dissolution. Sri Ramanujacharya contended oneness of this Nirguna and Saguna Brahmn related each other as Soul and body respectively. Brahmn-Universe relationship is explained by Shankaracharya through the well-known example of a snake-rope analogy where illusion (Maya) is caused by mistaking a rope for a snake.

According to Bhagavatam all divine incarnations are either plenary expansions or parts of the Supreme God – the Sagun Brahmn, the manifestation of the Nirgum Brahmn. Each of these divine incarnations has been perceived as the Supreme Personality of God-head not only by the Vedic Sages like Vyasa, Narada, Vashishtha and others but also by the modern spiritual philosophers (acharyas) like Sri Aurobindo, Sri Adi Shankaracharya, Sri Ramanujacharya and Sri Madhavacharya among others. Like Rama, Krishna, Shirdi Sai and Sri Sathya Sai Baba came to teach the humankind the lesson that every human being is immortal by nature, being a soul, and as such, everybody is a part and parcel of the same Godhead. Like Rama, and Krishna, Sai Baba says, "**I am God. You are also God. The difference is that I know I am God, but you do not know this**". Earlier, Krishna declared, "**Although, I am the Lord of all living entities, I still appear in every millennium in my original transcendental form**". This is indeed the purpose of the Sai Trinity: Shirdi Sai, Sathya Sai and Prema Sai. Like Rama and Krishna, Sri Sathya Sai Baba descended for the specific purpose of mitigating the anxieties of pure devotees who has been always anxious to see Him in His saffron robe, and to re-establish the ideals of Truth (Satya), Righteousness (Dharma), Love (Prema), Peace (Shanti) and Non-violence (Ahimsa).

An important aspect calls for an attention of the seekers both in science and spirituality. Science ventures to explore the physical universe. But, what about the search of truth for the metaphysical? What the world knows today as the scientific knowledge is confined to the things related to matter. But what about the area of search that remains the metaphysical in particular? Albert Einstein, among others, could think of new horizons of research or invention pointing towards the unexplored metaphysics. The supreme creative force masterminds the known and the unknown – that manifests itself in the miraculous works of the superhuman beings. Thus, when one thinks of miracles in the realm of science, one has to look to the frontiers of man's changing knowledge. The miraculous inventions contributed by science create a hope that today's miracles of the divine souls, which look to be impossible to an ordinary human being, may reappear as possible when science peeps into supernatural powers. Indeed, scientists, philosophers and parapsychologists have already started the exploratory efforts into the phenomenon what they term as extra-sensory perceptual powers of human beings and their extraordinary abilities of mental visions to see things which the physical eyes cannot see or the supernatural powers to hear mentally what physical ears cannot listen to recognize *i.e.* the power to know what will happen or the ability to reshape the matter into energy or to transform energy into matter or the power to shift objects from one place to another by wish or use telepathy *i.e.* the power of mental communication at any distance. These are some of the new inventions in the realm of human mind. It may take a long time to analyze the mysteries of the miracles. But it does not mean that the modern scientists or parapsychologists or philosophers will still keep on rejecting miracles as myths. The miracles of Sri Sathya Sai Baba presents a mighty challenge to the scientific minds, rationalists and the intellectuals either to explain the reasons behind Sai Baba's miracles or accept the might of some divine power God.

Indeed, God Realization requires the inner vision of the divine power within every living being. This means the celestial vision and the metaphysical experience of the Supreme Brahmn. This equally means the inward journey of the spiritual seeker perceiving the light of the soul, and a continuous exploration of pure consciousness which together take closer to the ultimate union with God and meditating upon any of His several forms. God, being omni-potent, omni-scient and omni-present can take a form. Seeing God in any form is experiencing the divine light. Lord Krishna was all along with and beside Arjuna in human form. Yet, Krishna advised Arjuna through the divine light of His elemental and metaphysical forms. Thus, seeing the light form of God is the first step towards the goal of God-Realization.

Invention of God is a supersensous experience of divine light, divine voice, pious name and holy nectar. This is beyond all reasoning, logic and intellectual perception. It is a search beyond the sense-domain. It is a journey into the metaphysical world of the ultimate reality. It surpasses all knowledge of the phenomenal world of physical objects and matter. It is delving deep into the inner world. Nobody can invent God unless and until God is Himself willing to be invented.

A Departing Tribute and Homage to Bhagwan Sri Sathya Sai Baba

If the human history is the story of search for truth, never before has the quest been so intense and inspiring as generated by the **Sai Phenomenon**. If ever an ideal role model glittered like the glowing sunshine, never before has a Divine Incarnation like **Sri Sathya Sai Baba** been so brightened and adored. If ever an aeon found its protector in a Rama or a Krishna, never before has the expression **'Sai Ram'** been rolled off the tongue with so much reverence and relief. If ever a preceptor led people on the spiritual path embodying love and compassion, never has the Sai Message been found to be more crucial to the survival of human values. If ever a lighthouse emerged in a epoch to guide the human society, never before has the **Cosmic Consciousness** under the veil of **Sai Legacy** enlightened the universe. If ever a motherland proudly glorified its progeny, never before Bharat Mata gave birth to a son like Sathya Sai equipped with infinite divine love and glory. If people from various religions and cults adhered to their respective beliefs and faiths, never before has the recognition in the unison of genuine secular humanism been extolled by a system called **Sai Value System**. If ever the abbreviation SSS stood for Sri Sathya Sai, never before has it been emphatically described by **Spirituality**, **Secularism** and **Service.**

In the modern era of aggressive rationality, rabid materialism and excessive faithlessness in the divine power, the spiritual awareness generated by the Sai phenomenon through its divine manifestation in the form of Bhagwan Sri Sathya Sai Baba is the true revelation of the Supreme Brahmn that pervades and sustains the whole universe. God, the Absolute and formless (Nirakaar) has been appearing on the earth in the human forms (Sakaar) as Rama in the Treta Yuga, as Krishna in the Dwapar Yuga while the latest in the sequence of cosmic Sai incarnations in the human form as Shirdi Sai in the 19th century, as Sri Sathya Sai in the 20th century and predicted 'Prema Sai' in the 21st century is the super-human phenomenon for creating spiritual renaissance. Bhagwan Sri Sathya Sai Baba, the latest human form of God, has been the:

- Amazing incarnation (Avataar) of God with the supreme goal of re-establishing Universal Religion (Sanathan Dharma) through the spiritual ideals of Truth (Sathya), Righteousness (Dharma), Peace (Shanti), Love (Prema) and Non-violence (Ahimsa);
- Unique Human – God equipped with miracle-making divine powers of invariably producing Vibhuti (sacred ash) out of thin air, materializing with a mere wave of hand, several types of watches, jewellery items and other articles by converting energy into matter;
- Greatest Reformer of the human society by way of emphasing the value system, preaching spiritual values and axiomatizing the ideals of Axiology;
- Omni-Doctor and a great healer who has been curing patients of many incurable ailments and even terminating the terminal diseases;
- Profound Philosopher with a mission to generate spiritual awareness in the human kind through His discourses full of spiritual philosophy and religious teachings;
- Dexterous Technologist using spirituality as the latest Transformation Technology for human transformation to human perfection;
- Excellent Manager emphasizing Dharmic Management of human beings through the spiritual ethos, values and culture; and
- Eternal Educator who has designed an education edifice 'Educare' based on human values through the harmonious development of the faculties of head, hand and heart.

Bhagwan Sri Sathya Sai Baba has been a super-charged magnetic force attracting millions of people from all over the world and from all types of creeds and cults. He has openly and categorically not only declared but also proved Himself as God's complete incarnation (Poorna Avataar) of the present epoch (Kaliyuga) – the God personified in flesh, bones and blood, whom one could see, hear, touch, feel and experience, with whom one could have conversation and get spiritually enlightened. He has been continuously operationalizing the much-desired value-system through the Vedic philosophy of idealism (spiritualism) which begins from where the western philosophy of materialism ends, by explaining the basic meaning of universal and spiritual values of truth, righteousness, peace, love and non-violence espoused by the earlier divine incarnations Rama and Krishna, and reiterated by various divine personalities like Zorashtra, Jesus Christ, Buddha, Mohammed and Nanak. According to Bhagwan Sri Sathya Sai Baba, the search for Truth and Totality, Unity and Purity, Intellect and Intuition, Science and Spirituality, Astrophysics and Metaphysics, and Analysis and Synthesis leads to holistic harmony of body, mind and soul leading to God-realization.

Such has been an impression on the minds of the devotees of Sai Baba which include among others the world fame personalities, eminent philosophers, spiritual scholars, doctors, lawyers, industrialists, scientists, professionals and educationists.

About two decades prior to India's independence, on 23 November 1926, in a remote village of Puttaparthy in district Ananthpur of the Indian (Southern) State of Andhra Pradesh (Rayealseema Region), mother Easwaramma and father Shri Venkamma Raju welcomed their fourth child Sathyanarayana. No one ever envisaged how his happy family event would impact the destiny of the human race. During the next eight and half decades, spiritual seekers from all over the world have been streaming into Puttaparthy, the birth place of Bhagwan Sri Sathya Sai Baba and the abode of His ashram – Prashanti Nilayam. Aeroplanes, trains and all types of automobiles have been bringing in countless pilgrims from all over world including simple villagers, grateful patients of His free hospitals, beneficiaries of His numerous social uplift and welfare projects, adoring devotees, spiritualists, scholars, philosophers, policy makers, young and old for having a glimpse of His Holy Darshans and for seeking His Divine Grace. Sai Baba's gospel of pure and unconditional love expressed through selfless service has been warmly received by all races, religions, cultures and communities, creating a global movement of true secular humanisms without any check posts or barriers. **What is it that has been compelling millions of people from all over the world to undertake long and arduous journeys, at great cost and inconvenience to come to the pilgrimage centre of Prashanti Nilayam**? It is because of the simple reason that Sai Baba, through His unprecedented philanthropy, demonstrated that human and spiritual values are the missing link in the chain of human love and harmonious social order. Sri Sathya Sai Baba used to say, "**God is Love, Love is God, Live in Love**". His life and message can best be summed up as **Pure and Pious Love**. In a historic letter dated 25 May 1947 addressed to His elder brother Seshma Raju, the then twenty year old Sai Baba declared, "**I have a task – to foster all mankind and ensure everyone lives a life full of bliss – to remove the sufferings of the poor and grant them what they lack**". In fulfilling this vow, Baba has been working continuously to give the joyous experience of love and compassion to all everywhere ever since the declaration of His Incarnation (Avtaarhood) on 20 October 1940.

Sai Baba never asked anybody for any donations. Instead, He strictly prohibited His enthusiastic devotees from asking funds for donations. Devotees all over the world voluntarily of their own sweet will would feel obliged if they ever were able to give donations to Sri Sathya Sai Central Trust those also through the Bank. Every penny received in donation would be accounted for and the trust's funds-management appropriately audited. Sai Baba utilized these funds for several social welfare projects including free treatment at several Sai Hospitals, providing highly subsidized food in the Ashram, and periodically free food and clothing to the needy in the name of Narayanseva, giving free education in schools and university's campuses at various places and occasionally helping the unemployed to earn by themselves by giving auto-rickshaws free of cost, sewing machines to the dependent ladies and providing various other means of livelihood.

Sri Sathya Sai Baba has been a truly outstanding divine humanitarian. The Sai Trust's facilities include among others free education from KG to PhD under Sri Sathya Sai University; free medical and surgical treatment under Sri Sathya Sai Institutes of Higher Medicines and Research, and Super Specialty Hospitals; various welfare schemes of water projects, and rural welfare programmes (which) are some of the most outstanding examples of Sai Baba's vision of total human development. Sai Baba never asked the people to renounce the world, but to live in the world and serve the poor and needy selflessly while surrendering wholly to the will of God. Baba exhorts all human beings to overcome the differences of races, religions, languages, castes or communities and seek their underlying oneness. Indeed, Sri Sathya Sai Baba has been a ray of light and hope in humanity's search for peace and understanding with His message of universal love, tolerance and unity which need to be imbibed by all. His enlightened vision, dexterous leadership, strong emphasis on character building, integrity, civility and compassion, with His focus on inculcating the principles and ideals of all religions and cultures, amply demonstrated the critical importance of His idea of thinking and working together as one human family – the only way to fulfil the mission of peaceful and prosperous global society.

Popularly known among the devotees as Bhagwan (God) and generally addressed as Swami (Lord) by the devotees and followers, Sri Sathya Sai Baba has always been adored and worshipped all over the world as the human incarnation of God. He used to say, "**Service is the highest spiritual discipline much more than what prayer and meditation, scriptures and Vedanta can help you reach the goal. Service has a double effect; it extinguishes the ego and gives bliss**". Sai Baba, being a genuine secularist, attracted and embraced followers of all faiths and religions spread across the world who would often say, **"I have come to confirm each in his own faith – so that the Christian becomes a better Christian, the Muslim, a better Muslim and the Hindu, a better Hindu**". From curing sick patients suffering from terminal diseases like cancer, appearing at several places at the same time as reported by several devotees, communicating with His followers through dreams, producing lingams both by waving His hand and from His mouth and doing several such other miracles almost on daily basis, have been some of the confirmed manifestations of His divine power. Sai Baba would always tell His devotees and followers that He is the embodiment of divine love; love is the instrument, there can be no being without love. He would invariably declare by saying, "**I am God, you, too, are God. The only difference between you and me is that while I am aware of it, you are completely unaware, yet**". His philanthropic work is unparalled in the world. He has set examples and demonstrated models of social welfare for emulation by the people particularly the moneyed and mighty who are capable of doing social welfare work by providing water to thirsty, food for the hungry, medicare to the patients and educare to the students.

All the Avtaars like Rama, Krishna and Shirdi Sai Baba had to leave their physical bodies. Sri Sathya Sai Baba had earlier declared, "**My body is not immortal, my message is**". The body withers away but the message remains for ever. Sri Sathya Sai Baba has been the human divine walking on the earth and moving among the people guiding them from within, and transforming them silently. He has been an expression of truth, righteousness, peace, love and non-violence which have come to be accepted as the five ethical norms in all areas of human growth and development. The universality of Sai Baba embraces the ideals of all faiths, all religions, all philosophies, transcending all boundaries with a global appeal crossing all borders of class, caste, community, country and culture. Baba's teachings constitute true **love-In-Action** which manifests through selfless service and eternal joy. Sai's boundless love is evident in His unparalleled and unqualified philanthropic manifestations in aiding the poor and the suffering. Sai's spiritual (atmic) power always inspired and continued motivating the learned scholars, thinkers and philosophers in writing books on various aspects of divinity and spirituality. His programmes on Educare, Rural care and Health care are unprecedented true examples of non-dual cosmic love for His creation. Indeed, one can see and feel Sri Sathya Sai Baba as God in human form and realize God in human form as Sri Sathya Sai Baba.

An ordinary human-being is bound by the limitations of his five senses each of which manifests in relation to his/her physical, mental and social needs. It is because of these sense-limitations, a human being cannot look beyond his immediate individual needs, family commitments and worldly obligations. Also, because of these limited attributes, a human-being's level of spiritual evolution gets limited as compared to the unlimited faculties or unbounded attributes of a divine-being like Sri Sathya Sai Baba. The spiritual evolutionary level of a divine-being surpasses that of every individual human-being and goes beyond the needs of his/her individual body, family, community, culture and country. Sri Sathya Sai Baba, a divine-being, never distinguished between human-beings on the basis of communities, castes, cults, cultures or countries. Life and death, sunrise and sunset, sound and silence, light and darkness never affected Him. His mission, for Him, was the most important – the mission of human-transformation to human-perfection through the mode of spiritual evolution. Sai Baba dwells in everybody's heart and lives in everybody's mind. His physical departure from the earthly world has, thus, given a deep and sudden shock which is becoming unbelievable and unbearable. All His devotees and His followers are stunned with bewilderment and are mourning with pain His departure from them. Our tribute and homage to the divine soul of Bhagwan Sri Sathya Sai Baba and our profound salutation to Him for His vision of humanity. The vacuum created by Sai Baba can be filled only none other than by Sai Baba Himself. His legacy is His message.

> "O Lord, if the blue mountain be the ink and
> if the ocean be that ink pot,
> if the biggest branch of the heavenly tree be the pen, and
> if the earth be the writing leaf; and taking these,
> if the Goddess of Learning Writes for Eternity,
> even then, the limit of Thy Virtues will not be reached"

References

1. Brunton Paul : The Inner Reality; Samuel Weiser, New York 1972, U.S.A.
2. Dass M.N. : Miracles of Mankind's Great Saviours; Zoroaster to Sathya Sai Konark Publishers Pvt. Ltd., 1992, New Delhi (India).
3. Hislop, John S. DR : **Conversations with Bhagwan Sri Sathya Sai Baba** Sri Sathya Sai Sadhana Trust Publications Division, Prasanthi Nilayam, Andhra Pradesh (India)
4. Holy Scriptures : Sri Ramakrishna Math Mylapore, Chennai, India
5. India – 2001 : **Spirituality**; Reference Encyclopedia Indmark & Mermaid Centre, Bangalore, Karnataka (India)
6. Karanjia, R.K. : **God Lives in India** Sai Towers Publishing, Bangalore (India), 2005
7. Kasturi, N. : **Sathyam Sivam Sundaram,** I, II, III, IV Sri Sathya Sai Sadhana Trust Publications Division, Prasanthi Nilayam, Andhra Pradesh (India), 2003

8. Kasturi, N. : **Siva Sakthi Swarupa**: **Bhagwan Sri Sathya Sai Baba**
Miracle Divine; Sri Sathya Sai Sadhana Trust Publications Division, Prasanthi Nilayam, Andhra Pradesh (India), November 2004

9. **Message of the Lord As a Practical Philosophy** : Sathya Sai Publications of New Zealand, Auckland, 1998, New Zealand

10. Murphet, Howard : Where the Road Ends
Macmillan India Limited, 1993, Delhi, India

11. **Sanathan Sarathi Series** : From 2000 to 2012
Sri Sathya Sai Sadhana Trust Publications Division, Prasanthi Nilayam, Andhra Pradesh (India)

12. "Santisri" – Sastry, Jandhyala Venkateswara : **Tapovanam**;
Prasanthi Nilayam – 2002, 2nd Edition published by the Author

13. Schultz, M : **The Hindu Philosophy**:
Classical Publications, 1978, New Delhi (India)

14. **Service – Ideals and Aspects** : Sri Ramakrishna Math
Mylapore, Chennai, India

15. Sharma, R.P. : **Human Personality in Ancient Indian Thought**, 2001
Kanishka Publishers, Distributors, New Delhi (India)

16. Swami Bhutreshanand : **Ramakrishna and His Gospel**
Vedanta Press, Hollywood California, U.S.A.

17. Swami Mukhyananda : Sri Shankaracharya – Life and Philosophy; Advaita Ashrama, Kolkata, India

18. Swami Prabhuvananda and Christopher Isherwood : The **Bhagavad Gita : The Song of God** (Translated version)

19.	Swami Shradhananda	:	**Seeing God Everywhere; A Practical Guide to Spiritual Living;** Vedanta Press Hollywood, California, U.S.A.
20.	Times of India	:	Week Days Edition; Speaking Tree Column from 2000 to 2012
21.	Times of India	:	Weekly Edition of Speaking Tree 2010-12
22.	Times of India	:	The Best of Speaking Tree Series, Volumes 1, 2, 3, 4, 5, 6 Times Group Books, Bennet, Coleman & Co. Ltd., New Delhi, India
23.	Vrekham, Georges Van	:	Evolution, Religion and the Unknown God Amaryllis, New Delhi, India

Prof. V.D. Madan, author of this book, retired in January 1998 from the Indira Gandhi National Open University (IGNOU) of India as an Officer on Special Duty with a professional experience of 30 years in higher education. His special interest include among others, the areas of Mathematic and Quality in distance education for which he has also been closely associated with the University of Delhi (India), University of Sokoto (Nigeria) and the UK Open University (England) both as a regular faculty member and visiting academic.

Professor Madan has contributed over four dozen research publications in both Mathematics and Distance Education and developed more than three dozen self-learning course materials in Mathematics for distance learners. He has presented several theme-based research papers at various reputed National and International level conferences including the two world conferences of the International Council for Distance Education (IVDE) held at Caracas (Venezuela) in 1990, Birmingham (UK) in 1995, and the one that of the International Council for Mathematics Education (ICME) at Sevilla (Spain) in 1997. His earlier published monographs, entitled: ***"An Omni-Tech Approach for Higher Education with a Focus on Distance Learning"*** *(two parts) and* ***"Quality Assurance in Higher Education: An Omni-Systemic Approach"*** *(three volumes) are innovative educational ventures both aimed at the comprehensive and holistic paradigms for technology-based quality education.*